Praise for work by Tony Okoromadu

It is hard to imagine a more colorful and comprehensive reference book. This is a staggeringly detailed compilation. Tony Okoromadu offers Post-it Note style commentary on most of the tables, with occasional pauses for longer analysis. Clearly a massive undertaking.

AACSB
The Association to Advance Collegiate Schools of Business
USA

Tony Okoromadu has done a great deal of work and an extraordinary job in assembling this vast amount of interesting material and data. And he presents these in an imaginative and innovative way. The book is reminiscent of the style of The Economist's World in Figures and would sit well in that class.

Michael Hay
Professor of Management and Entrepreneurship
London Business School

Tony Okoromadu has created a well-researched and clearly presented encyclopaedia of economic and commercial information. It is an excellent contribution to a better understanding of these countries and their economic potential.

Richard Dowden
Director
The Royal African Society
Former Africa Editor
The Economist

Good information is always important. When one is looking to do business in unfamiliar places, it is essential. Tony Okoromadu has done a remarkable job. The information is also beautifully and imaginatively displayed. This is a remarkable piece of work.

Martin Wolf
Chief Economics Commentator
Financial Times
London

The book both sheds light on the commercial realities of an important region of the continent and provides a guiding hand to investors.

Drawing on verified sources of information, Tony Okoromadu has added value to these with a lively, colourful and insightful interpretation. His novel approach both sets today's statistics in a recognisable context and clearly improves the landscape for decision-making. International investors and governments alike should welcome this as an important contribution.

Baroness Lynda Chalker
Former Cabinet Minister
United Kingdom Government

Not only does this study bring all the essential data together in one place, it makes sense of the statistics, pointing out the trends, strengths and weaknesses that lie behind the figures. Here at last is reliable factual material, superbly presented and interpreted in a way that makes it immediately understandable. Anyone with a serious interest in the region will need and value this rare commodity.

David White
Former Africa Editor
Financial Times
London

Tony Okoromadu has compiled an indispensable tool. The target audience is foreign investors, government and development agencies. The format is easy-to-use, making the content readily comprehensible to a wider public.

The value added here is that you have all key indicators of performance between the covers of one book. The information, culled from the multilateral development agencies, is presented in the form of indicators, tables and charts.

This manual deserves to become a standard reference for many years to come.

Jonathan Story
Emeritus Professor of International Political Economy
INSEAD, France

This is a unique and impressive compendium of key business environmental indicators. The information will be invaluable to a wide audience including economists, investment analysts, government departments, foreign investors etc. It is up to date and presented in a user-friendly and non-technical manner, representing a new and refreshing approach to country analyses.

Joe Nellis
Professor of International Management Economics
Cranfield University School of Management
United Kingdom

An Unconventional Introduction to

DEVELOPMENT ECONOMICS

A lively and user-friendly case studies method using hundreds of real-life macroeconomic scenarios from 52 countries

15 years **200** socio-economic concepts and indicators **600** full-color charts **200** full-color tables **100,000** data points **100's** of empirical analyses

Tony Okoromadu

To Lisa - my wife, belovéd, best friend, and indispensable accomplice at life

frontdesk@graffiticoncept.com

ISBN 9780956452610

All the information and data applied in the book are available in the public domain, and acknowledgement of source has been made at every turn.

:Graffiti:

Contents

Contents

Contents

Indicators & Sources

Continent Overview

GDP real growth
GDP real growth, % change
GDP per person ($US)
Growth in $US GDP per person
GDP per person ($PPP)
Growth in $PPP GDP per person
GNI per person ($US)
Growth in $US GNI per person
GNI per person ($PPP)
Growth in $PPP GNI per person
Value added in agriculture as % of GDP
Growth in value added in agriculture
Value added in agriculture as $US per person
Growth in $US value added in agriculture per person
Value added in industry as % of GDP
Growth in value added in industry
Value added in industry as $US per person
Growth in $US value added in industry per person
Value added in services as % of GDP
Growth in value added in services
Value added in services as $US per person
Growth in $US value added in services per person
Average interest on new external debt commitments
Average maturity on new external debt commitments
Debt service on external debt as $US per person
Interest payments on external debt (% of GNI)
Interest payments on external debt as $US per person
Exchange rate volatility
Inflation level, average annual (CPI)
Inflation, year-on-year change
Debt service as % of exports
Debt service: interest and amortization, as $US per person
General government gross debt as % of GDP
General government revenue as % of GDP
General government total expenditure as % of GDP
General government surplus/deficit as % of GDP
Exports of goods and services as % of GDP
Exports of goods and services as $US per person
Imports of goods and services as % of GDP
Imports of goods and services as $US per person
External debt stocks as % of GNI
Net official development assistance as % of GNI
Net official development assistance and aid as $US/person
Total reserves as % of total external debt
Total reserves as months of imports
Total reserves as $US per person
Growth in per person $US total reserves
Current account balance as % of GDP
Current account balance as $US per person
Gross national savings as % of GDP
Terms of trade in goods and services
Terms of trade in goods and services, year-on-year change
Bank liquid reserves to assets ratio
Commercial bank branches per 100,000 adults
Domestic credit provided by financial sector as % of GDP
Domestic credit to private sector as % of GDP
Domestic credit to private sector by banks as % of GDP
Foreign direct investment, $US
Foreign direct investment per person, $US
Growth in $US foreign direct investment per person
Foreign direct investment as % of GDP
Year-on-year change of %GDP Foreign direct investment
Foreign direct investment as % of gross fixed capital formation
Year-on-year change of %GFCF foreign direct investment
Foreign direct investment as % of goods and services trade
Year-on-year change of %goods and services fdi
Foreign direct investment as % of goods trade
Year-on-year change of %goods fdi
Gross private sector capital formation as $US per person
Growth in per person $US private sector capital formation
Gross private sector capital formation as % of GDP
Price level ratio of PPP to market exchange rate
Year-on-year change in price level ratio
Household final consumption in $US per person
Growth in $US household final consumption per person
Household final consumption as % of GDP
Year-on-year change in %GDP Household final consumption
Wired broadband subscriptions per 100 people
Fixed telephone subscriptions per 100 people
Mobile cellular subscriptions per 100 people
Secure internet servers per 1 million people
Internet users per 1,000 people
Cost of business start-up procedures as % of per person GNI
Cost to export, in $US per container
Cost to import, in $US per container
CPIA economic management cluster average
CPIA financial sector rating
CPIA property rights and rule-based governance rating
CPIA quality of budgetary and financial management rating
CPIA public sector transparency, accountability and corruption rating
World Bank ease of doing business ranking in the world
Total tax rate as % of commercial profits

West Africa & its Countries

Land mass
Population
Population age profile: percentages
Population age profiles: numbers
Population density
Urban population: percentages
Urban population: numbers
Urban population: growth rates
Rural population: percentages
Rural population: numbers
Rural population: growth rates
GDP, $PPP
Productivity index
Population: % of Sub-Saharan Africa
GDP: % of Sub-Saharan GDP
Female % of labour force

Quality of Life

Human development ranking
Life expectancy
Under-5 child mortality
% of 1-yr olds immunized against measles
% of 1-yr olds immunized against tuberculosis
% of Population with access to safe water
% of Population with access to sanitation
Phones per population (fixed & mobiles)
Mobile phones per population
Total adult literacy rate
Number of internet users
Personal computers per population
Net migration

Economic Strength

GDP contribution of Nigeria in Sub-Saharan Africa
GDP contribution of Nigeria in West Africa
GDP per person, $PPP
Growth in GDP per person
GNI per person, $PPP
Growth in GNI per person
Real GDP growth
Real non-oil GDP growth
Inflation
Movement of consumer prices
Exchange rate stability
Movement of real exchange rate

4. Economic Productivity

Country "productivity index"
Country economy "development status": GDP breakdown into the 3 sectors
Productivity in agriculture as % of GDP
Productivity in agriculture as $PPP per person
Growth in agriculture productivity
Productivity in industry as % of GDP
Productivity in industry as $PPP per person
Growth in industry productivity
Productivity in industry as $US per person
Breakdown of industry productivity into manufacturing and other industry productivity: %
Growth in $US industry productivity
Growth in $US manufacturing productivity
Growth in $US other industry productivity
Build-up of manufacturing productivity

Build-up of other industry productivity
Productivity in services as % of GDP
Productivity in services as $PPP per person
Growth in services productivity
Build-up of Agriculture productivity
Build-up of Industry productivity
Build-up of Services productivity

Govt. Earnings & Spending

Fiscal deficit/surplus, % of GDP
Fiscal deficit/surplus as $PPP per person
Govt. earnings as % of GDP
Govt. earnings as $PPP per person
Govt. spending as % of GDP
Govt. spending as $PPP per person
Growth in govt. earnings per person
Build-up in govt. earnings
Build-up in govt. spending
Current account balance as % of GDP
Debt service as % of GNI
Build-up in debt service
Build-up in GNI

Spending on Health

Total spending on health as % of GDP
Govt. spending on health as % of GDP
Private spending on health as % of GDP
Total spending on health as $PPP per person
Govt. spending on health as $PPP per person
Private spending on health as $PPP per person
Build-up of govt. spending on health
Build-up of private spending on health
Govt. spending on health as % of total govt. spending
Out-of-pocket spending on health as % of total health spending
Out-of-pocket spending on health as part of total spending on health per person, $PPP
Out-of-pocket spending on health as % of private health spending

Purchasing Power

Govt. consumption as % of GDP
Household consumption as % of GDP
Govt. consumption as $PPP per person
Household consumption as $PPP per person
Growth of govt. consumption per person
Growth of household consumption per person
Build-up of govt. consumption per person
Build-up of household consumption per person

Self-Reliance

Total exports per person of population
Total imports per person of population
Goods and services exports, %
Goods and services imxports, %
Total exports as % of GDP
Total imports as % of GDP
Growth in goods exports per person
Growth in goods imports per person
Build-up of goods exports per person
Build-up of goods imports per person
Growth in services exports per person
Growth in services imports per person
Build-up of services exports per person
Build-up of services imports per person
Net goods exports per person
Net services exports per person
Composition of goods exports and imports
Composition of services exports and imports
Foreign reserves as months of imports
Foreign debt as % of GDP
Foreign debt as $PPP per person
Service of foreign debt as % of exports
Growth rate of debt
Growth rate of income
Build-up of debt
Build-up of income
Foreign aid as % of GDP
Foreign aid as $PPP per person

Investor Confidence

FDI as % of GDP
FDI as $US per person
Growth in FDI per person
FDI as % of total capital investment
Total capital investment as % of GDP
Total capital investment as $US per person
Growth in total capital investment per person
Private component of TCI as % of GDP
Public component of TCI as % of GDP
Private component of TCI as $PPP per person
Public component of TCI as $PPP per person
Growth of private component of TCI
Growth of public component of TCI
Build-up of private component of TCI
Build-up of public component of TCI
Domestic credit to the private sector as % of GDP
Domestic credit to the private sector in $PPP
Growth in domestic credit to the private sector

Regulatory Environment

Ease of starting a business: rank
Ease of starting a business: no. of days
Ease of starting a business: no. of procedures
Ease of dealing with construction permits: rank
Ease of dealing with construction permits: no. of days
Ease of dealing with construction permits: no. of procedures
Ease of employing workers: rank
Ease of employing workers: ease of hiring
Ease of employing workers: flexibility of hours
Ease of employing workers: ease of firing
Ease of employing workers: cost of firing
Ease of registering property: rank
Ease of registering property: no. of procedures
Ease of registering property: no. of days
Ease of registering property: cost
Ease of getting credit: rank
Extent of investor protection: rank
Extent of investor protection: disclosure index
Extent of investor protection: liability index
Extent of investor protection: shareholder suits index
Ease of paying taxes: rank
Ease of paying taxes: no. of payments
Ease of paying taxes: time required
Ease of paying taxes: % tax on profits
Ease of paying taxes: % labour tax and contributions
Ease of paying taxes: other taxes
Ease of paying taxes: total tax rate
Ease of external trade: rank
Ease of external trade: cost to export one container
Ease of external trade: cost to import one container
Ease of external trade: no. of documents needed to export
Ease of external trade: no. of documents needed to import
Ease of external trade: no. of days for export
Ease of external trade: no. of days for import
Ease of enforcing contracts: rank
Ease of enforcing contracts: no. of procedures
Ease of enforcing contracts: time in days
Ease of enforcing contracts: cost
Ease of closing a business: rank
Ease of closing a business: recovery rate
Ease of doing business: rank

Business Friendliness

Index of economic freedoms: rank
Personal income tax rate
Corporate tax rate
Voice and accountability: rank
Political stability: rank
Govt. effectiveness: rank
Regulatory quality: rank
Rule of law: rank
Control of corruption: rank

(Shown in red are the indicators that go towards the BiA Index, Rankings and Ratings. Introduced and explained in both the book's introduction and its appendices.)

Sources:

African Development Bank AfDB
The Heritage Foundation/The Wall Street Journal
International Bank for Reconstruction and Development IBRD
International Finance Corporation IFC
International Monetary Fund IMF
International Telecommunication Union ITU
United Nations Children's Fund UNICEF
United Nations Conference on Trade and Development UNCTAD
United Nations Development Programme UNDP
United Nations Population Division UNPD
The World Bank
World Health Organisation WHO
World Trade Organisation WTO

Abstract

Rather than present development economics by introducing and explaining theories and concepts, this volume introduces the topic through the lens of a business investor exploration. Using the 52 developing countries of Africa as background, the reader is led to explore and analyze the major aspects of their economic environments over a combined period of 15 years. In so doing, various mechanisms, concepts and theories are utilized and they are introduced and explained at every step. This way, the reader becomes acquainted with the intricacies of development economics in a practical manner that involves real-life economic and business scenarios. Not only do they learn and grasp economic concepts and theories, they also learn how these work and when to deploy them. They should come away with a vivid understanding of development economics and developing countries characteristics, all of this experienced in an engaging, vibrant, graphically attractive and user-friendly process.

The book starts out with the conviction and basic premise that economic concepts are too often portrayed as nuclear science equivalent subject matter: they are presented as overly complicated and become perceived as an area that is closed off to anyone without an advanced degree in complex sounding fields like Game and Bargaining Theory and Experimental Quantitative Mathematical Econometrics. Whereas, even though some reasonable foundation in economic concepts is necessary and useful, a good chunk of economics (especially macroeconomics) is accessible to anyone with the interest and curiosity. It is the intent of this book to introduce macroeconomics to the reader and show that economics can indeed be a good friend with interesting stories to tell. The book has been devised as an innovative way of understanding basic applied macroeconomics in a quantitative context rather than theoretical burrowing, all this done in the background of a development economics framework.

Possibly the first things noticed about this volume are its vivid colors and exciting appearance. That is deliberate. A pivotal plank on which the project was built is that it had to be invigorating and inviting to read. It had to win the first challenge, which is to pull the observer inwards – quickly – and to keep them there. In this light, of particular consequence are the incisive and pithy commentaries that accompany the analyses outcomes on every page.

The second pivotal plank was this: that the project's aesthetics and engagement with the reader must not compromise its depth, exhaustiveness and thoroughness. That its contents, side-by-side with their engaging presentation, must be of the highest and most rigorous academic and analytical standards. We are confident the book works well on both counts, firmly supported and kept confidently upright by those two pivots.

Introduction

Development Economics or *Economics of Development*? Sometimes these two framings come across as different propositions. But they need not. Nevertheless, when they are merged into one same definition, they still appear unclear and their contents and boundaries somewhat ambiguous. In our view (which is the formulation followed in this book), while the two formulations might indeed be distinct (especially when one approaches the topics involved to a microscopically detailed level), usually they would be essentially the same. This would be the case for the audience to which this book is addressed.

Development Economics examines the characteristics found among countries that are classified as "developing" or "emerging" or, stretching it a bit, "transition". These countries tend to face challenges and operating contexts that are not found in the developed countries/economies. One such glaring characteristic, for example, is the challenge posed by the absence of reliable socio-economic data on many fronts. Another is poorly developed infrastructure. Yet another is a fragile system of government stability and structure; and another, a fragile system of institutions, legal and commercial structures, socio-political foundations, and so on. All these combined make their economic experiences and trajectories considerably different and somewhat less predictable than those obtaining in the developed countries. On the one hand, this makes their study considerably taxing (or frustrating, as some might rather characterize it), but on another, it makes it compellingly more interesting, which is the perspective we take in this book.

When studying each country as a standalone, it is possible to encounter results that are in themselves insightful and hugely important. Yet, we argue that this isn't enough: it is just as vital to study these economies in the context of their geographical and cultural counterparts: the other countries that are linked to them by geography, culture, proximity, language or other characteristics that combine to have them usually considered as country blocs. Hence, a Brazil should be studied within the context of Latin America, and a Nigeria within the context of sub-Saharan Africa. This is important – and we allude to this several times in this book – because studying a Brazil would be incomplete without comparatively assessing it within the context of the other countries in its bloc.

In other words, for an accurate evaluation of a developing country's economic outcomes, it is our view that the country must be evaluated within the context of its continent (or whatever is its conventional countries aggregate bloc). Our way of approaching this is to develop an empirical index that aggregates country socio-economic indices as proportionate outcomes with respect to the general performance of the country group. So, for example, we develop the BiA (Business in Africa) Index that will express the performance of each country relative to the rest of the continent. This (general economy) Index will have sub-Indices that go further and express the performance of each country in specific areas: for example, economic strength, self-reliance, depth of financial sector, foreign investment, etc. Together, these indices and the consequent country rankings will provide observers with a holistic picture of what each country's economic and business prospects are. By having a historical portrait of country Index performance, a clear outline can be obtained of how each country has measured up to its counterparts in its country bloc over time.

This approach to development economics is unusual but, in our opinion, long overdue. It proposes an in-depth study and evaluation of a country's socio-economic experience, while placing this in the comparative context of the country's counterparts in order to present a more accurate and precise assessment of that country's success, failure or underperformance, and the lessons to be drawn from these.

That said, it is hugely important that this system accommodates and adjusts for issues that might otherwise distort results, such as:

- country level internal positive or negative factors that might heavily distort the picture of country performance (for example, civil unrest during the period)
- systemic external positive or negative factors that might do similar (for example, the 80s debt crises, 00s world recession, etc.), and
- internal socio-economic factors that might pose significant but distorting advantages (for example, a particular country's lucrative natural resources that might mask internal structural inefficiencies)

The ensuing process and methods towards these ends are further explained in Part I - Continent Overview, as well as in the Appendices.

In a word, to carry out proper development economics work, countries should not be studied in isolation but must be placed in the context of their counterparts and the defining perimeters of time and events. We hope this book illustrates a way of doing that. As earlier mentioned, it confronts the topic from the platform of the African countries, examining each one of the 52 (more often, the 48 of sub-Saharan Africa, as will be explained) in depth, while evaluating them within the context of the group's experience, trajectory and performance.

The book's structure

The book is divided into 3 areas. Part I: Continent Overview; Part II: Economic and Business Analyses; and Part III: Appendices

Continent Overview section puts the continent in world context and presents the economic and social conditions of the 52 countries to some specific detail. This section will serve as a brief general introduction to the typical socioeconomic context within which developing countries operate. In this instance, the 52 African countries are assessed across a 15-year period using dozens of social, economic and business indicators, and then situated in a world context by comparing them alongside aggregate outcomes for Europe, USA and Latin America. The section presents a first opportunity to encounter some major economic and business concepts and introduces the country performance index mentioned in the introduction.

One of its chapters - **The Subcontinent** - dives down into general introductory details about the 48 sub-Saharan Africa countries and their socioeconomic situations.

Most of the book proceeds by focusing to greater detail on the 48 countries of sub-Saharan Africa (SSA) instead of all 52 countries of Africa, for the following reason. Africa is generally divided into 5 regions: Central Africa (9 countries), East Africa* (19 countries), North Africa (5 countries), Southern Africa (5 countries) and West Africa (16 countries). These regions together, with the exception of North Africa, make up sub-Saharan Africa. For economics and business purposes, by convention, the World Bank and other multilateral agencies consider the 5 North Africa countries (Algeria, Egypt, Libya, Morocco, Tunisia) alongside the countries of the Middle East, since they are considered to share more in common (socially, culturally, etc) with those countries than with the rest of Africa (sub-Saharan Africa). Hence the acronym often seen in economic, business and other international circles: MENA - Middle East and North Africa. In that wise, sub-Saharan Africa is usually studied as its own subcontinent, since it is considered to be more homogenous for comparison purposes.

Some knotty issues are also briefly explored in this section, as they affect the continent's 48 economies. Issues like the effect of population growth, the experienced relationship between foreign aid and economic development, the effect of economic growth on quality of life, and so on. That sub-chapter is called *Tricky Relations* and what it does is compile and compare data on those various connections and then draw conclusions from the emerging picture.

Economic and Business Analyses: 11 Chapters with closing analyses and submissions. This section is the largest part of the book and the most detailed. It analyses the 48 sub-Saharan Africa countries across hundreds of socio-economic and business indicators, and again across a number of years. This is important, as it helps identify trends and avoids the possible inaccuracy of interpreting development economics material by inspecting only static points in time. The section often proceeds by assuming the study is being done from the perspective of West Africa; this allows the opportunity to delve into even greater subject matter detail for a section of the continent; proceeding to the same level of detail for every country of the continent would require many more pages, unrealistic for a book of this already considerable size. Thus, the narrator, as it were, is the group of 16 countries who compare their economic outcomes to the rest of the continent and either applaud or lament, all the while guiding the reader through their stories and explaining the economic concepts and criteria.

Much of this sub-continent's trajectory is tracked from the perspective of its largest economy - Nigeria. In many cases, the country's trajectory over the time period is traced and illustrated with charts that timeline its progress. For every indicator, Nigeria's performance and position in Africa and West Africa is highlighted. The "running commentary" that trails through every chapter is a guided tour telling West Africa's story from the Nigeria perspective. Also, Nigeria being a major oil exporter, another set of tables compares its experience with that of Africa's other major oil exporters during the same time periods.

This part of the book is divided into 11 chapters that serve like stops on a tour around development economics. The many economic terms and concepts have been separated across the chapters as deemed appropriate. So, for example, the Economic Strength chapter involves GDP, GNI, inflation, exchange rates, etc; while the Productivity chapter involves industry output, agriculture output, services output, etc; Purchasing Power involves government and household consumption; Self-Reliance involves exports, imports, foreign debt, aid dependency; and so on.

Each chapter begins with a "Primer" section that explains the theory behind the economic concepts to be used in that chapter and is designed to be brief and concise. The scrupulous data-crunching of the myriad indices follows in the sub-chapters and the outcomes are every time illustrated in an engaging way.

The major implications and deductions from the charts and trends that emerge are explained with pithy yet incisive running commentaries, as it were, usually in the style of Post-it notes or even phone text message exchanges. But these deductions are by no means exhaustive: closer and closer scrutiny will almost always throw up yet more inferences.

We do not expect that every step will come easy to the reader, but the chapters presentation is such that anybody with a fundamental appreciation of broad economic concepts should feel carried along through every stage. Every chapter has a very strong user-friendly feel to it.

The chapters close with two one-page summation sections:

- *Leaders & Stragglers*: a section that involves the evaluation and ranking of country performance across the chapter's indicators. It leads to the rankings table at the chapter's end. (At the end of the book, all the countries are again evaluated and ranked, this time according to their performance across all of the so-labelled "critical" indices involved in all of the book's chapters.)

- *Wrap-up*: a closing and broad look at the chapter, tracing the overall performance of Nigeria by comparing it with the best overall performing country from West Africa. It does so by comparing the two countries' outcomes across all the major indicators in that chapter.

The Appendices collect together in one place, divided along chapter lines, the comprehensive ranking of all 48 sub-Saharan Africa countries after their stress tests and comprehensive analyses as covered in the preceding chapters. Every major economic indicator introduced and used throughout the book is included here, with the performance of each country within the analysis time frame shown under it. They are 66 pages with 264 tables. The appendices also start out with a section explaining some of the methodology involved in the country aggregate performance Index evaluation.

200 Indicators, 660+ Tables, 200+ Charts, 48 Countries, 12 Years

These case studies are quite possibly the most comprehensive and in-depth body of country analyses ever attempted for Sub-Saharan Africa.

They employ data from the multilateral development agencies like the World Bank, IMF, UNDP, UNCTAD, etc., and analyze this across several hundreds of macro and socio-economic indicators. In the end they produce a body of work that is a comparative dissection and examination of the trends within these country-economies during the respective time period. The sources of data employed are always identified at every turn.

Perhaps the most striking feature of this work is the way it presents and analyses the myriad economic sectors and activities; the way it employs specific and seemingly complex barometers and indicators, and yet makes certain that the procedures and import of their findings are as easily understood by the reader as is feasible.

Rather than use one year's performance as basis for assessment, blocks of 4-year moving averages are used almost everywhere, instead. It is considered that these moving averages should produce a more accurate and balanced reading of country performance.

Whatever the case, the eventual outcomes provide reliable enough grounds on which to assess a particular country's comparative strengths and weaknesses in the short to medium term.

Per-Capita Calibration

As much as possible, the indices and quantities used have been expressed in ratios, usually percentages of GDP and per person bases; reason being that applying solely absolute size could easily be misleading.

For example, ranking countries according to the total volume of foreign direct investment might well bring out the countries with the largest FDI portfolios, but it would say little about whether these countries are matching their potential, or about what scope there might still be for growth, until the same FDI is expressed as investment per person of population, or as a percentage of country GDP.

The same is perhaps even more easily seen in the evaluation of country output, GDP. Absolute size does matter (large economies have the advantages of their huge resources outlays being readily available) but only to a point; because it speaks much more about the respective economy and its efficiency and potential, when that GDP is expressed in per person terms. Both senses (per population and as percentage GDP) are used throughout the book and help provide more balanced and representative conclusions.

Purchasing Power Parity Dollars

Wherever possible, monetary value has been expressed in $PPP. This is the format most favored in economic evaluations when cross-country comparisons are to be made.

$PPP represents a (theoretical) monetary currency that has the same value everywhere, because it weeds out the effects of price movements and so on, across borders. Thus, one PPP dollar would have exactly the same value in every country. In other words, one PPP dollar in the Republic of Congo would purchase the exact same quantities of goods as it would in Sierra Leone and South Africa.

More about this is explained in the introduction to chapter 8, Economic Strength.

The BiA Index ™

The Business in Africa - BiA [Bee-eye-ay] - Index, as a measure, is explained in Appendix A. It is evaluated using the 56 indicators classed as "critical" among the 200 involved in the overall analyses in this volume. These 56 are identified in their respective chapters by the BiA sign rendered in white inside a small red rectangular box.

—-

* Sometimes Sudan is considered part of East Africa; at other times, especially for economic data, it is considered on its own. For most of this book, it is considered on its own but grouped (as it were, "caucusing") along with Southern Africa. It also comprises both the present-day Sudan and the (new) breakout country South Sudan, since there wasn't enough reliable data for South Sudan at the time of the analyses to consider it separately.

The IMF tends to include Sudan, Djibouti and Mauritania in "Middle East and Central Asia". While the World Bank includes all three in sub-Saharan Africa. We have followed the Bank's classification here.

Sub-Saharan Africa aggregate data often do not include Zimbabwe and Somalia, because of the volatile and out-of-sync situations there during the time period.

How to use this book

The book's purpose is to teach the foundations of development economics, employing the countries of Africa as case studies. Using real data and real territories and real time period snapshots of these economies, the teaching platform is a macroeconomic country competition in which the countries compete for the most robust economy, according to 56 determined "critical" socio-economic indicators chosen as parameters from the overall 200 socio-economic and business indicators involved in the book.

Most of the book is dedicated to a deep exploration of individual countries as well as country groups and should help communicate the socio-economic and business dynamics often encountered in development economics. While this branch of economic study will vary in its specific characteristics from one region of the world to another, the basic features that describe and distinguish them from developed economies are common across continents.

The specific studies shown in this book may not correspond to more recent calendar periods, but that is unimportant. What is important is that the studies and comparisons and trends illustrate how to approach the assessment of developing economies. Once those skills of contextualizing, measuring, analytically interpreting, etc., are cultivated, it will not be difficult to understand and evolve policy for developing countries, thinking innovatively and out-of-the-box when necessary.

Teachers and instructors might take advantage of the country comparative studies and charts to illustrate how to read a country's economy and how to determine which quantitative measures might be relevant, and which not. It will also help illustrate when and how improvisation must be done where information is inadequate – a predicament not as prevalent in the case of developed economies.

Students will benefit from spotting and interpreting scenarios gleaned from the data and charts, and attempting to devise socio-economic policy based on the country's trajectory and experiences.

While the book is not heavy on theory material, the fact that it introduces, explains and deploys the necessary theoretical foundations is an advantage: the student quickly comes to grips with the tools required and immediately applies that foundational conceptual basis to the economic outcomes represented and illustrated in the tables, figures and charts. It should help them learn the tools of reading a developing country's characteristics, travel direction, immediate versus non-critical shortcomings and enunciate policy strategies arising from there.

The different sections of the book can be approached as if they were submissions made by commissioned consultants. The student may wear the cap of client, consultant, student, policy formulator, government official, or whatever appropriate function. The book should also serve as an effective tool for instructor-led class discussions as well as assignments and essay research tasks.

That said, besides the education sector, this volume will also be useful to business, government and development agency communities.

Part I

Continent Overview

1. Where would your business go in Africa?

Background

You are Chief of Strategy at a large corporate organization and your team is considering expanding into Africa. This is a region of the world classified as "developing economies" (sometimes also as "emerging economies"). You know there are 54 countries within that continent and you need to familiarize yourself with the economic characteristics of developing regions in order to inform your strategy choices.

You employ consultants who prepare the following material for you. They expect that it will be detailed yet broad enough to present the important characteristics of that section of the world such that your team may make adequately informed decisions. They also are assuming that members of your team have the basics of economics grounding, but are not taking that for granted. So, they say they have prepared their material in such a manner that it can be understood with a minimum of economics foundation.

Where Should Your Business Go in Africa?

The 12 most robust economies on the continent

An in-depth examination of the macroeconomic and business environments of 52 countries and their performance over 15 years, using 96 stress-test parameters.

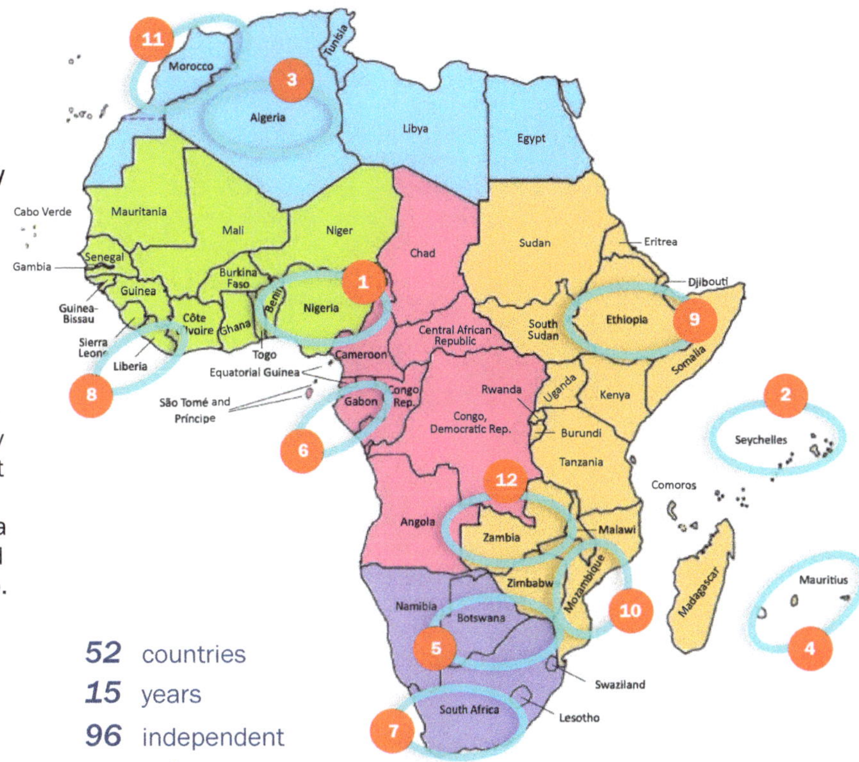

52 countries
15 years
96 independent parameters
100,000 data points
100's of empirical analyses

Twenty years ago, that question might have been deemed superfluous: only oil extracting conglomerates and other commodity hunters sailed for Africa, and they packed plenty lifeboats; they only half-expected — by some miracle — to land and set up in that mystifying business environment safely.

Then things started happening and, suddenly (well, not quite; "steadily" might be a better word) the "dark" continent didn't look so dark after all. For the past 15 years at least, Africa has outpaced the developed countries in economic growth rates. In the past 10 or so, those rates have been accompanied by a growing awareness within Africa that their continent must embrace better and sturdier institutional frameworks, for their own good. The result has been a solid march towards policies and practices that would only have been remotely glanced at, twenty years ago. True, there remain big impediments, and there are still one too many African strongmen in power; nevertheless, this looks to be the continent's time. And more and more international businesses are warming to that theme.

"Tick, tock, said the clock"

Since 2000, Africa has been growing at least twice as fast as the United States and the countries of the European Union. That trend doesn't look like stopping soon. The thirsty virgin territory that telecommunications investors have exposed has caught the eye of other industry sectors and there is a recognition now that, in spite of the poverty levels that attend the continent, there exist thriving middle class markets with ample consumer power. However, even though foreign investment has multiplied impressively over the recent decade, investment per person of population still indicates that there remain huge gaps to be serviced; and there is already a race to fill them. Yet the task, many fear, isn't for the fainthearted: "Where do we start?" is a question we often get, "There isn't reliable information out of that continent".

"Data, data, everywhere, yet not a drop to trust"

Or so it seems. We have been following Africa's economies closely for the past ten years and can confidently suggest that the quality of information out of the continent has been markedly improving. True, they are not at the levels of Europe or America, but there is enough information upon which to assess its countries and base sound business decisions. That is what this study has done: the **Business in Africa (BiA) Index** is a composite empirical evaluation of each country's macroeconomic and business conditions. It involves more than one hundred thousand data points, fifteen years, ninety-six independent parameters and hundreds of mathematical and empirical analyses. This is quite possibly the most thorough comparative evaluation of the continent's 54 countries currently available. To maintain accuracy and objectivity of the evaluations, we have not used data from national statistics offices (usually their Office of Statistics and Central Banks); instead we have restricted information to four multilateral agencies — the World Bank, IMF, United Nations Conference on Trade and Development (UNCTAD) and, for a relatively much smaller sample, the African Development Bank (AfDB) — hoping in this way to avoid biases that might be expected from information collected by national agencies about themselves.

"One king to rule them all"

The purpose here is an ambitious one: to develop an empirical Index by which the economic performance of African countries can be evaluated. Our **Business in Africa Index** expresses the overall performance of each country relative to the rest of the continent. It has sub-Indices that express each country's performance in ten major areas: general size, economic productivity, economic agility, government finances, self-reliance, depth of financial sector, investor confidence, purchasing power, infrastructure, and business friendliness. Together, they provide a holistic picture of what each country's economic and business prospects are. The overall **BiA Index** expresses, in clear, objective and empirical terms, the robustness of each country's economy relative to its 51 counterparts on the continent. All of Africa's 54 economies are involved here, except South Sudan (too recent, it's a new country) and Somalia (non-functioning state). All of them have been put through a rigorous wringer and explored upwards, downwards, sideways and edgeways: quite likely the most rigorous macro stress tests you will come across involving the continent.

GDP Growth per Year (%)			2000-2004
USA	Europe	Latin America	sub-Sah Africa
2.7	*2.3*	*2.5*	*5.0*

			2005-2009
USA	Europe	Latin America	sub-Sah Africa
0.9	*0.9*	*3.4*	*5.2*

			2010-2014
USA	Europe	Latin America	sub-Sah Africa
2.2	*1.0*	*3.4*	*4.4*

Primary data: World Bank

The criteria are 96 adjudged critical economic indicators, chosen from a collection of more than 400, spanning more than 20 years. The analyses, by their methods, have protected against country level internal positive or negative factors that might heavily distort the picture of country performance (for example, civil unrest during the period), systemic external positive or negative factors that might do similar (for example, the 80s debt crises, 00s world recession, etc.), and internal socio-economic factors that might pose significant but distorting advantages (for example, a particular country's lucrative natural resources that might mask internal structural inefficiencies).

Foreign Investment as % of GDP:			2000-2004
USA	Europe	Latin America	sub-Sah Africa
1.4	*4.0*	*3.7*	*2.4*

			2005-2009
USA	Europe	Latin America	sub-Sah Africa
1.4	*3.6*	*3.8*	*3.5*

			2010-2014
USA	Europe	Latin America	sub-Sah Africa
1.2	*2.0*	*4.4*	*2.7*

Primary data: UNCTAD

In almost every case, these critical indicators are adapted and analyzed to enable a comparative evaluation of each country in the context of the continent. For example, rather than absolute numbers (say, GDP or FDI), ratios are employed (GDP per person, FDI per person, FDI as % of GDP). And so on. For the most part, ratios are the appropriate platform for comparison. Also importantly, rather than a snapshot of the countries' positions at a particular year or point in time, the countries are assessed across the preceding five years every time.

"Whoops, there it is!"

The result is an index that allows the objective comparing and ranking of 52 African countries according to their robustness and thus, investment potential. It is an assessment of each country's economic development and will serve as a verdict on their economic scoresheet. This brief report, in the coming sections, focuses on the Top 12: those countries that rank from 1 to 12 in the final performance stress-tests composite **BiA Index**. They are, in our estimation, the destinations that should earn rights of "first refusal" in terms of business investments or expansion. We have also tried to show, at each stage, comparable information for the USA, Europe (countries of the European Union) and Latin America (which here also includes the Caribbean).

And so, the top 6 economies are: Nigeria, The Seychelles, Algeria, Mauritius, Botswana and Gabon; followed by a next 6 of South Africa, Liberia, Ethiopia, Mozambique, Morocco and Zambia. All have been assessed based on their performance during 2010 to 2014. Nigeria on top isn't surprising and lends credence to what is by now — surely — one of the most labored clichés in international socio-economy: sort out Nigeria's corruption and inefficiency problems and that country will soar. South Africa is in 7th place mostly because of its poor performance in Productivity, Agility (particularly its currency's volatility) and the state of its Government Finances.

Liberia beats 44 other countries, admittedly thanks to essentially starting from zero and so, no-place-to-go-but-up; yet you have to admire the sound work of economy management that its leaders have carried out, because things could just as easily have gone the opposite way. In the Investor Confidence category, Liberia bested all the other 51 countries, Mozambique was second. The Seychelles were better than every other in Productivity, while of the overall Top 12, Gabon's Government Finances were in the best shape, even though The Republic of Congo and Comoros were ahead of it in first and second place in that category.

The bottom 12 overall were Malawi, Burundi, Comoros, Democratic Republic of Congo, Chad, Guinea, Guinea-Bissau, Zimbabwe, The Gambia, Eritrea, Central African Republic, and Djibouti.

This study is not a critique: it does not seek to provide remedies. What it does is offer a snapshot of the continent's economies as they stood in 2015, based on their stress-tested performance in the preceding years. In so doing, it will provide decision makers with a platform on which to plan the future by reviewing the past.

To the best of our knowledge, there isn't yet anywhere else, as comprehensive and rigorous a ranking as our **Business in Africa Index**. None provides a level comparable to its exhaustive macro-economy wide evaluations of country performance in Africa.■

Business in Africa Index

	2015	2014	Country	Region	score
	1	1	Nigeria	West Africa	0.523
▲	2	4	Seychelles	East Africa	0.511
▼	3	2	Algeria	North Africa	0.501
▼	4	3	Mauritius	East Africa	0.501
▲	5	6	Botswana	Southern Africa	0.494
▲	6	8	Gabon	Central Africa	0.488
▼	7	5	South Africa	Southern Africa	0.481
▲	8	12	Liberia	West Africa	0.478
▲	9	11	Ethiopia	East Africa	0.471
▲	10	13	Mozambique	East Africa	0.468
▼	11	7	Morocco	North Africa	0.466
▲	12	19	Zambia	East Africa	0.464
▼	13	9	Egypt	North Africa	0.462
▼	14	10	Ghana	West Africa	0.456
▼	15	14	Tanzania	East Africa	0.455
▲	16	18	Congo, Rep.	Central Africa	0.454
	17	17	Kenya	East Africa	0.454
▼	18	15	Rwanda	East Africa	0.453
▲	19	29	Sierra Leone	West Africa	0.450
▼	20	16	Cabo Verde	West Africa	0.448
▼	21	20	Tunisia	North Africa	0.446
▲	22	23	Benin	West Africa	0.437
▲	23	34	Mauritania	West Africa	0.433
▼	24	21	Uganda	East Africa	0.433
▲	25	28	Burkina Faso	West Africa	0.433
▼	26	24	Cameroon	Central Africa	0.431
▼	27	25	Niger	West Africa	0.428
▲	28	37	Togo	West Africa	0.425
▼	29	26	Angola	Central Africa	0.425
	30	30	Senegal	West Africa	0.423
▼	31	27	Mali	West Africa	0.422
▼	32	22	Libya	North Africa	0.420
▼	33	32	Lesotho	Southern Africa	0.420
▲	34	38	Cote d'Ivoire	West Africa	0.419
▲	35	42	Sao Tome & Prin.	Central Africa	0.419
▼	36	31	Namibia	Southern Africa	0.414
▼	37	36	Sudan	East Africa	0.414
▼	38	35	Swaziland	Southern Africa	0.412
▲	39	40	Madagascar	East Africa	0.402
▼	40	33	Equatorial Guinea	Central Africa	0.399
	41	41	Malawi	East Africa	0.391
▲	42	44	Burundi	East Africa	0.391
	43	43	Comoros	East Africa	0.389
▲	44	47	Congo, Dem. Rep.	Central Africa	0.388
	45	45	Chad	Central Africa	0.384
▲	46	48	Guinea	West Africa	0.379
▲	47	49	Guinea-Bissau	West Africa	0.372
▼	48	39	Zimbabwe	East Africa	0.372
▲	49	50	Gambia, The	West Africa	0.368
▼	50	46	Eritrea	East Africa	0.358
	51	51	Central African Rep.	Central Africa	0.325
	52	52	Djibouti	East Africa	0.324

Central Africa
East Africa
North Africa
Southern Africa
West Africa

Top 6 African economies for 2015
Next 6 African economies for 2015
Remainder 40 economies for 2015

1.1 General Size

One-fifth of the continent's economic output emanates from Nigeria. Between Nigeria, South Africa and Algeria, they produce half the continent's GDP.

Annual GDP during 2010-2014

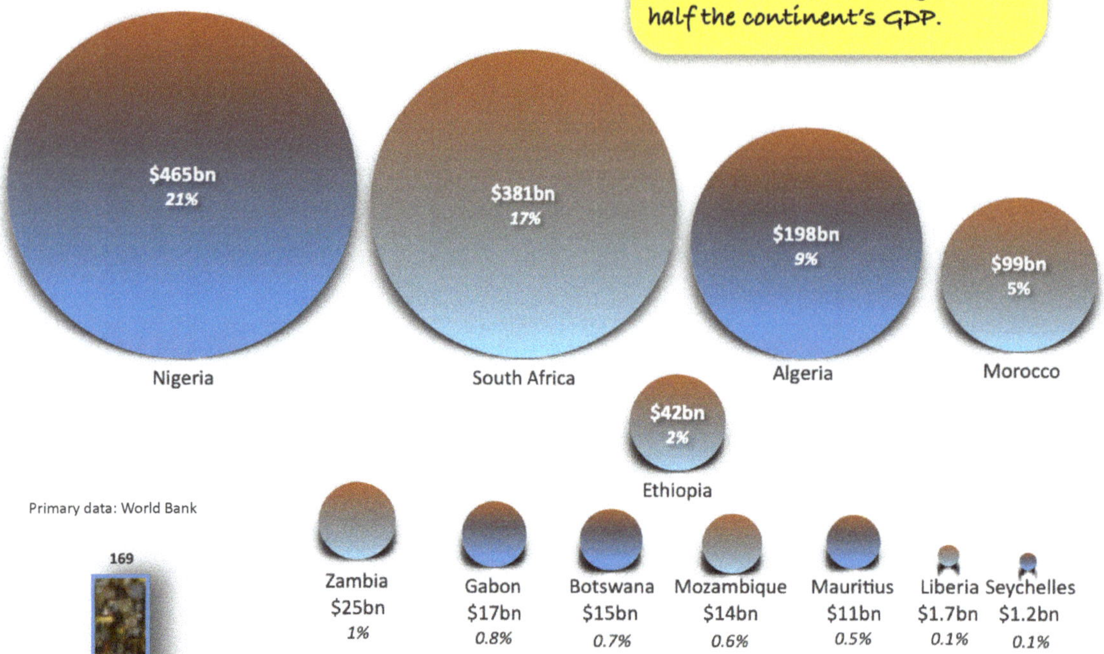

Primary data: World Bank

Average population during 2010-2014
millions

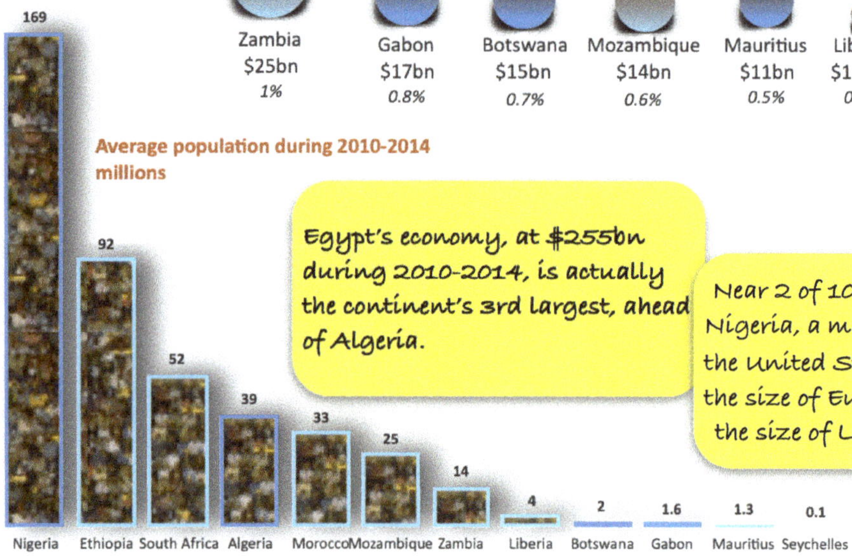

Egypt's economy, at $255bn during 2010-2014, is actually the continent's 3rd largest, ahead of Algeria.

Near 2 of 10 Africans lives in Nigeria, a market 1/2 the size of the United States, more than 1/3 the size of Europe, & more than 1/4 the size of Latin America.

Overall performance across all General Size parameters during the past 15 years

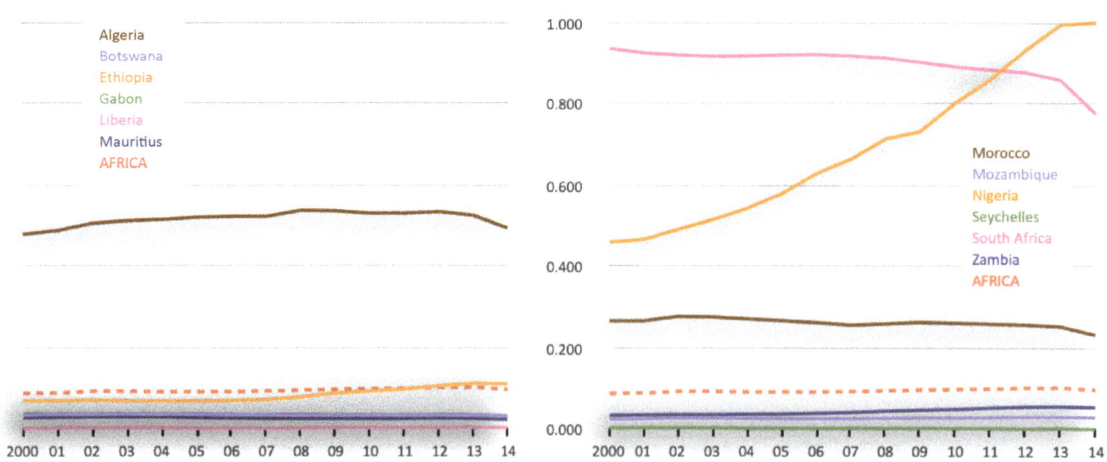

	2015	score
1	Nigeria	1.000
2	South Africa	0.776
3	Egypt	0.761
4	Algeria	0.494
5	Morocco	0.233
6	Angola	0.198
7	Sudan	0.154
8	Libya	0.134
9	Kenya	0.119
10	Ethiopia	0.111
11	Tunisia	0.111
12	Tanzania	0.102
13	Ghana	0.095
14	Cote d'Ivoire	0.064
15	Cameroon	0.063
16	Uganda	0.057
17	Zambia	0.055
18	Congo, Dem. Rep.	0.053
19	Botswana	0.033
20	Senegal	0.033
21	Gabon	0.032
22	Mozambique	0.030
23	Madagascar	0.028
24	Chad	0.027
25	Equatorial Guinea	0.026
26	Burkina Faso	0.026
27	Congo, Rep.	0.026
28	Zimbabwe	0.025
29	Namibia	0.025
30	Mali	0.025
31	Mauritius	0.024
32	Benin	0.018
33	Rwanda	0.017
34	Niger	0.016
35	Guinea	0.013
36	Mauritania	0.013
37	Malawi	0.012
38	Sierra Leone	0.009
39	Togo	0.009
40	Swaziland	0.008
41	Eritrea	0.007
42	Burundi	0.007
43	Lesotho	0.006
44	Central African Rep.	0.004
45	Cabo Verde	0.004
46	Liberia	0.004
47	Gambia, The	0.003
48	Seychelles	0.002
49	Guinea-Bissau	0.002
50	Djibouti	0.001
51	Comoros	0.001
52	Sao Tome & Prin.	0.001

- Top 6 African economies for 2015
- Next 6 African economies for 2015
- Remainder 40 economies for 2015

Parameters:
- GDP ($US)
- GDP ($PPP)
- GNI ($US)
- GNI ($PPP)

1.2 Productivity

In this section, 22 economic parameters went into assessing the economic output efficiency of the 52 countries, the most rigorous of the 10 sections in terms of running these countries through the analyses grinder.

Africa grew faster than the United States, Europe and Latin America during 2010-2014; the trend is poised to continue.

Liberia probably could go nowhere else but up, seeing as the country has had to be virtually rebuilt. Still, the impressive rates are a testament to the quality of economic mgt.

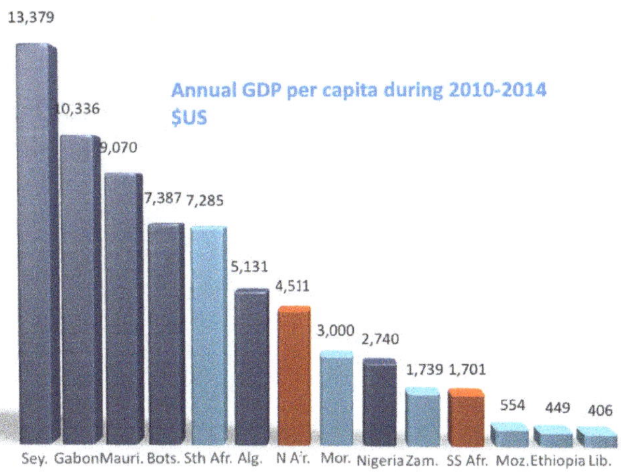

Primary data: World Bank

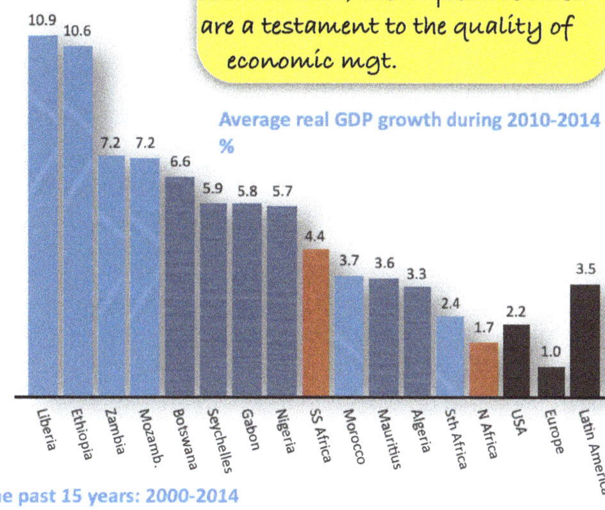

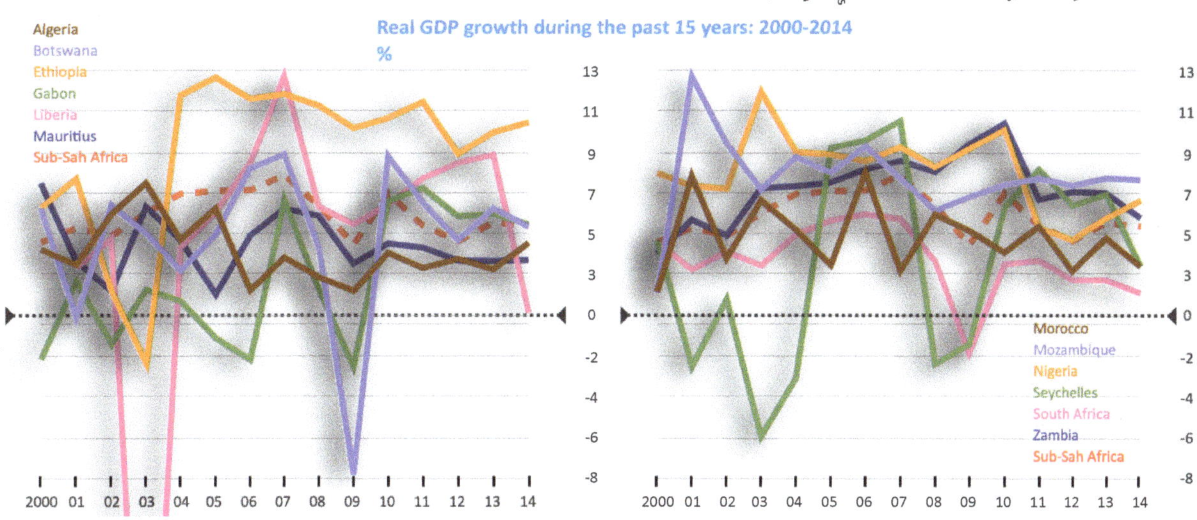

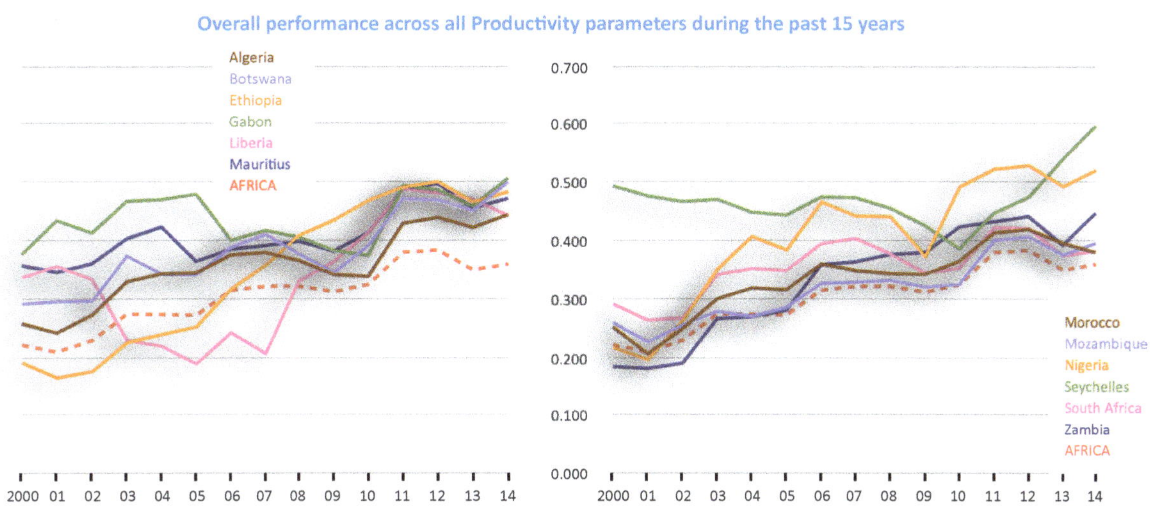

	2015	score
1	Seychelles	0.597
2	Nigeria	0.520
3	Gabon	0.507
4	Botswana	0.500
5	Ethiopia	0.483
6	Mauritius	0.472
7	Angola	0.462
8	Sierra Leone	0.458
9	Zambia	0.447
10	Algeria	0.444
11	Liberia	0.442
12	Ghana	0.440
13	Namibia	0.426
14	Zimbabwe	0.416
15	Congo, Rep.	0.410
16	Kenya	0.399
17	Tanzania	0.399
18	Mozambique	0.395
19	Egypt	0.395
20	Rwanda	0.394
21	Tunisia	0.389
22	Congo, Dem. Rep.	0.383
23	South Africa	0.382
24	Morocco	0.380
25	Togo	0.377
26	Sudan	0.373
27	Niger	0.373
28	Burkina Faso	0.373
29	Cote d'Ivoire	0.366
30	Lesotho	0.363
31	Mauritania	0.362
32	Cameroon	0.351
33	Uganda	0.335
34	Chad	0.334
35	Benin	0.334
36	Burundi	0.332
37	Swaziland	0.329
38	Cabo Verde	0.324
39	Mali	0.305
40	Comoros	0.295
41	Sao Tome & Prin	0.294
42	Guinea-Bissau	0.290
43	Malawi	0.281
44	Guinea	0.279
45	Senegal	0.278
46	Eritrea	0.258
47	Libya	0.252
48	Madagascar	0.244
49	Equatorial Guinea	0.240
50	Gambia, The	0.188
51	Djibouti	0.141
52	Central African Rep.	0.103

Top 6 African economies for 2015
Next 6 African economies for 2015
Remainder 40 economies for 2015

Parameters:
- GDP real growth
- GDP real growth, % change
- GDP per person ($US)
- Growth in $US GDP per person
- GDP per person ($PPP)
- Growth in $PPP GDP per person
- GNI per person ($US)
- Growth in $US GNI per person
- GNI per person ($PPP)
- Growth in $PPP GNI per person
- Value added in agriculture as % of GDP
- Growth in value added in agriculture
- Value added in agriculture as $US per person
- Growth in $US value added in agriculture per person
- Value added in industry as % of GDP
- Growth in value added in industry
- Value added in industry as $US per person
- Growth in $US value added in industry per person
- Value added in services as % of GDP
- Growth in value added in services
- Value added in services as $US per person
- Growth in $US value added in services per person

1.3 Agility

Exchange rate volatility is a bigger problem for South Africa & Zambia than for Nigeria, Morocco or Gabon. Only the last 2 had their currencies end 2014 higher than year 2000 levels.

This attempts to capture the flexibility with which the country can act in economic affairs, using mostly debt repayment burdens as criteria, along with inflation and exchange rates. It should be interpreted with caution, as Central African Republic tops the list most likely because of generous repayment terms it is offered due to its poverty levels. Nonetheless, Economic Agility is an asset that can be exploited for judicious economic planning. Strenuous debt repayment schedules can be huge weights dragging overall country performance back or, at the least, slowing it down. That said, debt leverage is an unavoidable economic necessity, even though that nimbleness is a good quality to have where possible: a jumbo jetliner may be less nimble than a small 12-seater plane, but it packs more people and is incomparably more powerful.

	2015	score
1	Central African Rep.	0.938
2	Burkina Faso	0.935
3	Mali	0.928
4	Niger	0.925
5	Benin	0.921
6	Uganda	0.911
7	Cameroon	0.909
8	Madagascar	0.908
9	Rwanda	0.908
10	Togo	0.899
11	Algeria	0.895
12	Kenya	0.894
13	Tanzania	0.893
14	Liberia	0.893
15	Senegal	0.889
16	Comoros	0.883
17	Nigeria	0.881
18	Congo, Rep.	0.877
19	Burundi	0.876
20	Cabo Verde	0.873
21	Mozambique	0.872
22	Djibouti	0.863
23	Equatorial Guinea	0.859
24	Lesotho	0.850
25	Morocco	0.850
26	Sao Tome & Prin.	0.844
27	Sierra Leone	0.842
28	Chad	0.841
29	Mauritania	0.838
30	Botswana	0.836
31	Eritrea	0.835
32	Zambia	0.832
33	Ethiopia	0.827
34	Gambia, The	0.824
35	Swaziland	0.818
36	Cote d'Ivoire	0.814
37	Ghana	0.806
38	Egypt	0.798
39	Guinea	0.785
40	Malawi	0.784
41	Congo, Dem. Rep.	0.780
42	Guinea-Bissau	0.767
43	Tunisia	0.754
44	Gabon	0.735
45	Namibia	0.726
46	Sudan	0.715
47	Angola	0.715
48	Mauritius	0.714
49	Zimbabwe	0.711
50	Libya	0.675
51	Seychelles	0.620
52	South Africa	0.607

Top 6 African economies for 2015
Next 6 African economies for 2015
Remainder 40 economies for 2015

Currency movements against the US dollar during the past 15 years: 2000=100

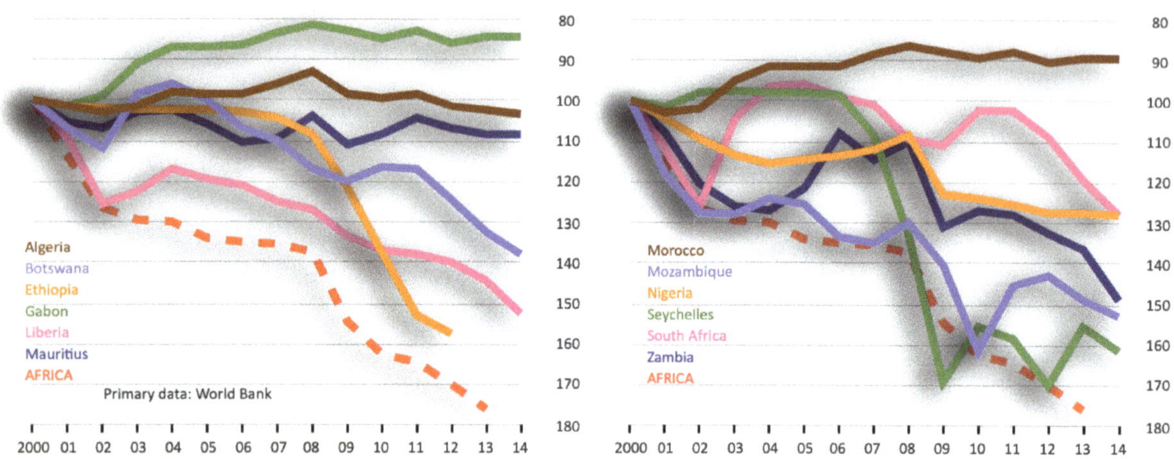

It should be noted that near half of the Latin America/ Caribbean countries have their currencies pegged to the US dollar, which does provide some relative stability.

Consumer prices movement during the past 15 years: 2000=100

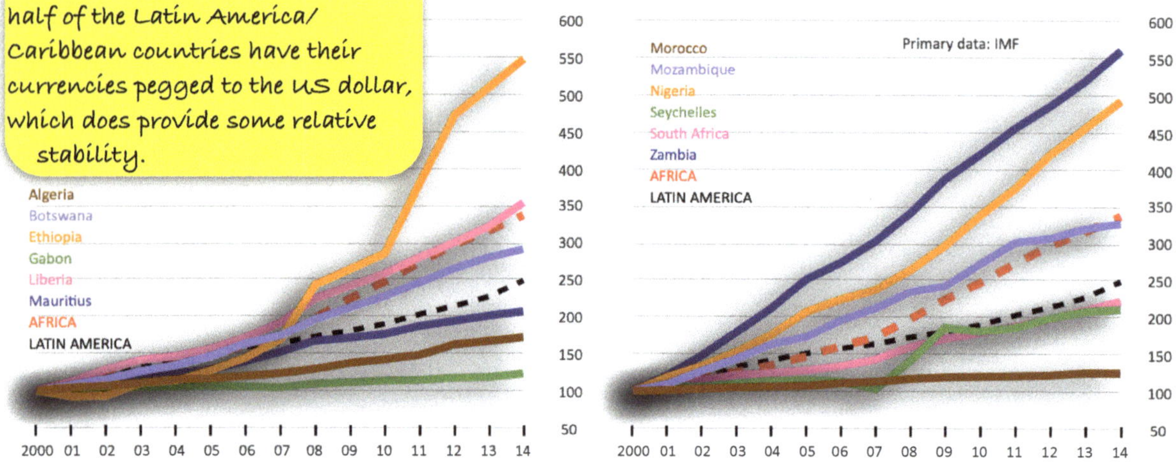

Overall performance across all Agility parameters during the past 15 years

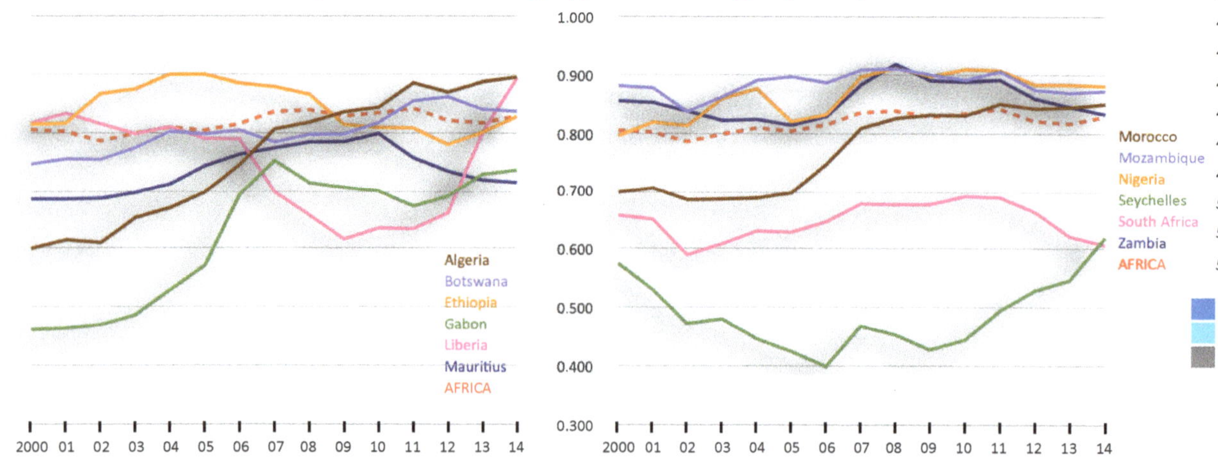

Parameters:
- Average interest on new external debt commitments
- Average maturity on new external debt commitments
- Debt service on external debt as $US per person
- Interest payments on external debt (% of GNI)
- Interest payments on external debt as $US per person
- Exchange rate volatility
- Inflation level, average annual (CPI)
- Inflation, year-on-year change
- Debt service as % of exports
- Debt service: interest and amortization, as $US per person

1.4 Govt. Finances

Government spending is a notoriously tricky — and volatile — subject every side of the Atlantic, but constitutional checks and balances in more developed economies generally keep it on a studied, even if delicate, keel. African economies seem to have gradually embraced more discipline, despite the absence in many instances of adequate institutional checks. It should be remembered here that racking up debt is not necessarily an ugly thing, and so, not an absolute measure of proficiency or the lack of it. The important factor is the use to which debt is put. If put to efficient ends, the results would tend to show in other areas of country **performance. For example, major** infrastructure is often capital intensive but can (should) result in improved efficiency of economic production, even if through roundabout means **(such as, for example,** improved living and work conditions producing improve**ments in labor productivity).**

Gabon has consistently run a surplus (it is a major oil producer). Botswana, the Seychelles and Nigeria just about keep it in there.

Since 2010 - except, perhaps, for Mozambique & Algeria - all Top 12 seem to have run a tight ship, not plunging significantly deeper into deficits.

General government gross debt as % of GDP during the past 5 years: 2010-2014

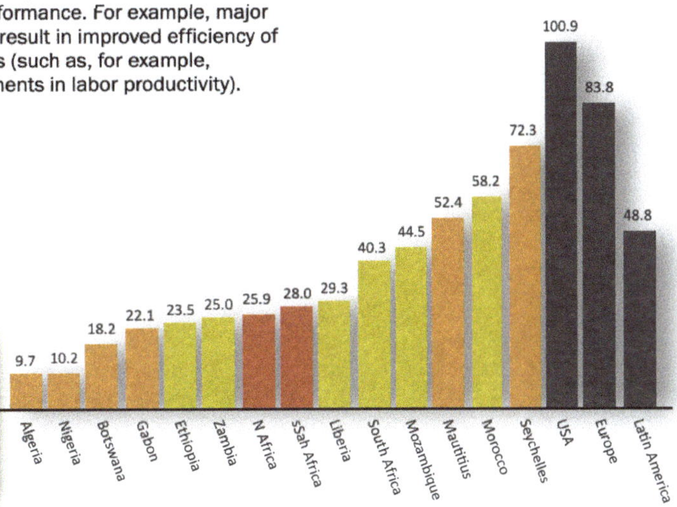

General government surplus/deficit as % of GDP during the past 15 years

Primary data: IMF

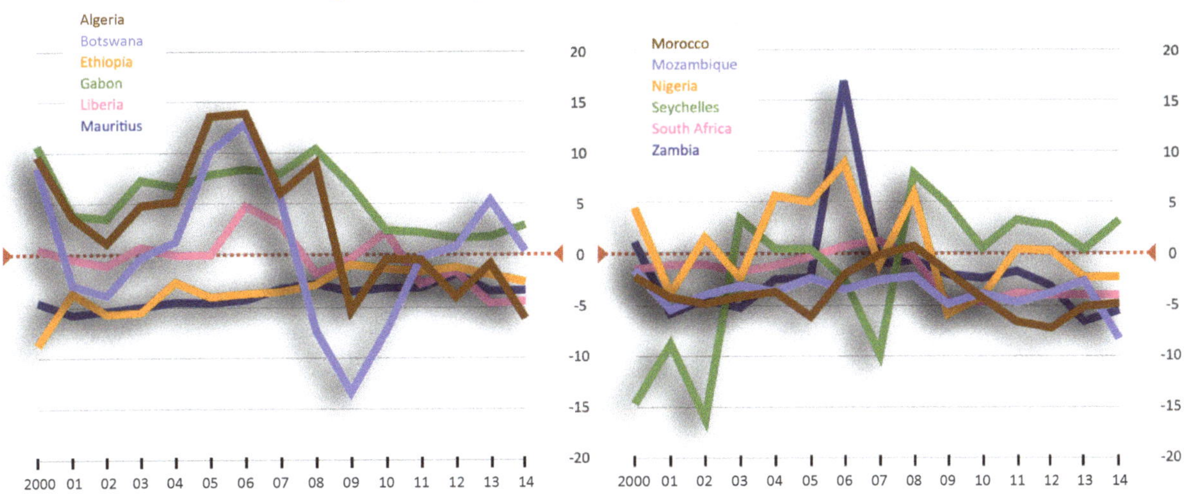

Overall performance across all Govt. Finances parameters during the past 15 years

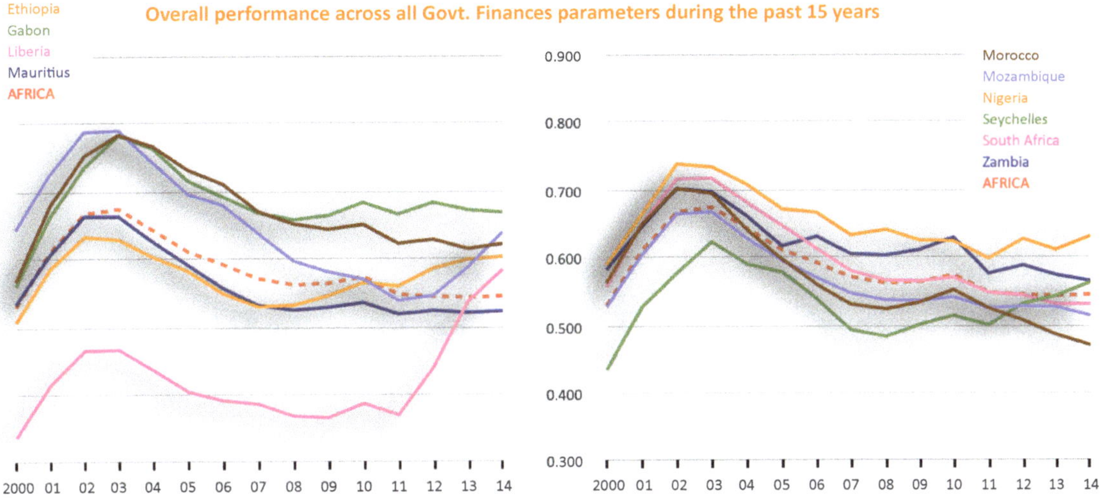

	2015	score
1	Congo, Rep.	0.764
2	Comoros	0.698
3	Gabon	0.668
4	Congo, Dem. Rep.	0.663
5	Angola	0.650
6	Botswana	0.639
7	Nigeria	0.631
8	Algeria	0.622
9	Chad	0.613
10	Swaziland	0.611
11	Ethiopia	0.603
12	Cameroon	0.599
13	Rwanda	0.598
14	Benin	0.597
15	Liberia	0.584
16	Libya	0.582
17	Niger	0.579
18	Burkina Faso	0.577
19	Central African Rep.	0.575
20	Madagascar	0.571
21	Mali	0.569
22	Zambia	0.565
23	Namibia	0.564
24	Uganda	0.564
25	Equatorial Guinea	0.563
26	Seychelles	0.563
27	Burundi	0.556
28	Tanzania	0.553
29	Guinea-Bissau	0.552
30	Zimbabwe	0.550
31	Lesotho	0.548
32	Sierra Leone	0.532
33	South Africa	0.531
34	Mauritania	0.530
35	Tunisia	0.527
36	Mauritius	0.523
37	Cote d'Ivoire	0.518
38	Djibouti	0.514
39	Mozambique	0.514
40	Kenya	0.507
41	Malawi	0.507
42	Togo	0.503
43	Senegal	0.503
44	Sudan	0.493
45	Guinea	0.472
46	Morocco	0.470
47	Ghana	0.416
48	Sao Tome & Prin.	0.412
49	Gambia, The	0.412
50	Cabo Verde	0.348
51	Egypt	0.335
52	Eritrea	0.191

Top 6 African economies for 2015
Next 6 African economies for 2015
Remainder 40 economies for 2015

Parameters:

- General government gross debt as % of GDP
- General government revenue as % of GDP
- General government total expenditure as % of GDP
- General government surplus/deficit as % of GDP

1.5 Self-Reliance

A misnomer, perhaps, as no country can actually be self-reliant. But this section tries to estimate the extent to which the economies have grown their exports strengths and reduced dependence on imports. Closed economies experimenting with "technology transfer" (that is, attempting to replicate industries domestically and focus primarily on producing home-grown goods, closing out imports) was a 70s and 80s trend, **Africa's governments have mostly ditched it by now. Playing to their comparative advantage strengths is the modus operandi that they (rightly) espouse — at least on paper.**

2015		score
1	Libya	0.723
2	Algeria	0.700
3	Gabon	0.643
4	Angola	0.592
5	Congo, Rep.	0.590
6	Ethiopia	0.574
7	Botswana	0.569
8	Equatorial Guinea	0.565
9	Nigeria	0.562
10	Chad	0.539
11	Zambia	0.538
12	Sudan	0.521
13	Mauritania	0.513
14	Cote d'Ivoire	0.505
15	Cameroon	0.496
16	South Africa	0.489
17	Rwanda	0.477
18	Swaziland	0.477
19	Congo, Dem. Rep.	0.475
20	Egypt	0.474
21	Benin	0.471
22	Madagascar	0.471
23	Mali	0.470
24	Morocco	0.468
25	Kenya	0.468
26	Uganda	0.467
27	Malawi	0.466
28	Eritrea	0.463
29	Guinea-Bissau	0.458
30	Niger	0.457
31	Senegal	0.453
32	Tanzania	0.453
33	Central African Rep.	0.446
34	Ghana	0.441
35	Tunisia	0.441
36	Guinea	0.430
37	Lesotho	0.428
38	Togo	0.425
39	Mauritius	0.424
40	Gambia, The	0.421
41	Burundi	0.419
42	Burkina Faso	0.418
43	Comoros	0.416
44	Mozambique	0.412
45	Sierra Leone	0.404
46	Namibia	0.400
47	Cabo Verde	0.379
48	Sao Tome & Prin.	0.352
49	Zimbabwe	0.335
50	Seychelles	0.298
51	Liberia	0.292
52	Djibouti	0.206

Top 6 African economies for 2015
Next 6 African economies for 2015
Remainder 40 economies for 2015

Seychelles and Mauritius are services-driven economies. Most of the others are commodities driven. South Africa is an admirable blend of the two.

Exports of goods and services as $US per person during the past 5 years: 2010-2014

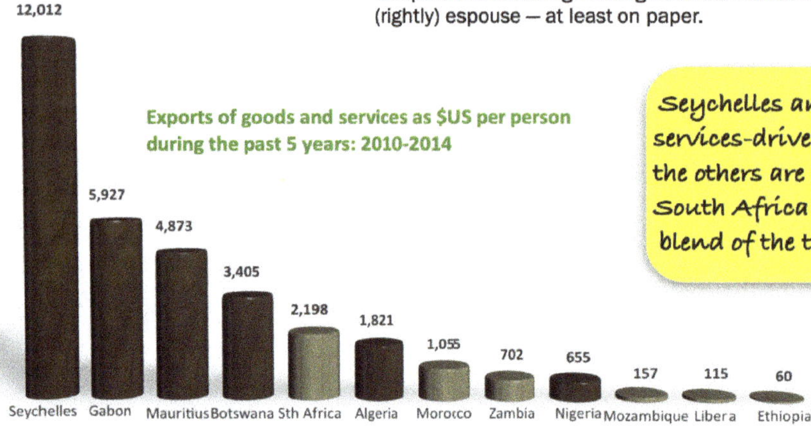

Primary data: World Bank

Algeria blows everyone else out of the water here. Still, the Top 12's collective "credit worthiness" outstrips Latin America's.

Total reserves as % of total external debt during the past 5 years: 2010-2014

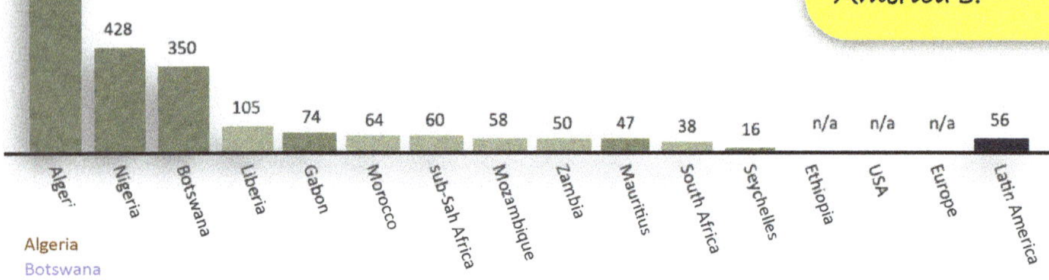

Overall performance across all Self-Reliance parameters during the past 15 years

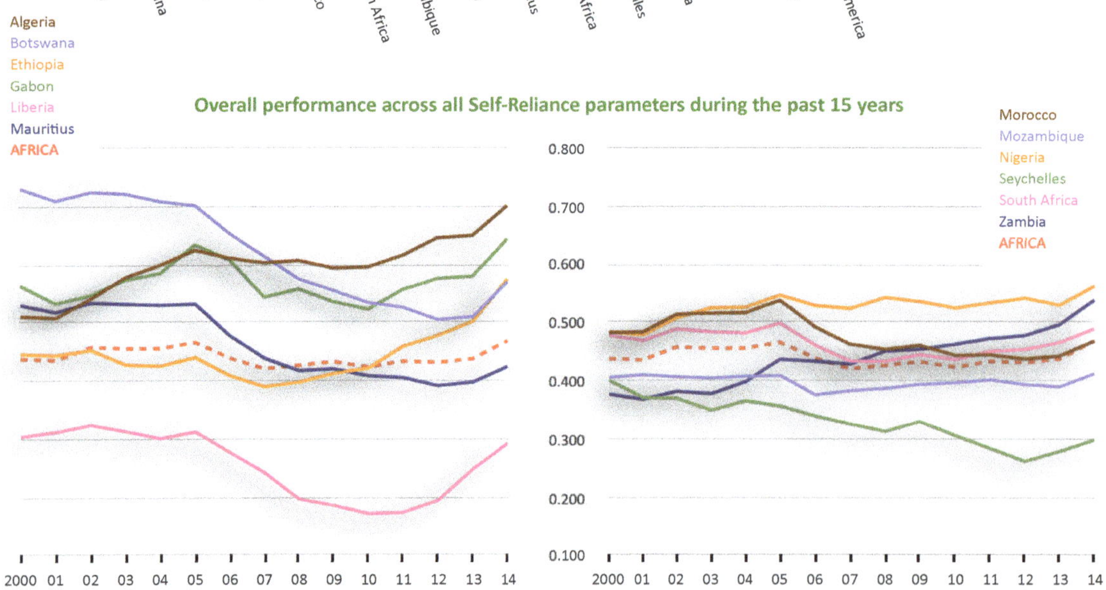

Parameters:

- Exports of goods and services as % of GDP
- Exports of goods and services as $US per person
- Imports of goods and services as % of GDP
- Imports of goods and services as $US per person
- External debt stocks as % of GNI
- Net official development assistance as % of GNI
- Net official development assistance and aid as $US/person
- Total reserves as % of total external debt
- Total reserves as months of imports
- Total reserves as $US per person
- Growth in per person $US total reserves
- Current account balance as % of GDP
- Current account balance as $US per person
- Gross national savings as % of GDP
- Terms of trade in goods and services
- Terms of trade in goods and services, year-on-year change

1.6 Depth of Financial Sector

Financial sectors the world over are still contending with the aftermath of the 2008 crisis which showed up deeply concerning systemic imbalances. While the shock waves did not leave African countries unscathed, for one reason or another – perhaps the fact that consumer credit tends not to be huge portions of their debt portfolios (otherwise a sign of a lack of development or sophistication of their finance industry, but in this instance a fortunate shortcoming) – banks in Africa didn't reel in the flurry of critical blows that western banks had to. Nonetheless, financial sector depth is crucial in estimating economy robustness, and there were structures put in place to ward off scenarios like the 2008 crisis, a popular one was the tightening of regulations that stipulated minimum liquid reserves banks must hold.

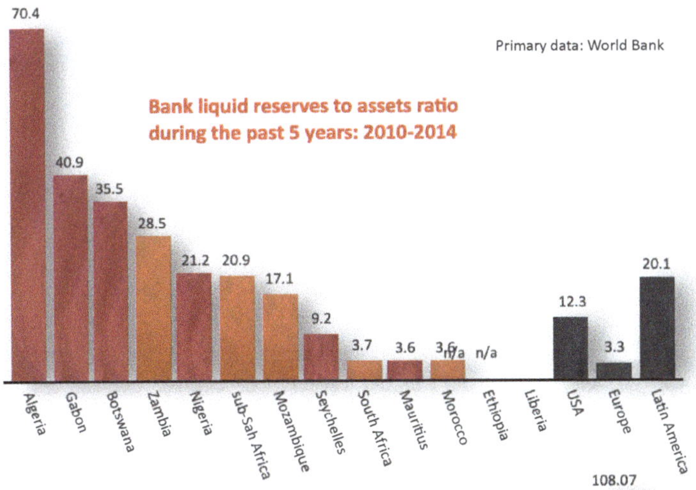

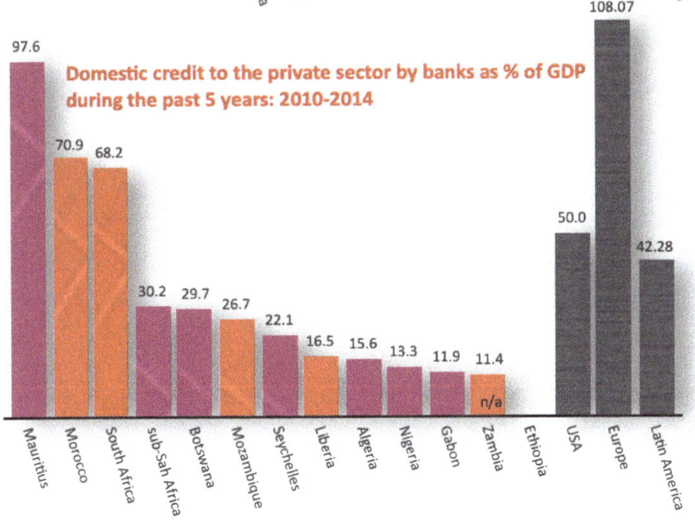

Most of the Top 12 maintain comparatively "safe" sizes of liquid reserves meant to ensure they are able to cover their loan portfolios without risking customer deposits.

How productively banks aid businesses with access to finance is a moot point anywhere, but Africa lags behind Europe and the USA and, possibly, Latin America.

South Africa & Mauritius have the strongest financial sectors, and Mauritius is doing a slow-but-steady upward, while South Africa has seen the sector weaken.

Overall performance across all Financial Sector Depth parameters during the past 15 years

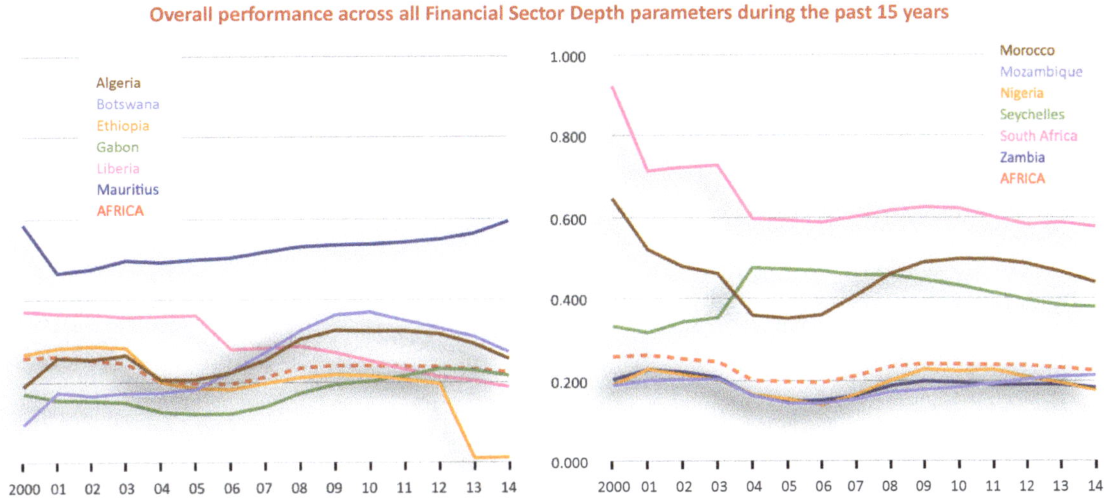

Parameters:

- Bank liquid reserves to assets ratio
- Commercial bank branches per 100,000 adults
- Domestic credit provided by financial sector as % of GDP
- Domestic credit to private sector as % of GDP
- Domestic credit to private sector by banks as % of GDP

	2015	score
1	Mauritius	0.594
2	South Africa	0.577
3	Cabo Verde	0.526
4	Tunisia	0.510
5	Morocco	0.441
6	Eritrea	0.413
7	Seychelles	0.381
8	Sao Tome & Prin.	0.339
9	Namibia	0.327
10	Equatorial Guinea	0.302
11	Egypt	0.280
12	Botswana	0.273
13	Angola	0.262
14	Algeria	0.257
15	Togo	0.254
16	Senegal	0.253
17	Comoros	0.250
18	Djibouti	0.245
19	Kenya	0.231
20	Mauritania	0.221
21	Gambia, The	0.220
22	Gabon	0.215
23	Mozambique	0.213
24	Benin	0.207
25	Ghana	0.202
26	Swaziland	0.201
27	Congo, Rep.	0.200
28	Mali	0.199
29	Burkina Faso	0.190
30	Cote d'Ivoire	0.189
31	Liberia	0.188
32	Malawi	0.187
33	Zambia	0.183
34	Cameroon	0.181
35	Sudan	0.179
36	Nigeria	0.176
37	Burundi	0.159
38	Tanzania	0.157
39	Uganda	0.154
40	Niger	0.137
41	Central African Rep.	0.137
42	Guinea-Bissau	0.134
43	Guinea	0.134
44	Chad	0.133
45	Lesotho	0.133
46	Madagascar	0.132
47	Sierra Leone	0.111
48	Congo, Dem. Rep.	0.093
49	Libya	0.067
50	Zimbabwe	0.054
51	Rwanda	0.050
52	Ethiopia	0.015

Top 6 African economies for 2015
Next 6 African economies for 2015
Remainder 40 economies for 2015

1.7 Investor Confidence

14 parameters this time try to estimate the zest with which foreign investment, especially, enters into the various countries' business sectors. Emphasis is given to private capital – rather than government – as this is always made with the confident expectation of desired returns. Government investment (in roads, for example) might well be made without expectation of profit and wouldn't be deemed as a confidence measure. Indeed, public sector investment is often made with the intention of boosting private sector consumption, even when these investments are financially non-rewarding in the strict sense. Also, only fixed investment is considered here; investments via stocks aren't, for the reason that they can be very short-term and fleeting, and so not necessarily a confidence vote on the economy's structural fundamentals.

The "high-risk, high-returns" reputation of Africa perhaps precedes it, explaining why the gulf in investment levels compared to, say, Latin America.

Foreign direct investment as $US per person during the past 5 years: 2010-2014

Primary data: UNCTAD

This is fast changing and that gulf is often seen now as a willing market just waiting – sometimes, begging – to be tapped, as telecom multinationals, for example, have happily learnt.

Foreign direct investment as % of Gross Fixed Capital Formation during the past 5 years: 2010-2014

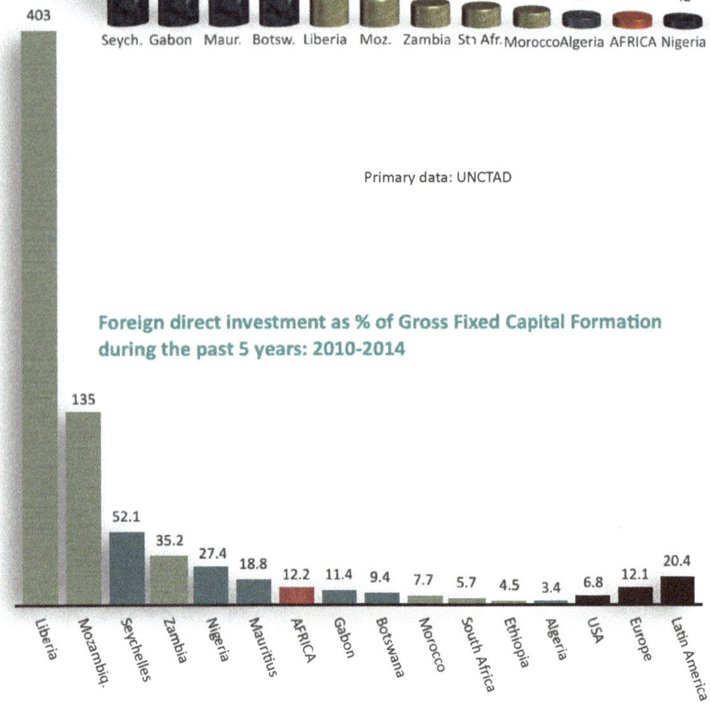

Again, steady improvement within the Top 12 is the story for much of the past 15 years.

Overall performance across all Investor Confidence parameters during the past 15 years

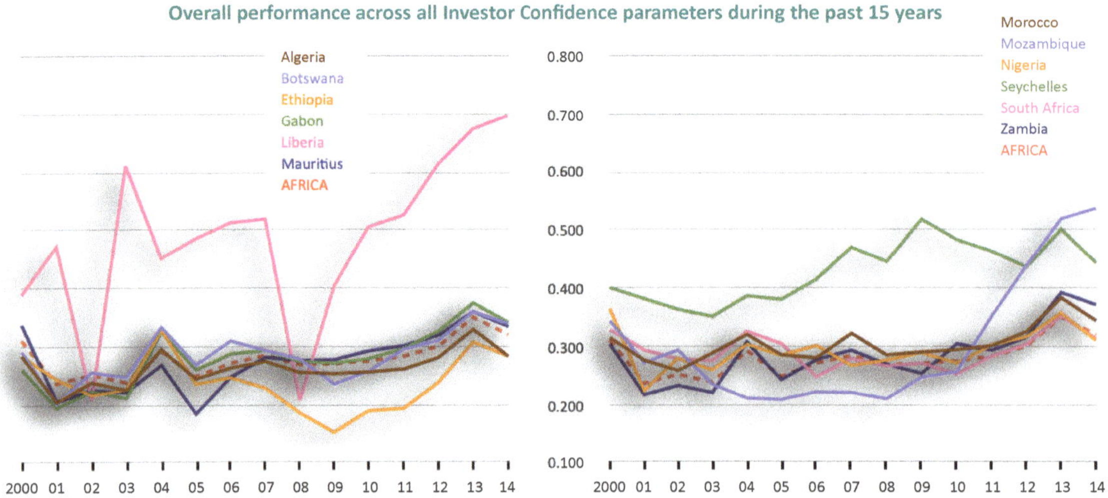

	2015	score
1	Liberia	0.696
2	Mozambique	0.537
3	Sao Tome & Prin.	0.471
4	Equatorial Guinea	0.455
5	Seychelles	0.443
6	Sierra Leone	0.380
7	Djibouti	0.371
8	Zambia	0.371
9	Congo, Rep.	0.368
10	Congo, Dem. Rep.	0.366
11	Libya	0.346
12	Morocco	0.344
13	Gabon	0.341
14	Botswana	0.339
15	Sudan	0.336
16	Mauritius	0.334
17	Tanzania	0.330
18	Niger	0.326
19	Mauritania	0.324
20	Ghana	0.323
21	Uganda	0.320
22	Namibia	0.318
23	South Africa	0.313
24	Nigeria	0.310
25	Togo	0.302
26	Guinea	0.301
27	Benin	0.296
28	Zimbabwe	0.295
29	Burkina Faso	0.289
30	Cabo Verde	0.288
31	Kenya	0.286
32	Senegal	0.285
33	Chad	0.285
34	Algeria	0.283
35	Ethiopia	0.283
36	Tunisia	0.283
37	Burundi	0.281
38	Madagascar	0.279
39	Comoros	0.278
40	Cameroon	0.278
41	Egypt	0.272
42	Malawi	0.268
43	Cote d'Ivoire	0.264
44	Gambia, The	0.262
45	Mali	0.260
46	Rwanda	0.258
47	Swaziland	0.256
48	Central African Rep.	0.247
49	Lesotho	0.246
50	Guinea-Bissau	0.241
51	Eritrea	0.222
52	Angola	0.181

Top 6 African economies for 2015
Next 6 African economies for 2015
Remainder 40 economies for 2015

Parameters:
- Foreign direct investment, $US
- Foreign direct investment per person, $US
- Growth in $US foreign direct investment per person
- Foreign direct investment as % of GDP
- Year-on-year change of %GDP Foreign direct investment
- Foreign direct investment as % of gross fixed capital formation
- Year-on-year change of %GFCF foreign direct investment
- Foreign direct investment as % of goods and services trade
- Year-on-year change of %goods and services fdi
- Foreign direct investment as % of goods trade
- Year-on-year change of %goods fdi
- Gross private sector capital formation as $US per person
- Growth in per person $US private sector capital formation
- Gross private sector capital formation as % of GDP

1.8 Purchasing Power

Again, private consumption is a more realistic measure of consumer demand viability (disposable income available) than government (or public) consumption. Population size should be taken into account when interpreting these results: lower per person spending does not necessarily imply an unattractive market: large population sizes enter into the final $US per person results. In Nigeria's case, for example, it may never reach the $ per person levels of a small population country like Mauritius, but the size of its middle class market is large enough to absorb investments and sustain strong demand. Consumption as a percentage of GDP helps to place the volume of that available disposable income in perspective.

Large GDP countries like Nigeria and South Africa offer comparatively larger markets for the same level of %GDP. Mauritius hits 74%GDP but still smaller market than Algeria.

That said, Africa disposable income %GDP levels in the Top 12 compare favorably with trends in the USA, Europe and Latin America.

And then GDP absolute size begins to make all the difference.

The almost effectively flat trends of Purchasing Power performance probably says more about the wealth gap within the countries, where spending is still restricted to a small group.

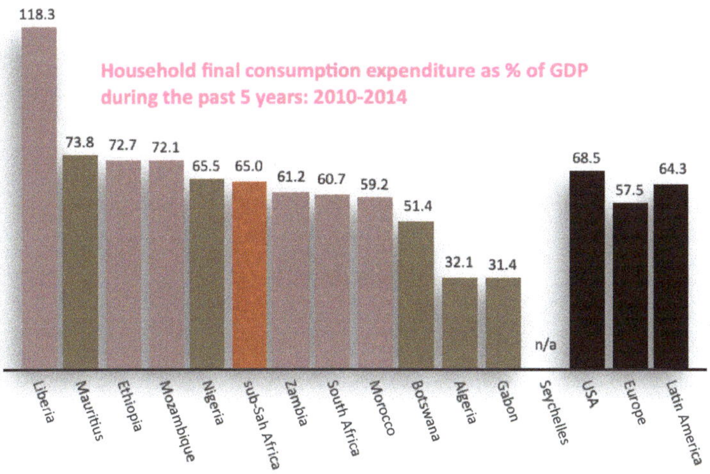

Primary data: World Bank

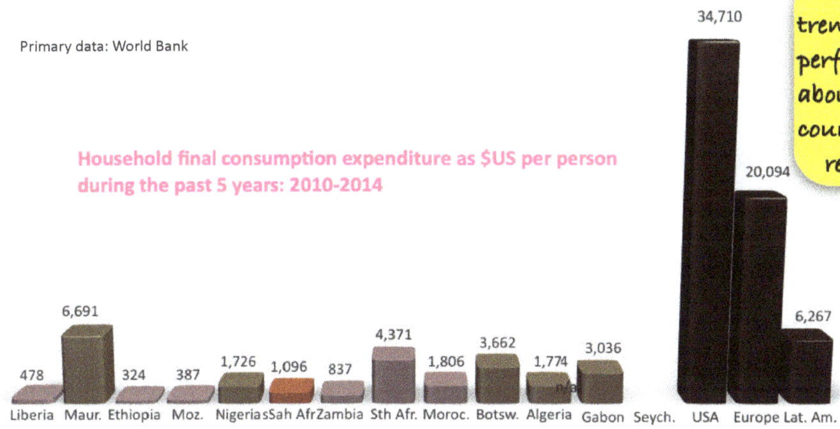

Overall performance across all Purchasing Power parameters during the past 15 years

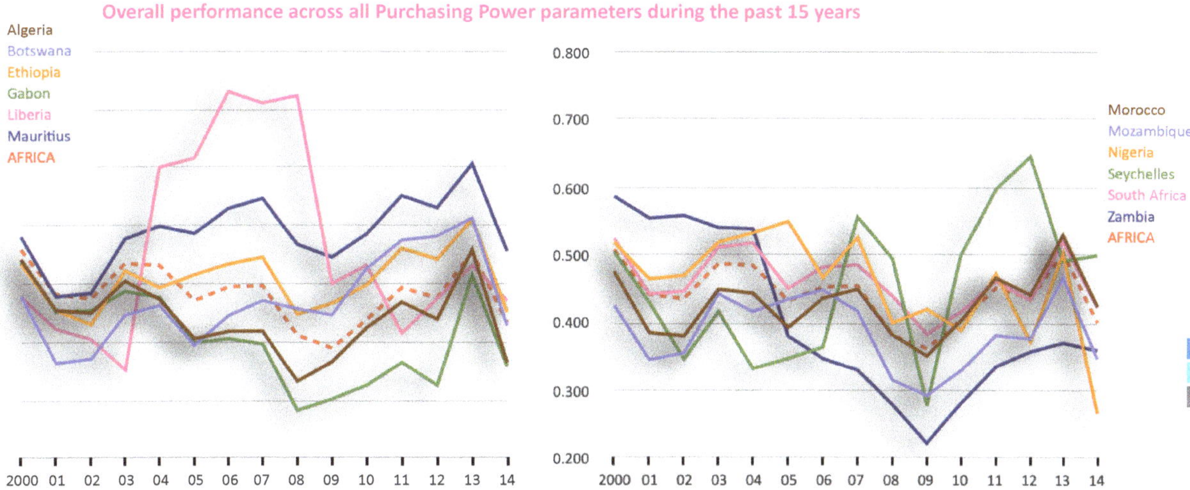

Parameters:

- Price level ratio of PPP to market exchange rate
- Year-on-year change in price level ratio
- Household final consumption in $US per person
- Growth in $US household final consumption per person
- Household final consumption as % of GDP
- Year-on-year change in %GDP Household final consumption

	2015	score
1	Sierra Leone	0.521
2	Egypt	0.507
3	Mauritius	0.505
4	Gambia, The	0.504
5	Seychelles	0.499
6	Tunisia	0.484
7	Togo	0.479
8	Guinea	0.473
9	Malawi	0.471
10	Madagascar	0.470
11	Mali	0.433
12	Liberia	0.432
13	Lesotho	0.426
14	Guinea-Bissau	0.425
15	Kenya	0.424
16	Morocco	0.424
17	South Africa	0.422
18	Swaziland	0.420
19	Sudan	0.416
20	Ethiopia	0.415
21	Comoros	0.413
22	Benin	0.407
23	Tanzania	0.406
24	Uganda	0.405
25	Rwanda	0.403
26	Cameroon	0.399
27	Senegal	0.397
28	Botswana	0.395
29	Ghana	0.394
30	Libya	0.389
31	Central African Rep.	0.389
32	Mauritania	0.386
33	Namibia	0.386
34	Djibouti	0.385
35	Burundi	0.385
36	Sao Tome & Prin.	0.385
37	Cote d'Ivoire	0.376
38	Cabo Verde	0.375
39	Chad	0.372
40	Zimbabwe	0.370
41	Zambia	0.359
42	Niger	0.358
43	Mozambique	0.346
44	Burkina Faso	0.346
45	Algeria	0.341
46	Gabon	0.335
47	Eritrea	0.306
48	Congo, Dem. Rep.	0.303
49	Congo, Rep.	0.302
50	Nigeria	0.266
51	Equatorial Guinea	0.263
52	Angola	0.230

Top 6 African economies for 2015
Next 6 African economies for 2015
Remainder 40 economies for 2015

1.9 Infrastructure

This has for a very long time been the bane of Africa's economic climate but strong advances have been made in recent years. For one, telecommunications infrastructure has completely transformed business in Africa and the continent is even a pioneer in transactions like mobile payment platforms, especially the East African countries. Utilities is also a big growth sector on the continent as more and more governments realize it is in their overall social and political interests to establish conducive living and social environments.

Projects involving the provision of physical infrastructure for telecoms are growing in size and scope in Africa everyday. It is a burgeoning investment area.

The International Telecommunications Union (ITU) states that Africa led the world in mobile broadband growth (40%), twice world average in 2014.

By end 2014, mobile-broadband penetration in Africa was projected to hit 40%, up from 2% in as recent as 2010.

ITU: Africa and Asia/the Pacific are the regions of the world with the strongest mobile-cellular growth and lowest penetration rates [thus a yet vastly unsaturated market].

Telecommunications infrastructure will continue to transform African business environments rapidly and in an enduring manner.

Fixed (wired) broadband subscriptions per 1,000 people during 2010-2014

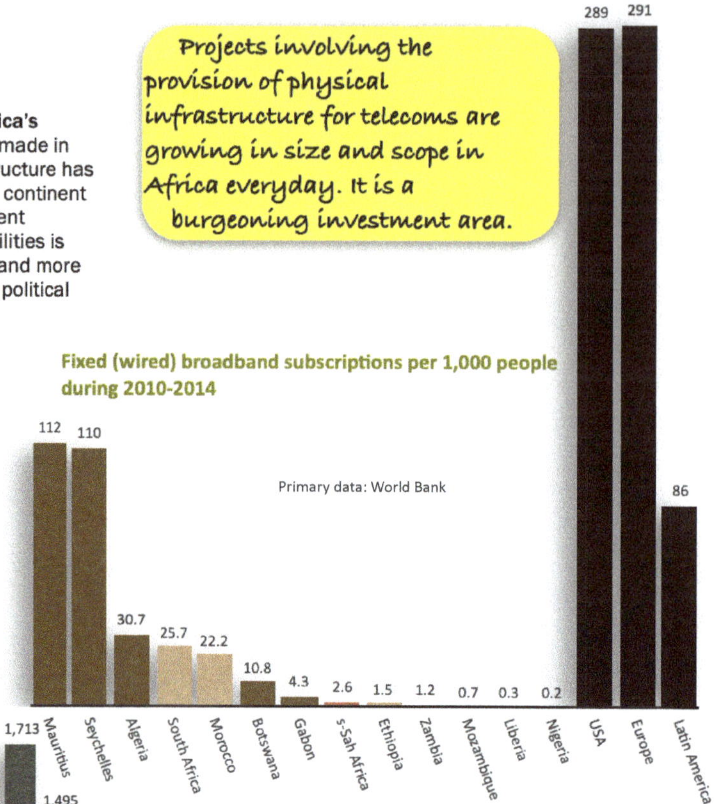

Mobile (cellular) subscriptions per 1,000 people during 2010-2014

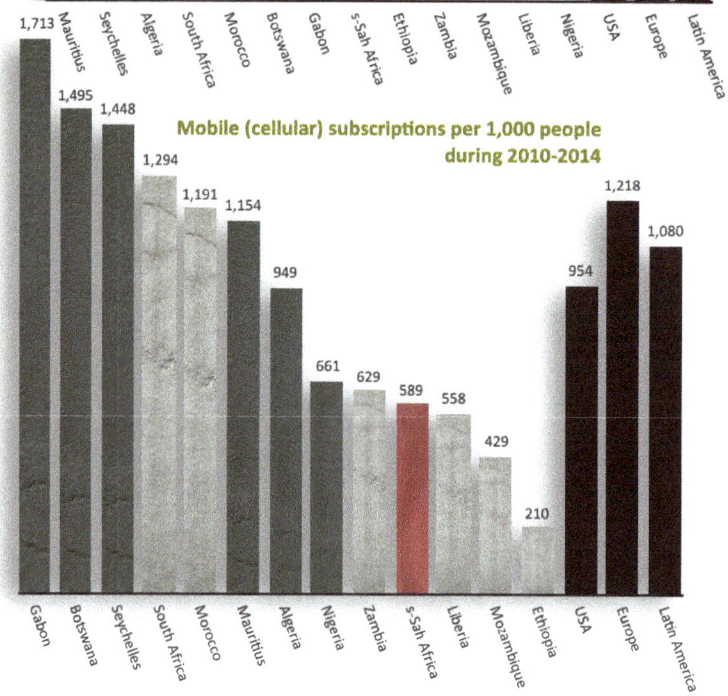

	2015	score
1	Seychelles	0.895
2	Mauritius	0.691
3	South Africa	0.396
4	Cabo Verde	0.395
5	Morocco	0.294
6	Botswana	0.280
7	Gabon	0.249
8	Tunisia	0.247
9	Namibia	0.241
10	Egypt	0.232
11	Libya	0.189
12	Senegal	0.188
13	Sao Tome & Prin.	0.186
14	Nigeria	0.183
15	Kenya	0.177
16	Swaziland	0.175
17	Zimbabwe	0.172
18	Gambia, The	0.171
19	Ghana	0.171
20	Sudan	0.153
21	Mauritania	0.139
22	Congo, Rep.	0.137
23	Angola	0.132
24	Equatorial Guinea	0.131
25	Mali	0.129
26	Benin	0.129
27	Cote d'Ivoire	0.128
28	Algeria	0.127
29	Zambia	0.121
30	Lesotho	0.116
31	Tanzania	0.110
32	Uganda	0.109
33	Cameroon	0.109
34	Comoros	0.086
35	Rwanda	0.085
36	Togo	0.083
37	Burkina Faso	0.081
38	Liberia	0.075
39	Guinea-Bissau	0.072
40	Mozambique	0.066
41	Guinea	0.063
42	Sierra Leone	0.060
43	Madagascar	0.056
44	Djibouti	0.047
45	Malawi	0.046
46	Chad	0.044
47	Niger	0.043
48	Congo, Dem. Rep.	0.040
49	Central African Rep.	0.035
50	Ethiopia	0.032
51	Burundi	0.028
52	Eritrea	0.008

Top 6 African economies for 2015
Next 6 African economies for 2015
Remainder 40 economies for 2015

Overall performance across all Infrastructure parameters during the past 15 years

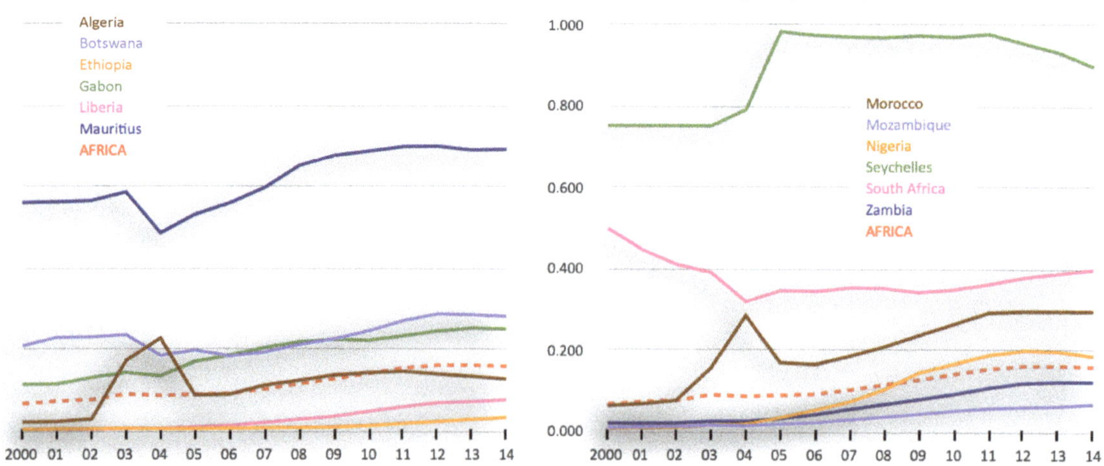

Parameters:
- Wired broadband subscriptions per 100 people
- Fixed telephone subscriptions per 100 people
- Mobile cellular subscriptions per 100 people
- Secure internet servers per 1 million people
- Internet users per 1,000 people

1.10 Business Friendliness

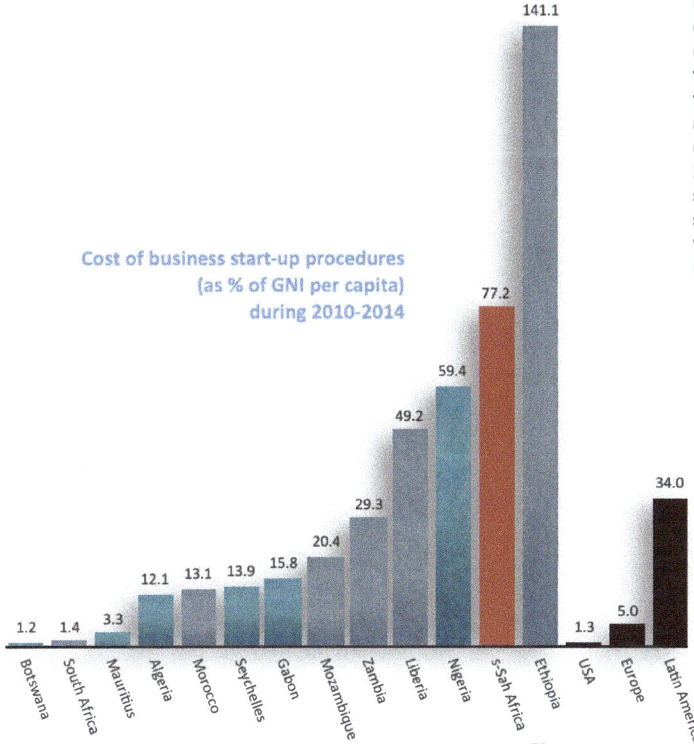

In the end, this is the brunt. The 1990s and early 2000s were often characterized by tales of woe regarding companies who ventured onto the continent and the hoops they had to jump through. Eastern Europe was just opening up as well, and money tended to move in that direction, instead. Not so anymore. The late 2000s have been characterized by efforts to streamline the investment processes and swing previously shuttered doors wide open with a smile. But a lot still — admittedly — remains to be done.

Ethiopia has the most red tape.

Primary data: World Bank

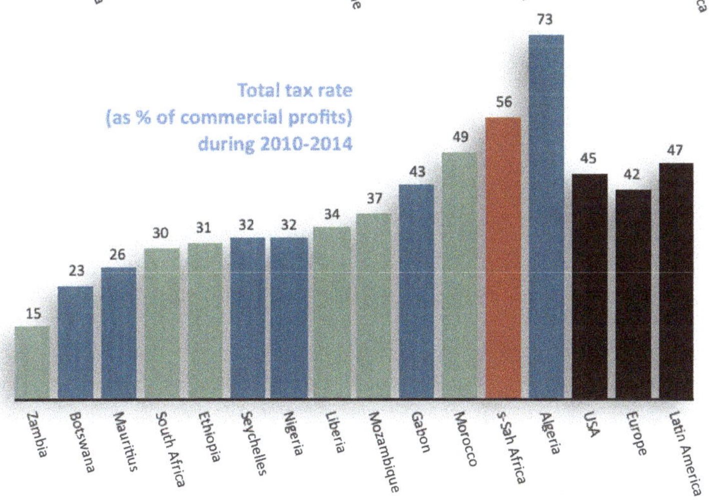

Once you get past that, though, as in much of the Top 12, the tax regimes are comparatively friendlier than in USA, Europe or Latin America.

High flyers, most. Mauritius tops it. But there's a spring in the steps of Seychelles, Morocco and Mozambique.

	2015	score
1	Mauritius	0.985
2	South Africa	0.902
3	Seychelles	0.901
4	Cabo Verde	0.876
5	Namibia	0.847
6	Morocco	0.837
7	Tunisia	0.834
8	Ghana	0.815
9	Egypt	0.806
10	Swaziland	0.793
11	Botswana	0.788
12	Mozambique	0.775
13	Rwanda	0.772
14	Tanzania	0.769
15	Gabon	0.749
16	Senegal	0.744
17	Lesotho	0.737
18	Kenya	0.727
19	Burkina Faso	0.717
20	Equatorial Guinea	0.709
21	Benin	0.691
22	Nigeria	0.676
23	Sierra Leone	0.672
24	Libya	0.668
25	Uganda	0.662
26	Algeria	0.656
27	Ethiopia	0.650
28	Sao Tome & Prin.	0.648
29	Mali	0.647
30	Zambia	0.625
31	Cameroon	0.622
32	Malawi	0.607
33	Liberia	0.607
34	Mauritania	0.603
35	Niger	0.603
36	Madagascar	0.599
37	Cote d'Ivoire	0.590
38	Togo	0.573
39	Gambia, The	0.559
40	Djibouti	0.555
41	Burundi	0.533
42	Guinea	0.531
43	Guinea-Bissau	0.495
44	Angola	0.473
45	Sudan	0.458
46	Congo, Rep.	0.452
47	Comoros	0.452
48	Eritrea	0.381
49	Central African Rep.	0.344
50	Zimbabwe	0.339
51	Congo, Dem. Rep.	0.300
52	Chad	0.282

Top 6 African economies for 2015
Next 6 African economies for 2015
Remainder 40 economies for 2015

Overall performance across all Business Friendliness parameters during the past 15 years

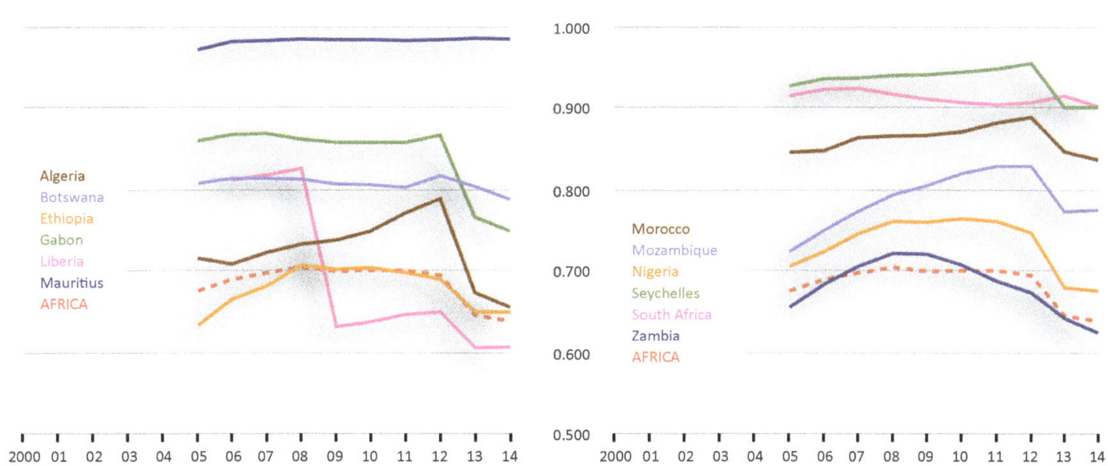

Parameters:

- Cost of business start-up procedures as % of per person GNI
- Cost to export, in $US per container
- Cost to import, in $US per container
- CPIA economic management cluster average
- CPIA financial sector rating
- CPIA property rights and rule-based governance rating
- CPIA quality of budgetary and financial management rating
- CPIA public sector transparency, accountability and corruption rating
- World Bank ease of doing business ranking in the world
- Total tax rate as % of commercial profits

Appendix 1 - Parameters

1. General Size

1 GDP ($US)
2 GDP ($PPP)
3 GNI ($US)
4 GNI ($PPP)

2. Productivity

1 GDP real growth
2 GDP real growth, % change
3 GDP per person ($US)
4 Growth in $US GDP per person
5 GDP per person ($PPP)
6 Growth in $PPP GDP per person
7 GNI per person ($US)
8 Growth in $US GNI per person
9 GNI per person ($PPP)
10 Growth in $PPP GNI per person
11 Value added in agriculture as % of GDP
12 Growth in value added in agriculture
13 Value added in agriculture as $US per person
14 Growth in $US value added in agriculture per person
15 Value added in industry as % of GDP
16 Growth in value added in industry
17 Value added in industry as $US per person
18 Growth in $US value added in industry per person
19 Value added in services as % of GDP
20 Growth in value added in services
21 Value added in services as $US per person
22 Growth in $US value added in services per person

3. Agility

1 Average interest on new external debt commitments
2 Average maturity on new external debt commitments
3 Debt service on external debt as $US per person
4 Interest payments on external debt (% of GNI)
7 Interest payments on external debt as $US/person
8 Exchange rate stability
9 Inflation level, average annual (CPI)
10 Inflation, year-on-year change
11 Debt service as % of exports
12 Debt service: interest and amortization, as $US/person

4. Government Finances

1 General government gross debt as % of GDP
2 General government revenue as % of GDP
3 General government total expenditure as % of GDP
4 General government surplus/deficit as % of GDP

5. Self-Reliance

1 Exports of goods and services as % of GDP
2 Exports of goods and services as $US per person
3 Imports of goods and services as % of GDP
4 Imports of goods and services as $US per person
5 External debt stocks as % of GNI
6 Net official development assistance as % of GNI
7 Net official development assist. & official aid as $US/pers
8 Total reserves as % of total external debt
9 Total reserves as months of imports
10 Total reserves as $US per person
11 Growth in per person $US total reserves
12 Current account balance as % of GDP
13 Current account balance as $US per person
14 Gross national savings as % of GDP
15 Terms of trade in goods & services
16 Terms of trade in goods & services, yr-on-yr change

6. Financial Sector Depth

1 Bank liquid reserves to assets ratio
2 Commercial bank branches per 100,000 adults
3 Domestic credit provided by financial sector as % of GDP
4 Domestic credit to private sector as % of GDP
5 Domestic credit to private sector by banks as % of GDP

7. Investor Confidence

1 Foreign direct investment, $US
2 Foreign direct investment per person, $US
3 Growth in $US foreign direct investment per person
4 Foreign direct investment as % of GDP
5 Year-on-year change of %GDP Foreign direct investment
6 Foreign direct investment as % of gross fixed capital
7 Year-on-year change of %GFCF foreign direct investment
8 Foreign direct investment as % of goods and services trade
9 Year-on-year change of %goods and services fdi
10 Foreign direct investment as % of goods trade
11 Year-on-year change of %goods fdi
12 Gross private sector capital formation as $US per person
13 Growth in per person $US private sector capital formation
14 Gross private sector capital formation as % of GDP

8. Purchasing Power

1 Price level ratio of PPP to market exchange rate
2 Year-on-year change in price level ratio
3 Household final consumption in $US per person
4 Growth in $US household final consumption per person
5 Household final consumption as % of GDP
6 Yr-on-yr change in %GDP Household final consumption

9. Infrastructure

1 Wired broadband subscriptions per 100 people
2 Fixed telephone subscriptions per 100 people
3 Mobile cellular subscriptions per 100 people
4 Secure internet servers per 1 million people
5 Internet users per 1,000 people

10. Business Friendliness

1 Cost of business start-up procedures as % of per pers GNI
2 Cost to export, in $US per container
3 Cost to import, in $US per container
4 CPIA economic management cluster average
5 CPIA financial sector rating
6 CPIA property rights and rule-based governance rating
7 CPIA quality of budgetary and financial management rating
8 CPIA public sector transparency, accountability, corruption
9 World Bank ease of doing business ranking in the world
10 Total tax rate as % of commercial profits

Appendix 2 - Countries of Africa

Central Africa	East Africa	North Africa	Southern Africa	West Africa
1 Angola	1 Burundi	1 Algeria	1 Botswana	1 Benin
2 Cameroon	2 Comoros	2 Egypt	2 Lesotho	2 Burkina Faso
3 Central African Republic	3 Djibouti	3 Libya	3 Namibia	3 Cabo Verde
4 Chad	4 Eritrea	4 Morocco	4 South Africa	4 Côte d'Ivoire
5 Congo, Democratic Rep.	5 Ethiopia	5 Tunisia	5 Swaziland	5 Gambia, The
6 Congo, Republic	6 Kenya			6 Ghana
7 Equatorial Guinea	7 Madagascar			7 Guinea
8 Gabon	8 Malawi			8 Guinea-Bissau
9 São Tomé and Principe	9 Mauritius			9 Liberia
	10 Mozambique			10 Mali
	11 Rwanda			11 Mauritania
	12 Seychelles			12 Niger
	13 Somalia			13 Nigeria
	14 South Sudan			14 Senegal
	15 Sudan			15 Sierra Leone
	16 Tanzania			16 Togo
	17 Uganda			
	18 Zambia			
	19 Zimbabwe			

2. The Subcontinent

2.1 Sub-Saharan Africa

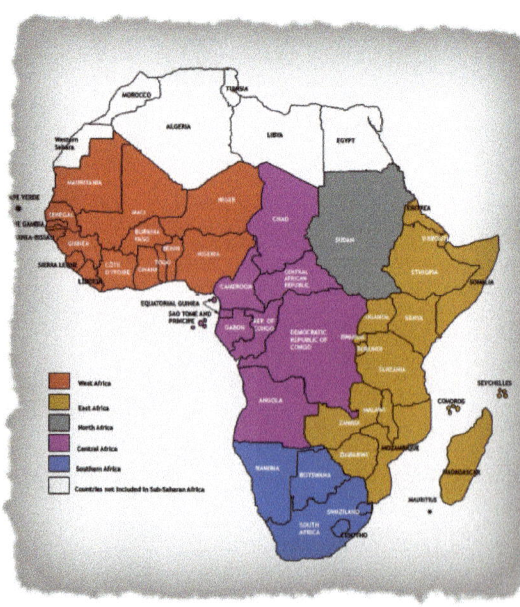

- Central Africa
- East Africa
- Southern Africa
- Sudan
- West Africa

	Country	Years since Independence 2009	Population 2007 (millions)	Population Density 2005-2010 (pers/ sq.km.)	GDP 2007 ($US, millions)	GDP per Person 2007 ($US)	Region
1	• Angola	34	16	14	59,263	3,629	Central Africa
2	• Benin	49	8	82	5,554	707	West Africa
3	• Botswana	43	2	3	12,339	7,005	Southern Africa
4	• Burkina Faso	49	14	55	6,769	493	West Africa
5	• Burundi	47	8	313	975	125	East Africa
6	• Cameroon	49	19	39	20,433	1,084	Central Africa
7	• Cape Verde	34	1	134	1,513	3,080	West Africa
8	• Central African Rep.	49	4	7	1,700	398	Central Africa
9	• Chad	49	10	9	7,018	739	Central Africa
10	• Comoros	34	1	381	466	729	East Africa
11	• Congo, Dem. Rep.	49	61	27	10,013	164	Central Africa
12	• Congo, Rep.	49	4	12	7,657	2,159	Central Africa
13	• Côte d'Ivoire	49	20	61	19,824	983	West Africa
14	• Djibouti	32	1	37	848	1,108	East Africa
15	• Equatorial Guinea	41	1	18	12,576	10,437	Central Africa
16	• Eritrea	16	5	42	1,316	271	East Africa
17	• Ethiopia	n/a	77	77	19,535	253	East Africa
18	• Gabon	49	1	5	11,571	8,076	Central Africa
19	• Gambia, The	44	2	153	651	410	West Africa
20	• Ghana	52	22	99	15,014	683	West Africa
21	• Guinea	51	10	39	4,157	417	West Africa
22	• Guinea-Bissau	36	2	48	382	225	West Africa
23	• Kenya	46	35	66	27,102	782	East Africa
24	• Lesotho	43	2	66	1,672	694	Southern Africa
25	• Liberia	162	4	35	745	199	West Africa
26	• Madagascar	49	20	34	7,343	373	East Africa
27	• Malawi	45	13	120	3,586	268	East Africa
28	• Mali	49	13	10	7,156	548	West Africa
29	• Mauritania	49	3	3	2,819	952	West Africa
30	• Mauritius	41	1	621	6,927	5,494	East Africa
31	• Mozambique	34	20	27	8,102	398	East Africa
32	• Namibia	19	2	3	8,831	4,355	Southern Africa
33	• Niger	49	13	11	4,252	318	West Africa
34	• Nigeria	49	144	162	165,921	1,153	West Africa
35	• Rwanda	47	9	377	3,412	363	East Africa
36	• São Tomé & Príncipe	34	0.2	165	145	923	Central Africa
37	• Senegal	49	12	64	11,300	924	West Africa
38	• Seychelles	33	0.1	191	912	10,728	East Africa
39	• Sierra Leone	48	6	82	1,664	290	West Africa
40	• Somalia	49	n/a	n/a	n/a	n/a	East Africa
41	• South Africa	78	48	40	283,381	5,922	Southern Africa
42	• Sudan	53	37	16	46,531	1,252	North Africa
43	• Swaziland	41	1	66	2,946	2,892	Southern Africa
44	• Tanzania	45	39	44	16,691	428	East Africa
45	• Togo	49	7	118	2,503	387	West Africa
46	• Uganda	47	31	131	11,916	385	East Africa
47	• Zambia	45	12	16	11,411	990	East Africa
48	• Zimbabwe	29	12	35	3,583	305	East Africa

2.2 Central Africa

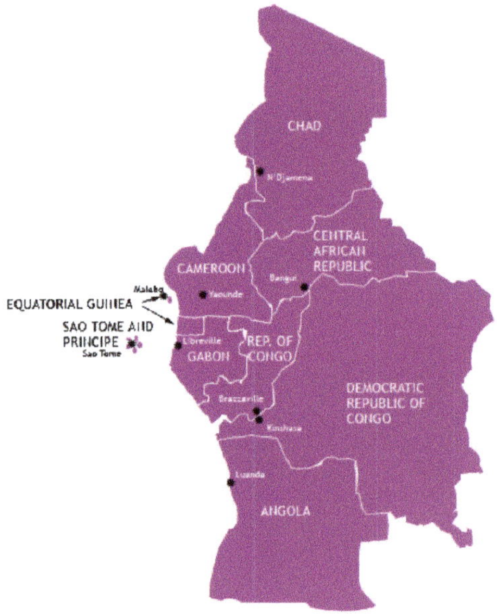

Primary Data: IMF

	Country	Population 2007 (millions)	Average GDP per Person 2004-07 ($US)	Average Annual Real GDP Growth 2004-07 (%)	Average Annual Inflation Rate 2004-07 (%)	National Currency	Exchange Rate 2009 (currency oer $US)	Exchange Rate Stability relative to rest of S-S Africa during 2004-09 (0=least stable; 10=most stable)	Official Language
1	•Angola	16	2,447	17.7	23.0	Kwanza	79	8.7	Portuguese
2	•Cameroon	19	976	3.1	2.1	Central African CFA Franc	478	6.9	English, French
3	•Central African Rep.	4.3	349	2.7	2.1	Central African CFA Franc	478	5.6	French, Sangho
4	•Chad	9.5	643	10.5	-0.2	Central African CFA Franc	478	4.7	French, Arabic
5	•Congo, Dem. Rep.	61	139	6.6	13.8	Congolese Franc	784	0.4	French
6	•Congo, Rep.	3.5	1,913	4.0	3.3	Central African CFA Franc	478	4.9	French
7	•Equatorial Guinea	1.2	7,650	17.6	4.3	Central African CFA Franc	480	7.8	Spanish, French
8	•Gabon	1.4	6,664	2.7	1.3	Central African CFA Franc	478	6.7	French
9	•São Tomé & Príncipe	0.2	800	6.2	17.9	Dobra	16,336	0.7	Portuguese

2.3 East Africa

Primary Data: IMF

	Country	Population 2007 (millions)	Average GDP per Person 2004-07 ($US)	Average Annual Real GDP Growth 2004-07 (%)	Average Annual Inflation Rate 2004-07 (%)	National Currency	Exchange Rate 2009 (currency oer $US)	Exchange Rate Stability relative to rest of S-S Africa during 2004-09 (0=least stable; 10=most stable)	Official Language
1	•Burundi	8	111	3.6	8.1	Burundian Franc	1,208	3.8	Kirundi, French
2	•Comoros	1	653	1.4	3.8	Comorian Franc	358	6	Arabic, French
3	•Djibouti	0.8	1,010	4.0	3.7	Djiboutian Franc	178	9.8	French, Arabic
4	•Eritrea	4.9	260	1.1	15.5	Nafka	15	9.1	Tigrinya, Arabic, English
5	•Ethiopia	77	191	11.4	10.9	Birr	10	3.3	Amharic
6	•Kenya	34.7	624	6.0	11.5	Kenyan Shilling	80	6.2	English, Kiswahili
7	•Madagascar	19.7	293	5.3	13.4	Ariary	1,972	4	French, Malagasy
8	•Malawi	13.4	232	6.0	12.2	Malawian Kwacha	141	2.4	English, Nyanja
9	•Mauritius	1.3	5,124	3.8	6.9	Mauritian Rupee	29	8.2	English, French
10	•Mozambique	20.3	348	8.0	10.1	Metical	27,037	4.2	Portuguese
11	•Rwanda	9.4	290	6.9	9.7	Rwandan Franc	574	9.6	Rwanda, French, English
12	•Seychelles	0.1	10,755	5.0	2.0	Seychellois Rupee	14	0	English, French
13	•Somalia	n/a	n/a	n/a	n/a	Somali Shilling	n/a	n/a	Somali
14	•Tanzania	39.0	383	7.3	5.7	Tanzanian Shilling	1,325	3.6	Kiswahili, Kiunguju, English
15	•Uganda	30.9	331	8.1	6.6	Ugandan Shilling	1,905	8.9	English
16	•Zambia	11.5	754	5.8	14.0	Zambian Kwacha	5,182	2.2	English
17	•Zimbabwe	11.7	322	-5.2	10.6	Zimbabwean	n/a	n/a	English

2.4 Southern Africa & Sudan

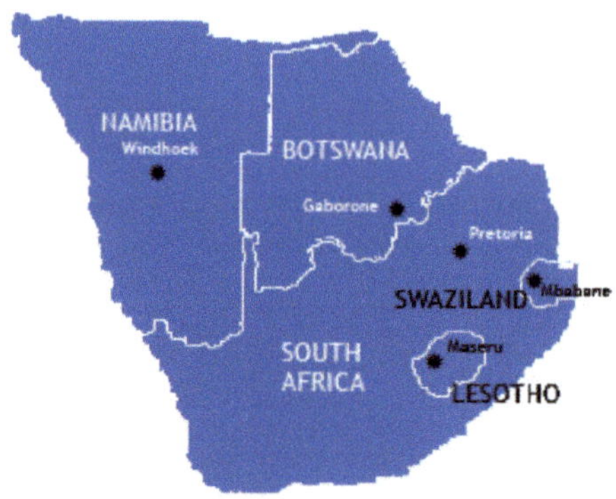

Primary Data: IMF

	Country	Population 2007 (millions)	Average GDP per Person 2004-07 ($US)	Average Annual Real GDP Growth 2004-07 (%)	Average Annual Inflation Rate 2004-07 (%)	National Currency	Exchange Rate 2009 (currency oer $US)	Exchange Rate Stability relative to rest of S-S Africa during 2004-09 (0=least stable; 10=most stable)	Official Language
1	•Sudan	37	916	8.2	8.0	Sudanese Pound	2	3.1	Arabic
1	•Botswana	1.8	6,331	4.3	8.6	Pula	7	1.1	Setswana,
2	•Lesotho	2.4	624	4.6	5.6	Loti	9	1.8	Sesotho, English
3	•Namibia	2	3,841	6.8	4.5	Namibian Dollar	9	1.6	English
4	•South Africa	47.9	5,299	5.1	4.1	Rand	8	2	English and 10 others
5	•Swaziland	1.0	2,608	2.7	5.4	Lilangeni	9	1.3	English, siSwati

2.5 West Africa

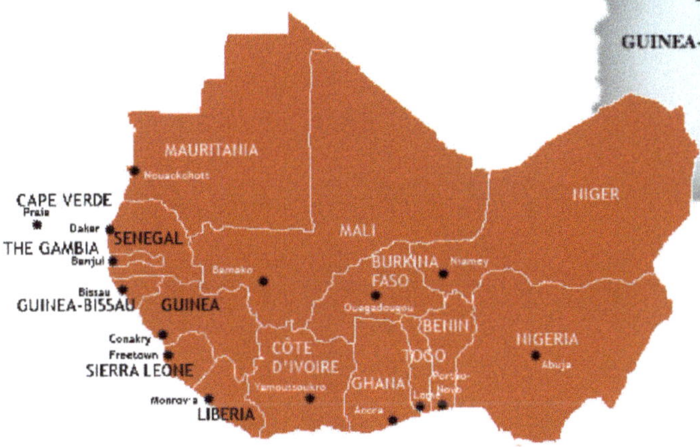

Primary Data: IMF

	Country	Population 2007 (millions)	Average GDP per Person 2004-07 ($US)	Average Annual Real GDP Growth 2004-07 (%)	Average Annual Inflation Rate 2004-07 (%)	National Currency	Exchange Rate 2009 (currency oer $US)	Exchange Rate Stability relative to rest of S-S Africa during 2004-09 (0=least stable; 10=most stable)	Official Language
1	•Benin	8	622	3.6	2.8	West African CFA Franc	501	8	French
2	•Burkina Faso	14	433	5.2	2.0	West African CFA Franc	490	7.6	French
3	•Cape Verde	0.5	2,399	7.3	1.9	Escudo	80	4.4	Portuguese
4	•Côte d'Ivoire	20.2	893	1.4	2.4	West African CFA Franc	477	5.8	French
5	•Gambia, The	2	329	6.3	6.7	Dalasi	27	2.7	English
6	•Ghana	22.0	557	5.9	12.2	Cedi	14,617	0.9	English
7	•Guinea	10.0	360	2.4	26.6	Guinean Franc	4,997	0.2	French
8	•Guinea-Bissau	1.7	198	2.2	2.4	West African CFA Franc	484	7.3	Portuguese
9	•Liberia	3.8	165	6.3	7.9	Liberian Dollar	n/a	n/a	English
10	•Mali	13.1	469	4.2	1.6	West African CFA Franc	478	5.3	French
11	•Mauritania	3.0	771	5.8	9.0	Ouguiya	247	9.3	Arabic
12	•Niger	13.4	277	4.2	2.1	West African CFA Franc	478	5.1	French
13	•Nigeria	143.9	918	7.3	11.6	Naira	152	2.9	English
14	•Senegal	12.2	791	4.7	2.5	West African CFA Franc	480	6.4	French
15	•Sierra Leone	5.7	244	7.1	11.9	Leone	3,150	8.4	English
16	•Togo	6.5	352	2.4	2.6	West African CFA Franc	484	7.1	French

3. Size, Populations, Ages, Economic Vigor

3.1a Land Mass of the Regions

their surface areas

	Country	sq. km.
1	Sudan	2,505,810
2	Congo, DR	2,344,860
3	Chad	1,284,000
4	Niger	1,267,000
5	Angola	1,246,700
6	Mali	1,240,190
7	South Africa	1,219,090
8	Ethiopia	1,104,300
9	Mauritania	1,025,520
10	Tanzania	945,090
11	Nigeria	923,770
12	Namibia	824,290
13	Mozambique	801,590
14	Zambia	752,610
15	Somalia	637,660
16	Central African Rep.	622,980
17	Madagascar	587,040
18	Botswana	581,730
19	Kenya	580,370
20	Cameroon	475,440
21	Zimbabwe	390,760
22	Congo, Rep.	342,000
23	Côte d'Ivoire	322,460
24	Burkina Faso	274,000
25	Gabon	267,670
26	Guinea	245,860
27	Uganda	241,040
28	Ghana	238,540
29	Senegal	196,720
30	Malawi	118,480

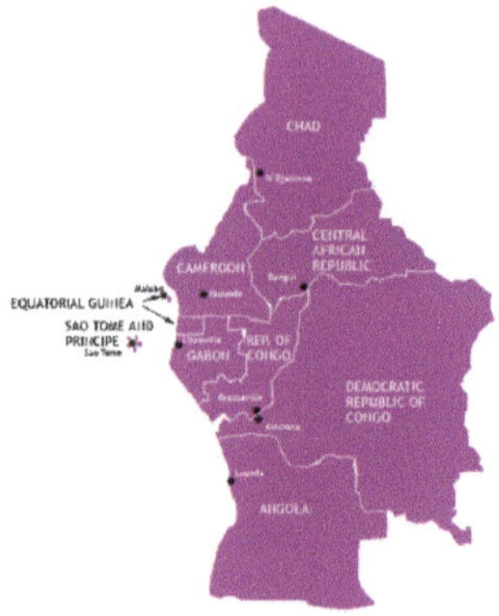

Central Africa
6,612,660 sq.km.

East Africa
6,335,440 sq.km.

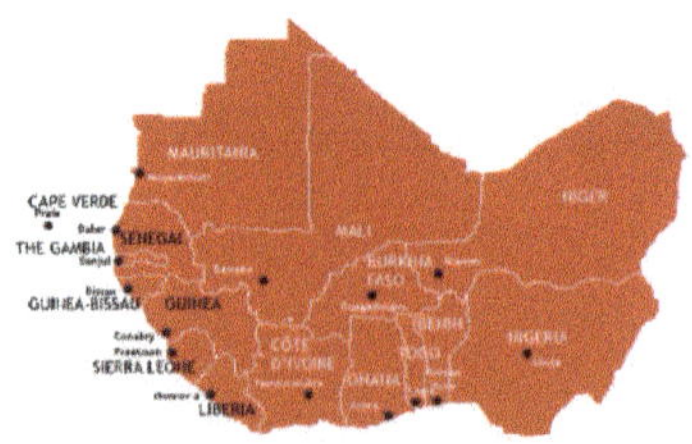

West Africa
6,138,030 sq.km.

Southern Africa
2,672,820 sq.km.

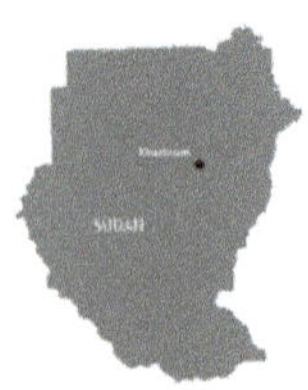

Sudan
2,505,810 sq.km.

3.1b Land Mass in SSA: Top 10

1
Sudan
2,505,810 sq.km.
10%

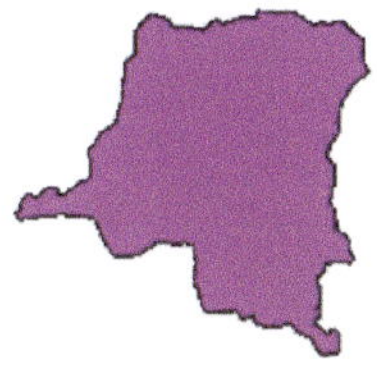

2
Congo, Dem. Rep.
2,344,860 sq.km.
10%

3
Chad
1,284,000 sq.km
5%

4
Niger
1,267,000 sq.km
5%

5
Angola
1,246,700 sq.km.
5%

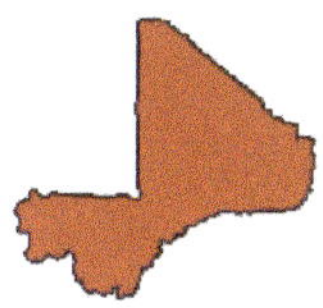

6
Mali
1,240,190 sq.km.
5%

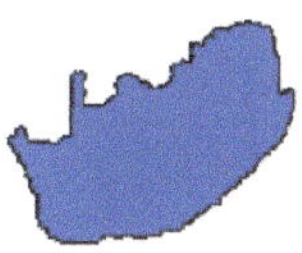

7
South Africa
1,219,090 sq.km.
5%

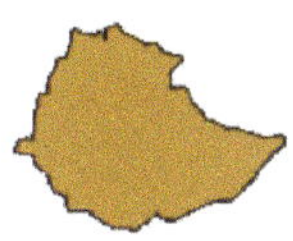

8
Ethiopia
1,104,300 sq.km.
4.5%

9
Mauritania
1,025,520 sq.km.
4%

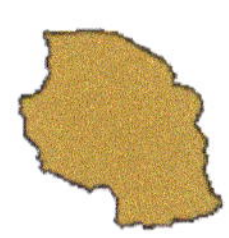

10
Tanzania
945,090 sq.km.
4%

the large 10 in SSA

	Country	sq. km.
31	Eritrea	117,600
32	Benin	112,620
33	Liberia	117,370
34	Sierra Leone	71,740
35	Togo	56,790
36	Guinea-Bissau	36,120
37	Lesotho	30,350
38	Equatorial Guinea	28,050
39	Burundi	27,830
40	Rwanda	26,340
41	Djibouti	23,200
42	Swaziland	17,360
43	Gambia	11,300
44	Cape Verde	4,030
45	Comoros	2,230
46	Mauritius	2,040
47	Sao Tome and Principe	960
48	Seychelles	460

- Central Africa
- East Africa
- Southern Africa
- North Africa
- West Africa

3.2a Population of the Regions

their populations

#	Country	2009
1	Nigeria	151,874,000
2	Ehiopia	81,238,000
3	Congo, DR	64,772,000
4	South Africa	48,812,000
5	Tanzania	40,538,000
6	Sudan	39,117,000
7	Kenya	35,884,000
8	Uganda	33,195,000
9	Ghana	23,108,000
10	Mozambique	21,456,000
11	Cameroon	19,926,000
12	Côte d'Ivoire	19,317,000
13	Madagascar	17,894,000
14	Angola	17,312,000
15	Burkina Faso	14,365,000
16	Niger	14,191,000
17	Malawi	13,931,000
18	Mali	13,667,000
19	Senegal	12,820,000
20	Zambia	12,749,000
21	Guinea	10,564,000
22	Chad	9,973,000
23	Rwanda	9,792,000
24	Benin	8,334,000
25	Burundi	8,108,000
26	Togo	6,793,000
27	Sierra Leone	6,040,000
28	Eritrea	4,973,000
29	Central African Rep.	4,442,000
30	Liberia	4,134,000

2009 IMF estimates

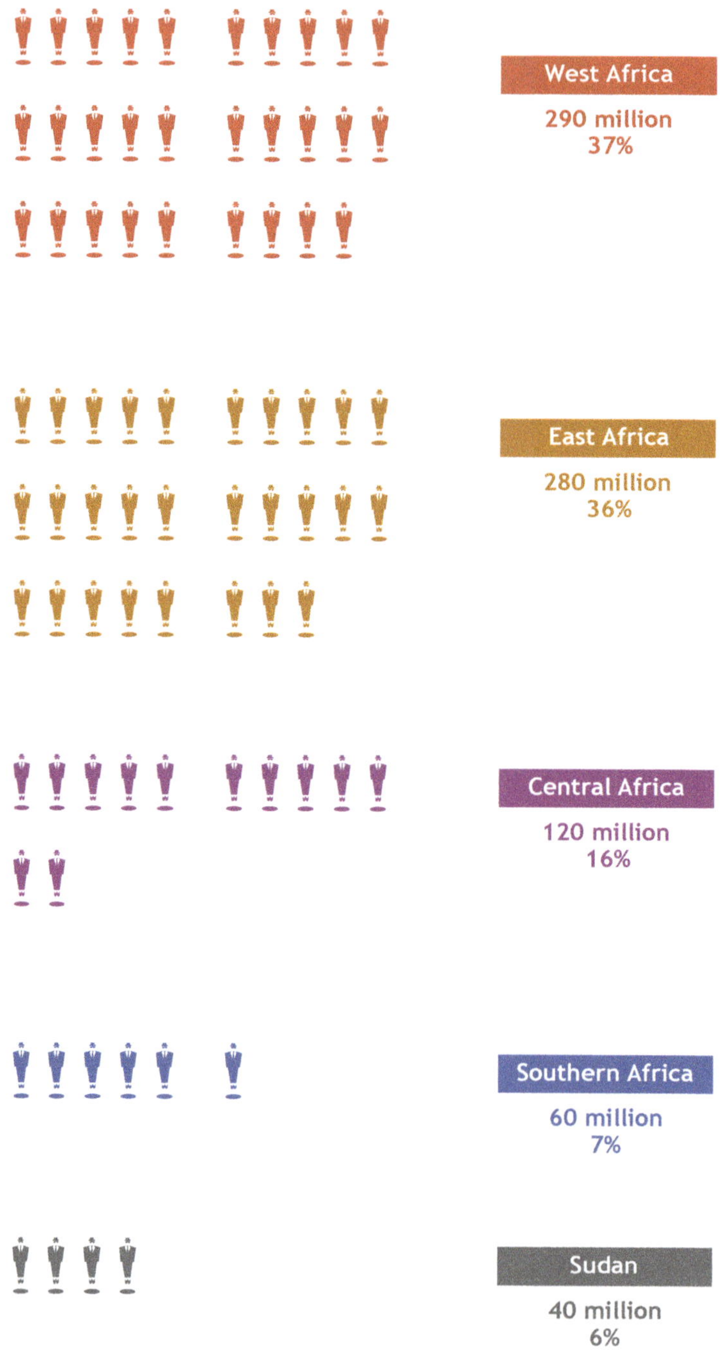

- Central Africa
- East Africa
- Southern Africa
- North Africa
- West Africa

3.2b Share of Population in SSA: Top 10

the swarming 10 in SSA

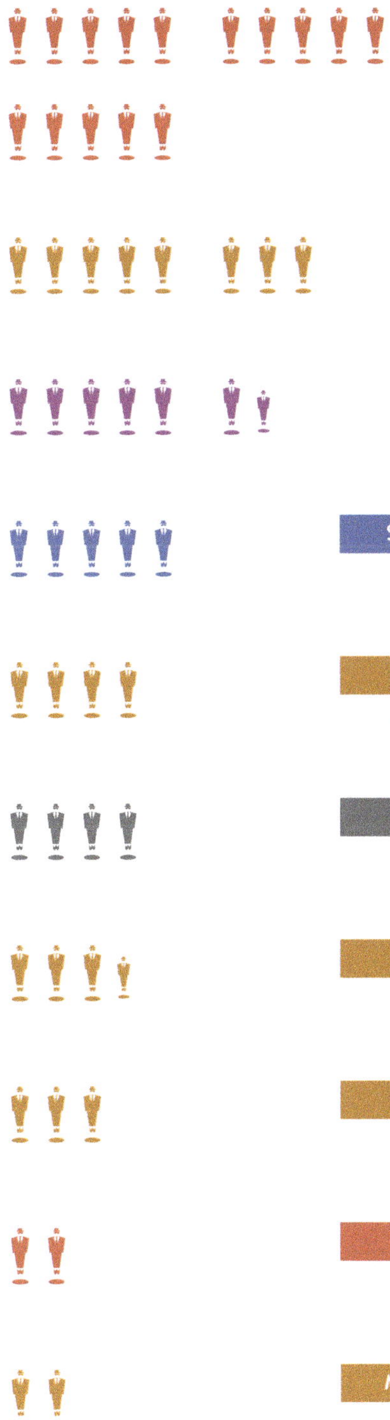

1. Nigeria — 150 million, 20%
2. Ethiopia — 80 million, 10%
3. Congo, DR — 65 million, 8%
4. South Africa — 50 million, 6%
5. Tanzania — 40 million, 5%
6. Sudan — 40 million, 56%
7. Kenya — 35 million, 4.5%
8. Uganda — 30 million, 4%
9. Ghana — 20 million, 3%
10. Mozambique — 20 million, 3%

Central Africa
East Africa
Southern Africa
North Africa
West Africa

	Country	2009
31	Congo, Rep.	3,756,000
32	Mauritania	3,105,000
33	Lesotho	2,496,000
34	Namibia	2,100,000
35	Guinea-Bissau	1,767,000
36	Gambia	1,672,000
37	Botswana	1,530,000
38	Gabon	1,475,000
39	Mauritius	1,281,000
40	Equatorial Guinea	1,276,000
41	Swaziland	1,195,000
42	Djibouti	804,000
43	Comoros	666,000
44	Cape Verde	513,000
45	Sao Tome and Principe	171,000
46	Seychelles	83,000
47	Somalia	n/a
48	Zimbabwe	n/a

3.3a Population Age Profiles of the Regions: %s

their ages

UNPD estimates for 2005-10

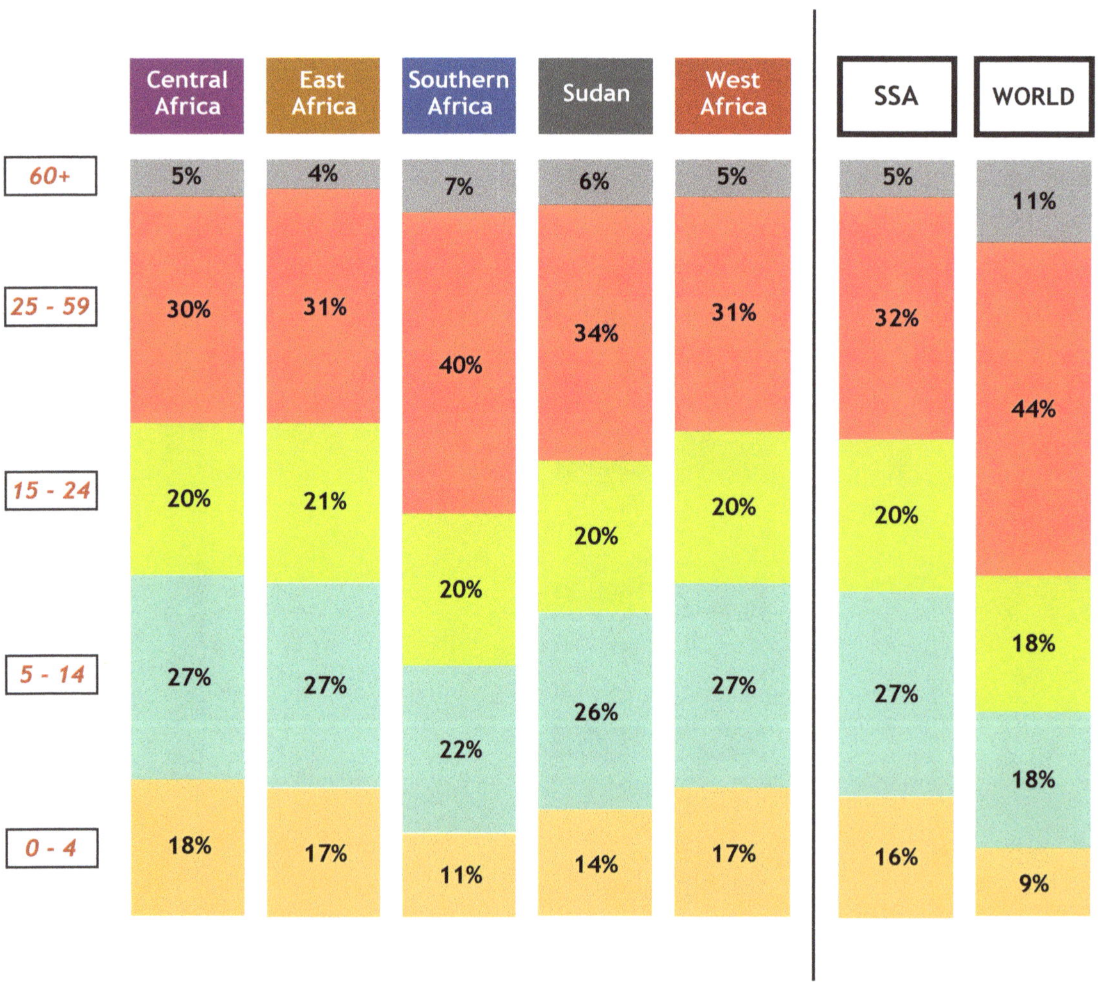

3.3b Population Age Profiles of the Regions: numbers

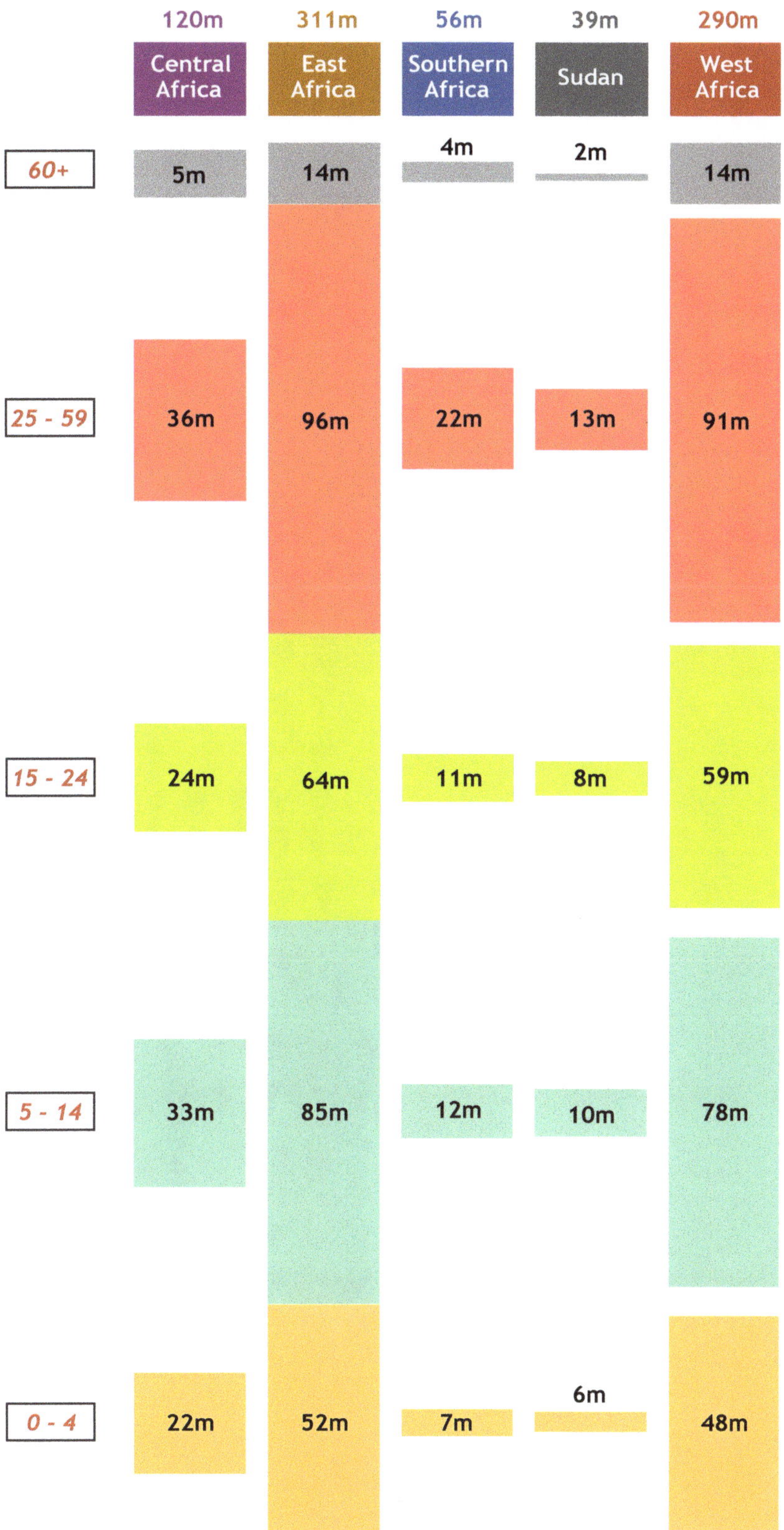

the numbers, this time

UNPD estimates for 2005-10

Total figure for East Africa differs from that in section 2.2 because the IMF estimates there exclude Somalia and Zimbabwe.

3.4a Population Density of the Regions

their people per square kilometer

	Country	2005-10
1	Mauritius	621
2	Comoros	381
3	Rwanda	377
4	Burundi	313
5	Seychelles	191
6	Sao Tome & Principe	165
7	Nigeria	162
8	Gambia	153
9	Cape Verde	134
10	Uganda	131
11	Malawi	120
12	Togo	118
13	Ghana	99
14	Sierra Leone	82
15	Benin	82
16	Ethiopia	77
17	Lesotho	66
18	Swaziland	66
19	Kenya	66
20	Senegal	64
21	Côte d'Ivoire	61
22	Burkina Faso	55
23	Guinea-Bissau	48
24	Tanzania	44
25	Eritrea	42
26	South Africa	40
27	Cameroon	39
28	Guinea	39
29	Djibouti	37
30	Liberia	35

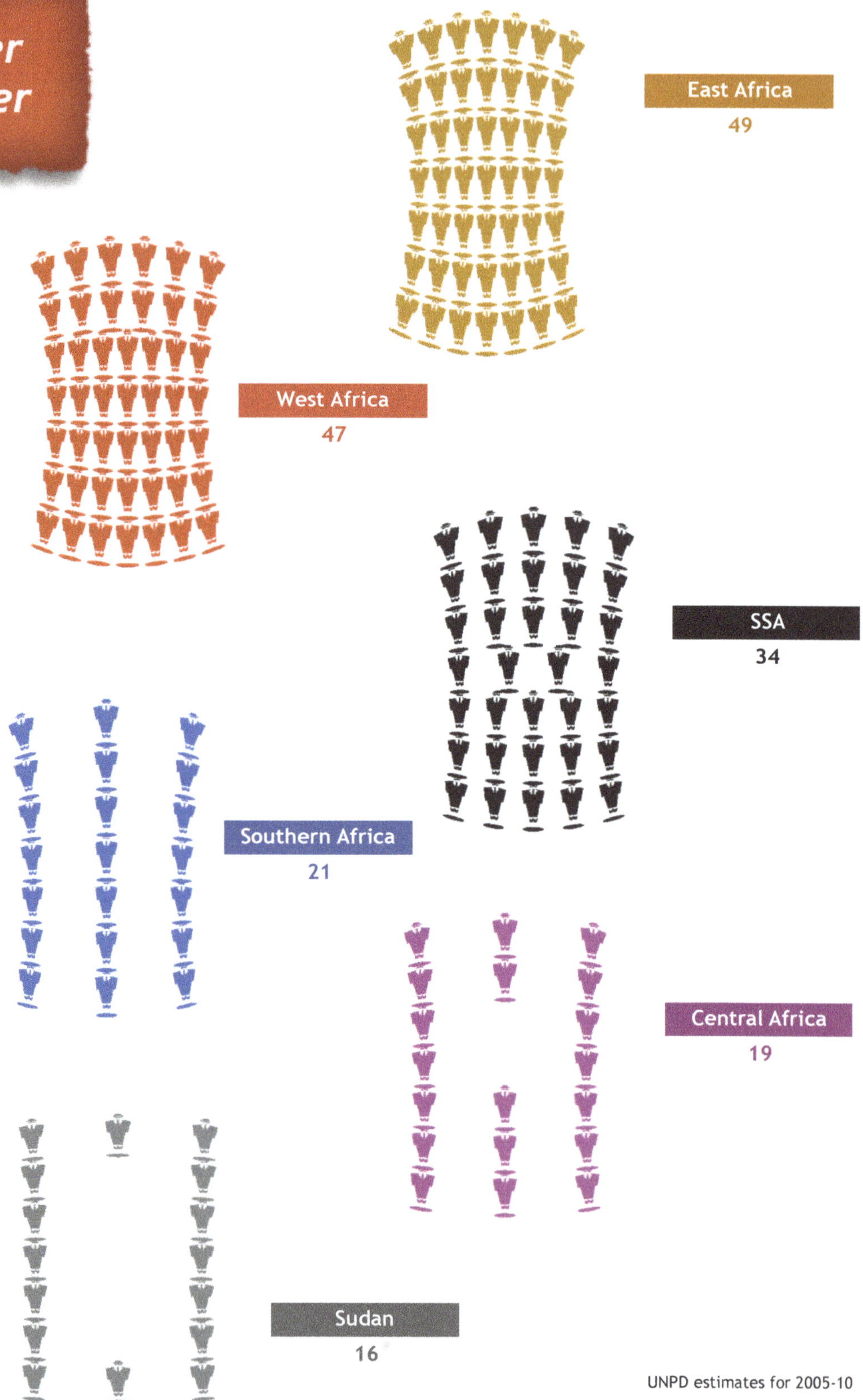

UNPD estimates for 2005-10

3.4b Population Density in the Countries: Top 10

the packed 10 in SSA

UNPD estimates for 2005-10

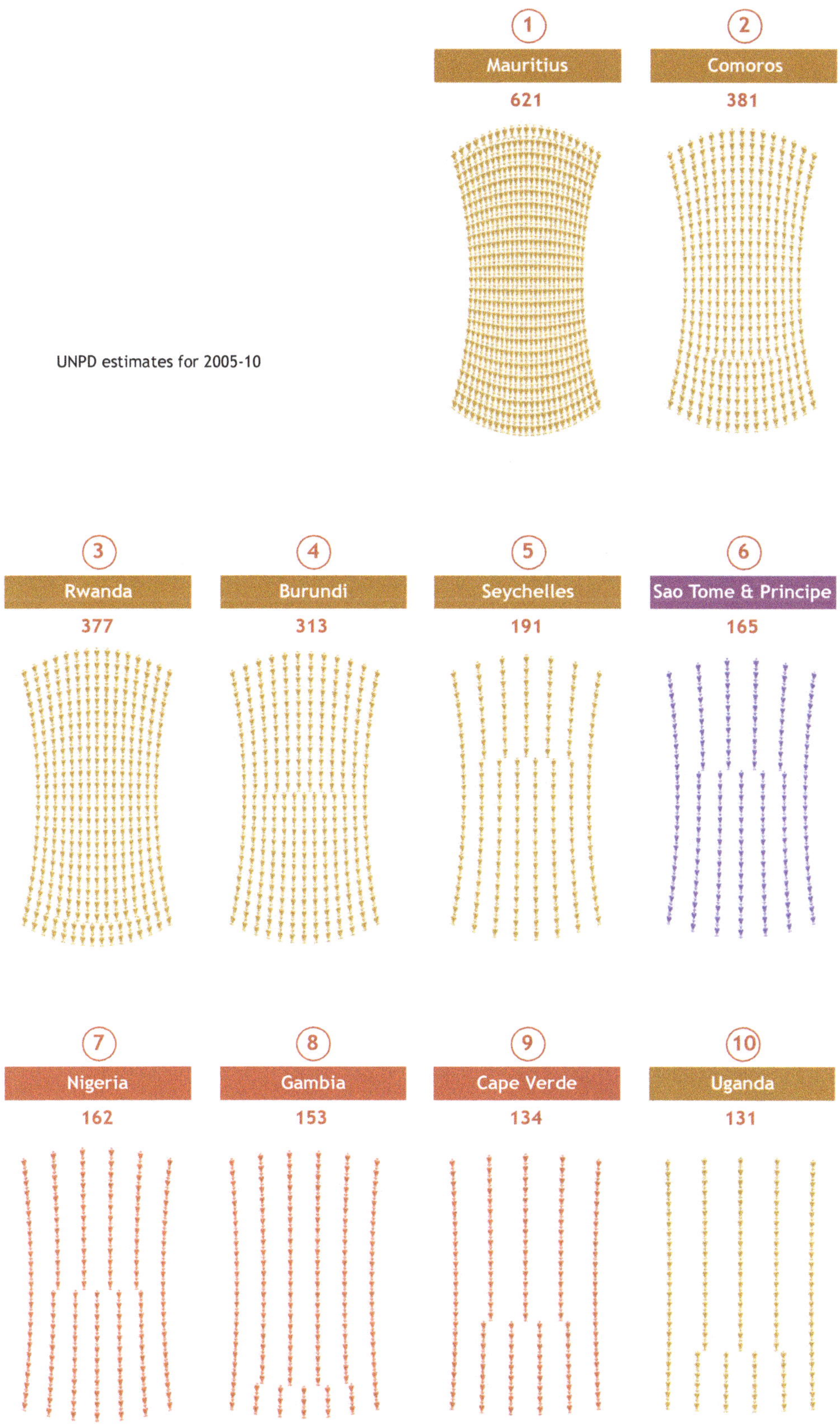

Central Africa
East Africa
Southern Africa
North Africa
West Africa

	Country	2005-10
31	Zimbabwe	35
32	Madagascar	34
33	Congo, D.R.	27
34	Mozambique	27
35	Equatorial Guinea	18
36	Zambia	16
37	Sudan	16
38	Angola	14
39	Somalia	14
40	Congo, Rep.	12
41	Niger	11
42	Mali	10
43	Chad	9
44	Central African Rep.	7
45	Gabon	5
46	Botswana	3
47	Mauritania	3
48	Namibia	3

3.5a Urban Population in the Regions: % and numbers

Urban Population as % of
Total Population
2005-10

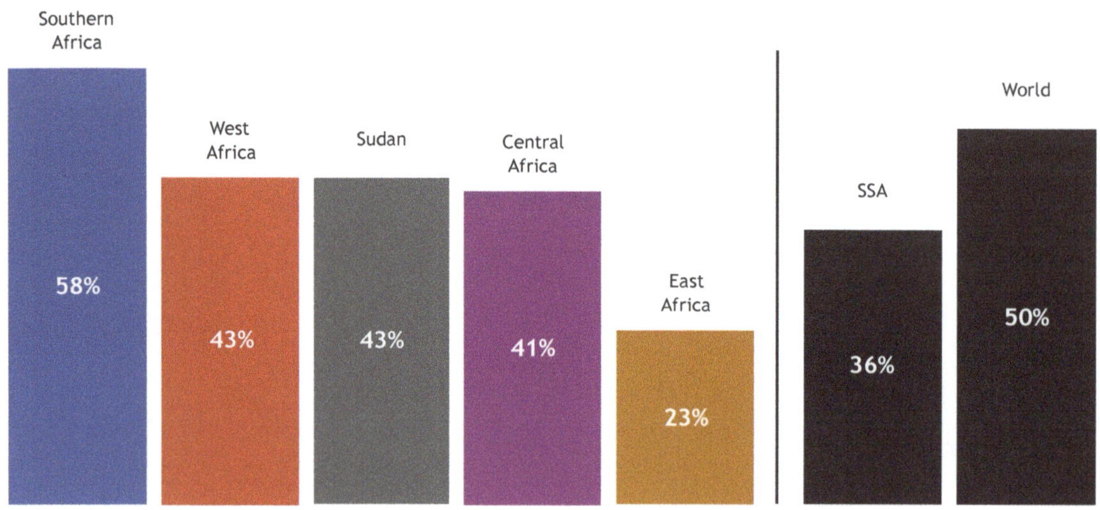

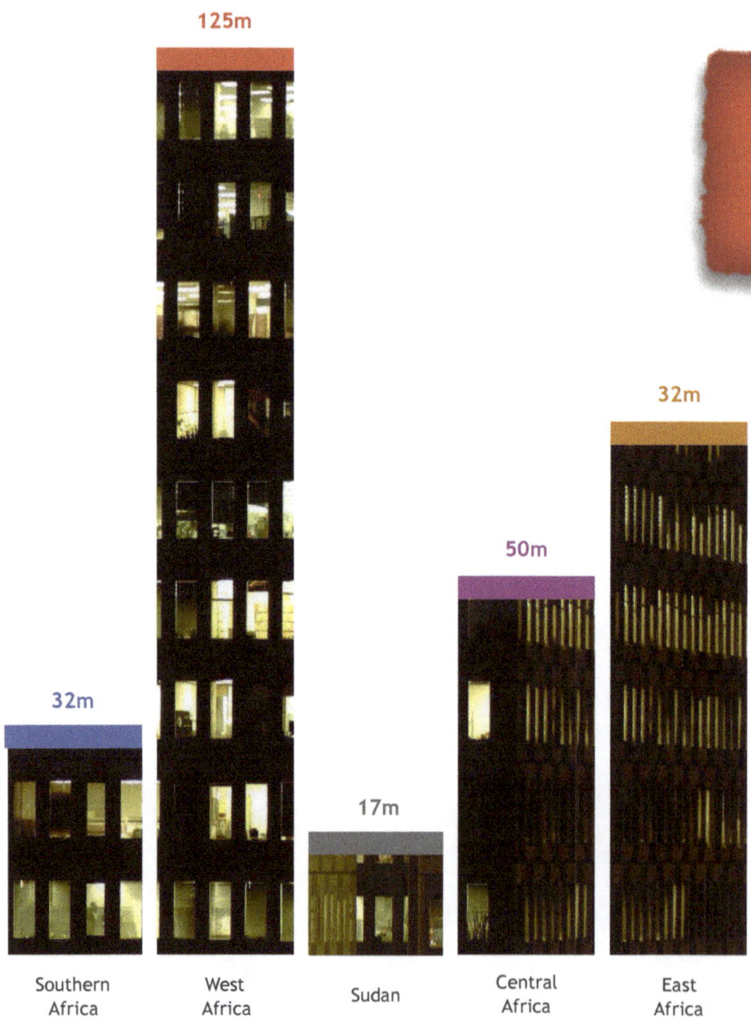

the city slickers within

Total Urban Population
2005-10

UNPD estimates

3.5b Urban Population in SSA: %. Top 10

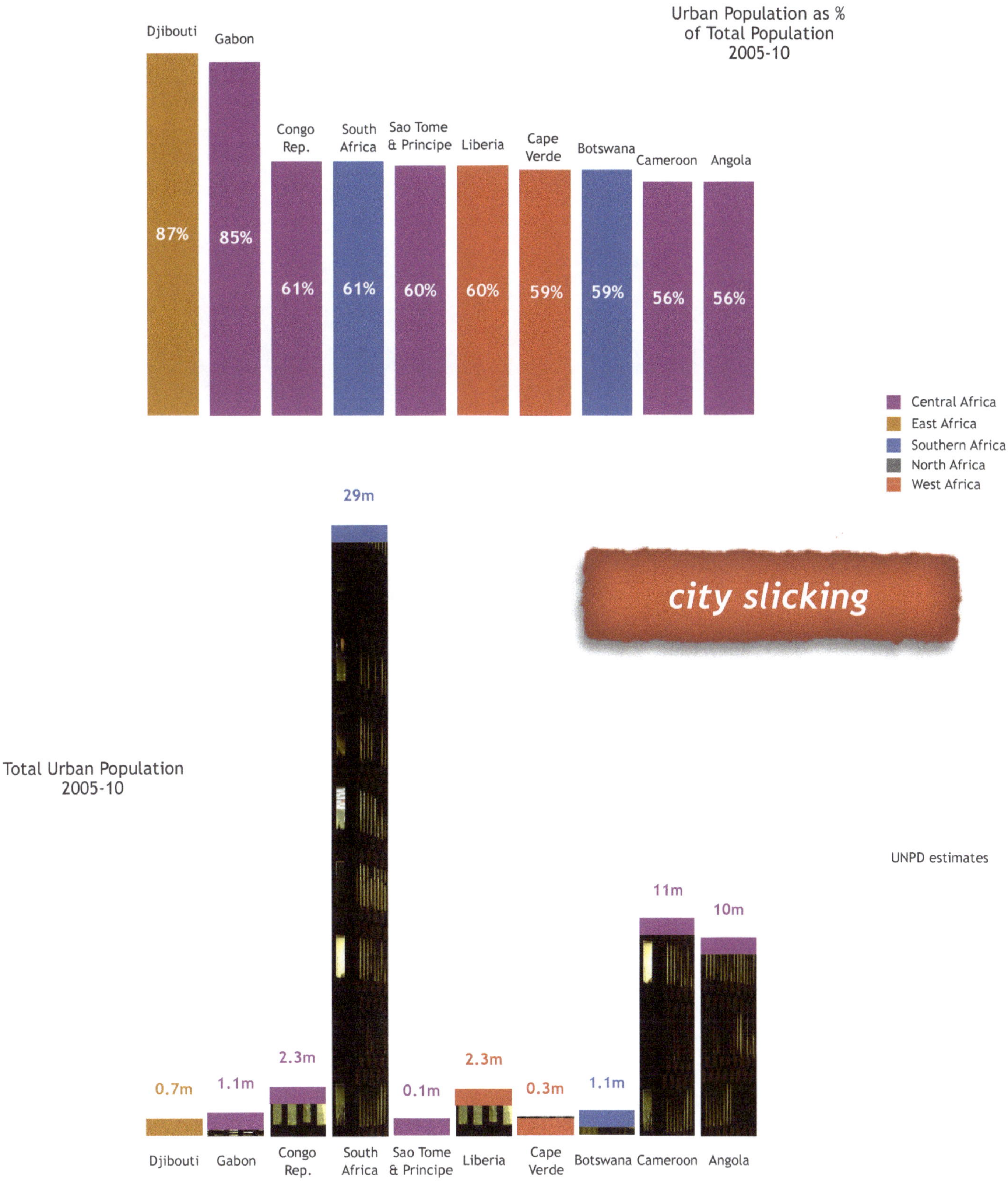

3.6a Rural Population in the Regions: % and numbers

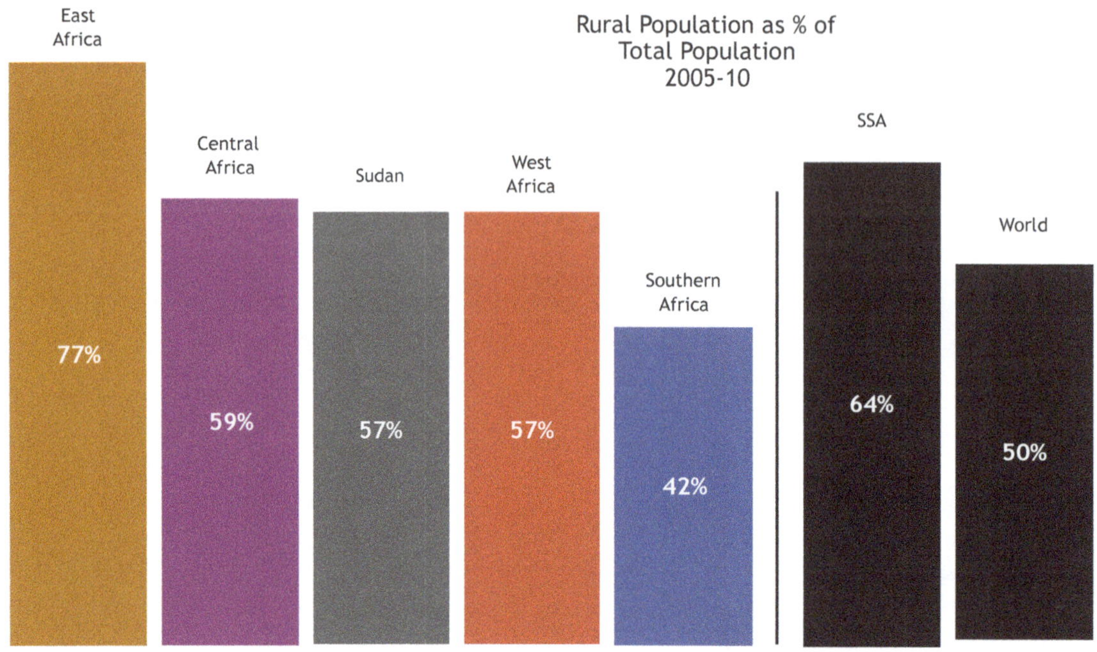

the country folk within

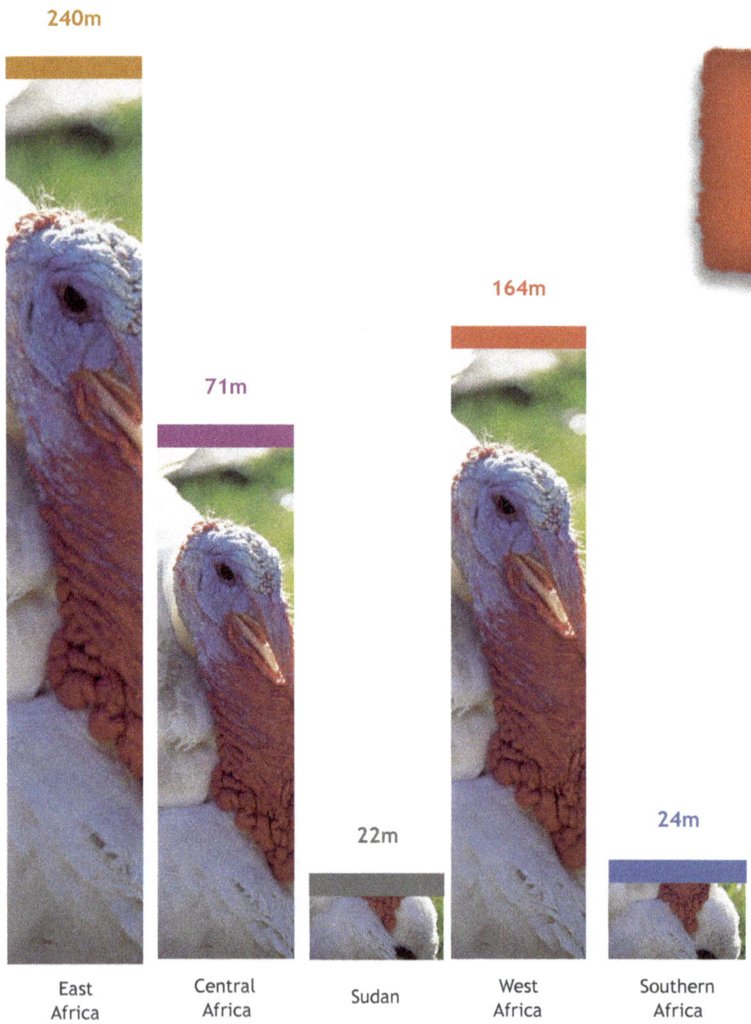

Total Rural Population 2005-10

UNPD estimates

3.6b Rural Population in SSA: %. Top 10

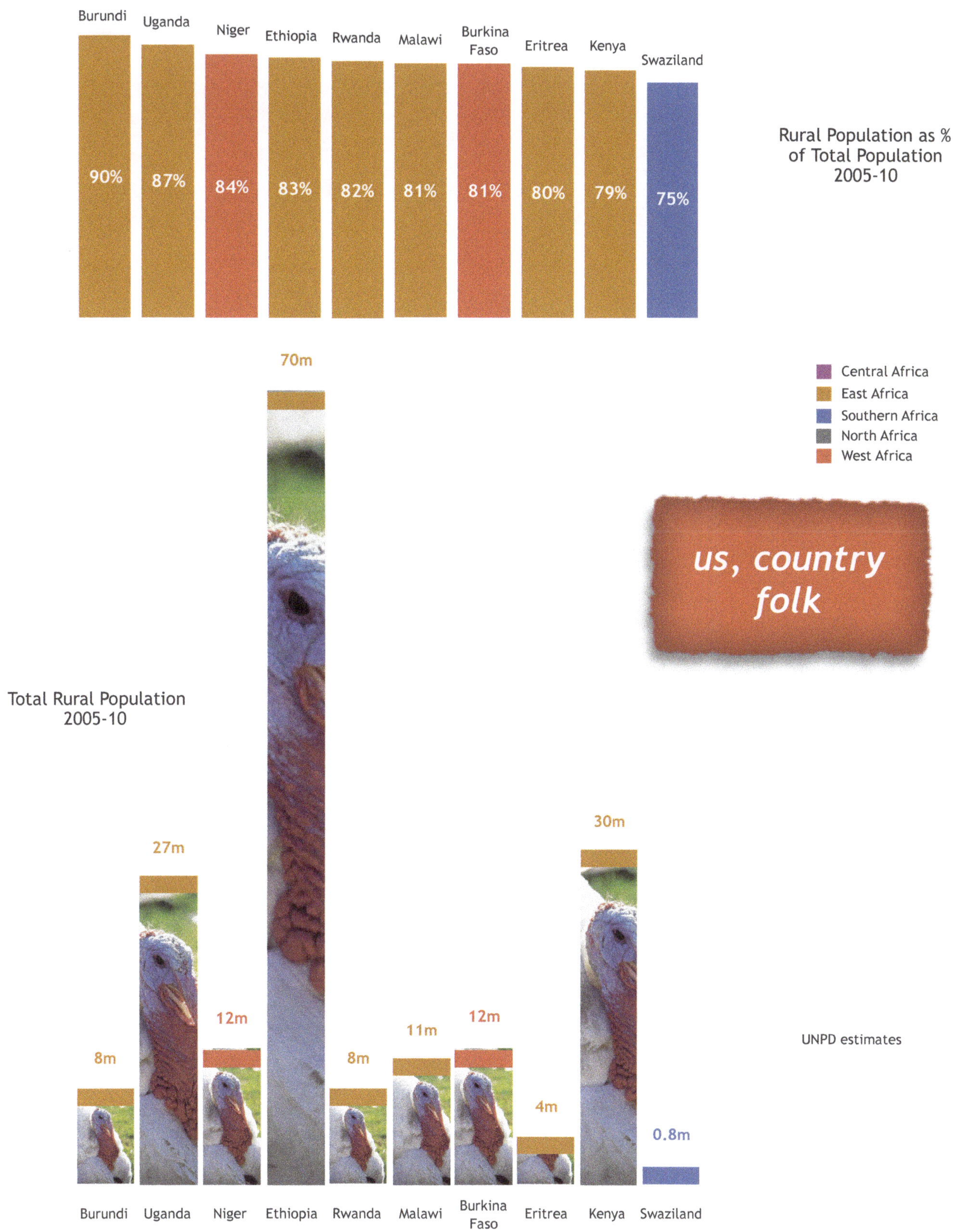

3.7 GDP in Sub-Saharan Africa's Regions ($PPP)

GDP of Sub-Saharan Africa during 1999/2002

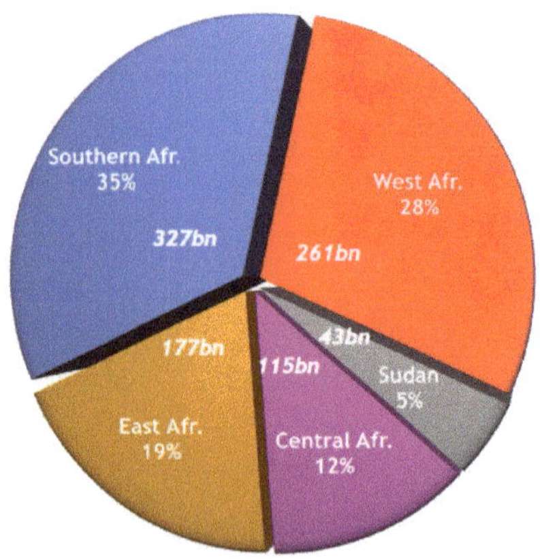

this is how they stack up

GDP of Sub-Saharan Africa during 2003/06

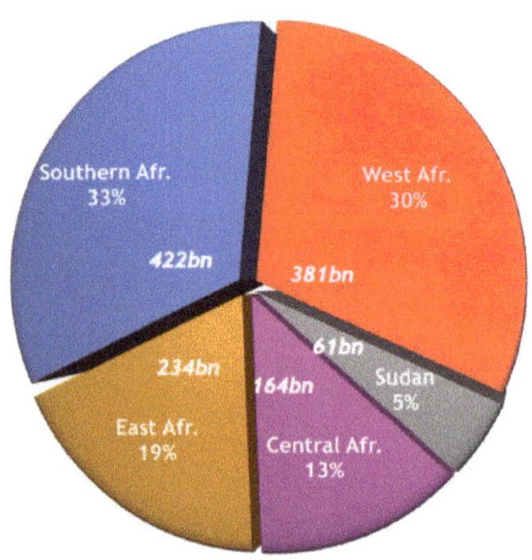

GDP of Sub-Saharan Africa during 2007/10

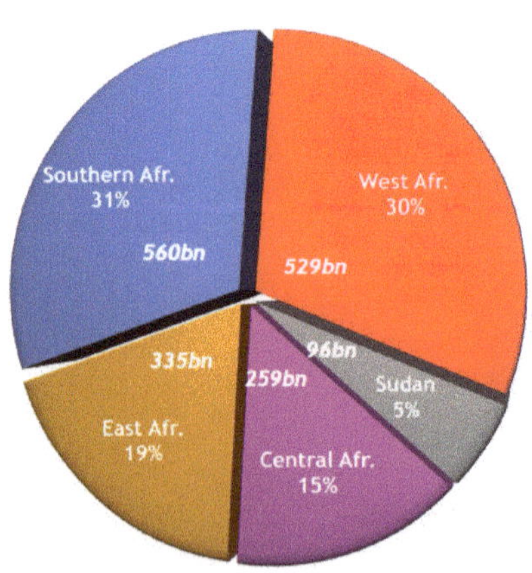

Contribution to the continent's GDP in 2009

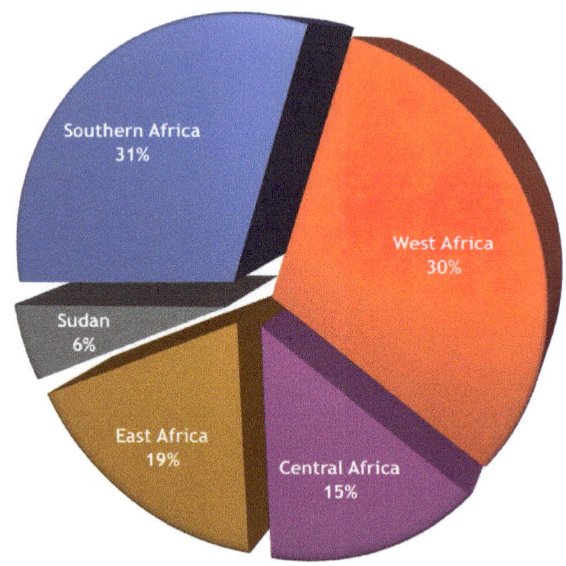

2009	GDP $PPP billions	GDP per Person $PPP
Southern Africa	574	10,229
West Africa	552	1,890
East Africa	345	1,219
Central Africa	272	2,208
Sudan	102	2,597

Primary data: IMF

4. The Size of Foreign Direct Investment

4.1 FDI Outcome in the World's Development Groups

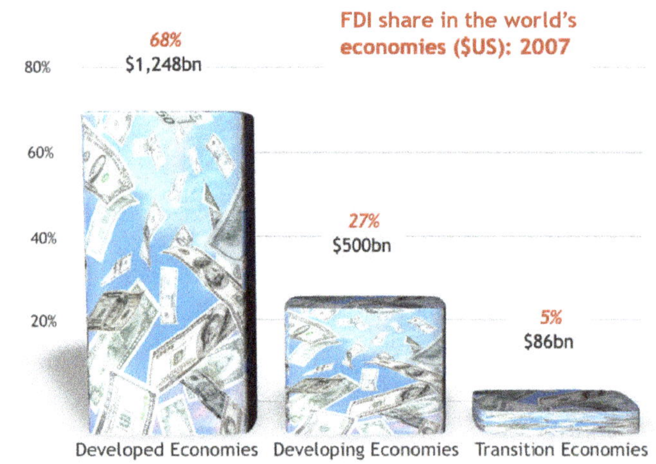

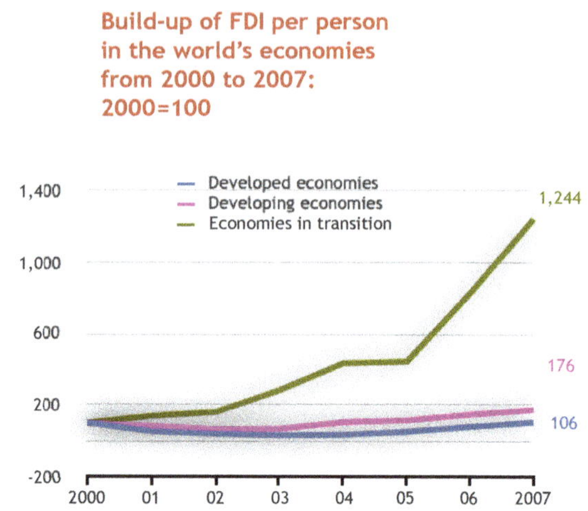

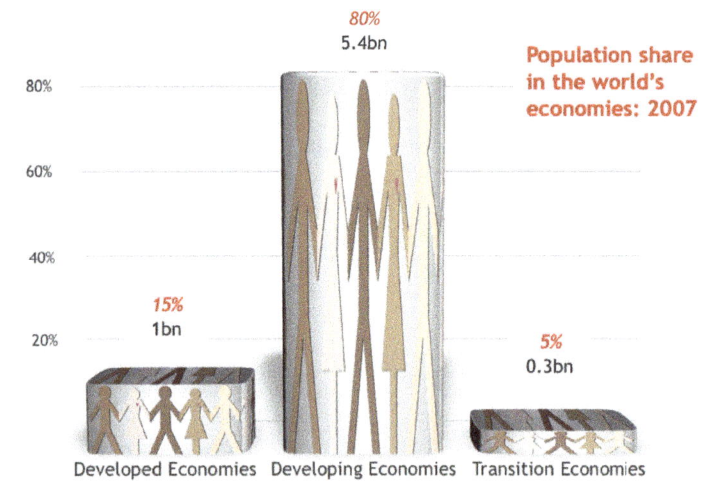

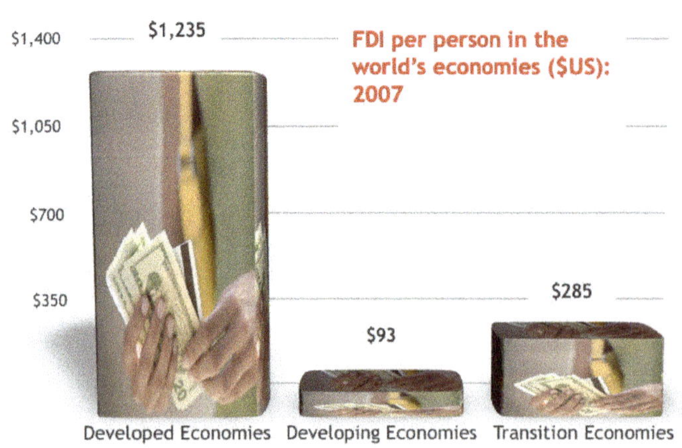

- Not a surprising picture, perhaps. Most of the world's foreign investment by far, went to the developed nations. And the smallest (when measured per person of population) effectively ended up in the developing economies of the world.
- Partly because these developing economies have the largest population (5-and-a-half times the developed world's) and partly because they attracted a too small share of the world's FDI.
- The transition economies (mainly in eastern Europe and parts of south-east Asia) were a favorite destination between 2000 and 2007, with investment per person taking off and leaving both the developed and developing countries in its wake. Even though the latter two groups built on their year 2000 levels, albeit only marginally so.

Primary Data: UNCTAD

4.2 FDI Outcome in the Developing Economies

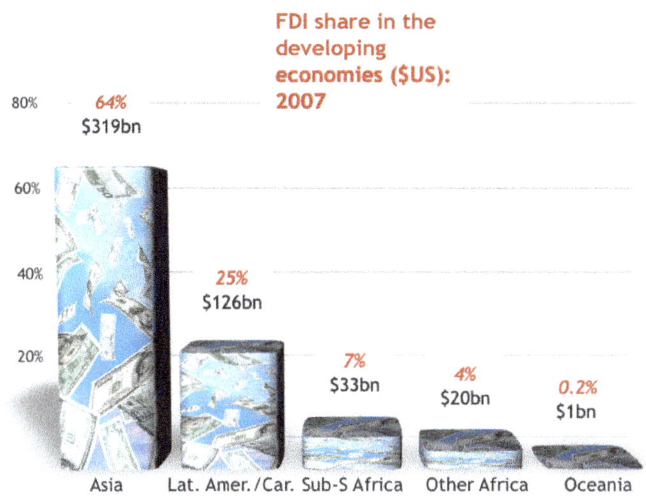

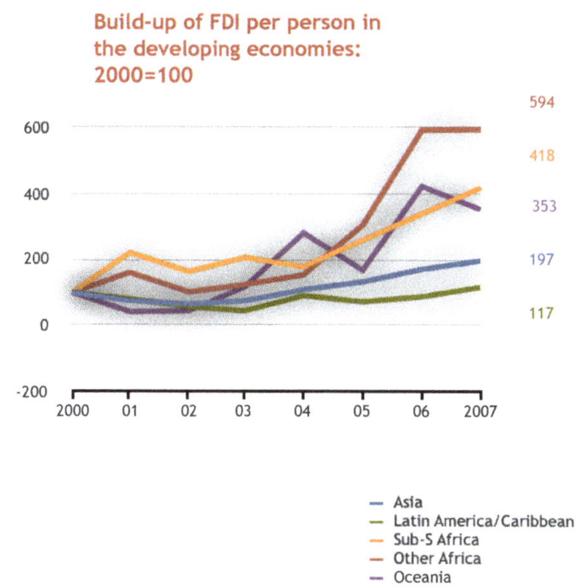

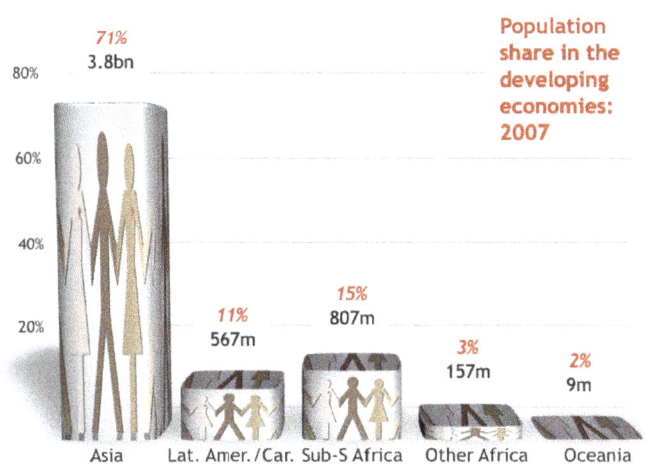

- Among the developing economies, Asian countries attracted the most FDI by a distance. But they also hold the highest number of residents, leaving them with only a moderate investment per person.
- That figure was still high, though, compared to the Sub-Saharan Africa level.
- Only Latin America/Caribbean & Other Africa attracted a share of developing world FDI larger than their shares of its population.
- Sub-Saharan Africa had the smallest FDI per resident.
- Africa was gaining ground, though, building up on foreign investment faster than the rest of the developing world.

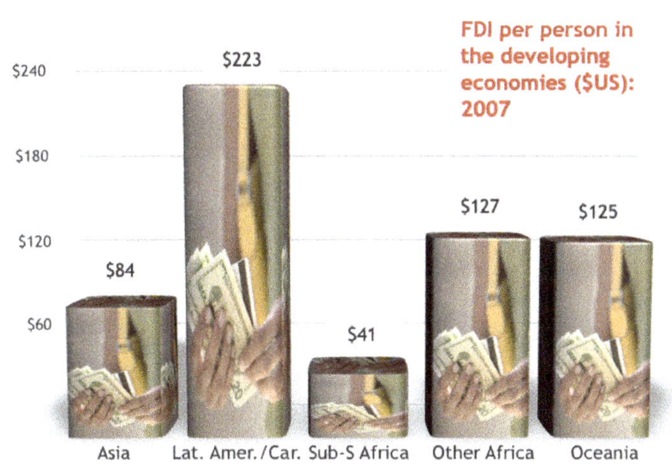

Primary Data: UNCTAD

4.3 FDI Outcome in the 5 Continents

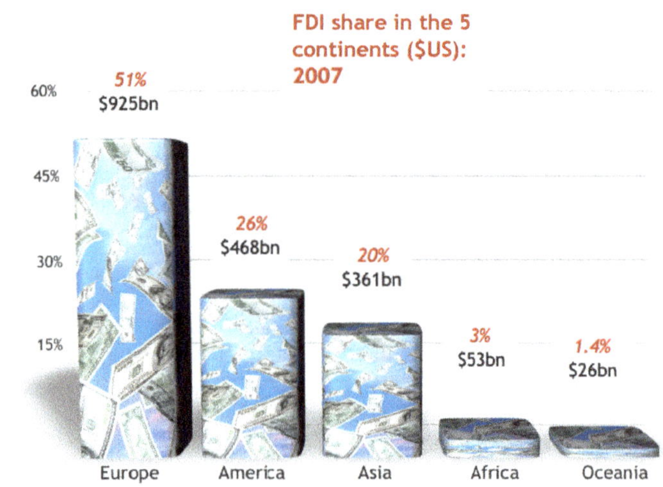

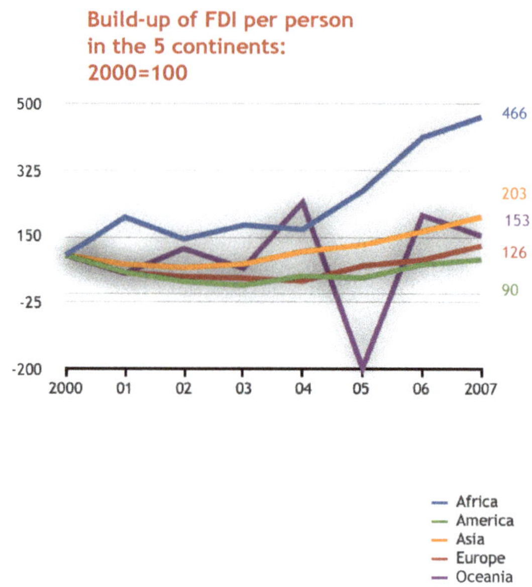

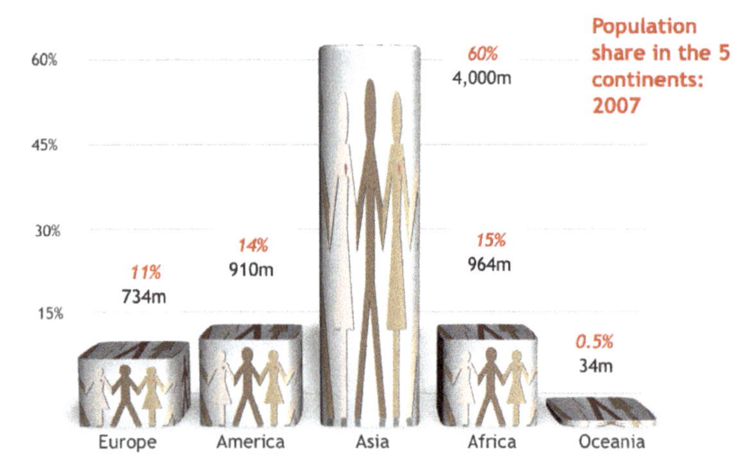

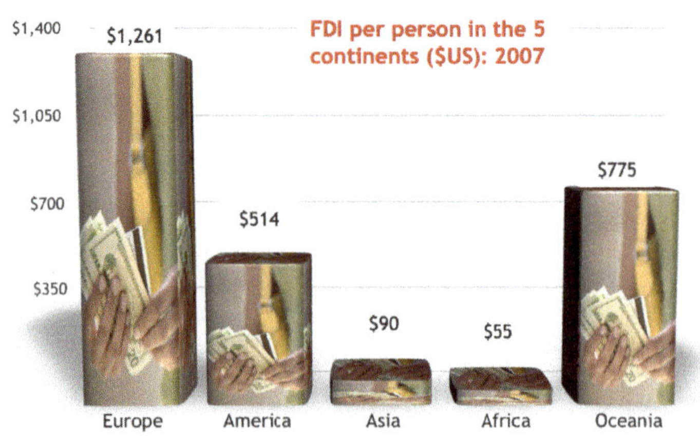

- Asia is the most populous of the 5 continents, commanding the third largest volume of foreign direct investment; behind Europe and both Americas.
- Africa is the 2nd most populous, behind Asia and ahead of America, Europe and Oceania. It cornered the least investment per person.
- That situation seems on course to change, though: Africa was building up FDI per population faster than the rest of the world, since the year 2000.

Primary Data: UNCTAD

4.4 FDI Outcome in Sub-Saharan Africa

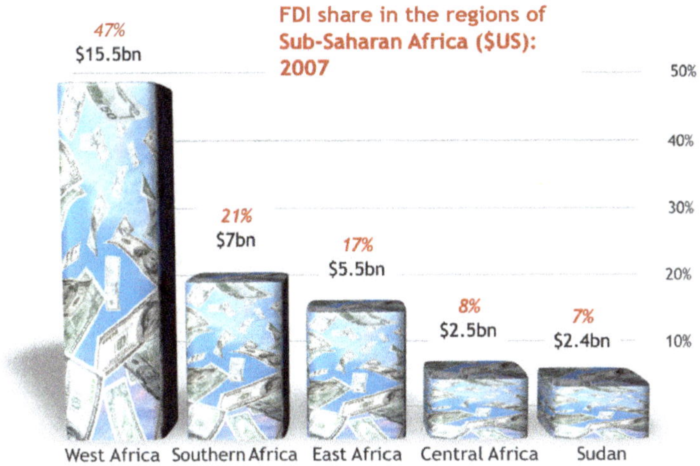

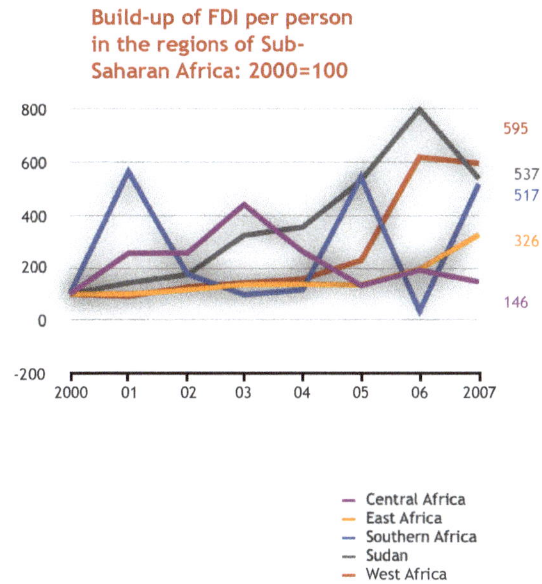

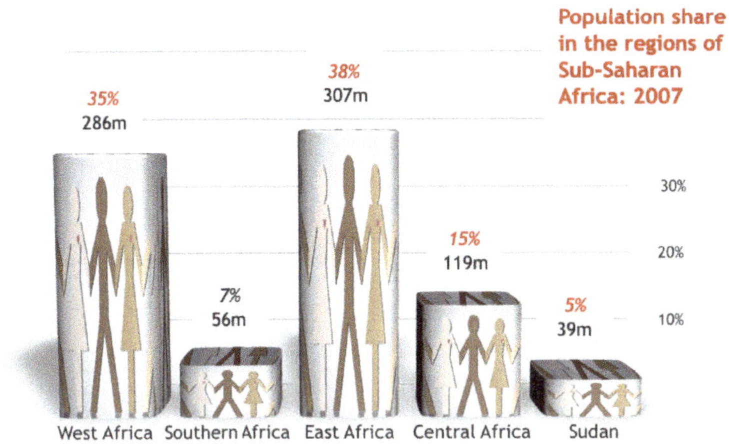

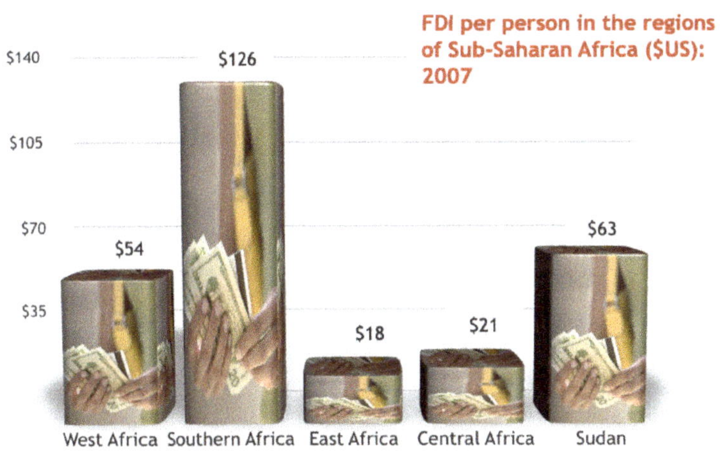

- Within Sub-Saharan Africa itself, West Africa was the final destination of most FDI, 47% of total. The next region was Southern Africa, with 21%, less than half West Africa's.
- Nevertheless, Southern Africa still ends up with the highest investment per resident, because its population is much smaller than West Africa's. Indeed, it had the highest FDI per person in the continent.
- Southern Africa was followed by Sudan in 2nd place, and West Africa in 3rd. Then Central Africa and East Africa in 4th and 5th place, respectively.
- In terms of levels of investment since the year 2000, West Africa was doing best, as at 2007. But it had been surpassed for many years by Sudan, until 2007. Southern Africa had varied haphazardly and Central Africa – of the 5 regions – had performed worst.

4.5 Share of FDI & Share of Population in S.S. Africa

03-06

Share of FDI ▲	bottom tier of population	middle tier of population	top tier of population
TOP TIER FDI: ranks 1 - 16	• Equat. Guinea • Botswana • Mauritania • Namibia	• Chad • Zambia • Congo, Rep.	• Nigeria • Sudan • South Africa • Angola • Ethiopia • Tanzania • Uganda • Cameroon • Côte d'Ivoire
MIDDLE TIER FDI: ranks 17 - 32	• Gabon • Seychelles • Cape Verde • Djibouti • Lesotho • Mauritius	• Mali • Senegal • Guinea • Togo • Malawi • Benin • Sierra Leone	• Ghana • Mozambique • Madagascar
BOTTOM TIER FDI: ranks 33 - 48	• Gambia • Sao Tome & Prin. • Guinea-Bissau • Comoros • Swaziland • Liberia	• Somalia • Niger • Central Afr. Rep. • Rwanda • Eritrea • Burundi	• Kenya • Zimbabwe • Burkina Faso • Congo, Dem. R.

Share of Population ▶

- Central Africa
- East Africa
- Southern Africa
- North Africa
- West Africa

Primary Data: UNCTAD

	% Share: 03-06	FDI	Popn
1	Nigeria	31.6	18.4
2	Sudan	11.8	4.8
3	South Africa	10.4	6.3
4	Equatorial Guinea	9.0	0.1
5	Angola	4.9	2.1
6	Chad	3.4	1.3
7	Ethiopia	2.5	10.3
8	Tanzania	2.3	5.0
9	Zambia	2.3	1.5
10	Botswana	2.1	0.2
11	Mauritania	2.0	0.4
12	Congo, Rep.	1.9	0.5
13	Uganda	1.7	3.8
14	Cameroon	1.7	2.3
15	Namibia	1.5	0.3
16	Côte d'Ivoire	1.5	2.4

	% Share: 03-06	FDI	Popn
17	Ghana	1.4	2.9
18	Mozambique	1.1	2.7
19	Gabon	1.0	0.2
20	Madagascar	0.8	2.4
21	Mali	0.7	1.5
22	Senegal	0.5	1.5
23	Guinea	0.5	1.2
24	Seychelles	0.4	0.0
25	Cape Verde	0.4	0.1
26	Djibouti	0.4	0.1
27	Togo	0.3	0.8
28	Lesotho	0.3	0.3
29	Malawi	0.3	1.7
30	Mauritius	0.3	0.2
31	Benin	0.3	1.1
32	Sierra Leone	0.3	0.7

	% Share: 03-06	FDI	Popn
33	Kenya	0.3	4.6
34	Gambia, The	0.2	0.2
35	Zimbabwe	0.2	1.7
36	Somalia	0.2	1.1
37	Niger	0.2	1.7
38	Burkina Faso	0.2	1.8
39	Central African Rep	0.1	0.5
40	Sao Tome &	0.1	0.0
41	Rwanda	0.1	1.2
42	Guinea-Bissau	0.0	0.2
43	Eritrea	0.0	0.6
44	Comoros	0.0	0.1
45	Burundi	0.0	1.0
46	Swaziland	0.0	0.1
47	Congo, Dem. Rep.	0.0	7.6
48	Liberia	-1.3	0.4

	FDI per Person ($US)	2007
1	Equatorial Guinea	3,402
2	Seychelles	2,861
3	Namibia	336
4	Cape Verde	334
5	Mauritius	269
6	Botswana	263
7	Djibouti	235
8	Sao Tome & Principe	224
9	Gabon	202
10	South Africa	117
11	Congo, Rep.	93
12	Nigeria	84
13	Zambia	83
14	Sudan	63
15	Chad	56
16	Lesotho	53
17	Madagascar	51
18	Mauritania	49
19	Burkina Faso	41
20	Gambia, The	37
21	Ghana	36
22	Swaziland	33
23	Mali	29
24	Côte d'Ivoire	22
25	Mozambique	20
26	Kenya	19
27	Somalia	16
28	Cameroon	15
29	Tanzania	15
30	Sierra Leone	14
31	Uganda	12
32	Guinea	12
33	Congo, Dem. Rep.	11
34	Liberia	11
35	Togo	10
36	Rwanda	7
37	Senegal	6
38	Central African Rep.	6
39	Benin	5
40	Zimbabwe	5
41	Guinea-Bissau	4
42	Malawi	4
43	Ethiopia	3
44	Niger	2
45	Comoros	1
46	Burundi	0
47	Eritrea	-1
48	Angola	-88

4.6 Share of FDI & Share of Population in West Africa

this is how it worked out

2003 - 2006:

- Nigeria, expectedly, gulped the greatest part of the foreign direct investment in West Africa.
- Only 4 countries of the 16 cornered a larger share of West Africa's foreign direct investment than their share of its population size: Nigeria, Mauritania, Cape Verde, and – marginally – The Gambia.

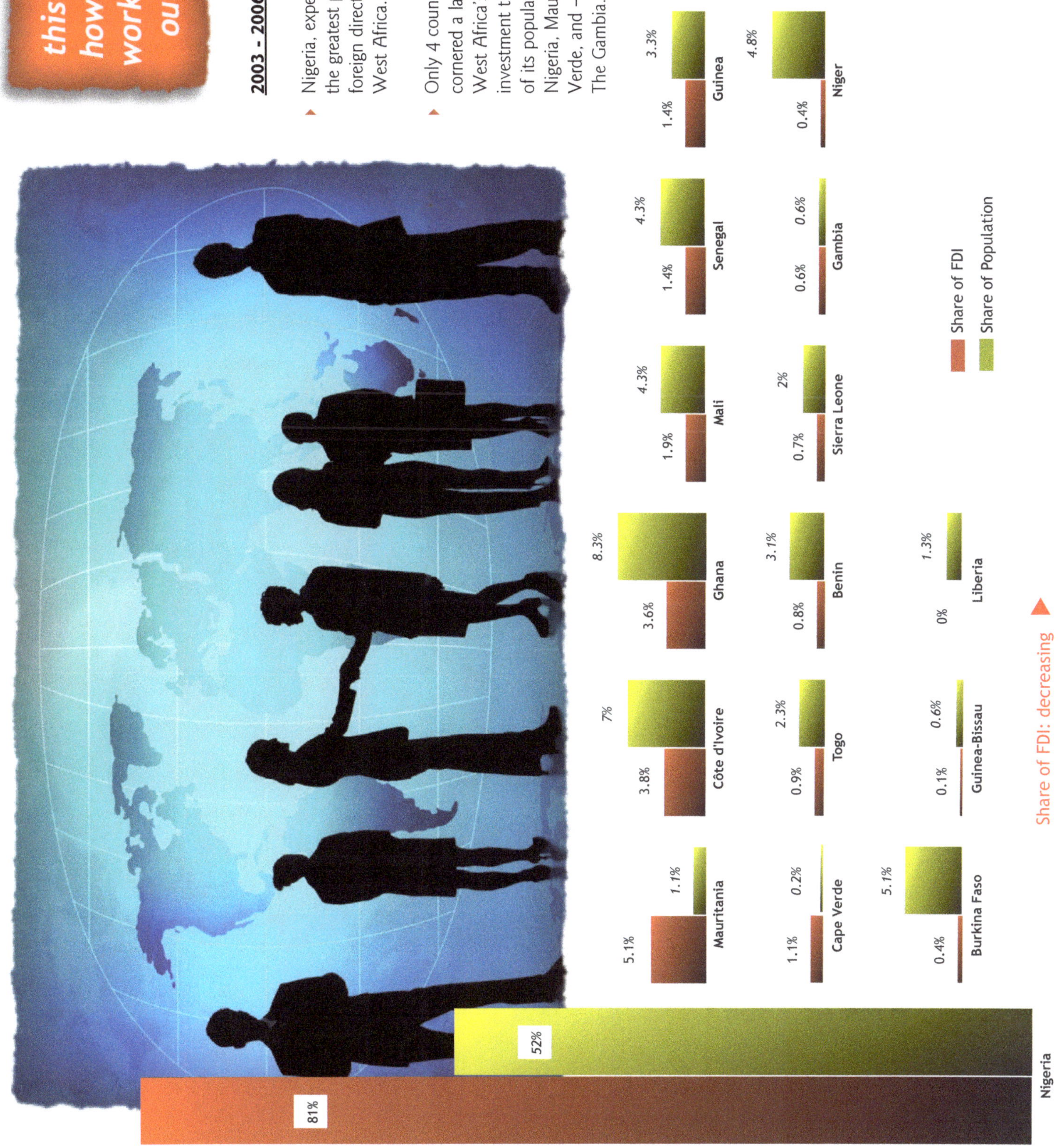

5. Tricky Relations

5.1 Tricky Relations: Foreign Aid & Quality of Life

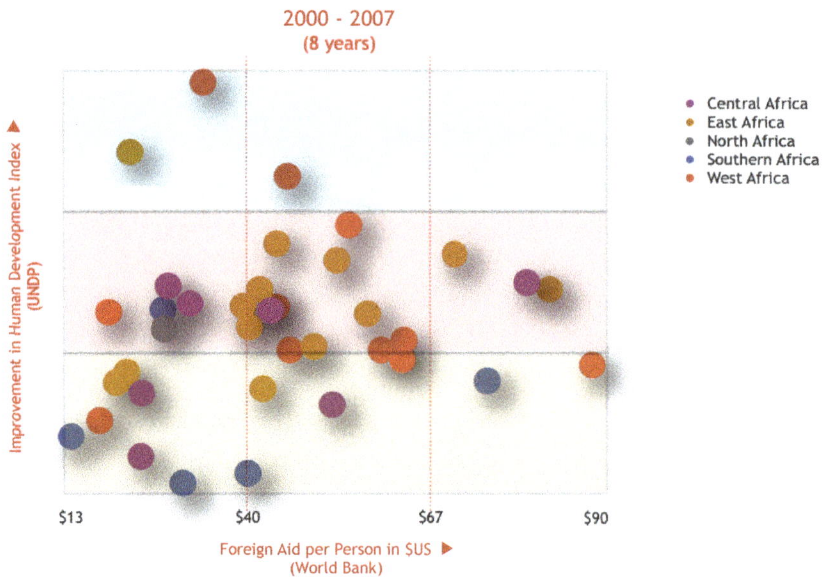

% distribution:

A 5%	D 3%	G 0%	8%
B 16%	E 27%	H 8%	51%
C 19%	F 17%	I 5%	41%
40%	47%	13%	

A: low aid, high improvement in quality of life
B: low aid, medium improvement in quality of life
C: low aid, low improvement in quality of life

D: medium aid, high improvement in quality of life
E: medium aid, medium improvement in quality of life
F: medium aid, low improvement in quality of life

G: high aid, high improvement in quality of life
H: high aid, medium improvement in quality of life
I: high aid, low improvement in quality of life

A
1. Niger
2. Ethiopia

2

D
1. Burkina Faso

1

G

0

B
1. Chad
2. Congo, D.R.
3. Burundi
4. Botswana
5. Nigeria
6. Sudan

6

E
1. Mali
2. Tanzania
3. Rwanda
4. Uganda
5. Benin
6. Equat. Guinea
7. Eritrea
8. Madagascar
9. Guinea-Bissau
10. Comoros

10

H
1. Mozambique
2. Congo, Rep.
3. Zambia

3

C
1. Mauritius
2. Kenya
3. Gabon
4. Côte d'Ivoire
5. South Africa
6. Central Afr. R.
7. Swaziland

7

F
1. Senegal
2. Ghana
3. Liberia
4. Malawi
5. Cameroon
6. Lesotho

6

I
1. Mauritania
2. Namibia

2

	Country	Improvemt in Qlty of Life	Aid per Pers.
		(%)	(US$)
1	•Niger	3.92	33
2	•Ethiopia	3.13	22
3	•Burkina Faso	2.85	45
4	•Mali	2.3	54
5	•Tanzania	2.09	43
6	•Mozambique	1.97	69
7	•Rwanda	1.9	52
8	•Congo, Rep.	1.65	80
9	•Chad	1.61	27
10	•Uganda	1.57	41
11	•Zambia	1.57	83
12	•Congo, Dem. Rep.	1.41	31
13	•Burundi	1.38	38
14	•Benin	1.37	43
15	•Botswana	1.34	27
16	•Equatorial Guinea	1.33	42
17	•Nigeria	1.31	19
18	•Eritrea	1.29	57
19	•Madagascar	1.14	39
20	•Sudan	1.12	27
21	•Guinea-Bissau	0.99	62
22	•Comoros	0.92	49
23	•Ghana	0.88	45
24	•Senegal	0.88	59
25	•Liberia	0.77	62
26	•Mauritania	0.71	90
27	•Cape Verde	0.71	270
28	•Mauritius	0.63	21
29	•Namibia	0.53	74
30	•Kenya	0.51	20
31	•Malawi	0.44	41
32	•Gabon	0.39	24
33	•Cameroon	0.26	51
34	•Côte d'Ivoire	0.08	17
35	•Seychelles	0.06	137
36	•South Africa	-0.1	13
37	•Central African Rep.	-0.33	23
38	•Lesotho	-0.52	39
39	•Swaziland	-0.63	30

- Data on foreign aid here is as provided by the World Bank. Improvement in quality of life is as assessed by the United Nations Development Program (UNDP) through its Human Development Index. 39 Sub-Saharan Africa countries had enough data to compare the two indices, but 2 countries had unusually high foreign aid per person, which flew way beyond the other countries, so they were left out of the chart-comparison here, leaving 37 countries. Those two countries are Cape Verde, with $270 per capita, and Seychelles, with $137. They would both have fallen within the "low improvement in quality of life" sector.

- It should be borne in mind that low improvement in quality of life does not necessarily translate into low quality of life. The progress made during these 8 years (2000-2007) might very well be smaller in country Y compared to country Z, but country Y's level of quality of life might very well be vastly superior to Z's, even though the leap in level across the 8 years is smaller. (Indeed, the leap might be smaller precisely because there isn't much more room to improve from the subsisting level. Hence South Africa and Mauritius fall into the bottom quality of life improvement group. Nonetheless, for the majority of African economies, the improvement levels shown would still be an appropriate reflection of the existing levels of quality of life.)

- It turns out that there isn't an obvious pattern to the foreign aid received and the ensuing level of quality of life. Most countries ended up in the average levels: 47% received medium aid, and 51% turned up with medium improvements in quality of life. The scattered dots show the absence of any clearly defined pattern.

- However, it can be seen that of the 3 countries with the best improvement in quality of life, 2 are from West Africa (Niger, followed by Burkina Faso) and 1 from East Africa (Ethiopia). It is also interesting to note that Niger received less aid than Burkina Faso, but outdid it in quality of life improvement, as did Ethiopia as well.

- In the medium segment of quality of life improvement, a West African country also comes out tops: Mali, and it received average foreign aid amounts.

- Mauritania received the most aid ($90) but didn't make much progress in quality of life.

- Even though most of Southern Africa fell into the bottom quality of life improvement category, as explained above, they still had high absolute levels of quality of life. Nonetheless, South Africa, Lesotho and Swaziland, actually recorded deterioration in quality of life, albeit to small extents.

- ***Hence, no apparent relationship between foreign aid and improvement in quality of life. There must be other stronger factors at play.***

5.2 Tricky Relations: Foreign Aid & Economic Growth

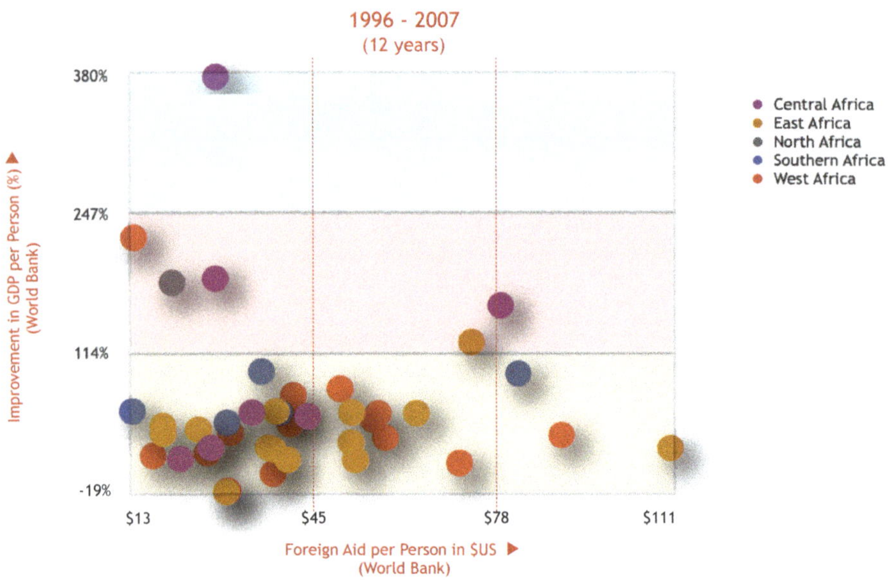

% distribution:

A 2%	D 0%	G 0%	2%
B 7%	**E 2%**	**H 2%**	**11%**
C 58%	**F 22%**	**I 7%**	**87%**
67%	24%	9%	

A: low aid, high economic growth
B: low aid, medium economic growth
C: low aid, low economic growth

D: medium aid, high economic growth
E: medium aid, medium economic growth
F: medium aid, low economic growth

G: high aid, high economic growth
H: high aid, medium economic growth
I: high aid, low economic growth

A
1. Angola

1

D

0

G

0

B
1. Nigeria
2. Chad
3. Sudan

3

E
1. Zambia

1

H
1. Congo, Rep.

1

C
1. Botswana
2. Burkina Faso
3. Benin
4. South Africa
5. Tanzania
6. Lesotho
7. Gabon
8. Cameroon
9. Swaziland
10. Ghana
11. Ethiopia
12. Mauritius
13. Niger
14. Kenya
15. Uganda
16. Central Afr. R.
17. Madagascar
18. Côte d'Ivoire
19. Togo
20. Congo, D.R.
21. Malawi
22. Gambia
23. Guinea
24. Burundi

24

F
1. Mali
2. Comoros
3. Mozambique
4. Senegal
5. Liberia
6. Sierra Leone
7. Eritrea
8. Rwanda
9. Guinea-Bissau

9

I
1. Namibia
2. Mauritania
3. Djibouti

3

	Country	Improvement in GDP/pers	Aid/pers.
		(%)	(US$)
1	•Angola	379	28
2	•Nigeria	225	13
3	•Chad	186	28
4	•Sudan	182	20
5	•Congo, Rep.	160	80
6	•Zambia	124	74
7	•Cape Verde	102	278
8	•Botswana	96	36
9	•Namibia	94	83
10	•Mali	80	50
11	•Burkina Faso	73	42
12	•Benin	60	41
13	•South Africa	59	13
14	•Tanzania	58	39
15	•Comoros	57	52
16	•Lesotho	57	39
17	•Gabon	57	34
18	•Mozambique	56	64
19	•Senegal	56	57
20	•Cameroon	54	45
21	•Seychelles	52	170
22	•Liberia	50	56
23	•Swaziland	47	30
24	•Ghana	46	41
25	•Ethiopia	45	18
26	•Mauritius	41	25
27	•Niger	38	30
28	•Kenya	37	18
29	•Mauritania	35	91
30	•Sierra Leone	33	59
31	•Eritrea	28	52
32	•Uganda	23	37
33	•Central African Rep.	23	27
34	•Djibouti	23	111
35	•Madagascar	22	38
36	•Côte d'Ivoire	18	26
37	•Togo	16	16
38	•Congo, Dem. Rep.	12	21
39	•Malawi	12	41
40	•Rwanda	11	53
41	•Guinea-Bissau	8	72
42	•Gambia, The	-2	38
43	•Guinea	-18	30
44	•Burundi	-19	30

- This time, the comparison is possible for a period as long as 12 years: the average foreign aid per capita during 1996-2007 is compared with the change in GDP per capita during the same years. That change is evaluated by taking the moving 3-year average at the period's start and comparing it with the closing moving 3-year average at its end.

- 44 countries in total, but two are dropped from the chart because of their extreme aid-per-person figures. They are Cape Verde ($278) and the Seychelles ($170). They would both have fallen into the low economic growth segment, hardly altering the conclusion.

- The majority of countries by far (87%) ended up in the low economic growth group. Even making allowances for the large economies among them (few, like South Africa) that may not be able – and may not need – to grow as rapidly as counterpart smaller economies, the outcome nevertheless strongly suggests that foreign aid has borne little connection to economic outcomes.

- The economies that grew fastest, ending up in the top two rows, were mainly oil exporters: Angola in the top row, then Nigeria, Chad, Sudan, and Republic of the Congo. Zambia is the only non-oil economy among them. Of these six, the leading four received less foreign aid than most of the continent.

- Indeed, the highest aid recipient on the chart is Djibouti, and that doesn't seem to have affected its rate of economic growth during the 12 year period.

- It doesn't seem that there are geographical peculiarities, either: the bottom row is awash with countries from all corners of the region.

- ***Tricky relations? Perhaps. But it does seem that volume of foreign aid received does not affect the pace of economic change.***

5.3 Tricky Relations: Foreign Aid & Child Mortality

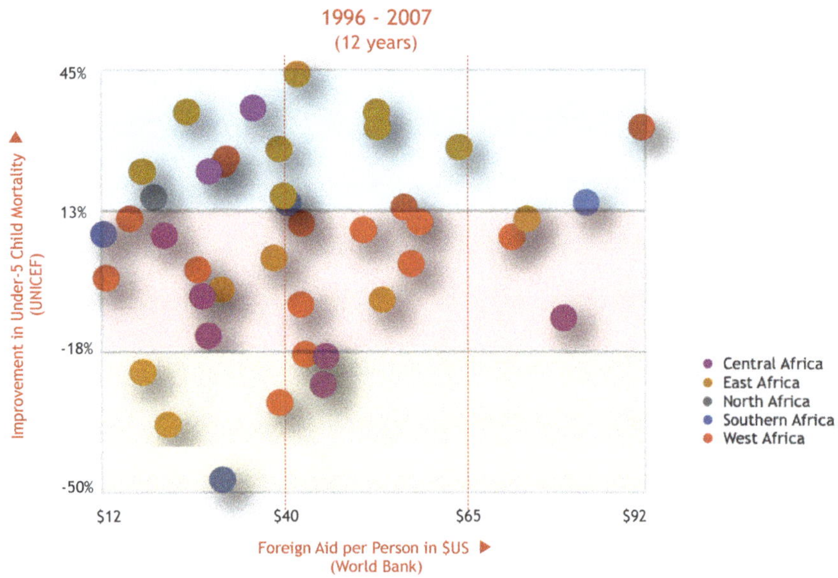

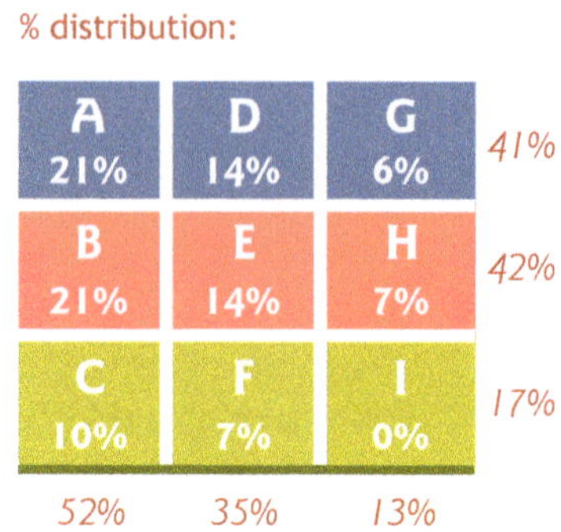

A: low aid, best improvement in child mortality
B: low aid, average improvement in child mortality
C: low aid, least improvement in child mortality

D: medium aid, best improvement in child mortality
E: medium aid, average improvement in child mortality
F: medium aid, least improvement in child mortality

G: high aid, best improvement in child mortality
H: high aid, average improvement in child mortality
I: high aid, least improvement in child mortality

A

1. Gabon
2. Mauritius
3. Madagascar
4. Niger
5. Guinea
6. Ethiopia
7. Angola
8. Tanzania
9. Sudan

9

D

1. Malawi
2. Eritrea
3. Comoros
4. Mozambique
5. Lesotho
6. Liberia

6

G

1. Mauritania
2. Namibia

2

B

1. Togo
2. South Africa
3. Congo, D.R.
4. Uganda
5. Côte d'Ivoire
6. Nigeria
7. Burundi
8. Central Afr. R.
9. Chad

9

E

1. Sierra Leone
2. Benin
3. Mali
4. Senegal
5. Rwanda
6. Ghana

6

H

1. Zambia
2. Guinea-Bissau
3. Congo, Rep.

3

C

1. Kenya
2. Gambia
3. Zimbabwe
4. Swaziland

4

F

1. Burkina Faso
2. Equat. Guinea
3. Cameroon

3

I

0

	Country	Improvement in U-5 Mortality	Aid/pers.
		(%)	($US)
1	•Cape Verde	54	278
2	•Malawi	45	41
3	•Gabon	37	34
4	•Mauritius	36	25
5	•Eritrea	36	52
6	•Comoros	33	52
7	•Mauritania	33	91
8	•Seychelles	29	170
9	•Mozambique	28	64
10	•Madagascar	28	38
11	•Niger	26	30
12	•Guinea	24	30
13	•Ethiopia	23	18
14	•Angola	23	28
15	•Tanzania	17	39
16	•Djibouti	17	111
17	•Sudan	17	20
18	•Lesotho	16	39
19	•Namibia	16	83
20	•Liberia	15	56
21	•Zambia	12	74
22	•Togo	12	16
23	•Sierra Leone	11	59
24	•Benin	11	41
25	•Mali	9	50
26	•South Africa	8	13
27	•Congo, Dem. Rep.	8	21
28	•Guinea-Bissau	8	72
29	•Uganda	3	37
30	•Senegal	2	57
31	•Côte d'Ivoire	0	26
32	•Nigeria	-2	13
33	•Burundi	-4	30
34	•Central African Rep.	-6	27
35	•Rwanda	-7	53
36	•Ghana	-8	41
37	•Congo, Rep.	-11	80
38	•Chad	-15	28
39	•Burkina Faso	-19	42

	Country	Improvement in U-5 Mortality	Aid/pers.
		(%)	($US)
40	•Equatorial Guinea	-20	45
41	•Kenya	-23	18
42	•Cameroon	-26	45
43	•Gambia, The	-30	38
44	•Sao Tome & Principe	-33	231
45	•Zimbabwe	-35	22
46	•Swaziland	-48	30
47	•Botswana	-93	36

- Data is available this time for all 48 countries except Somalia. Under-5 child mortality, here provided by UNICEF, refers to the number of children out of 1,000 who die before their 5th birthday. We measured improvement by comparing the opening 3-yr moving average (1996-1998) of the mortality figure, to the closing 3-yr moving average (2005-2007).

- Within those 47 countries, 5 fell around the chart extremes and were left out of it for better analysis. Four of them had extreme aid per person figures: Cape Verde ($278), Sao Tome & Principe ($231), the Seychelles ($170) and Djibouti ($111). All of them, except Sao Tome & Principe, would have landed in the top row of improvement in child mortality, as can be gleaned from the table at left. Botswana is the 5th country removed, this time for the extremity of its mortality deterioration, 93%.

- It turns out that there might indeed be a trend towards a bigger improvement in mortality figures with the increase of foreign aid. The countries which suffered the worst improvement were generally those which had received less aid. As aid increased, the mortality situation seemed to improve alongside it.

- It can be noted, though, that among the least aid recipients were to be found some countries that nonetheless posted the best improvements in under-5 mortality: Gabon and Mauritius, particularly, among 7 others. The most improvement was notched by Malawi, and it received less than the average aid per capita on the continent.

- ***Still, there seems to be a trend towards improvement in mortality figures with the increase of foreign aid. Perhaps these specific aid tranches were aimed directly at health targets.***

5.4 Tricky Relations: Foreign Aid & Life Expectancy

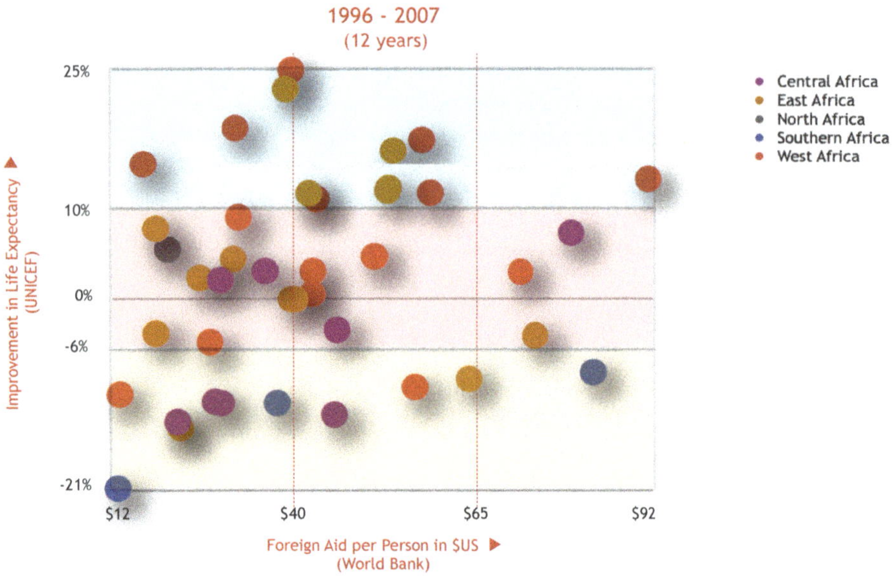

% distribution:

A 10%	D 17%	G 2%	29%
B 28%	E 10%	H 7%	45%
C 17%	F 7%	I 2%	26%
55%	34%	11%	

A: low aid, best improvement in life expectancy
B: low aid, average improvement in life expectancy
C: low aid, least improvement in life expectancy

D: medium aid, best improvement in life expectancy
E: medium aid, average improvement in life expectancy
F: medium aid, least improvement in life expectancy

G: high aid, best improvement in life expectancy
H: high aid, average improvement in life expectancy
I: high aid, least improvement in life expectancy

A

1. Gambia
2. Uganda
3. Guinea
4. Togo

4

D

1. Senegal
2. Rwanda
3. Comoros
4. Eritrea
5. Sierra Leone
6. Malawi
7. Burkina Faso

7

G

1. Mauritania

1

B

1. Niger
2. Ethiopia
3. Sudan
4. Burundi
5. Gabon
6. Mauritius
7. Chad
8. Tanzania
9. Madagascar
10. Kenya
11. Côte d'Ivoire

11

E

1. Mali
2. Benin
3. Ghana
4. Equat. Guinea

4

H

1. Congo, Rep.
2. Guinea-Bissau
3. Zambia

3

C

1. Nigeria
2. Central Afr. R.
3. Botswana
4. Angola
5. Congo, D.R.
6. Zimbabwe
7. South Africa

7

F

1. Mozambique
2. Liberia
3. Cameroon

3

I

1. Namibia

1

	Country	Improvmt in Life Exp.	Aid per Pers.
		(%)	($US)
1	•Gambia, The	25	38
2	•Uganda	23	37
3	•Guinea	18.7	30
4	•Senegal	17.4	57
5	•Rwanda	16.2	53
6	•Togo	14.8	16
7	•Mauritania	13.1	91
8	•Comoros	12.1	52
9	•Eritrea	11.8	52
10	•Malawi	11.6	41
11	•Sierra Leone	11.6	59
12	•Burkina Faso	10.9	42
13	•Niger	9	30
14	•Ethiopia	7.7	18
15	•Congo, Rep.	7.3	80
16	•Djibouti	7.3	111
17	•Cape Verde	5.9	278
18	•Sudan	5.5	20
19	•Mali	4.7	50
20	•Burundi	4.4	30
21	•Gabon	3.1	34
22	•Benin	3.1	41
23	•Guinea-Bissau	3	72
24	•Mauritius	2.3	25
25	•Chad	2.1	28
26	•Ghana	0.6	41
27	•Tanzania	0	39
28	•Madagascar	0	38
29	•Sao Tome & Principe	-2	231
30	•Equatorial Guinea	-3.4	45
31	•Kenya	-3.8	18
32	•Zambia	-4	74
33	•Côte d'Ivoire	-4.7	26
34	•Namibia	-8	83
35	•Mozambique	-8.7	64
36	•Liberia	-9.6	56
37	•Nigeria	-10.4	13
38	•Central African Rep.	-11.2	27
39	•Angola	-11.3	28
40	•Botswana	-11.3	36
41	•Cameroon	-12.6	45
42	•Congo, Dem. Rep.	-13.4	21
43	•Zimbabwe	-14.1	22
44	•South Africa	-20.7	13
45	•Lesotho	-31.8	39
46	•Swaziland	-38.5	30

- Data was available this time for all 48 countries except Somalia and the Seychelles. Cape Verde ($278), Sao Tome & Principe ($231) and Djibouti ($111) were removed from the chart, for extremity of aid data. Cape Verde and Djibouti reported improvement in life expectancy (Cape Verde: 6%, Djibouti: 7.3%) and would have qualified for the middle row of average improvement. Sao Tome & Principe, however, reported a deterioration (-2%) but would still have qualified in the middle row. Their absence doesn't alter the chart outcome much.

- On the contrary, the other two countries omitted from the chart might have done. Lesotho and Swaziland had the worst performance by far, clocking -32% and -39%, respectively. Southern Africa had the worst life expectancy deterioration figures: South Africa (-21%), Lesotho (-32%) and Swaziland (-39%) had the worst drops.

- Of the countries that received average aid, a greater number ended up in the top improvement bracket, than ended up in the bottom. It was almost the same for those that received the highest aid. Unlike those that received the least aid (more of them ended up at bottom than did at the top). Small bias towards concluding that more aid brought better advancement in life expectancy, but probably valid, nonetheless.

- West Africa made more progress in life expectancy than any other region, squeezing 7 of its 16 countries into the top row. No Central African country made top row. All Southern Africa fell into the bottom row; they were hardest hit by the pace of deterioration in life expectancy.

- ***Close call, but aid seems to have helped life expectancy outcomes.***

5.5 Tricky Relations: Foreign Aid & Emigration

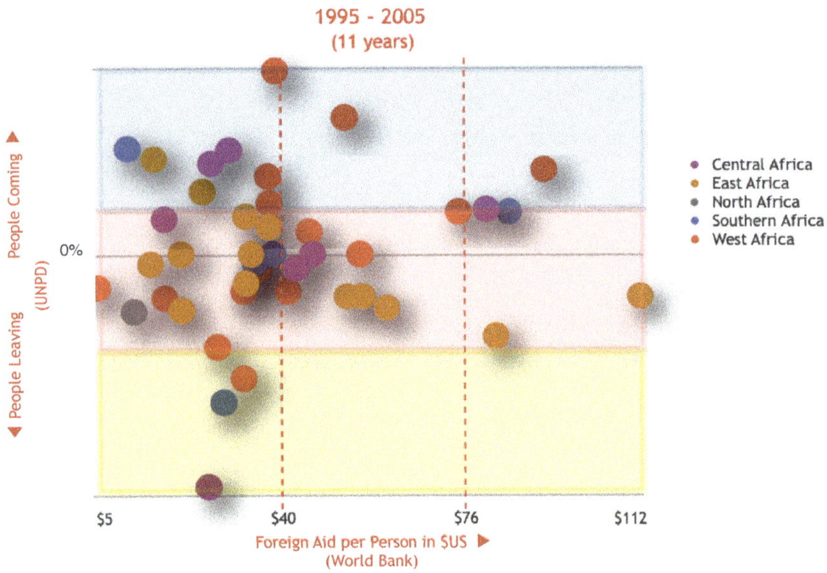

% distribution:

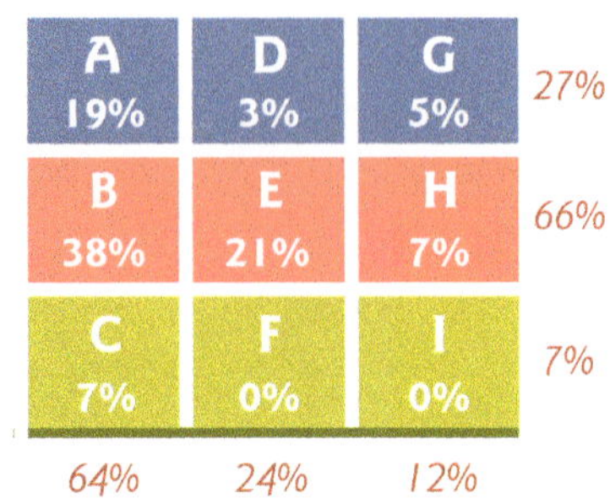

A: low aid, best migration situation
B: low aid, average migration situation
C: low aid, worst migration situation

D: medium aid, best migration situation
E: medium aid, average migration situation
F: medium aid, worst migration situation

G: high aid, best migration situation
H: high aid, average migration situation
I: high aid, worst migration situation

A

1. South Africa
2. Angola
3. Kenya
4. Chad
5. Burkina Faso
6. Burundi
7. Ghana

7

D

1. Sierra Leone

1

G

1. Mauritania
2. Congo, Rep.

2

B

1. Uganda
2. Congo, D.R.
3. Malawi
4. Lesotho
5. Madagascar
6. Mauritius
7. Botswana
8. Ethiopia
9. Gambia
10. Tanzania
11. Nigeria
12. Guinea
13. Togo
14. Zimbabwe
15. Sudan
16. Niger

16

E

1. Guinea-Bissau
2. Mali
3. Senegal
4. Equat. Guinea
5. Gabon
6. Liberia
7. Rwanda
8. Comoros
9. Mozambique

9

H

1. Namibia
2. Djibouti
3. Zambia

3

C

1. Côte d'Ivoire
2. Swaziland
3. Central Afr. R.

3

F

0

I

0

	Country	Improvemt in Migration	Aid per Pers.
		(%)	($US)
1	•Eritrea	2400	56
2	•Benin	433	40
3	•Sierra Leone	323	54
4	•South Africa	250	12
5	•Angola	246	31
6	•Kenya	225	17
7	•Chad	214	28
8	•Mauritania	200	93
9	•Burkina Faso	183	39
10	•Burundi	148	26
11	•Ghana	120	39
12	•Congo, Rep.	106	81
13	•Namibia	100	86
14	•Guinea-Bissau	100	76
15	•Uganda	89	34
16	•Congo, Dem. Rep.	83	19
17	•Malawi	65	39
18	•Mali	53	47
19	•Equatorial Guinea	0	48
20	•Sao Tome & Principe	0	279
21	•Madagascar	0	36
22	•Mauritius	0	22
23	•Lesotho	0	40
24	•Senegal	0	57
25	•Botswana	-20	36
26	•Ethiopia	-24	16
27	•Gabon	-33	44
28	•Gambia, The	-33	37
29	•Cape Verde	-50	273
30	•Tanzania	-68	35
31	•Nigeria	-79	6
32	•Liberia	-89	43
33	•Guinea	-89	34
34	•Rwanda	-100	57
35	•Comoros	-100	54
36	•Djibouti	-100	111
37	•Togo	-104	19
38	•Mozambique	-127	62
39	•Zimbabwe	-133	22

	Country	Improvemt in Migration	Aid per Pers.
		(%)	($US)
40	•Sudan	-136	13
41	•Zambia	-194	83
42	•Niger	-220	29
43	•Côte d'Ivoire	-294	34
44	•Swaziland	-350	30
45	•Central African Rep.	-550	27

- Aid per person is as assessed by the World Bank, and migration numbers are provided by the United Nations Population Division (UNPD) and computed every five years. For this comparison, change in net migration is computed for the period 1995 - 2005 by evaluating the percentage change in net migration figures for 1995 - 2000 and 2000 - 2005. A positive percentage would indicate a net movement of people into the country (immigration) and a negative percentage would indicate a net exodus of people (emigration) for the period.

- 45 countries with data available this time, and 3 removed from the chart for their extremity: Sao Tome & Principe ($279) and Cape Verde ($273) for their aid per capita, and Eritrea for its extreme net positive migration change (2,400%); most likely the return of its peoples after the long war years.

- At first glance, it appears that an increase in foreign aid brings with it a higher possibility that populations would return rather than leave. Countries completely disappear from the lowest band of the chart as aid increases, meaning immigrant rather than emigrant populations.

- Most of the 26 countries with small aid per person end up having average migration numbers (16 of them; mostly below zero, meaning emigration), the next highest is the batch of high returnees (7 countries), followed lastly by those with exiting populations (3 countries).

- No country with average aid per capita has high emigration numbers, and most end up in the average migration band.

- More of the 5 countries with high aid per capita turned out to encourage returnees rather than emigrants.

- ***Perhaps, in the end, foreign aid does influence migration figures by discouraging populations from leaving. Caution should be exercised with that conclusion, though. The relationship between both factors may not be a direct one.***

5.6 Tricky Relations: Economic Growth & Qlty of Life

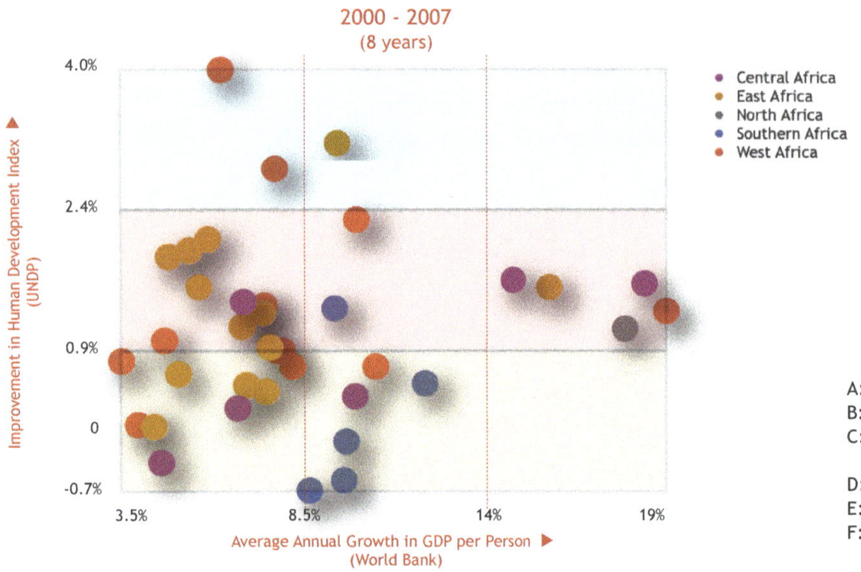

% distribution:

A 5%	D 3%	G 0%	8%
B 27%	E 5%	H 14%	46%
C 30%	F 16%	I 0%	46%
62%	24%	14%	

A: low econ. growth, high improvement in quality of life
B: low econ. growth, medium improvement in quality of life
C: low econ. growth, low improvement in quality of life

D: medium econ. growth, high improvement in quality of life
E: medium econ. growth, medium improvement in quality of life
F: medium econ. growth, low improvement in quality of life

G: high econ. growth, high improvement in quality of life
H: high econ. growth, medium improvement in quality of life
I: high econ. growth, low improvement in quality of life

A
1. Niger
2. Burkina Faso

2

D
1. Ethiopia

1

G

0

B
1. Tanzania
2. Mozambique
3. Rwanda
4. Uganda
5. Congo, D.R.
6. Benin
7. Eritrea
8. Madagascar
9. Guinea-Bissau
10. Comoros

10

E
1. Mali
2. Botswana

2

H
1. Congo, Rep.
2. Chad
3. Zambia
4. Nigeria
5. Sudan

5

C
1. Ghana
2. Senegal
3. Liberia
4. Mauritania
5. Mauritius
6. Kenya
7. Malawi
8. Cameroon
9. Côte d'Ivoire
10. Seychelles
11. Central Afr. R.

11

F
1. Cape Verde
2. Namibia
3. Gabon
4. South Africa
5. Lesotho
6. Swaziland

6

I

0

	Country	Improvemt in Qlty of Life	Growth in GDP/pers
		(%)	(%)
1	•Niger	3.92	6.4
2	•Ethiopia	3.13	9.7
3	•Burkina Faso	2.85	7.9
4	•Mali	2.3	10.2
5	•Tanzania	2.09	6.0
6	•Mozambique	1.97	5.5
7	•Rwanda	1.9	4.9
8	•Congo, Rep.	1.65	14.6
9	•Chad	1.61	18.4
10	•Uganda	1.57	5.8
11	•Zambia	1.57	15.7
12	•Congo, Dem. Rep.	1.41	7.0
13	•Burundi	1.38	0.4
14	•Benin	1.37	7.6
15	•Botswana	1.34	9.6
16	•Equatorial Guinea	1.33	36.8
17	•Nigeria	1.31	19.0
18	•Eritrea	1.29	7.6
19	•Madagascar	1.14	7.0
20	•Sudan	1.12	17.8
21	•Guinea-Bissau	0.99	4.8
22	•Comoros	0.92	7.8
23	•Ghana	0.88	8.1
24	•Senegal	0.88	8.0
25	•Liberia	0.77	3.6
26	•Cape Verde	0.71	10.7
27	•Mauritania	0.71	8.4
28	•Mauritius	0.63	5.2
29	•Namibia	0.53	12.1
30	•Kenya	0.51	7.1
31	•Malawi	0.44	7.7
32	•Gabon	0.39	10.2
33	•Cameroon	0.26	6.9
34	•Côte d'Ivoire	0.08	4.1
35	•Seychelles	0.06	4.5
36	•South Africa	-0.1	9.9
37	•Central African Rep.	-0.33	4.7
38	•Lesotho	-0.52	9.8
39	•Swaziland	-0.63	8.9

- Intuitive wisdom would expect that these two components would share a simple relationship: quality of life moving up as economic growth improved or took root. But the resulting picture doesn't fit that structure.

- It might also be that 8 years are too few for such an analysis, but they were the best the data could afford for the majority of countries. A quite feasible explanation for the non-relationship might be a simple one: that the benefits of economic growth have not been well harnessed to translate into better educational and health infrastructure in the main, which would have had a direct and even immediate impact on the population's living conditions.

- Equatorial Guinea and Burundi are left out of the chart on account of extreme values of GDP growth rates, 37% and 0.4% respectively. They both ended up in the middle band of life improvement.

- There are some interesting observations from the chart, though. 4 of the 5 countries posting the fastest rate of economic growth in those 8 years are oil exporters; only Zambia isn't. And they all return medium quality of life improvements; none of them does worse – or better – than that.

- All 5 Southern African countries post medium growth rates of GDP, but only 1 makes reasonable progress in quality of life. Most countries of West and East Africa show bottom-third rates of GDP growth, but 2 of those countries (Niger & Burkina Faso, West Africa) nevertheless report very high (top 3) improvements in quality of life over the period. Ethiopia is the only other African country that revealed high quality of life improvements.

- As for trends – if at all there are any – of the 23 countries posting low economic growth, most (11) return the lowest life improvements, followed by the medium improvements (10).

- By the time focus shifts a step higher to the mid-level economic growth countries – 9 of them in total – most (6) still return poor life improvement, followed by the middle improvement band (2).

- As said already, the 5 fastest-growing economies manage only average improvements in the quality of their populations' life conditions.

- ***No visible direct relationship between economic growth rate and quality of life in Africa. A striking disconnect.***

5.7 Tricky Relations: Population & Economic Growth

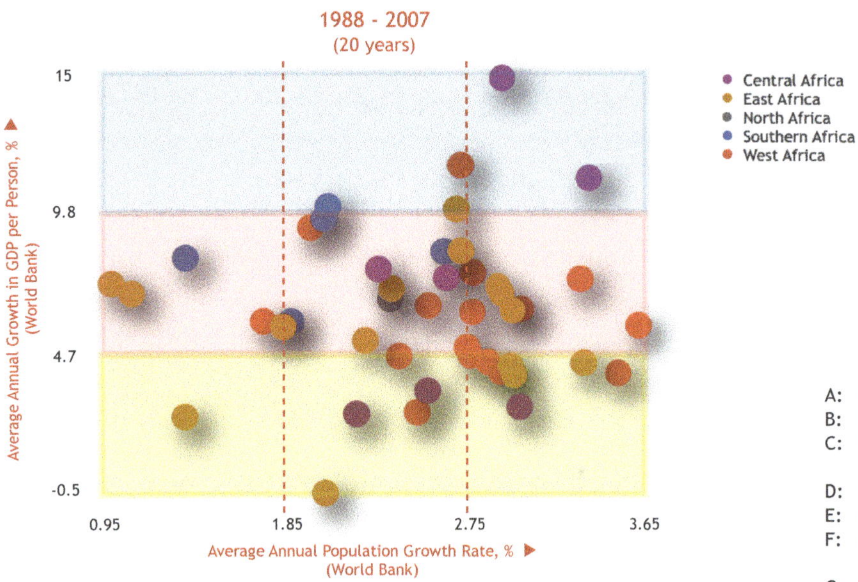

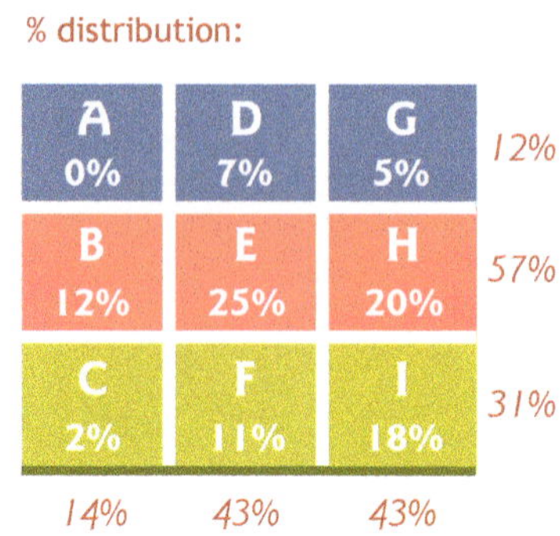

A: low population growth, high GDP/pers growth
B: low population growth, medium GDP/pers growth
C: low population growth, low GDP/pers growth

D: medium population growth, high GDP/pers growth
E: medium population growth, medium GDP/pers growth
F: medium population growth, low GDP/pers growth

G: high population growth, high GDP/pers growth
H: high population growth, medium GDP/pers growth
I: high population growth, low GDP/pers growth

A

0

D

1. Nigeria
2. Botswana
3. Zambia

3

G

1. Angola
2. Chad

2

B

1. Lesotho
2. Mauritius
3. Seychelles
4. Sierra Leone
5. Rwanda

5

E

1. Swaziland
2. Cape Verde
3. Malawi
4. Namibia
5. Congo, Rep.
6. Gabon
7. Mozambique
8. Sudan
9. Ghana
10. South Africa
11. Comoros

11

H

1. Mali
2. Benin
3. Kenya
4. Tanzania
5. Burkina Faso
6. Madagascar
7. Mauritania
8. Gambia
9. Senegal

9

C

1. Zimbabwe

1

F

1. Guinea-Bissau
2. Cameroon
3. Liberia
4. Central Afr. R.
5. Burundi

5

I

1. Guinea
2. Togo
3. Uganda
4. Ethiopia
5. Côte d'Ivoire
6. Niger
7. Djibouti
8. Congo, D.R.

8

	Country	Growth in GDP/pers	Growth in Population
		(%)	(%)
1	•Angola	14.8	2.9
2	•Nigeria	11.6	2.7
3	•Chad	11.2	3.4
4	•Botswana	10.1	2.1
5	•Zambia	10.0	2.7
6	•Swaziland	9.7	2.1
7	•Cape Verde	9.4	2.0
8	•Malawi	8.5	2.7
9	•Namibia	8.5	2.6
10	•Lesotho	8.3	1.4
11	•Congo, Rep.	7.9	2.3
12	•Mali	7.7	2.8
13	•Gabon	7.6	2.7
14	•Benin	7.5	3.3
15	•Mauritius	7.3	1.0
16	•Kenya	7.2	2.9
17	•Mozambique	7.2	2.4
18	•Tanzania	7.0	2.9
19	•Seychelles	7.0	1.1
20	•Sudan	6.8	2.4
21	•Ghana	6.5	2.6
22	•Burkina Faso	6.4	3.0
23	•Madagascar	6.4	3.0
24	•Mauritania	6.3	2.8
25	•South Africa	6.0	1.9
26	•Sierra Leone	6.0	1.8
27	•Gambia, The	5.8	3.6
28	•Rwanda	5.8	1.9
29	•Comoros	5.3	2.3
30	•Senegal	5.0	2.8
31	•Guinea	4.7	2.8
32	•Guinea-Bissau	4.7	2.4
33	•Togo	4.5	2.9
34	•Uganda	4.5	3.3
35	•Ethiopia	4.4	3.0
36	•Côte d'Ivoire	4.2	2.9
37	•Niger	4.1	3.5
38	•Djibouti	4.0	3.0
39	•Cameroon	3.5	2.6

	Country	Growth in GDP/pers	Growth in Population
		(%)	(%)
40	•Congo, Dem. Rep.	2.9	3.0
41	•Liberia	2.7	2.5
42	•Central African Rep.	2.6	2.2
43	•Zimbabwe	2.5	1.4
44	•Burundi	-0.3	2.1

Movement of *Population, GDP* and *GDP/pers* in Sub-Saharan Africa across 20 Years from 1987 to 2007: 1987=100

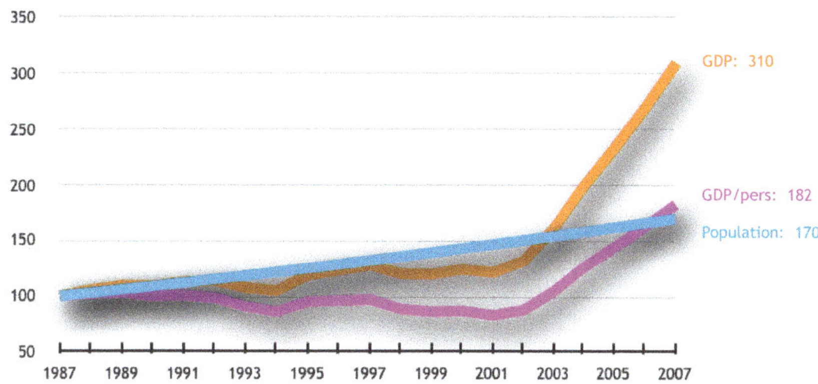

- Comparing growth of population to growth of GDP would help address the query of population being a spur or an impediment to economic development, or being entirely extraneous to it. Perhaps it will not provide a definitive answer, but compiling and comparing such data could only help elucidate any relationship, where present.

- In that regard, it might be more appropriate to compare growth of population not with growth of GDP, but with growth of GDP-per-Person. GDP growth could only be regarded as adequate if it outstrips the nation's rate of population growth. In other words, the country might indeed grow GDP, but unless this GDP is adequate for its growing number of residents, it should still be regarded as a decline in economic performance.

- Equatorial Guinea was left out of the chart because of its extreme GDP per Person growth rate: 30%. Its population growth rate (3.2%) would have placed it in sector G, high population growth accompanied by high GDP per person growth.

- As it is, the continent is just about equal in number of countries with medium and high population growth rate (43% both ways). There were only 6 countries with low population growth.

- None of those 6 attains high GDP growth; they mainly do medium, save for Zimbabwe which returns a low GDP per person growth rate.

- Of the 19 countries (43% of total) that fall into the medium population growth category, more than half attain medium GDP rates or better: 14 (32% of total).

- And of the 19 that fall into the high population growth category, 11 (25% of total) do medium GDP growth rates or better.

- During the nineties, GDP struggled to keep up with the rate of population growth on the continent as a whole. It began to pick up around 2001. By 2005, it was soaring away, outdoing population in build-up. GDP per person took longer to catch up with population estimates, but had in turn begun to outdo it by 2006.

- ***Seems too close to call, regarding the demerits or otherwise of the effects of fast growing populations on GDP build-up. It does look certain, though, that slow growing populations across the past 20 years in Africa have not gained much of an advantage in cranking out their GDP.***

6. West Africa in Sub-Saharan Africa

placing them in context

Primer

West Africa is the most populous region of Sub-Saharan Africa, with 37% of overall population, followed by East Africa on 36%. It isn't the largest of the regions in surface area, though, but 2nd largest, behind Central Africa. In terms of people density, it comes second (47 pers/sq km) after East Africa (49 pers/sq km). And so on.

This chapter attempts to present the sub-region in the context of its constituent countries. Where possible, West Africa is also placed in the context of the other sub-regions of the continent also.

The result should be a commencement to the rest of the book's body of analyses on a convenient footing.

For this chapter, various start-off indices are used, most of which do not require much elaboration.

- **Land mass (in square kilometers)**
- **Population**
- **The age profiles of the population**
- **Population density**
- **Urban population**
- **Rural population**
- **GDP**
- **Economic Vigor**
- **Percentage of females in the labour force**

"Economic Vigor" is an attempt to quantify the efficiency of a country's economy in broad terms. We define it as the percentage share of the continent's GDP compared to the percentage share of its population. In other words, we ask the question: has the country contributed a larger share to the continent's output (GDP) than its share of the continent's population might warrant? Does the country supply a larger percentage of GDP to the continent than the percentage of the continent's population it contains?

It is important to get an empirical sense of this vigor, so we devised the Productivity Index, a metric that attempts to quantify it and is obtained by dividing a country's share of the continent GDP by its share of the continent population.

The chapter closes with a broad evaluation of the countries' basic strengths in population size and GDP output, illustrated in the Leaders & Stragglers section. This provides a ranking of 41 Sub-Saharan African countries for which most of the 200 indicators in this study were available.

Subsequent chapters will provide a closing section called "Wrap-up", where Nigeria will be benchmarked against the best performing West African country in that chapter of the economy under consideration, according to the key indicators employed in the chapter.

Sources of Primary Data: IMF, World Bank, UNPD

Charts

Tables

6.1 Land Mass: The Large 5

Niger

1,267,000 sq.km.

Mali

1,240,190 sq.km.

Mauritania

1,025,520 sq.km.

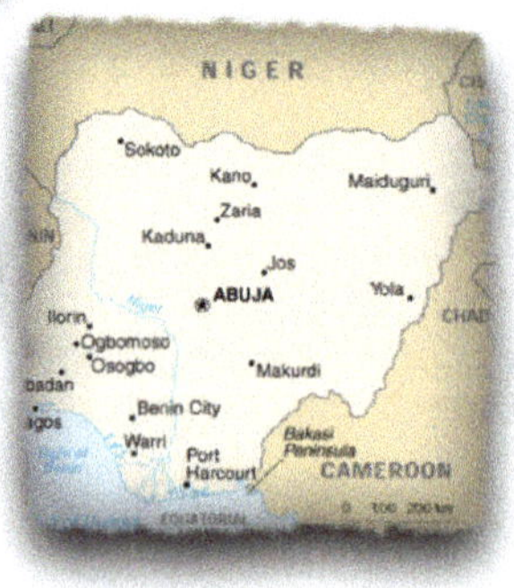

Nigeria

923,770 sq.km.

Côte d'Ivoire

322,460 sq.km.

		Land Mass (sq.km)
6	Burkina Faso	274,000
7	Guinea	245,860
8	Ghana	238,540
9	Senegal	196,720
10	Benin	112,620
11	Liberia	111,370
12	Sierra Leone	71,740
13	Togo	56,790
14	Guinea-Bissau	36,120
15	Gambia, The	11,300
16	Cape Verde	4,030

+1-800-help

any need to explain population density, urban/ rural population, etc?

No, thanks

You bet

6.2 Population: The Swarming 5

	2009	Population (millions)	% of West Africa
6	Mali	13.6	4.7%
7	Senegal	13	4.4%
8	Guinea	11	3.6%
9	Benin	8	2.9%
10	Togo	7	2.3%
11	Sierra Leone	6	2.1%
12	Liberia	4	1.4%
13	Mauritania	3	1.1%
14	Guinea-Bissau	1.8	0.6%
15	Gambia, The	1.7	0.6%
16	Cape Verde	0.5	0.2%

1 in 2 West Africans is Nigerian. The country isn't the largest of the 16, but it holds more than half of the sub-region's population.

2009 IMF estimates

6.3 Population Age Profiles: 2005-2010

Everywhere, near 90% of the population are younger than 60; & about 60% are younger than 25.

Again, the numbers for Nigeria in every age band completely eclipse the rest of West Africa.

UNPD estimates

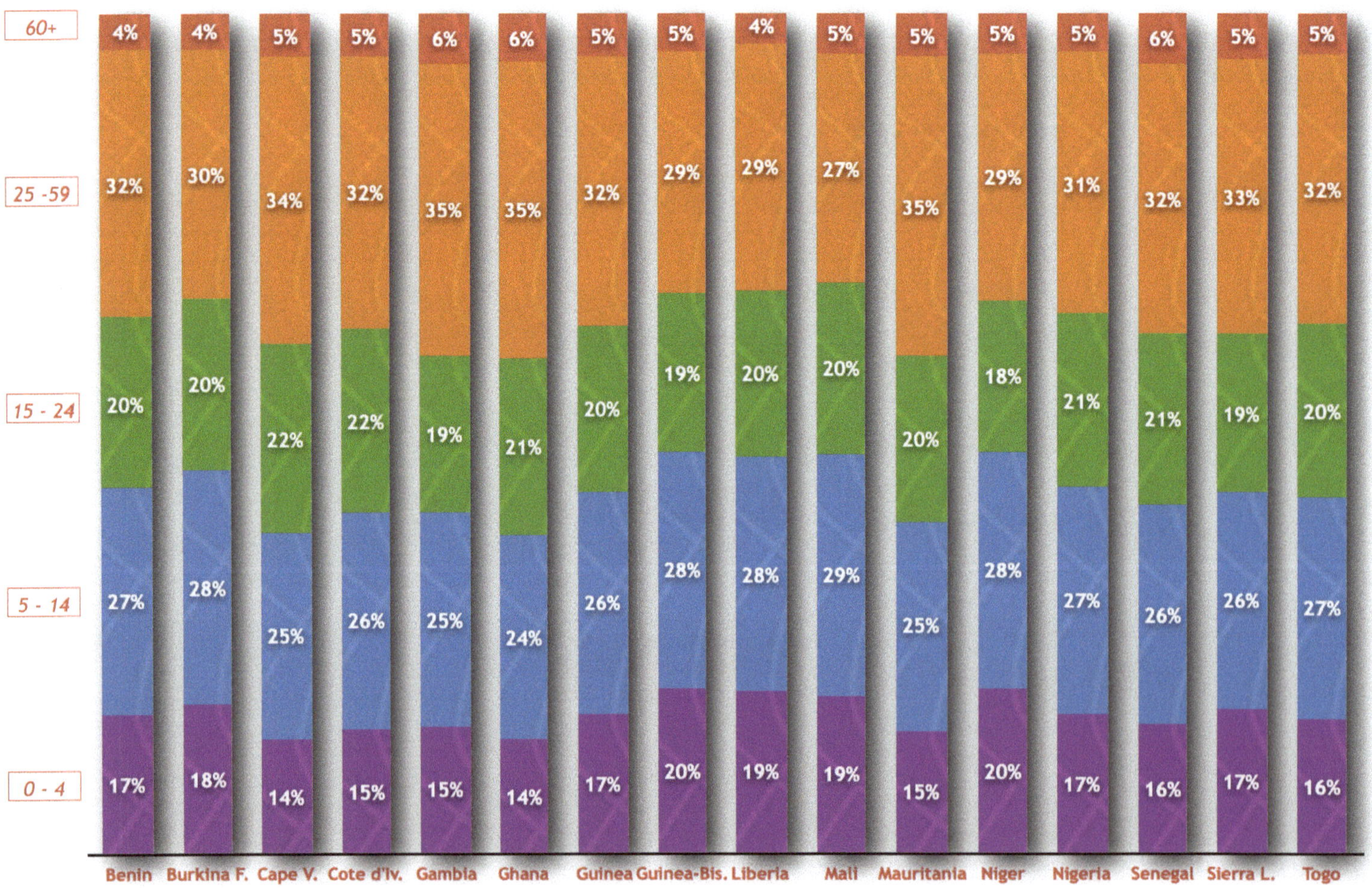

6. West Africa in Sub-Saharan Africa

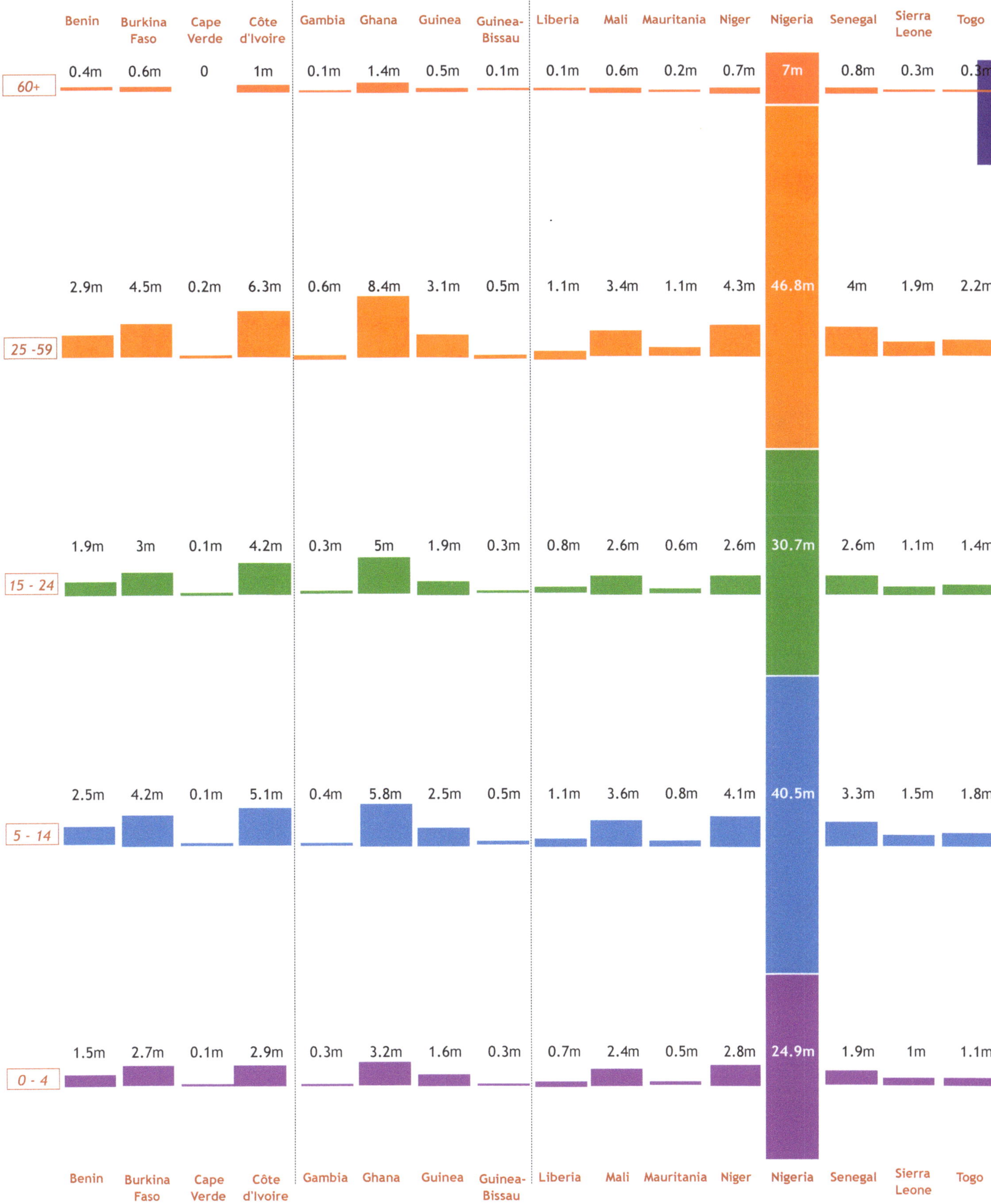

6.4 Population Density: 2005-2010

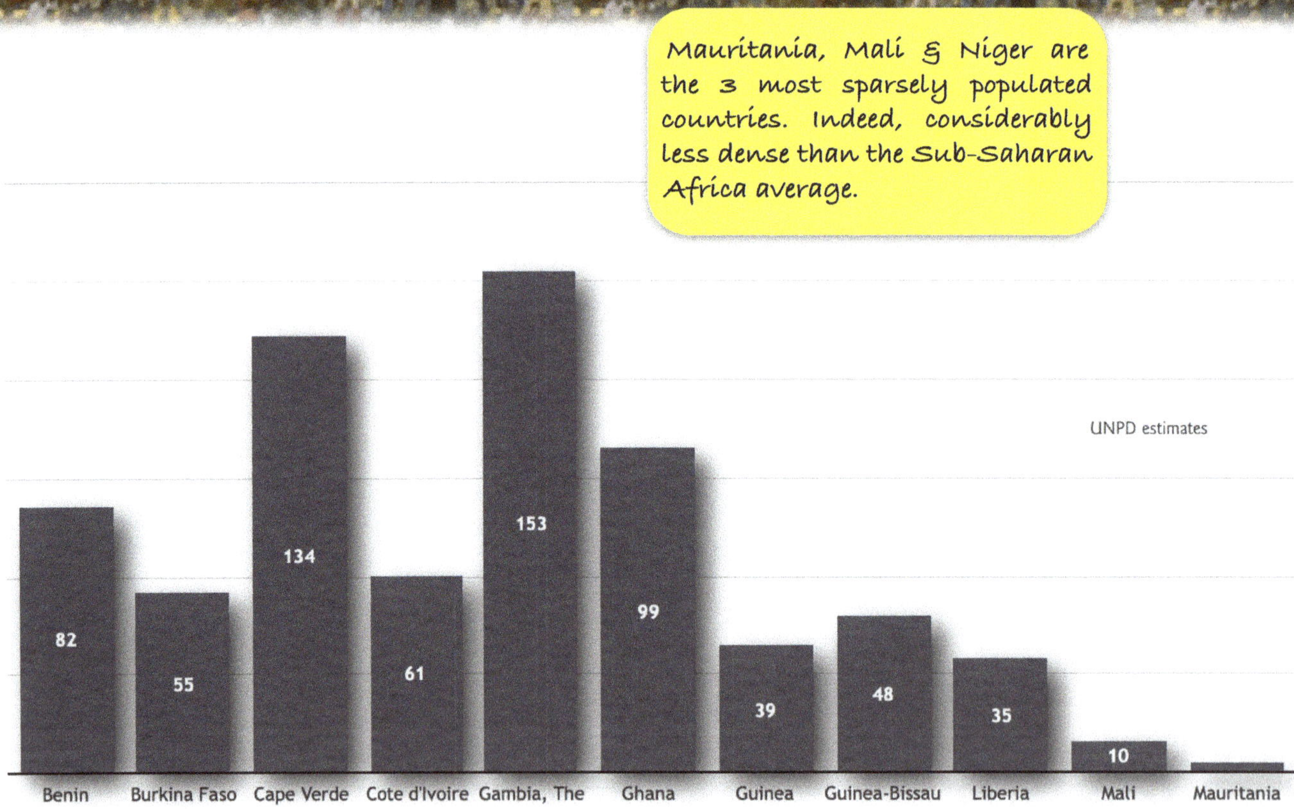

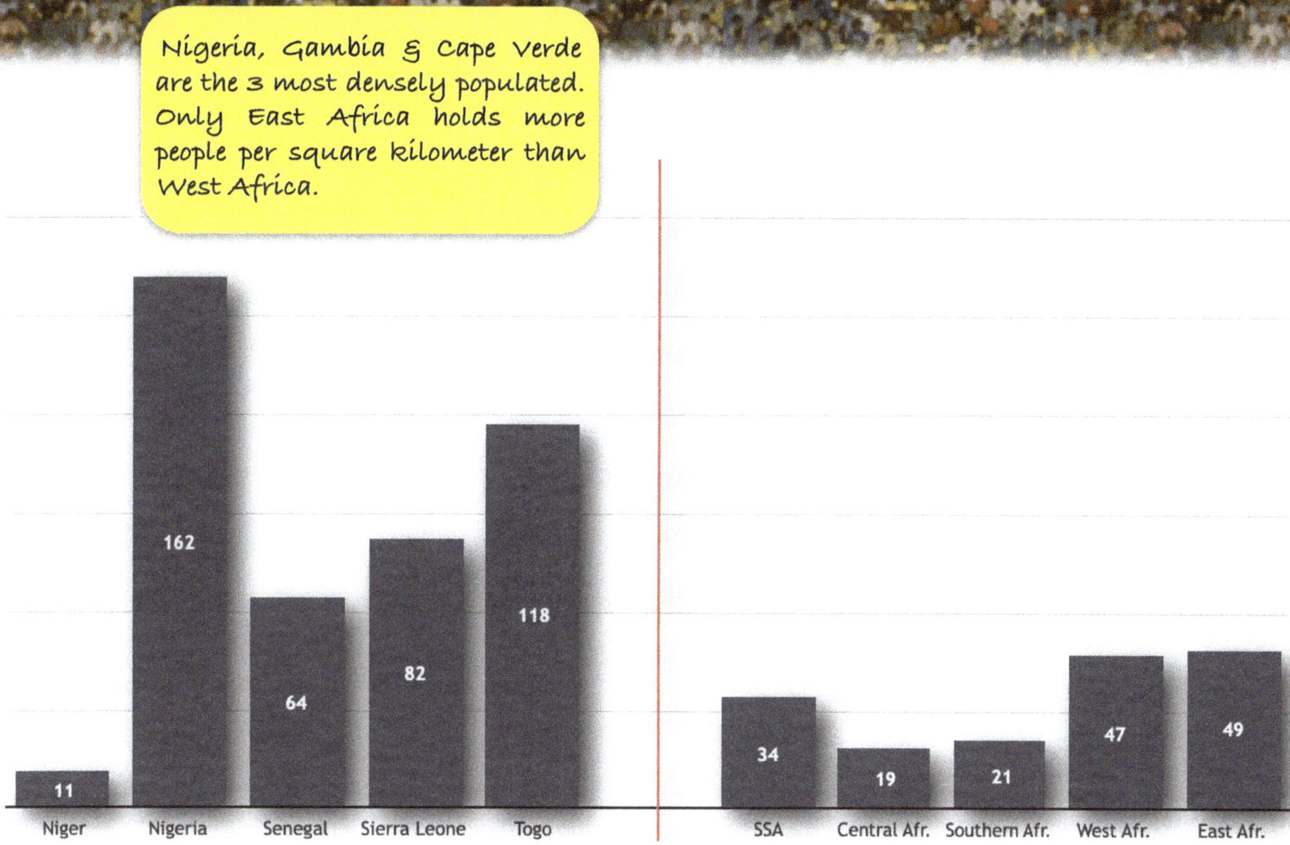
Nigeria, Gambia & Cape Verde are the 3 most densely populated. Only East Africa holds more people per square kilometer than West Africa.
11
162
64
82
118
34
19
21
47
49
Niger
Nigeria
Senegal
Sierra Leone
Togo
SSA
Central Afr.
Southern Afr.
West Afr.
East Afr.

6.5 Urban Population: 2005-2010

Urban population is growing fastest in Liberia, Burkina Faso & Mali. But the most urban dwellers are in Nigeria, Ghana & Côte d'Ivoire.

UNPD estimates

Urban Populations in the Countries of West Africa during 2005 - 2010. (millions)

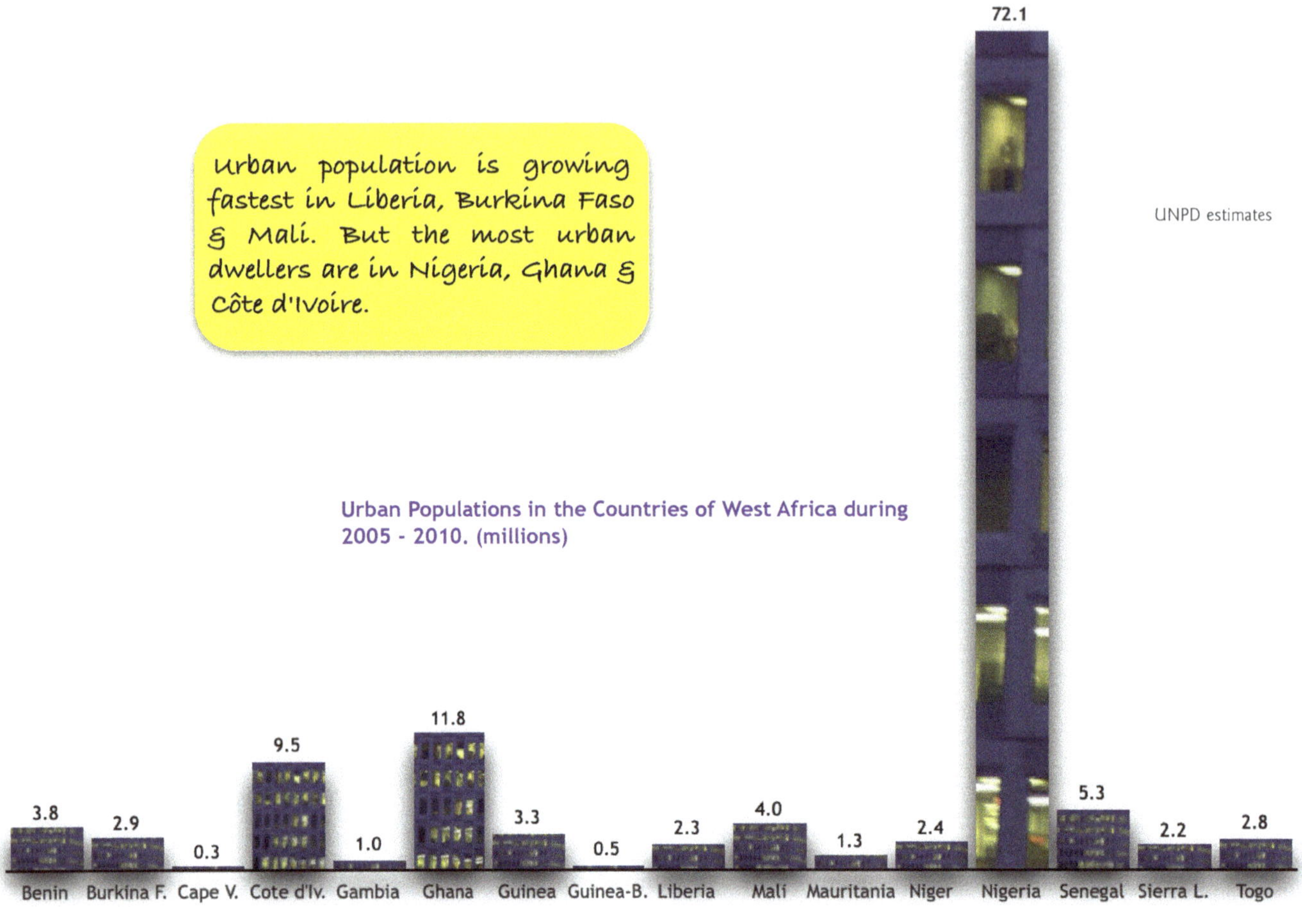

Urban % of the Populations in the Countries of West Africa during 2005 - 2010.

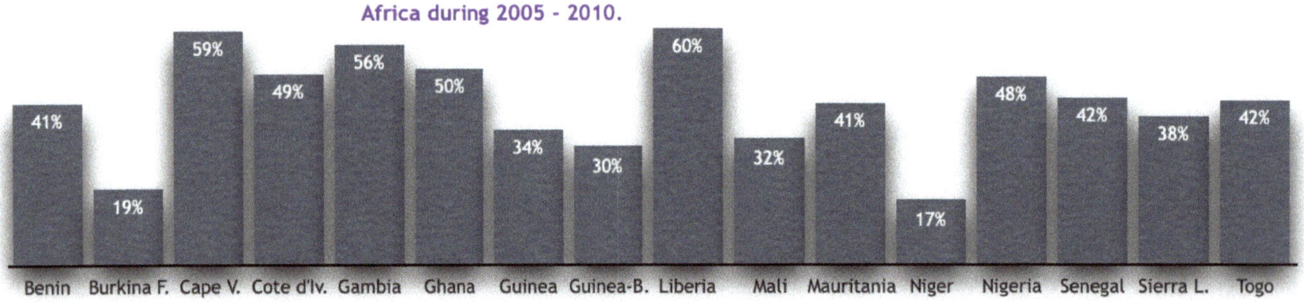

Growth Rate of the Urban Populations in the Countries of West Africa during 2005 - 2010.

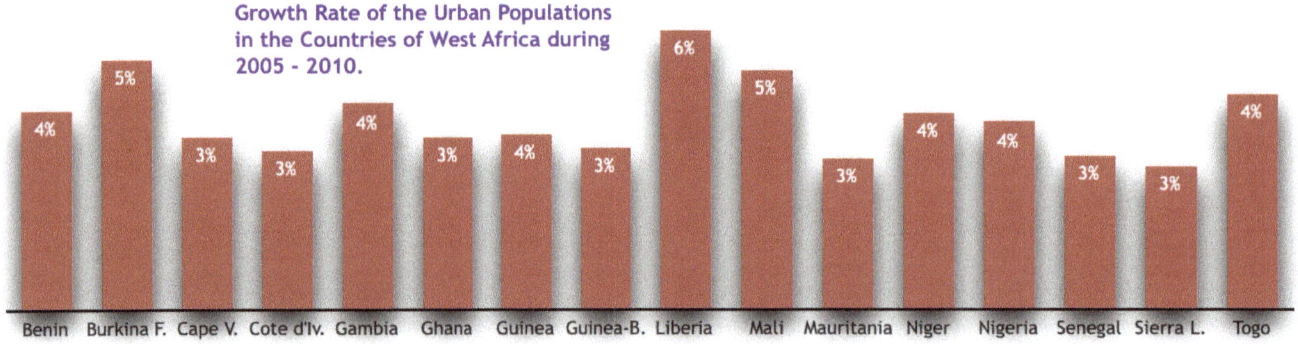

6.6 Rural Population: 2005-2010

Rural populations are growing everywhere, but slower than urban growth. Again, Nigeria, Ghana & Côte d'Ivoire hold the most rural dwellers.

UNPD estimates

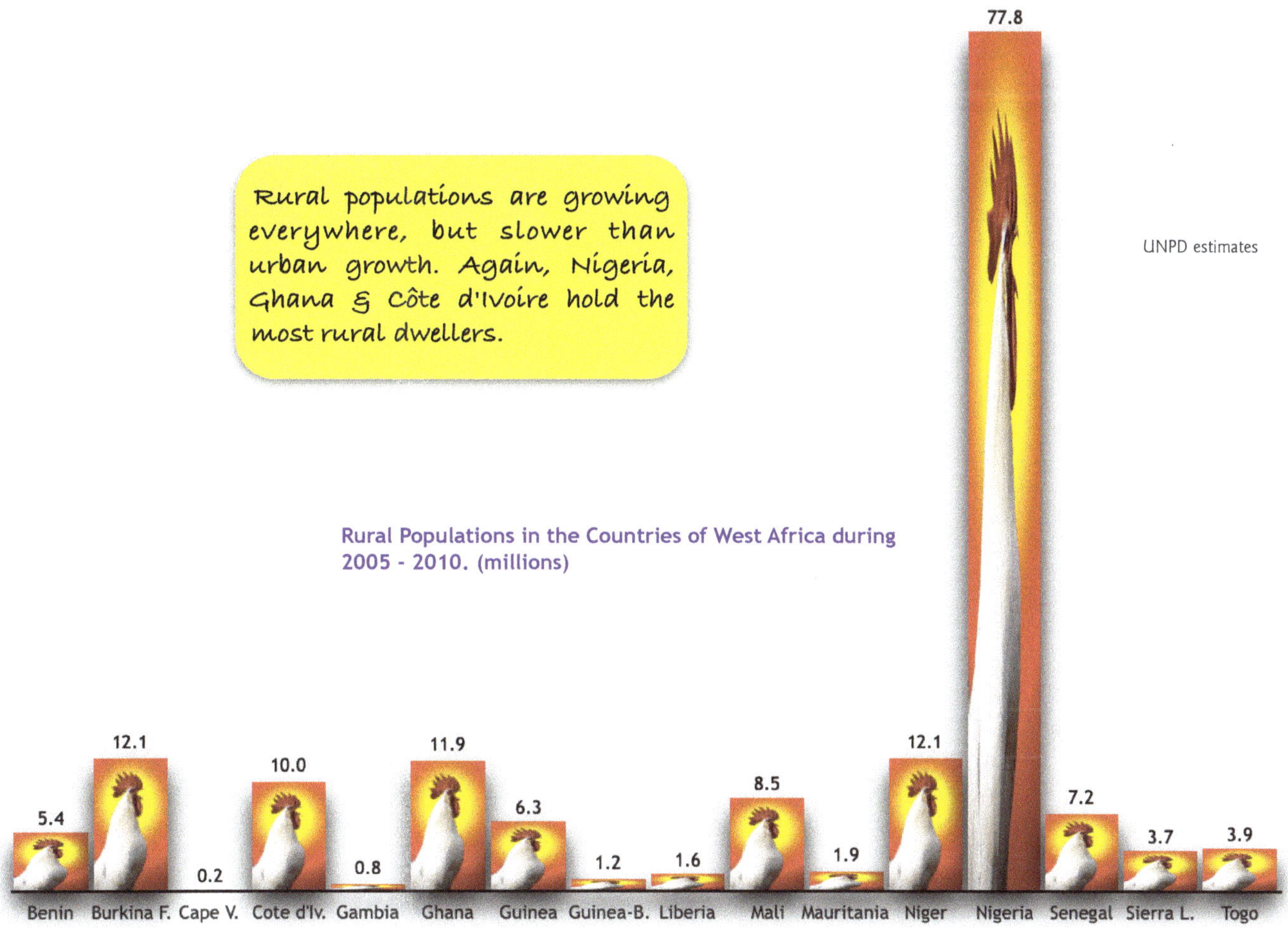

Rural Populations in the Countries of West Africa during 2005 - 2010. (millions)

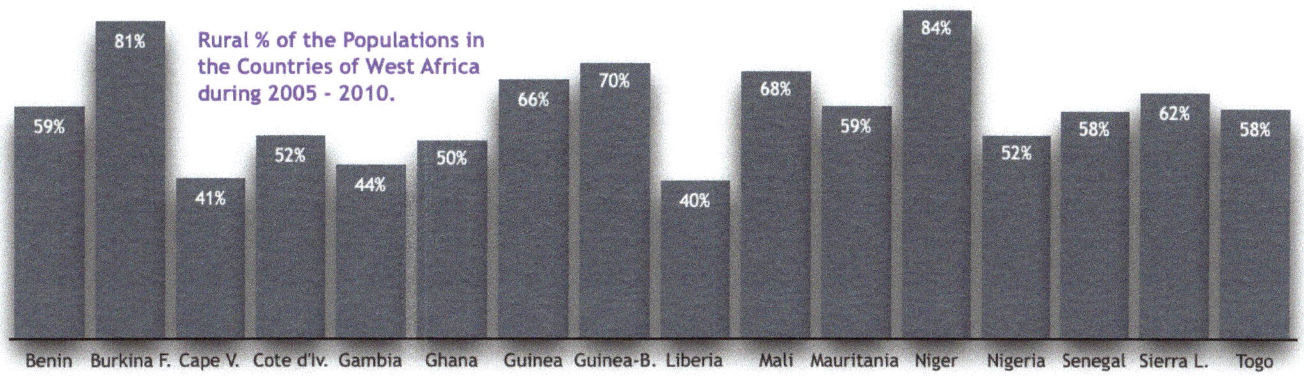

Rural % of the Populations in the Countries of West Africa during 2005 - 2010.

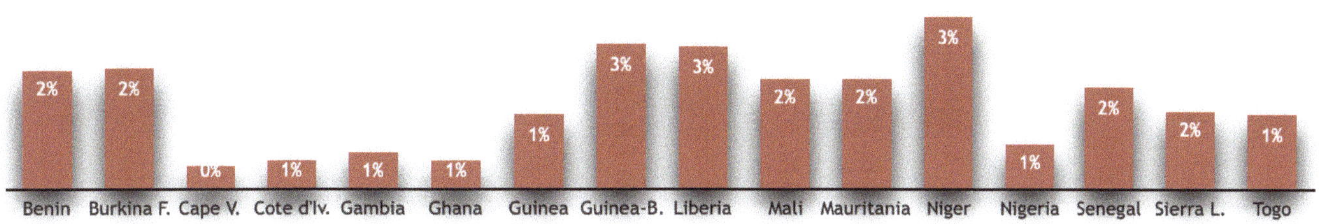

Growth Rate of the Rural Populations in the Countries of West Africa during 2005 - 2010.

6.7 GDP: The Top 5

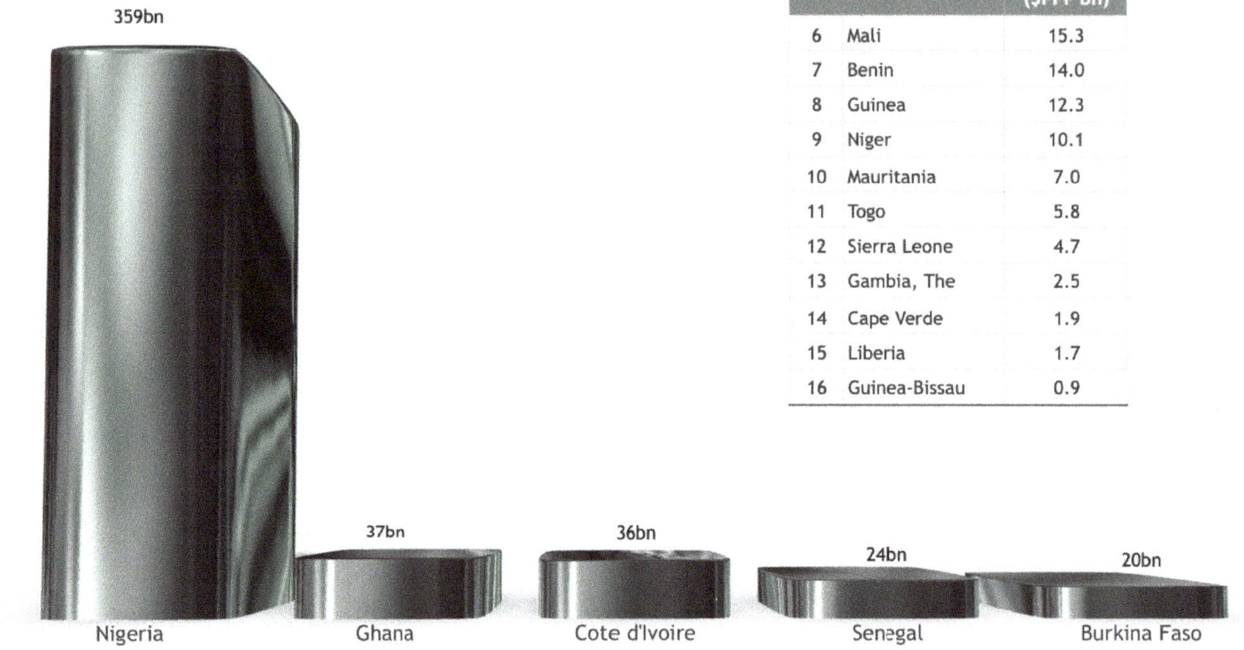

	2009	GDP ($PPP bn)
6	Mali	15.3
7	Benin	14.0
8	Guinea	12.3
9	Niger	10.1
10	Mauritania	7.0
11	Togo	5.8
12	Sierra Leone	4.7
13	Gambia, The	2.5
14	Cape Verde	1.9
15	Liberia	1.7
16	Guinea-Bissau	0.9

As with population, so with GDP; Nigeria, Ghana and Côte d'Ivoire provide the bulk. Nigeria's GDP is nearly twice that of the rest of West Africa.

IMF estimates

6.8 Economic Vigor

Productivity Index of the Countries of West Africa during 2009

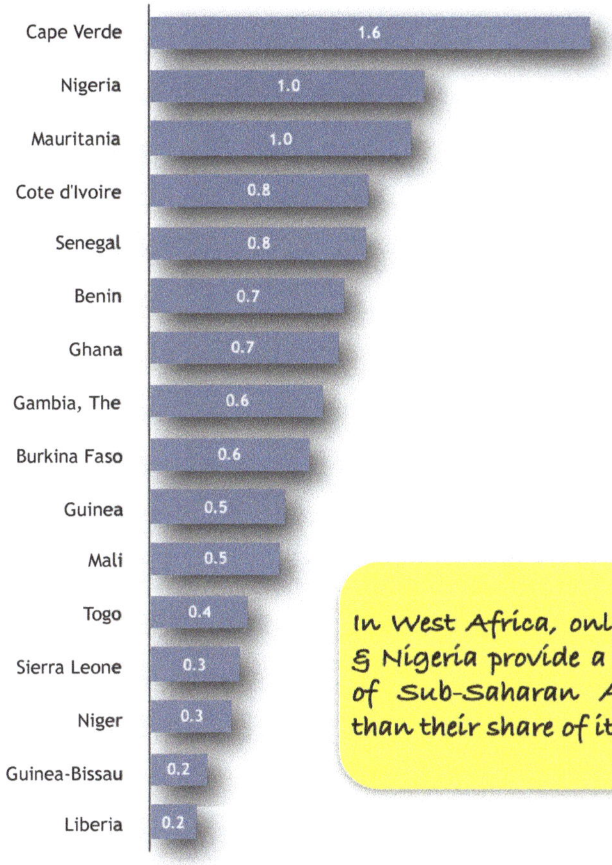

	2009	% of SSA Population	% of SSA GDP
1	Cape Verde	0.06	0.10
2	Nigeria	19.15	19.47
3	Mauritania	0.39	0.38
4	Côte d'Ivoire	2.44	1.96
5	Senegal	1.62	1.29
6	Benin	1.05	0.76
7	Ghana	2.91	2.03
8	Gambia, The	0.21	0.13
9	Burkina Faso	1.81	1.07
10	Guinea	1.33	0.66
11	Mali	1.72	0.83
12	Togo	0.86	0.31
13	Sierra Leone	0.76	0.25
14	Niger	1.79	0.55
15	Guinea-Bissau	0.22	0.05
16	Liberia	0.52	0.09

In West Africa, only Cape Verde & Nigeria provide a greater share of Sub-Saharan Africa's GDP than their share of its population.

Primary data: IMF

6.9 Female % of Labor Force

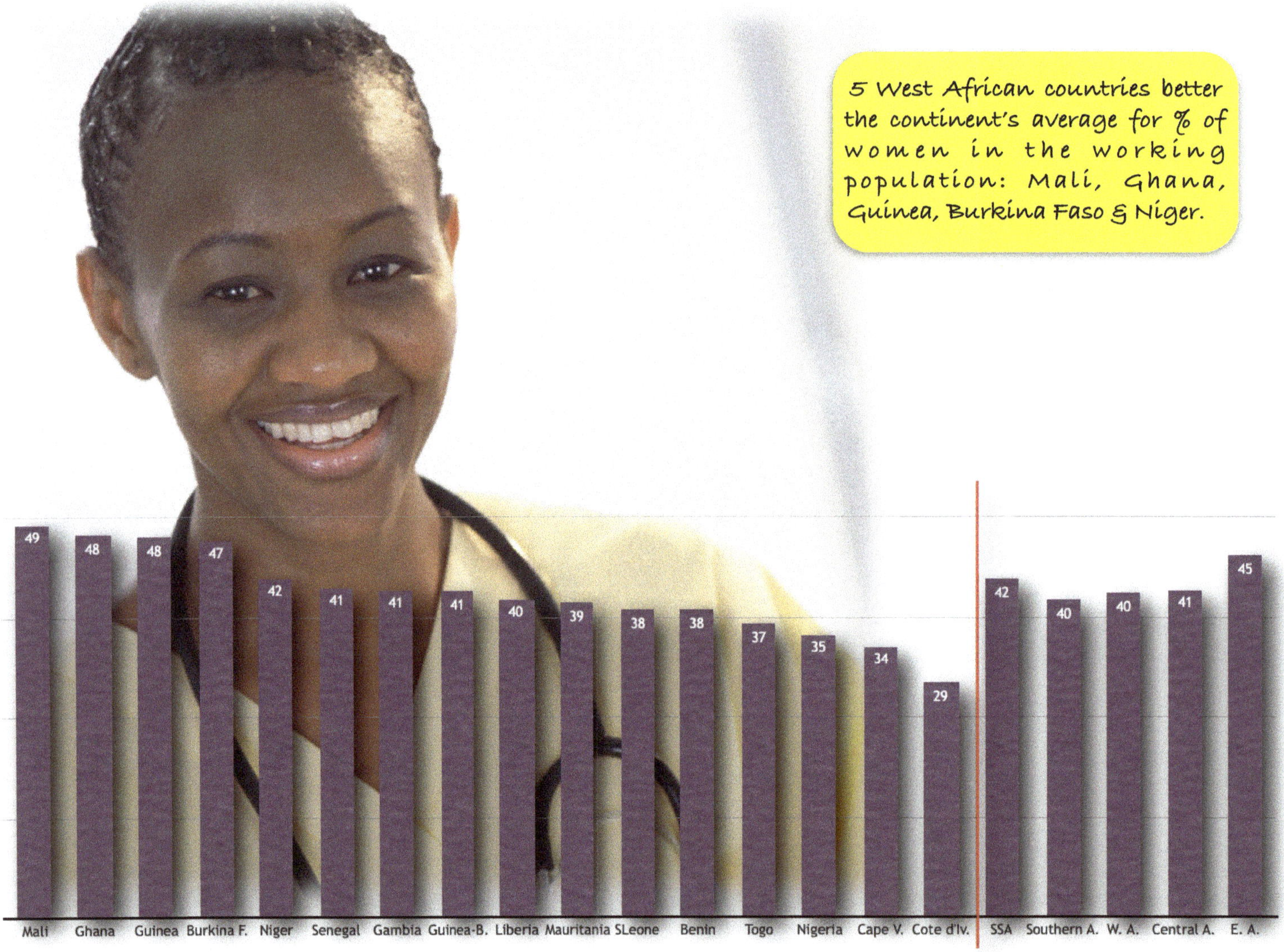

2006: World Bank

first impressions

This ranking is only an introductory one, basing its outcome on two criteria: relative size of population and relative size of GDP.

But it is of significance, as size of population might point to potential size of market. Size of GDP might point to size of wealth.

The ensuing end-of-chapter tables in the rest of the book will provide the more robust and comprehensive diverse bases for consequent sector rankings.

General-Size Rankings: 2009

Rank	Country
1	Nigeria
2	South Africa
3	Ethiopia
4	Kenya
	Tanzania
5	Angola
	Congo, Dem. Rep.
	Ghana
6	Cameroon
	Uganda
7	Côte d' Ivoire
8	Mozambique
9	Madagascar
10	Senegal

TOP

Rank	Country
11	Burkina Faso
12	Zambia
13	Mali
14	Chad
	Malawi
15	Niger
16	Botswana
17	Guinea
18	Benin
19	Gabon
20	Congo, Rep.
21	Rwanda
22	Equatorial Guinea
	Togo

MIDDLE

Rank	Country
23	Mauritius
	Namibia
	Sierra Leone
24	Burundi
	Eritrea
25	Central Afr. Rep.
26	Lesotho
27	Swaziland
28	Gambia
29	Guinea-Bissau
30	Cape Verde
31	Comoros
	Seychelles

BOTTOM

Primary Data: IMF

Central Africa
East Africa
Southern Africa
West Africa

Part II

Economic and Business Analyses

7. Quality of Life

last things first

Primer

Usually, the condition of an economy's people is discussed at the study's end, preceded by chapters that describe the (technical) macro-economic character of the group of countries and then lead from there to the standards of living as outcomes of that character. We have opted to place quality of life early on here, simply to reiterate the point that an economy exists for the people and not the other way round. That is, management of an economy has one sole defining purpose: to improve the welfare of its constituent population. It is on that (overriding) basis that performance may be assessed.

Various indices have been employed here to assess the standard of living of the population and the quality of life that this represents.

Human Development Ranking: based on the "human development index" as evaluated by the United Nations Development Program. It is the most widely respected evaluation of the quality of life in the different countries of the world and is an amalgamation of various parameters to rate and compare standards of living across countries.

Life Expectancy at Birth: the number of years newborn children would live if subject to the mortality risks prevailing for the cross-section of population at the time of their birth.

Child Mortality (Under-5): the probability of dying between birth and exactly five years of age, based on actual recorded number of deaths. It is usually expressed per 1,000 live births.

Babies Immunization: Measles percentage of 1-year old children who have been immunized against measles.

Babies Immunization: Tuberculosis percentage of 1-year old children who have been immunized against tuberculosis.

Population with Access to Safe Water: percentage of population with access to clean water: i.e. "population using improved drinking water sources". Improved water sources include household connections, public standpipes, boreholes, protected dug wells, protected springs, and rainwater collections – UNICEF/WHO

Population with Access to Sanitation: percentage of population using adequate sanitation facilities; adequate sanitation includes connection to public sewers, connection to septic systems, and [efficient] latrine systems – UNICEF/WHO

Phones per Population (Fixed & Mobile): the number of phone lines (fixed and mobile) per 100 inhabitants.

Number of Mobile Phone Users: the number of mobile phone lines per 100 inhabitants.

Number of Internet Users: out of every 1,000 persons.

Personal Computers per Population: out of every 1,000 persons.

Migration: net migration: the number of immigrants less the number of emigrants.

Sources of Primary Data: UNDP, UNICEF, AfDB, ITU, UNPD

Charts

Tables

1999-2002; 2003-2006:
- *self-comparison to preceding period;*
- *performance in S-Saharan Africa;*
- *performance in West Africa;*
- *performance among oil-exporters;*

for:

Human Development Ranking*

Life Expectancy

Child Mortality

Babies Immunization: Measles

Babies Immunization: Tuberculosis

1990; 2004-2006:
- *self-comparison to preceding period;*
- *performance in S-Saharan Africa;*
- *performance in West Africa;*
- *performance among oil-exporters;*

for:

Population with Access to Safe Water

Population with Access to Sanitation

2000; 2007:
- *self-comparison to preceding period;*
- *performance in S-Saharan Africa;*
- *performance in West Africa;*
- *performance among oil-exporters;*

for:

Phones per Population (Fixed & Mobiles)

Number of Mobile Phone Users

Literacy

Number of Internet Users

Personal Computers per Population**

Net Migration per Population***

- Human Development Index in Sub-Saharan Africa during 2003-05: Rankings
- Life Expectancy in Sub-Saharan Africa during 2003-06: Rankings
- Under-5 Child Mortality in Sub-Saharan Africa during 2003-06: Rankings
- Phones (Fixed & Mobiles) per Population in Sub-Saharan Africa during 2007: Rankings
- Internet Users per Population in Sub-Saharan Africa during 2007: Rankings
- Personal Computers per Population in Sub-Saharan Africa during 2006: Rankings
- **Quality of Life Rankings: 2003-07**

* 1999-2002; 2003-2005

** 2001; 2006

*** 2000-2005

7.1 Human Development Ranking

smile, their beloved country

	99-02	03-05
Self-comparison to Preceding Period		▼
Performance in Sub-Saharan Africa	▼	▼
Performance in West Africa	▲	▲
	Cape Verde	Cape Verde
	Ghana	Ghana
	Togo	Togo
	Nigeria	Mauritania
	Mauritania	Gambia, The
	Senegal	Senegal
	Gambia, The	**Nigeria**
	Côte d'Ivoire	Guinea
	Benin	Benin
	Guinea	Côte d'Ivoire
	Guinea-Bissau	Guinea-Bissau
	Mali	Mali
	Burkina Faso	Burkina Faso
	Niger	Niger
	Sierra Leone	Sierra Leone
Performance among Oil-Exporters	▼	▼
	Equatorial Guinea	Gabon
	Gabon	Equatorial Guinea
	Cameroon	Congo, Rep.
	Congo, Rep.	Sudan
	Sudan	Cameroon
	Nigeria	**Nigeria**
	Côte d'Ivoire	Angola
	Angola	Côte d'Ivoire
	Chad	Chad

7.1

Quality of Life Ranking in West Africa among 46 Sub-Saharan Africa Countries during 2003-2005 (1=best, 46=worst)

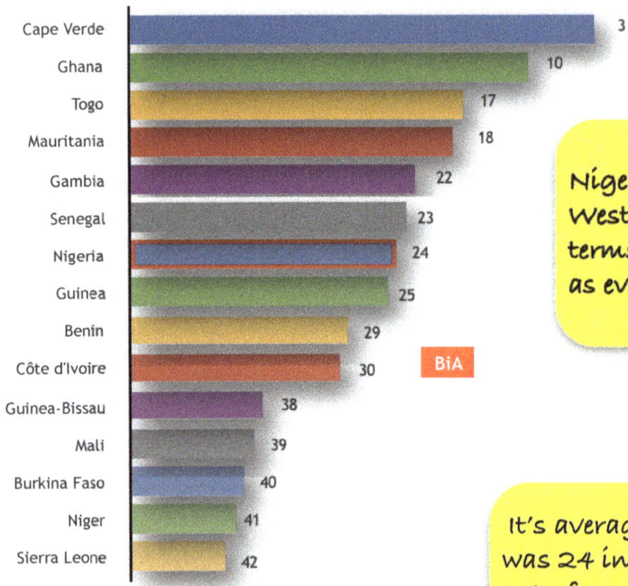

Nigeria placed 7th in 16-nation West Africa during 2003-05 in terms of "human development", as evaluated by the UNDP.

It's average rank for those years was 24 in Sub-Saharan Africa, out of 46. Cape Verde was best in West Africa, and 3rd best on the continent.

Primary Data: UNDP

▲	improved *or* better than average
▼	worsened *or* worse than average
◁▷	no change *or* average

7.2

Human Development Index Rankings of West African Countries among 46 Sub-Saharan Africa Countries during 1999 to 2006

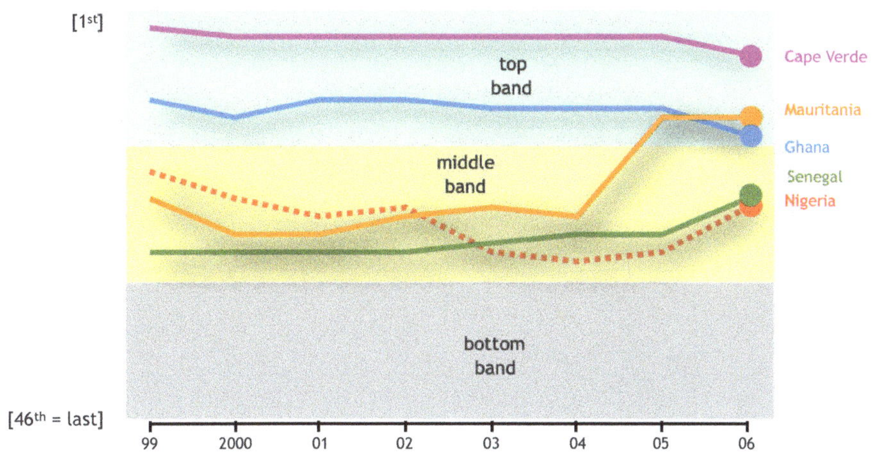

Nigeria's position might have been stronger if the country hadn't returned worse Human Development indices for 03-05 than the preceding 99-02 period.

It fell back within Sub-Saharan Africa and West Africa as well. Among the oil economies it stayed worse than average.

Cape Verde and Ghana were the only countries of West Africa to consistently stay in the top band of SSA performance throughout the 8 years of 99-06.

7.2

Human Development Index Rankings of West African Countries among 46 Sub-Saharan Africa Countries during 1999 to 2006

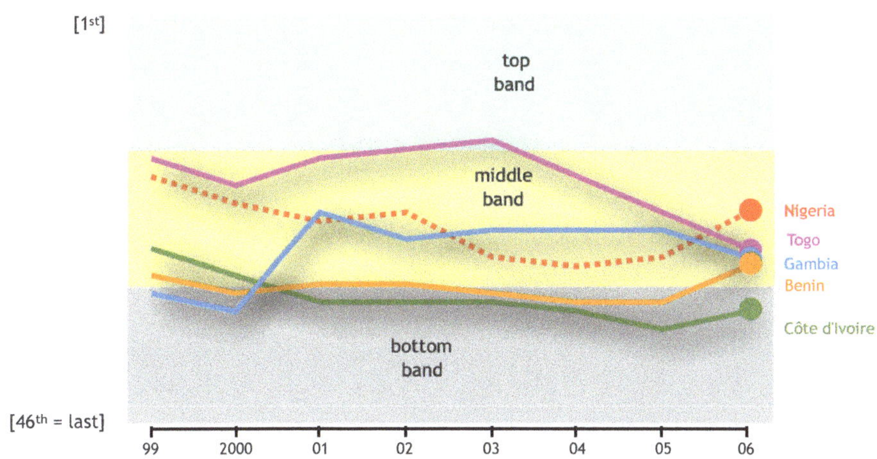

Mauritania joined the top band in 2005, and Togo was there for a brief stay in 2003 but dived back down alarmingly thereafter.

Nigeria remained firmly in the SSA middle band. Senegal and Gambia overtook it after 2003, but Gambia fell behind again after 2005.

Primary Data: UNDP

As such, the best living conditions in West Africa during 1999-2006 were to be found in Cape Verde and Ghana.

7.2

Human Development Index Rankings of West African Countries among 46 Sub-Saharan Africa Countries during 1999 to 2006

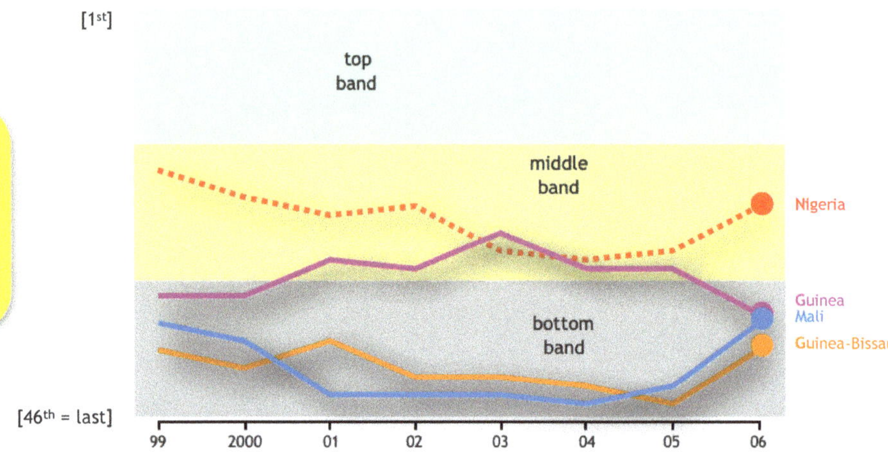

Besides those two, and Mauritania and Senegal, the rest of West Africa performed at a lower level than Nigeria throughout 1999-2006.

7.2

Human Development Index Rankings of West African Countries among 46 Sub-Saharan Africa Countries during 1999 to 2006

By 2006, Sierra Leone was 45th (2nd from the bottom) in SSA. Burkina Faso & Niger were 40th and 41st respectively.

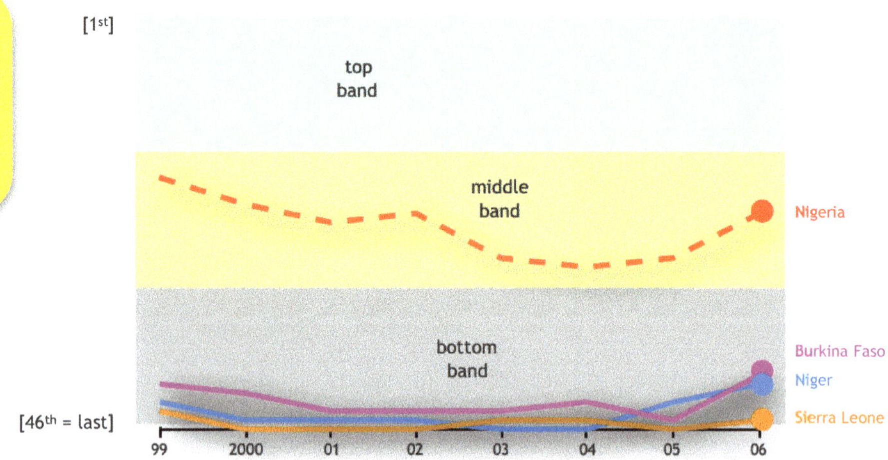

Primary Data: UNDP

Seychelles had the best index in Africa, followed by Mauritius, Cape Verde, South Africa and Gabon in the top-5 bracket. War-ravaged Sierra Leone was bottom.

In West Africa, 2 countries made the top band: Cape Verde & Ghana; 7 made middle; and 5 made bottom.

Human Development Index in Sub-Saharan Africa during 2003-05: Rankings

Rank	Country	Rank	Country	Rank	Country
1	Seychelles	15	Lesotho	29	Congo, Dem. Rep.
2	Mauritius	16	Togo	30	Burundi
3	Cape Verde		Uganda	31	Mozambique
4	South Africa	17	Kenya	32	Ethiopia
5	Gabon	18	Gambia, The	33	Central Afr. Rep.
6	Equatorial Guinea	19	Senegal		Chad
7	Namibia	20	Eritrea	34	Guinea-Bissau
8	Botswana		Nigeria	35	Mali
9	Comoros	21	Guinea	36	Burkina Faso
10	Ghana	22	Rwanda	37	Niger
11	Congo, Rep.	23	Angola	38	Sierra Leone
12	Madagascar	24	Tanzania		
13	Swaziland	25	Benin		
14	Cameroon	26	Côte d' Ivoire		
		27	Malawi		
		28	Zambia		
TOP		MIDDLE		BOTTOM	

Primary Data: UNDP

7.2 Life Expectancy

running on extra-time?

	99-02	03-06
Self-comparison to Preceding Period		▼
Performance in Sub-Saharan Africa	▲	▼
Performance in West Africa	▲	▼
	Cape Verde	Cape Verde
	Ghana	Ghana
	Senegal	Senegal
	Benin	Gambia, The
	Mauritania	Mauritania
	Mali	Togo
	Nigeria	Benin
	Togo	Guinea
	Gambia, The	Mali
	Guinea	Burkina Faso
	Liberia	Niger
	Niger	**Nigeria**
	Burkina Faso	Côte d'Ivoire
	Côte d'Ivoire	Guinea-Bissau
	Guinea-Bissau	Liberia
	Sierra Leone	Sierra Leone
Performance among Oil-Exporters	▲	▼
	Sudan	Sudan
	Gabon	Gabon
	Nigeria	Congo, Rep.
	Cameroon	Cameroon
	Equatorial Guinea	Equatorial Guinea
	Congo, Rep.	**Nigeria**
	Chad	Chad
	Côte d'Ivoire	Côte d'Ivoire
	Angola	Angola

7.3

Life Expectancy at Birth in West Africa during 2003-2006

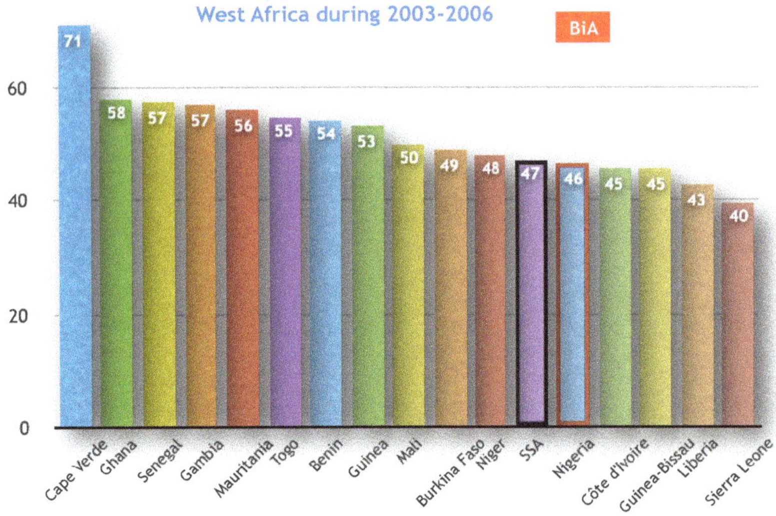

Primary Data: UNICEF

If born in Nigeria, you were likely to live shorter than you would being born in 11 countries of West Afr., and just a shade shorter if born elsewhere in Africa.

You were likely to live longest in Cape Verde, followed by Ghana, within West Africa.

▲	improved *or* better than average
▼	worsened *or* worse than average
◁▷	no change *or* average

You might expect to live longer in Nigeria, though, if you were born before 2003.

After that point, chances of a long life fell behind most of West Africa and Sub-Saharan Africa, and also behind most of the oil countries.

7.4

Life Expectancy at Birth in Nigeria and Sub-Saharan Africa from 1999 to 2007

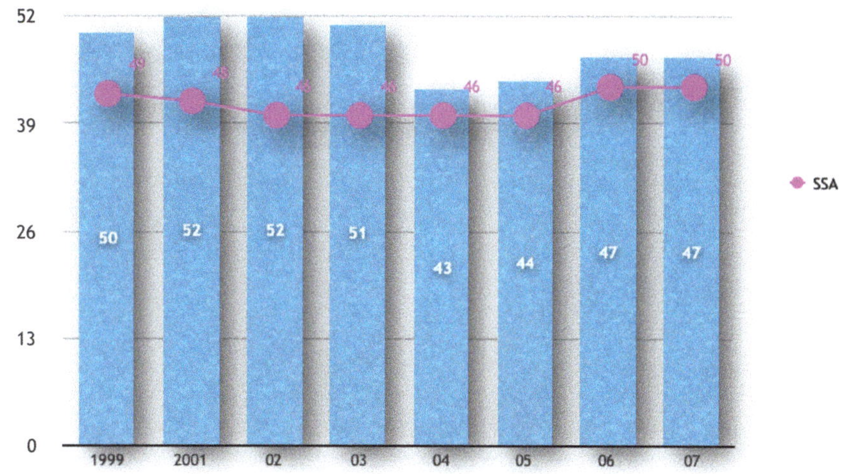

+1-800-help

"Life Expectancy" not to be confused with "Average Life Span", mind.

Why?

Life expectancy, remember, is the number of years newborn children are expected to live if they were subject to the mortality risks prevailing within the country's population at the time of their birth.

While average life span would be the statistical average of actual number of years lived within a population. One is a prediction, the other a historical statistic.

Life Expectancy in Sub-Saharan Africa during 2003-06: Rankings

HIGHEST

Rank	Country
1	Mauritius
2	Cape Verde
3	Comoros
4	Ghana
5	Senegal
6	Gambia, The
7	Madagascar
8	Gabon
9	Eritrea
	Togo

BOTTOM

Rank	Country
19	Burundi
20	Congo, Dem. Rep.
21	Rwanda
22	Angola
	Malawi
	Mozambique
23	Central Afr. Rep.
24	Botswana
	Sierra Leone
25	Zambia
26	Lesotho
27	Swaziland
N/A	Seychelles

MIDDLE

Rank	Country
10	Benin
11	Guinea
12	Congo, Rep.
13	Mali
14	Burkina Faso
	Ethiopia
	Kenya
	Niger
	Uganda
15	Cameroon
	Namibia
	South Africa
	Tanzania
16	Equatorial Guinea
	Nigeria
17	Chad
18	Côte d' Ivoire
	Guinea-Bissau

Primary Data: UNICEF

7.3 Child Mortality (Under-5 year olds)

infant survival

	99-02	03-06
Self-comparison to Preceding Period		▼
Performance in Sub-Saharan Africa	▼	▼
Performance in West Africa	▼	▼
	Cape Verde	Cape Verde
	Ghana	Ghana
	Gambia, The	Gambia, The
	Senegal	Senegal
	Togo	Togo
	Benin	Mauritania
	Guinea	Benin
	Côte d'Ivoire	Guinea
	Mauritania	Côte d'Ivoire
	Nigeria	Nigeria
	Burkina Faso	Burkina Faso
	Guinea-Bissau	Guinea-Bissau
	Mali	Mali
	Liberia	Liberia
	Niger	Niger
	Sierra Leone	Sierra Leone
Performance among Oil-Exporters	▼	▼
	Sudan	Sudan
	Congo, Rep.	Gabon
	Gabon	Congo, Rep.
	Equatorial Guinea	Cameroon
	Cameroon	Côte d'Ivoire
	Côte d'Ivoire	Equatorial Guinea
	Nigeria	Nigeria
	Chad	Chad
	Angola	Angola

Primary Data: UNICEF

7.5

Under-5 Child Mortality in West Africa during 2003-06

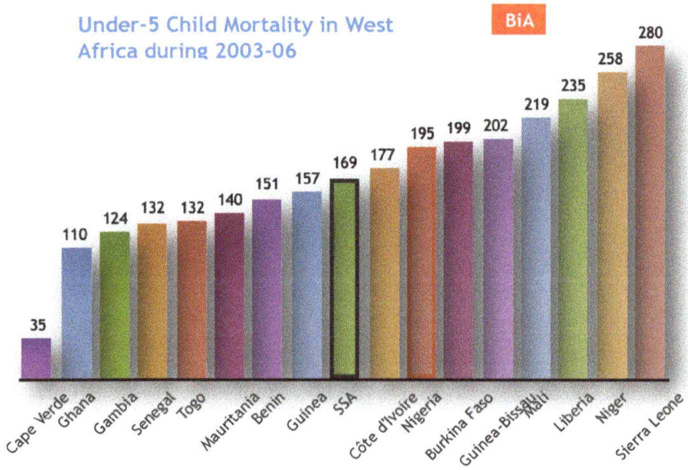

▲	improved *or* better than average
▼	worsened *or* worse than average
◁▷	no change *or* average

Effective increase in child mortality in Nigeria across 99/07, although numbers began to dip; slightly first in 04, but consistently from then on to 07.

However, it still stayed worse than the Africa average during that 8-yr period of 99-07.

7.6

Under-5 Child Mortality in Nigeria and Sub-Saharan Africa from 1999 to 2007

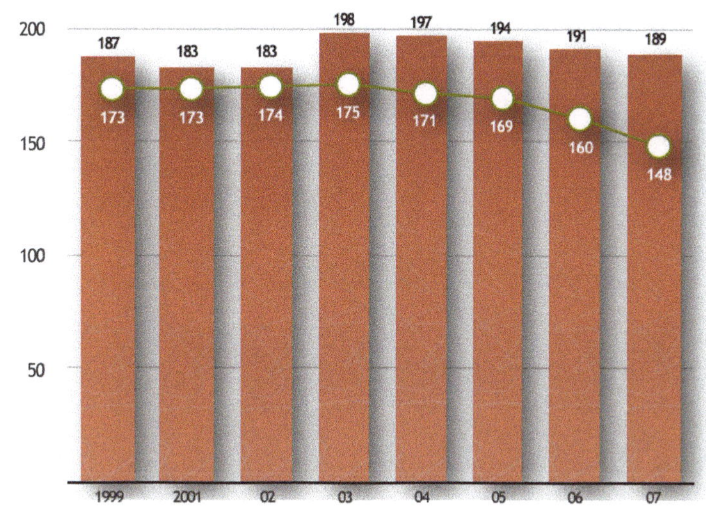

Primary Data: UNICEF

The best child care obtained in the Seychelles.

Under-5 Child Mortality in Sub-Saharan Africa during 2003-06: Rankings

Rank	Country	Rank	Country	Rank	Country
1	Seychelles	14	Gambia, The	27	Central Afr. Rep.
2	Mauritius	15	Senegal	28	Burundi
3	Cape Verde		Togo	29	Equatorial Guinea
4	Namibia	16	Tanzania	30	Rwanda
5	South Africa	17	Uganda	31	Nigeria
6	Comoros	18	Mozambique	32	Burkina Faso
7	Eritrea	19	Malawi	33	Guinea-Bissau
8	Gabon	20	Benin	34	Chad
9	Lesotho	21	Cameroon	35	Congo, Dem. Rep.
10	Ghana	22	Ethiopia	36	Mali
11	Congo, Rep.	23	Guinea	37	Niger
12	Botswana	24	Swaziland	38	Angola
13	Kenya	25	Côte d' Ivoire	39	Sierra Leone
	Madagascar	26	Zambia		
BEST		AVERAGE		BOTTOM	

Central Africa
East Africa
Southern Africa
West Africa

7.4 Babies Immunization: Measles

got my jabs;
did you get yours?

	99-02	03-06
Self-comparison to Preceding Period		▲
Performance in Sub-Saharan Africa	▼	▼
Performance in West Africa	▼	▼
	Gambia, The	Gambia, The
	Benin	Benin
	Ghana	Ghana
	Cape Verde	Burkina Faso
	Mauritania	Mali
	Côte d'Ivoire	Liberia
	Liberia	Guinea-Bissau
	Togo	Togo
	Senegal	Senegal
	Guinea	Sierra Leone
	Burkina Faso	Niger
	Mali	Cape Verde
	Sierra Leone	Mauritania
	Niger	Guinea
	Guinea-Bissau	Côte d'Ivoire
	Nigeria	Nigeria

Primary Data: UNICEF

	99-02	03-06
Performance among Oil-Exporters	▼	▼
	Sudan	Cameroon
	Angola	Sudan
	Côte d'Ivoire	Congo, Rep.
	Cameroon	Côte d'Ivoire
	Equatorial Guinea	Gabon
	Chad	Angola
	Gabon	Equatorial Guinea
	Nigeria	Nigeria
	Congo, Rep.	Chad

7.7

% of 1-yr olds Immunized against Measles in West Africa during 2003-06

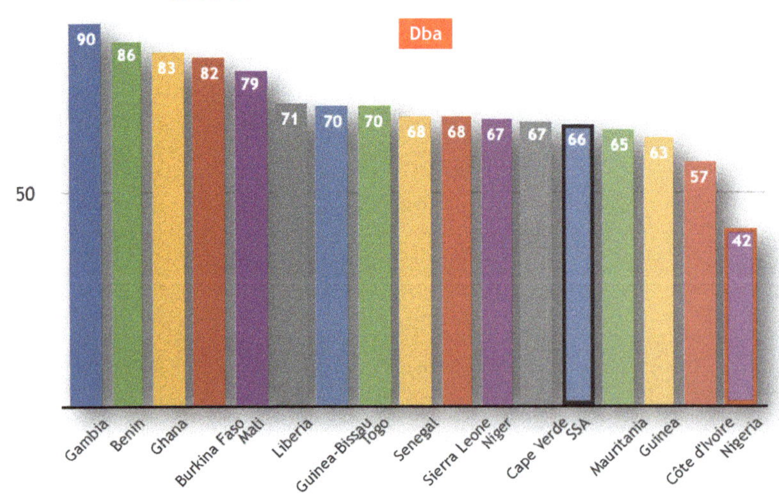

▲	improved *or* better than average
▼	worsened *or* worse than average
◁▷	no change *or* average

Only 42% of 1-yr olds in Nigeria got their measles inoculation during 2003-2006.

The average in Africa was 66%, and Nigeria's was the worst index within West Africa.

7.8

% of 1-yr olds Immunized against Measles in Nigeria and Sub-Saharan Africa from 1997 to 2007

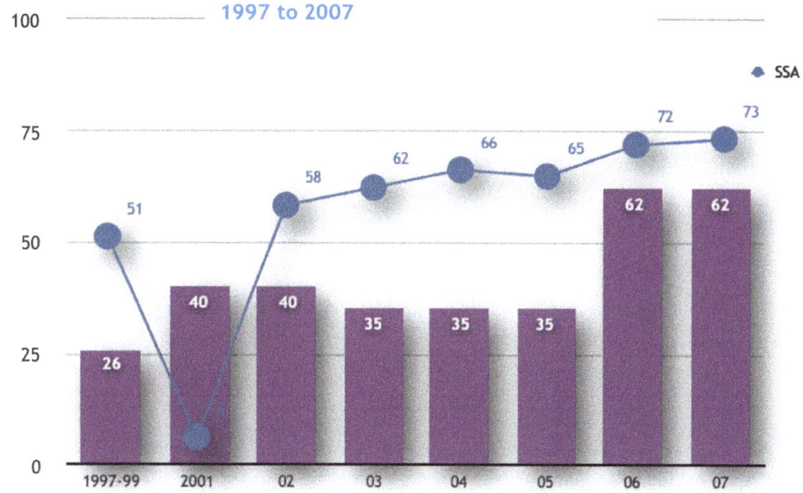

Primary Data: UNICEF

Nigeria made a concerted positive climb in 2006, which was sustained during 2007. But it still lagged behind most of Africa.

% of 1-yr olds Immunized against Measles in Sub-Saharan Africa during 2003-06: Rankings

Rank	Country
1	Seychelles
2	Mauritius
3	Tanzania
4	Botswana
5	Gambia, The
6	Rwanda
7	Uganda
8	Eritrea
9	Benin
10	Zambia
11	Ghana
	South Africa
12	Burkina Faso
13	Malawi

TOP

Rank	Country
14	Mali
15	Lesotho
16	Mozambique
17	Burundi
18	Kenya
19	Comoros
20	Guinea-Bissau
	Swaziland
	Togo
21	Namibia
22	Senegal
	Sierra Leone
23	Niger
24	Cape Verde
25	Cameroon
26	Congo, Dem. Rep.

MIDDLE

Rank	Country
27	Guinea
28	Ethiopia
29	Congo, Rep.
30	Madagascar
31	Côte d' Ivoire
32	Gabon
33	Angola
34	Equatorial Guinea
35	Nigeria
36	Chad
37	Central Afr. Rep.

BOTTOM

Central Africa
East Africa
Southern Africa
West Africa

7.5 Babies Immunization: Tuberculosis

don't leave it late

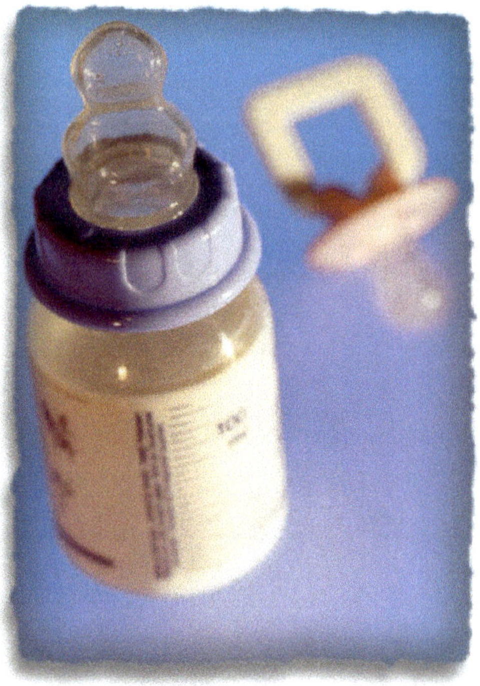

	99-02	03-06
Self-comparison to Preceding Period		▲
Performance in Sub-Saharan Africa	▼	▼
Performance in West Africa	▼	▼
	Gambia, The	Benin
	Benin	Gambia, The
	Ghana	Ghana
	Cape Verde	Burkina Faso
	Senegal	Togo
	Mauritania	Senegal
	Togo	Mauritania
	Mali	Sierra Leone
	Côte d'Ivoire	Guinea-Bissau
	Guinea	Guinea
	Burkina Faso	Cape Verde
	Sierra Leone	Mali
	Liberia	Niger
	Guinea-Bissau	Liberia
	Nigeria	Côte d'Ivoire
	Niger	**Nigeria**

Primary Data: UNICEF

7.9

% of 1-yr olds Immunized against Tuberculosis in West Africa during 2003-06

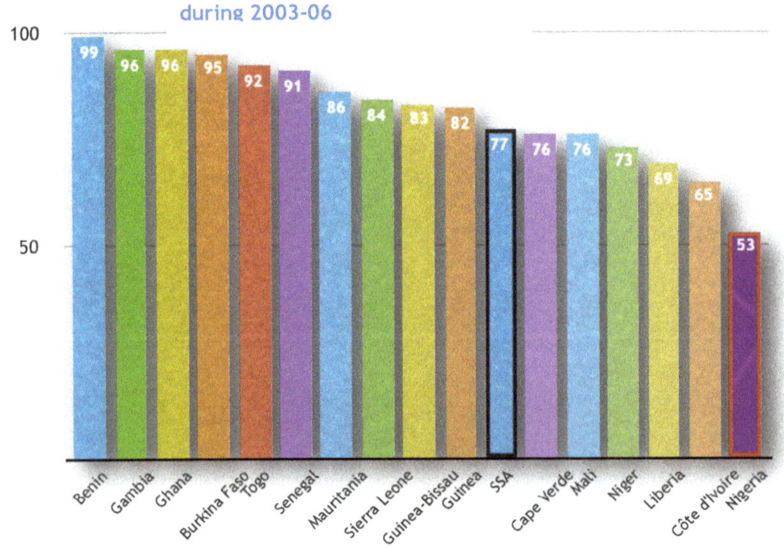

	99-02	03-06
Performance among Oil-Exporters	▼	▼
	Gabon	Gabon
	Côte d'Ivoire	Cameroon
	Angola	Congo, Rep.
	Cameroon	Equatorial Guinea
	Equatorial Guinea	Angola
	Sudan	Côte d'Ivoire
	Chad	Sudan
	Congo, Rep.	**Nigeria**
	Nigeria	Chad

▲	improved *or* better than average
▼	worsened *or* worse than average
◁▷	no change *or* average

7.10

% of 1-yr olds Immunized against Tuberculosis in Nigeria and Sub-Saharan Africa from 1997 to 2007

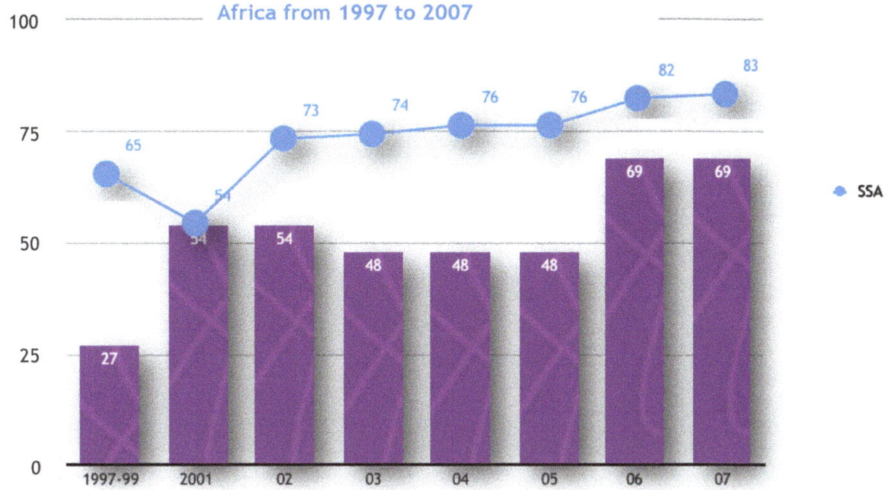

Primary Data: UNICEF

A story not dissimilar to that of measles inoculation, with the same poor trend up to 2005 and sharp improvement thereafter.

Again, most of Africa did better throughout 1999-2007.

7.6 Population with Access to Safe Water

some water runs through it

	1990	04-06
Self-comparison to Preceding Period		▲
Performance in Sub-Saharan Africa	▼	▼
Performance in West Africa	◁▷	▼
	Côte d'Ivoire	Côte d'Ivoire
	Senegal	Gambia, The
	Benin	Cape Verde
	Ghana	Senegal
	Togo	Ghana
	Nigeria	Benin
	Guinea	Liberia
	Niger	Burkina Faso
	Burkina Faso	Guinea-Bissau
	Mauritania	Sierra Leone
	Mali	Mauritania
		Togo
		Nigeria
		Guinea
		Mali
		Niger

Primary Data: AfDB

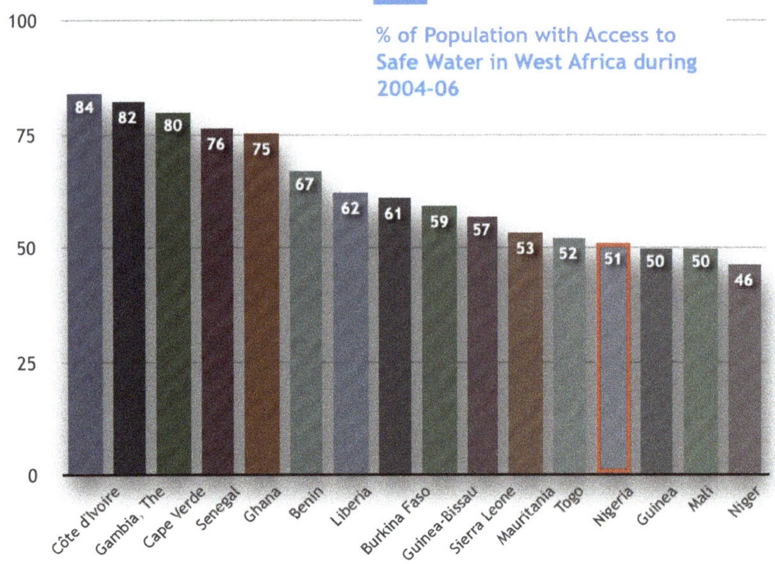

7.11 % of Population with Access to Safe Water in West Africa during 2004-06

	1990	04-06
Performance among Oil-Exporters	▼	▼
	Côte d'Ivoire	Gabon
	Sudan	Côte d'Ivoire
	Cameroon	Sudan
	Nigeria	Cameroon
	Angola	Congo, Rep.
	Chad	Angola
		Nigeria
		Equatorial Guinea
		Chad

Nigerians' access to potable water improved during 04-06, compared to 1990 levels.

But they were worse off than most other West Africans, Africans, and residents of companion oil economies.

▲	improved *or* better than average
▼	worsened *or* worse than average
◁▷	no change *or* average

7.7 Population with Access to Sanitation

but it's being sorted

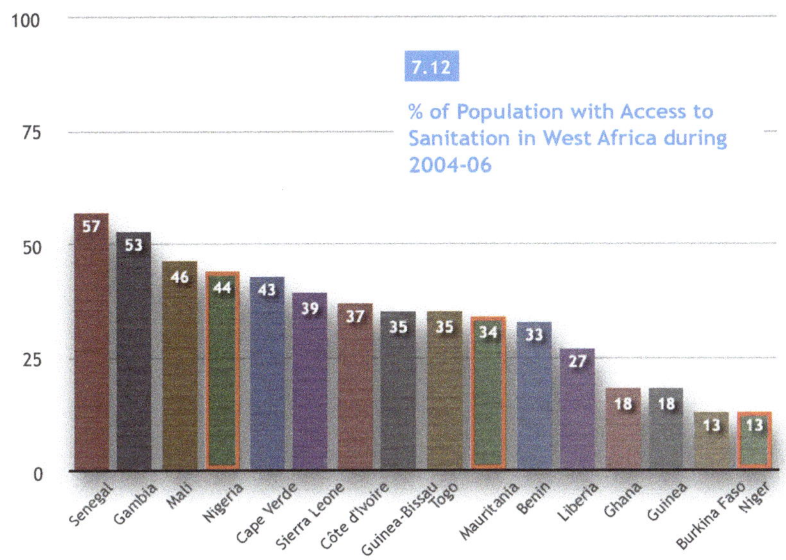

7.12

% of Population with Access to Sanitation in West Africa during 2004-06

This time, Nigeria stays among the top ranks within the entire continent, oil economies inclusive.

	1990	04-06
Self-comparison to Preceding Period		▲
Performance in Sub-Saharan Africa	▲	▲
Performance in West Africa	▲	▲
	Nigeria	Senegal
	Liberia	Gambia, The
	Togo	Mali
	Mali	**Nigeria**
	Senegal	Cape Verde
	Mauritania	Sierra Leone
	Côte d'Ivoire	Côte d'Ivoire
	Ghana	Guinea-Bissau
	Guinea	Togo
	Benin	Mauritania
	Burkina Faso	Benin
	Niger	Liberia
		Ghana
		Guinea
		Burkina Faso
		Niger

Primary Data: AfDB

	1990	04-06
Performance among Oil-Exporters	▲	▲
	Cameroon	Equatorial Guinea
	Nigeria	Cameroon
	Sudan	**Nigeria**
	Angola	Côte d'Ivoire
	Côte d'Ivoire	Gabon
	Chad	Sudan
		Angola
		Congo, Rep.
		Chad

▲	improved *or* better than average
▼	worsened *or* worse than average
◁▷	no change *or* average

7.8 Phones per Population (Fixed & Mobiles)

interconnected

Primary Data: ITU

	2000	2007
Self-comparison to Preceding Period		▲
Performance in Sub-Saharan Africa	▼	▲
Performance in West Africa	▼	▲
	Cape Verde	Cape Verde
	Côte d'Ivoire	Gambia, The
	Senegal	**Nigeria**
	Gambia, The	Senegal
	Togo	Ghana
	Ghana	Côte d'Ivoire
	Benin	Togo
	Mauritania	Benin
	Guinea-Bissau	Mauritania
	Guinea	Burkina Faso
	Burkina Faso	Mali
	Sierra Leone	Guinea
	Nigeria	Guinea-Bissau
	Mali	Niger
	Liberia	
	Niger	
Performance among Oil-Exporters	▼	▲
	Gabon	**Nigeria**
	Côte d'Ivoire	Gabon
	Congo, Rep.	Equatorial Guinea
	Equatorial Guinea	Côte d'Ivoire
	Sudan	Sudan
	Cameroon	Cameroon
	Angola	Angola
	Nigeria	Congo, Rep.
	Chad	Chad

▲	improved *or* better than average
▼	worsened *or* worse than average
◁▷	no change *or* average

7.13

Phones (fixed & mobile) for every 100 Persons of Population in West Africa during 2000 & 2007

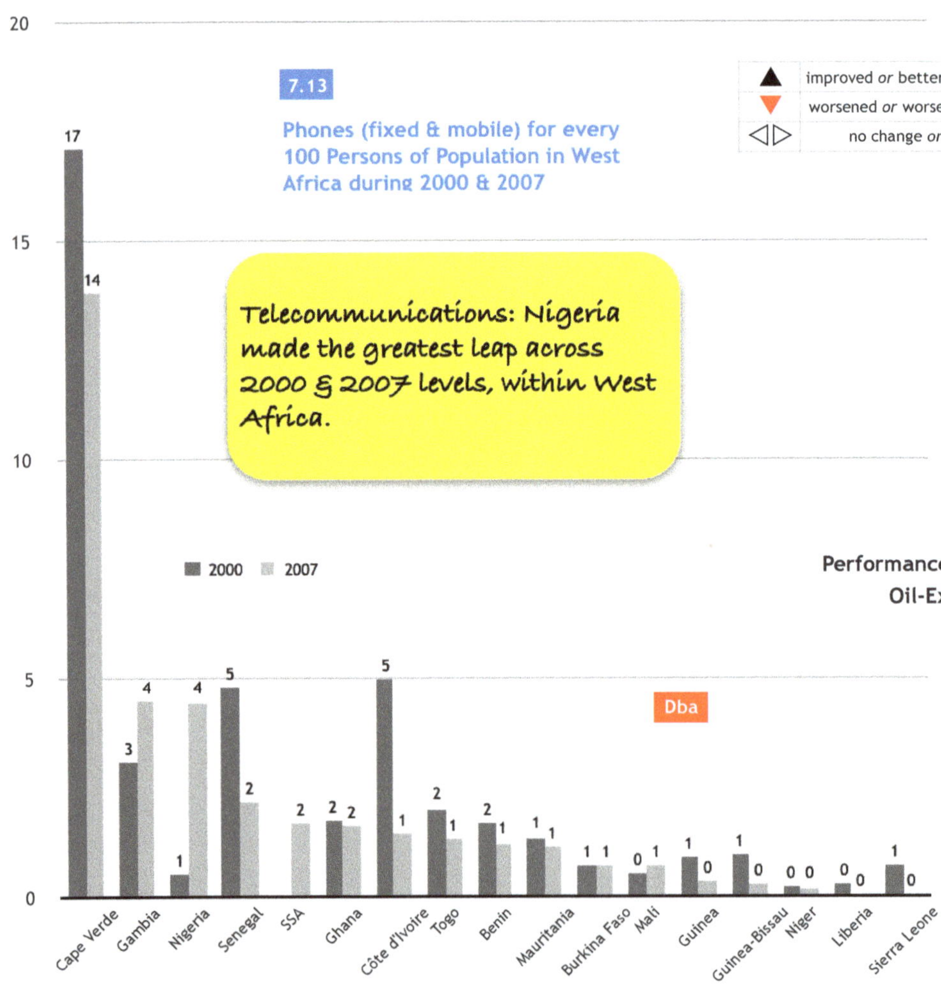

Phones (Fixed & Mobiles) per Population in Sub-Saharan Africa during 2007: Rankings

Rank	Country	Rank	Country	Rank	Country
1	Mauritius	15	Ghana	29	Tanzania
2	Seychelles	16	Côte d' Ivoire	30	Uganda
3	Cape Verde	17	Togo	31	Burundi
4	South Africa	18	Malawi	32	Congo, Rep.
5	Botswana	19	Benin	33	Guinea
6	Namibia	20	Ethiopia	34	Mozambique
7	Gambia, The	21	Eritrea	35	Central Afr. Rep.
8	Nigeria	22	Cameroon	36	Guinea-Bissau
9	Swaziland	23	Zambia	37	Rwanda
10	Lesotho	24	Kenya	38	Niger
11	Gabon	25	Burkina Faso	39	Chad
12	Comoros	26	Mali	40	Congo, Dem. Rep.
13	Senegal	27	Madagascar	N/A	Sierra Leone
14	Equatorial Guinea	28	Angola		
TOP		MIDDLE		BOTTOM	

Central Africa
East Africa
Southern Africa
West Africa

Primary Data: ITU

It climbed swiftly within the rest of Africa, too; and it topped the oil exporters group.

Nigeria was 8th best among 40 African countries as at 2007. In West Africa, Cape Verde and Gambia edged ahead of it.

7.9 Number of Mobile Phone Users

	2000	2007
Self-comparison to Preceding Period		▲
Performance in Sub-Saharan Africa	▼	▲
Performance in West Africa	▼	▲
	Cape Verde	Gambia, The
	Côte d'Ivoire	Mauritania
	Senegal	Côte d'Ivoire
	Togo	Senegal
	Benin	Ghana
	Ghana	Cape Verde
	Mauritania	**Nigeria**
	Guinea	Benin
	Gambia, The	Mali
	Sierra Leone	Togo
	Burkina Faso	Guinea-Bissau
	Mali	Liberia
	Liberia	Sierra Leone
	Nigeria	Burkina Faso
	Niger	Niger
		Guinea
Performance among Oil-Exporters	▼	◁▷
	Gabon	Gabon
	Côte d'Ivoire	Equatorial Guinea
	Congo, Rep.	Côte d'Ivoire
	Equatorial Guinea	Congo, Rep.
	Cameroon	**Nigeria**
	Angola	Cameroon
	Chad	Angola
	Sudan	Sudan
	Nigeria	Chad

▲	improved *or* better than average
▼	worsened *or* worse than average
◁▷	no change *or* average

7.14

Mobile Phones for every 100 Persons of Population in West Africa during 2000 & 2007

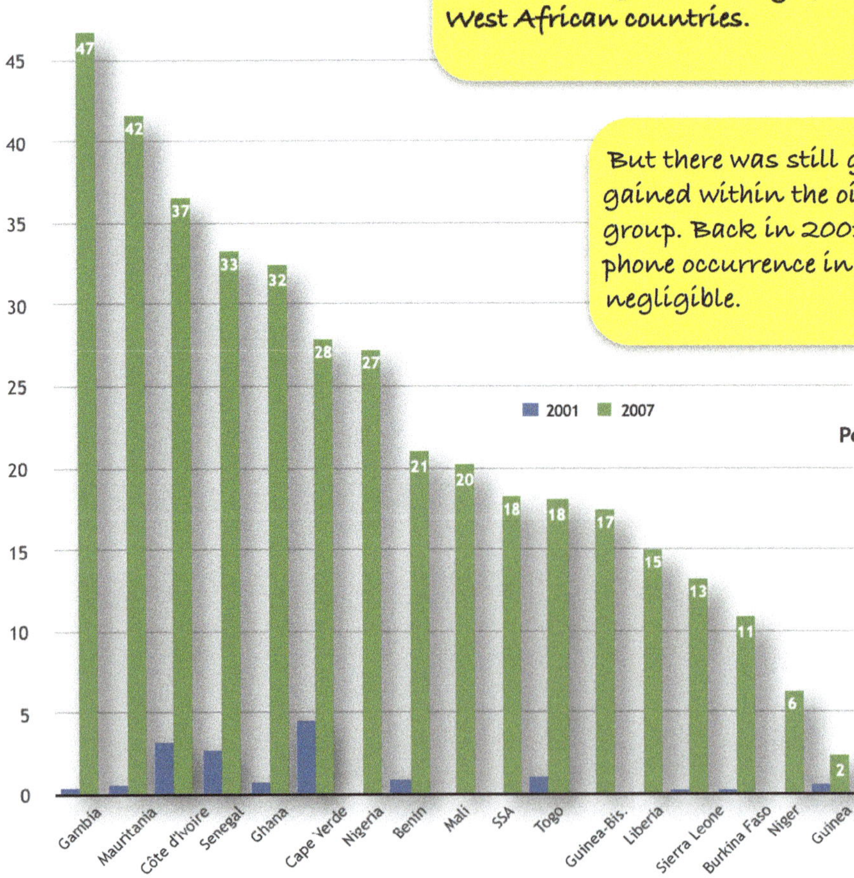

Concerning mobile phones specifically, by 2007 Nigeria had the 7th highest density of 16 West African countries.

But there was still ground to be gained within the oil exporters group. Back in 2001, mobile phone occurrence in Nigeria was negligible.

Primary Data: ITU

7.10 Literacy

that's his favorite book

	2000	2007
Self-comparison to Preceding Period		▲
Performance in Sub-Saharan Africa	▲	▲
Performance in West Africa	▲	▲
	Cape Verde	Cape Verde
	Ghana	Ghana
	Nigeria	Nigeria
	Togo	Togo
	Liberia	Liberia
	Côte d'Ivoire	Côte d'Ivoire
	Mauritania	Guinea-Bissau
	Guinea-Bissau	Benin
	Benin	Gambia, The
	Senegal	Senegal
	Gambia, The	Mauritania
	Mali	Mali
	Burkina Faso	Burkina Faso
	Niger	Niger
Performance among Oil-Exporters	◁▷	◁▷
	Equatorial Guinea	Equatorial Guinea
	Congo, Rep.	Congo, Rep.
	Cameroon	Cameroon
	Nigeria	Nigeria
	Sudan	Sudan
	Côte d'Ivoire	Côte d'Ivoire
	Chad	Chad

▲	improved *or* better than average
▼	worsened *or* worse than average
◁▷	no change *or* average

Primary Data: AfDB

3rd best literacy levels in West Afr., bettered by only Cape Verde & Ghana. Average in the oil group, where the table stayed the same for 2007 as for 2000.

7.15

Total Adult Literacy Rate (%) in West Africa during 2000 & 2007

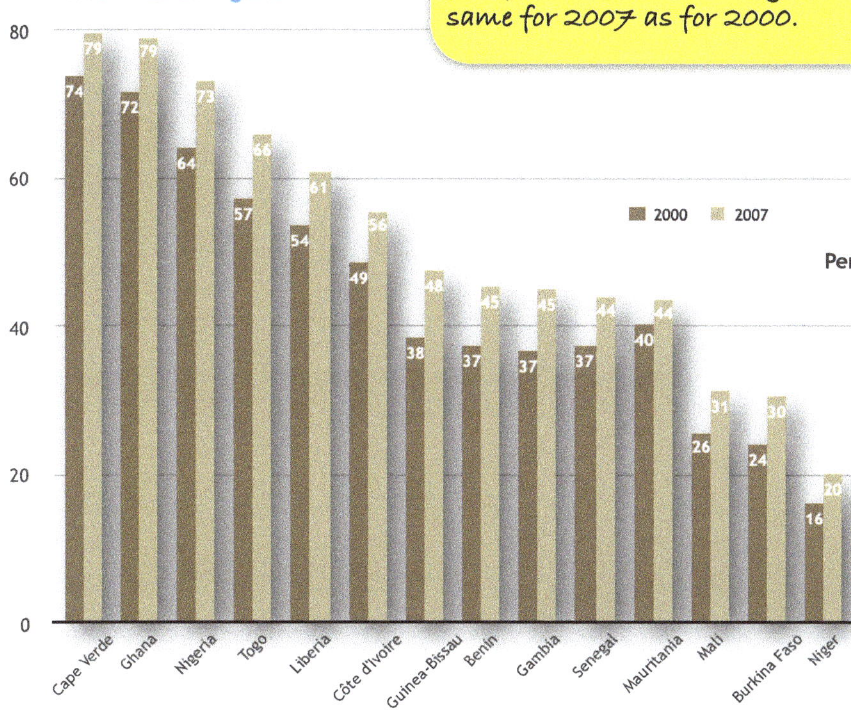

7.11 Number of Internet Users

	2000	2007
Self-comparison to Preceding Period		▲
Performance in Sub-Saharan Africa	▼	▲

Performance in West Africa

2000 ▼	2007 ▲
Togo	**Nigeria**
Cape Verde	Senegal
Gambia, The	Cape Verde
Senegal	Gambia, The
Côte d'Ivoire	Togo
Guinea-Bissau	Ghana
Benin	Guinea-Bissau
Mauritania	Benin
Ghana	Côte d'Ivoire
Mali	Mauritania
Guinea	Mali
Sierra Leone	Burkina Faso
Burkina Faso	Guinea
Nigeria	Niger
Niger	Sierra Leone
Liberia	

Primary Data: ITU

▲	improved *or* better than average
▼	worsened *or* worse than average
◁▷	no change *or* average

7.16

Internet Users out of every 1,000 Persons of Population in West Africa during 2000 & 2007

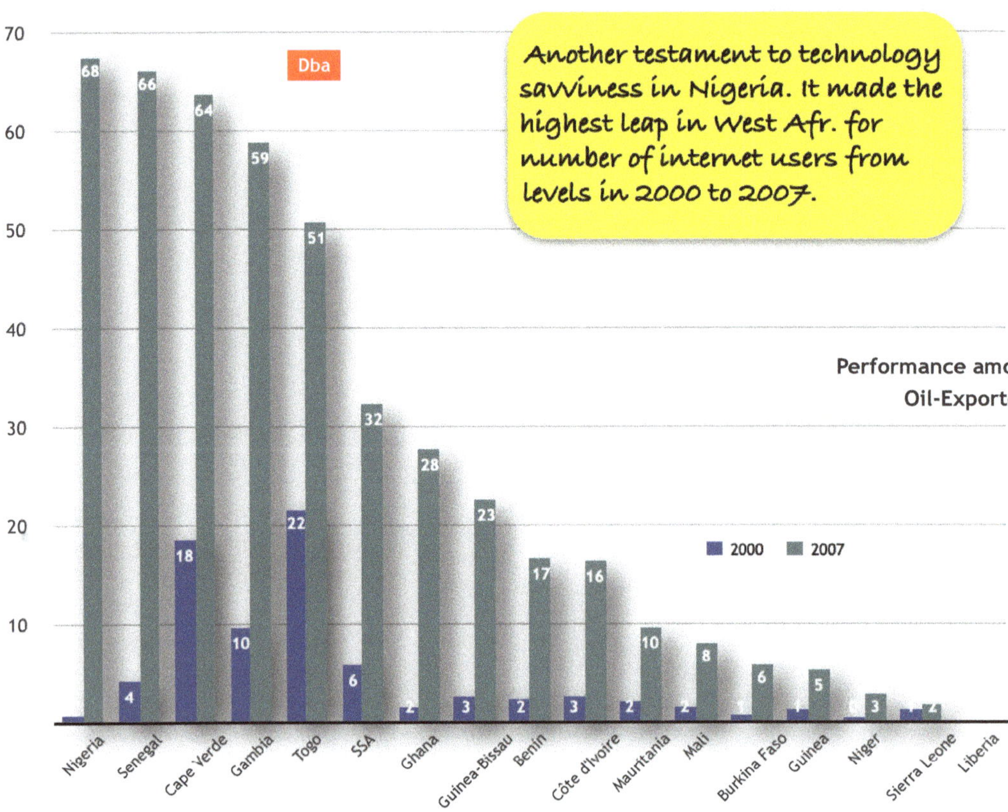

Performance among Oil-Exporters

2000 ▼	2007 ▲
Gabon	**Nigeria**
Cameroon	Gabon
Côte d'Ivoire	Sudan
Equatorial Guinea	Cameroon
Angola	Congo, Rep.
Sudan	Côte d'Ivoire
Nigeria	Equatorial Guinea
Chad	Angola
Congo, Rep.	Chad

Internet Users per Population in Sub-Saharan Africa during 2007: Rankings

TOP

Rank	Country
1	Seychelles
2	Mauritius
3	South Africa
4	Kenya
5	Nigeria
6	Senegal
7	Uganda
8	Cape Verde
9	Gambia, The
10	Gabon
11	Togo
12	Namibia
13	Botswana

MIDDLE

Rank	Country
14	Zambia
15	Swaziland
16	Lesotho
17	Ghana
18	Comoros
19	Guinea-Bissau
20	Cameroon
21	Eritrea
22	Congo, Rep.
23	Benin
24	Côte d' Ivoire
25	Equatorial Guinea
26	Rwanda

BOTTOM

Rank	Country
27	Malawi
	Tanzania
28	Mozambique
29	Mali
30	Burundi
31	Angola
	Chad
32	Burkina Faso
33	Madagascar
34	Guinea
35	Congo, Dem. Rep.
36	Ethiopia
37	Central Afr. Rep.
38	Niger
39	Sierra Leone

Primary Data: ITU

Central Africa
East Africa
Southern Africa
West Africa

It also made the biggest climb within the oil group, jumping from 7th to top place among the 9 countries.

In Africa, it was 5th out of 41 countries, bettered only by Seychelles, Mauritius, South Africa and Kenya.

7.12 Personal Computers per Population

they know their gigabytes

	2001	2006
Self-comparison to Preceding Period		▲
Performance in Sub-Saharan Africa	▼	▼
Performance in West Africa	▲	▲
	Cape Verde	Cape Verde
	Togo	Togo
	Senegal	Mauritania
	Gambia, The	Senegal
	Mauritania	Gambia, The
	Côte d'Ivoire	Côte d'Ivoire
	Nigeria	**Nigeria**
	Guinea	Benin
	Ghana	Ghana
	Guinea-Bissau	Guinea
	Benin	Mali
	Burkina Faso	Burkina Faso
	Mali	Guinea-Bissau
	Niger	Niger
Performance among Oil-Exporters	▲	▼
	Gabon	Sudan
	Côte d'Ivoire	Gabon
	Nigeria	Equatorial Guinea
	Equatorial Guinea	Côte d'Ivoire
	Cameroon	Cameroon
	Congo, Rep.	**Nigeria**
	Sudan	Angola
	Chad	Congo, Rep.
	Angola	Chad

▲	improved *or* better than average
▼	worsened *or* worse than average
◁▷	no change *or* average

7.17

Number of Personal Computers for every 1,000 Persons of Population in West Africa during 2001 & 2006

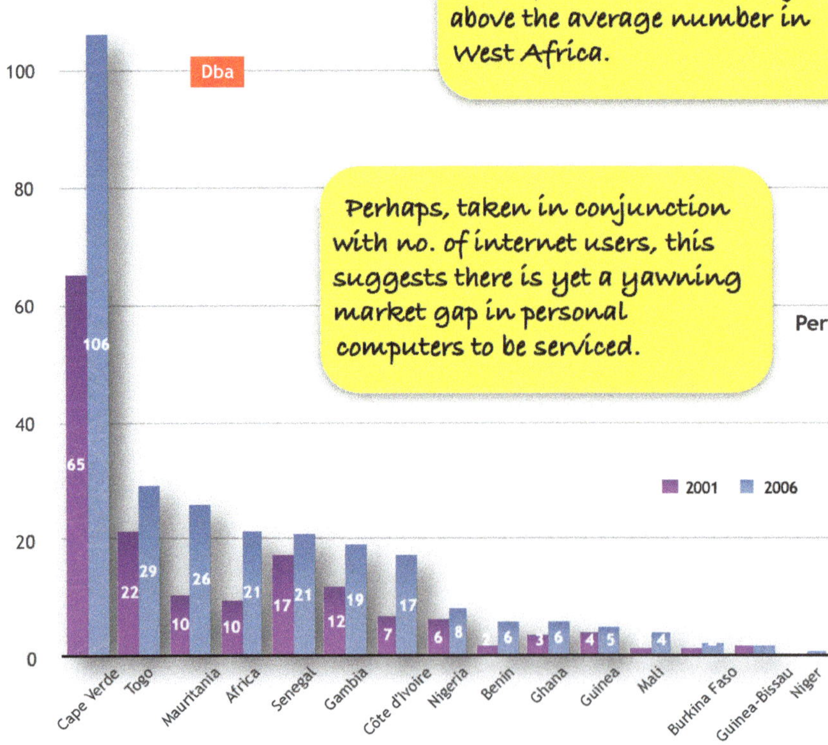

However, people owned fewer computers in Nigeria than in most of the continent; but just above the average number in West Africa.

Perhaps, taken in conjunction with no. of internet users, this suggests there is yet a yawning market gap in personal computers to be serviced.

Primary Data: AfDB

Personal Computers per Population in Sub-Saharan Africa during 2006: Rankings

Rank	Country
1	Seychelles
2	Mauritius
3	Namibia
4	Cape Verde
5	South Africa
6	Botswana
7	Swaziland
8	Gabon
9	Togo
10	Senegal
11	Gambia, The
12	Equatorial Guinea

TOP

Rank	Country
13	Côte d' Ivoire
14	Uganda
15	Kenya
	Mozambique
16	Zambia
17	Cameroon
18	Tanzania
19	Nigeria
20	Angola
	Burundi
21	Comoros
22	Eritrea
23	Benin
24	Ghana

MIDDLE

Rank	Country
25	Madagascar
26	Congo, Rep.
27	Guinea
28	Mali
29	Ethiopia
30	Central Afr. Rep.
31	Burkina Faso
32	Rwanda
33	Guinea-Bissau
	Malawi
34	Chad
35	Lesotho
	Niger
36	Congo, Dem. Rep.
N/A	Sierra Leone

BOTTOM

Primary Data: AfDB

Central Africa
East Africa
Southern Africa
West Africa

In Africa, unlike the top band for internet users, Nigeria falls in the middle band for incidence of personal computers.

Again, a possible pointer to the market that is still available for computers there.

7.13 Net Migration

their bags are packed, they're ready to go

2000-2005

Self-comparison to Preceding Period

Performance in Sub-Saharan Africa: ◁▷

Performance in West Africa: ▼

- Sierra Leone
- Gambia, The
- Benin
- Mauritania
- Burkina Faso
- Guinea-Bissau
- Ghana
- Togo
- **Nigeria**
- Niger
- Senegal
- Cape Verde
- Mali
- Côte d'Ivoire
- Liberia
- Guinea

Primary Data: UNPD

7.18

Net Migration out of every one million Persons of Population in West Africa during 2000-05

300 persons in every million left Nigeria during 2000-2005. The same as the Africa average, but just below average for West Africa.

The highest no. of emigrants went out of Guinea & the highest no. of immigrants went to Sierra Leone, quite likely returnees after the cessation of civil war.

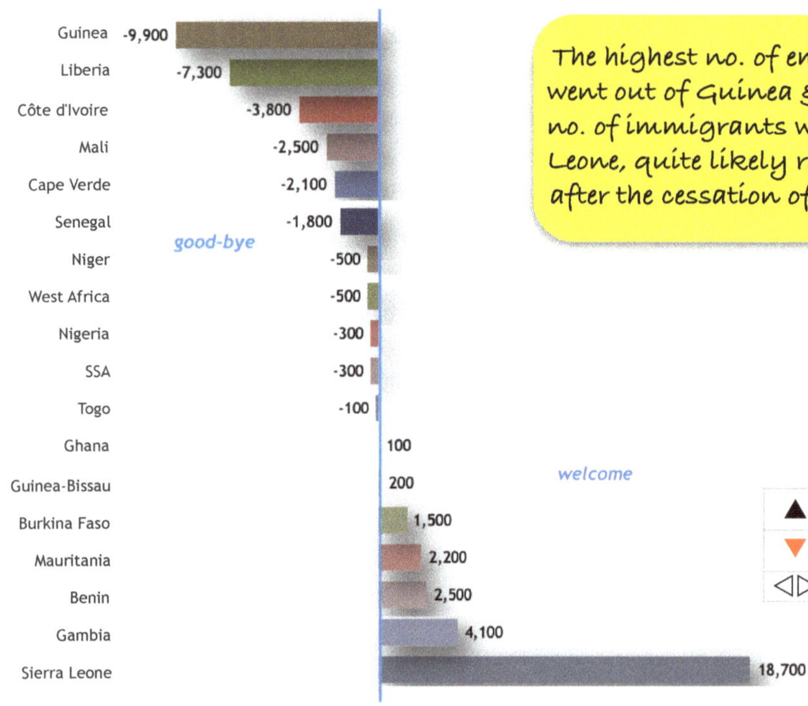

Performance among Oil-Exporters: ▼

- Chad
- Angola
- Gabon
- Cameroon
- Equatorial Guinea
- **Nigeria**
- Congo, Rep.
- Sudan
- Côte d'Ivoire

▲	better = less people leaving *or* more people coming in
▼	worse = more people leaving *or* less people coming in
◁▷	no change *or* average

Leaders & Stragglers

and they lived happily ever after

Quality of Life Rankings: 2003-07

Rank	Country	Rank	Country	Rank	Country
1	Mauritius	15	Eritrea	29	Guinea
2	Seychelles	16	Swaziland	30	Rwanda
3	Cape Verde	17	Benin	31	Burundi
4	South Africa	18	Tanzania	32	Mali
5	Gambia, The	19	Lesotho	33	Ethiopia
6	Namibia	20	Cameroon	34	Burkina Faso
7	Botswana	21	Nigeria	35	Guinea-Bissau
8	Gabon	22	Equatorial Guinea	36	Angola
9	Comoros	23	Congo, Rep.	37	Niger
10	Senegal	24	Madagascar	38	Congo, Dem. Rep.
11	Ghana	25	Zambia	39	Chad
12	Togo	26	Côte d' Ivoire	40	Central Afr. Rep.
13	Uganda	27	Malawi	41	Sierra Leone
14	Kenya	28	Mozambique		
TOP		MIDDLE		BOTTOM	

Central Africa
East Africa
Southern Africa
West Africa

Bang in the middle of Africa, Nigeria wasn't the best place to live during 2003-2007, but it was far from being the worst.

Within West Africa, it stood firmly in the very centre: 8th out of 15 listed countries; 7 better than it, and 7 worse.

Mauritius, Seychelles, Cape Verde, South Africa and Gambia were best in Africa.

Wrap-up: Quality of Life

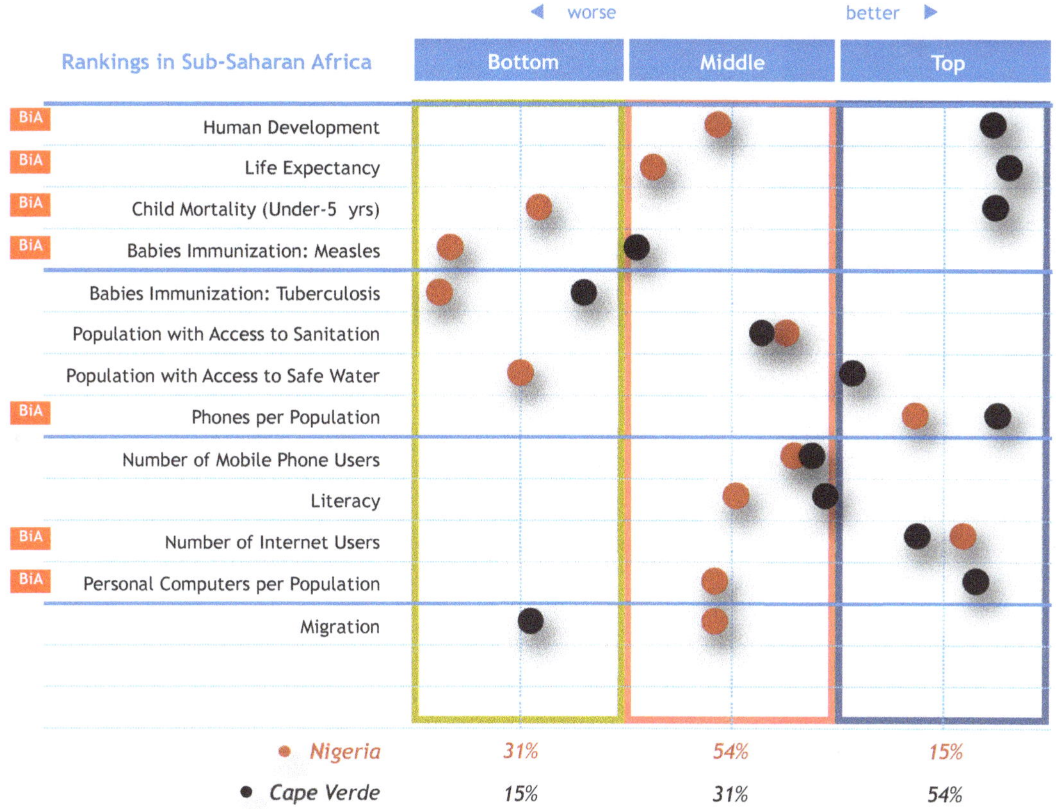

- The best West Africa performance was Cape Verde's; 3rd place in the Africa rankings. Nigeria was almost bang in the middle, at 21st position.

- Of the 13 socio-economic indicators, Nigeria had 31% falling into the bottom-third category in Africa, with the highest proportion qualifying for only average (middle-band) performance; 54%.

- In contrast, Cape Verde had most of its indicators performance, 54%, qualifying for top-third; followed by 31% in the middle-third. The smallest portion of its indicators, 15%, fell into the bottom third of Sub-Saharan Africa.

- The particularly bad Nigeria report-card belongs to babies' immunization, population's access to safe water, and child mortality. All of them health issues.

- Whereas its best showing came from one sector only: information & communication technology. Cape Verde's best came in almost all "life issues": life expectancy, child mortality, access to safe water, and human development in general. Even though they had a strong score-card in technology sectors, too.

8. Economic Strength

built to last

Primer

GDP

The muscle power of an economy is usually expressed as Gross Domestic Product (GDP), which is a measure of a country's economic activity and resulting output. It comprises the total of all economic activity in the country, across all sectors of activity. The United States is the world's largest economy since it has the highest output (GDP) year after year.

GDP per person

However, a country might have a large GDP but also an accompanying large population. So, in strict terms, the muscle power of the economy would more accurately be expressed in per capita (per person of population) bases. GDP per capita would indicate the capacity of an economy to optimally make use of its factors of production, chief of which is population (labour). Then again, a high GDP per person will not necessarily indicate a success in production; some countries are endowed with natural resources that will continuously swell their GDP and could mask existing and gravely damaging inefficiencies. Usually, though, this can be discerned and accurately separated from genuine efficiency in the economy.

Purchasing Power Parity (PPP)

For more accurate country comparisons, GDP is often expressed in "Purchasing Power Parity" dollars, because this allows for a more realistic and representative comparison of economic output between countries. It puts the countries on a common platform, by cancelling out domestic financial and social peculiarities affecting the US dollar in these different environments, and using a "common currency", $PPP, instead. One PPP dollar would theoretically have the same power in each country, because it would purchase the same basket of goods in every economy. Unlike comparisons at market exchange rates, PPP reflects the real purchasing power of each country's residents and allows for more balanced comparisons across borders.

Gross National Income

(Formerly known as GNP, gross national product.) GNI is more a measure of a country's (and population's) wealth. It comprises the total of incomes earned by the country's residents both from home and from abroad, and indicates the capacity of an economy to provide for the needs of its residents.

GNI per Person

GNI per Person in mature economies tends to grow at a slower rate than in semi-developed or developing economies. However, the GNI per person in mature economies is much higher. Usually, a strong and viable economy would have a growing GNI per capita adequate to maintain or increase consumption levels. Nevertheless, GNI does not necessarily reflect the purchasing power of the citizens; issues like distribution of wealth, gap between rich and poor (and even corruption) come into play.

Growth Rates

In an efficient economy, GDP and GNI will grow continually, but it is interesting to note that economies will not grow indefinitely. Economic recessions will occur in cycles and redress balances. Statistically, they tend to occur every ten years or so. GDP and GNI will grow at slower rates in developed economies (because these have exploited most of the production avenues open to them) than in developing ones (where new avenues are easier to come by). But developed world GNI will still be larger in size. The challenge for developing economies is to grow GDP as quickly (by efficiently maximizing resources) and sustainably as possible.

Real Growth Rates

The important factor, however, is not merely the absolute GDP or GDP Growth, but the GDP per person and its annual growth. If GDP is not growing faster than population the economy is actually in recession. And so, Real GDP Growth is what is usually evaluated. Assessing real growth also allows taking into account the erosion of value that inflation brings.

Inflation

This is the rate at which the costs of goods and services increase in an economy, essentially due to demand outstripping supply. This would usually reflect the ability of the country to manage all economic sectors efficiently so that demand for goods does not overwhelm the available supply, meaning growth of demand will be a profit incentive that draws out a corresponding and sustainable increase in production; rather than the opposite (falling demand, thus falling prices) which would lead producers to hold back by not investing more money to produce more goods since there isn't a profit imperative for them to do so. That, in turn, would lead to a slump in economic activity and the consequent negative effects on growth.

Yet, some inflation need not be a bad thing. Inflation helps to ensure that there is a continuous demand and supply of goods. The opposite, (deflation: falling demand, too many goods) does not encourage increased output and further investment, leading – as pointed out earlier – to economic downturn because, among other things, it will lead to increased unemployment, as industries would shed staff since production levels will keep falling. However, inflation must be well controlled otherwise it spirals and leads to, for example, further problems of exchange rates and disincentives for saving, leading to insufficient funds for investment, etc.

The target for inflation is usually low single digits, about 1% to 3%.

Movement of Consumer Prices

This shows the trend in the cost of a select basket of the same goods as it is affected by the inflation rate in the country from year to year. Countries with the highest inflation rates (usually a bad sign) end up with identical goods costing more there than in another country with lower inflation rates. If cost of living is continuously rising, it makes planning more challenging, and renders the economy unattractive.

Exchange Rate Swings

This is the fluctuation in the national currency's exchange rate with – usually – the US dollar. Ordinarily, a low value for a nation's currency aids exports (because buyers find their foreign currencies going a longer distance in the markets of the exporting country in terms of purchasing power, since they find the goods affordable) and hence these "low" currency values hold a certain attraction. Nevertheless, beyond a certain point, it may actually make production (and, hence, economic growth) difficult, especially where raw materials input are largely imported from abroad: the low-value local currency is unable to pay for the raw materials required.

It must be noted, though, that the main challenge may not necessarily be to keep the currency's value constant. Sometimes, especially in developing economies, circumstances might advise a devaluing. However, a one-time big-drop devaluation that occurs and holds the new exchange rate for several years, might be more desirable than the same big-drop devaluation occurring in fits and starts across the same number of years. Uncertainty is usually disdained by business.

(Note: Economy growth rates shown here are those pre-dating the worst period of the persisting global financial crisis and recession. And new rates were still constantly being revised and released by the various multilateral agencies. Nevertheless, the comparative conclusions drawn here remain appropriate, since the crisis is not limited to a particular geography or sector within Sub-Saharan Africa.)

Sources of Primary Data: IMF, World Bank

Charts

Tables

1999-2002; 2003-2006; 2007-2010:

- *self-comparison to preceding period;*
- *performance in S-Saharan Africa;*
- *performance in West Africa;*
- *performance among oil-exporters;*

for:

GDP per Person ($PPP)

Growth in GDP per Person

Real GDP Growth

Real Non-Oil GDP Growth*

Inflation

1999-2002; 2003-2006:

- *self-comparison to preceding period;*
- *performance in S-Saharan Africa;*
- *performance in West Africa;*
- *performance among oil-exporters;*

for:

GNI per Person ($PPP)

Growth in GNI per Person

2000-2007; 2003-2010:

- *self-comparison to preceding period;*
- *performance in S-Saharan Africa;*
- *performance in West Africa;*
- *performance among oil-exporters;*

for:

Exchange Rate Stability

- GDP per Person of Population ($PPP) in Sub-Saharan Africa during 2003-06: Rankings
- Growth in GDP per Person of Population in Sub-Saharan Africa during 2003-06: Rankings
- GNI per Person of Population ($PPP) in Sub-Saharan Africa during 2003-06: Rankings
- Growth in GNI per Person of Population in Sub-Saharan Africa during 2003-06: Rankings
- Real GDP Growth in Sub-Saharan Africa during 2003-06: Rankings
- Consumer Price Movement in West Africa in 2007 and 2010: 2000=100
- Inflation in Sub-Saharan Africa during 2003-06: Rankings
- Exchange Rate Stability in Sub-Saharan Africa during 2003-06: Rankings
- Movement of Real Exchange Rates in West Africa in 2007, 2010: 2000=100

- **Economic Strength Rankings: 2003-06**

* only for the oil-exporters

8.1 Nigeria GDP in Sub-Saharan Africa ($PPP)

Besides growing in absolute size since 1999, Nigeria's GDP has also grown as a proportion of the continent's. From 15% in 1999 to 19% in 2007.

That proportion is expected to hit close to 20% of Sub-Saharan Africa GDP by 2010.

8.1

GDP contribution of Nigeria in Sub-Saharan Africa during 1999/02, 2003/06, 2007/10

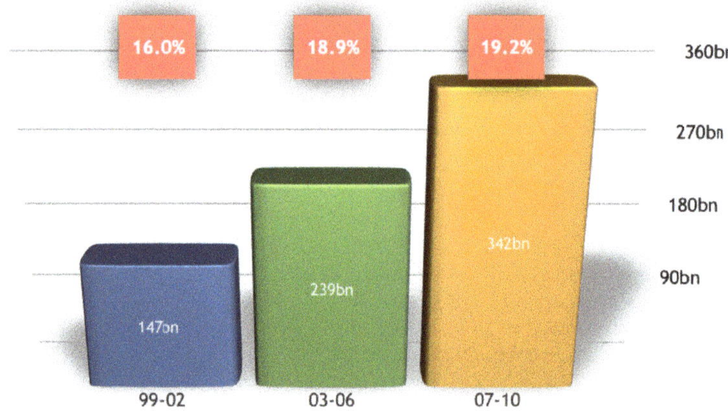

8.2

GDP contribution of Nigeria in Sub-Saharan Africa from 1999 to 2010

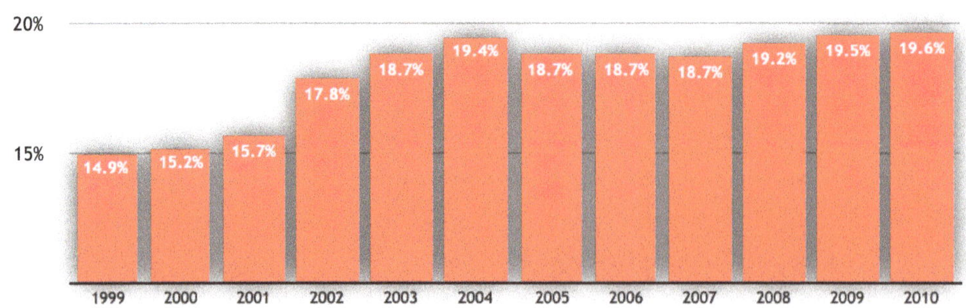

8.2 Nigeria GDP in West Africa ($PPP)

and this is how this stacks up

As expected, Nigeria's is the largest economy in West Africa. It has cornered more and more of the sub-region's output over the past ten years: 55% in 2000, to 65% by 2010.

8.3

GDP contribution of Nigeria in West Africa during 1999/02, 2003/06, 2007/10

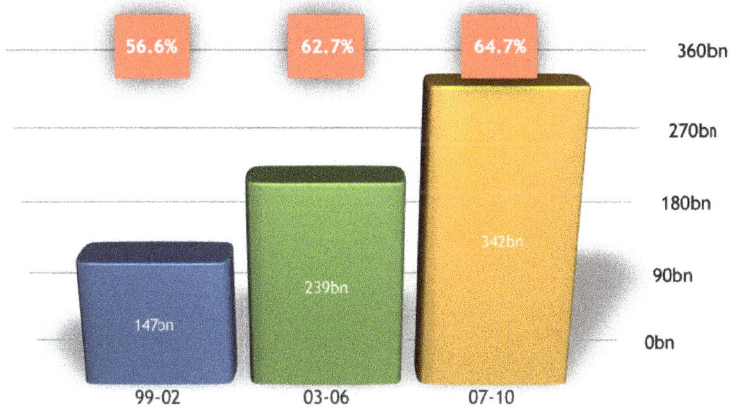

8.4

GDP contribution of Nigeria in West Africa from 1999 to 2010

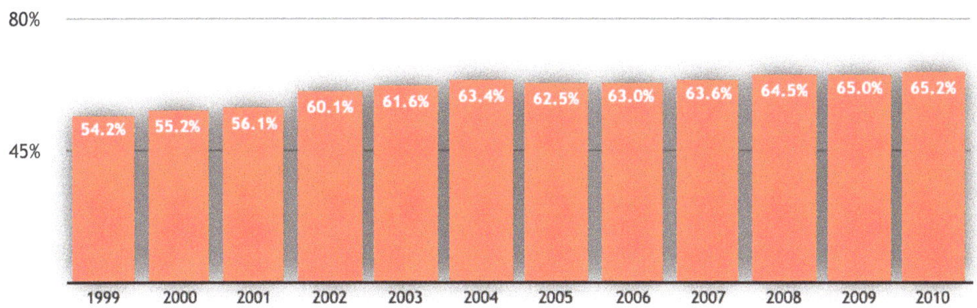

+1-800-help

Why insist on $PPP and not just use $US?

Purchasing Power Parity dollars ($PPP) lets you compare across countries on an equal footing, as it were. Otherwise $US (or any other currency) wouldn't, because the value changes from country to country.

I see.

One $PPP has the same strength in every country: it would buy the exact same number of apples everywhere.

8.3 GDP per Person ($PPP)

what she's bringing to the party

	99-02	03-06	07-10
Self-comparison to Preceding Period		▲	▲
Performance in Sub-Saharan Africa	▼	▲	▲
Performance in West Africa	▲	▲	▲
	Cape Verde	Cape Verde	Cape Verde
	Côte d'Ivoire	**Nigeria**	**Nigeria**
	Mauritania	Mauritania	Mauritania
	Senegal	Côte d'Ivoire	Côte d'Ivoire
	Nigeria	Senegal	Senegal
	Benin	Benin	Benin
	Ghana	Ghana	Ghana
	Gambia, The	Gambia, The	Gambia, The
	Guinea	Burkina Faso	Burkina Faso
	Burkina Faso	Guinea	Guinea
	Mali	Mali	Mali
	Togo	Togo	Togo
	Niger	Niger	Sierra Leone
	Guinea-Bissau	Sierra Leone	Niger
	Liberia	Guinea-Bissau	Guinea-Bissau
	Sierra Leone	Liberia	Liberia
Performance among Oil-Exporters	▼	▼	▼
	Gabon	Gabon	Gabon
	Equatorial Guinea	Equatorial Guinea	Equatorial Guinea
	Congo, Rep.	Angola	Angola
	Angola	Congo, Rep.	Congo, Rep.
	Cameroon	Cameroon	Sudan
	Côte d'Ivoire	**Nigeria**	**Nigeria**
	Sudan	Sudan	Cameroon
	Nigeria	Côte d'Ivoire	Côte d'Ivoire
	Chad	Chad	Chad

Despite its very large population, Nigeria scores quite high in output per inhabitant, in West Africa. Before 2003, it had posted only weak reports.

That improved performance is tainted, though, when Nigeria is compared to fellow oil-sustained economies. It performs below average.

Primary Data: IMF

▲	improved *or* better than average
▼	worsened *or* worse than average
◁▷	no change *or* average

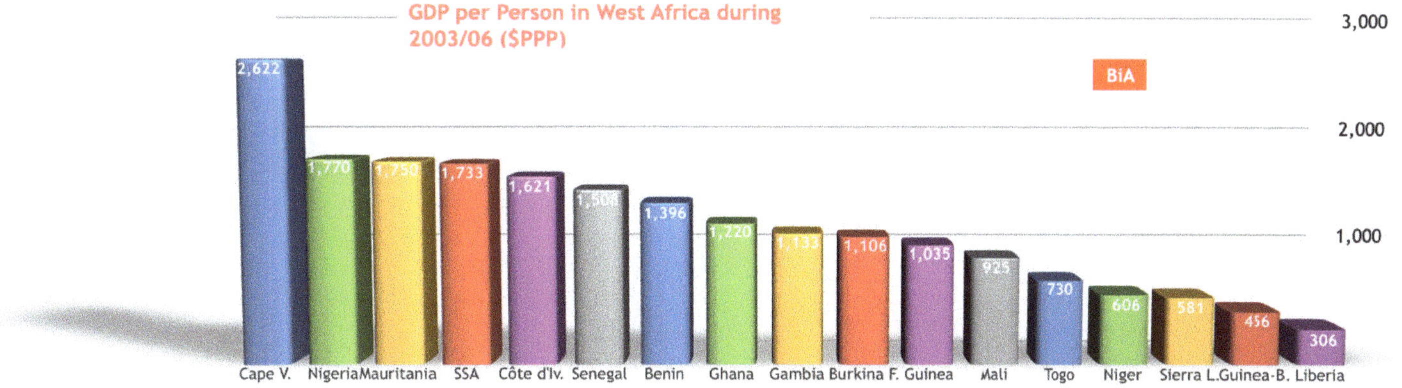

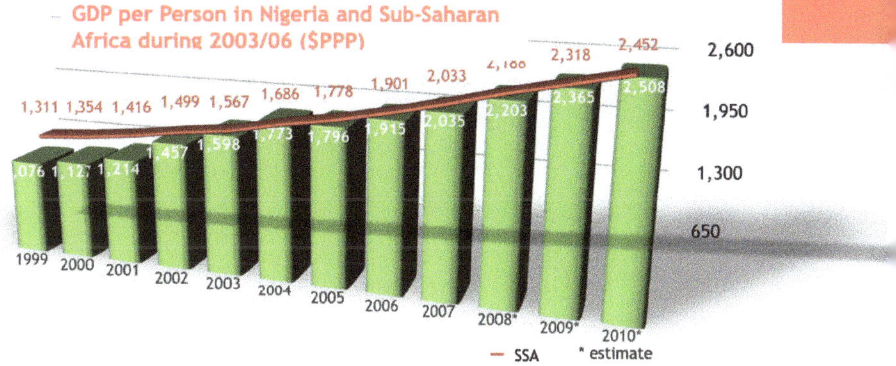

On the continent level, Nigeria stays just above average, coming from behind in 2000 to surpass continental performance by 2003.

Primary Data: IMF

GDP per Person of Population ($PPP) in Sub-Saharan Africa during 2003-06: Rankings

Rank	Country	Rank	Country	Rank	Country
1	Seychelles	15	Senegal	29	Uganda
2	Botswana	16	Chad	30	Eritrea
3	Gabon	17	Kenya	31	Rwanda
4	Equatorial Guinea	18	Benin	32	Togo
5	Mauritius	19	Ghana	33	Mozambique
6	South Africa	20	Zambia	34	Malawi
7	Namibia	21	Gambia, The	35	Central Afr. Rep.
8	Swaziland	22	Lesotho	36	Ethiopia
9	Angola	23	Burkina Faso	37	Niger
10	Congo, Rep.	24	Comoros	38	Sierra Leone
11	Cape Verde	25	Tanzania	39	Guinea-Bissau
12	Cameroon	26	Guinea	40	Burundi
13	Nigeria	27	Mali	41	Congo, Dem. Rep.
14	Côte d' Ivoire	28	Madagascar		
TOP		MIDDLE		BOTTOM	

Central Africa
East Africa
Southern Africa
West Africa

It does just enough to stay above water from then onwards, finishing in 13th place, out of 41 countries. Close shave.

8.4 Growth in GDP per Person

loaded on vitamins

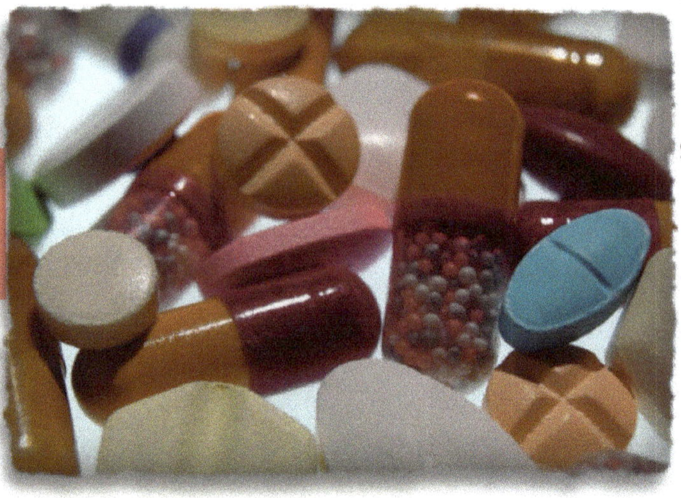

Growth rate of GDP per Person for Nigeria was falling across the 2000 to 2007 years. It did worse in 2003/07, and is projected to do relatively worse again in 2007/10.

Still, a first-rate showing in West Africa, which may suggest that the other countries faced similar climates and challenges. Or that they failed to pull their weight effectively.

A tottering performance among oil-exporters. Nigeria dropped in position during 03/06; it had done significantly better in 1999/02. But it is expected to pick up in 2007/10.

	00-02	03-06	07-10
Self-comparison to Preceding Period		▼	▼
Performance in Sub-Saharan Africa	▲	▲	▲
Performance in West Africa	▲	▲	▲
	Sierra Leone	Sierra Leone	Liberia
	Nigeria	Mauritania	Cape Verde
	Cape Verde	**Nigeria**	**Nigeria**
	Mali	Cape Verde	Ghana
	Ghana	Gambia, The	Sierra Leone
	Benin	Ghana	Gambia, The
	Burkina Faso	Mali	Senegal
	Guinea	Burkina Faso	Burkina Faso
	Liberia	Togo	Mauritania
	Senegal	Senegal	Côte d'Ivoire
	Niger	Niger	Benin
	Gambia, The	Benin	Mali
	Mauritania	Guinea-Bissau	Guinea
	Côte d'Ivoire	Côte d'Ivoire	Niger
	Togo	Guinea	Togo
	Guinea-Bissau	Liberia	Guinea-Bissau

	00-02	03-06	07-10
Performance among Oil-Exporters	▲	◁▷	▲
	Equatorial Guinea	Chad	Angola
	Nigeria	Equatorial Guinea	Sudan
	Sudan	Angola	Equatorial Guinea
	Angola	Sudan	**Nigeria**
	Chad	**Nigeria**	Congo, Rep.
	Congo, Rep.	Congo, Rep.	Gabon
	Cameroon	Cameroon	Côte d'Ivoire
	Gabon	Gabon	Cameroon
	Côte d'Ivoire	Côte d'Ivoire	Chad

Primary Data: IMF

▲	improved *or* better than average
▼	worsened *or* worse than average
◁▷	no change *or* average

8.7

Growth in GDP per Person in West Africa during 2003-06 (%)

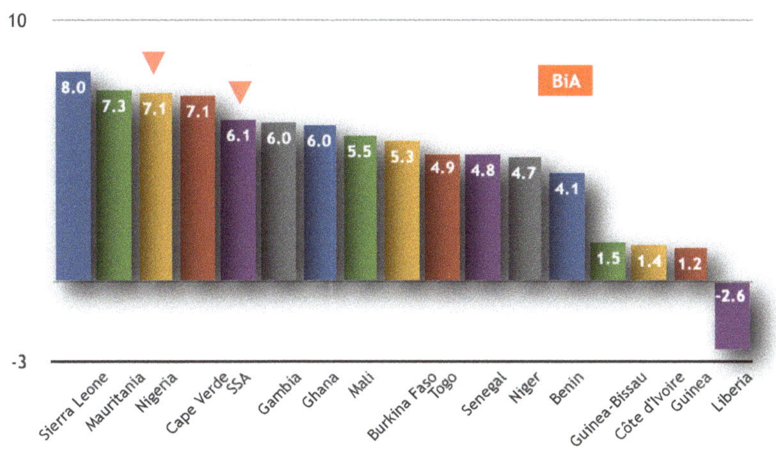

8.8

Growth in GDP per Person in Nigeria and Sub-Saharan Africa during 2003/06 (%)

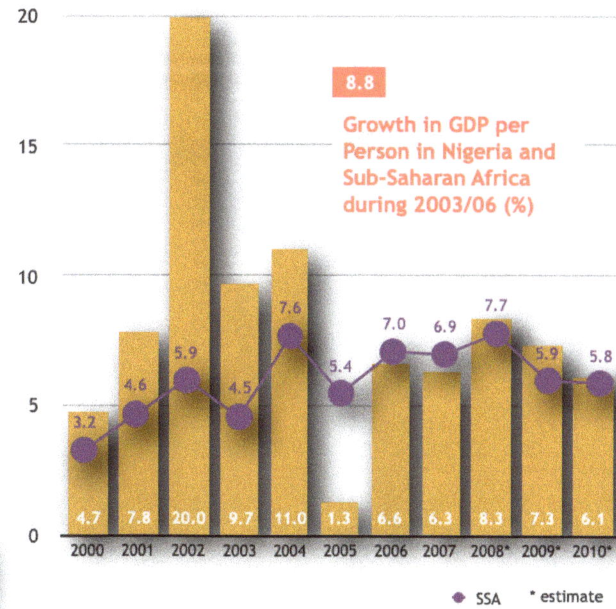

Primary Data: IMF

2000 to 2004 saw Nigeria growing its output per person by several notches faster than the rest of Africa.

But, even though that rate would not afterwards fall as spectacularly as in 2005, it has struggled since then to keep up with the Africa average.

Growth in GDP per Person of Population in Sub-Saharan Africa during 2003-06: Rankings

Rank	Country	Rank	Country	Rank	Country
1	Chad	15	Malawi	29	Swaziland
2	Equatorial Guinea	16	Congo, Dem. Rep.	30	Lesotho
3	Angola	17	Gambia, The	31	Benin
4	Madagascar	18	Ghana	32	Burundi
5	Ethiopia	19	Zambia	33	Cameroon
6	Botswana	20	Mauritius	34	Comoros
7	Sierra Leone	21	Mali	35	Gabon
8	Mozambique	22	Congo, Rep.	36	Central Afr. Rep.
9	Tanzania	23	Burkina Faso	37	Guinea-Bissau
10	Nigeria	24	Kenya	38	Côte d' Ivoire
11	Cape Verde	25	Togo	39	Guinea
12	South Africa	26	Senegal	40	Seychelles
13	Namibia	27	Uganda	41	Eritrea
14	Rwanda	28	Niger		
HIGHEST		MIDDLE		BOTTOM	

Central Africa
East Africa
Southern Africa
West Africa

8.5 GNI per Person ($PPP)

she's earned it

GNI per capita: Nigeria improved in 03/06, compared to 99/02. But that rally wasn't strong enough to lift it above average in the continent.

That it was good enough for an upper West Africa performance might again point to a dismal showing across the entire sub-region...

...It could also be that there were systemic challenges peculiar to West Africa & absent in the rest of the continent. More likely the former, though.

Something gravely amiss with Nigeria's GNI, as the oil-exporters' table confirms:

Nigeria isn't squeezing what it can from domestic economic output and earnings from investments, etc., outside its borders.

	99-02	03-06
Self-comparison to Preceding Period		▲
Performance in Sub-Saharan Africa	▼	▼
Performance in West Africa	▲	▲
	Cape Verde	Cape Verde
	Côte d'Ivoire	Mauritania
	Mauritania	Côte d'Ivoire
	Senegal	Senegal
	Nigeria	**Nigeria**
	Benin	Benin
	Guinea	Ghana
	Ghana	Guinea
	Gambia, The	Burkina Faso
	Burkina Faso	Gambia, The
	Mali	Mali
	Togo	Togo
	Niger	Niger
	Guinea-Bissau	Sierra Leone
	Sierra Leone	Guinea-Bissau
	Liberia	Liberia
Performance among Oil-Exporters	▼	▼
	Gabon	Equatorial Guinea
	Equatorial Guinea	Gabon
	Angola	Angola
	Congo, Rep.	Congo, Rep.
	Cameroon	Cameroon
	Côte d'Ivoire	Sudan
	Sudan	Côte d'Ivoire
	Nigeria	**Nigeria**
	Chad	Chad

Primary Data: World Bank

▲	improved *or* better than average
▼	worsened *or* worse than average
◁▷	no change *or* average

8.9

GNI per Person in West Africa during 2003/06 ($PPP)

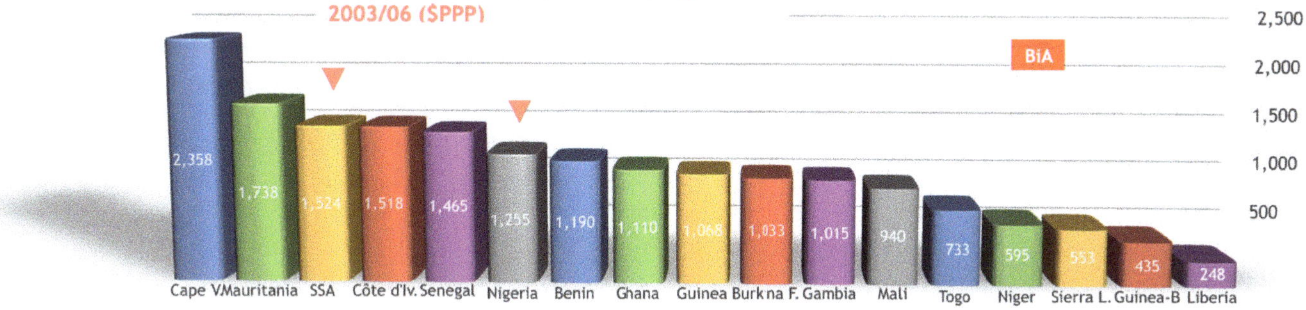

8.10

GNI per Person in Nigeria and Sub-Saharan Africa from 1999 to 2006 ($PPP)

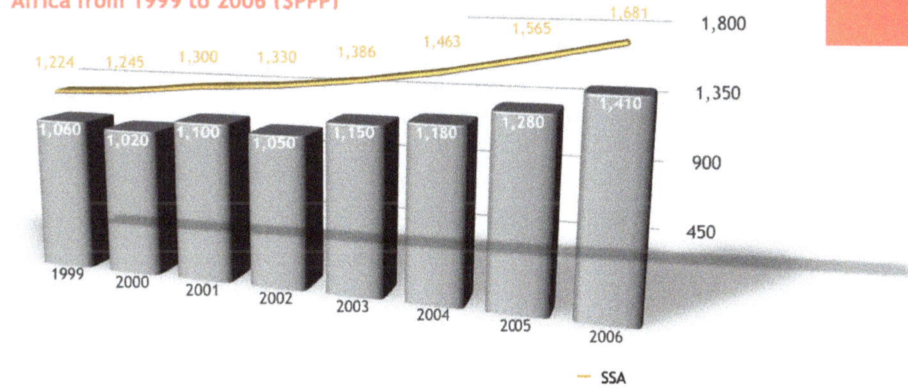

The rest of Africa left Nigeria in their wake throughout 1999-2006.

GNI per Person of Population ($PPP) in Sub-Saharan Africa during 2003-06: Rankings

Rank	Country	Rank	Country	Rank	Country
1	Seychelles	15	Senegal	28	Madagascar
2	Equatorial Guinea	16	Kenya	29	Togo
3	Gabon	17	**Nigeria**	30	Eritrea
4	Botswana	18	Benin	31	Rwanda
5	Mauritius	19	Ghana	32	Central Afr. Rep.
6	South Africa	20	Chad	33	Malawi
7	Namibia		Comoros	34	Mozambique
8	Swaziland	21	Guinea	35	Niger
9	Angola	22	Zambia	36	Sierra Leone
10	Cape Verde	23	Burkina Faso	37	Ethiopia
11	Congo, Rep.	24	Gambia, The	38	Guinea-Bissau
12	Cameroon	25	Mali	39	Burundi
13	Lesotho	26	Tanzania	40	Congo, Dem. Rep.
14	Côte d' Ivoire	27	Uganda		
HIGHEST		MIDDLE		BOTTOM	

To place the outcomes in perspective, Seychelles posted $13,500, Senegal $1,500, Nigeria $1,300, and Madagascar $800. The continent average was $1,500.

Primary Data: World Bank

Central Africa
East Africa
Southern Africa
West Africa

8.6 Growth in GNI per Person

but is she growing it?

A seemingly desperate attempt by Nigeria to make up for lost ground in GNI per inhabitant.

& it pulls it off, somewhat: it jumps several notches during 2003/06, within West Africa, among the oil-exporters, and within the entire continent, too.

	00-02	03-06
Self-comparison to Preceding Period		▲
Performance in Sub-Saharan Africa	▼	▲
Performance in West Africa	▼	▲
	Sierra Leone	**Nigeria**
	Liberia	Ghana
	Cape Verde	Sierra Leone
	Mauritania	Gambia, The
	Guinea	Burkina Faso
	Benin	Cape Verde
	Ghana	Mali
	Mali	Mauritania
	Burkina Faso	Senegal
	Senegal	Niger
	Niger	Guinea
	Gambia, The	Benin
	Togo	Togo
	Guinea-Bissau	Guinea-Bissau
	Nigeria	Côte d'Ivoire
	Côte d'Ivoire	Liberia
Performance among Oil-Exporters	▼	◁▷
	Equatorial Guinea	Equatorial Guinea
	Angola	Angola
	Sudan	Sudan
	Congo, Rep.	Chad
	Chad	**Nigeria**
	Cameroon	Congo, Rep.
	Gabon	Cameroon
	Nigeria	Côte d'Ivoire
	Côte d'Ivoire	Gabon

Primary Data: World Bank

▲	improved *or* better than average
▼	worsened *or* worse than average
◁▷	no change *or* average

8.11

Growth in GNI per Person in West Africa during 2003/06 (%)

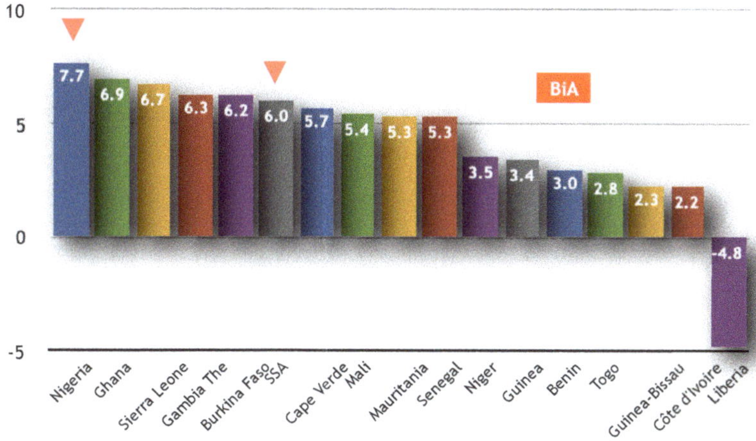

8.12

Growth in GNI per Person in Nigeria and Sub-Saharan Africa from 2000 to 2006 (%)

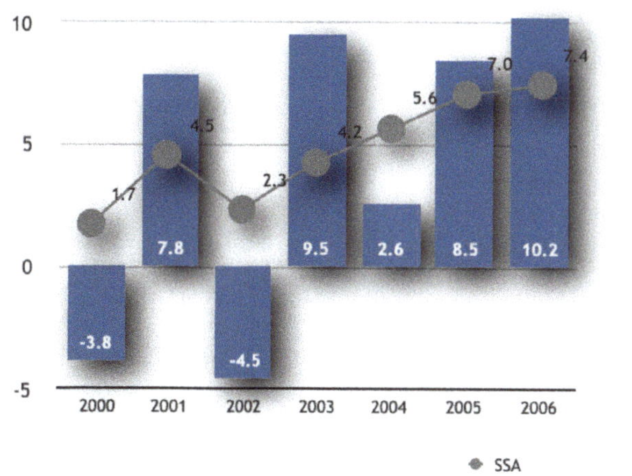

Primary Data: World Bank

But there still was an unsteady showing: fits and starts rather than consistency.

Growth in GNI per Person of Population in Sub-Saharan Africa during 2003-06: Rankings

Rank	Country	Rank	Country	Rank	Country
1	Equatorial Guinea	15	Mauritius	29	Swaziland
2	Angola	16	Burkina Faso	30	Niger
3	Chad	17	Mozambique	31	Guinea
4	Botswana	18	Malawi	32	Seychelles
5	Nigeria	19	Cape Verde	33	Benin
6	Ethiopia	20	Mali	34	Togo
7	Lesotho	21	Kenya	35	Comoros
8	Ghana	22	Namibia	36	Guinea-Bissau
9	Sierra Leone	23	Congo, Rep.	37	Côte d' Ivoire
10	Tanzania	24	Senegal	38	Central Afr. Rep.
11	Congo, Dem. Rep.	25	Cameroon	39	Burundi
12	Madagascar	26	Uganda	40	Eritrea
13	South Africa	27	Rwanda	41	Gabon
14	Gambia, The	28	Zambia		
TOP		MIDDLE		BOTTOM	

Central Africa
East Africa
Southern Africa
West Africa

8.7 Real GDP Growth

bull's-eye!

When stripped of adornments, growth in core GDP was mixed news for Nigeria. 03/06 was worse than 99/02. And 07/10 is likely to fare, in turn, worse than 03/06.

Yet in inter-country comparisons, Nigeria comes out better than most in West Africa and in the entire Africa, as well.

Nonetheless, oil-exporters put up a better struggle: Nigeria still does better than average, but it is outranked by 2 more countries in 03/06 and 07/10, than was the case previous to 03/06.

	99-02	03-06	07-10
Self-comparison to Preceding Period		▼	▼
Performance in Sub-Saharan Africa	▲	▲	▲
Performance in West Africa	▲	▲	▲
	Liberia	**Nigeria**	Liberia
	Sierra Leone	Sierra Leone	**Nigeria**
	Nigeria	Mauritania	Cape Verde
	Cape Verde	Gambia, The	Ghana
	Benin	Cape Verde	Sierra Leone
	Burkina Faso	Burkina Faso	Gambia, The
	Ghana	Ghana	Senegal
	Mali	Mali	Benin
	Guinea	Senegal	Burkina Faso
	Senegal	Niger	Mauritania
	Gambia, The	Benin	Mali
	Mauritania	Togo	Niger
	Niger	Guinea	Guinea
	Guinea-Bissau	Guinea-Bissau	Côte d'Ivoire
	Togo	Côte d'Ivoire	Togo
	Côte d'Ivoire	Liberia	Guinea-Bissau

Primary Data: IMF

	99-02	03-06	07-10
Performance among Oil-Exporters	▲	▲	▲
	Equatorial Guinea	Chad	Angola
	Nigeria	Angola	Sudan
	Angola	Equatorial Guinea	Equatorial Guinea
	Sudan	**Nigeria**	**Nigeria**
	Chad	Sudan	Congo, Rep.
	Cameroon	Congo, Rep.	Cameroon
	Congo, Rep.	Cameroon	Gabon
	Côte d'Ivoire	Gabon	Côte d'Ivoire
	Gabon	Côte d'Ivoire	Chad

▲	improved *or* better than average
▼	worsened *or* worse than average
◁▷	no change *or* average

8.13

Real GDP Growth in West Africa during 2003/06 (%)

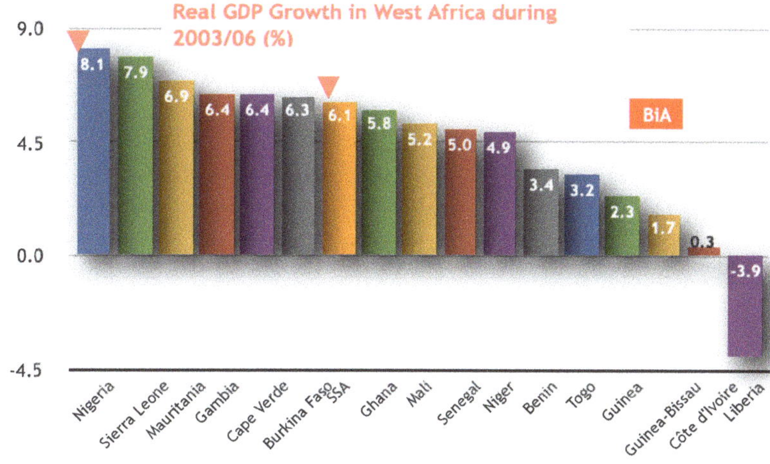

The years from 2005 to 2007 are beginning to look like bogey years for Nigeria...

...Performance again dropped during that 3-year period, even though 2008-2010 is expected to witness a bounce-back, relative to the rest of the continent.

8.14

Real GDP Growth in Nigeria and Sub-Saharan Africa from 1999 to 2006 (%)

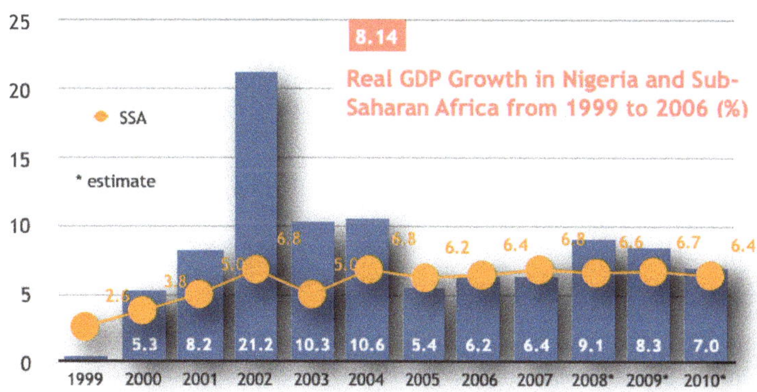

Primary Data: IMF

Real GDP Growth in Sub-Saharan Africa during 2003-06: Rankings

Rank	Country	Rank	Country	Rank	Country
1	Chad	15	Zambia	29	Benin
2	Angola	16	Uganda	30	Cameroon
3	Equatorial Guinea	17	Mali	31	Togo
4	**Nigeria**	18	Botswana	32	Swaziland
5	Sierra Leone	19	Senegal	33	Burundi
6	Mozambique	20	Niger	34	Guinea
7	Ethiopia	21	Malawi	35	Gabon
8	Tanzania	22	Kenya	36	Comoros
9	Congo, Dem. Rep.	23	Namibia	37	Guinea-Bissau
10	Madagascar	24	South Africa	38	Côte d' Ivoire
11	Gambia, The	25	Congo, Rep.	39	Eritrea
12	Cape Verde	26	Rwanda	40	Central Afr. Rep.
13	Burkina Faso	27	Lesotho	41	Seychelles
14	Ghana	28	Mauritius		
TOP		MIDDLE		BOTTOM	

Central Africa
East Africa
Southern Africa
West Africa

8.8 Real Non-Oil GDP Growth

Expectedly, this area is more critical for the oil economies than it is for the rest. Nigeria does worse in 03/06 than previous, and just about stays at the same level for 07/08.

Among oil-exporters, it is outflanked by Equatorial Guinea in 99/02, and then also by Angola in 03/06 and 07/08. But it still keeps its head above average.

	97-02	03-06	07-08
Self-comparison to Preceding Period		▼	◁▷
Performance among Oil-Exporters	▲	▲	▲
	Equatorial Guinea	Equatorial Guinea	Equatorial Guinea
	Nigeria	Angola	Angola
	Angola	**Nigeria**	**Nigeria**
	Cameroon	Chad	Chad
	Chad	Congo, Rep.	Congo, Rep.
	Congo, Rep.	Cameroon	Cameroon
	Gabon	Gabon	Gabon
	Côte d'Ivoire	Côte d'Ivoire	Côte d'Ivoire
	Sudan	Sudan	Sudan

▲	improved *or* better than average
▼	worsened *or* worse than average
◁▷	no change *or* average

Primary Data: IMF

how fragile is that economy?

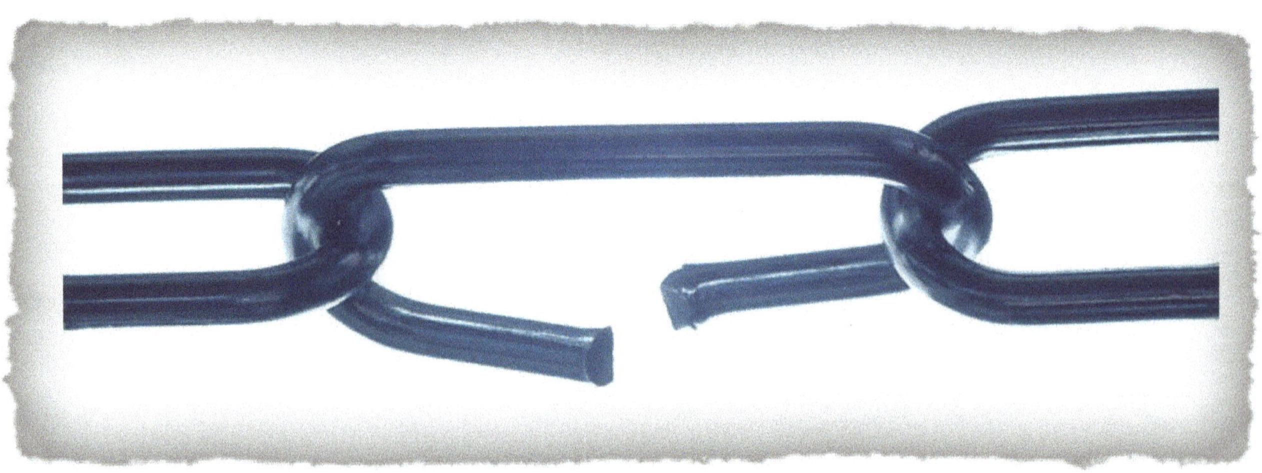

8.15

Real Non-Oil GDP Growth in West Africa during 2003/06

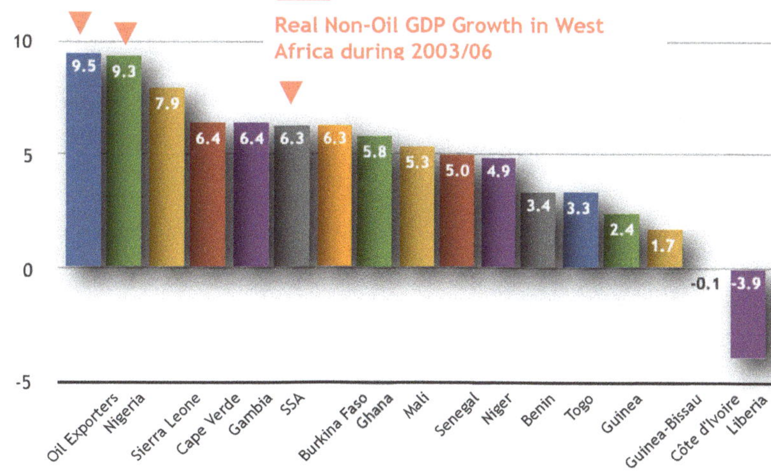

Again, the bogey years of 2005-2007. And 2008 is expected to be a further decline from 2007.

8.16

Real Non-Oil GDP Growth in Nigeria and Sub-Saharan Africa from 1997 to 2008

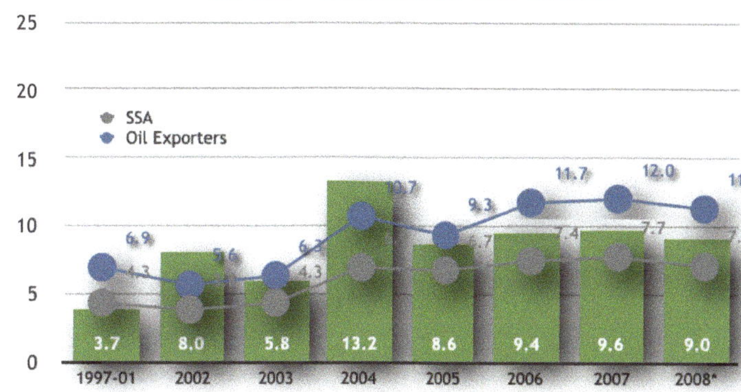

Nigeria does better than most of Africa, but worse than the oil-exporters, who — alas — are the crucial measurement standard.

* estimate

Primary Data: IMF

8.9 Inflation

cash overload

Poor showing. Incremental improvements only expected during 2007/10.

Below par in Africa from 2003 to 2010. Below par in West Africa from 1999 to 2010. Below par among oil economies from 1999 to 2010.

	99-02	03-06	07-10
Self-comparison to Preceding Period		▼	▲
Performance in Sub-Saharan Africa	▲	▼	▼
Performance in West Africa	▼	▼	▼
	Burkina Faso	Guinea-Bissau	Niger
	Senegal	Mali	Benin
	Niger	Senegal	Mali
	Cape Verde	Cape Verde	Burkina Faso
	Mali	Niger	Côte d'Ivoire
	Togo	Togo	Guinea-Bissau
	Côte d'Ivoire	Burkina Faso	Cape Verde
	Benin	Côte d'Ivoire	Togo
	Guinea-Bissau	Benin	Senegal
	Gambia, The	Liberia	Gambia, The
	Guinea	Mauritania	Mauritania
	Mauritania	Gambia, The	**Nigeria**
	Sierra Leone	Sierra Leone	Ghana
	Liberia	**Nigeria**	Liberia
	Nigeria	Ghana	Sierra Leone
	Ghana	Guinea	Guinea
Performance among Oil-Exporters	▼	▼	▼
	Gabon	Gabon	Chad
	Congo, Rep.	Cameroon	Cameroon
	Côte d'Ivoire	Chad	Côte d'Ivoire
	Cameroon	Côte d'Ivoire	Congo, Rep.
	Chad	Congo, Rep.	Gabon
	Equatorial Guinea	Equatorial Guinea	Equatorial Guinea
	Sudan	Sudan	Sudan
	Nigeria	**Nigeria**	**Nigeria**
	Angola	Angola	Angola

Primary Data: IMF

▲	improved *or* better than average
▼	worsened *or* worse than average
◁▷	no change *or* average

8.17

Inflation in West Africa during 2003/06 (%)

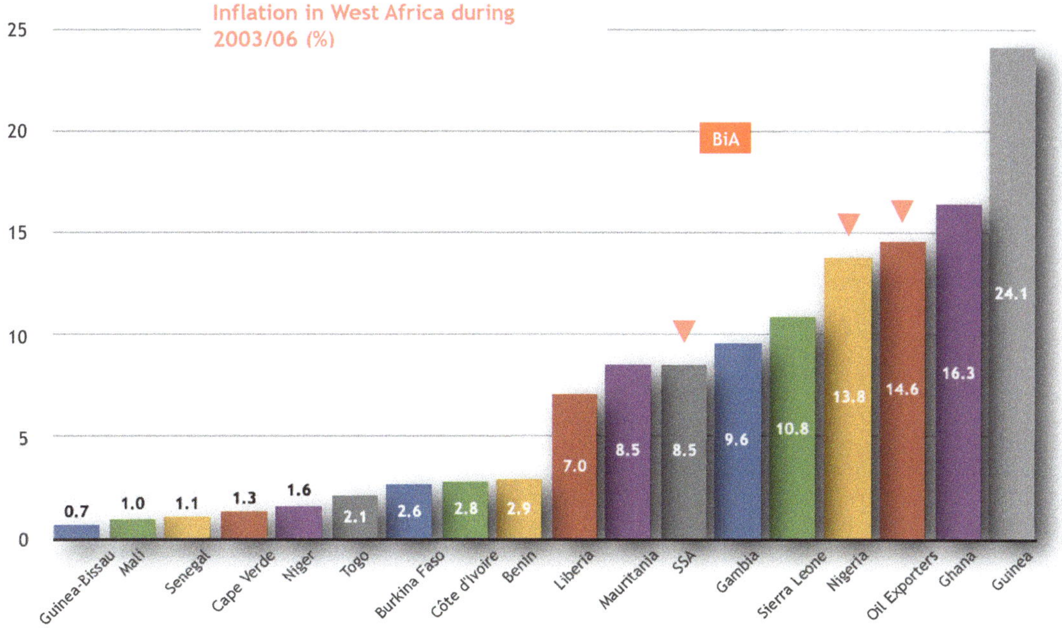

The oil exporters crashed their inflation rates from 20% in 2003 to 6% in 2007 [a 14% drop]. Nigeria's slowed more gradually from 14% to 6% [an 8% drop].

2008 to 2010 may see Nigeria faring worse than the rest of Africa again, with a rising inflation rate.

Primary Data: IMF

8.18

Inflation in Nigeria and Sub-Saharan Africa from 1999 to 2010

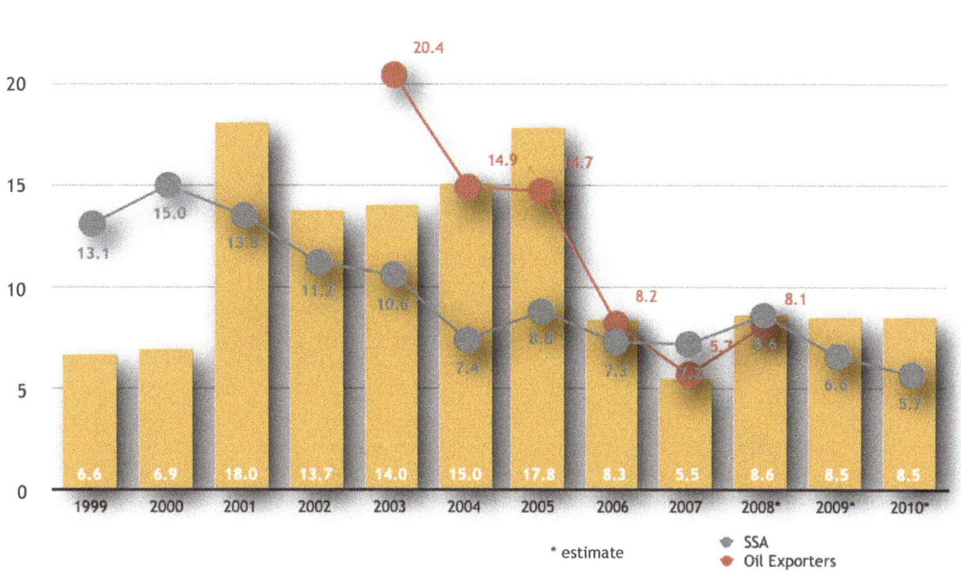

8.10 Movement of Consumer Prices

we'll be needing a larger bag

Primary Data: IMF
Figures for 2008-10 are estimates

An item costing 100 currency units everywhere in 2000, by 2007 would cost: 240 in Nigeria and 120 in Benin, 300 in Ghana, and 170 in Mauritania.

8.19

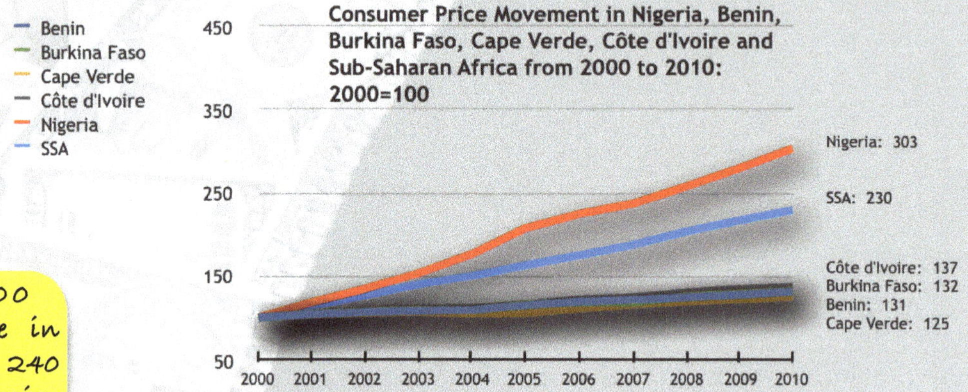

Consumer Price Movement in Nigeria, Benin, Burkina Faso, Cape Verde, Côte d'Ivoire and Sub-Saharan Africa from 2000 to 2010: 2000=100

8.20

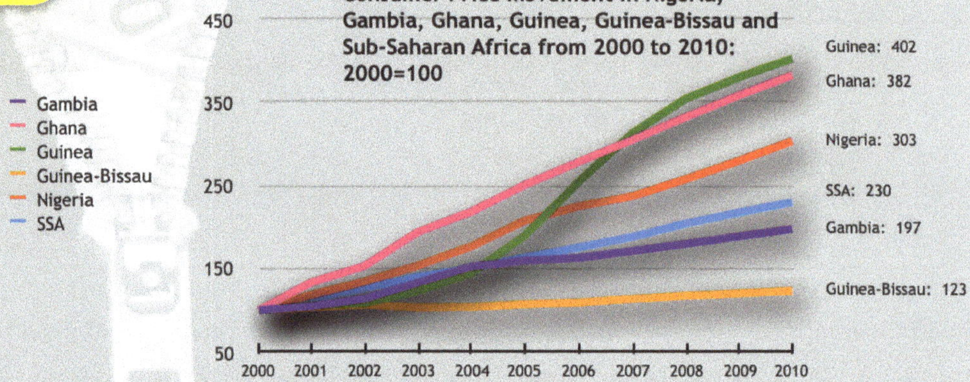

Consumer Price Movement in Nigeria, Gambia, Ghana, Guinea, Guinea-Bissau and Sub-Saharan Africa from 2000 to 2010: 2000=100

8.21

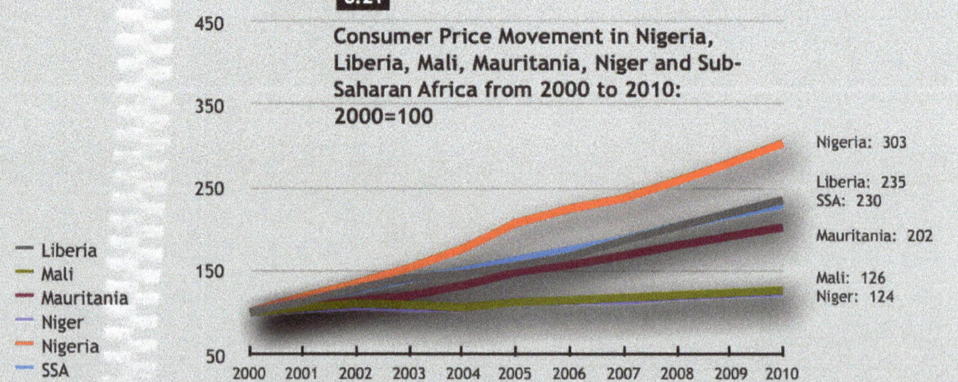

Consumer Price Movement in Nigeria, Liberia, Mali, Mauritania, Niger and Sub-Saharan Africa from 2000 to 2010: 2000=100

Consumer Price Movement in West Africa in 2007 and 2010: 2000=100

	2000	2007	2010
Benin	100	122	131
Burkina Faso	100	118	132
Cape Verde	100	116	125
Côte d'Ivoire	100	125	137
Gambia, The	100	171	197
Ghana	100	305	382
Guinea	100	313	402
Guinea-Bissau	100	113	123
Liberia	100	187	235
Mali	100	117	126
Mauritania	100	169	202
Niger	100	114	124
Nigeria	100	237	303
Senegal	100	116	127
Sierra Leone	100	166	221
Togo	100	117	131
SSA	100	188	230

8.22

Consumer Price Movement in Nigeria, Senegal, Sierra Leone, Togo and Sub-Saharan Africa from 2000 to 2010: 2000=100

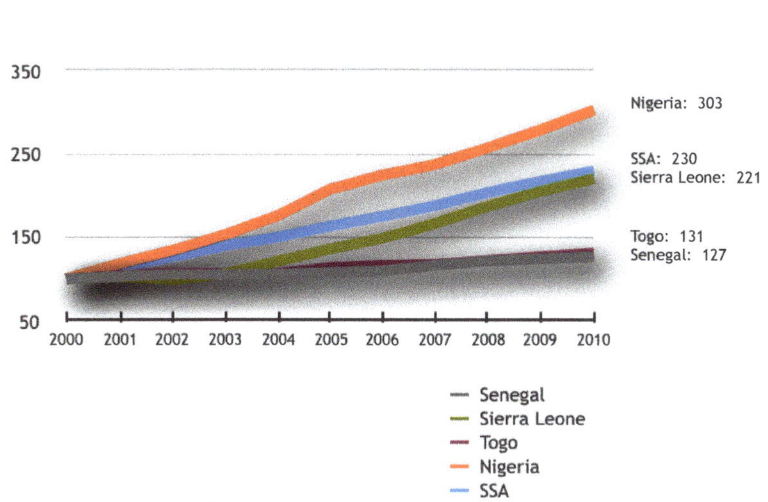

By 2010, the cost would have risen to 230 currency units as continental average, but 300 units in Nigeria.

Primary Data: IMF

Inflation in Sub-Saharan Africa during 2003-06: Rankings

Rank	Country	Rank	Country	Rank	Country
1	Gabon	15	Congo, Rep.	29	Madagascar
2	Guinea-Bissau	16	Comoros	30	Ethiopia
3	Mali	17	South Africa	31	Sierra Leone
4	Senegal	18	Namibia	32	Mozambique
5	Cape Verde	19	Mauritius	33	Kenya
6	Niger	20	Tanzania	34	Malawi
7	Seychelles	21	Swaziland	35	Congo, Dem. Rep.
8	Cameroon	22	Equatorial Guinea	36	Nigeria
9	Togo	23	Lesotho	37	Ghana
10	Chad	24	Uganda	38	Zambia
11	Burkina Faso	25	Burundi	39	Eritrea
12	Côte d' Ivoire	26	Botswana	40	Guinea
13	Benin	27	Rwanda	41	Angola
14	Central Afr. Rep.	28	Gambia, The		
BEST		AVERAGE		BOTTOM	

Central Africa
East Africa
Southern Africa
West Africa

8.11 Exchange Rate Stability

turbulence

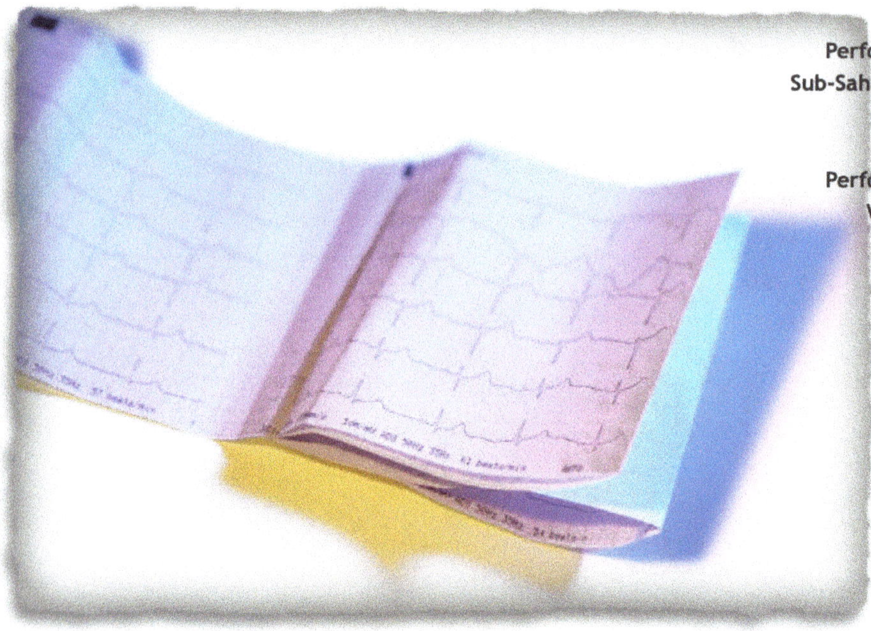

	00-07	03-10
Self-comparison to Preceding Period		▼
Performance in Sub-Saharan Africa	▼	▼
Performance in West Africa	▼	▼

00-07	03-10
Senegal	Benin
Benin	Mali
Mali	Guinea-Bissau
Côte d'Ivoire	Senegal
Cape Verde	Côte d'Ivoire
Niger	Niger
Burkina Faso	Burkina Faso
Guinea-Bissau	Togo
Togo	Cape Verde
Liberia	Liberia
Sierra Leone	Gambia, The
Mauritania	Sierra Leone
Gambia, The	Mauritania
Nigeria	**Nigeria**
Guinea	Ghana
Ghana	Guinea

Primary Data: IMF

A rougher ride for the Nigerian Naira than for the currencies of 13 of the 15 other West African States, for the 8 years between 2000 and 2007.

	00-07	03-10
Performance among Oil-Exporters	▼	▼
	Cameroon	Cameroon
	Côte d'Ivoire	Côte d'Ivoire
	Gabon	Gabon
	Congo, Rep.	Congo, Rep.
	Chad	Chad
	Sudan	Sudan
	Equatorial Guinea	Equatorial Guinea
	Nigeria	**Nigeria**
	Angola	Angola

The same story expected for the 8 years from 2003 to 2010.

Within the oil-exporters league, only Angola did worse.

▲	improved *or* better than average
▼	worsened *or* worse than average
◁▷	no change *or* average

8.23

Exchange Rate Stability in West Africa during 2003/06

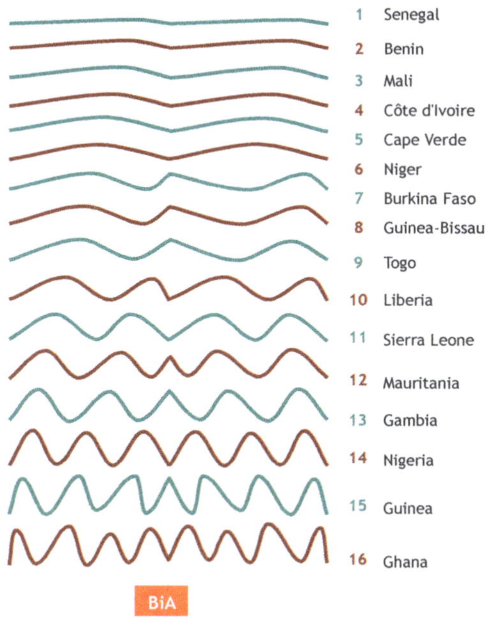

8.24

Movement of Real Exchange Rate in Nigeria, Ghana and Senegal from 2000 to 2010: 2000=100

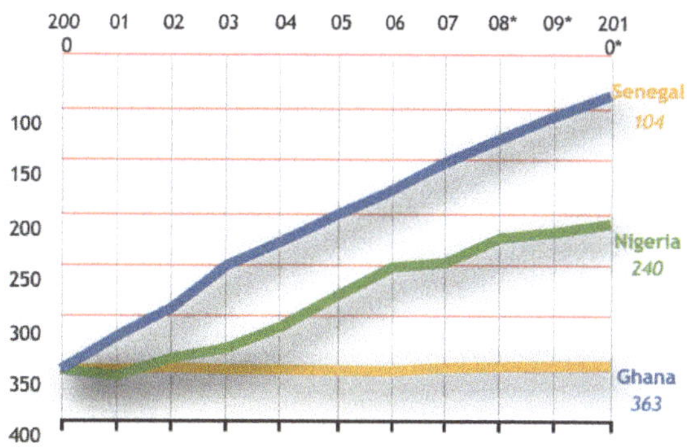

* estimate

Primary Data: IMF

From 100 currency units to one dollar everywhere in 2000, by 2007 it was 98 units in Benin, 181 in Gambia, 171 in Mauritania, 298 in Ghana.

In Nigeria it was 203 in 2007. Further declines to follow from then on to 2010.

Central Africa
East Africa
Southern Africa
West Africa

Exchange Rate Stability in Sub-Saharan Africa during 2003-06: Rankings

Rank	Country	Rank	Country	Rank	Country
1	Cameroon	15	Gabon	29	Sierra Leone
2	Senegal	16	Lesotho	30	Rwanda
3	Benin	17	Uganda	31	Equatorial Guinea
4	Mali	18	Namibia	32	Madagascar
5	Côte d' Ivoire	19	South Africa	33	Gambia
6	Cape Verde	20	Kenya	34	Nigeria
7	Niger	21	Swaziland	35	Eritrea
8	Burkina Faso	22	Ethiopia	36	Zambia
9	Guinea-Bissau	23	Tanzania	37	Guinea
10	Central Afr. Rep.	24	Congo, Rep.	38	Ghana
11	Comoros	25	Botswana	39	Malawi
12	Seychelles	26	Mozambique	40	Congo, Dem. Rep.
13	Togo	27	Chad	41	Angola
14	Mauritius	28	Burundi		
	BEST		MIDDLE		BOTTOM

Movement of Real Exchange Rates in West Africa in 2007, 2010: 2000=100

	2000	2007	2010
Benin	100	98	101
Burkina Faso	100	105	112
Cape Verde	100	99	105
Côte d'Ivoire	100	105	109
Gambia, The	100	181	198
Ghana	100	298	363
Guinea	100	258	300
Guinea-Bissau	100	92	95
Liberia	100	119	120
Mali	100	99	103
Mauritania	100	171	171
Niger	100	99	103
Nigeria	100	203	240
Senegal	100	102	104
Sierra Leone	100	144	176
Togo	100	91	91

Stormy waters indeed for the Naira in Africa. 34th out of 41.

fit and nimble

Overall, Nigeria fits in the top third in terms of economic strength displayed between 2003 and 2006.

Some smaller countries though, like Burkina Faso and Senegal, exhibited niftier muscles.

Economic Strength Rankings: 2003-06

Rank	Country	Rank	Country	Rank	Country
1	Equatorial Guinea	15	Congo, Rep.	29	Niger
2	Cape Verde	16	Gabon	30	Uganda
3	Chad	17	Seychelles	31	Togo
4	Botswana	18	Lesotho	32	Comoros
5	South Africa	19	Madagascar	33	Zambia
6	Senegal	20	Ethiopia	34	Rwanda
7	Mauritius	21	Benin	35	Congo, Dem. Rep.
8	Angola	22	Swaziland	36	Malawi
9	Namibia	23	Gambia	37	Guinea-Bissau
10	Burkina Faso	24	Kenya	38	Central Afr. Rep.
11	Mali	25	Ghana	39	Guinea
12	Nigeria	26	Sierra Leone	40	Burundi
13	Cameroon	27	Mozambique	41	Eritrea
14	Tanzania	28	Côte d' Ivoire		
TOP		MIDDLE		BOTTOM	

Central Africa
East Africa
Southern Africa
West Africa

Wrap-up: Economic Strength

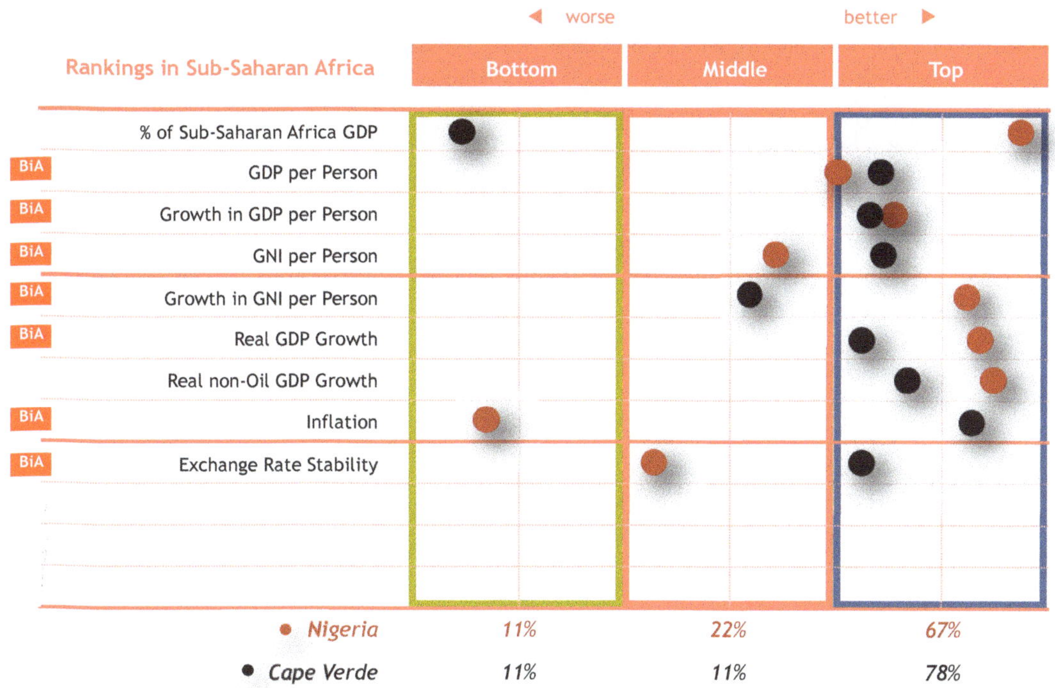

- Again, Cape Verde was the strongest economy in West Africa and 2nd strongest on the continent. Nigeria was 5th in West Africa and 12th on the continent.
- Nigeria clearly supplies a bigger chunk of the continent's economy than Cape Verde does, by a distance.
- Earnings per population (GDP, GNI) has Cape Verde better off, but it is close. However, Nigeria was growing both these (GDP & GNI) faster.
- Nigeria also grew Real GDP and non-Oil GDP faster, too. Even though non-Oil GDP isn't relevant in Cape Verde's case.
- So, it would seem a sturdy display by Nigeria on the whole. Except that Inflation and Exchange Rate Stability of the Naira did it in, and both those indicators are critical to the rankings (BiA).

9. Economic Productivity

efficiency counts for much

Primer

The whole spectrum of economic activity is divided into 3 broad groups – **Agriculture, Industry, Services** – for ease and convenience of not just tabulation, but also categorization of economic activities according to their nature and interconnection. This aids greatly at the point of analyzing, structuring and understanding systems of different countries and groupings that would otherwise be perplexingly disparate.

The convention used for this demarcation is the International Standard Industrial Classification of All Economic Activities (ISIC), as moderated and maintained by the United Nations. It is presently structured into major groupings as follows below. The more detailed breakdown is shown at the end of this introduction.

Agriculture (A - B)

A - Agriculture, hunting and forestry
B - Fishing

Industry (C - F)

C - Mining and quarrying
D - Manufacturing
E - Electricity, gas and water supply
F - Construction

Services (G - Q)

G - Wholesale and retail trade; repair of motor vehicles, motorcycles and personal and household goods
H - Hotels and restaurants
I - Transport, storage and communications
J - Financial intermediation
K - Real estate, renting and business activities
L - Public administration and defense; compulsory social security
M - Education
N - Health and social work
O - Other community, social and personal service activities
P - Activities of private households as employers and undifferentiated production activities of private households
Q - Extraterritorial organizations and bodies

By separating economic activity into sectors like these, it becomes possible to calibrate the quality of economic development and growth within and across countries.

Productivity (or Value Added)

The contribution of each of the three sectors (agriculture, industry, services) to the overall economy is assessed by evaluating their "Value Added": simply the value of production output less the cost of input, roughly meaning "profit" or "net output".

Productivity can be measured in money terms (the monetary value of net output) or as percentages of the total value of economic output, GDP. Expressing productivity as money per person of population – rather than as just the size of the net output alone – gives a better indication of efficiency in the sectors. Expressing it as a percentage of GDP will bring to light the sectors on which an economy relies most strongly.

"Productivity Index"

This is our innovative attempt to calibrate the working efficiency with which countries exploit their comparative endowments of population size. It rates the countries by comparing their share of the continent's total population with their share in the continent's GDP output. A country that produced a larger ratio of the continent's GDP than its ratio of the continent's population, would have an index greater than 1. While, "under-performing" by producing a smaller percentage of GDP than percentage of population size, would return an index less than 1.

Economic "Advancement"

Underdeveloped economies have larger agricultural sectors (relative to industry and services) and so a large "Productivity in Agriculture" component to their GDP. Mid-stage economies tend to have a predominant Industry component; while more mature economies have Services as the largest input into GDP. (For this reason, some economists hold that Japan should not be classified as an advanced economy, seeing that its industrial sector outstretches the services one.)

This is not to imply, though, that African economies with predominant services sectors are "mature"; there are, of course, other major socio-economic (and even, political) factors that play a role. But these countries may be said to be the more developed of the economies in their bracket.

Growth in Productivity

Growth in Productivity is also more accurately evaluated as growth in the productivity-per-person of population indices.

Industry Productivity split into *Manufacturing* and *Other Industry*

For better evaluation and further precision, Industry sector of economic activity is often divided into two areas: **manufacturing** (as contained in D in the demarcation above) and **other industry** (groups C, E and F). Isolating manufacturing from other segments helps to evaluate the health of the "real sector", as manufacturing is often called: generally, an increase in manufacturing activity – and consequently, output of manufactures – would indicate a healthy economy where manufacturing activity is continuous because there is a market for the products, implying that consumer spending is healthy, in turn indicating the presence of suitable aggregate demand. And so, the trend in manufacturing activity, when separated from the rest of the industry segment, often points to the state of the whole economy. Just as it also gives a rough indication of capacity utilization in factories, as well as of their efficiency of production.

In economies heavily dependent on commodities (segment C "mining and quarrying") such as the oil exporters and exporters of precious metals, activity in that "other industry" sector can mask a deterioration in manufacturing output, if Industry Activity is not separated into the two groups. Trade in commodities is often easy and lucrative. Easy, because of the straightforward process involved (essentially extraction from the earth, and direct sale afterwards, without further industrial or manufacturing procedures going into the final product); and lucrative because of the existence of cartels such as OPEC in the oil sector. But these factors also make such commodities susceptible to perilous swings in the international market. Consequently, an economy that relies overwhelmingly on productivity in the "Other Industry" segment is more vulnerable to peaks and troughs and more likely to suffer systemic damage at the first signs of a downturn, since they are not diversified enough and cannot cushion those blows.

Build-up of Productivity

By tying all these sectors down to a common start-point (e.g., 100 units for the year 2000), and tracing their build-up using the actual growth rates as ensued during the consequent years, a picture of the various trajectories can be clearly seen and also extrapolated. The level and quality of activity is well illustrated by these paths, and comparisons can also be made between the different segments of economic output. For example, with the Industry Sector, the trajectory of productivity between the Manufacturing and Other Industry segments would show how much development is taking place across those spheres of activity. The gap between the two groups at a particular year would indicate the disparity (or otherwise) in quality of output and activity in those areas. Detailed structure and explanatory notes follow.

Sources of Primary Data: AfDB, IMF, World Bank

International Standard Industrial Classification of all Economic Activities

ISIC Rev.3.1

(As published by the United Nations. Note: the numbers are category codes and not serial numbers.)

A - Agriculture, hunting and forestry

01 Agriculture, hunting and related service activities
02 Forestry, logging and related service activities

B - Fishing

05 Fishing, aquaculture and service activities incidental to fishing

C - Mining and quarrying

10 Mining of coal and lignite; extraction of peat
11 Extraction of crude petroleum and natural gas; service activities incidental to oil and gas extraction, excluding surveying
12 Mining of uranium and thorium ores
13 Mining of metal ores
14 Other mining and quarrying

D - Manufacturing

15 Manufacture of food products and beverages
16 Manufacture of tobacco products
17 Manufacture of textiles
18 Manufacture of wearing apparel; dressing and dyeing of fur
19 Tanning and dressing of leather; manufacture of luggage, handbags, saddlery, harness and footwear
20 Manufacture of wood and of products of wood and cork, except furniture; manufacture of articles of straw and plaiting materials
21 Manufacture of paper and paper products
22 Publishing, printing and reproduction of recorded media
23 Manufacture of coke, refined petroleum products and nuclear fuel
24 Manufacture of chemicals and chemical products
25 Manufacture of rubber and plastics products
26 Manufacture of other non-metallic mineral products
27 Manufacture of basic metals
28 Manufacture of fabricated metal products, except machinery and equipment
29 Manufacture of machinery and equipment n.e.c.
30 Manufacture of office, accounting and computing machinery
31 Manufacture of electrical machinery and apparatus n.e.c.
32 Manufacture of radio, television and communication equipment and apparatus
33 Manufacture of medical, precision and optical instruments, watches and clocks
34 Manufacture of motor vehicles, trailers and semi-trailers
35 Manufacture of other transport equipment
36 Manufacture of furniture; manufacturing n.e.c.
37 Recycling

E - Electricity, gas and water supply

40 Electricity, gas, steam and hot water supply
41 Collection, purification and distribution of water

F - Construction

45 Construction

G Wholesale and retail trade; repair of motor vehicles, motorcycles and personal and household goods

50 Sale, maintenance and repair of motor vehicles and motorcycles; retail sale of automotive fuel
51 Wholesale trade and commission trade, except of motor vehicles and motorcycles
52 Retail trade, except of motor vehicles and motorcycles; repair of personal and household goods

H Hotels and restaurants

55 Hotels and restaurants

I - Transport, storage and communications

60 Land transport; transport via pipelines
61 Water transport
62 Air transport
63 Supporting and auxiliary transport activities; activities of travel agencies
64 Post and telecommunications

J - Financial intermediation

65 Financial intermediation, except insurance and pension funding
66 Insurance and pension funding, except compulsory social security
67 Activities auxiliary to financial intermediation

K - Real estate, renting and business activities

70 Real estate activities
71 Renting of machinery and equipment without operator and of personal and household goods
72 Computer and related activities
73 Research and development
74 Other business activities

L - Public administration and defense; compulsory social security

75 Public administration and defense; compulsory social security

M - Education

80 Education

N - Health and social work

85 Health and social work

O - Other community, social and personal service activities

90 Sewage and refuse disposal, sanitation and similar activities
91 Activities of membership organizations n.e.c.
92 Recreational, cultural and sporting activities
93 Other service activities

P - Activities of private households as employers and undifferentiated production activities of private households

95 Activities of private households as employers of domestic staff
96 Undifferentiated goods-producing activities of private households for own use
97 Undifferentiated service-producing activities of private households for own use

Q - Extraterritorial organizations and bodies

99 Extraterritorial organizations and bodies

Charts

Tables

1999-2002; 2003-2006; 2007-2010:
- *self-comparison to preceding period;*
- *performance in S-Saharan Africa;*
- *performance in West Africa;*
- *performance among oil-exporters;*

for:

Country Productivity Index

1999-2002; 2003-2006:
- *self-comparison to preceding period;*
- *performance in S-Saharan Africa;*
- *performance in West Africa;*
- *performance among oil-exporters;*

for:

Productivity in Agriculture as % of GDP

Productivity in Agriculture as $PPP per Person

Growth in Agriculture Productivity

Productivity in Industry as % of GDP

Productivity in Industry as $PPP per Person

Growth in Industry Productivity

Productivity in Services as % of GDP

Productivity in Services as $PPP per Person

Growth in Services Productivity

- Productivity in Agriculture as $PPP per Person in Sub-Saharan Africa during 2003-06: Rankings
- Growth in Agriculture Productivity in Sub-Saharan Africa during 2003-06: Rankings
- Productivity in Industry as $PPP per Person in Sub-Saharan Africa during 2003-06: Rankings
- Growth in Industry Productivity in Sub-Saharan Africa during 2003-06: Rankings
- Gap between *Manufacturing* and *Other Industry* Productivity levels: 2000=100
- Productivity in Services as $PPP per Person in Sub-Saharan Africa during 2003-06: Rankings
- Growth in Services Productivity in Sub-Saharan Africa during 2003-06: Rankings
- **Economic Productivity Rankings: 2003-06**

9.1 Country "Productivity Index"

lifting above their weight

+1-800-help

"Productivity" vs "Value Added"?

The same meaning. Think of it like the profit you make when you sell a modified product; you added value to the original item.

Interesting

But why express it "per person"? That's not usually the case.

We believe it helps measure efficiency better. Absolute numbers don't tell much on their own.

Although Nigeria is poised to do worse in 2007-2010, it was squeezing out more from its population potential than most of West Africa. But not better than the majority of oil exporters.

Primary Data: IMF

	99-02	03-06	07-10
Self-comparison to Preceding Period		▲	▼
Performance in Sub-Saharan Africa	▼	▲	▲
Performance in West Africa	▲	▲	▲
	Cape Verde	Cape Verde	Cape Verde
	Côte d'Ivoire	**Nigeria**	**Nigeria**
	Mauritania	Mauritania	Mauritania
	Senegal	Côte d'Ivoire	Côte d'Ivoire
	Nigeria	Senegal	Senegal
	Benin	Benin	Benin
	Ghana	Ghana	Ghana
	Gambia, The	Gambia, The	Gambia, The
	Guinea	Burkina Faso	Burkina Faso
	Burkina Faso	Guinea	Guinea
	Mali	Mali	Mali
	Togo	Togo	Togo
	Niger	Niger	Sierra Leone
	Guinea-Bissau	Sierra Leone	Niger
	Liberia	Guinea-Bissau	Guinea-Bissau
	Sierra Leone	Liberia	Liberia
Performance among Oil-Exporters	▼	▼	▼
	Gabon	Gabon	Gabon
	Equatorial Guinea	Equatorial Guinea	Equatorial Guinea
	Congo, Rep.	Angola	Angola
	Angola	Congo, Rep.	Congo, Rep.
	Cameroon	Cameroon	Sudan
	Côte d'Ivoire	**Nigeria**	**Nigeria**
	Sudan	Sudan	Cameroon
	Nigeria	Côte d'Ivoire	Côte d'Ivoire
	Chad	Chad	Chad

▲	improved *or* better than average
▼	worsened *or* worse than average
◁▷	no change *or* average

9.1 BiA

Country "Productivity Index" in West Africa during 2003/06

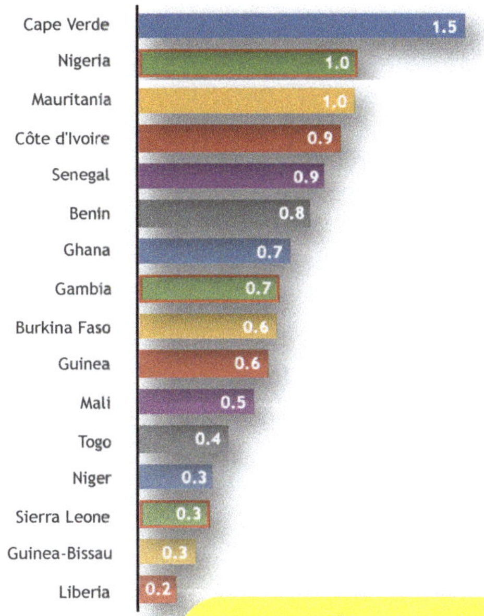

9.2

Country "Productivity Index" in West Africa during 2007/2010

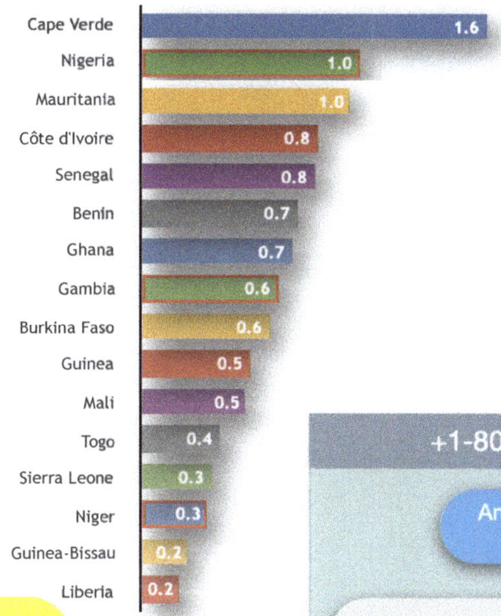

West Africa stayed much the same across 03/06 and 07/10 in terms of country economy efficiency, save for Niger and Sierra Leone, who jostled for 3rd from bottom.

+1-800-help

And "Productivity Index"?

Our attempt to gauge the actual efficiency of a country, compared to its counterpart countries. Somewhat like measuring Return on Investment: how much of the continent's resources did this country have and how much of the continent's eventual output was it responsible for?

Ingenious

We hope so 😊

9.3

Country "Productivity Index" in Nigeria from 1999 to 2010

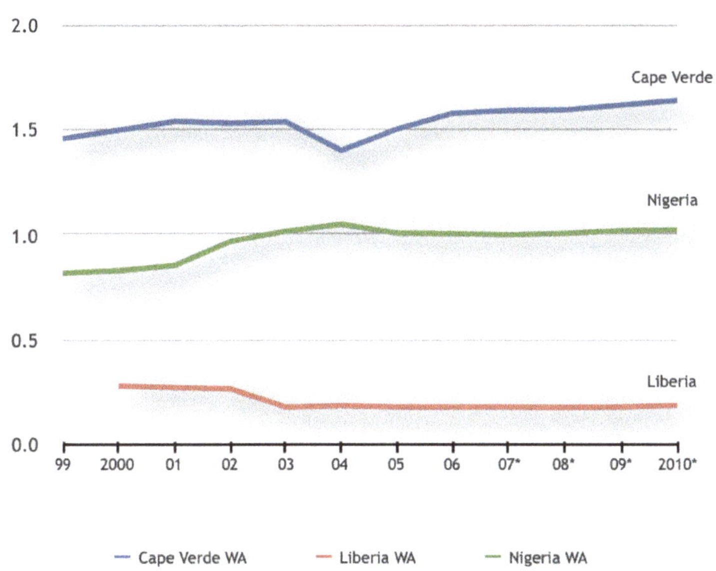

* estimate

Compared to West Africa's best performer, Cape Verde, Nigeria's "efficiency trajectory" was not dissimilar. A generally steady upward gradient.

Primary Data: IMF

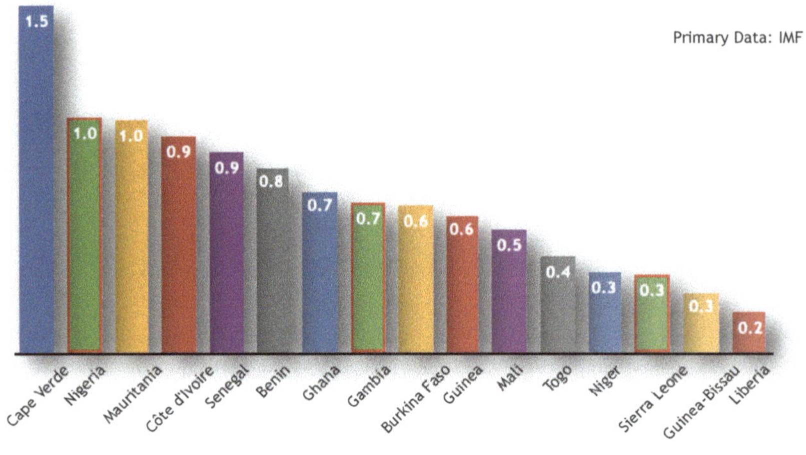

9.4

Country "Productivity Index" [above] & corresponding country share of continent population [below] in West Africa during 2003/06

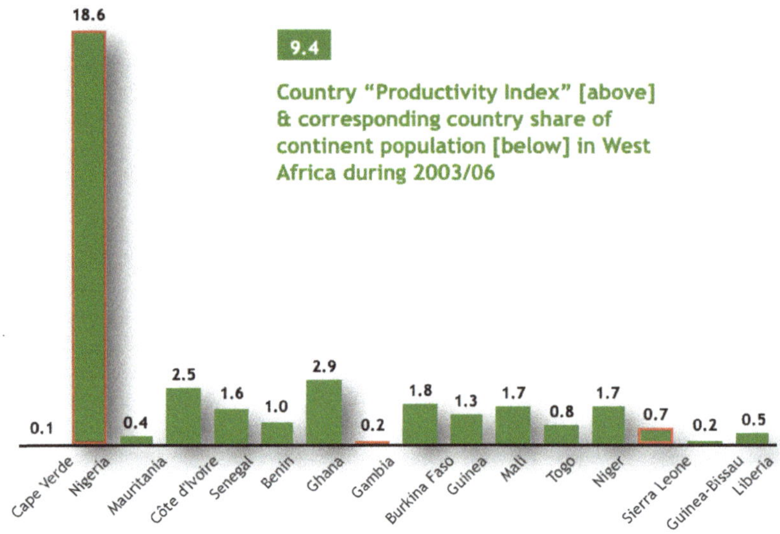

Cape Verde's outstanding performance is illustrated here. With 0.06% of Sub-Saharan Africa's population, it supplied 0.09% of its GDP; 1.5 times.

Nigeria had 18.6% of the population and supplied 18.9% of the GDP. Giving it a productivity index of 1.

Going by its small share of population, Mauritania comes out looking particularly well.

Country Productivity Index in Sub-Saharan Africa during 2003-06: Rankings

Rank	Country	Region
1	Seychelles	East Africa
2	Botswana	Southern Africa
3	Gabon	Central Africa
4	Equatorial Guinea	Central Africa
5	Mauritius	East Africa
6	South Africa	Southern Africa
7	Namibia	Southern Africa
8	Swaziland	Southern Africa
9	Angola	Central Africa
10	Congo, Rep.	Central Africa
11	Cape Verde	West Africa
12	Cameroon	Central Africa
13	Nigeria	West Africa
14	Côte d' Ivoire	West Africa

TOP

Rank	Country	Region
15	Senegal	West Africa
16	Chad	Central Africa
17	Kenya	East Africa
18	Benin	West Africa
19	Ghana	West Africa
20	Zambia	East Africa
21	Gambia, The	West Africa
22	Lesotho	Southern Africa
23	Burkina Faso	West Africa
24	Comoros	East Africa
25	Tanzania	East Africa
26	Guinea	West Africa
27	Mali	West Africa
28	Madagascar	East Africa

MIDDLE

Rank	Country	Region
29	Uganda	East Africa
30	Eritrea	East Africa
31	Rwanda	East Africa
32	Togo	West Africa
33	Mozambique	East Africa
34	Malawi	East Africa
35	Central Afr. Rep.	Central Africa
36	Niger	West Africa
37	Ethiopia	East Africa
38	Sierra Leone	West Africa
39	Guinea-Bissau	West Africa
40	Burundi	East Africa
41	Congo, Dem. Rep.	Central Africa

BOTTOM

Legend (cell colours): Central Africa; East Africa; Southern Africa; West Africa

Nigeria just about makes it into the top segment. The best performer in West Africa, Cape Verde, was 11th in Africa. The Seychelles top the group.

9.2 Country Economy "Development Status"

eggs in one basket

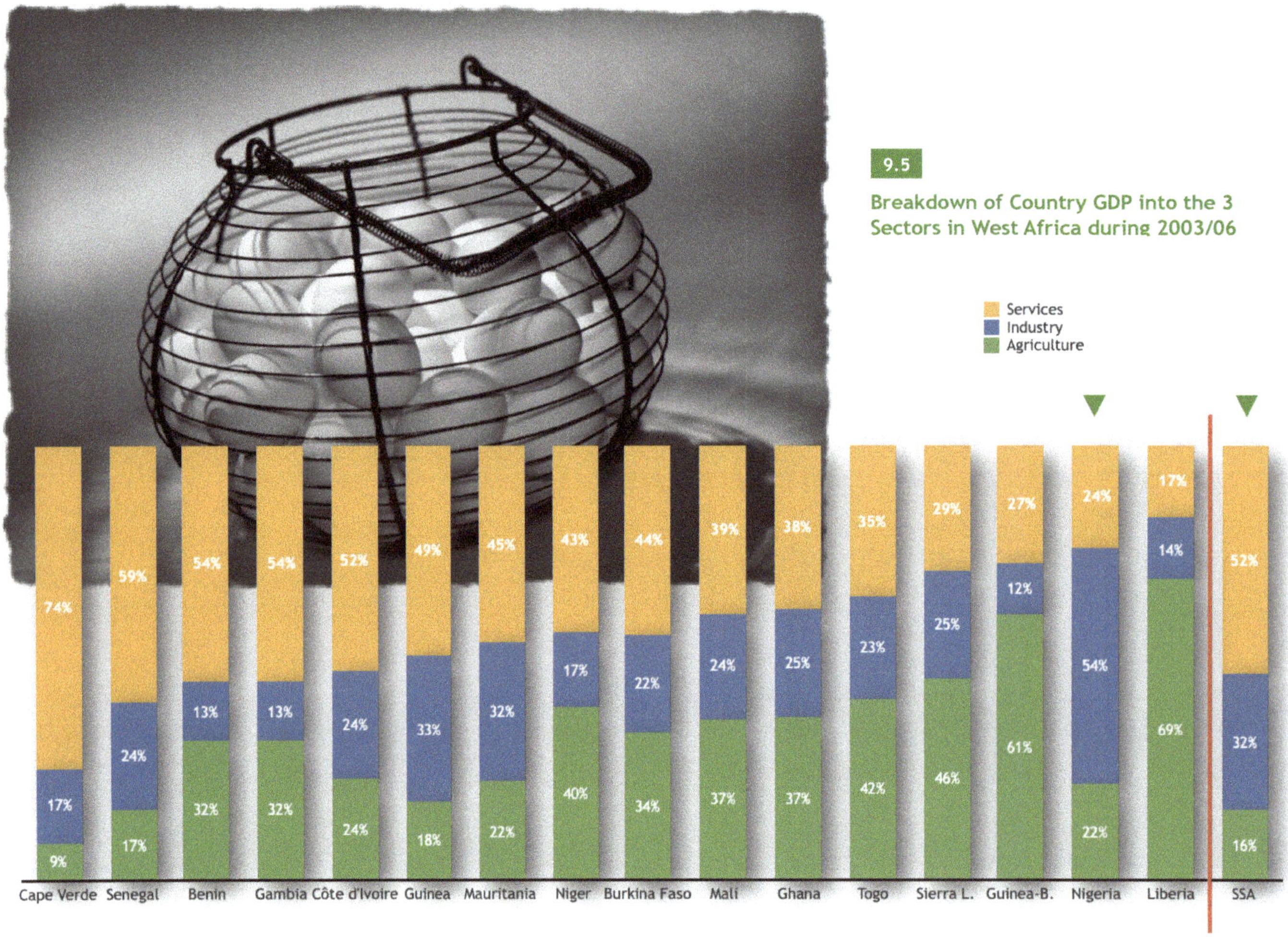

9.5

Breakdown of Country GDP into the 3 Sectors in West Africa during 2003/06

Primary Data: World Bank

Arranged in decreasing size of their services sector. Nigeria is 2nd from bottom in West Africa; suggesting that it is likely the least "developed" economy in the region.

At 24% of GDP, its services sector is less than half the Africa average.

In Africa, the services sector grew across 1999/2006, largely at the expense of agriculture, which dropped by 4%. Industry generally hovered around 30%.

Nigeria does have the largest industry sector, which is due largely to its dominating oil industry. Its agriculture sector, at 22% of GDP, is slightly larger than the Africa average.

For Nigeria, the industry sector ballooned up till 2005. Services and agriculture shrank; services by 8% and agriculture by 14%.

9.6

Breakdown of GDP into the 3 Sectors in Nigeria from 1999 to 2006

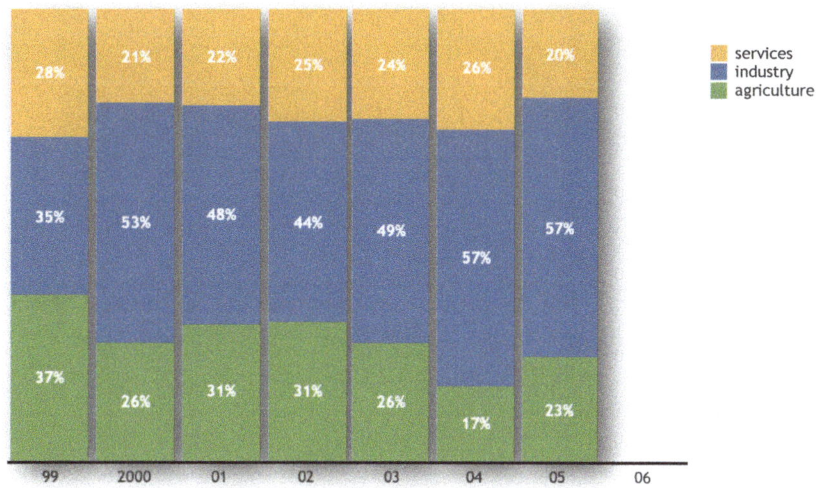

9.7

Breakdown of GDP into the 3 Sectors in Sub-Saharan Africa from 1999 to 2006

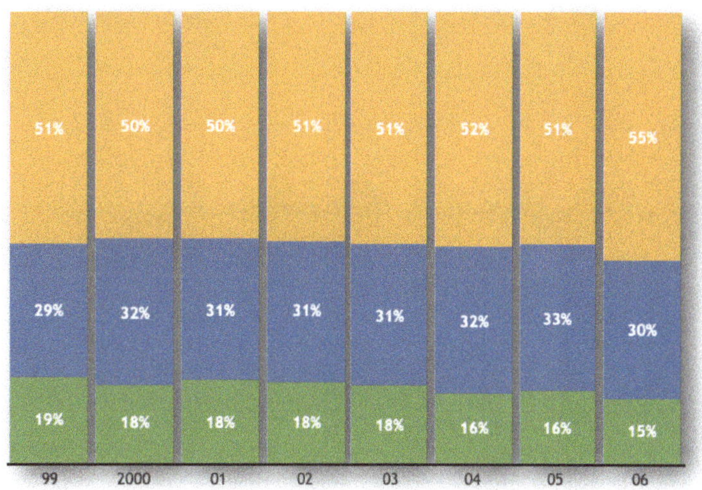

9.3 Productivity in Agriculture as % of GDP

looks like a good harvest

Primary Data: World Bank

	99-02	03-06
Self-comparison to Preceding Period		▼
Performance in ub-Saharan Africa	▲	▲
Performance in West Africa	▼	▼
	Liberia	Liberia
	Guinea-Bissau	Guinea-Bissau
	Sierra Leone	Sierra Leone
	Mali	Togo
	Niger	Niger
	Togo	Ghana
	Benin	Mali
	Ghana	Gambia, The
	Gambia, The	Benin
	Burkina Faso	Burkina Faso
	Nigeria	Côte d'Ivoire
	Mauritania	Mauritania
	Côte d'Ivoire	**Nigeria**
	Guinea	Guinea
	Senegal	Senegal
	Cape Verde	Cape Verde
Performance among Oil-Exporters	▲	▲
	Sudan	Sudan
	Chad	Chad
	Nigeria	Côte d'Ivoire
	Côte d'Ivoire	**Nigeria**
	Cameroon	Cameroon
	Equatorial Guinea	Angola
	Angola	Gabon
	Gabon	Congo, Rep.
	Congo, Rep.	Equatorial Guinea

9.8

Productivity in Agriculture as % of GDP in West Africa during 2003/06

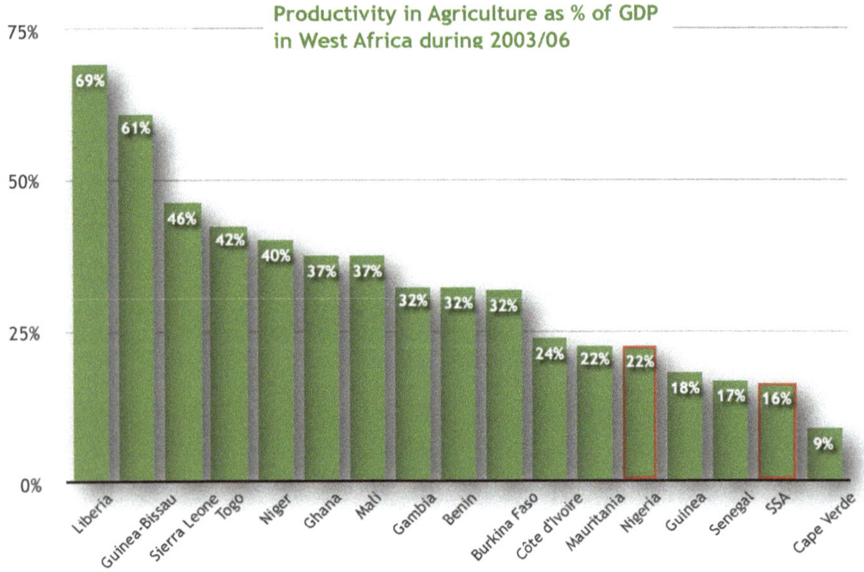

▲	improved *or* better than average
▼	worsened *or* worse than average
◁▷	no change *or* average

9.9

Productivity in Agriculture as % of GDP in Nigeria and Sub-Saharan Africa from 1999 to 2006

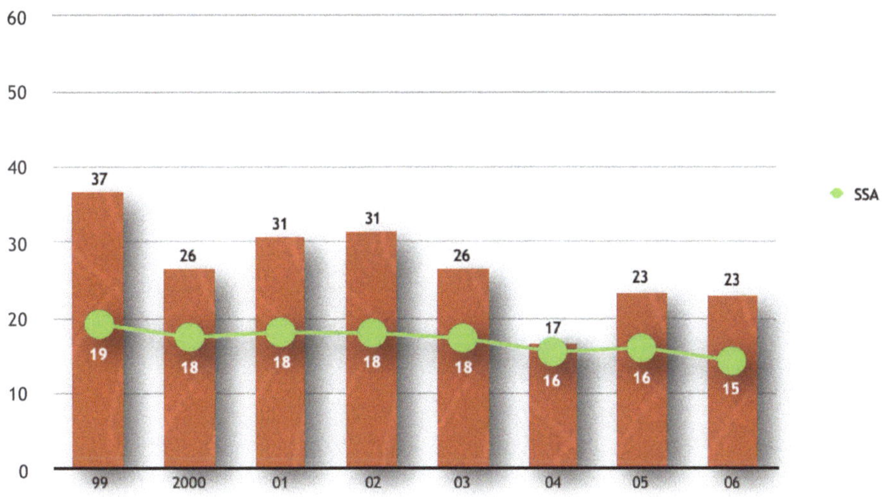

It could be argued that agriculture's part in Africa's GDP output hovered healthily between 15% and 20%. While Nigeria's swung wildly between 23% and 37%.

Agriculture is not a big player in Nigeria's GDP. 03/06 is incontrovertibly worse than 99/02. Yet, better than the Africa average.

Agriculture's share of Sub-Saharan Africa's GDP also slips downwards from 1992 through 2006, a straight fall of 4%. But Nigeria's was a fall of 14%.

9.4 Productivity in Agriculture as $PPP per Person

more grains to their elbows

But, quantify productivity as money generated per person of population, and Nigeria improves significantly.

Top-half finishes in West Africa during both 99/02 and 03/06, even though within the oil exporters fraternity it doesn't excel. Average there in 03/06.

	99-02	03-06
Self-comparison to Preceding Period		▲
Performance in Sub-Saharan Africa	▲	▲
Performance in West Africa	▲	▲
	Benin	Ghana
	Mauritania	Benin
	Côte d'Ivoire	**Nigeria**
	Nigeria	Mauritania
	Ghana	Côte d'Ivoire
	Gambia, The	Gambia, The
	Mali	Burkina Faso
	Burkina Faso	Mali
	Liberia	Togo
	Guinea-Bissau	Guinea-Bissau
	Togo	Sierra Leone
	Senegal	Senegal
	Guinea	Niger
	Niger	Cape Verde
	Cape Verde	Liberia
	Sierra Leone	Guinea
Performance among Oil-Exporters	▼	◁▷
	Gabon	Gabon
	Sudan	Sudan
	Equatorial Guinea	Equatorial Guinea
	Cameroon	Cameroon
	Chad	**Nigeria**
	Côte d'Ivoire	Côte d'Ivoire
	Nigeria	Chad
	Angola	Angola
	Congo, Rep.	Congo, Rep.

Primary Data: World Bank, IMF

▲	improved *or* better than average
▼	worsened *or* worse than average
◁▷	no change *or* average

9. Economic Productivity

9.10

Productivity in Agriculture per Person of Population in West Africa during 2003/06 ($PPP)

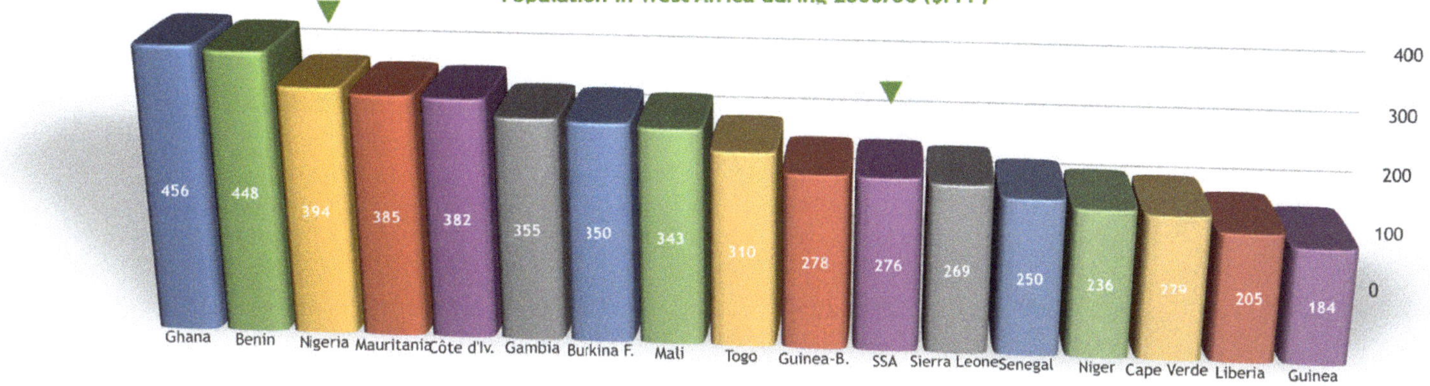

9.11

Productivity in Agriculture per Person of Population in Nigeria and Sub-Saharan Africa from 1999 to 2006 ($PPP)

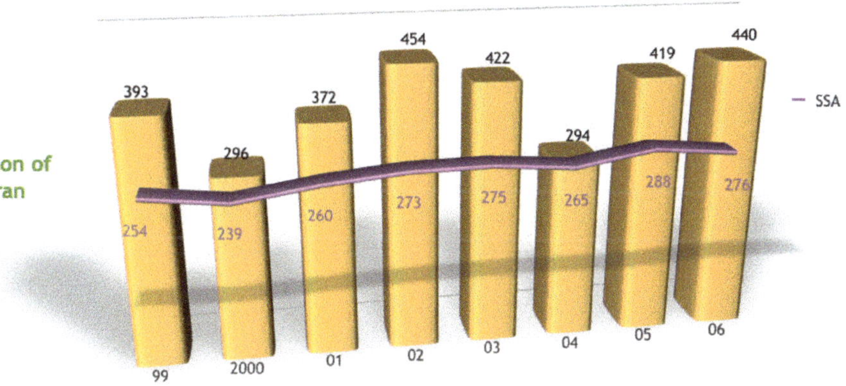

Here again, Nigeria outperforms most of Africa, just about finding room in the top band.

Productivity in Agriculture as $PPP per Person in Sub-Saharan Africa during 2003-06: Rankings

Rank	Country	Rank	Country	Rank	Country
1	Gabon	15	Central Afr. Rep.	29	Zambia
2	Mauritius	16	Chad	30	Senegal
3	Comoros	17	Gambia, The	31	South Africa
4	Swaziland	18	Burkina Faso	32	Niger
5	Namibia	19	Mali	33	Malawi
6	Tanzania	20	Angola	34	Cape Verde
7	Ghana	21	Rwanda	35	Mozambique
8	Benin	22	Togo	36	Lesotho
9	Seychelles	23	Botswana	37	Guinea
10	Equatorial Guinea	24	Ethiopia	38	Congo, Rep.
11	Cameroon	25	Guinea-Bissau	39	Eritrea
12	Kenya	26	Uganda	40	Congo, Dem. Rep.
13	Nigeria	27	Sierra Leone	41	Burundi
14	Côte d' Ivoire	28	Madagascar		
TOP		MIDDLE		BOTTOM	

Central Africa
East Africa
Southern Africa
West Africa

9.5 Growth in Agriculture Productivity

something to crow about

	99-02	03-06
Self-comparison to Preceding Period		▼
Performance in Sub-Saharan Africa	▲	▲
Performance in West Africa	▲	▼

The bad news, though, is that the Nigeria agriculture sector wasn't growing robustly. It slowed significantly from 99/02 to 03/06. Bottom half of West Africa.

That malaise was shared by other oil exporters, who — except for Angola — actually fared worse. This highlights the much feared neglect of non-oil sectors.

99-02	03-06
Liberia	Cape Verde
Nigeria	Gambia, The
Gambia, The	Togo
Ghana	Ghana
Sierra Leone	Mali
Burkina Faso	Sierra Leone
Togo	Senegal
Guinea	Niger
Benin	Guinea-Bissau
Côte d'Ivoire	Burkina Faso
Niger	Benin
Senegal	**Nigeria**
Mauritania	Côte d'Ivoire
Mali	Guinea
Cape Verde	Mauritania
Guinea-Bissau	Liberia

9.12 Growth in Agriculture Productivity in West Africa during 2003/06 (%)

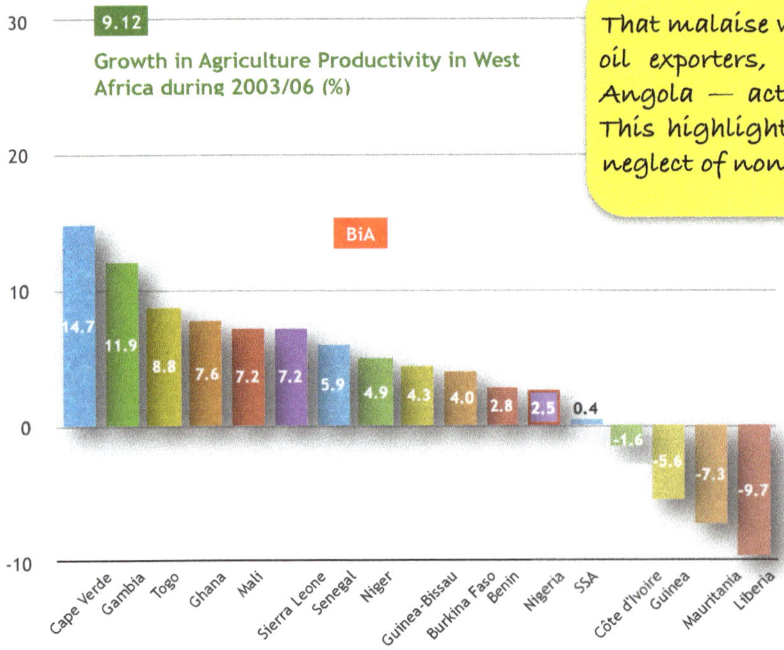

Performance among Oil-Exporters	99-02	03-06
	▲	▲
	Nigeria	Angola
	Chad	**Nigeria**
	Sudan	Sudan
	Côte d'Ivoire	Cameroon
	Cameroon	Côte d'Ivoire
	Angola	Gabon
	Gabon	Congo, Rep.
	Equatorial Guinea	Chad
	Congo, Rep.	Equatorial Guinea

Primary Data: World Bank, IMF

▲	improved *or* better than average
▼	worsened *or* worse than average
◁▷	no change *or* average

9.13

Growth in Agriculture Productivity in Nigeria and Sub-Saharan Africa from 1999 to 2006 (%)

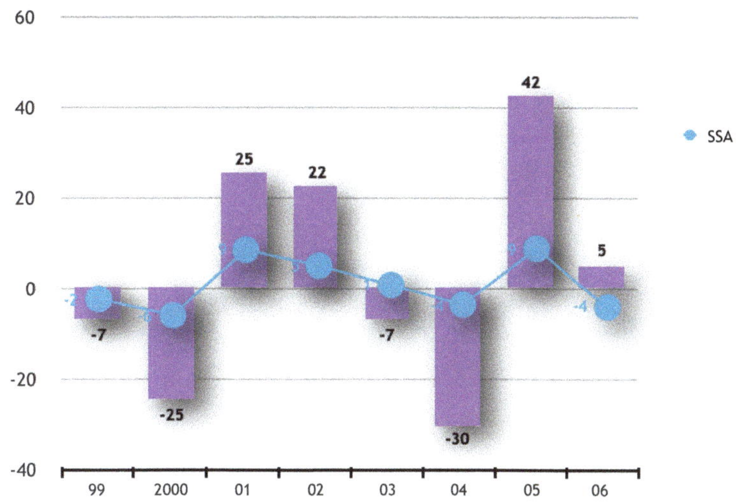

Angola, oil producer though it is, led the charge ahead of the rest of the continent. The only oil economy in the top segment.

All the other oil exporters made bottom, save for Nigeria, who just made into the middle band.

Growth in Agriculture Productivity in Sub-Saharan Africa during 2003-06: Rankings

Rank	Country	Rank	Country	Rank	Country
1	Angola	15	Uganda	29	Seychelles
2	Cape Verde	16	Senegal	30	Comoros
3	Ethiopia	17	Zambia	31	Cameroon
4	Gambia, The	18	Niger	32	Mauritius
5	Eritrea	19	Guinea	33	Burundi
6	Togo	20	Lesotho	34	Swaziland
7	Mozambique	21	Burkina Faso	35	Côte d' Ivoire
8	Tanzania	22	Malawi	36	Gabon
9	Ghana	23	Congo, Dem. Rep.	37	South Africa
10	Mali	24	Botswana	38	Congo, Rep.
11	Sierra Leone	25	Kenya	39	Chad
12	Namibia	26	Benin	40	Guinea-Bissau
13	Madagascar	27	Nigeria	41	Equatorial Guinea
14	Rwanda	28	Central Afr. Rep.		
TOP		MIDDLE		BOTTOM	

Central Africa
East Africa
Southern Africa
West Africa

9.6 Productivity in Industry as % of GDP

churning them out...

	99-02	03-06
Self-comparison to Preceding Period		▲
Performance in Sub-Saharan Africa	▲	▲
Performance in West Africa	▲	▲
	Nigeria	Nigeria
	Guinea	Guinea
	Mauritania	Mauritania
	Sierra Leone	Sierra Leone
	Ghana	Ghana
	Senegal	Senegal
	Côte d'Ivoire	Côte d'Ivoire
	Mali	Mali
	Burkina Faso	Burkina Faso
	Togo	Togo
	Niger	Niger
	Cape Verde	Cape Verde
	Benin	Benin
	Gambia, The	Gambia, The
	Guinea-Bissau	Guinea-Bissau
	Liberia	Liberia
Performance among Oil-Exporters	◁▷	◁▷
	Equatorial Guinea	Equatorial Guinea
	Angola	Angola
	Congo, Rep.	Congo, Rep.
	Gabon	Gabon
	Nigeria	Nigeria
	Cameroon	Chad
	Côte d'Ivoire	Cameroon
	Sudan	Sudan
	Chad	Côte d'Ivoire

Primary Data: World Bank

Industry is the largest of the Nigeria sectors, at 55% of GDP. Considerably larger than the Africa average (32%).

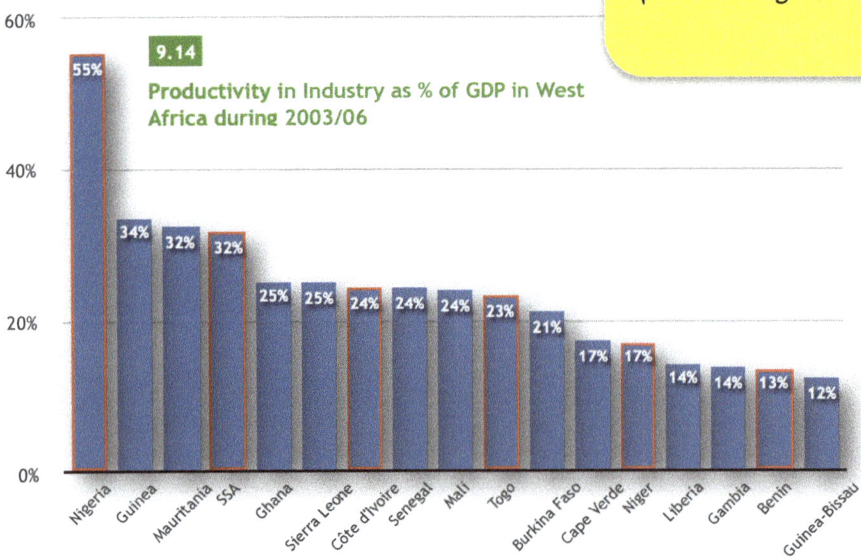

9.14 Productivity in Industry as % of GDP in West Africa during 2003/06

▲	improved *or* better than average
▼	worsened *or* worse than average
◁▷	no change *or* average

9.15

Productivity in Industry as % of GDP in Nigeria and Sub-Saharan Africa from 1999 to 2006

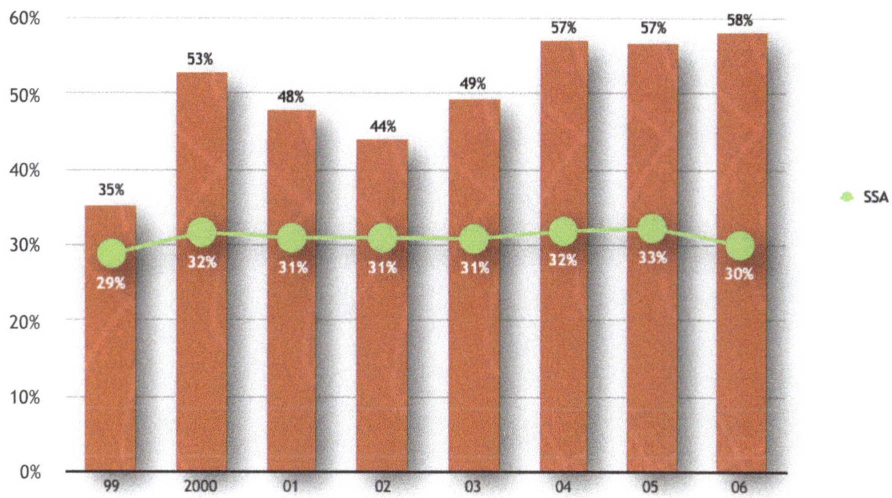

This time, Africa hovers around 30% Industry in its GDP. Nigeria grew Industry from 35% of GDP in 1999 to 58% in 2006.

Yet, Nigeria was only average among the oil countries. Suggesting either that the other economies are more heavily tilted towards industry, or are able to achieve more efficient output.

This may be a positive trend, or it may not. That would depend on how much of this growth was driven by the relatively easy trade in oil exports ...

... rather than an increasing capacity utilization in its manufacturing sector.

Examined in chapter 9.9 - 9.11 below.

9.7 Productivity in Industry as $PPP per Person

... and churning this out...

Primary Data: World Bank, IMF

	99-02	03-06
Self-comparison to Preceding Period		▲
Performance in Sub-Saharan Africa	▲	▲
Performance in West Africa	▲	▲
	Nigeria	**Nigeria**
	Mauritania	Mauritania
	Côte d'Ivoire	Cape Verde
	Cape Verde	Côte d'Ivoire
	Senegal	Senegal
	Guinea	Guinea
	Ghana	Ghana
	Burkina Faso	Burkina Faso
	Mali	Mali
	Benin	Benin
	Gambia, The	Togo
	Togo	Gambia, The
	Sierra Leone	Sierra Leone
	Niger	Niger
	Guinea-Bissau	Guinea-Bissau
	Liberia	Liberia
Performance among Oil-Exporters	▼	◁▷
	Gabon	Equatorial Guinea
	Equatorial Guinea	Gabon
	Congo, Rep.	Angola
	Angola	Congo, Rep.
	Cameroon	**Nigeria**
	Nigeria	Chad
	Côte d'Ivoire	Cameroon
	Sudan	Sudan
	Chad	Côte d'Ivoire

Almost the same trend in industry productivity output per person, as for industry productivity % GDP. Top of West Africa; better than most Africa; average among oil exporters.

▲	improved *or* better than average
▼	worsened *or* worse than average
◁▷	no change *or* average

9. Economic Productivity

9.16

Productivity in Industry per Person of Population in West Africa during 2003/06 ($PPP)

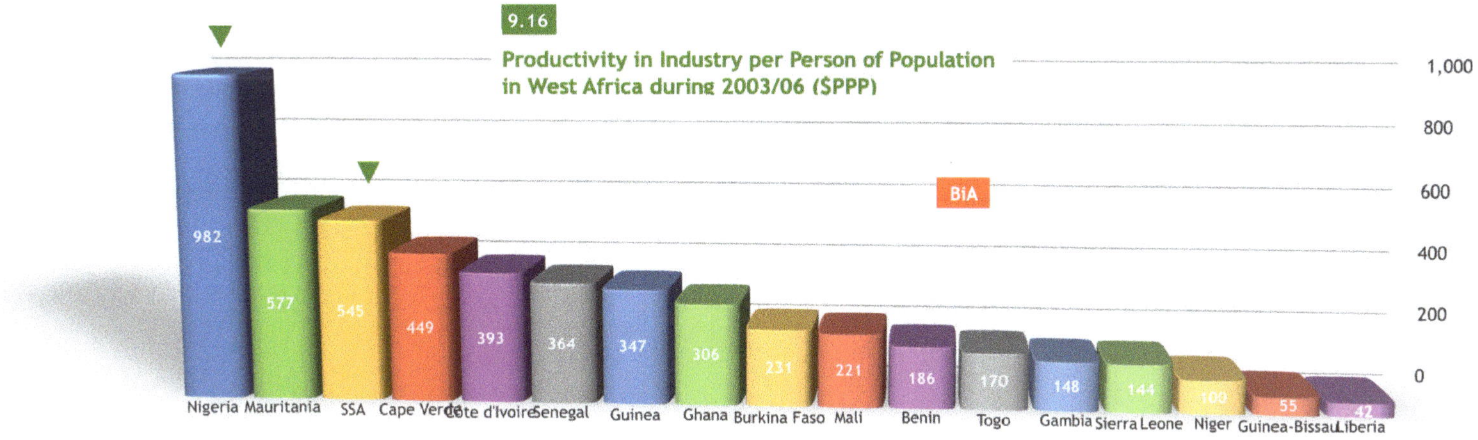

9.17

Productivity in Industry per Person of Population in Nigeria and Sub-Saharan Africa from 1999 to 2006 ($PPP)

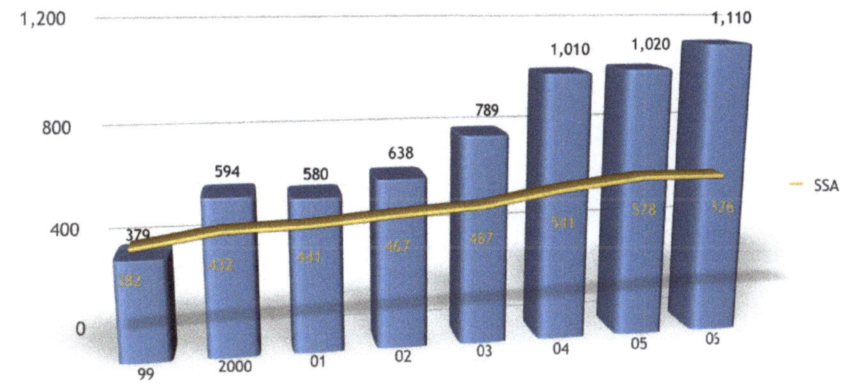

In West Africa, only Mauritania and Nigeria produced more industry output per person than the rest of Africa.

Here again, as it was for industry in % GDP, Nigeria grew industry output per person rapidly from 99 to 2006. But no celebrating until we've checked its manufacturing sector out.

Productivity in Industry as $PPP per Person in Sub-Saharan Africa during 2003-06: Rankings

Rank	Country	Rank	Country	Rank	Country
1	Equatorial Guinea	15	Cape Verde	29	Uganda
2	Gabon	16	Côte d' Ivoire	30	Rwanda
3	Botswana	17	Senegal	31	Gambia, The
4	Seychelles	18	Guinea	32	Sierra Leone
5	Mauritius	19	Zambia	33	Madagascar
6	Angola	20	Ghana	34	Comoros
7	South Africa	21	Kenya	35	Malawi
8	Congo, Rep.	22	Burkina Faso	36	Niger
9	Swaziland	23	Mali	37	Central Afr. Rep.
10	Namibia	24	Eritrea	38	Ethiopia
11	Nigeria	25	Benin	39	Congo, Dem. Rep.
12	Chad	26	Mozambique	40	Burundi
13	Cameroon	27	Tanzania	41	Guinea-Bissau
14	Lesotho	28	Togo		
TOP		MIDDLE		BOTTOM	

Central Africa
East Africa
Southern Africa
West Africa

9.8 Growth in Industry Productivity

... but how fast?

However, many West Africans also grew industry output per person fairly rapidly. Half the sub-region did better than the Africa average.

	99-02	03-06
Self-comparison to Preceding Period		▼
Performance in Sub-Saharan Africa	▲	▲
Performance in West Africa	▲	▲
	Mali	Mauritania
	Nigeria	Liberia
	Sierra Leone	**Nigeria**
	Burkina Faso	Togo
	Cape Verde	Cape Verde
	Senegal	Sierra Leone
	Benin	Burkina Faso
	Gambia, The	Ghana
	Ghana	Côte d'Ivoire
	Guinea	Guinea
	Mauritania	Niger
	Niger	Benin
	Togo	Senegal
	Côte d'Ivoire	Mali
	Guinea-Bissau	Gambia, The
	Liberia	Guinea-Bissau
Performance among Oil-Exporters	▲	▲
	Equatorial Guinea	Chad
	Nigeria	Sudan
	Sudan	**Nigeria**
	Congo, Rep.	Equatorial Guinea
	Angola	Angola
	Chad	Congo, Rep.
	Cameroon	Gabon
	Gabon	Côte d'Ivoire
	Côte d'Ivoire	Cameroon

Primary Data: World Bank, IMF

9.18

Growth in Industry Productivity in West Africa during 2003/06 (%)

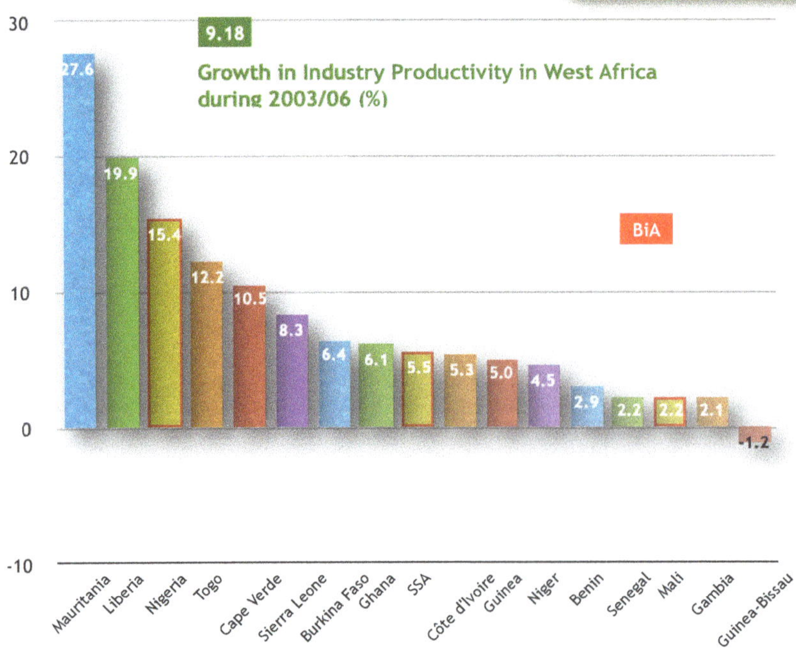

▲	improved *or* better than average
▼	worsened *or* worse than average
◁▷	no change *or* average

Nigeria's industry output grew fastest during 2000: 57%. It thereafter put the brakes on; only attempting another spike in 2004; but this time at 28%, half the previous pace.

Three of the four fastest growing industry sectors in Africa belonged to oil economies.

9.19

Growth in Industry Productivity in Nigeria and Sub-Saharan Africa from 1999 to 2006 (%)

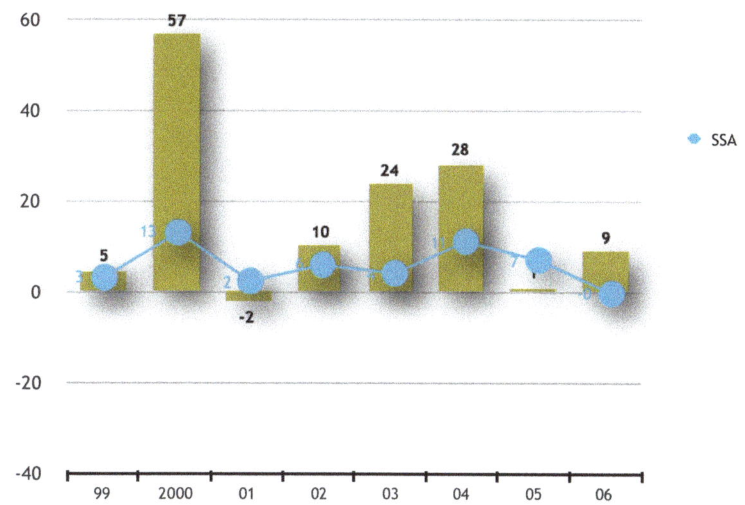

Growth in Industry Productivity in Sub-Saharan Africa during 2003-06: Rankings

Rank	Country	Rank	Country	Rank	Country
1	Chad	15	Ethiopia	29	Swaziland
2	Nigeria	16	Botswana	30	Cameroon
3	Congo, Dem. Rep.	17	Kenya	31	Comoros
4	Equatorial Guinea	18	Gabon	32	Benin
5	Togo	19	Burkina Faso	33	Senegal
6	Zambia	20	Rwanda	34	Mauritius
7	Angola	21	Ghana	35	Mali
8	Madagascar	22	Namibia	36	Gambia, The
9	Mozambique	23	Côte d' Ivoire	37	Central Afr. Rep.
10	Cape Verde	24	Guinea	38	Uganda
11	Malawi	25	Lesotho	39	Guinea-Bissau
12	Congo, Rep.	26	Burundi	40	Seychelles
13	Tanzania	27	South Africa	41	Eritrea
14	Sierra Leone	28	Niger		
TOP		MIDDLE		BOTTOM	

Central Africa
East Africa
Southern Africa
West Africa

9.9 *Manufacturing* and *Other Industry* Productivity

we've got to know which is which

Primary Data: AfDB, World Bank

Crunch time.

Nigeria's high industry productivity turns out to comprise mostly of non-manufacturing activities.

As suspected, oil activity would constitute a huge chunk (part of the 92% "other industry").

In Nigeria, manufacturing accounted for only 8% of industry output: the smallest among West Africans.

The only other oil exporter in West Africa, Côte d'Ivoire, had manufacturing at 71% of its industry sector output.

The proportions hardly changed in Nigeria during 1999-2006. Manufacturing continued to constitute about 8% of industry output throughout.

The rest would be made up largely of oil industry activity.

9. Economic Productivity

9.20

Productivity in Industry per Person of Population in West Africa during 2003/06 ($US)

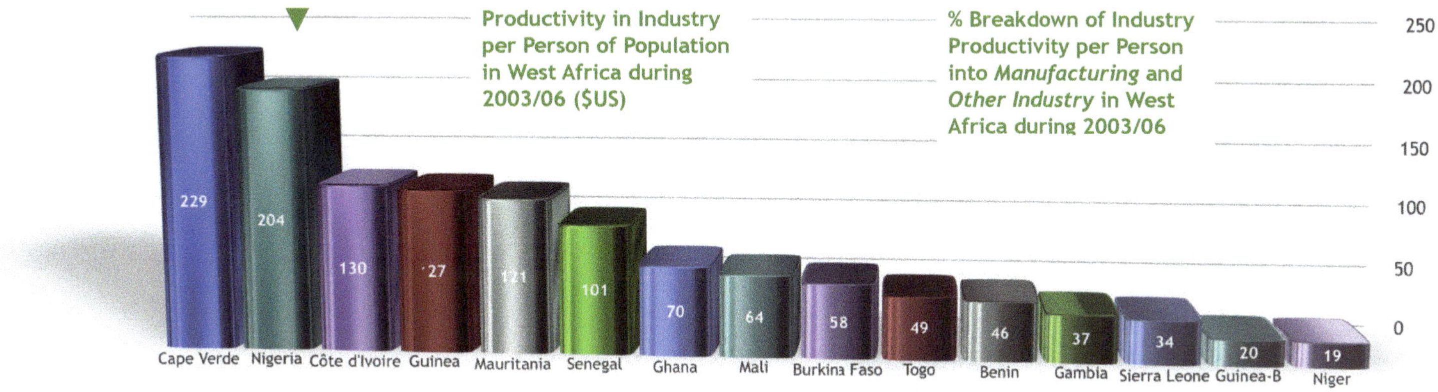

9.21

% Breakdown of Industry Productivity per Person into *Manufacturing* and *Other Industry* in West Africa during 2003/06

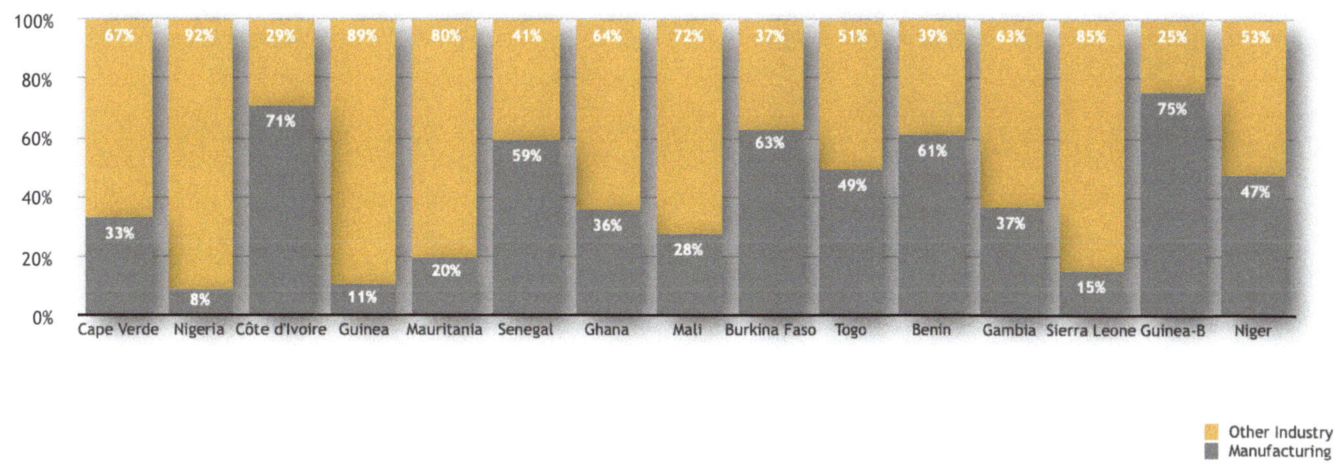

9.22

Productivity in Industry per Person of Population in Nigeria from 1999 to 2006 ($US)

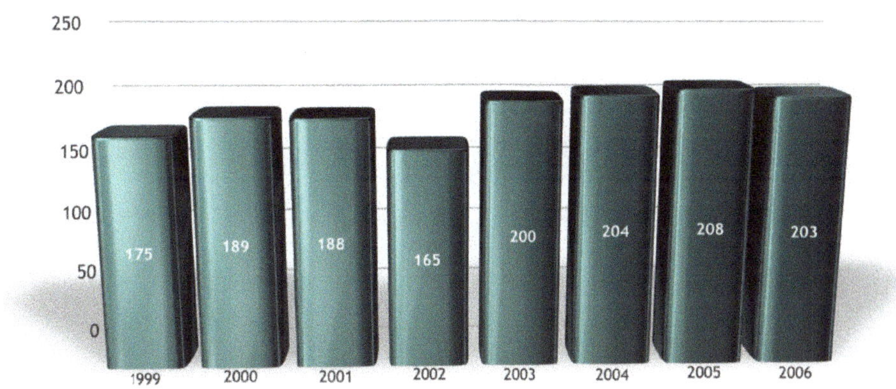

9.23

% Breakdown of Industry Productivity per Person into *Manufacturing* and *Other Industry* in Nigeria from 1999 to 2006

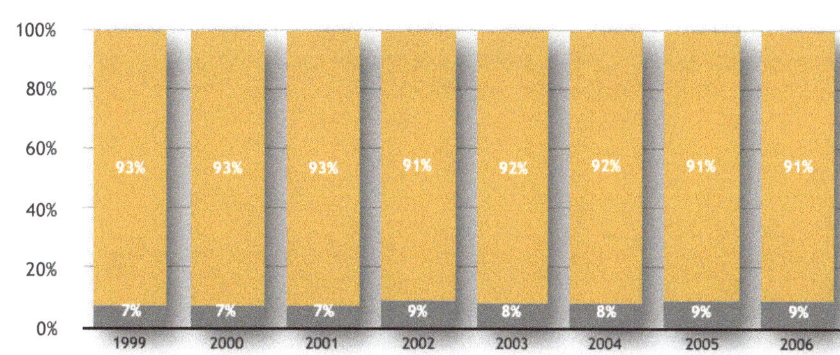

9.10 Growth in *Man.* and *Other Industry* Productivity

and we've got to tell what's going where

9.26

Growth in $US Industry Productivity in Nigeria from 1999 to 2006 (%)

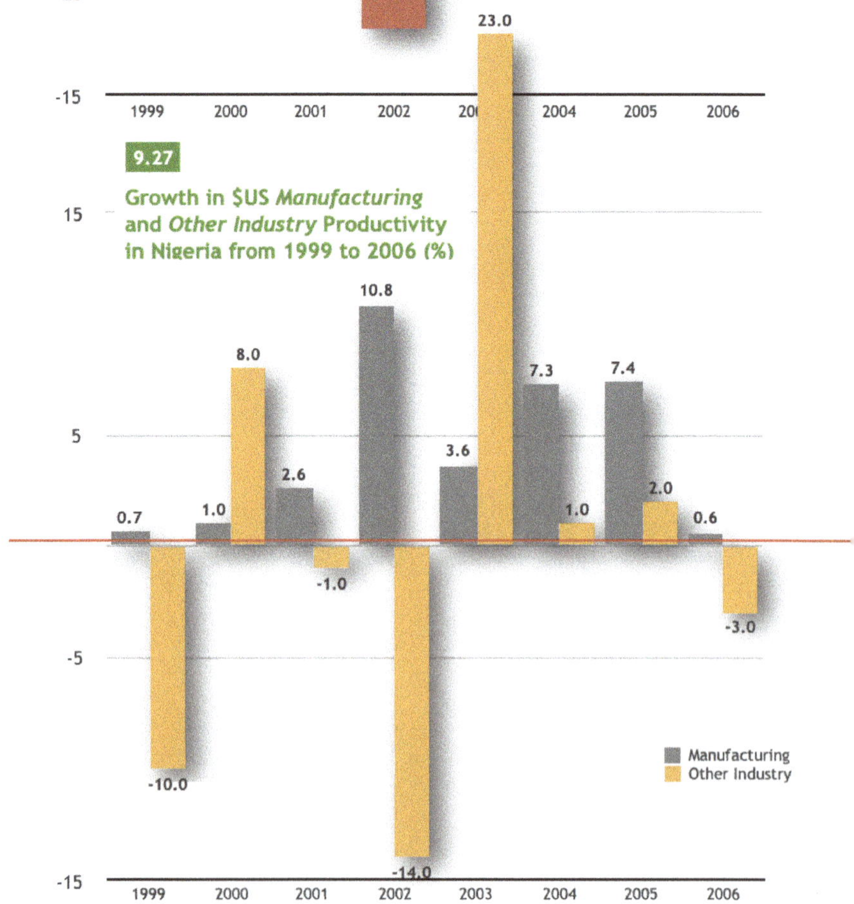

9.27

Growth in $US *Manufacturing* and *Other Industry* Productivity in Nigeria from 1999 to 2006 (%)

Nigeria's "Other Industry" grew in fits and starts. Whereas, manufacturing began to grow from 1999, then slowed during 2003. A good climb in 2004-05, but sharp drop in 2006.

Primary Data: AfDB, World Bank

9.24

Growth in $US Industry Productivity in West Africa during 2003/06 (%)

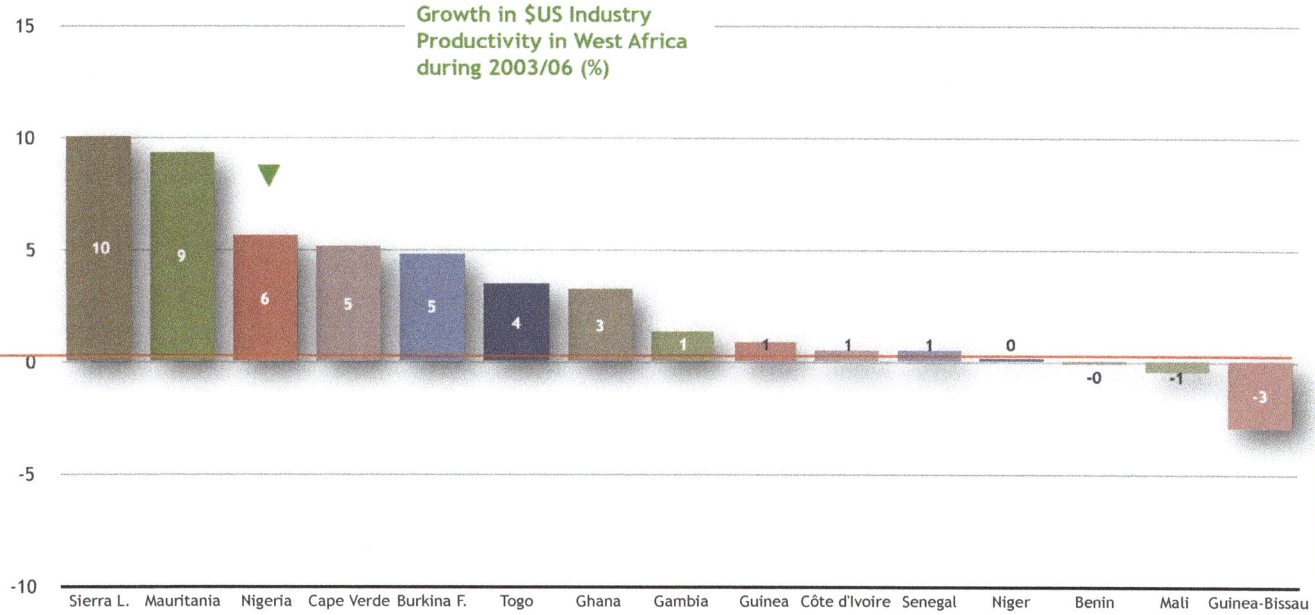

9.25

Growth in $US *Manufacturing* and *Other Industry* Productivity in West Africa during 2003/06 (%)

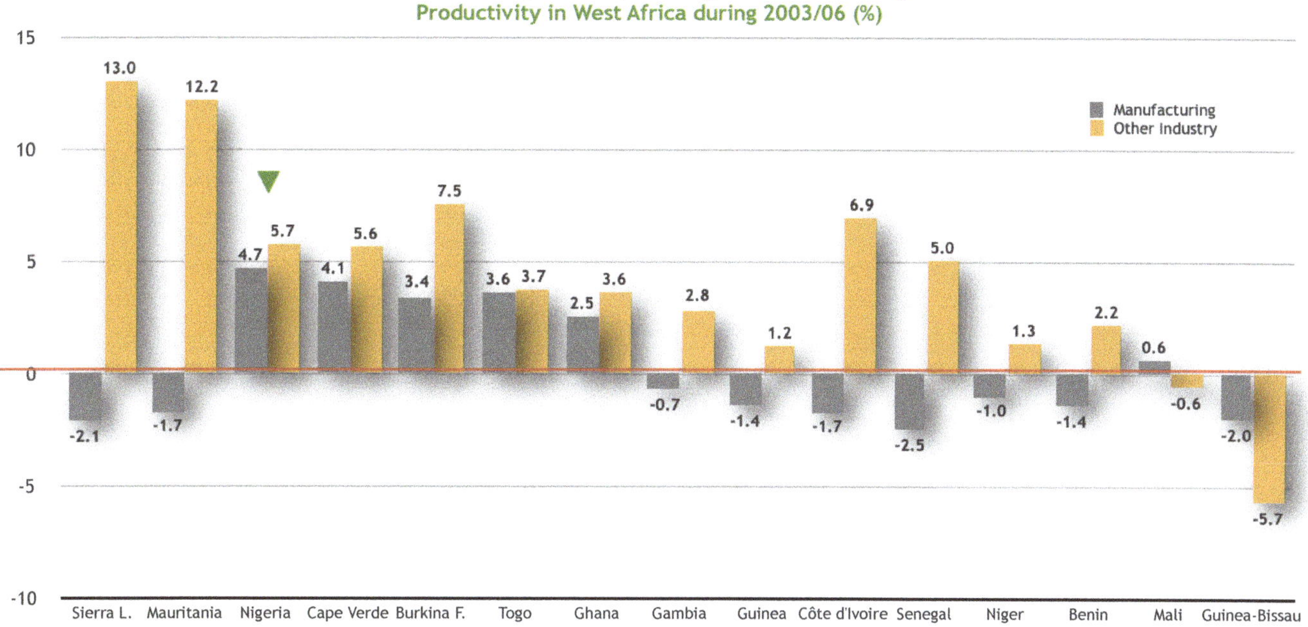

Growth patterns within the industry sector yield a similar story: high growth in general, and faster growth for "other industry" (read "oil"), at 5.7%, than for manufacturing, 4.7%.

9.11 Build-up in *Man.* and *Other Industry* Productivity

or is it all just talk, talk?

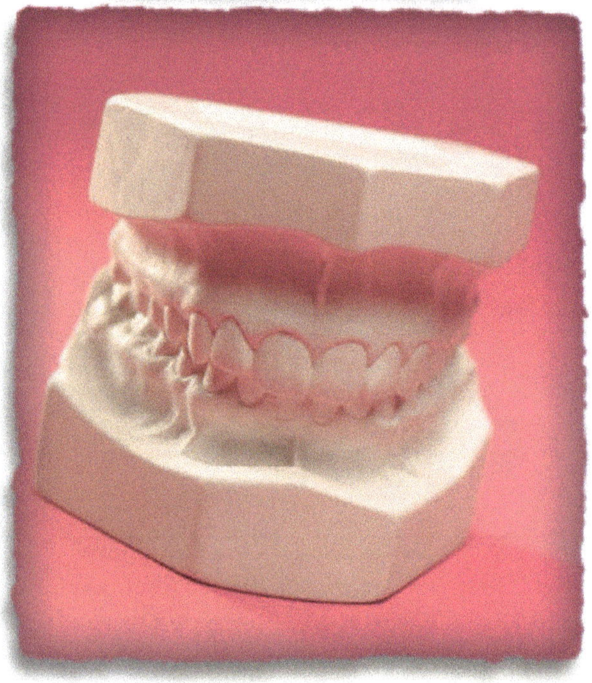

Gap between *Manufacturing* and *Other Industry* Productivity levels: 2000=100

	West Africa	2006
1	Burkina Faso	2.7
2	Ghana	3.9
3	Guinea	10.1
4	Niger	11.3
5	Benin	17.6
6	Guinea-Bissau	18.3
7	Cape Verde	18.4
8	Togo	21.0
9	Gambia	22.6
10	Nigeria	31.3
11	Senegal	33.1
12	Mali	50.4
13	Côte d'Ivoire	52.1
14	Sierra Leone	56.0
15	Mauritania	88.2
16	Liberia	n/a

	oil exporters	2006
1	Angola	14.2
2	Gabon	16.7
3	Cameroon	21.4
4	Nigeria	31.3
5	Côte d'Ivoire	52.1
6	Congo, Rep.	78.6
7	Equatorial Guinea	118.6
8	Sudan	157.3
9	Chad	1203.2

Primary Data: AfDB, World Bank

This section demonstrates the travel trajectories of industry sector growth, in its manufacturing and "other industry" components.

Burkina Faso made the best job of keeping both components moving apace. Mauritania made the worst of it. As at 2006, its industry sector components were 88 percentage points apart.

full lines: manufacturing
dotted lines: other industry

9.28

Build-up of *Manufacturing* and *Other Industry* Productivity from 2000 to 2006: Nigeria, Benin, Burkina Faso. 2000=100

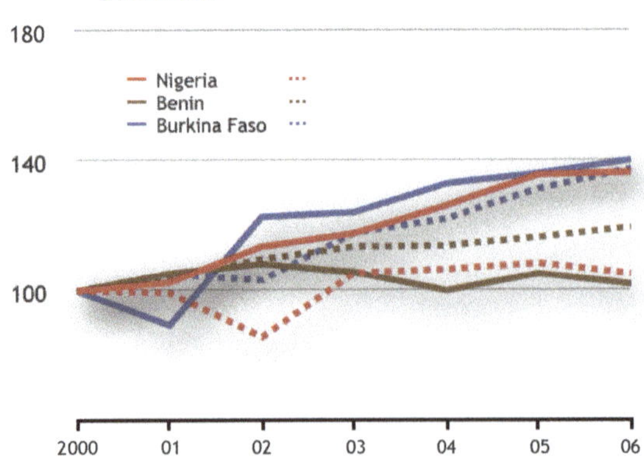

full lines: manufacturing
dotted lines: other industry

9.29

Build-up of *Manufacturing* and *Other Industry* Productivity from 2000 to 2006: Nigeria, Cape Verde, Côte d'Ivoire. 2000=100

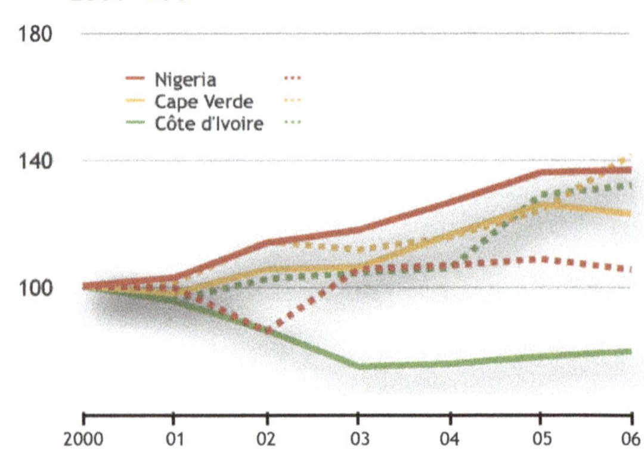

9.30

Build-up of *Manufacturing* and *Other Industry* Productivity from 2000 to 2006: Nigeria, Gambia, Ghana. 2000=100

full lines: manufacturing
dotted lines: other industry

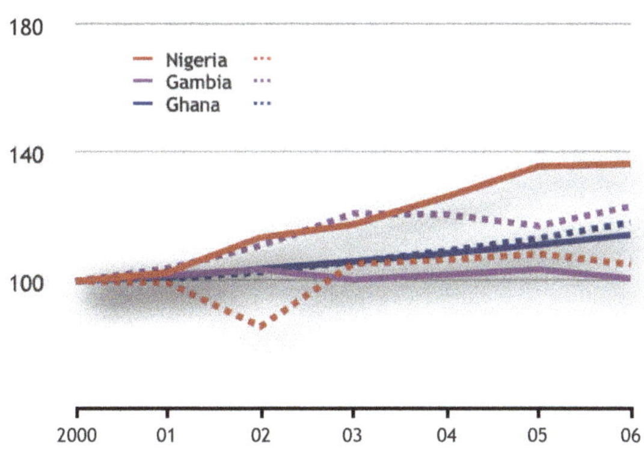

9.31

Build-up of *Manufacturing* and *Other Industry* Productivity from 2000 to 2006: Nigeria, Guinea, Guinea-Bissau. 2000=100

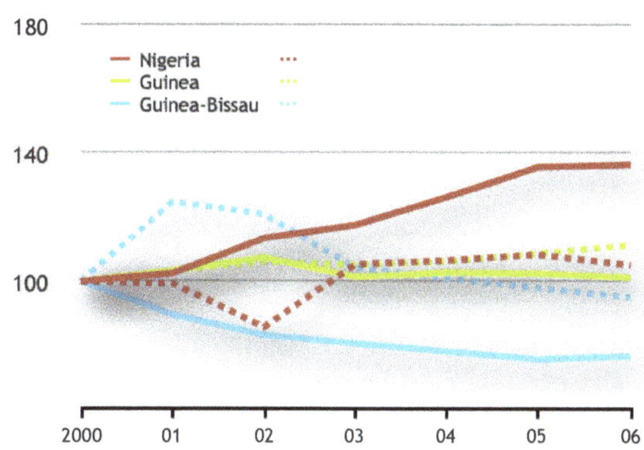

9.32

Build-up of *Manufacturing* and *Other Industry* Productivity from 2000 to 2006: Nigeria, Mali, Mauritania. 2000=100

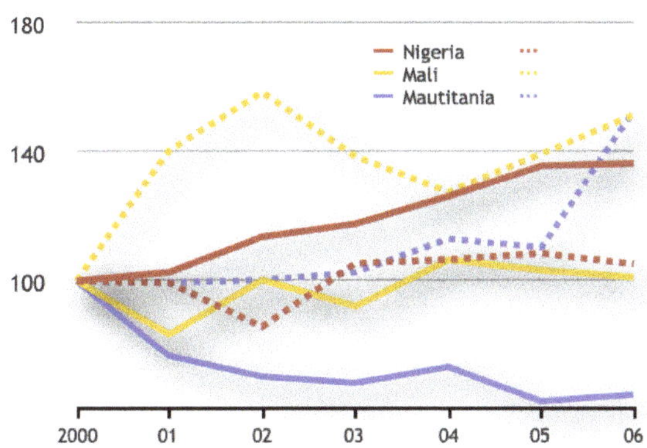

9.33

Build-up of *Manufacturing* and *Other Industry* Productivity from 2000 to 2006: Nigeria, Niger, Senegal. 2000=100

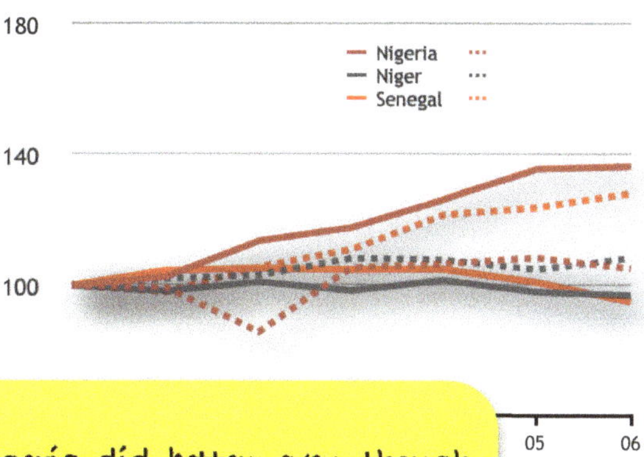

Nigeria did better, even though, at 31 percentage points, its gap is one of the worse ones in West Africa.

9.34

Build-up of *Manufacturing* and *Other Industry* Productivity from 2000 to 2006: Nigeria, Sierra Leone, Togo. 2000=100

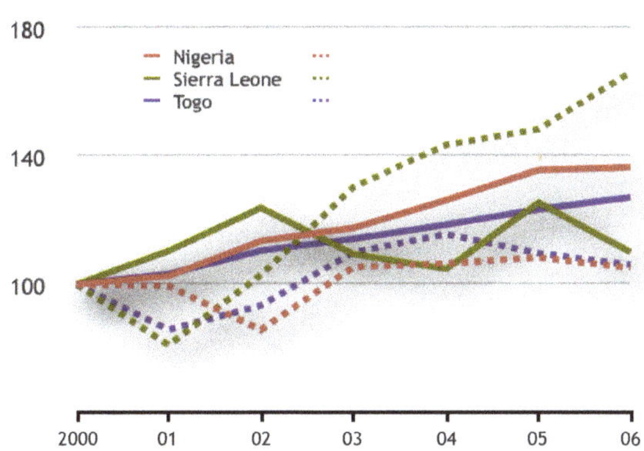

But, among the oil exporters, it was something of a triumph (finishing in the top half): Chad closed the group with a 1,203 percentage points gap!

A starker neglect of manufacturing for the easy but precarious attention to oil exports, is hardly conceivable.

9.12 Productivity in Services as % of GDP

it's lunch break, that's why

	99-02	03-06
Self-comparison to Preceding Period		▼
Performance in Sub-Saharan Africa	▼	▼
Performance in West Africa	▼	▼

Primary Data: World Bank

99-02	03-06
Cape Verde	Cape Verde
Senegal	Senegal
Gambia, The	Benin
Côte d'Ivoire	Gambia, The
Benin	Côte d'Ivoire
Guinea	Guinea
Togo	Mauritania
Mauritania	Niger
Niger	Burkina Faso
Burkina Faso	Mali
Ghana	Ghana
Mali	Togo
Guinea-Bissau	Sierra Leone
Nigeria	Guinea-Bissau
Sierra Leone	**Nigeria**
Liberia	Liberia

Performance among Oil-Exporters	99-02	03-06
	▼	▼
	Côte d'Ivoire	Côte d'Ivoire
	Chad	Cameroon
	Cameroon	Sudan
	Gabon	Gabon
	Sudan	Chad
	Congo, Rep.	Congo, Rep.
	Nigeria	Angola
	Angola	**Nigeria**
	Equatorial Guinea	Equatorial Guinea

9.35

Productivity in Services as % of GDP in West Africa during 2003/06

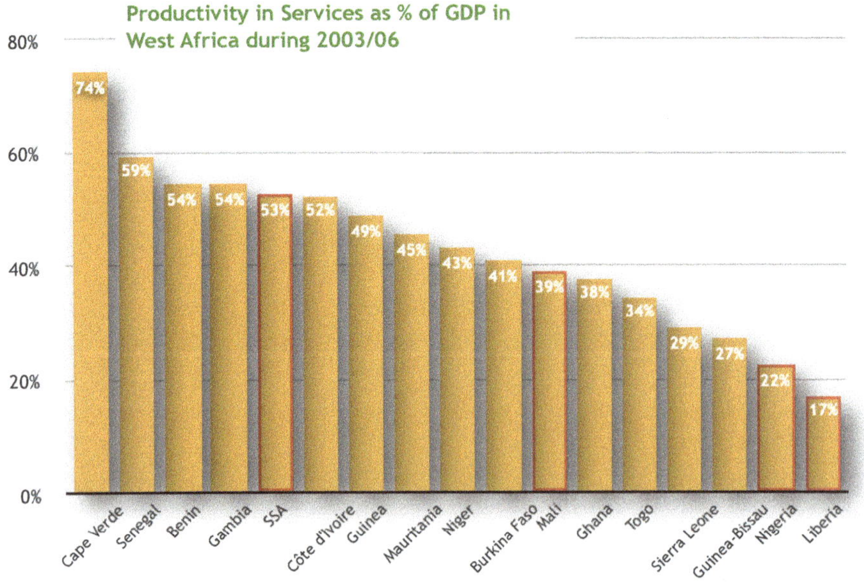

▲	improved *or* better than average
▼	worsened *or* worse than average
◁▷	no change *or* average

9.36

Productivity in Services as % of GDP in Nigeria and Sub-Saharan Africa from 1999 to 2006

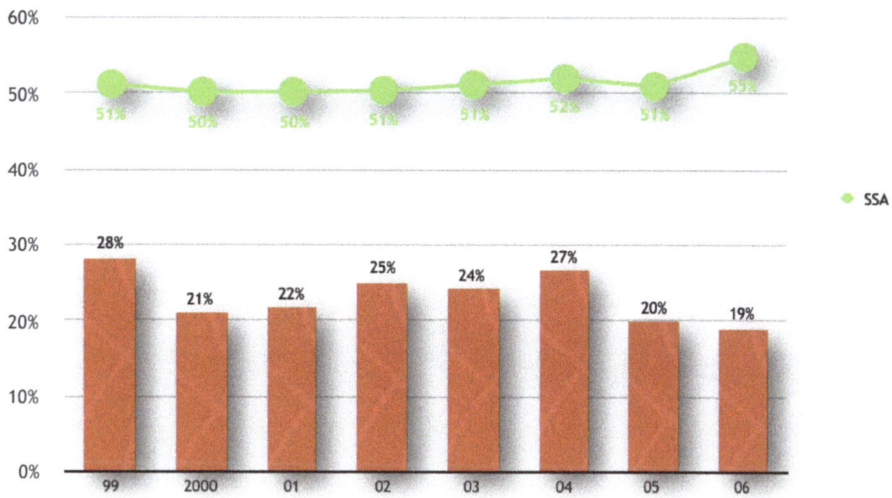

A graphic depiction of the distance between services size on the continent and services size in Nigeria. As much as 36% in 2006.

Nigeria's services sector is small indeed. It was only larger than Liberia's in West Africa, and was bottom also among the oil economies. It shrunk in 03/06 from its level in 99/02.

9.13 Productivity in Services as $PPP per Person

unlock the value within

Primary Data: World Bank, IMF

	99-02	03-06
Self-comparison to Preceding Period		▲
Performance in Sub-Saharan Africa	▼	▼
Performance in West Africa	▼	▼
	Cape Verde	Cape Verde
	Côte d'Ivoire	Senegal
	Senegal	Côte d'Ivoire
	Mauritania	Mauritania
	Benin	Benin
	Gambia, The	Gambia, The
	Guinea	Guinea
	Ghana	Ghana
	Burkina Faso	Burkina Faso
	Togo	**Nigeria**
	Nigeria	Mali
	Mali	Niger
	Niger	Togo
	Guinea-Bissau	Sierra Leone
	Sierra Leone	Guinea-Bissau
	Liberia	Liberia
Performance among Oil-Exporters	▼	▼
	Gabon	Gabon
	Côte d'Ivoire	Congo, Rep.
	Congo, Rep.	Cameroon
	Cameroon	Angola
	Angola	Côte d'Ivoire
	Sudan	Sudan
	Chad	Chad
	Nigeria	**Nigeria**
	Equatorial Guinea	Equatorial Guinea

As with services % GDP, so with services as output per person. 03/06 worse than 99/02; Nigeria worse than Africa; Nigeria worse than West Africa; Nigeria bottom of oil group.

▲	improved *or* better than average
▼	worsened *or* worse than average
◁▷	no change *or* average

9.37

Productivity in Services per Person of Population in West Africa during 2003/06 ($PPP)

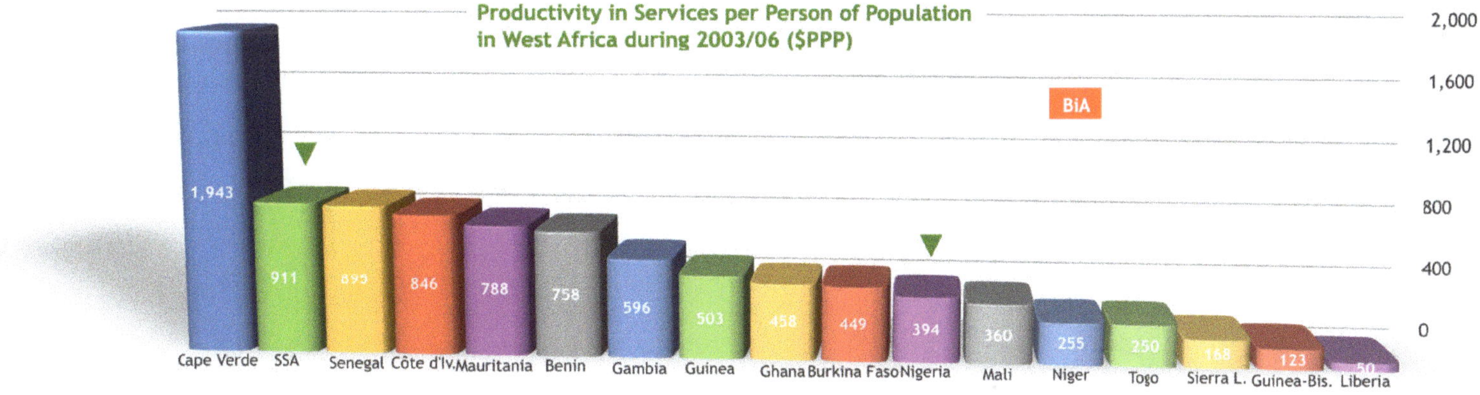

9.38

Productivity in Services per Person of Population in Nigeria and Sub-Saharan Africa from 1999 to 2006 ($PPP)

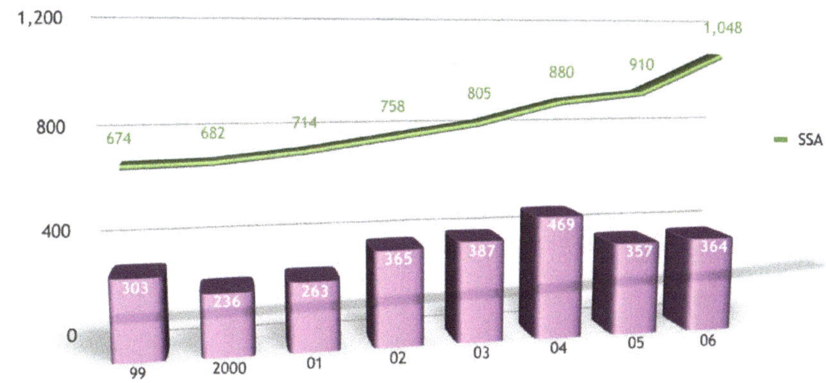

But, among Africa's oil economies, Gabon, Congo Rep., Cameroon, Angola and Côte d'Ivoire made it into Africa's top third. Everyone, that is, except Nigeria and 2 others.

Productivity in Services as $PPP per Person in Sub-Saharan Africa during 2003-06: Rankings

Rank	Country	Rank	Country	Rank	Country
1	Seychelles	15	Benin	29	Equatorial Guinea
2	Mauritius	16	Gambia, The	30	Mali
3	Botswana	17	Zambia	31	Mozambique
4	South Africa	18	Madagascar	32	Malawi
5	Gabon	19	Guinea	33	Rwanda
6	Namibia	20	Lesotho	34	Niger
7	Cape Verde	21	Eritrea	35	Togo
8	Swaziland	22	Ghana	36	Ethiopia
9	Congo, Rep.	23	Burkina Faso	37	Central Afr. Rep.
10	Cameroon	24	Chad	38	Sierra Leone
11	Senegal	25	Comoros	39	Burundi
12	Angola	26	Uganda	40	Guinea-Bissau
13	Côte d' Ivoire	27	**Nigeria**	41	Congo, Dem. Rep.
14	Kenya	28	Tanzania		
	TOP		MIDDLE		BOTTOM

Central Africa
East Africa
Southern Africa
West Africa

9.14 Growth in Services Productivity

force majeure

	99-02	03-06
Self-comparison to Preceding Period		▼
Performance in Sub-Saharan Africa	▲	▼
Performance in West Africa	▲	▼
	Sierra Leone	Sierra Leone
	Cape Verde	Mali
	Nigeria	Cape Verde
	Mauritania	Senegal
	Benin	Burkina Faso
	Burkina Faso	Benin
	Guinea-Bissau	Ghana
	Mali	Niger
	Ghana	Gambia, The
	Senegal	Guinea
	Guinea	Mauritania
	Niger	**Nigeria**
	Liberia	Côte d'Ivoire
	Gambia, The	Guinea-Bissau
	Côte d'Ivoire	Liberia
	Togo	Togo

Not encouraging news about the pace of services sector growth. Doesn't look like Nigeria will be catching up in a hurry.

Primary Data: World Bank, IMF

9.39

Growth in Services Productivity in West Africa during 2003/06 (%)

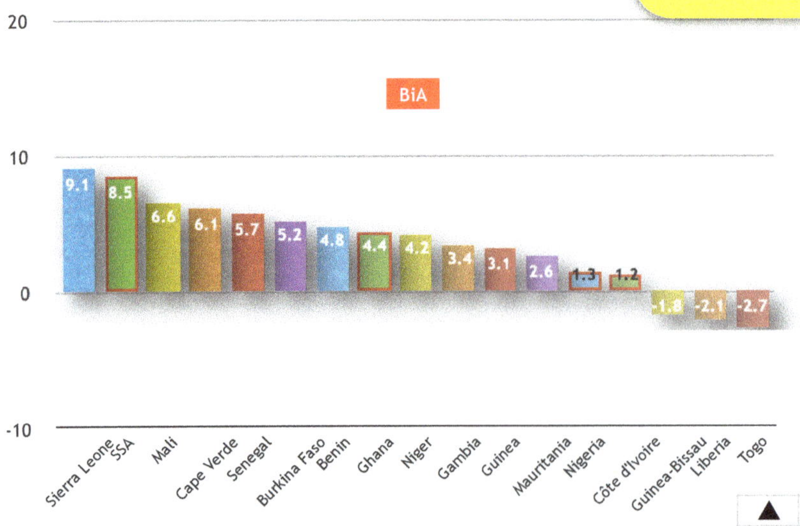

	99-02	03-06
Performance among Oil-Exporters	▲	▲
	Equatorial Guinea	Angola
	Nigeria	Sudan
	Sudan	Cameroon
	Chad	**Nigeria**
	Cameroon	Côte d'Ivoire
	Angola	Congo, Rep.
	Côte d'Ivoire	Equatorial Guinea
	Congo, Rep.	Gabon
	Gabon	Chad

▲	improved *or* better than average
▼	worsened *or* worse than average
◁▷	no change *or* average

"Shall we grow, or shall we not?", Nigeria's services growth seems to ponder.

9.40

Growth in Services Productivity in Nigeria and Sub-Saharan Africa from 1999 to 2006 (%)

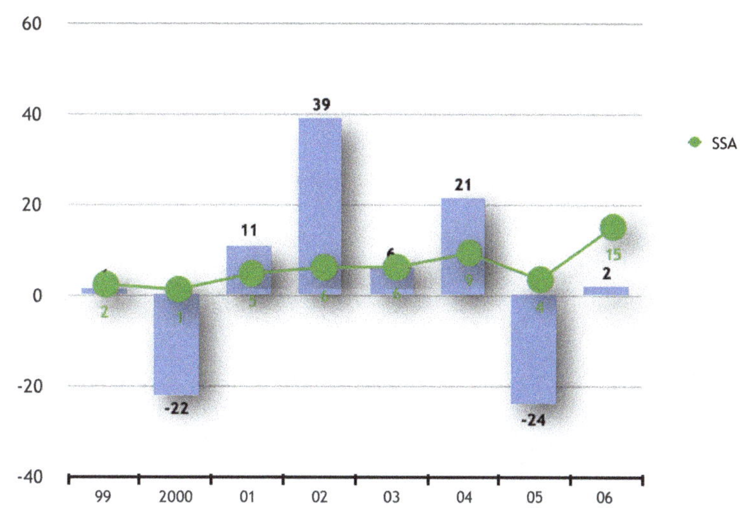

Bottom third in Africa.

Growth in Services Productivity in Sub-Saharan Africa during 2003-06: Rankings

Rank	Country	Rank	Country	Rank	Country
1	Madagascar	15	Uganda	29	Seychelles
2	Botswana	16	Senegal	30	Comoros
3	Sierra Leone	17	Mozambique	31	Zambia
4	Angola	18	Burundi	32	Nigeria
5	Mauritius	19	Congo, Dem. Rep.	33	Côte d' Ivoire
6	South Africa	20	Kenya	34	Central Afr. Rep.
7	Ethiopia	21	Burkina Faso	35	Guinea-Bissau
8	Namibia	22	Benin	36	Congo, Rep.
9	Swaziland	23	Ghana	37	Equatorial Guinea
10	Malawi	24	Lesotho	38	Togo
11	Rwanda	25	Niger	39	Eritrea
12	Mali	26	Gambia, The	40	Gabon
13	Cape Verde	27	Cameroon	41	Chad
14	Tanzania	28	Guinea		
TOP		MIDDLE		BOTTOM	

Central Africa
East Africa
Southern Africa
West Africa

9.15 Build-up in Productivity in the 3 Sectors

they'll need putting together

full lines: Nigeria
dotted lines: SSA

9.41

Build-up of Agriculture Productivity in Nigeria and Sub-Saharan Africa from 2000 to 2006. 2000=100

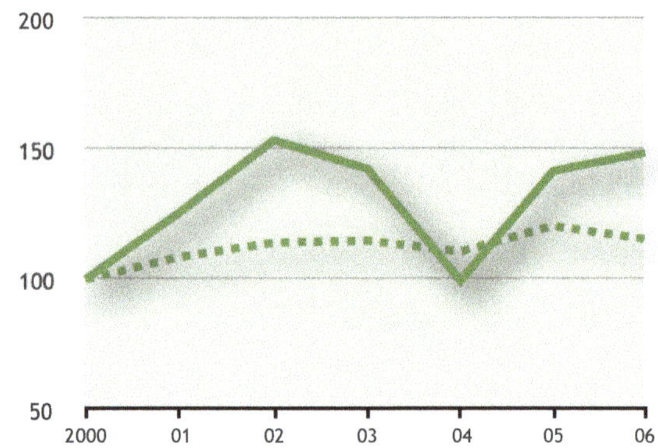

9.42

Build-up of Industry Productivity in Nigeria and Sub-Saharan Africa from 2000 to 2006. 2000=100

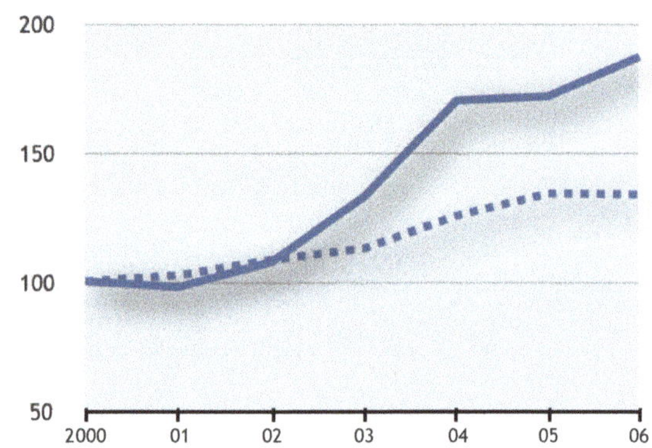

9.43

Build-up of Services Productivity in Nigeria and Sub-Saharan Africa from 2000 to 2006. 2000=100

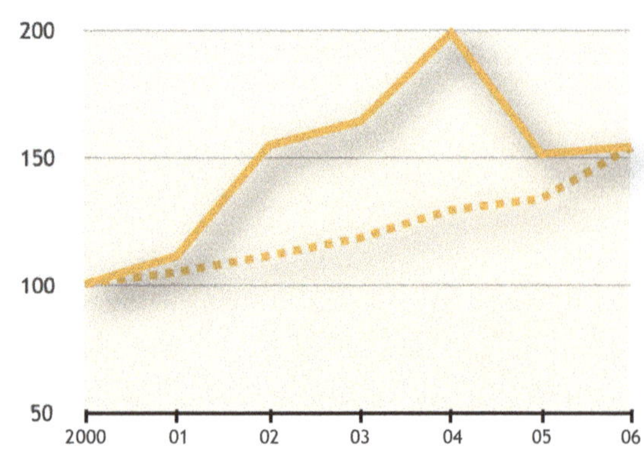

Compared to Africa, Nigeria's productivity growth in the 3 sectors has at more than one point outstripped the continent's. But never definitively — except in the industry sector.

Primary Data: World Bank

9.44

Build-up of Productivity in Agriculture, Industry and Services in Nigeria from 2000 to 2006. 2000=100

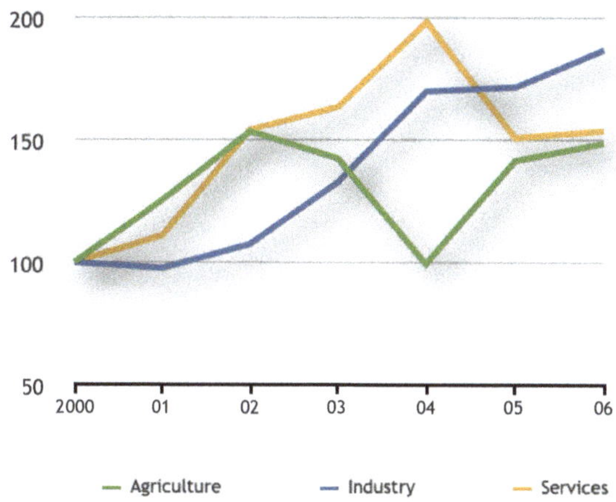

9.45

Build-up of Productivity in Agriculture, Industry and Services in Sub-Saharan Africa from 2000 to 2006. 2000=100

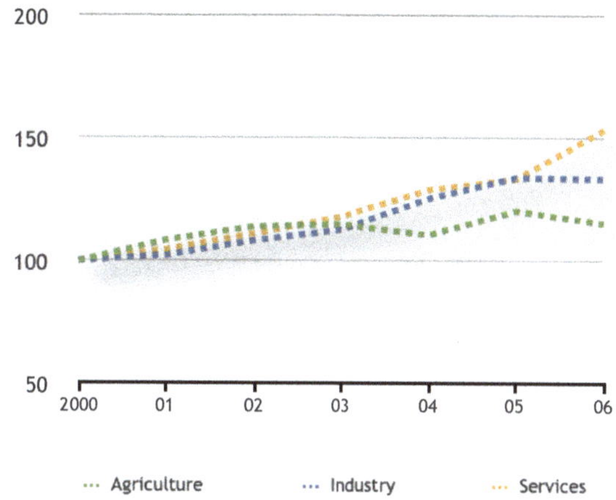

In effect, most of Africa has built up output in the 3 sectors steadily but definitively; climbing throughout, except for a small temporary dip in agriculture during 2004.

Nigeria's progress has been shaky and lacking in confidence. Clearly seen in chart 9.44.

Meantime, the rest of Africa built up productivity with some self-assurance; while Nigeria charted rougher paths. Even though it indeed made effective general upward movement.

On the whole, despite the petrifying hiccups, Nigeria does manage to build in 2006 on levels in 1999. But at no point did it look reassuringly sustainable.

That fast industry growth may not be cause for cheer, because it is down to the easy-money, postpone-the-evil-day, oil industry.

milk, anyone?

Nigeria squeezes into the top third. Better than most of the oil states. Albeit without a look of confidence to the job.

Economic Productivity Rankings: 2003-06

- Central Africa
- East Africa
- Southern Africa
- West Africa

Rank	Country
1	Angola
2	Namibia
3	Botswana
4	Mauritius
5	Cape Verde
6	Swaziland
7	Gabon
8	Seychelles
9	South Africa
10	Ghana
	Tanzania
11	Nigeria
12	Kenya
	Equatorial Guinea

TOP

Rank	Country
13	Madagascar
14	Cameroon
15	Senegal
16	Zambia
17	Benin
18	Burkina Faso
19	Côte d' Ivoire
20	Chad
21	Congo, Rep.
	Gambia, The
22	Mali
23	Mozambique
24	Ethiopia
	Rwanda

MIDDLE

Rank	Country
25	Lesotho
26	Sierra Leone
27	Togo
28	Comoros
	Malawi
29	Uganda
30	Guinea
31	Eritrea
32	Congo, Dem. Rep.
33	Niger
34	Central Afr. Rep.
35	Burundi
36	Guinea-Bissau

BOTTOM

Wrap-up: Economic Productivity

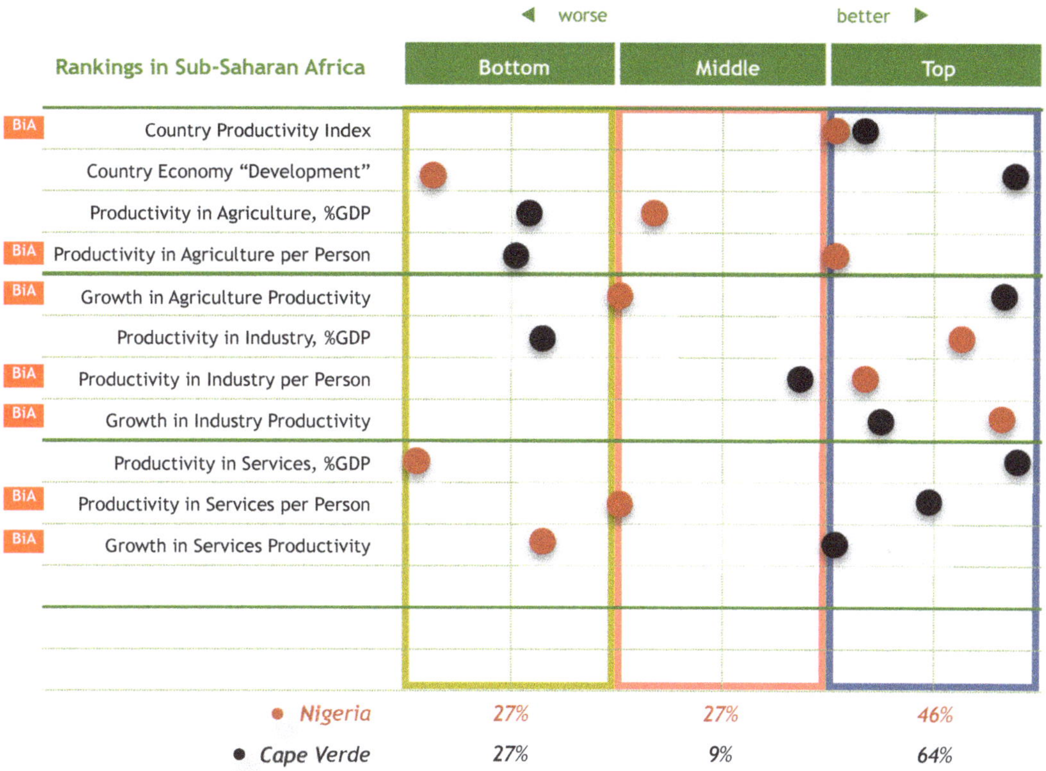

- Cape Verde, no. 1 in West Africa and no. 5 in Africa. Nigeria, no. 3 in West Africa and no. 11 in Africa.
- Nigeria has most of the indicators in the top segment (46%), as does Cape Verde (64%).
- Indeed, Nigeria performs well in the agriculture sector, but it needs to grow that productivity with greater urgency.
- In industry Nigeria is in top shape. However, near 92% of this is made up of oil extraction and exports, while manufacturing constitutes the remaining 8%.
- It is in services that Nigeria plunges. It doesn't manage to leave the bottom section. Cape Verde, by contrast, is in its element there.

10. Govt. Earnings & Spending

cutting the coat, or growing the cloth?

Primer

The indices in this section involve the principal financial balances of the government. It is an area of macro-economic study that often appears confusing, but its overall intents and significance may be reasonably understood without complication.

Government Earnings

Governments generally get their income from taxes and duties on goods and services produced within their shores or acquired via importation from the outside. Usually, it may be safely assumed that this is the case, even though there might be instances where a government derives revenue directly from the goods and services it itself produces (e.g., nationalized industries and businesses). However, the more common trend is for "profit-focused" corporations to be run by the private sector, while the public sector generally renders those services that would otherwise generate profit only at inappropriately great cost to the end users (health, roads, and basic education, for example). Still, these services would not be significant earners of revenue for government, and government earnings would still largely be made up of taxes and duties of diverse sorts.

Government Spending

Instead, those "unappealing" services borne by the government would often comprise government expenditure. Government spending would then often be services such as health mentioned above, and other infrastructure which only organizations the size and position of governments can provide: education, law & order establishments (security, police, armed forces, etc), and capital projects such as roads, and so on. Rather than a direct revenue-yielding expenditure, these outlays are often indirect incentives that boost aggregate demand (the consumer's purchase of products and services) by providing an enabling environment for the country's economic sectors to churn out products and services that its inhabitants would be financially enabled to purchase. That would usually be because those investments have led to job creation and increase in the inhabitants' purchasing power, and so on, in a production cycle (investment leading to production leading to consumption, and over again, in a continuity).

Fiscal Deficit/Surplus

Also known as Fiscal Balance and Budget Deficit/Surplus. This is the left-over after government spending is deducted from its earnings, and is an important indicator of government performance.

The deficit or surplus sometimes expresses a government's ability to function on its own resources. Here, the desirable state is a surplus, but a deficit is permissible and, indeed, preferable, if it is due to government investment that will eventually drive domestic consumption (residents' purchase of goods and services) and, consequently, domestic production (provision by industry of those goods and services to meet rising demand).

The size of a surplus or deficit is often expressed as a portion of GDP. In addition, we have expressed it here as surplus/deficit per inhabitant of population in order to develop a picture of the level of government spending per inhabitant and its potential impact on their quality of life, and so qualify the deficit/surplus more accurately.

Grants

Here, too, we have chosen the option of including grants – where present – as part of government revenue (they usually come in the shape of non-interest bearing foreign aid), rather than leaving them out. Our reasoning being that, in appraising a government's fiscal performance and discipline, the government should be assessed on the basis of all income at its disposal; and more so when such incomes come at no financial cost. (The volume of these grants is considered in more detail in chapter 13, "Self-Reliance".)

Which: deficit or surplus?

There isn't an immediate good or bad, desirable or undesirable, interpretation to deficits and surpluses; it all depends on the reasons and purposes behind the shortfall or surplus. Deficits are indeed very good, as explained above, when they indicate a rise in spending by government that spurs on individual and industry spending or investment, because it thereby leads to economic growth. At the same time, though, a deficit might be evocative of financial recklessness.

Debt Service

The matter of foreign debt is treated more exhaustively in chapter 8, "Self-Reliance". Here, we attempt to express the ability of the economies to sustain their debt levels, with respect to their earning power. Debt levels are usually expressed as percentages of GDP (to assess their size in relation to the overall economy) and as percentages of exports (to assess the ability of the country to offset these foreign debts, since exports are the main source of foreign currency earnings).

We have, instead, chosen to express debt service here as a percentage of GNI (Gross National Income, formerly GNP: Gross National Product), because this would involve both GDP and export earnings, and would also take into account other sources of a country's income besides those two, namely incomes such as remittances and investment earnings from abroad. Our idea being to evaluate the country's debt service levels by comparing it to the economy's total earnings, as it were.

Current Account Balance

Current Account Balance is surplus or deficit that arises from the external trade transactions involving a country's residents interacting with non-residents. It is the part of "Balance of Payments" record of transactions that does not involve capital projects and investments across borders (e.g., Foreign Direct Investment, addressed in chapter 14). It rather measures the ease or otherwise, with which an economy can generate needed revenue from external trade (imports and exports) in goods and services.

Again, a current account deficit is not necessarily a malaise, but it has to be kept within appropriate limits, if a deficit is inevitable. Oil exporters, for example, will generally have stronger current account balances than their non-oil counterparts. It becomes incumbent on them to use these accumulated savings effectively.

Build-up of Debt Service and GNI

By tying down both parameters to 100 in a common year (2000 here) and depicting their progress thereafter according to the actual rates of growth recorded during the subsequent years (here, 2001 to 2006), we provide an illustration of the appropriateness or otherwise of the country's pace of debt accumulation, and whether this debt has been transformed into revenue-yielding or value-generating assets and operations. The wider the distance between levels of debt service and levels of GNI build-up, the greater the possibility that debt accumulation has been reckless or ill-advised. At the same time, though, a large gulf might be the result of a deliberate – even if, audacious – move by the country to wipe debt off its books.

Sources of Primary Data: AfDB, IMF, World Bank

Charts

Tables

1997-2002; 2003-2006; 2007-2008:
- *self-comparison to preceding period;*
- *performance in S-Saharan Africa;*
- *performance in West Africa;*
- *performance among oil-exporters;*

for:

Fiscal Deficit & Surplus as % of GDP

Fiscal Deficit & Surplus per Person ($PPP)

Govt. Earnings as % of GDP

Govt. Earnings per Person ($PPP)

Current Account Balance as % of GDP

2003-2006; 2007-2008:
- *self-comparison to preceding period;*
- *performance in S-Saharan Africa;*
- *performance in West Africa;*
- *performance among oil-exporters;*

for:

Growth in Govt. Earnings per Person

1999-2002; 2003-2006:
- *self-comparison to preceding period;*
- *performance in S-Saharan Africa;*
- *performance in West Africa;*
- *performance among oil-exporters;*

for:

Debt Service as % of GNI

- Govt. Earnings as % of GDP in Sub-Saharan Africa during 2003-06: Rankings
- Govt. Earnings per Person ($PPP) in Sub-Saharan Africa during 2003-06: Rankings
- Growth in Govt. Earnings per Person in Sub-Saharan Africa during 2003-06: Rankings
- Gap between GNI and Debt Service Build-up Levels by 2006 in West Africa and among Africa's Oil Exporters: 2000=100
- **Govt. Earnings & Spending Rankings: 2003-06**

10.1 Fiscal Deficit & Surplus as % of GDP

is it good news, or bad?

	97-02	03-06	07-08
Self-comparison to Preceding Period		▲	▼
Performance in Sub-Saharan Africa	▲	▲	▲
Performance in West Africa	▲	▲	▲
	Benin	Niger	Sierra Leone
	Senegal	Mali	**Nigeria**
	Côte d'Ivoire	**Nigeria**	Liberia
	Nigeria	Burkina Faso	Guinea
	Togo	Liberia	Côte d'Ivoire
	Guinea	Sierra Leone	Gambia, The
	Mali	Togo	Benin
	Burkina Faso	Benin	Niger
	Niger	Côte d'Ivoire	Togo
	Gambia, The	Senegal	Cape Verde
	Ghana	Ghana	Mali
	Sierra Leone	Guinea	Guinea-Bissau
	Cape Verde	Cape Verde	Senegal
	Guinea-Bissau	Gambia, The	Burkina Faso
	Liberia	Guinea-Bissau	Ghana

Even though Nigeria's balance during 07-08 is a step-down from the preceding years', it still outperformed almost all of West Africa during the 11 years from 1997.

	97-02	03-06	07-08
Performance among Oil-Exporters	▼	▼	▼
	Equatorial Guinea	Equatorial Guinea	Equatorial Guinea
	Gabon	Cameroon	Congo, Rep.
	Cameroon	Congo, Rep.	Gabon
	Côte d'Ivoire	Gabon	Angola
	Nigeria	**Nigeria**	**Nigeria**
	Chad	Angola	Cameroon
	Congo, Rep.	Chad	Chad
	Angola	Côte d'Ivoire	Côte d'Ivoire

Primary Data: IMF

Something missing, though, when ranked alongside other oil exporters. Nigeria didn't outperform the majority. Rather, it was sat rigidly in the bottom half.

▲	"movement towards surplus" OR "above average"
▼	"movement towards deficit" OR "below average"
◁▷	no change *or* average

10.1

Fiscal Deficit/Surplus in West Africa (% GDP) during 03/06

10.2

Fiscal Deficit/Surplus in West Africa (% GDP) during 07/08

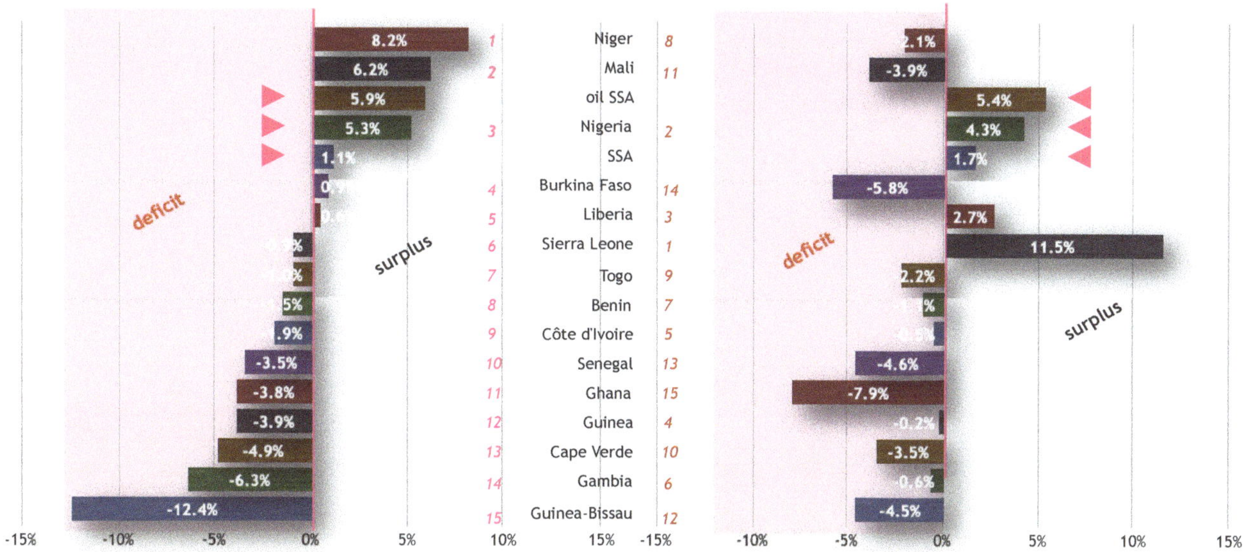

A third of West Africa (5 countries) spent within their means in 03/06. By 07/08, they dropped to 3. Nigeria & Liberia were the only countries running a surplus during both periods.

On the average, across Africa, most govts seemed to exercise fiscal discipline, with surpluses of about 1.1% and 1.7% during 03-06 and 07-08, respectively.

The oil countries, not unexpectedly, ran a high surplus.

10.3

Fiscal Deficit/Surplus in Nigeria and Sub-Saharan Africa (% GDP) from 1997 to 2008

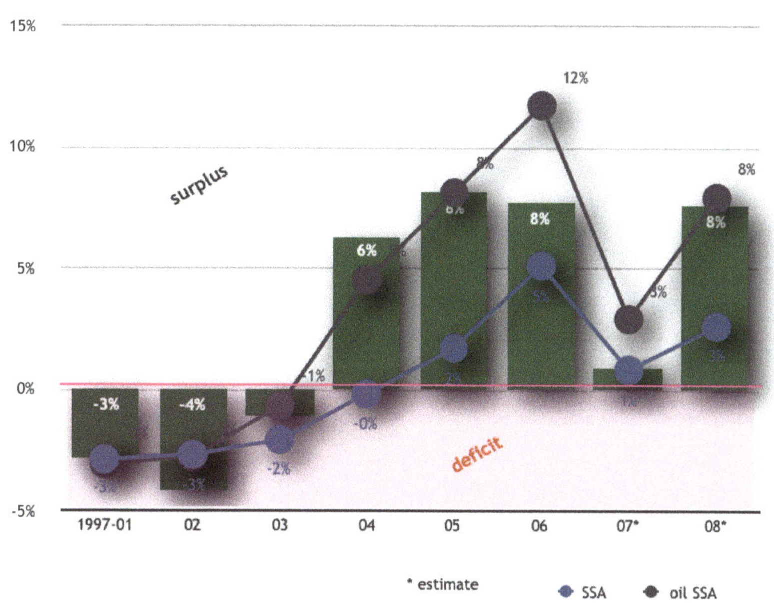

In an interesting group-play, all of Africa seemed to follow an identical trajectory during 1997-2008: deficits in 97-03, surpluses in 04 to 08, but with a big dip in 07.

It is likely this reflects the movement of commodity prices in the international market, particularly in oil and agricultural products.

10.2 Fiscal Deficit & Surplus per Person ($PPP)

it's all he's been left with

	97-02	03-06	07-08
Self-comparison to Preceding Period		▲	▼
Performance in Sub-Saharan Africa	▲	▲	▲
Performance in West Africa	▲	▲	▲
	Benin	**Nigeria**	**Nigeria**
	Senegal	Mali	Sierra Leone
	Togo	Niger	Liberia
	Niger	Burkina Faso	Guinea
	Côte d'Ivoire	Liberia	Côte d'Ivoire
	Mali	Sierra Leone	Gambia, The
	Nigeria	Togo	Niger
	Guinea	Benin	Benin
	Burkina Faso	Côte d'Ivoire	Togo
	Sierra Leone	Guinea	Guinea-Bissau
	Gambia, The	Ghana	Mali
	Guinea-Bissau	Senegal	Burkina Faso
	Ghana	Guinea-Bissau	Senegal
	Cape Verde	Gambia, The	Ghana
	Liberia	Cape Verde	Cape Verde
Performance among Oil-Exporters	▼	▼	▼
	Equatorial Guinea	Equatorial Guinea	Equatorial Guinea
	Gabon	Gabon	Gabon
	Cameroon	Congo, Rep.	Congo, Rep.
	Côte d'Ivoire	Cameroon	Angola
	Nigeria	Angola	**Nigeria**
	Chad	**Nigeria**	Cameroon
	Congo, Rep.	Chad	Chad
	Angola	Côte d'Ivoire	Côte d'Ivoire

ta: IMF

▲	"movement towards surplus" OR "above average"
▼	"movement towards deficit" OR "below average"
◁▷	no change *or* average

When fiscal balance is expressed as $ per inhabitant, the same picture plays out, as did for balance expressed as % of GDP.

Nigeria better than most of West Africa, but not as good as its fellow oil exporters, and not keeping up in 07-08 with the pre-07 levels.

+1-800-help

Still don't get how govt deficit can be a good thing 😳

Projects like large infrastructure (roads, railways, power plants, etc) are not attractive — and sometimes just too big — for the private sector. Govt spends to build them, without making a "profit". But the new infrastructure spurs new businesses and improves efficiency at many levels, leading to increase in economic activity and GDP. Even if the govt books are in the red, the resulting growths in GDP, wages, standard of living, etc, more than compensate.

10.4

Fiscal Deficit/Surplus per Person in West Africa ($PPP) during 03/06

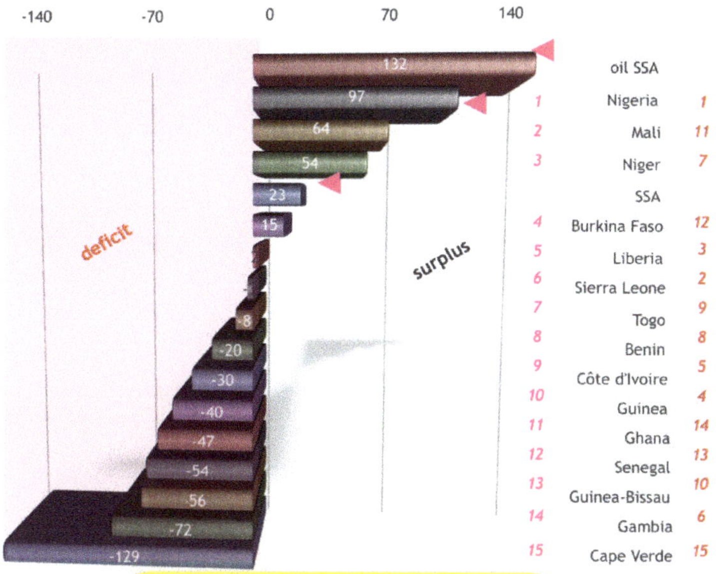

10.5

Fiscal Deficit/Surplus per Person in West Africa ($PPP) during 07/08

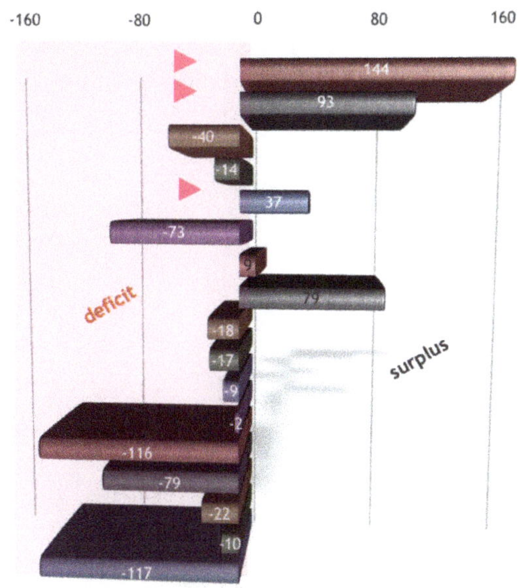

This time, fewer than 5 countries in West Africa spent within their means.

Across Africa, on average, govts ended up with a surplus of $23 and $37 per person in 03-06 and 07-08 respectively.

+1-800-help

Is that the same reasoning for foreign debt?

Essentially.

But remember, it all depends on how effectively the govt. deploys these borrowed funds, or how strategically it spends on infrastructure.

And don't forget to read the chapter intro, a lot of these issues are addressed there.

The highest surpluses were registered by the oil economies during both periods.

Again, during the years between 1997 & 2008, Nigeria & most of Africa followed the same trajectory of deficit, surplus, slump but still surplus, then recovery in surplus again.

10.6

Fiscal Deficit/Surplus per Person in Nigeria and Sub-Saharan Africa ($PPP) from 1997 to 2008

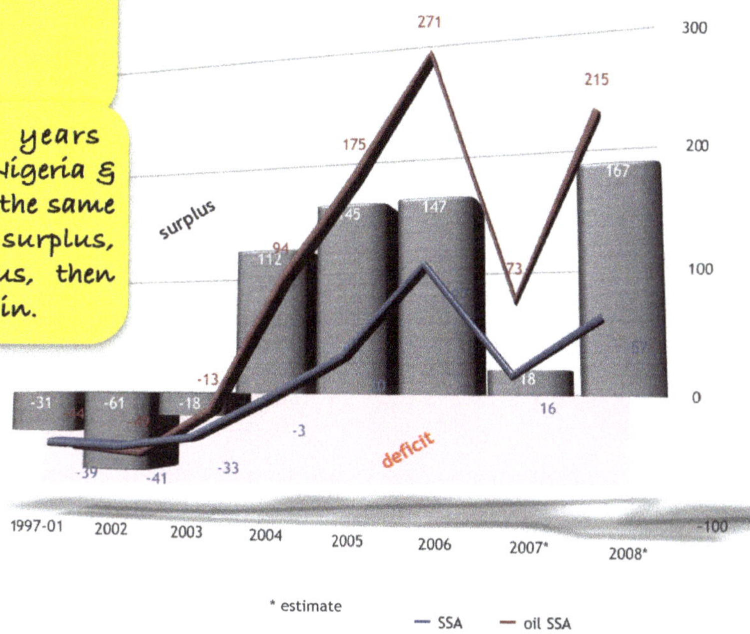

10.3 Govt. Earnings as % of GDP

there lies your fortune

	97-02	03-06	07-08
Self-comparison to Preceding Period		▲	▼
Performance in Sub-Saharan Africa	▼	▼	▼
Performance in West Africa	▲	▲	▼
	Cape Verde	Liberia	Liberia
	Gambia, The	Gambia, The	Guinea-Bissau
	Guinea-Bissau	Cape Verde	Gambia, The
	Ghana	Ghana	Cape Verde
	Nigeria	Guinea-Bissau	Ghana
	Senegal	**Nigeria**	Senegal
	Côte d'Ivoire	Senegal	Benin
	Benin	Mali	Côte d'Ivoire
	Sierra Leone	Benin	Mali
	Togo	Sierra Leone	Togo
	Mali	Togo	**Nigeria**
	Burkina Faso	Côte d'Ivoire	Burkina Faso
	Guinea	Burkina Faso	Niger
	Niger	Niger	Sierra Leone
	Liberia	Guinea	Guinea

Not good news about Nigeria's govt. receipts. If the country kept up surpluses (as the previous sections hold) it must be that it tightened its spending, since it didn't grow revenue.

	97-02	03-06	07-08
Performance among Oil-Exporters	▼	▼	▼
	Angola	Angola	Congo, Rep.
	Gabon	Equatorial Guinea	Equatorial Guinea
	Congo, Rep.	Congo, Rep.	Angola
	Equatorial Guinea	Gabon	Gabon
	Nigeria	**Nigeria**	Chad
	Côte d'Ivoire	Cameroon	Côte d'Ivoire
	Cameroon	Côte d'Ivoire	Cameroon
	Chad	Chad	**Nigeria**

Indeed, Nigeria's revenue, as a proportion of its economy size, fell to below West Africa and oil exporters levels.

Primary Data: IMF

▲	increased earnings *or* above average
▼	decreased earnings *or* below average
◁▷	no change *or* average

10.7

Govt. Earnings as % of GDP in West Africa during 2003/06

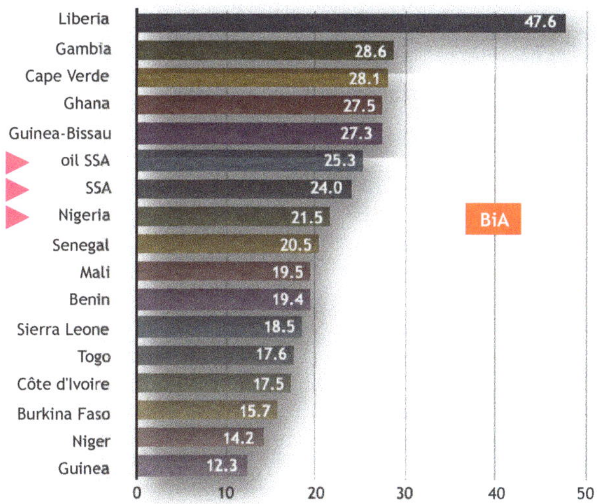

10.8

Govt. Earnings as % of GDP in Nigeria and Sub-Saharan Africa from 1997 to 2008

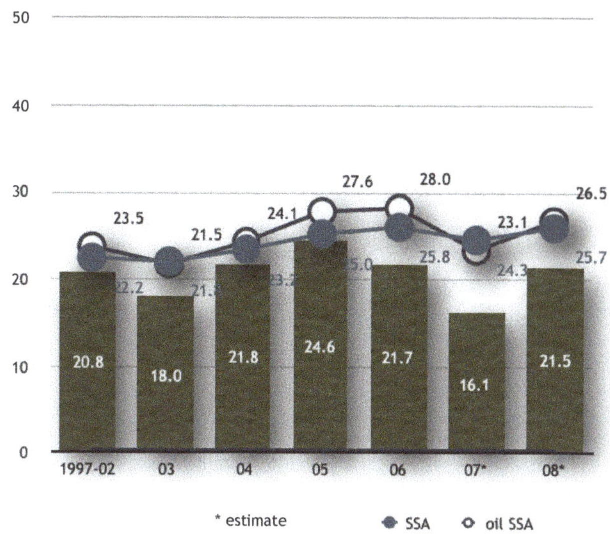

In the end, it sat bang in the middle of Sub-Saharan Africa.

This depleting revenue might have been due to any number of factors, including a possible lax regime of duties and tax collection.

Govt. Earnings as % of GDP in Sub-Saharan Africa during 2003-06: Rankings

Rank	Country	Rank	Country	Rank	Country
1	Lesotho	15	Guinea-Bissau	29	Sierra Leone
2	Seychelles	16	Malawi	30	Togo
3	Botswana	17	Rwanda	31	Cameroon
4	Swaziland	18	South Africa	32	Côte d' Ivoire
5	Namibia	19	Ethiopia	33	Congo, Dem. Rep.
6	Eritrea	20	Nigeria	34	Comoros
7	Angola	21	Kenya	35	Burkina Faso
8	Burundi	22	Uganda	36	Chad
9	Equatorial Guinea	23	Senegal	37	Tanzania
10	Congo, Rep.	24	Mauritius	38	Niger
11	Gabon	25	Mozambique	39	Madagascar
12	Gambia, The	26	Mali	40	Guinea
13	Cape Verde	27	Benin	41	Central Afr. Rep.
14	Ghana	28	Zambia		
TOP		MIDDLE		BOTTOM	

10.4 Govt. Earnings per Person ($PPP)

trickles, or pouring rain?

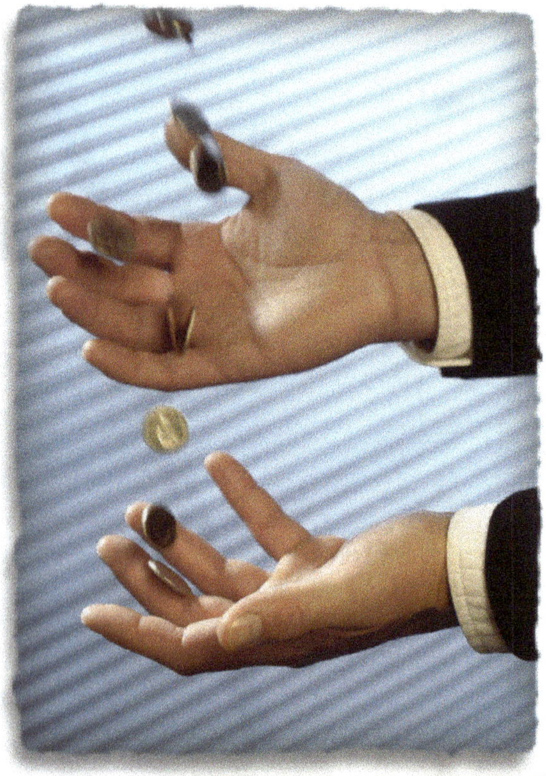

	97-02	03-06	07-08
Self-comparison to Preceding Period		▲	▲
Performance in Sub-Saharan Africa	▼	▼	▼
Performance in West Africa	▲	▲	▲
	Cape Verde	Cape Verde	Cape Verde
	Côte d'Ivoire	**Nigeria**	Gambia, The
	Gambia, The	Ghana	**Nigeria**
	Nigeria	Gambia, The	Ghana
	Senegal	Senegal	Senegal
	Benin	Côte d'Ivoire	Côte d'Ivoire
	Ghana	Benin	Benin
	Burkina Faso	Mali	Burkina Faso
	Guinea-Bissau	Burkina Faso	Mali
	Guinea	Liberia	Liberia
	Mali	Togo	Guinea-Bissau
	Togo	Guinea	Togo
	Niger	Guinea-Bissau	Guinea
	Sierra Leone	Sierra Leone	Niger
	Liberia	Niger	Sierra Leone
Performance among Oil-Exporters	▼	▼	▼
	Gabon	Equatorial Guinea	Equatorial Guinea
	Angola	Gabon	Gabon
	Equatorial Guinea	Angola	Angola
	Congo, Rep.	Congo, Rep.	Congo, Rep.
	Côte d'Ivoire	**Nigeria**	Cameroon
	Cameroon	Cameroon	**Nigeria**
	Nigeria	Côte d'Ivoire	Chad
	Chad	Chad	Côte d'Ivoire

Same verdict when assessed in money units: decline in Nigeria govt. earnings, although it was one of the better performers in West Africa. It did worse than most of the wider continent.

Nigeria ended up worse than the oil group, just as it did when earnings was measured in %GDP terms.

Primary Data: IMF

▲	increased earnings *or* above average
▼	decreased earnings *or* below average
◁▷	no change *or* average

10.9

Govt. Earnings per Person ($PPP) in West Africa during 2003/06

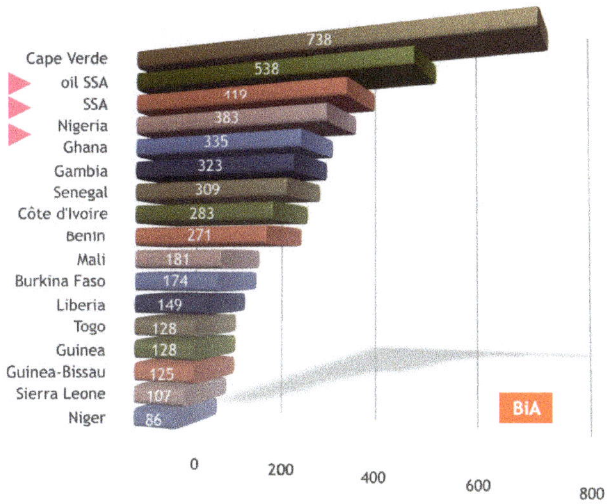

10.10

Govt. Earnings per Person ($PPP) in Nigeria and Sub-Saharan Africa from 1997 to 2008

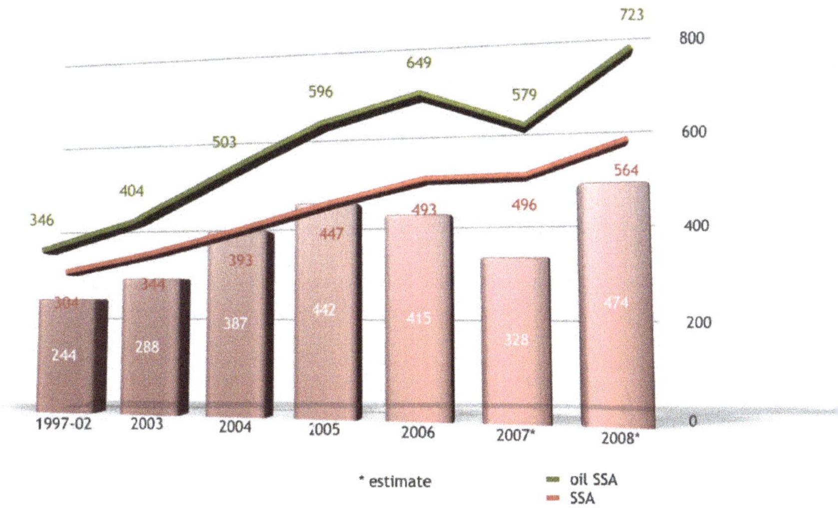

Interesting to see that earnings per person isn't hampered by Nigeria's large population. Indeed, the country ranks higher than when assessed by proportion of GDP.

Yet, it continued below the SSA & oilSSA levels, just as it did on the %GDP scale. Quite likely means that Nigeria isn't pulling its weight: chose to crawl rather than sprint.

A top-third finish for Nigeria within Sub-Saharan Africa, despite its below-average performance on the continent.

Only shows that a few countries on the continent led the pack by such a distance that their combined results put more than half the continent in the shade.

Seychelles: $7,600; Gabon: $4,000; Congo Rep: $1,300; Cape Verde: $740; Nigeria: $380. The first 10 countries pulled near 80% of the continent's total earnings per person.

Govt. Earnings per Person ($PPP) in Sub-Saharan Africa during 2003-06: Rankings

Rank	Country	Rank	Country	Rank	Country
1	Seychelles	15	Ghana	29	Uganda
2	Botswana	16	Eritrea	30	Tanzania
3	Equatorial Guinea	17	Gambia, The	31	Mozambique
4	Gabon	18	Senegal	32	Ethiopia
5	South Africa	19	Kenya	33	Togo
6	Mauritius	20	Côte d' Ivoire	34	Guinea
7	Swaziland	21	Benin	35	Burundi
8	Namibia	22	Chad	36	Guinea-Bissau
9	Angola	23	Zambia	37	Madagascar
10	Congo, Rep.	24	Rwanda	38	Sierra Leone
11	Lesotho	25	Mali	39	Niger
12	Cape Verde	26	Comoros	40	Central Afr. Rep.
13	Nigeria	27	Burkina Faso	41	Congo, Dem. Rep.
14	Cameroon	28	Malawi		
TOP		MIDDLE		BOTTOM	

10.5 Govt. Earnings & Spending as % of GDP

wayward cash?

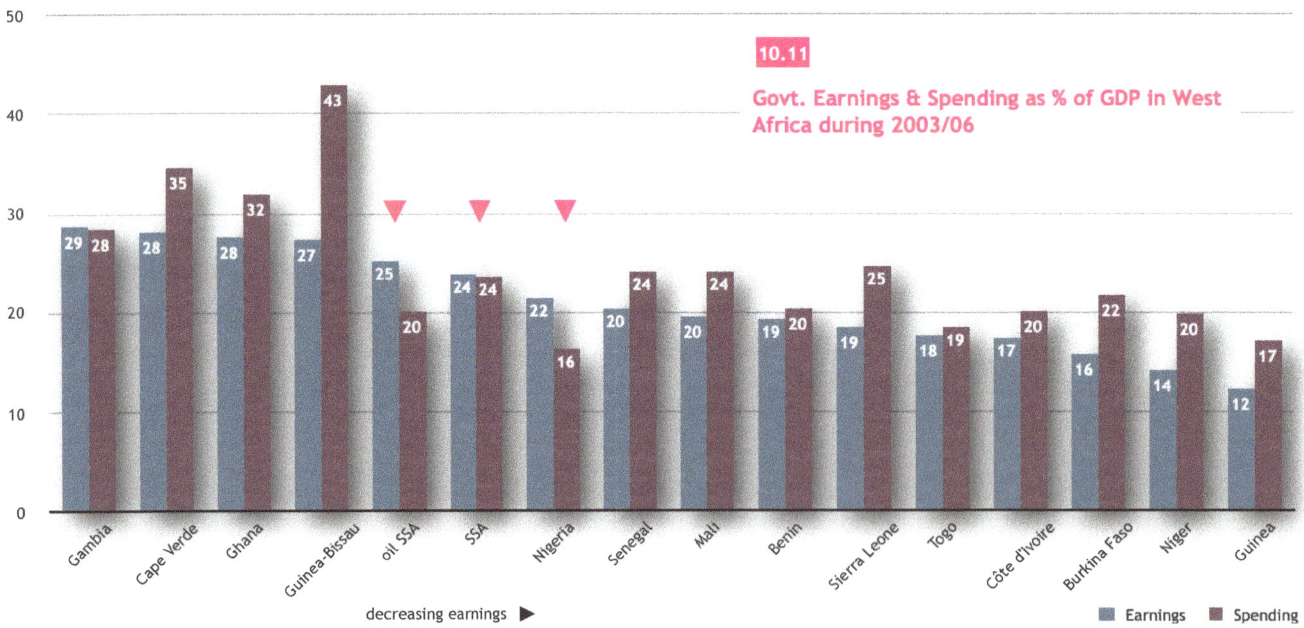

10.11

Govt. Earnings & Spending as % of GDP in West Africa during 2003/06

Primary Data: IMF

Note: figures in this section might differ slightly from those in the preceding ones. Data round-off at source, besides possible inaccuracies, might be to blame. But they do not at all alter the conclusions significantly.

As noted in the intro, not every case of deficit is down to reckless or inopportune spending. But we may still observe the countries where spending overshot earnings.

Only a very few in West Africa ran a surplus. But, while Guinea-Bissau's & Côte d'Ivoire's deficits, for example, did not return economic growth, Cape Verde's did. (See chap. 8)

10.6 Govt. Earnings & Spending per Person ($PPP)

guess which is the heavier

10.12

Govt. Earnings & Spending per Person ($PPP) in West Africa during 2003/06

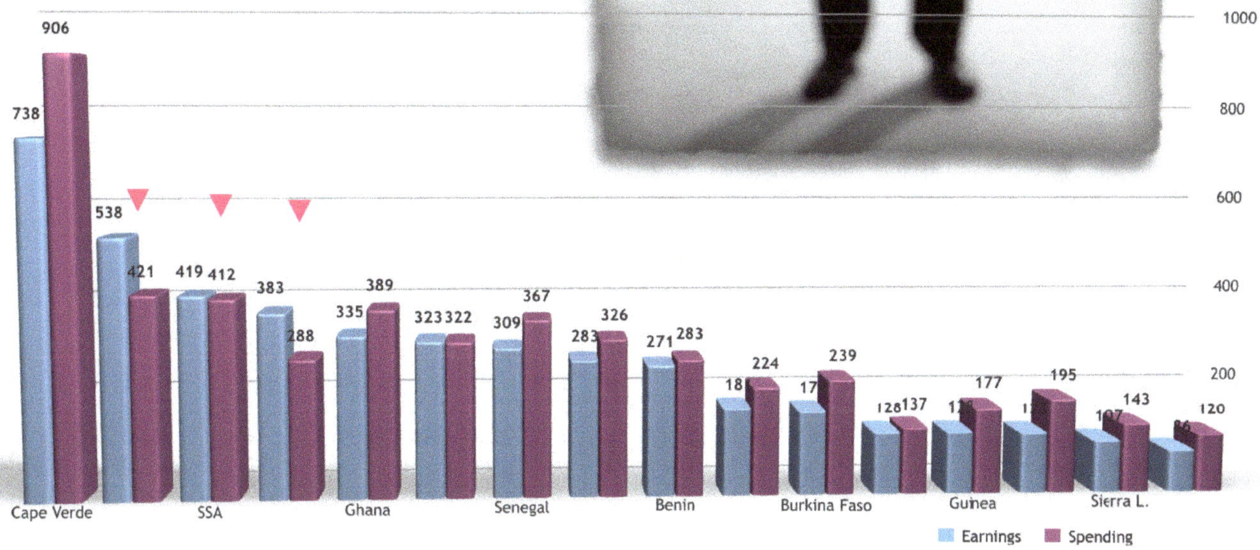

decreasing earnings ▶

Primary Data: IMF

An almost replica picture when earnings & spending are seen as $ per inhabitant. Sierra Leone, Cape Verde & Burkina Faso were the top converters of deficit into economic growth.

10.7 Growth in Govt. Earnings per Person

outgrown the tape measure, hopefully

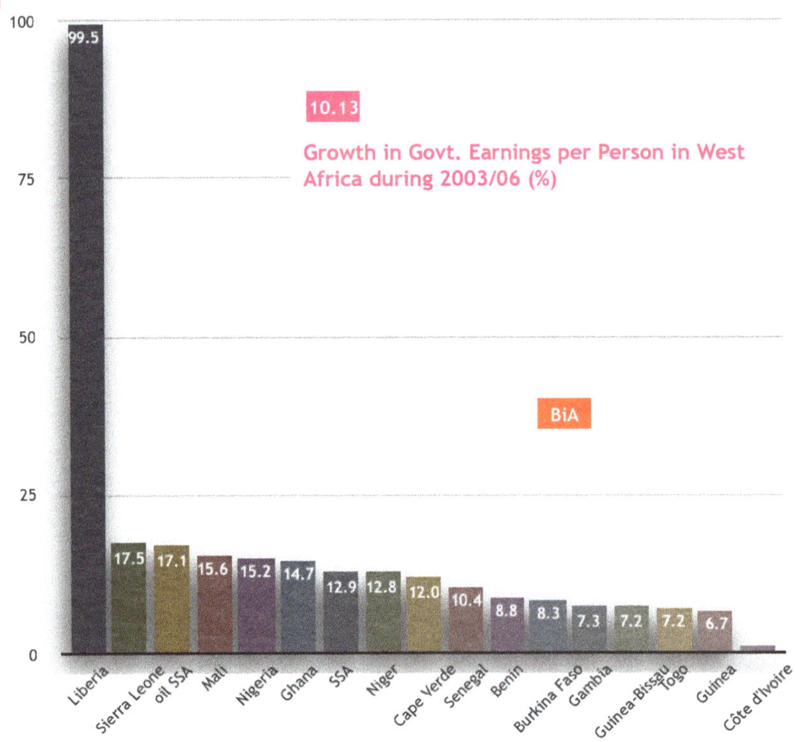

10.13

Growth in Govt. Earnings per Person in West Africa during 2003/06 (%)

	03-06	07-08
Self-comparison to Preceding Period		▼
Performance in Sub-Saharan Africa	▲	▲

Performance in West Africa	03-06 ▲	07-08 ▲
	Liberia	Guinea-Bissau
	Sierra Leone	Gambia, The
	Mali	**Nigeria**
	Nigeria	Ghana
	Ghana	Burkina Faso
	Niger	Côte d'Ivoire
	Cape Verde	Benin
	Senegal	Liberia
	Benin	Niger
	Burkina Faso	Guinea
	Gambia, The	Togo
	Guinea-Bissau	Senegal
	Togo	Cape Verde
	Guinea	Mali
	Côte d'Ivoire	Sierra Leone

Performance among Oil-Exporters	03-06 ▼	07-08 ▲
	Equatorial Guinea	**Nigeria**
	Chad	Chad
	Congo, Rep.	Côte d'Ivoire
	Angola	Angola
	Nigeria	Cameroon
	Cameroon	Congo, Rep.
	Côte d'Ivoire	Equatorial Guinea
	Gabon	Gabon

Primary Data: IMF

▲	improved *or* better than average
▼	worsened *or* worse than average
◁▷	no change *or* average

Liberia towers way above everybody else, understandably: reflects the in-pouring of vital economic aid after years of brutal civil war that razed the country to the ground.

Nigeria's growth rate was also in the higher bracket within West Africa, even if it wasn't as determined.

The country ends up in the top-third within the continent, reflecting the relative advantage the Nigeria govt. had with regard to financial resources available and at its disposal.

Growth in Govt. Earnings per Person in Sub-Saharan Africa during 2003-06: Rankings

Rank	Country	Rank	Country	Rank	Country
1	Equatorial Guinea	15	Madagascar	29	Benin
2	Chad	16	Ethiopia	30	Burkina Faso
3	Congo, Dem. Rep.	17	Malawi	31	Seychelles
4	Mozambique	18	Tanzania	32	Gambia, The
5	Congo, Rep.	19	Cameroon	33	Guinea-Bissau
6	Swaziland	20	Niger	34	Togo
7	Burundi	21	Cape Verde	35	Kenya
8	Sierra Leone	22	South Africa	36	Guinea
9	Angola	23	Rwanda	37	Zambia
10	Botswana	24	Namibia	38	Comoros
11	Mali	25	Senegal	39	Côte d' Ivoire
12	Nigeria	26	Mauritius	40	Gabon
13	Lesotho	27	Central Afr. Rep.	41	Eritrea
14	Ghana	28	Uganda		
TOP		MIDDLE		BOTTOM	

10.8 Build-up in Govt. Earnings & Spending

did they get their policies confused?

10.14

Build-up in Govt. Earnings & Spending in Nigeria and Sub-Saharan Africa from 2002 to 2008

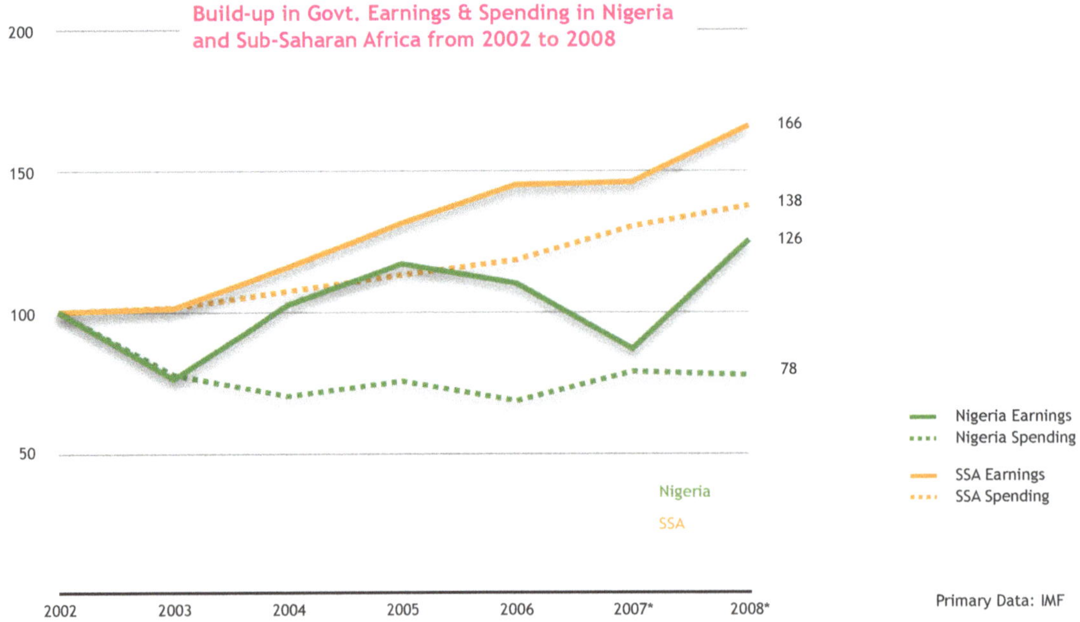

Primary Data: IMF

Sub-Saharan Africa made a steady climb of its earnings and its spending, almost in tandem, but with a widening surplus, from 2002 to 2008.

Nigeria's progress was an effective climb in earnings build-up, but through some twists and turns. Its spending didn't grow apace, but fell, also thereby widening its surplus.

So, 2 different roads to an end-surplus: Africa steadily spent, while growing earnings at the same time. Nigeria cut spending and grew earnings slower than the continent.

The oil-exporters' travel path is strikingly similar to Nigeria's, with the difference that their cut in spending was temporary, and their growth of earnings more resolute.

10.15

Build-up in Govt. Earnings & Spending in Nigeria and Oil Exporters in Sub-Saharan Africa from 2002 to 2008

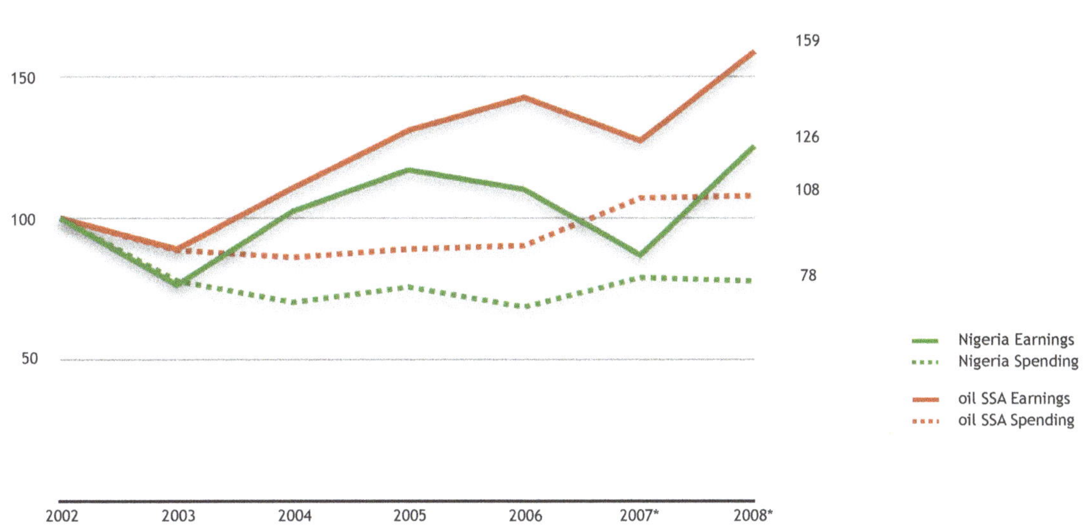

* estimate

10.9 Current Account Balance as % of GDP

that's what the machine said

Excellent, excellent, & excellent again, for Nigeria. But — to spoil the party — an all too easy performance, built on the straightforward trade in oil export.

Within the oil bloc, Nigeria makes it into the top half, yet you can't help the feeling, deep inside, that it could have done better.

	97-02	03-06	07-08
Self-comparison to Preceding Period		▲	▲
Performance in Sub-Saharan Africa	▲	▲	▲
Performance in West Africa	▲	▲	▲
	Côte d'Ivoire	**Nigeria**	**Nigeria**
	Nigeria	Côte d'Ivoire	Guinea-Bissau
	Gambia, The	Guinea-Bissau	Côte d'Ivoire
	Guinea	Togo	Sierra Leone
	Mauritania	Ghana	Benin
	Senegal	Guinea	Mali
	Ghana	Sierra Leone	Togo
	Sierra Leone	Benin	Ghana
	Niger	Mali	Guinea
	Togo	Senegal	Senegal
	Benin	Niger	Burkina Faso
	Mali	Cape Verde	Gambia, The
	Liberia	Gambia, The	Mauritania
	Burkina Faso	Burkina Faso	Niger
	Cape Verde	Liberia	Cape Verde
	Guinea-Bissau	Mauritania	Liberia
Performance among Oil-Exporters	▲	▲	▲
	Gabon	Gabon	Gabon
	Côte d'Ivoire	Angola	Angola
	Nigeria	Congo, Rep.	**Nigeria**
	Cameroon	**Nigeria**	Congo, Rep.
	Congo, Rep.	Côte d'Ivoire	Equatorial Guinea
	Angola	Cameroon	Côte d'Ivoire
	Sudan	Sudan	Cameroon
	Equatorial Guinea	Equatorial Guinea	Chad
	Chad	Chad	Sudan

Primary Data: IMF

▲	"movement towards surplus" OR "above average"
▼	"movement towards deficit" OR "below average"
◁▷	no change *or* average

10.16

Current Account Balance as % of GDP in West Africa during 2003/06

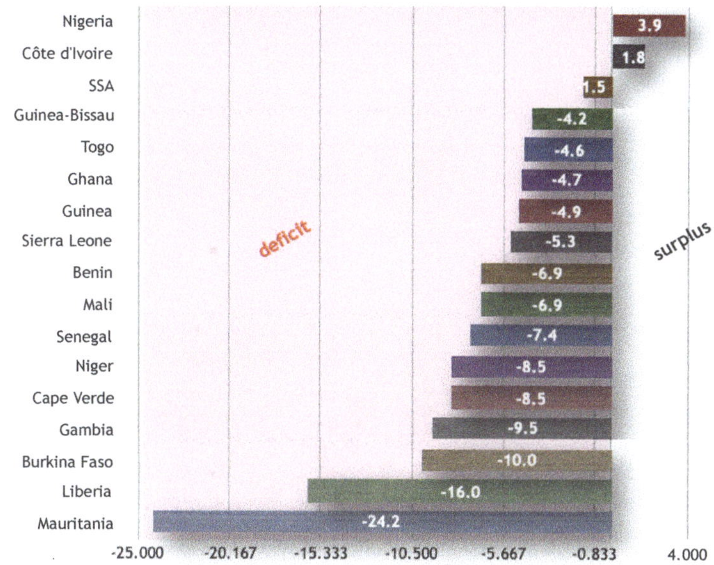

Only the oil producers in West Africa returned a current accounts surplus. The Africa average was a deficit. Oil trade seemed the only fast moving exports item during 03/06.

10.17

Current Account Balance as % of GDP in Nigeria and Sub-Saharan Africa from 1999 to 2010

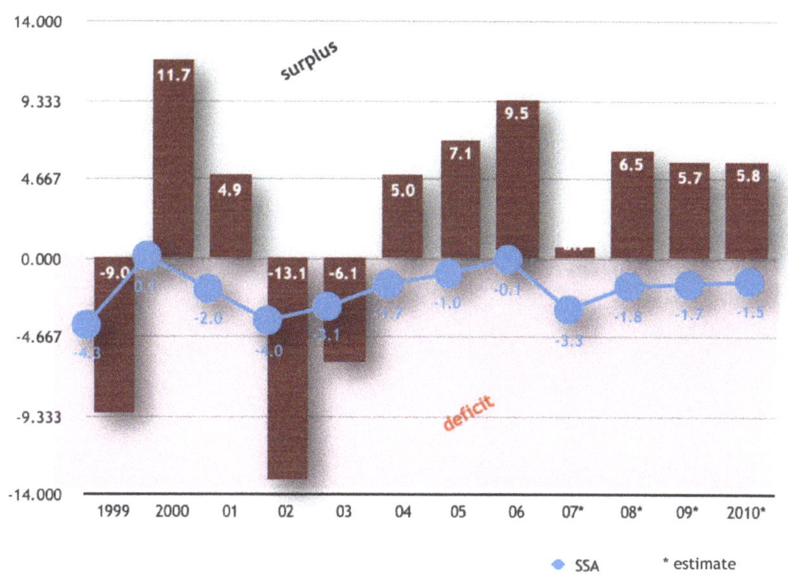

One can almost read the state of oil on the international market, from the current accounts balance of Nigeria: surplus means high price, deficit would imply an oil glut.

10.10 Debt Service as % of GNI

the debt trap

	99-02	03-06
Self-comparison to Preceding Period		▼
Performance in Sub-Saharan Africa	▼	▼
Performance in West Africa	▼	▼
	Niger	Togo
	Togo	Burkina Faso
	Burkina Faso	Côte d'Ivoire
	Benin	Niger
	Sierra Leone	Benin
	Mali	Mali
	Cape Verde	Sierra Leone
	Guinea	Ghana
	Ghana	Senegal
	Gambia, The	Cape Verde
	Senegal	Mauritania
	Nigeria	Guinea
	Mauritania	Gambia, The
	Côte d'Ivoire	**Nigeria**
	Guinea-Bissau	Guinea-Bissau
Performance among Oil-Exporters	▼	▼
	Equatorial Guinea	Equatorial Guinea
	Sudan	Côte d'Ivoire
	Chad	Chad
	Congo, Rep.	Sudan
	Cameroon	Cameroon
	Nigeria	Gabon
	Côte d'Ivoire	Congo, Rep.
	Gabon	**Nigeria**
	Angola	Angola

Nigeria went all out on debt repayment during 99-06, esp. during 03-06, when it outpaced all but one country in both West Africa & in the oil bloc, at rate of repayment.

Primary Data: AfDB, World Bank

▲	better = low debt service
▼	worse = high debt service
◁▷	no change *or* average

The wisdom behind such high outlays of debt repayment might only be glimpsed 2 or 3 years down the line for Nigeria.

It would have to be seen whether the commitment of such a high portion of GNI to settling otherwise mounting debt would free the economy up so that it flourishes with fresh vigor...

... or whether it would be a belt notch too far and stifle whatever energies might have been remaining for growth.

10.18

Debt Service as % of GNI in West Africa during 2003/06

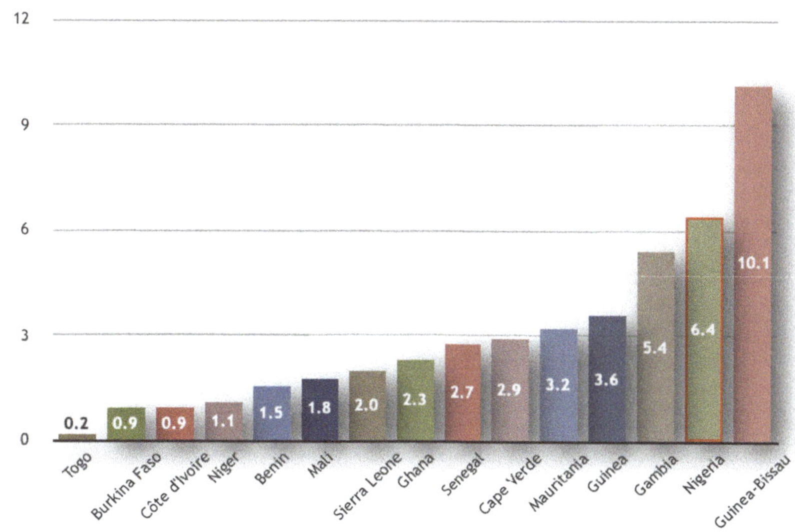

10.19

Debt Service as % of GNI in Nigeria from 1999 to 2006

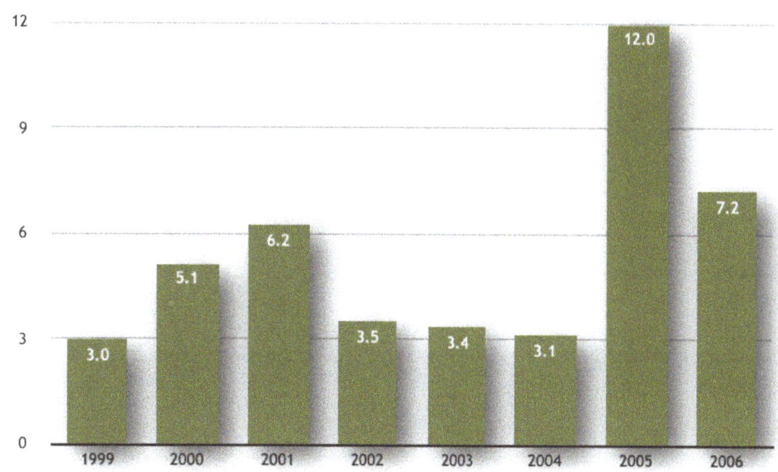

10.11 Build-up in Debt Service & GNI

let's see if they did their maths

Gap between *GNI* and *Debt Service* build-up levels by 2006: 2000=100
(negative = more debt service than GNI)

	West Africa	2006
1	Côte d'Ivoire	146
2	Liberia	126
3	Mali	123
4	Ghana	107
5	Togo	106
6	Senegal	99
7	Burkina Faso	91
8	Mauritania	86
9	Sierra Leone	76
10	Benin	57
11	Guinea	4
12	Cape Verde	4
13	Guinea-Bissau	-15
14	Gambia	-31
15	Niger	-89
16	Nigeria	-112

	oil exporters	2006
7	Equatorial Guinea	455
1	Angola	296
2	Gabon	165
8	Sudan	152
5	Côte d'Ivoire	146
9	Chad	113
3	Cameroon	112
4	Nigeria	-112
6	Congo, Rep.*	-615

* 2005

Republic of Congo's approach almost looks an aberration! The widest gap in the oil group, and the 2nd widest on the continent: Seychelles' was 860 percentage points.

Two contrasting approaches, waiting for the jury's verdict in another 4 years or so: Côte d'Ivoire sped up GNI growth faster than it did debt payback; Nigeria took the other road.

10.20

Build-up of Debt Service & GNI in Nigeria and Côte d'Ivoire from 2000 to 2006: 2000=100

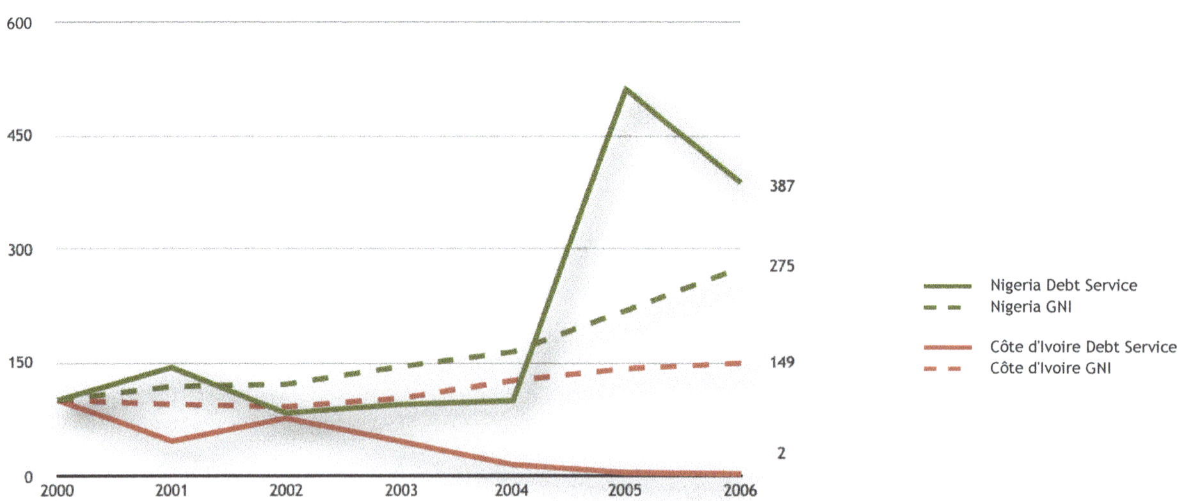

Primary Data: AfDB, World Bank

Leaders & Stragglers

were they the right moves?

In the end, the Nigeria govt. has maintained a level of discipline, compared to the rest of Africa. It tied with South Africa at 8th position. Only Ghana in West Africa did better.

Govt. Earnings & Spending Rankings: 2003-06

Rank	Country
1	Equatorial Guinea
2	Botswana
3	Swaziland
4	Angola
	Congo, Rep.
	Lesotho
5	Seychelles
6	Namibia
7	Ghana
8	**Nigeria**
	South Africa
9	Cape Verde
10	Burundi
11	Gabon

TOP

Rank	Country
12	Mauritius
13	Chad
	Mozambique
14	Gambia, The
	Malawi
15	Mali
16	Eritrea
17	Cameroon
	Rwanda
18	Senegal
19	Ethiopia
20	Kenya
	Sierra Leone
21	Benin
	Congo, Dem. Rep.

MIDDLE

Rank	Country
22	Uganda
23	Guinea-Bissau
24	Tanzania
25	Zambia
26	Côte d' Ivoire
	Madagascar
27	Burkina Faso
28	Niger
	Togo
29	Comoros
30	Central Afr. Rep.
31	Guinea

BOTTOM

Central Africa
East Africa
Southern Africa
West Africa

Wrap-up: Govt. Earnings & Spending

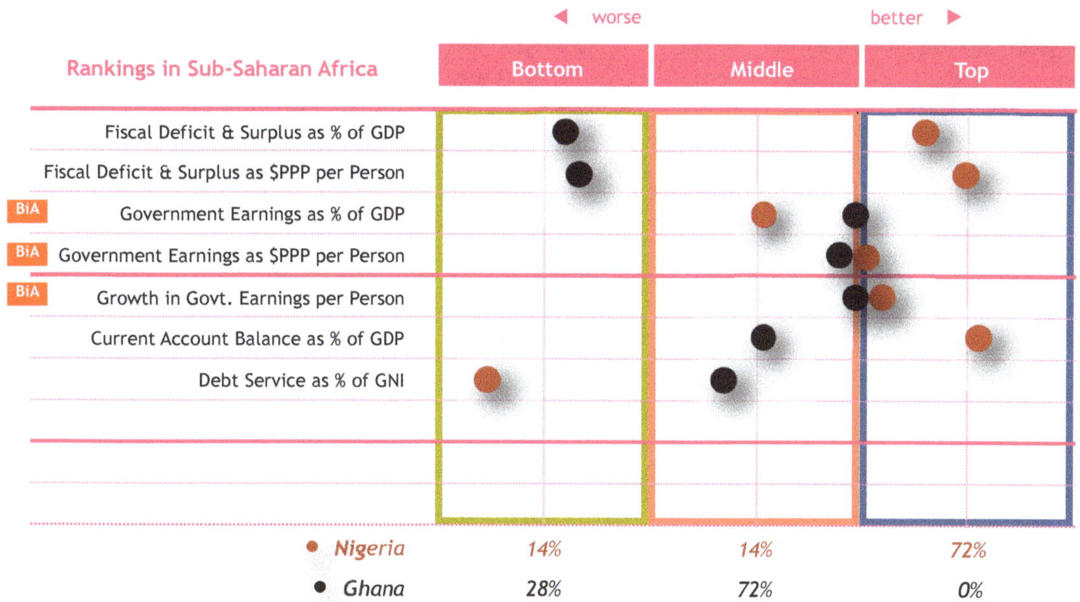

- Ghana just pips Nigeria to the best performer position in West Africa, coming 7th in Africa to Nigeria's 8th position.

- On the face of it, Nigeria does come off looking the prettier of the two countries; top bracket for 72% of the indicators to Ghana's 0%. Even though Ghana has 72% in the middle bracket to Nigeria's 14%, Nigeria still comes away second best.

- The reason for that is this: Nigeria excelled, but not in the right places. The fiscal balances looked good, but they were not the result of a push to grow earnings all round. It did better than Ghana in 2 of those 3 critical indicators, but not by the necessary margin. The gap in size of government earnings considered as %GDP for the 2 countries was too wide, so that it overshadowed the small margins to Nigeria's favor in the other 2 indicators.

11. Spending on Health

so that your staff will be working fit

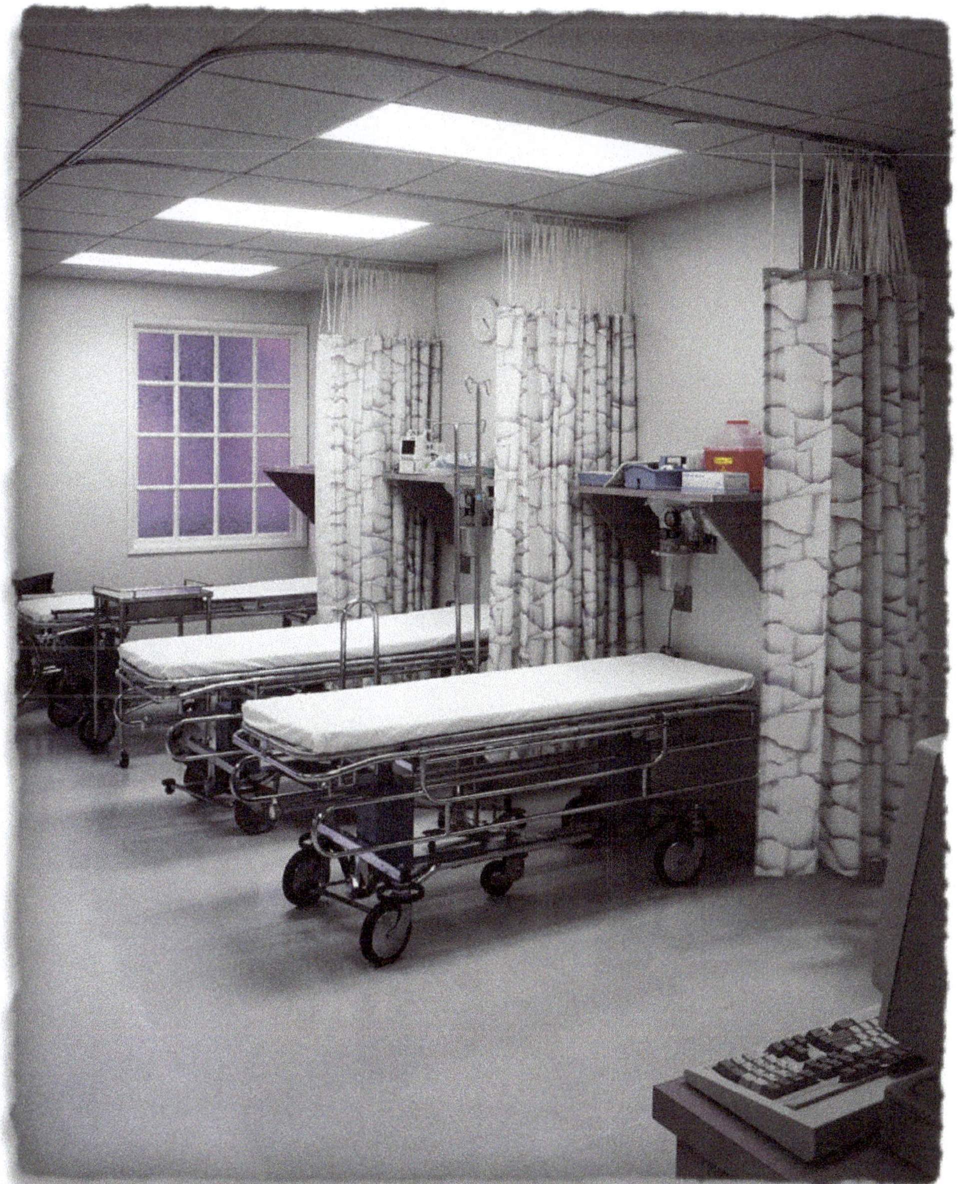

11.1 Total Spending (Govt. & Private) on Health as % GDP

11.2 Total Spending (G & P) on Health per Person

11.3 Build-up of Govt. & Private Spending on Health

11.4 Govt. Spending on Health as % of Total Govt. Spending

11.5 Out-of-Pocket Spending on Health as % of Total Health Spending

11.6 Out-of-Pocket Spending on Health as Part of Total Spending on Health per Person

11.7 Out-of-Pocket as % of Private Spending on Health

11.8 *Out-of-Pocket* & *Other Private* Spending on Health per Person

11.9 *Out-of-Pocket*, *Other Private* and *Govt.* Portions of Total Spending on Health per Person

Leaders & Stragglers

Wrap-up

Primer

It is easy to underestimate the impact of the domestic health sector on the economies of Africa. It isn't unlikely that man-hours lost to relatively common and treatable ailments (e.g., malaria) have not been properly quantified, and it isn't uncommon, either, to find that employees effectively are out of work – and so, rendered unproductive to the business and the economy – for considerable periods, compared to other economies, every work-year.

Much of that uncertainty is down to the paucity of accurate information. Health statistics of the working population isn't readily available, and because of the general state of health sectors and their service delivery, workers' efficiency may be hampered not only by direct illness to themselves, but illness to members of their family or household. The end-result is much the same: disruption to work and a dent on their effectiveness and output, which goes on to reflect – inevitably – on the larger economy, once accumulated.

This section attempts to show the quality of health resources available to a population. It compares levels of government and private expenditure on health and thus illustrates the degree of government commitment to the state of health of its residents, and the extent to which the private sector carries (or must carry) the burden of responsibility. It thus provides a snapshot of the challenges and liabilities that the different economies pose to employers and residents.

We have chosen to compare economies here by the expenditure on health undertaken by the two broad groups of providers: government and private sources. The private segment is here split into two major parts: *out-of-pocket* and *other private sector* expenses or outlays. Much of the data headings is self-explanatory, and where brief definitions follow, they are provided by the World Health Organization (WHO) from where the bulk of the data is sourced.

For the purposes here, a "household" is defined as an individual or a group of persons sharing the same living accommodation, which pool some or all of their income and wealth, and which consume certain types of goods and services collectively (mainly housing and food).

Total Spending on Health

The sum of government and private expenditure on health.

Government Spending on Health

The sum of expenditures for health maintenance, restoration or enhancement paid for in cash, or supplied in kind by government entities such as the Ministry of Health, other ministries, parastatals, or social security services.

Private Spending on Health

The sum of expenditures on health by households; by private entities such as commercial or mutual health insurance and non-profit institutions that serve households; and by resident corporations not controlled by government.

Out-of-Pocket Spending on Health

Private households' out-of-pocket payment: the expenditure on health by households as direct payments.

Other Private Spending on Health

The rest of health spending by the private sector after out-of-pocket expenditure. As mentioned above, consists largely of health insurance arrangements and direct expenses by corporations and businesses.

Sources of Primary Data: World Bank, WHO

Charts

Tables

2000-2002; 2003-2006:

- *self-comparison to preceding period;*
- *performance in S-Saharan Africa;*
- *performance in West Africa;*
- *performance among oil-exporters;*

for:

Total Spending (Govt. & Private) on Health as % of GDP

Total Spending (Govt. & Private) on Health per Person, $PPP

Govt. Spending on Health as % of Total Govt. Spending

Out-of-Pocket Spending on Health as % of Total Health Spending

Out-of-Pocket as % of Private Spending on Health

- Total Spending on Health as % of GDP during 2003-06: Rankings
- Total Spending on Health per Person ($PPP) during 2003-06: Rankings
- Govt. Spending on Health as % of Total Govt. Spending during 2003-06: Rankings
- Out-of-Pocket Spending on Health as % of Total Health Spending during 2003-06: Rankings
- Out-of-Pocket Spending as % of Private Spending on Health during 2003-06: Rankings
- **Spending on Health Rankings: 2003-06**

11.1 Total Spending (Govt. & Private) on Health as % of GDP

keeping everyone in working order

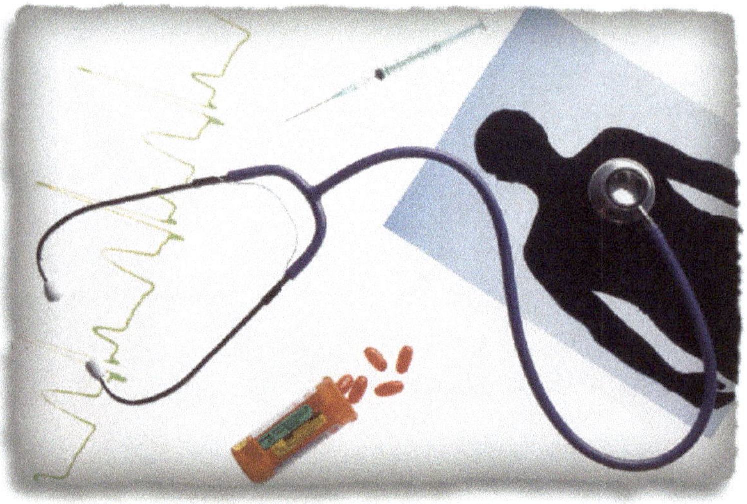

Health spending in Nigeria at all levels and by all quarters is the 3rd worst in West Africa, when compared to the size of the different economies.

Indeed, 03/06 was a big drop in total health spending from the preceding 4 yrs.

	00-02	03-06
Self-comparison to Preceding Period		▼
Performance in Sub-Saharan Africa	▼	▼
Performance in West Africa	▲	▼

Primary Data: World Bank

00-02	03-06
Ghana	Burkina Faso
Mali	Ghana
Guinea-Bissau	Togo
Guinea	Guinea-Bissau
Gambia, The	Guinea
Cape Verde	Mali
Burkina Faso	Senegal
Nigeria	Gambia, The
Togo	Cape Verde
Benin	Benin
Senegal	Sierra Leone
Côte d'Ivoire	Niger
Sierra Leone	Liberia
Niger	**Nigeria**
Liberia	Côte d'Ivoire
Mauritania	Mauritania

Performance among Oil-Exporters

00-02 ▲	03-06 ▲
Chad	Chad
Gabon	Gabon
Nigeria	Cameroon
Cameroon	**Nigeria**
Côte d'Ivoire	Côte d'Ivoire
Sudan	Sudan
Angola	Congo, Rep.
Equatorial Guinea	Angola
Congo, Rep.	Equatorial Guinea

11.1

Total Spending (Govt. & Private) on Health as %GDP in West Africa during 2003/06

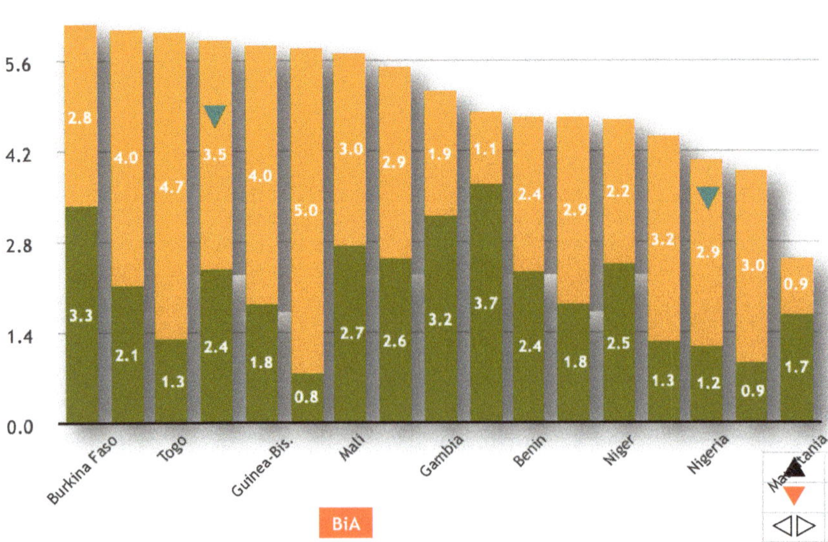

Private
Govt.

▲ improved *or* better than average
▼ worsened *or* worse than average
◁▷ no change *or* average

11. Spending on Health

11.2

Total Spending (Govt. & Private) on Health as %GDP in Nigeria from 2000 to 2006

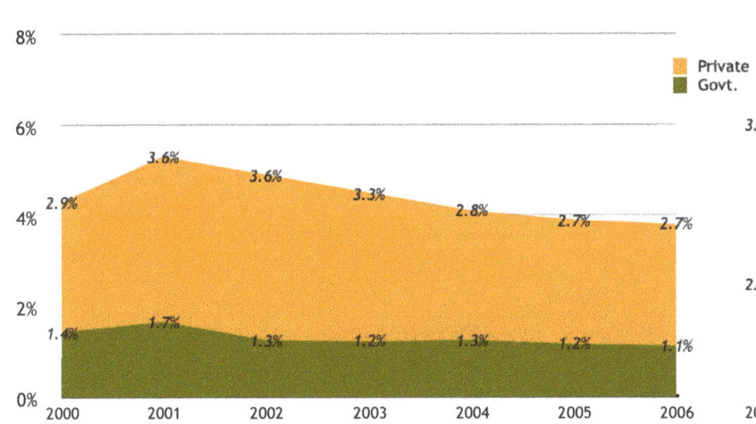

11.3

Total Spending (Govt. & Private) on Health as %GDP in Sub-Saharan Africa from 2000 to 2006

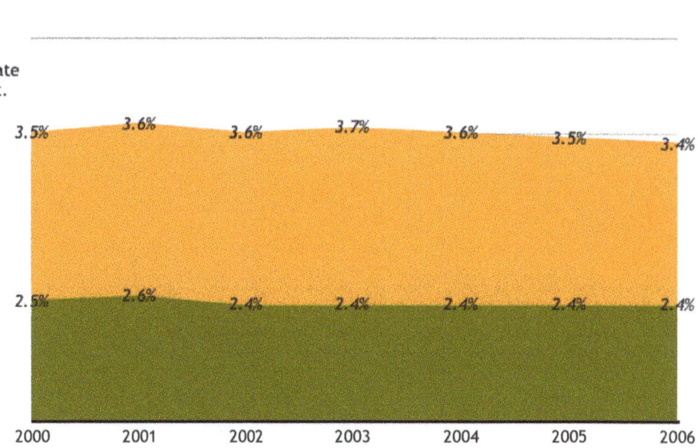

It probably says much for the oil countries that even with that dismal score, Nigeria still makes it into their top half. Too immersed in oil barrels to care?

Total expenditure on health dropped in 2006 from the 2000 level across Africa, but the drop was sharper in Nigeria, where it declined steeply after 2001.

Nigeria fell below 4% of GDP and never went near 6% in 7 yrs. Africa's broke the 6% mark in 2001 and fell just slightly below it in 2006.

Govt. health spending was consistently above 2% in Africa, but consistently less than 2% in Nigeria, dropping to 1% by 2006, compared to Africa's 2.4%.

Total Spending on Health as % of GDP during 2003-06: Rankings

Rank	Country
1	Malawi
2	Rwanda
3	Namibia
	South Africa
4	Botswana
5	Uganda
6	Burundi
7	Zambia
8	Lesotho
9	Swaziland
10	Burkina Faso
11	Seychelles
12	Ghana

TOP

Rank	Country
13	Togo
14	Congo, Dem. Rep.
15	Guinea-Bissau
16	Guinea
17	Mali
18	Senegal
19	Tanzania
	Chad
20	Gambia, The
21	Cape Verde
22	Benin
	Sierra Leone
23	Niger
24	Gabon

MIDDLE

Rank	Country
25	Mozambique
26	Kenya
	Cameroon
27	Ethiopia
28	Mauritius
29	Central Afr. Rep.
	Nigeria
30	Côte d' Ivoire
31	Eritrea
32	Madagascar
33	Comoros
34	Congo, Rep.
35	Angola
36	Equatorial Guinea

BOTTOM

Central Africa
East Africa
Southern Africa
West Africa

No surprises, therefore, that Nigeria is in the bottom sector of the Africa table, with health expenditure being worse than every other country, save 7.

11.2 Total Spending (Govt. & Private) on Health per Person, $PPP

who's actually coughing up?

	00-02	03-06
Self-comparison to Preceding Period		▼
Performance in Sub-Saharan Africa	▼	▼
Performance in West Africa	▼	▼
	Cape Verde	Cape Verde
	Guinea	Guinea
	Ghana	Ghana
	Côte d'Ivoire	Burkina Faso
	Togo	Senegal
	Mali	Togo
	Senegal	Côte d'Ivoire
	Burkina Faso	Mali
	Gambia, The	Gambia, The
	Nigeria	**Nigeria**
	Guinea-Bissau	Mauritania
	Mauritania	Benin
	Benin	Sierra Leone
	Sierra Leone	Guinea-Bissau
	Liberia	Liberia
	Niger	Niger
Performance among Oil-Exporters	◁▷	▼
	Gabon	Gabon
	Equatorial Guinea	Equatorial Guinea
	Côte d'Ivoire	Cameroon
	Cameroon	Côte d'Ivoire
	Nigeria	Sudan
	Angola	Angola
	Sudan	**Nigeria**
	Chad	Chad
	Congo, Rep.	Congo, Rep.

11.4

Total Spending (Govt. & Private) on Health per Person in West Africa during 2003/06 ($PPP)

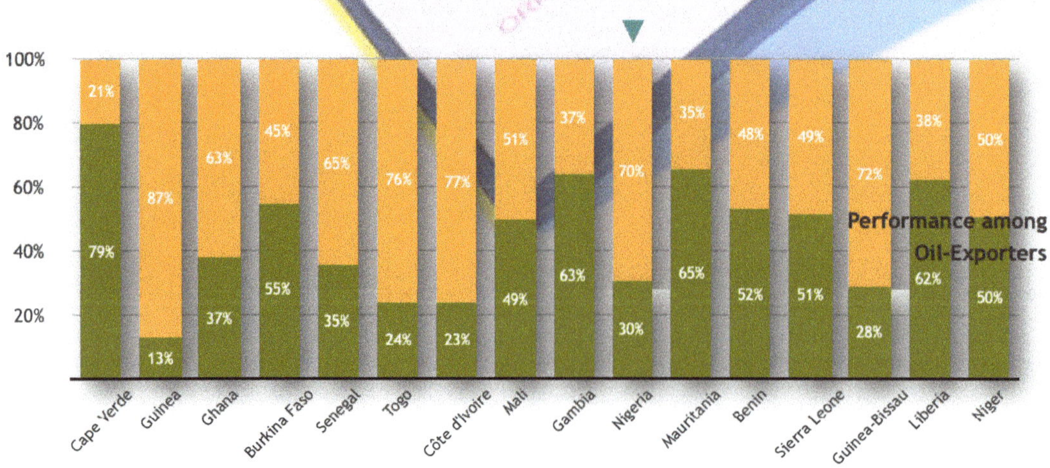

11.5

% Breakdown of Total Spending (Govt. & Private) on Health per Person in West Africa during 2003/06 ($PPP)

Private
Govt.

Primary Data: WHO

▲	improved *or* better than average
▼	worsened *or* worse than average
◁▷	no change *or* average

11.6

Total Spending (Govt. & Private) on Health per Person in Nigeria from 2000 to 2006 ($PPP)

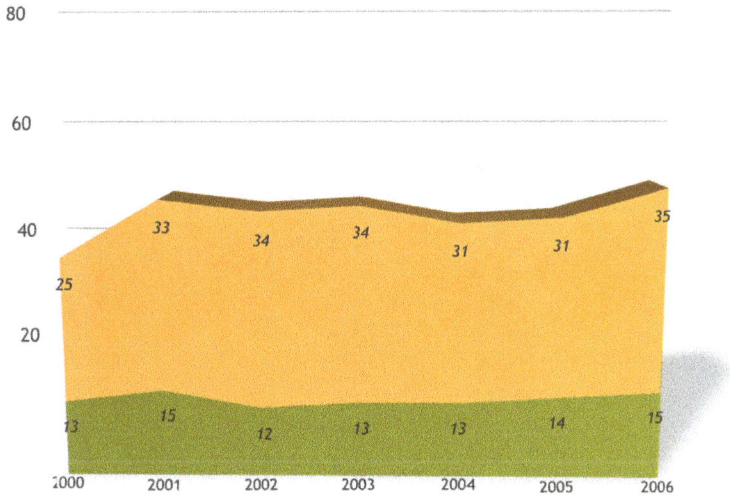

11.7

Total Spending (Govt. & Private) on Health per Person in Mali from 2000 to 2006 ($PPP)

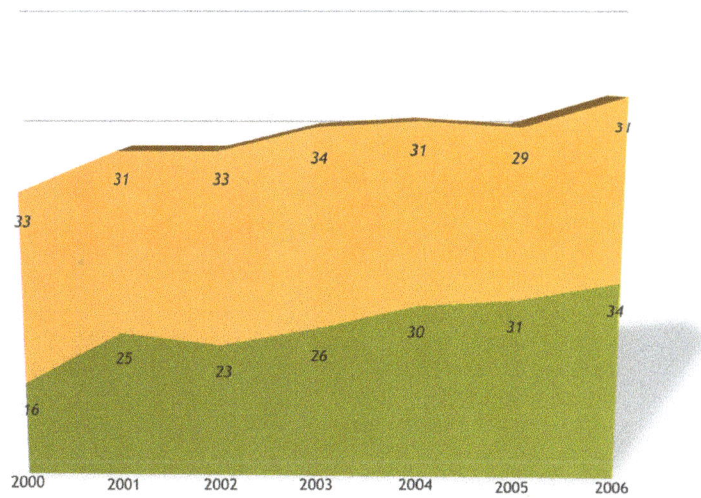

Primary Data: WHO

This time, the disparity between money spent on health in the country and in the rest of Sub-Saharan Africa is more noticeable.

In Mali for comparison (average in West Africa) govt. spending during 2000-06 grew by 9 times that in Nigeria: $18 per person, against Nigeria's $2.

During the same period, private health spending in Nigeria grew by $10 a head; in Mali it fell instead, by $2. Govt. shouldered more of the burden.

Throughout 2000-2006, in total health expenditure, Mali outspent Nigeria by an average of $13 per person.

Expressed in real money, Nigeria's total health spending is still worse than average in Africa, West Africa and, this time, in the oil club, too.

And much of that health responsibility is borne by private corporations and households. The govt. contributed just 30%: only better than 4 in West Africa.

11. Spending on Health

Total Spending on Health per Person ($PPP) during 2003-06: Rankings

Rank	Country	Rank	Country	Rank	Country
1	South Africa	15	Ghana	29	Benin
2	Seychelles	16	Burkina Faso	30	Chad
3	Botswana	17	Cameroon	31	Sierra Leone
4	Mauritius	18	Senegal	32	Guinea-Bissau
5	Namibia	19	Togo	33	Tanzania
6	Swaziland	20	Malawi	34	Eritrea
7	Gabon	21	Zambia	35	Madagascar
8	Equatorial Guinea	22	Côte d' Ivoire	36	Comoros
9	Cape Verde	23	Mali	37	Congo, Rep.
10	Rwanda	24	Gambia, The	38	Niger
11	Uganda	25	Central Afr. Rep.	39	Ethiopia
12	Lesotho	26	Angola	40	Congo, Dem. Rep.
13	Guinea	27	Mozambique	41	Burundi
14	Kenya	28	Nigeria		
	TOP		MIDDLE		BOTTOM

Central Africa
East Africa
Southern Africa
West Africa

And it just about jostles its way into the last position in the middle bracket on the continent. All 5 Southern Africa countries were in the top bracket.

11.3 Build-up of Govt. & Private Spending on Health

she's keeping a close eye on it

11.8

Build-up of Govt. & Private Spending on Health in Nigeria and Mali from 2000 to 2006: 2000=100

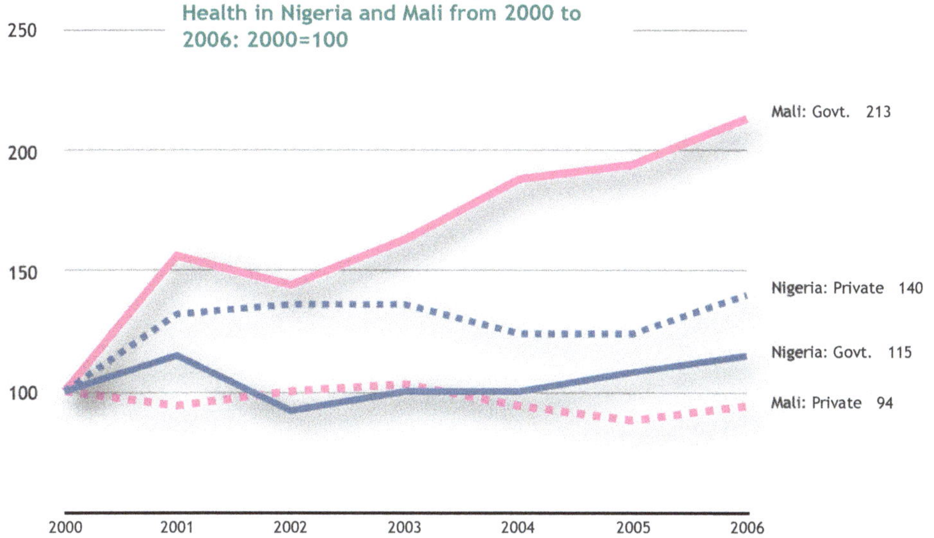

Primary Data: WHO

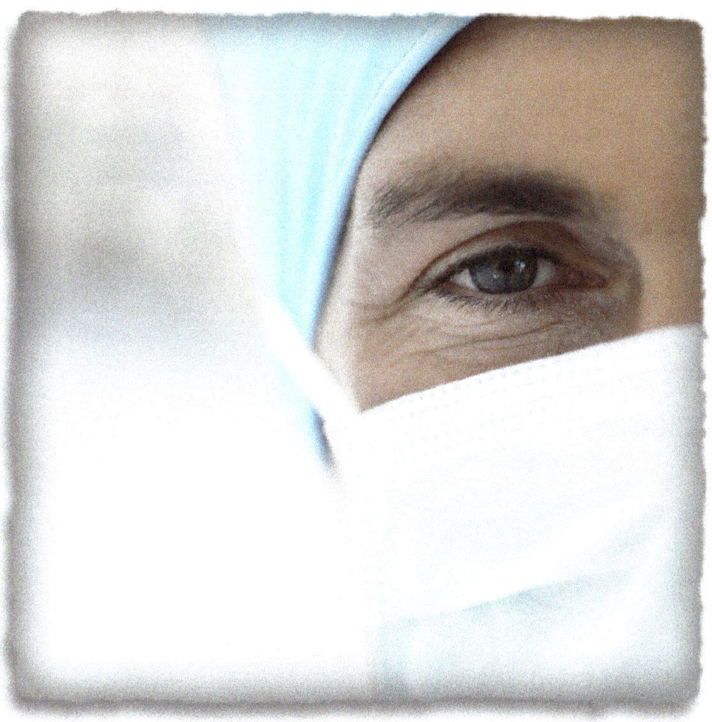

Using Mali again for comparison (average), growth of govt. spending outpaced Nigeria's during 2000-2006, by almost 100 percentage points.

Private sector shell-out in Mali dropped during the same period, by 6 points; in Nigeria it grew by 40 points...

... showing that individuals in Mali saw their health expenses dropping because the govt. shouldered more weight.

It was the opposite in Nigeria: while govt. and private health spending both grew, private spending surpassed the govt.'s by 25 points.

Whereas, Mali's govt. spent 120 percentage points more than the private sector per inhabitant in the 7 yrs from 2000 to 2006.

Their private sector shed weight, instead, during the period (from 100 down to 94 percentage points).

11.4 Govt. Spending on Health as % of Total Govt. Spending

the govt is your friend, sir

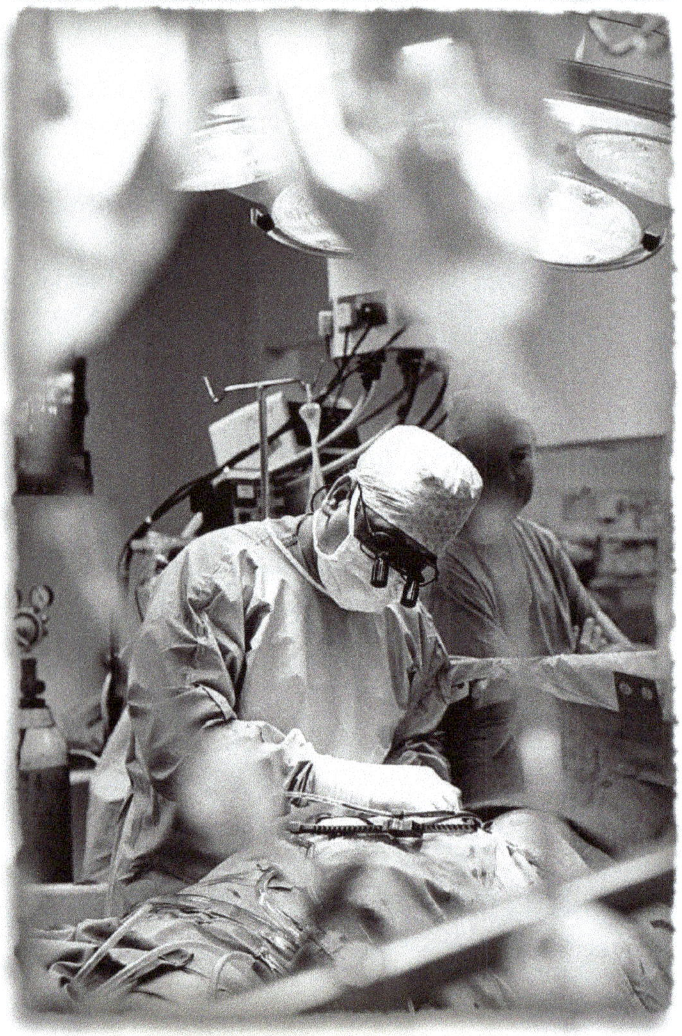

It might have been tempting to put Nigeria's poor per-capita govt. spending on health down to the country's large population.

But not so. Health mattered less and less across 00-06, taking up an increasingly smaller share of the govt. budget.

	00-02	03-06
Self-comparison to Preceding Period		▼
Performance in Sub-Saharan Africa	▼	▼
Performance in West Africa	▼	▼
	Benin	Liberia
	Niger	Burkina Faso
	Cape Verde	Benin
	Mali	Mali
	Ghana	Cape Verde
	Burkina Faso	Gambia, The
	Senegal	Niger
	Gambia, The	Sierra Leone
	Liberia	Senegal
	Sierra Leone	Ghana
	Togo	Togo
	Mauritania	Guinea
	Côte d'Ivoire	Mauritania
	Guinea	Côte d'Ivoire
	Guinea-Bissau	Guinea-Bissau
	Nigeria	**Nigeria**
Performance among Oil-Exporters	▼	▼
	Gabon	Gabon
	Chad	Cameroon
	Equatorial Guinea	Chad
	Cameroon	Equatorial Guinea
	Sudan	Sudan
	Côte d'Ivoire	Angola
	Congo, Rep.	Côte d'Ivoire
	Nigeria	Congo, Rep.
	Angola	**Nigeria**

Primary Data: WHO

▲	improved *or* better than average
▼	worsened *or* worse than average
◁▷	no change *or* average

11. Spending on Health

11.9

Govt. Spending on Health as % of Total Govt. Spending in West Africa during 2003/06

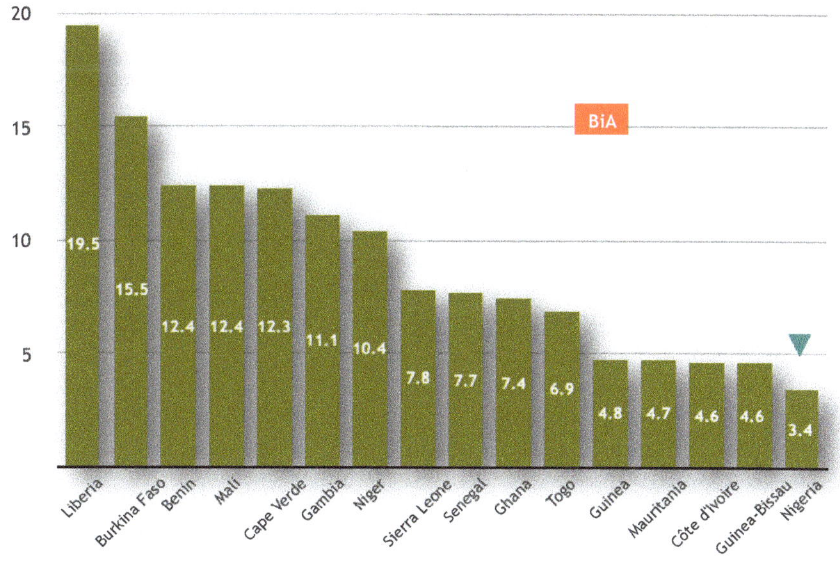

As a % of total govt. expenditure during the period, health wasn't on Nigeria's list of priorities.

It dedicated fewer resources to the health sector than all the other countries of West Africa and the countries of the oil group.

11.10

Govt. Spending on Health as % of Total Govt. Spending in Nigeria from 2000 to 2006

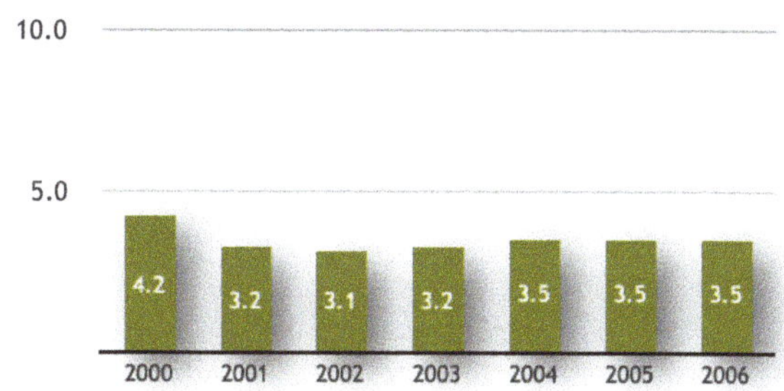

The charts at right are to the same scale. Other West African govts. had health sectors pulling larger chunks of spending; they towered over Nigeria's.

Again, rock-bottom on the continent, inevitably.

Govt. Spending on Health as % of Total Govt. Spending during 2003-06: Rankings

TOP

Rank	Country
1	Rwanda
2	Malawi
3	Botswana
4	Burkina Faso
5	Gabon
6	Benin
7	Mali
8	Cape Verde
9	Namibia
10	Tanzania
11	Mozambique
12	Zambia
13	Swaziland

MIDDLE

Rank	Country
14	Central Afr. Rep.
15	Gambia, The
16	Niger
17	Ethiopia
18	Cameroon
19	Uganda
20	Seychelles
21	Chad
	South Africa
22	Madagascar
23	Mauritius
24	Comoros
25	Lesotho
26	Sierra Leone

BOTTOM

Rank	Country
27	Senegal
28	Equatorial Guinea
29	Ghana
30	Congo, Dem. Rep.
31	Togo
32	Kenya
33	Guinea
34	Angola
35	Côte d' Ivoire
	Guinea-Bissau
36	Eritrea
37	Congo, Rep.
38	Nigeria
39	Burundi

Central Africa
East Africa
Southern Africa
West Africa

Primary Data: WHO

11.5 Out-of-Pocket Spending on Health as % of Total Health Spending

he's had to cough up

An increasingly familiar play-out: Nigeria outdone in health.

Nigerians shouldered the task of their health requirements themselves: they had to spend their own money directly, from their own disposable income.

The situation worsened across the 2000-2006 yrs.

	00-02	03-06
Self-comparison to Preceding Period		▼
Performance in Sub-Saharan Africa	▼	▼
Performance in West Africa	▼	▼
	Cape Verde	Cape Verde
	Mauritania	Gambia, The
	Niger	Mauritania
	Gambia, The	Liberia
	Guinea-Bissau	Niger
	Ghana	Burkina Faso
	Benin	Guinea-Bissau
	Sierra Leone	Benin
	Burkina Faso	Sierra Leone
	Senegal	Ghana
	Liberia	Mali
	Mali	Senegal
	Nigeria	**Nigeria**
	Togo	Togo
	Côte d'Ivoire	Côte d'Ivoire
	Guinea	Guinea
Performance among Oil-Exporters	▼	▼
	Gabon	Angola
	Equatorial Guinea	Equatorial Guinea
	Angola	Gabon
	Congo, Rep.	Congo, Rep.
	Chad	Chad
	Nigeria	Sudan
	Côte d'Ivoire	**Nigeria**
	Cameroon	Côte d'Ivoire
	Sudan	Cameroon

Primary Data: WHO

▲	improved *or* smaller than average
▼	worsened *or* higher than average
◁▷	no change *or* average

11.11

Out-of-Pocket Spending on Health as % of Total Health Spending in West Africa during 2003/06

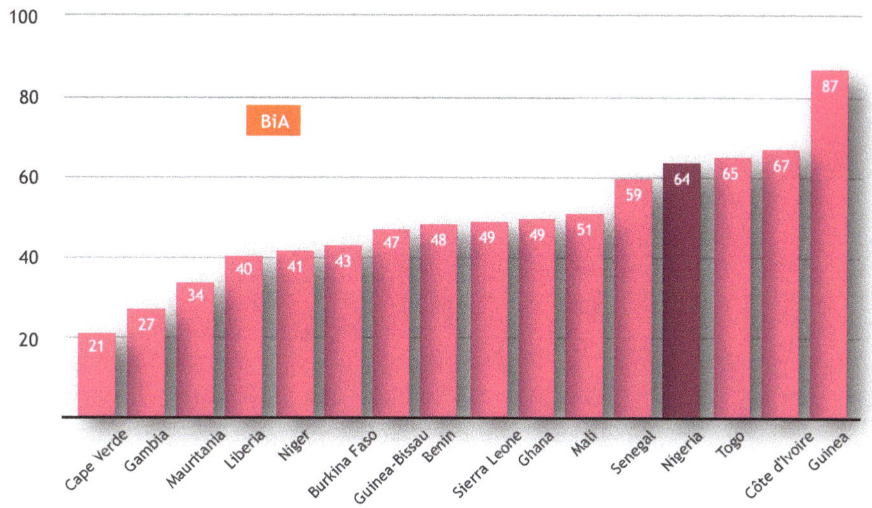

Indeed, the position is staggering: more than 60% of all health spending in Nigeria is funded by the people directly, from their income or savings.

Govt. clinics and medicines account for less than 40% of the citizens' requirements.

11.12

Out-of-Pocket Spending on Health as % of Total Health Spending in Nigeria from 2000 to 2006

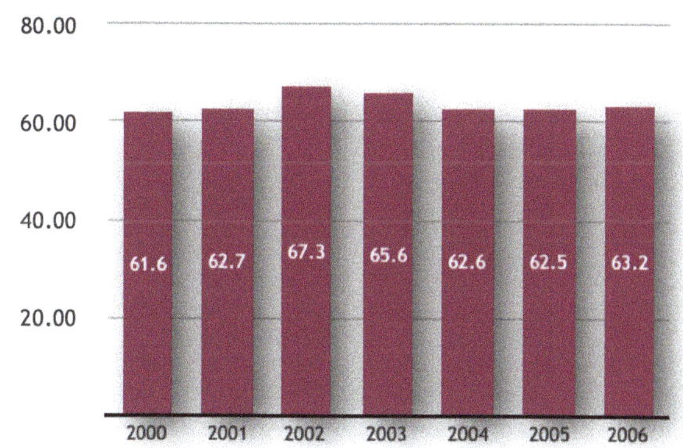

Out-of-Pocket Spending on Health as % of Total Health Spending during 2003-06: Rankings

Rank	Country	Rank	Country	Rank	Country
1	Namibia	15	Lesotho	29	Ghana
2	Botswana	16	Zambia	30	Mali
3	Malawi	17	Ethiopia	31	Congo, Rep.
4	South Africa	18	Uganda	32	Chad
5	Mozambique	19	Mauritius	33	Senegal
6	Swaziland	20	Tanzania	34	Central Afr. Rep.
7	Seychelles	21	Niger	35	Nigeria
8	Angola	22	Burkina Faso	36	Togo
9	Equatorial Guinea	23	Kenya	37	Côte d' Ivoire
10	Rwanda	24	Eritrea	38	Congo, Dem. Rep.
11	Madagascar	25	Comoros	39	Cameroon
12	Cape Verde	26	Guinea-Bissau	40	Burundi
13	Gambia, The	27	Benin	41	Guinea
14	Gabon	28	Sierra Leone		
LOWEST %		MIDDLE		LARGEST %	

Central Africa
East Africa
Southern Africa
West Africa

Primary Data: WHO

11.6 Out-of-Pocket Spending on Health as Part of Total Spending on Health per Person, $PPP

nice colors, yes?

The monies spent on health by individuals & households tally with the percentages illustrated in the previous section.

The focus in this section are the disparities in money volumes.

Even though Cape Verde has its people spending a lot more than other residents in all but 1 West African country, its total expenditure on health more than makes up for that extra weight.

At $30 per capita, Nigerians spent just about the West Africa average of personal money on their health. But that wasn't a desirable position, small though the amount was;

reason being that personal money represented the largest source for their health expenses. As seen in the preceding sections, their overall health spending was the worst on show.

11.13

Out-of-Pocket Spending on Health as part of Total Health Spending in West Africa during 2003/06 ($PPP)

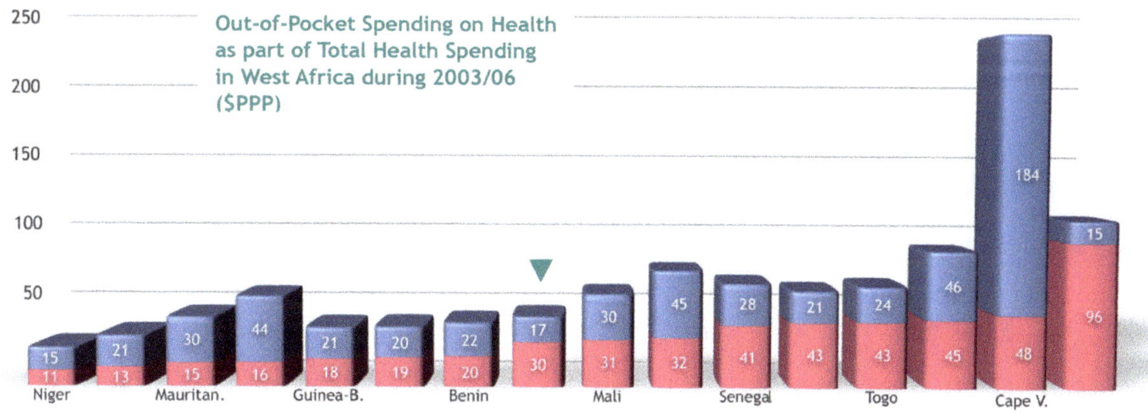

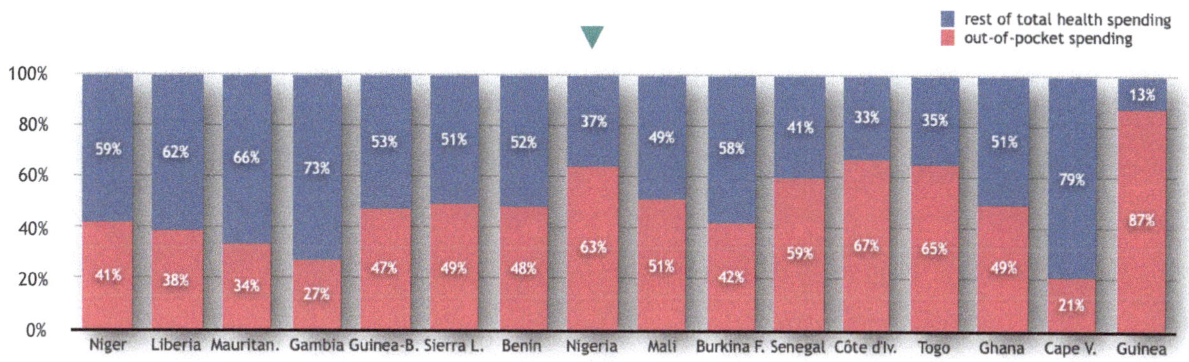

11.14

% Breakdown of Total Health Spending showing Out-of-Pocket Spending on Health in West Africa during 2003/06

Primary Data: WHO

11.15

Out-of-Pocket Spending on Health as part of Total Health Spending in Nigeria from 2000 to 2006 ($PPP)

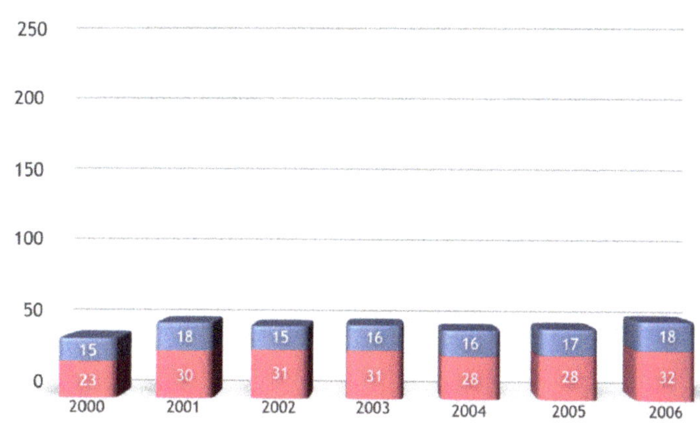

8.16

% Breakdown of Total Health Spending showing Out-of-Pocket Spending on Health in Nigeria from 2000 to 2006

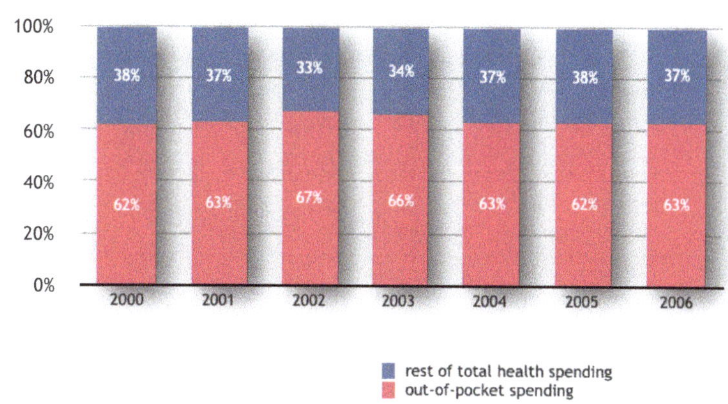

11.7 Out-of-Pocket as % of Private Spending on Health

do you love your insurance company?

Leaving total spending and looking at just private spending, personal expenditure on health made up a large part of Nigeria's private health spending.

Nigeria was bested by most of Africa, even though it came up average in West Africa.

Among the oil exporters the general situation is a dismal one, because in spite of Nigeria's poor showing, it still came up better than average there.

	00-02	03-06
Self-comparison to Preceding Period		◁▷
Performance in Sub-Saharan Africa	▼	▼
Performance in West Africa	▲	▲
	Guinea-Bissau	Guinea-Bissau
	Ghana	Gambia, The
	Gambia, The	Ghana
	Niger	Togo
	Togo	Niger
	Côte d'Ivoire	Côte d'Ivoire
	Senegal	Senegal
	Nigeria	**Nigeria**
	Burkina Faso	Burkina Faso
	Liberia	Liberia
	Guinea	Mali
	Mali	Guinea
	Cape Verde	Cape Verde
	Benin	Benin
	Mauritania	Mauritania
	Sierra Leone	Sierra Leone
Performance among Oil-Exporters	▲	▲
	Equatorial Guinea	Equatorial Guinea
	Côte d'Ivoire	Côte d'Ivoire
	Nigeria	**Nigeria**
	Cameroon	Cameroon
	Chad	Chad
	Sudan	Sudan
	Angola	Angola
	Congo, Rep.	Congo, Rep.
	Gabon	Gabon

Primary Data: WHO

▲	improved *or* smaller than average
▼	worsened *or* higher than average
◁▷	no change *or* average

11.17

Out-of-Pocket Spending as % of Private Spending on Health in West Africa during 2003/06

BiA

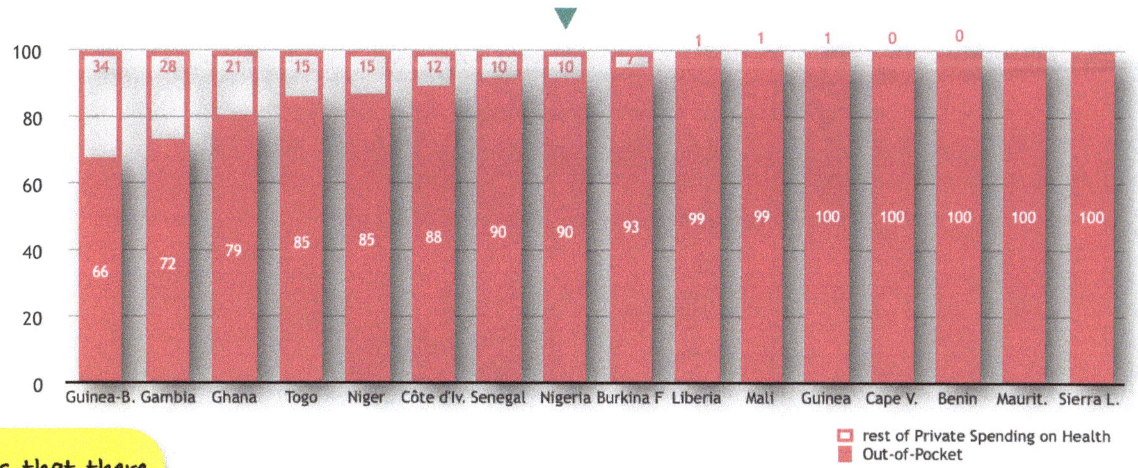

The other inference is that there is no health insurance arrangement through most of West Africa, & certainly through most of the oil exporters:

individuals are forced to pay for health directly, off their pockets, literally.

In West Africa, near half the countries have no support scheme for private spending: individuals carry the entire cost of private spending: 100%.

In Nigeria, 10% of private sector spending is provided by insurance schemes or corporate spending. That figure changed little across 2000-2006.

As is seen at right, a large proportion of African countries haven't effective private sector health arrangement schemes.

11.18

Out-of-Pocket Spending as % of Private Spending on Health in Nigeria from 2000 to 2006

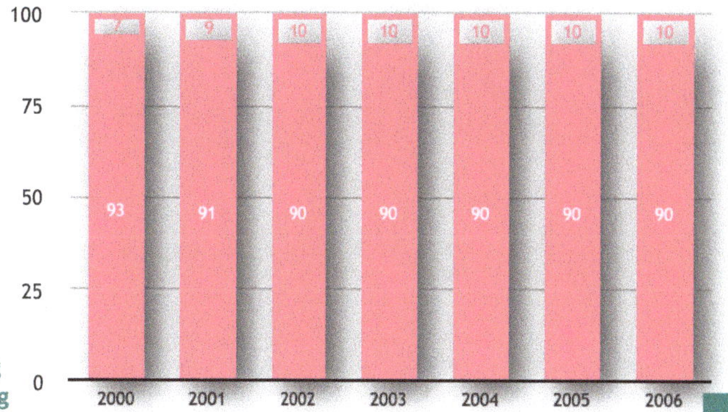

Out-of-Pocket Spending as % of Private Spending on Health during 2003-06: Rankings

Rank	Country	Rank	Country	Rank	Country
1	Namibia	13	Lesotho	25	Senegal
2	South Africa	14	Gambia, The	26	Nigeria
3	Botswana	15	Zambia	27	Burkina Faso
4	Malawi	16	Equatorial Guinea	28	Cameroon
5	Mozambique	17	Ghana	29	Central Afr. Rep.
6	Swaziland	18	Kenya	30	Chad
7	Rwanda	19	Mauritius	31	Mali
8	Uganda	20	Ethiopia	32	Guinea
9	Madagascar	21	Tanzania	33	Cape Verde
10	Seychelles	22	Togo	34	Benin
11	Eritrea	23	Niger	35	Angola
12	Guinea-Bissau	24	Côte d' Ivoire		Burundi
					Comoros
					Congo, Dem. Rep.
					Congo, Rep.
					Gabon
					Sierra Leone
	LOWEST %		MIDDLE		LARGEST %

Central Africa
East Africa
Southern Africa
West Africa

Primary Data: WHO

11.8 *Out-of-Pocket* & *Other Private* Spending on Health per Person

I paid for the ones on the top shelf

Much the same observations as in the preceding section. But here, the quantities of money spent can be appreciated better.

+1-800-help

Why such high out-of-pockets?

Health insurance is not usually a widely available recourse in developing economies, hence the large o.o.p. spending

Remind me: what is "other private" spending, again?

Largely health insurance arrangements and direct expenses by corporations and businesses.

Right!

11.19

Out-of-Pocket & other Private Spending on Health per Person in West Africa during 2003/06, $PPP

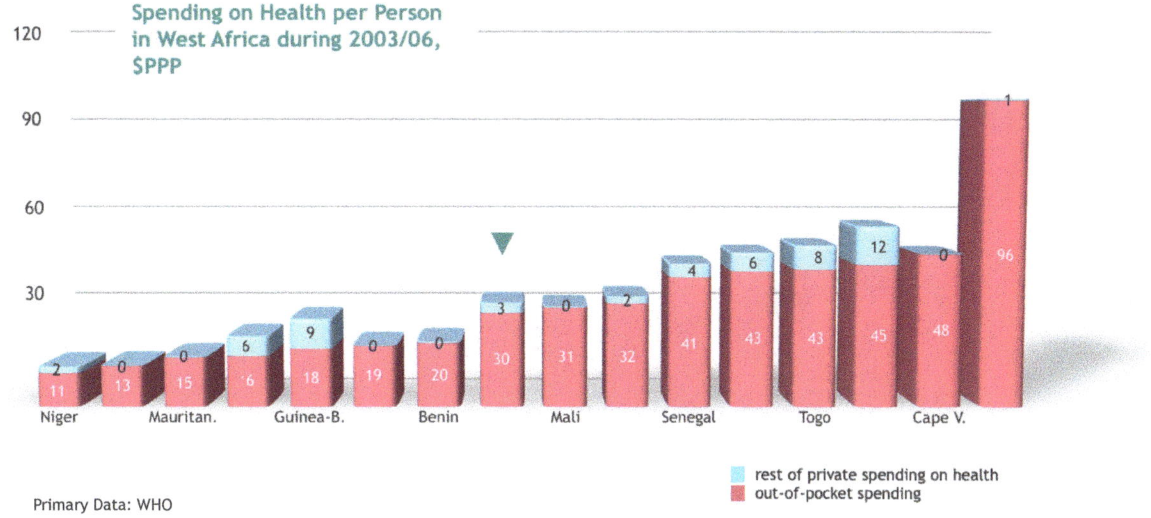

Primary Data: WHO

11.20

Out-of-Pocket & other Private Spending on Health per Person in Nigeria from 2000 to 2006, $PPP

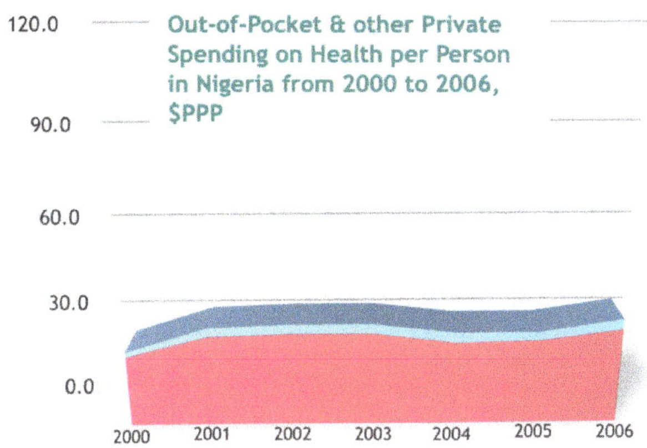

11.21

Out-of-Pocket & other Private Spending on Health per Person in Mali from 2000 to 2006, $PPP

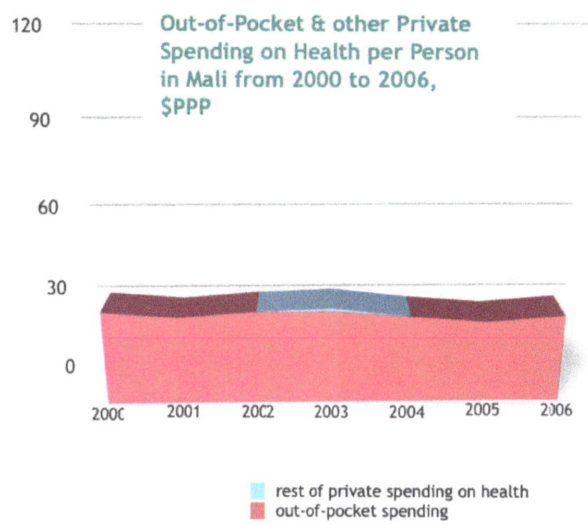

In most of West Africa, "other private sources" account for less than $5 of private spending on health.

The highest was $12 in Ghana, which nonetheless also had one of the highest out-of-pocket levels: $45.

11.9 *Out-of-Pocket*, *Other Private* and *Govt*. Portions of Total Spending on Health per Person

is there a problem here?

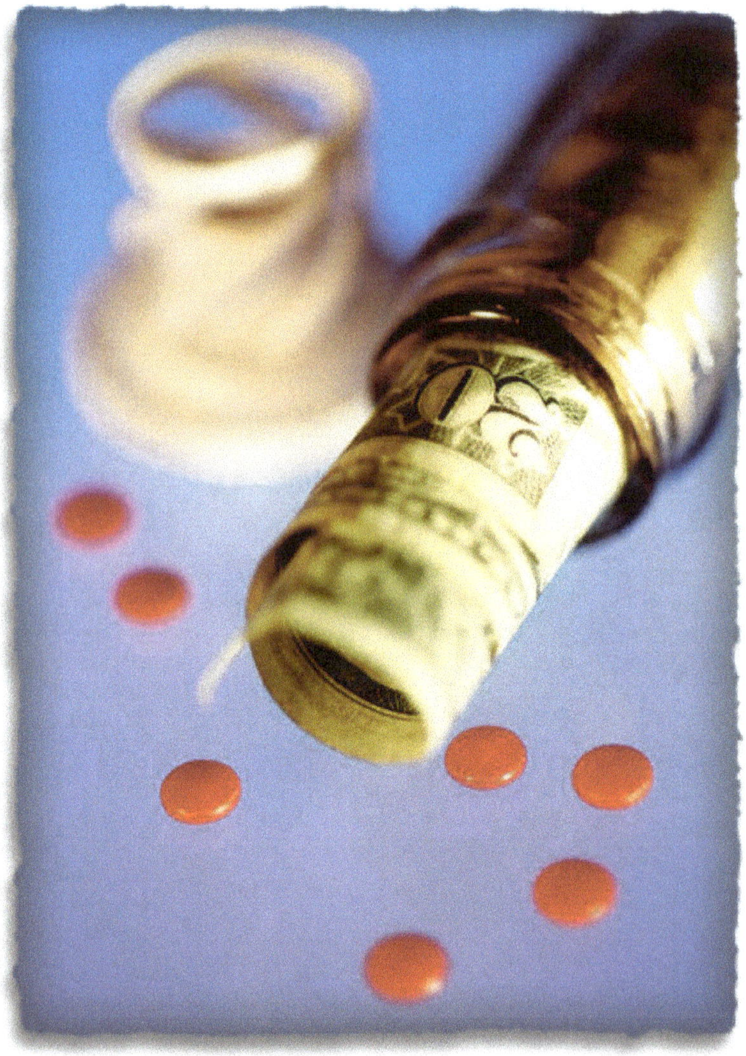

Ghana also had the 3rd highest total spending on health per capita, more of it coming from the private sector ($57) than the govt. ($34).

Guineans spend the most from private coffers ($97; 90%). They have the 2nd largest total spending on health ($111 per pers), after Cape Verde ($232).

In several countries, "other private" spending is near non-existent, their citizens having to shell out from their own pockets, for all non-govt. health expenses.

Nowhere did "other private" spending outweigh out-of-pocket.

Between 2000 & 2006, there was hardly any development in the health insurance sector in Nigeria; instead, out-of-pocket spending grew.

Nigeria govt. spending between 2000 & 2006: no movement. No change in govt. spending in 7 yrs.

Whatever was spent by the govt. in 2000 was just about maintained stagnant throughout the deteriorating sector, 7 yrs. on.

11.22

Breakdown of Total Health Spending into Out-of-Pocket, other Private & Govt. Spending per Person in West Africa during 2003/06, $PPP

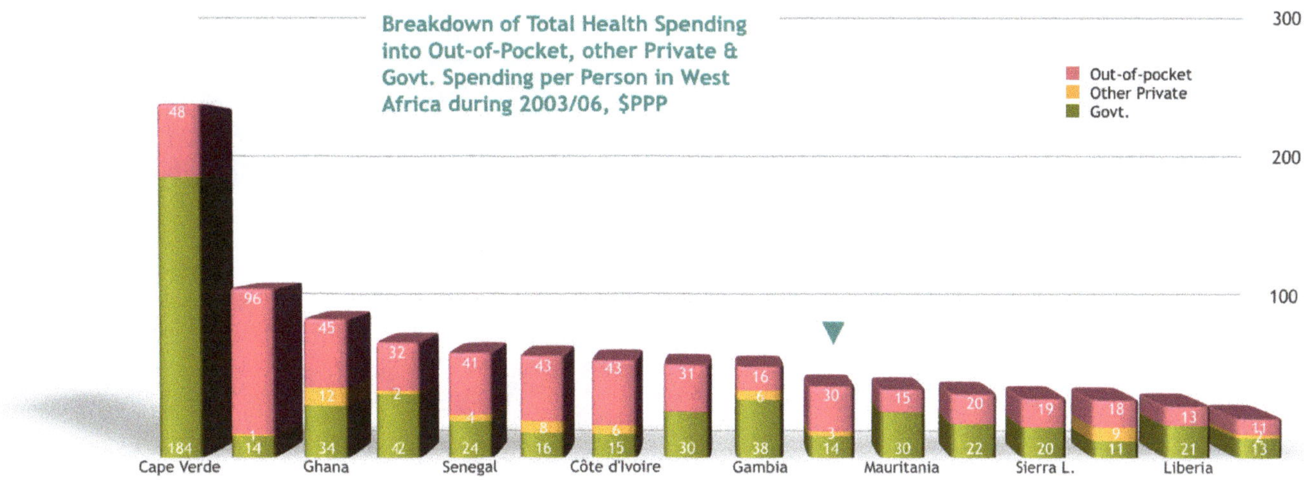

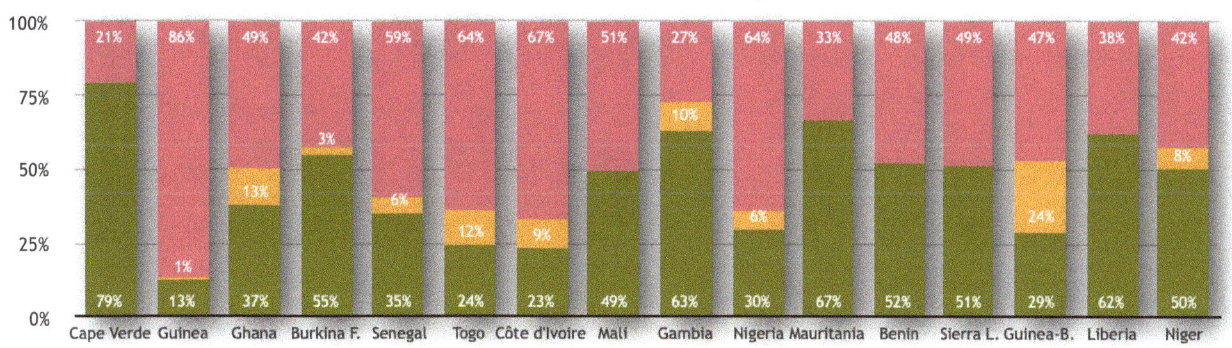

11.23

% Breakdown of Total Health Spending into Out-of-Pocket, other Private & Govt. Spending per Person in West Africa during 2003/06

Primary Data: WHO

Out-of-pocket
Other Private
Govt.

The most desirable West African country for health purposes is Cape Verde, by several miles.

11.24

Breakdown of Total Health Spending into Out-of-Pocket, other Private & Govt. Spending per Person in Nigeria from 2000 to 2006, $PPP

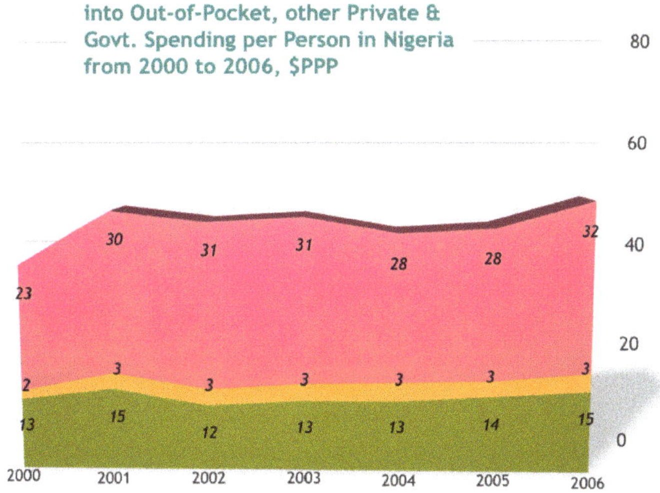

11.25

Breakdown of Total Health Spending into Out-of-Pocket, other Private & Govt. Spending per Person in Mali from 2000 to 2006, $PPP

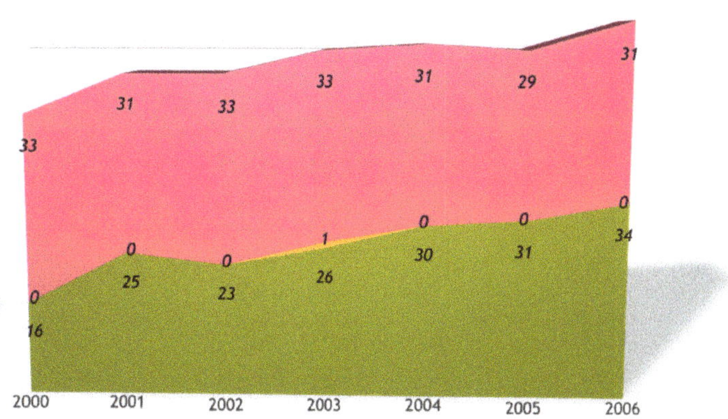

Leaders & Stragglers

is yours in working condition?

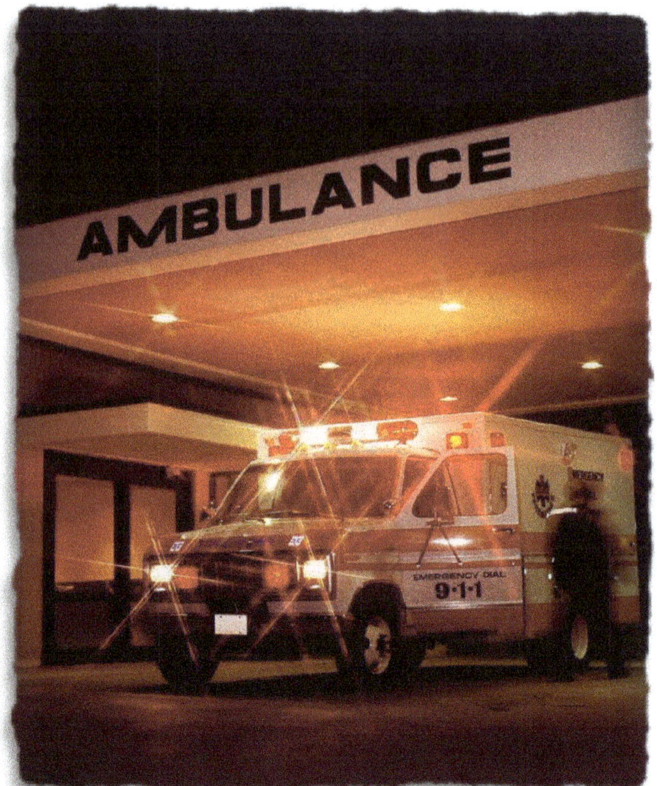

In Africa, the most desirable country for health is Botswana, then Namibia and Malawi. Nigeria is 4th from bottom.

Spending on Health Rankings: 2003-06

Rank	Country
1	Botswana
2	Namibia
3	Malawi
4	Rwanda
5	South Africa
6	Swaziland
7	Seychelles
8	Uganda
9	Zambia
10	Lesotho
11	Mozambique
12	Burkina Faso
13	Gambia, The
14	Cape Verde

TOP

Rank	Country
15	Gabon
16	Mauritius
17	Equatorial Guinea
18	Ghana
19	Tanzania
20	Mali
21	Madagascar
22	Kenya
23	Guinea-Bissau
24	Benin
25	Ethiopia
26	Togo
27	Niger
28	Senegal

MIDDLE

Rank	Country
29	Cameroon
30	Central Afr. Rep.
31	Chad
32	Eritrea
33	Guinea
34	Angola
35	Sierra Leone
36	Côte d' Ivoire
37	Comoros
38	Nigeria
39	Congo, Dem. Rep.
40	Burundi
41	Congo, Rep.

BOTTOM

Central Africa
East Africa
Southern Africa
West Africa

Wrap-up: Spending on Health

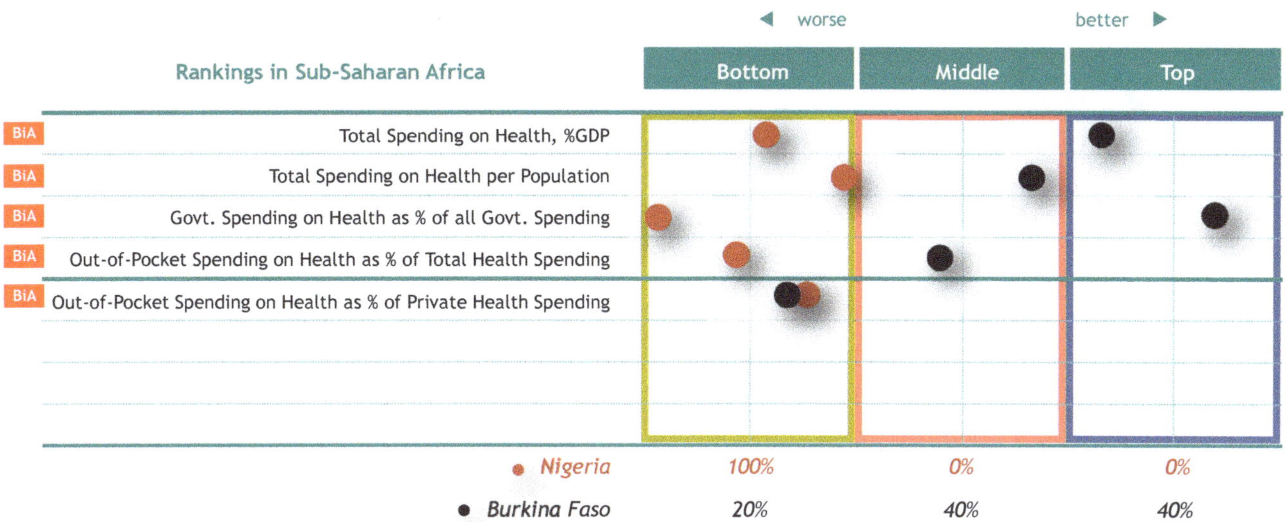

- Burkina Faso, best performer in West Africa, no. 12 in Africa. Nigeria was bottom in West Africa and no. 38 in Africa.
- The reason stands out in stark reality from the boxes: by all 5 measures, Nigeria fails in quality of health services. It spends less than Burkina Faso (and likely, the rest of West Africa) every time.
- Its citizens pay for too much of the services from their own pocket; the government spends too little of its GDP on health while the other expenses it spends on – whatever they are – seem to be of more urgency and take priority over healthcare.
- Whereas Burkina Faso spends bravely out of its public coffers.

12. Purchasing Power

depth of pocket

Primer

The purchasing power of a people is usually expressed by the term, "consumption". There are two parts to it: **government** (or public) consumption and **household** (or private) consumption. It is money spent on mainly recurrent expenditure, as distinct from, for example, capital expenditure like projects and investments.

Government Consumption

The level of government spending tends to reflect the role of the State in an economy. Generally, in mature economies, government consumption hovers between 10% and 20% of GDP. (Although in strongly welfarist societies, e.g., Scandinavia, it tends to be higher.) High expenditure levels are not automatically a positive sign: they could just as easily be beneficial to economic growth as they could be effectively wastes of funds.

Household Consumption

Usually considerably higher than government consumption, tending towards around 60% of GDP in more developed economies. It reflects the purchasing power and disposable income of the population. Household consumption plays an important role in economic development: it is the main factor that drives production which in turn spurs on investment that again drives production and consumption, in a continuous cycle.

Consumption per Person

And so, Household Consumption per Person in a virile economy would increase from year to year, or at least would not drop sharply. High private consumption levels usually indicate healthy economies. (In this section, we have again used per population ratios for expression. We believe this is crucial for an accurate assessment of consumption and purchasing power.)

Note: Government/Household Consumption should be distinguished from Government/Private Investments. They both make up spending, but consumption refers to non-capital expenditure, while investments mean capital or infrastructure spending. Dealt with in chapter 14.

Sources of Primary Data: IMF, World Bank

Charts

12.1 Govt. & Household Consumption as % of GDP in West Africa during 2003/06

12.2 Govt. & Household Consumption per Person ($PPP) in West Africa during 2003/06

12.3 Govt. & Household Consumption in Nigeria as % of GDP from 1999-2007

12.4 Govt. & Household Consumption in Sub-Saharan Africa as % of GDP from 1999-2007

12.5 Govt. & Household Consumption per Person in Nigeria ($PPP) from 1999-2007

12.6 Govt. & Household Consumption per Person in Sub-Saharan Africa ($PPP) from 1999-2007

12.7 Growth of Govt. & Household Consumption per Person in West Africa during 2003/06

12.8 Build-up of Govt. & Household Consumption per Person in Nigeria and Sub-Saharan Africa from 2000-07: 2000=100

- **Wrap-up**

Tables

1999-2002; 2003-2006:

- *self-comparison to preceding period;*
- *performance in S-Saharan Africa;*
- *performance in West Africa;*
- *performance among oil-exporters;*

for:

Government Consumption as % of GDP

Household Consumption as % of GDP

Government Consumption per Person ($PPP)

Household Consumption per Person ($PPP)

Growth in Government Consumption per Person

Growth in Household Consumption per Person

- Household Consumption per Person in Sub-Saharan Africa during 2003-06: Rankings
- Household Consumption as % of GDP in Sub-Saharan Africa during 2003-06: Rankings
- Growth of Household Consumption per Person in Sub-Saharan Africa during 2003-06: Rankings
- **Purchasing Power Rankings: 2003-06**

12.1 Government Consumption as % of GDP

was it all just a party?

	99-02	03-06
Self-comparison to Preceding Period		◁▷
Performance in Sub-Saharan Africa	▲	▲
Performance in West Africa	▲	▲
	Nigeria	Nigeria
	Cape Verde	Mauritania
	Mauritania	Ghana
	Sierra Leone	Guinea-Bissau
	Gambia, The	Benin
	Senegal	Senegal
	Niger	Cape Verde
	Burkina Faso	Sierra Leone
	Guinea-Bissau	Burkina Faso
	Benin	Niger
	Mali	Gambia, The
	Ghana	Togo
	Togo	Mali
	Côte d'Ivoire	Côte d'Ivoire
	Guinea	Guinea
Performance among Oil-Exporters	▲	▲
	Angola	Angola
	Nigeria	Nigeria
	Congo, Rep.	Congo, Rep.
	Gabon	Sudan
	Cameroon	Cameroon
	Sudan	Côte d'Ivoire
	Chad	Gabon
	Côte d'Ivoire	Chad

Primary Data: World Bank, IMF

12.1

Govt. & Household Consumption as % of GDP in West Africa during 2003/06

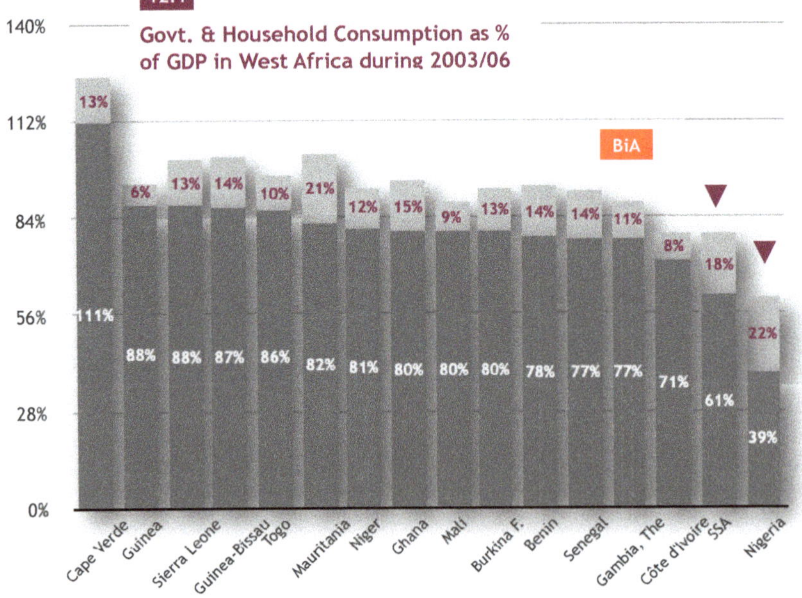

▲	improved *or* better than average
▼	worsened *or* worse than average
◁▷	no change *or* average

12.2 Household Consumption as % of GDP

money to burn

	99-02	03-06
Self-comparison to Preceding Period		▼
Performance in Sub-Saharan Africa	▼	▼
Performance in West Africa	▼	▼
	Cape Verde	Cape Verde
	Guinea-Bissau	Guinea
	Sierra Leone	Sierra Leone
	Togo	Guinea-Bissau
	Ghana	Togo
	Benin	Mauritania
	Niger	Niger
	Mauritania	Ghana
	Burkina Faso	Mali
	Guinea	Burkina Faso
	Mali	Benin
	Senegal	Senegal
	Gambia, The	Gambia, The
	Côte d'Ivoire	Côte d'Ivoire
	Nigeria	**Nigeria**
...ance among ...il-Exporters	▼	▼
	Chad	Sudan
	Sudan	Cameroon
	Côte d'Ivoire	Côte d'Ivoire
	Cameroon	Gabon
	Gabon	Chad
	Nigeria	Angola
	Congo, Rep.	**Nigeria**
	Angola	Congo, Rep.

Data: World Bank

▲	improved *or* better than average
▼	worsened *or* worse than average
◁▷	no change *or* average

A clear depiction of where purchasing power lies. Nigeria is tops in West Africa for govt. consumption, but bottom in household consumption.

A similar situation within the oil group.

Between 1999 and 2006, household consumption dips for Nigeria, while government consumption stays about equal to its preceding high levels.

These suggest Nigerians do not spend as much as their West Africa and oil counterparts in private, household, expenditure.

Reason might be that they are more frugal, but it's more likely that they have a smaller disposable income and are, on the whole, poorer than other Africans.

+1-800-help

"household consumption"?

also known as private consumption

??? 😐

money spent by individuals & families on "everyday" items (food, clothes, cars, rent, etc.) but not "capital" expenditure (house purchase, e.g.) which would be classified as household (or private) investment

Got it

it's a near similar logic for government (or public) consumption & government (public) investment

12.3 Government Consumption per Person ($PPP)

nice... but only if it nourishes

Primary Data: World Bank, IMF

	99-02	03-06
Self-comparison to Preceding Period		▲
Performance in Sub-Saharan Africa	▲	▲

Performance in West Africa	99-02	03-06
	▲	▲
	Cape Verde	Nigeria
	Nigeria	Mauritania
	Mauritania	Cape Verde
	Senegal	Senegal
	Benin	Benin
	Gambia, The	Ghana
	Côte d'Ivoire	Burkina Faso
	Burkina Faso	Côte d'Ivoire
	Ghana	Gambia, The
	Mali	Mali
	Niger	Sierra Leone
	Togo	Togo
	Guinea-Bissau	Niger
	Guinea	Guinea-Bissau
	Sierra Leone	Guinea

12.2

Govt. & Household Consumption per Person ($PPP) in West Africa during 2003/06

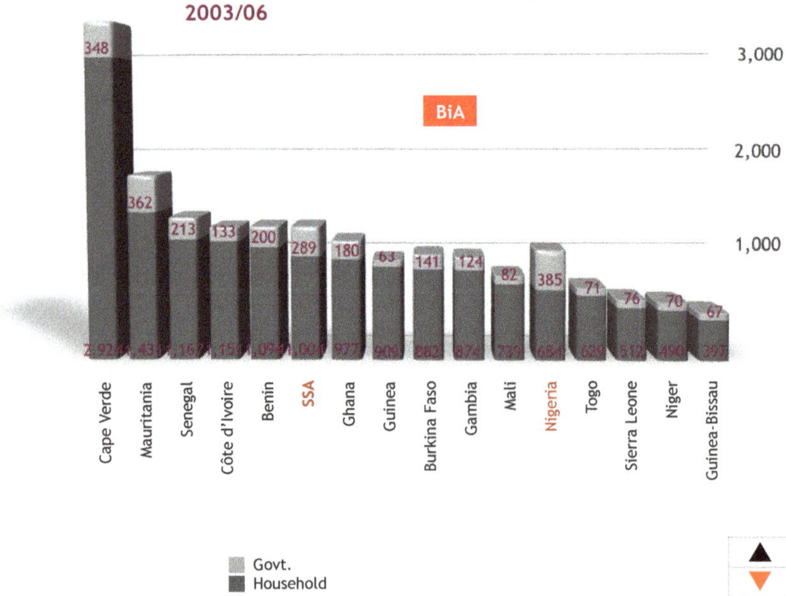

Performance among Oil-Exporters	99-02	03-06
	▲	▲
	Gabon	Angola
	Angola	Gabon
	Congo, Rep.	Congo, Rep.
	Nigeria	Nigeria
	Cameroon	Sudan
	Côte d'Ivoire	Cameroon
	Sudan	Côte d'Ivoire
	Chad	Chad

▲	improved *or* better than average
▼	worsened *or* worse than average
◁▷	no change *or* average

12.4 Household Consumption per Person ($PPP)

because they can afford it

In money terms per capita, the numbers tell a similar story: rich and spending govt., but a non-spending population, individually effectively poorer than other Africans.

	99-02	03-06
Self-comparison to Preceding Period		▲
Performance in Sub-Saharan Africa	▼	▼
Performance in West Africa	▼	▼
	Cape Verde	Cape Verde
	Mauritania	Mauritania
	Côte d'Ivoire	Senegal
	Benin	Côte d'Ivoire
	Senegal	Benin
	Ghana	Ghana
	Guinea	Guinea
	Burkina Faso	Burkina Faso
	Gambia, The	Gambia, The
	Nigeria	Mali
	Togo	**Nigeria**
	Mali	Togo
	Guinea-Bissau	Sierra Leone
	Niger	Niger
	Sierra Leone	Guinea-Bissau
Performance among Oil-Exporters	▼	▼
	Gabon	Gabon
	Cameroon	Angola
	Côte d'Ivoire	Cameroon
	Sudan	Sudan
	Congo, Rep.	Congo, Rep.
	Chad	Côte d'Ivoire
	Angola	Chad
	Nigeria	**Nigeria**

Primary Data: World Bank

▲	improved *or* better than average
▼	worsened *or* worse than average
◁▷	no change *or* average

12.5 Consumption from 1999 to 2007

12.3

Govt. & Household Consumption in Nigeria as % of GDP from 1999-2007

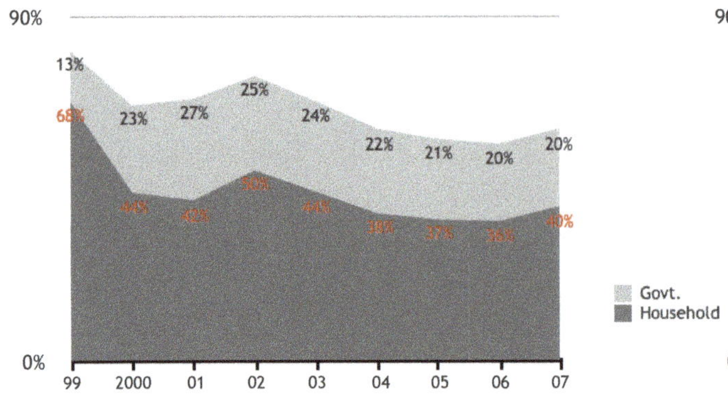

12.4

Govt. & Household Consumption in Sub-Saharan Africa as % of GDP from 1999-2007

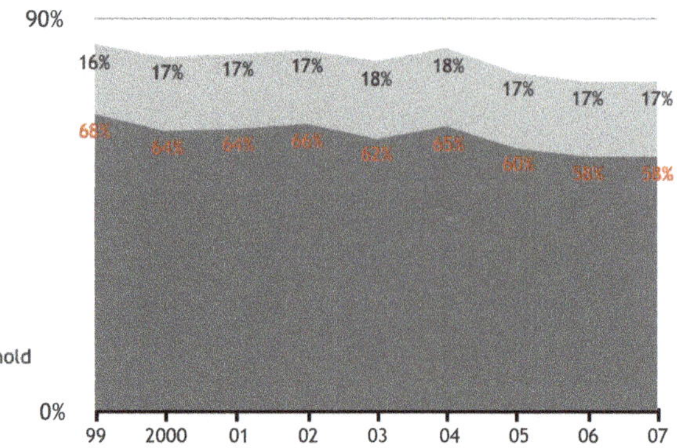

Total consumption, as a % of total economic output, fell across Africa (9%), but it fell deeper in Nigeria (21%).

The levels of personal consumption were every time higher in the rest of Africa (68% ending up as 58%) than Nigeria (68% ending up as 40%).

In money terms, consumption rose in Africa, suggesting a population growing in wealth. Nigeria's residents were poorer (smaller disposable income).

Consumption in GDP terms fell, & in money terms rose, suggesting that the economies can sustain higher spending levels, spurring growth; but only if managed more efficiently.

12.5

Govt. & Household Consumption per Person in Nigeria ($PPP) from 1999-2007

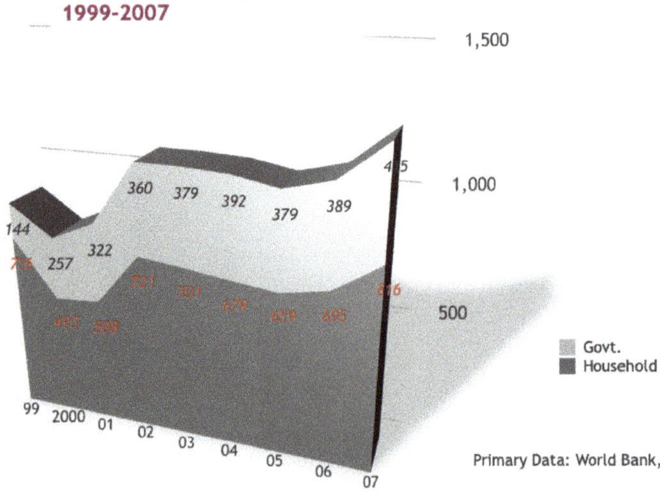

12.6

Govt. & Household Consumption per Person in Sub-Saharan Africa ($PPP) from 1999-2007

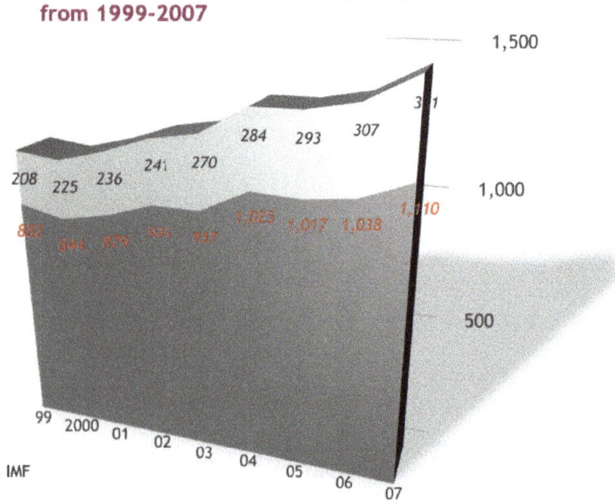

Primary Data: World Bank, IMF

Household Consumption per Person in Sub-Saharan Africa during 2003-06: Rankings

Rank	Country
1	Seychelles
2	Gabon
3	Mauritius
4	South Africa
5	Botswana
6	Cape Verde
7	Swaziland
8	Namibia
9	Angola
10	Cameroon
11	Senegal
12	Congo, Rep.
13	Côte d' Ivoire
14	Benin

TOP

Rank	Country
15	Kenya
16	Equatorial Guinea
17	Lesotho
18	Ghana
19	Comoros
20	Chad
21	Guinea
22	Burkina Faso
23	Gambia, The
24	Tanzania
25	Madagascar
26	Mali
27	Zambia
28	Nigeria

MIDDLE

Rank	Country
29	Eritrea
30	Uganda
31	Rwanda
32	Togo
33	Malawi
34	Central Afr. Rep.
35	Sierra Leone
36	Ethiopia
37	Mozambique
38	Niger
39	Guinea-Bissau
40	Burundi
41	Congo, Dem. Rep.

BOTTOM

Not surprising, then, that Nigeria is at best just about average in individual's purchasing power.

This is often camouflaged by the capacity of its huge market to absorb products and services thrown at it.

It should be remembered that its people may be poorer on the whole than other Africans, but even though the percentage of its relatively wealthy is small...

... because of its overall population, that small percentage is still larger in absolute size (no. of persons) than many countries' entire populations.

Household Consumption as % of GDP in Sub-Saharan Africa during 2003-06: Rankings

Rank	Country
1	Cape Verde
2	Malawi
3	Central Afr. Rep.
4	Lesotho
5	Congo, Dem. Rep.
6	Guinea
7	Comoros
	Sierra Leone
8	Guinea-Bissau
9	Togo
10	Rwanda
11	Madagascar
12	Ethiopia
13	Burundi
14	Eritrea

TOP

Rank	Country
15	Niger
16	Ghana
17	Mali
18	Burkina Faso
19	Benin
20	Senegal
21	Gambia, The
22	Uganda
23	Tanzania
24	Kenya
25	Mozambique
26	Cameroon
27	Côte d' Ivoire

MIDDLE

Rank	Country
28	Swaziland
29	Mauritius
30	Zambia
31	South Africa
32	Gabon
33	Chad
34	Seychelles
35	Namibia
36	Angola
37	Nigeria
38	Congo, Rep.
39	Botswana
40	Equatorial Guinea

BOTTOM

Primary Data: World Bank, IMF

- Central Africa
- East Africa
- Southern Africa
- West Africa

12.6 Growth in Government Consumption per Person

there's more where that came from

	99-02	03-06
Self-comparison to Preceding Period		▼
Performance in Sub-Saharan Africa	▲	▼

Performance in West Africa

99-02 ▲	03-06 ▼
Nigeria	Guinea-Bissau
Sierra Leone	Ghana
Guinea	Mali
Benin	Mauritania
Mauritania	Benin
Guinea-Bissau	Cape Verde
Senegal	Senegal
Cape Verde	Togo
Burkina Faso	Burkina Faso
Côte d'Ivoire	Niger
Gambia, The	Côte d'Ivoire
Ghana	Sierra Leone
Niger	**Nigeria**
Mali	Gambia, The
Togo	Guinea

The Nigerian govt. seems to have begun to cut down its expenses drastically during 2003-06, compared to 1999-02 levels.

Primary Data: World Bank, IMF

Performance among Oil-Exporters

99-02 ▲	03-06 ▼
Nigeria	Sudan
Angola	Gabon
Sudan	Cameroon
Chad	Chad
Cameroon	Côte d'Ivoire
Côte d'Ivoire	**Nigeria**
Congo, Rep.	Congo, Rep.
Gabon	Angola

▲	improved *or* better than average
▼	worsened *or* worse than average
◁▷	no change *or* average

12.7

Growth of Govt. & Household Consumption per Person in West Africa during 2003/06

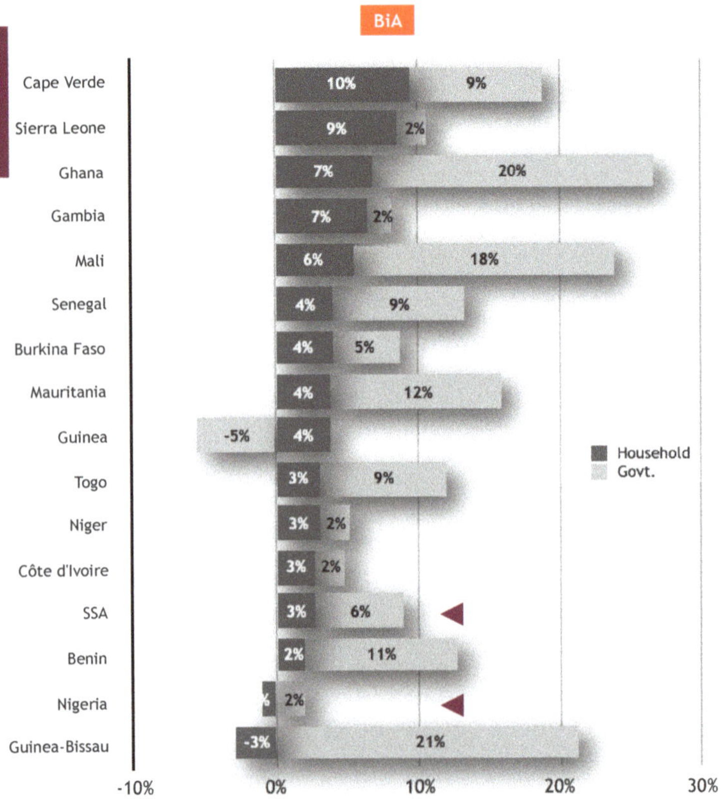

12.7 Growth in Household Consumption per Person

I'd like this... and that... and that...

	99-02	03-06
Self-comparison to Preceding Period		▼
Performance in Sub-Saharan Africa	▲	▼
Performance in West Africa	▼	▼
	Sierra Leone	Cape Verde
	Cape Verde	Sierra Leone
	Burkina Faso	Ghana
	Mali	Gambia, The
	Mauritania	Mali
	Guinea	Senegal
	Senegal	Burkina Faso
	Ghana	Mauritania
	Benin	Guinea
	Gambia, The	Togo
	Nigeria	Niger
	Niger	Côte d'Ivoire
	Togo	Benin
	Guinea-Bissau	**Nigeria**
	Côte d'Ivoire	Guinea-Bissau
Performance among Oil-Exporters	▼	▼
	Angola	Gabon
	Gabon	Angola
	Chad	Congo, Rep.
	Cameroon	Sudan
	Sudan	Côte d'Ivoire
	Nigeria	Cameroon
	Côte d'Ivoire	**Nigeria**
	Congo, Rep.	Chad

Primary Data: World Bank, IMF

▲	improved *or* better than average
▼	worsened *or* worse than average
◁▷	no change *or* average

But individuals' consumption was not growing, either (or, at best, was growing at a falling rate, and relatively much slower than elsewhere).

Not a good sign. Because it again highlights a progressively weaker private purchasing power.

Without consumption, industry won't grow, putting pressure on GDP, and ultimately shrinking the economy.

12.8 Build-up of Consumption from 1999 to 2007

Looks like there was a rally to an increased purchasing power in Nigeria between 2000 & 2007, if all the countries are put to the same start level in 2000.

Suggests that pre-2000 levels were so low that even later growth rates could not bring it to par in West Africa, as borne out by the preceding sections above.

12.8

Build-up of Govt. & Household Consumption per Person in Nigeria and Sub-Saharan Africa from 2000-07: 2000=100

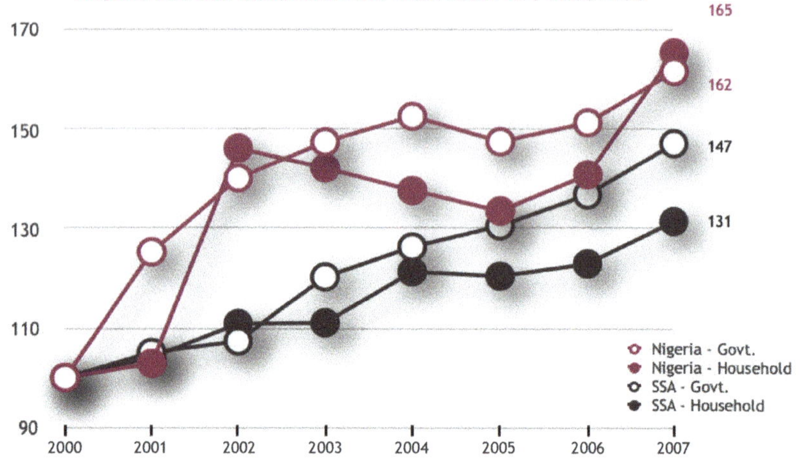

Primary Data: World Bank, IMF

Central Africa
East Africa
Southern Africa
West Africa

Growth of Household Consumption per Person in Sub-Saharan Africa during 2003-06: Rankings

Rank	Country	Rank	Country	Rank	Country
1	Gabon	15	Angola	29	Niger
2	Ethiopia	16	Congo, Rep.	30	Namibia
3	Madagascar	17	Mali	31	Côte d' Ivoire
4	Botswana	18	Comoros	32	Cameroon
5	Cape Verde	19	Congo, Dem. Rep.	33	Benin
6	Mauritius	20	Swaziland	34	Zambia
7	Sierra Leone	21	Rwanda	35	Burundi
8	Central Afr. Rep.	22	Senegal	36	Lesotho
9	South Africa	23	Burkina Faso	37	**Nigeria**
10	Kenya	24	Mozambique	38	Chad
11	Ghana	25	Guinea	39	Guinea-Bissau
12	Gambia, The	26	Uganda	40	Eritrea
13	Malawi	27	Togo	41	Equatorial Guinea
14	Tanzania	28	Seychelles		
TOP		MIDDLE		BOTTOM	

Poor growth in household consumption between 2003-06, again as illustrated by the build-up chart above.

Leaders & Stragglers

around the world in 80 days

Bleak verdict, indeed.

Bringing to question issues like:
- an impoverishing larger segment of population; or
- wealth being restricted to a small minority, so that their large consumption notwithstanding, data still reports poor overall purchasing power; or

... a mixture of both.

Purchasing Power Rankings: 2003-06

Rank	Country	Rank	Country	Rank	Country
1	Cape Verde	15	Senegal	29	Cameroon
2	Gabon	16	Swaziland	30	Côte d' Ivoire
3	Mauritius	17	Gambia, The	31	Namibia
4	Madagascar	18	Lesotho	32	Uganda
5	Comoros	19	Mali	33	Niger
6	South Africa	20	Angola	34	Eritrea
7	Central Afr. Rep.	21	Tanzania	35	Guinea-Bissau
8	Ghana	22	Rwanda	36	Mozambique
9	Malawi	23	Burkina Faso	37	Burundi
10	Botswana	24	Seychelles	38	Zambia
11	Sierra Leone	25	Congo, Dem. Rep.	39	Chad
12	Kenya	26	Benin	40	Equatorial Guinea
13	Ethiopia	27	Congo, Rep.	41	Nigeria
14	Guinea	28	Togo		
TOP		MIDDLE		BOTTOM	

Primary Data: World Bank, IMF

Central Africa
East Africa
Southern Africa
West Africa

Wrap-up: Purchasing Power

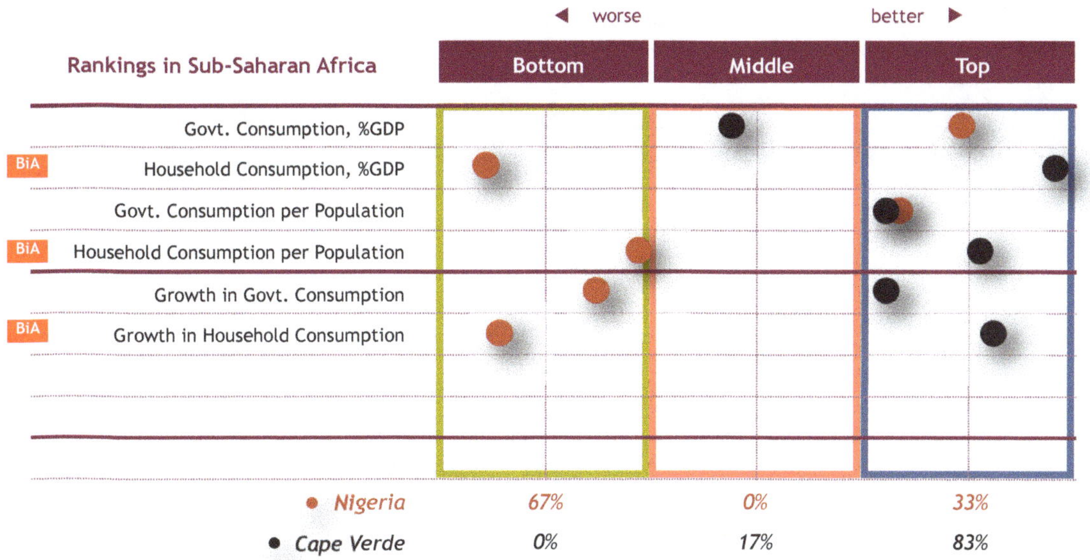

- The people of Cape Verde have the deepest pockets in West Africa and Africa, too. Nigeria is bottom of West Africa and Africa, too.

- Government consumption in Nigeria is healthy enough, the problem is private disposable income. The Nigeria government was cutting back its spending, though, growing it at a falling pace. The contrast couldn't be starker between Nigeria government spending and the purchasing power of the country's people.

- It might be proposed that this is because of its large population, but that won't entirely explain the dismal showing. Government consumption per person of population is very robust, despite that large population.

- Instead, it is more likely that there is a quickly growing gulf between sections of the population, between the rich and the poor, the ranks of the rich narrowing, while that at the other end is increasingly bloated.

13. Self-Reliance

doing it by themselves

Strictly speaking, no economy can be self-reliant. But the more developed the economy, the less reliant it is on external providers for products or services it can efficiently render by itself. Every economy is said to have areas of "competitive advantage": sectors in which it is well positioned (by natural endowments, for example, or specific skills, etc) to compete favorably with other countries. It would not make sense, for example, for Nigeria to depend on others for crude oil, or the United States to outsource its banking needs to foreign operators.

So, different sectors can be evaluated to see if the economy is operating as efficiently as should be possible in the circumstances. By expressing these indicators in per capita terms, a more accurate picture of self-reliance or the extent of dependence is achieved.

Imports dependence

The extent on which an economy depends on others to supply goods and services. Usually taken to be an unhealthy situation, unless inescapable. Holland, for example, cannot be expected to grow its own bananas, but would be inefficient if it relied overwhelmingly on others for its dairy needs.

Net exports: desirable status; means the country exports more than it imports; results in a positive trade balance.

Net imports: the country imports more than it exports; results in a negative trade balance.

By self-sufficient, we mean that the country exports more than it imports, not that it produces all the quantity of the particular products that its consumption level requires.

Composition of Goods Exports

Three broad sectors: agriculture, fuels & mining, and manufactures. Agriculture and fuels/mining are regarded as "primary" sectors because their products require relatively little further innovation before sale. Manufactures, on the other hand, require innovation and significant further added input or processing; and so, further alteration/transformation. Sturdier and more developed economies are supposed to rely more on the sectors that demand innovation and actual discernible value-added. These economies are generally less susceptible to the vagaries of international commodity prices, which tend to be more fickle since these commodities effectively are sold as-is, without the distinguishing qualities of end-processing or transformation that would provide comparatively more attractive value-added features.

Foreign Reserves

Countries usually hold money in foreign reserves, which can be deployed in a number of ways, for a variety of objectives. While huge foreign reserves is the better position, the continuous growing of reserves without appropriate deployment might augur negatively for the country. The volume of reserves is often measured by the number of months of imports it can finance at prevailing import levels. This helps put the amount of reserves in more accurate contexts, since imports would have to be paid for in foreign currency.

Foreign Debt

Again, strictly speaking, it would be unusual to come across a country (or government) that is without debt. Domestic debt is common and in order, because it is a convenient way for governments to source funds without "capital flight", that is, without having repayment funds leaving the country to creditors abroad. Domestic debt, besides incentives of specifically micro-economic sorts, ensures that the money circulates and stays within the country, stimulating economic development, rather than leaving the country's shores and stimulating economic growth in foreign lands.

However, only rarely do countries manage to source all funds internally. The danger, though, is to have foreign debt grow to unmanageable proportions that would compromise the country's ability to drive internal growth, because it would effectively become committed to an albatross of external debt repayment burdens. Countries in that position jeopardize domestic needs because a disproportionately large chunk of their earnings goes towards servicing foreign debt commitments. This is often a big danger with developing economies.

Growth of Income & Debt

Income here refers to GNI: Gross National Income, an estimation of the earnings of all of a country's residents and non-residents, i.e., it includes remittances from abroad. Comparing its growth with the growth of debt provides a rough assessment of the country's book balance and sustainability.

Aid Dependency

Foreign aid is not necessarily restricted to poor countries, although they – understandably – form the bulk of beneficiaries of aid. Usually, countries are either net donors or net recipients. While it would be unexpected for the United States, Switzerland or other west European countries to be beneficiaries of any sort of aid, it is accepted that Hungary, Jordan, Israel and Poland, for example, would be listed as aid recipients of one economic sort or another, despite being rich or developed economies. However, the danger here applies more accurately to the poorer countries of the developing world and the countries of the "transition" economies (mostly the former Soviet Republics and south-east Asia). Excessive dependency on aid is taken to be a sign of a weak economic base and rings alarm bells of fragility.

Aid Dependency and Country Development

There has been a lot of discussion lately about the appropriateness or otherwise of aid as a channel for the stimulation of social and economic development. Much has been said about the merits and otherwise of a continued pumping of aid into developing country economies. An attempt is made in the earlier part of this book (Part I) to view the question from an empirical perspective, by comparing the pace of economic and social development of African countries, with the amount of aid they received, across 8 to 12 years.

Sources of Primary Data: AfDB, IMF, World Bank, WTO

Charts

Tables

2000-2002; 2003-2006:
- *self-comparison to preceding period;*
- *performance in S-Saharan Africa;*
- *performance in West Africa;*
- *performance among oil-exporters;*

for:

Growth in Total Goods Exports per Population

Growth in Services Exports per Population

1999-2002; 2003-2006:
- *self-comparison to preceding period;*
- *performance in S-Saharan Africa;*
- *performance in West Africa;*
- *performance among oil-exporters;*

for:

Growth in Total Goods Exports per Population

Imports Dependence in Merchandise

Imports Dependence in Services

Service of Foreign Debt (as % of exports)

1997-2002; 2003-2006; 2007-2008:
- *self-comparison to preceding period;*
- *performance in S-Saharan Africa;*
- *performance in West Africa;*
- *performance among oil-exporters;*

for:

Foreign Reserves (months of imports)

Foreign Debt (as % of GDP)

Foreign Debt (as $PPP per person)

Aid Dependency (as % of GDP)

Aid Dependency (as $PPP per person)

- Total Exports and Imports per Person of Population in West Africa during 2003/06 ($US)
- Merchandise Imports Dependence per Person in Sub-Saharan Africa during 2003-06: Rankings
- Services Imports Dependence per Person in Sub-Saharan Africa during 2003-06: Rankings
- Foreign Reserves (as months of imports) in Sub-Saharan Africa during 2003-06: Rankings
- Foreign Debt as % of GDP in Sub-Saharan Africa during 2003-06: Rankings
- Foreign Debt per Person of Population in Sub-Saharan Africa during 2003-06: Rankings
- Service of Foreign Debt as % of Exports in Sub-Saharan Africa during 2003-06: Rankings
- Foreign Aid as % of GDP in Sub-Saharan Africa during 2003-06: Rankings
- Foreign Aid in Sub-Saharan Africa as $PPP per Person during 2003-06: Rankings
- Household Consumption as % of GDP in Sub-Saharan Africa during 2003-06: Rankings
- **Self-Reliance Rankings: 2003-06**

13.1 Exports & Imports of Goods & Services

outgoings & incomings

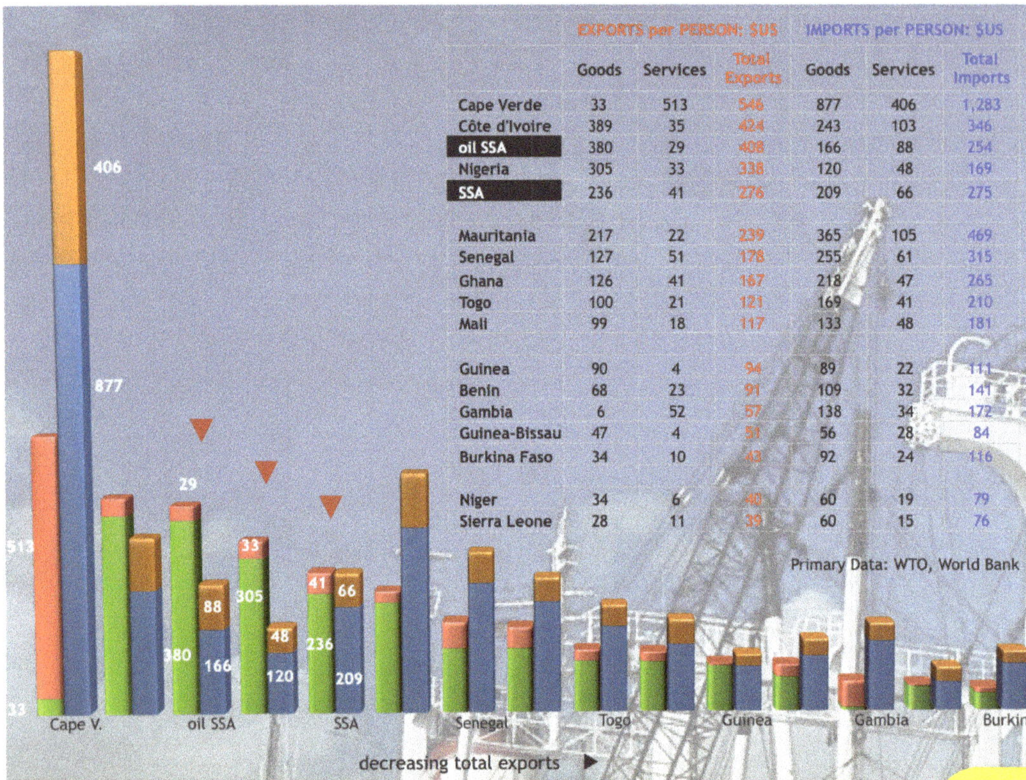

	EXPORTS per PERSON: $US			IMPORTS per PERSON: $US		
	Goods	Services	Total Exports	Goods	Services	Total Imports
Cape Verde	33	513	546	877	406	1,283
Côte d'Ivoire	389	35	424	243	103	346
oil SSA	380	29	408	166	88	254
Nigeria	305	33	338	120	48	169
SSA	236	41	276	209	66	275
Mauritania	217	22	239	365	105	469
Senegal	127	51	178	255	61	315
Ghana	126	41	167	218	47	265
Togo	100	21	121	169	41	210
Mali	99	18	117	133	48	181
Guinea	90	4	94	89	22	111
Benin	68	23	91	109	32	141
Gambia	6	52	57	138	34	172
Guinea-Bissau	47	4	51	56	28	84
Burkina Faso	34	10	43	92	24	116
Niger	34	6	40	60	19	79
Sierra Leone	28	11	39	60	15	76

Primary Data: WTO, World Bank

13.1

Total Exports and Imports per Person of Population in West Africa during 2003/06. ($US)

- Services Exports
- Goods Exports

- Services Imports
- Goods Imports

Nigeria has the 3rd highest volume of total exports per person in West Africa.

Most of the exports are merchandise (goods; 90%) and much of that merchandise is crude oil. Only a small % comes from the services sector (10%).

The same is true of Africa's oil bloc, 93% goods and 7% services. For the rest of Africa, the ratios were 85% and 15%.

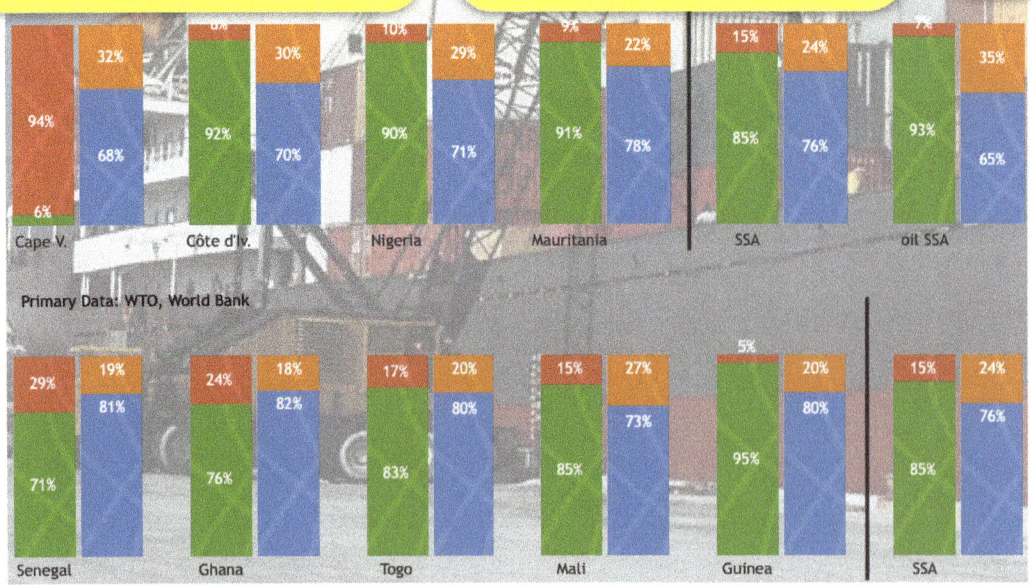

13.2

% Breakdown of Exports and Imports into Goods & Services in West Africa during 2003/06

- Services Exports
- Goods Exports

- Services Imports
- Goods Imports

13.3

Total Exports and Imports as % of GDP in West Africa during 2003/06.

If taken as a proportion of the country overall economy size, rather than $ per person, Nigeria has the highest volume of exports.

Cape Verde & Gambia are the only countries in West Africa that earn more exports revenue from services and not goods.

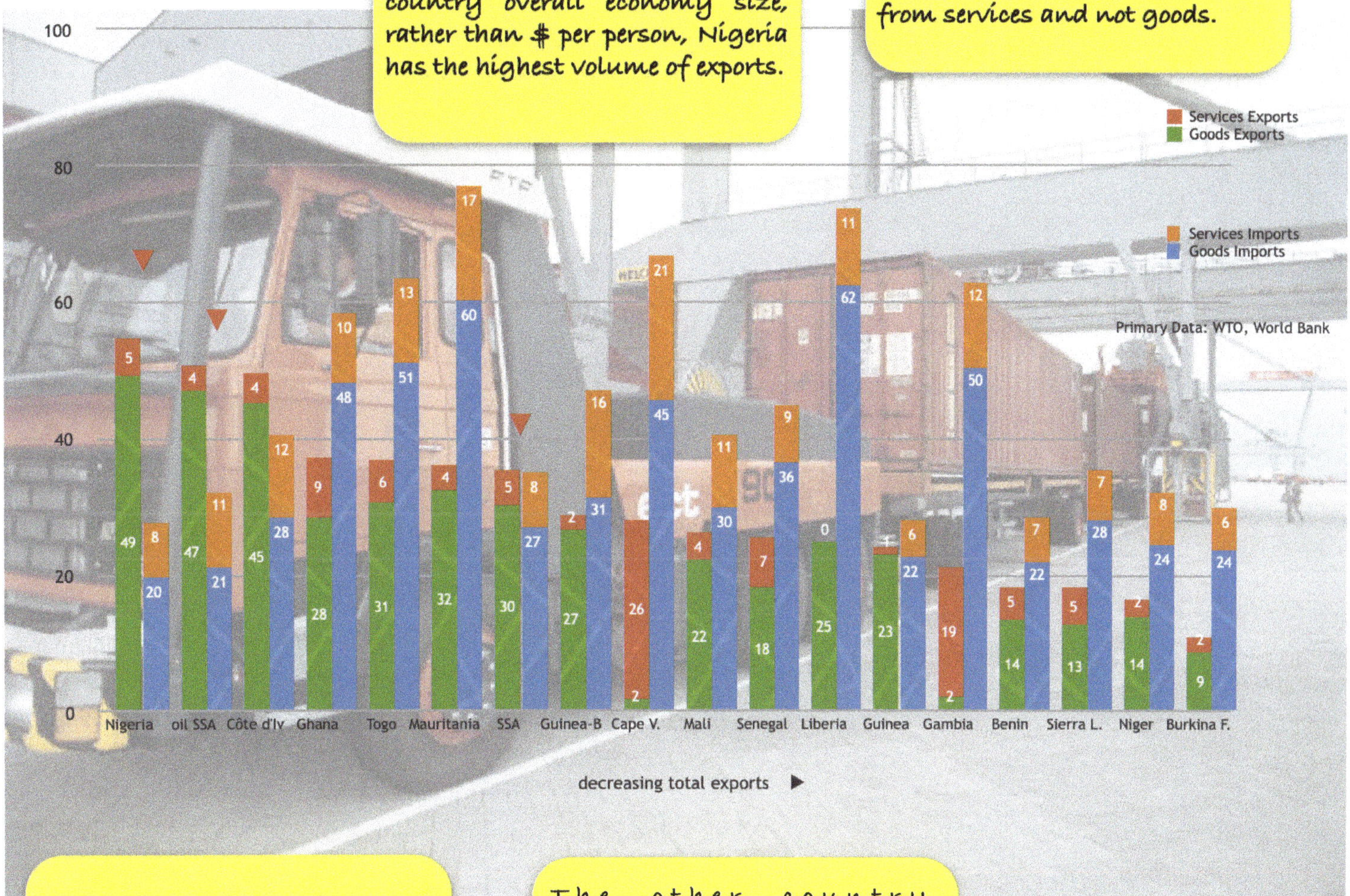

And Nigeria is 1 of only 2 countries in West Africa that export more than they import, as a proportion of economy.

The other country, unsurprisingly, is the only other oil country in the group: Côte d'Ivoire.

13.2

% Breakdown of Exports and Imports into Goods & Services in West Africa during 2003/06

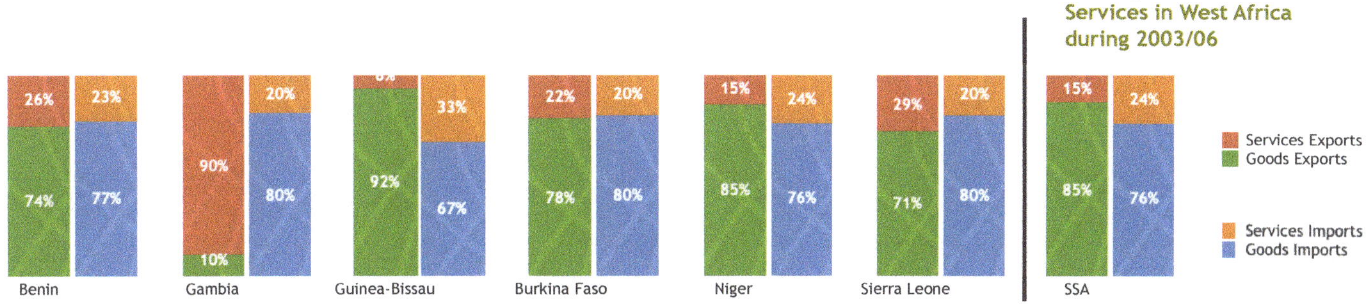

Exports per person in Nigeria has increased at a faster pace than in the rest of Africa. Again, largely oil exports.

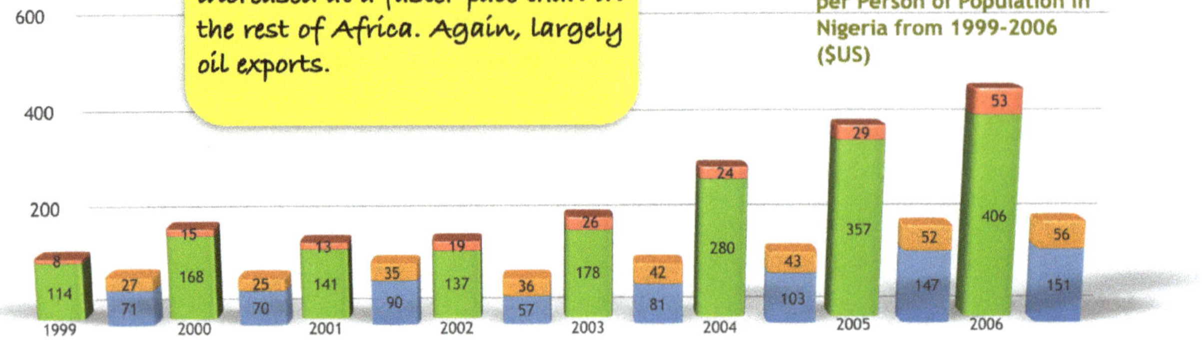

13.4
Total Exports and Imports per Person of Population in Nigeria from 1999-2006 ($US)

Nigeria also put increasing distance between exports and imports; good news for its trade balance; better than the Africa average.

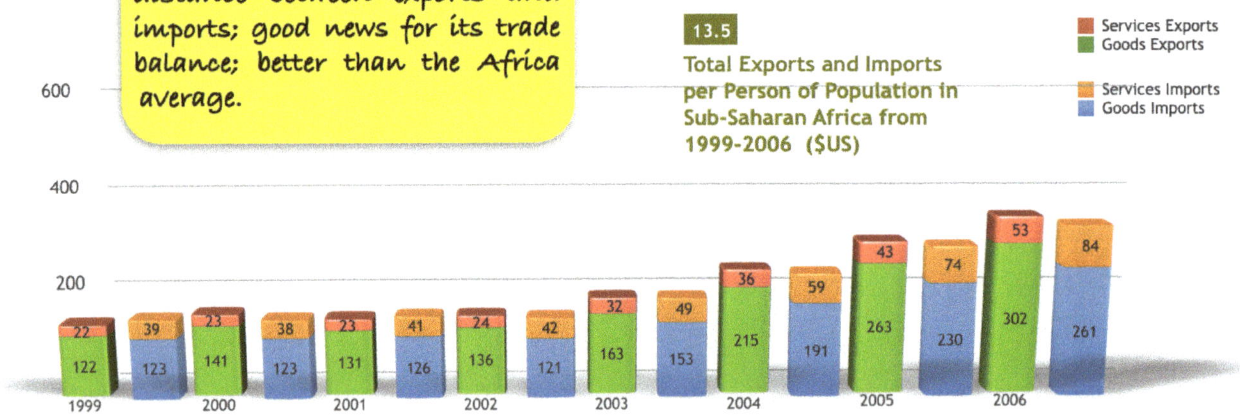

13.5
Total Exports and Imports per Person of Population in Sub-Saharan Africa from 1999-2006 ($US)

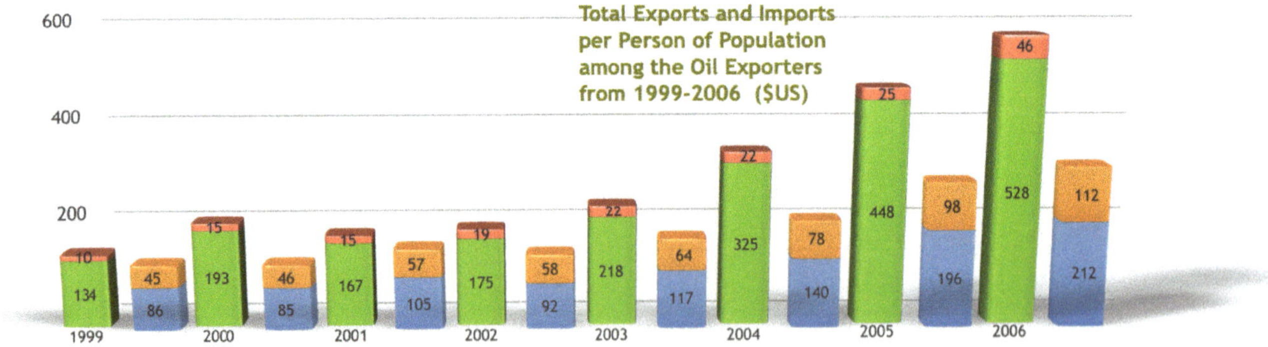

13.6
Total Exports and Imports per Person of Population among the Oil Exporters from 1999-2006 ($US)

Primary Data: WTO, World Bank

But the other oil economies in Sub-Saharan Africa had their exports growing higher and more rapidly than Nigeria's.

However, their imports have been less curtailed than Nigeria's, growing larger and quicker, too.

With respect to the overall size of the economy, exports have risen in Nigeria but not as rapidly as they did in per person terms.

13.7
Total Exports and Imports as % of GDP in Nigeria from 1999-2006

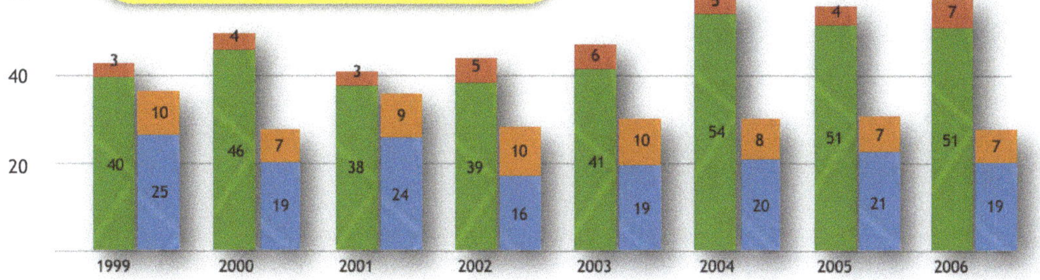

Which suggests that while exports have risen, the rest of the economy has risen as well, but at a slower rate, and so to a smaller extent.

13.8
Total Exports and Imports as % of GDP in Sub-Saharan Africa from 1999-2006

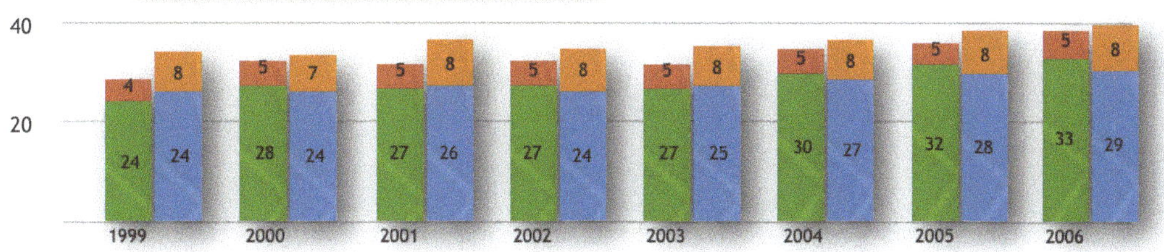

13.9
Total Exports and Imports as % of GDP among the Oil Exporters from 1999-2006

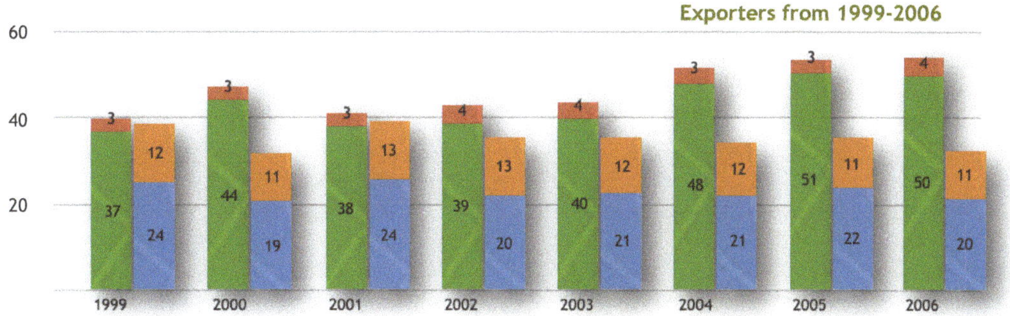

Primary Data: WTO, World Bank

Imports fell in Nigeria, and by more than it did in the other oil economies. While the rest of Africa increased imports levels.

Services Exports
Goods Exports
Services Imports
Goods Imports

13.2 Growth in Goods Exports and Imports

are they leaving faster than they are coming?

In West Africa, only Mauritania and Sierra Leone grew exports faster than Nigeria during 2003/06.

Among oil exporters, Nigeria stepped up one place, growing exports quicker than 5 of the 9 oil producers.

Growth in Total Goods Exports per Population	00-02	03-06
Self-comparison to Preceding Period		▲
Performance in Sub-Saharan Africa	▲	▲
Performance in West Africa	▲	▲
	Sierra Leone	Mauritania
	Mali	Sierra Leone
	Nigeria	**Nigeria**
	Côte d'Ivoire	Burkina Faso
	Guinea	Ghana
	Gambia, The	Cape Verde
	Togo	Niger
	Ghana	Mali
	Guinea-Bissau	Côte d'Ivoire
	Benin	Guinea
	Senegal	Togo
	Burkina Faso	Senegal
	Cape Verde	Guinea-Bissau
	Niger	Benin
	Mauritania	Gambia, The
	Liberia	Liberia

Primary Data: WTO, World Bank

Performance among Oil-Exporters	00-02	03-06
	◁▷	▲
	Sudan	Chad
	Equatorial Guinea	Equatorial Guinea
	Angola	Angola
	Congo, Rep.	**Nigeria**
	Nigeria	Sudan
	Côte d'Ivoire	Congo, Rep.
	Cameroon	Gabon
	Gabon	Cameroon
	Chad	Côte d'Ivoire

▲	improved *or* better than average
▼	worsened *or* worse than average
◁▷	no change *or* average

13.10

Growth on Previous Yr. of Goods Exports and Imports per Person in West Africa during 2003/06

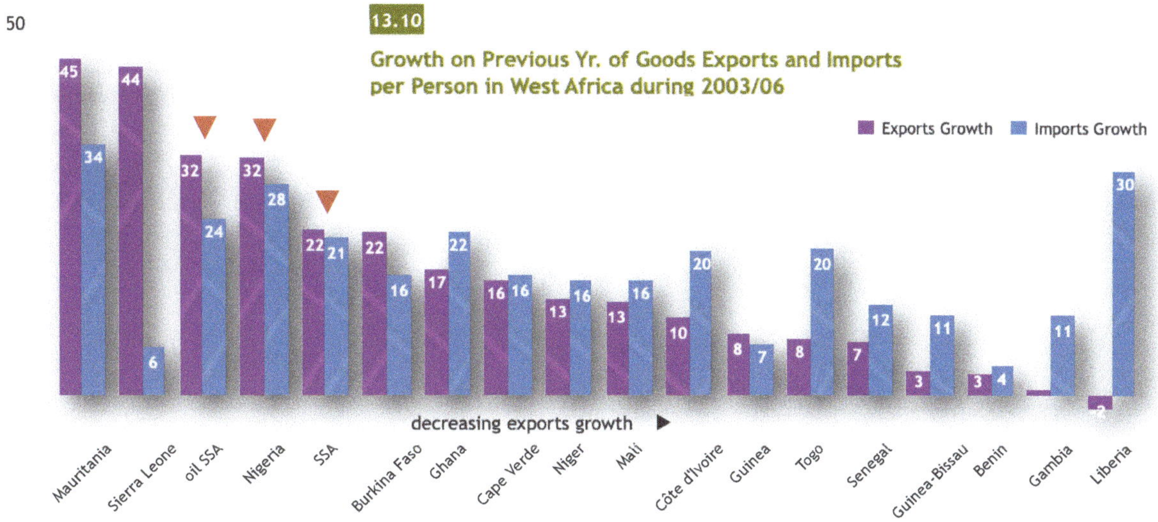

Primary Data: WTO, World Bank

Concretely, focusing on just the period between 2000 and 2007, Nigeria grew exports earnings by a larger volume than the Africa average.

13.11

Build-up of Goods Exports and Imports per Person in Nigeria and Sub-Saharan Africa from 2000-07: 2000=100

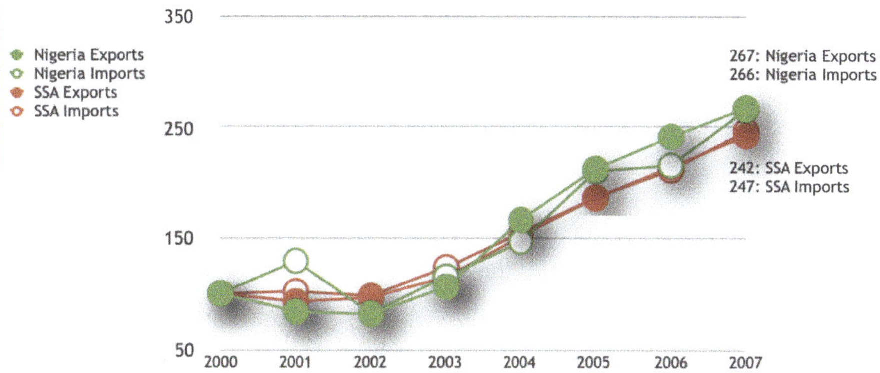

But it didn't do as well as the other oil economies, even though it kept its imports volume growth under tighter check than they did.

13.12

Build-up of Goods Exports and Imports per Person in Nigeria and Oil-Exporting Countries from 2000-07: 2000=100

13.3 Growth in Services Exports and Imports

are these coming faster than they are leaving?

Nigeria didn't grow services exports as ruggedly. The pace slowed in 03/06. Though that only cost it a drop of 1 place in West Africa, compared to 00/02.

Its drop among the oil exporters, however, was worse; the group seem to have grown their non-oil exports earnings by faster margins.

Growth in Services Exports per Population	00-02	03-06
Self-comparison to Preceding Period		▼
Performance in Sub-Saharan Africa	▲	▲
Performance in West Africa	▲	▲

00-02	03-06
Nigeria	Burkina Faso
Sierra Leone	**Nigeria**
Guinea	Togo
Guinea-Bissau	Cape Verde
Mauritania	Ghana
Mali	Guinea-Bissau
Niger	Mauritania
Cape Verde	Niger
Togo	Benin
Burkina Faso	Senegal
Ghana	Gambia, The
Senegal	Sierra Leone
Côte d'Ivoire	Côte d'Ivoire
Benin	Mali
Gambia, The	Guinea

Primary Data: WTO, World Bank

Performance among Oil-Exporters	00-02	03-06
	▲	▲
	Sudan	Angola
	Nigeria	Sudan
	Cameroon	Equatorial Guinea
	Equatorial Guinea	**Nigeria**
	Angola	Gabon
	Chad	Chad
	Congo, Rep.	Congo, Rep.
	Côte d'Ivoire	Côte d'Ivoire
	Gabon	Cameroon

▲	improved *or* better than average
▼	worsened *or* worse than average
◁▷	no change *or* average

13.13

Growth on Previous Yr. of Services Exports and Imports per Person in West Africa during 2003/06 (%)

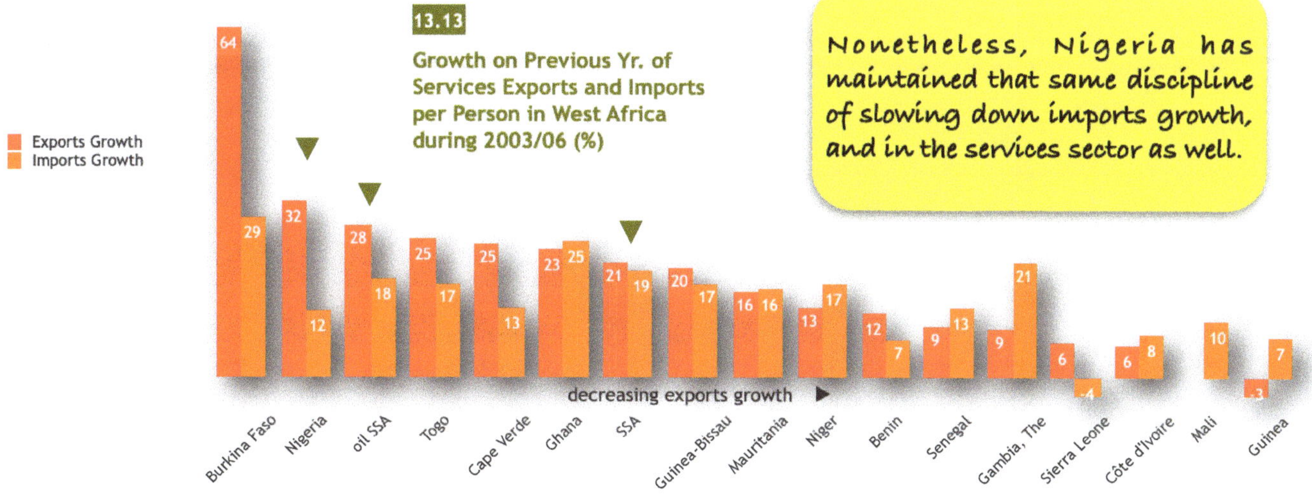

Primary Data: WTO, World Bank

Nonetheless, Nigeria has maintained that same discipline of slowing down imports growth, and in the services sector as well.

13.14

Build-up of Services Exports and Imports per Person in Nigeria and Sub-Saharan Africa from 2000-06: 2000=100

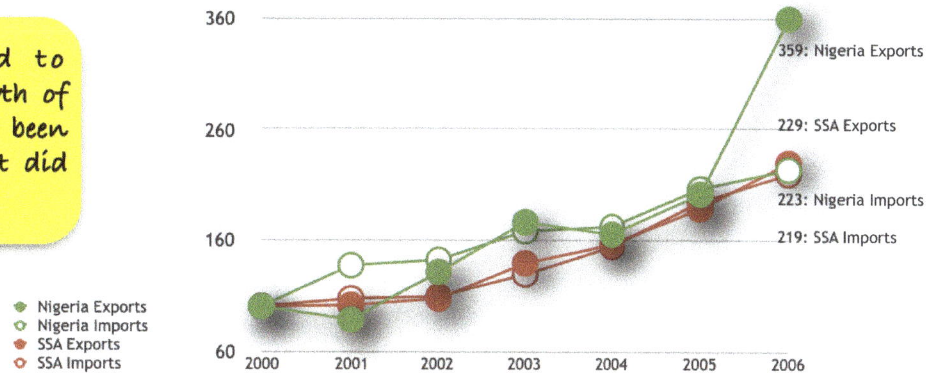

If focus is restricted to 2000-2006, Nigeria's growth of services exports might have been slow on the average, but it did spike in 2006.

13.15

Build-up of Services Exports and Imports per Person in Nigeria and Oil-Exporting Countries from 2000-06: 2000=100

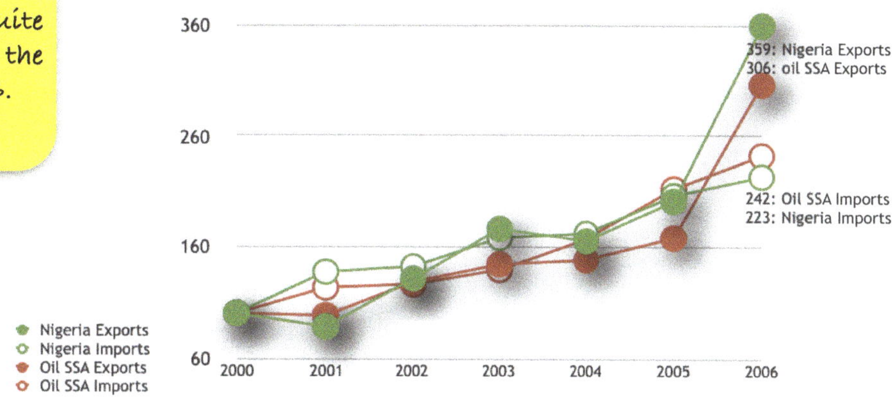

As it spiked in the other oil economies, too, indicating, quite likely, a spur common across the group between 2005 and 2006.

13.4 Imports Dependence in Merchandise

unable to do without

Nigeria was the best performer in West Africa in external trade of goods, selling more than it bought.

Among Africa's oil economies, it was out-done. But it saw a modest improvement, nonetheless, of 1 place up, to average position.

	99-02	03-06
Self-comparison to Preceding Period		▲
Performance in Sub-Saharan Africa	▲	▲
Performance in West Africa	▲	▲

Primary Data: WTO, World Bank

99-02	03-06
Côte d'Ivoire	**Nigeria**
Nigeria	Côte d'Ivoire
Guinea	Guinea
Guinea-Bissau	Guinea-Bissau
Niger	Niger
Mali	Sierra Leone
Mauritania	Mali
Sierra Leone	Benin
Togo	Liberia
Burkina Faso	Burkina Faso
Benin	Togo
Liberia	Ghana
Senegal	Senegal
Ghana	Gambia, The
Gambia, The	Mauritania
Cape Verde	Cape Verde

	99-02	03-06
Performance among Oil-Exporters	▼	◁▷
	Equatorial Guinea	Equatorial Guinea
	Gabon	Gabon
	Congo, Rep.	Congo, Rep.
	Angola	Angola
	Côte d'Ivoire	**Nigeria**
	Nigeria	Côte d'Ivoire
	Cameroon	Chad
	Sudan	Cameroon
	Chad	Sudan

▲	better = less imports dependent
▼	worse = more imports dependent
◁▷	no change *or* average

13. Self-Reliance

Only 3 countries in West Africa were "self-sufficient" in external trade during 2003/06: Nigeria, Côte d'Ivoire and Guinea.

13.16

Net Goods Exports per Person in West Africa during 2003/06

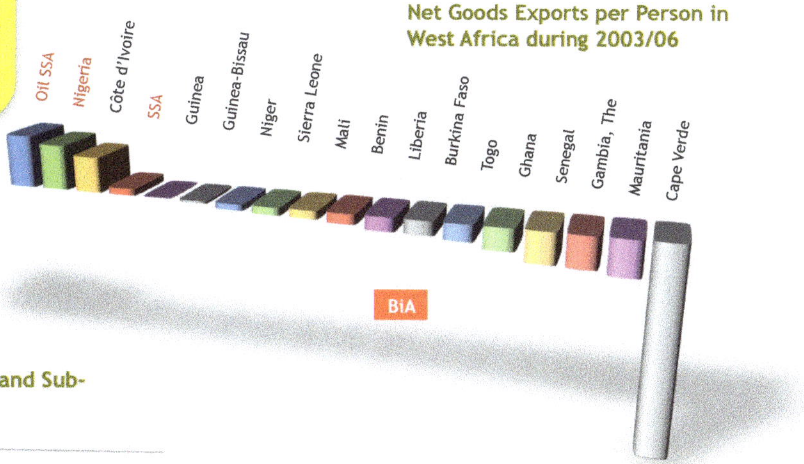

	$US
oil SSA	214
Nigeria	185
Côte d'Ivoire	146
SSA	27
Guinea	1
Guinea-Bissau	-9
Niger	-26
Sierra Leone	-32
Mali	-34
Benin	-41
Liberia	-58
Burkina Faso	-58
Togo	-69
Ghana	-91
Senegal	-128
Gambia, The	-132
Mauritania	-148
Cape Verde	-844

Primary Data: WTO, World Bank

13.17

Net Goods Exports per Person in Nigeria and Sub-Saharan Africa from 1999-2007

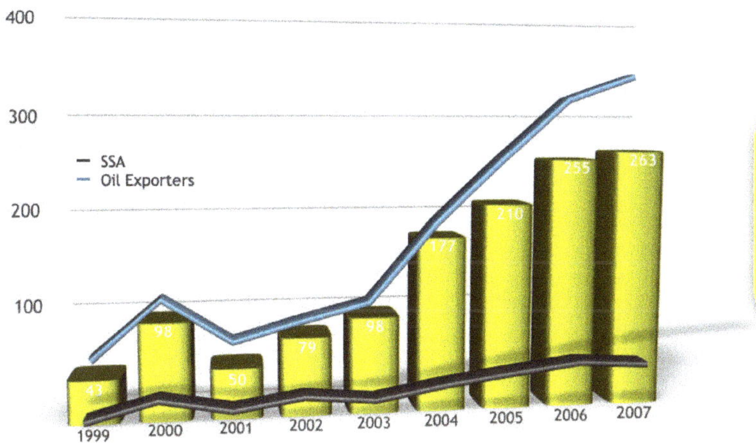

Indeed, Nigeria was more self-sufficient than most of the continent, save the other oil exporters.

Merchandise Imports Dependence per Person in Sub-Saharan Africa during 2003-06: Rankings

Rank	Country	Rank	Country	Rank	Country
1	Equatorial Guinea	15	Niger	29	Togo
2	Gabon	16	Burundi	30	Kenya
3	Congo, Rep.	17	Rwanda	31	Ghana
4	Angola	18	Zambia	32	Eritrea
5	Botswana	19	Mozambique	33	Comoros
6	Nigeria	20	Sierra Leone	34	Senegal
7	Côte d' Ivoire	21	Mali	35	Gambia, The
8	Chad	22	Ethiopia	36	South Africa
9	Cameroon	23	Madagascar	37	Namibia
10	Guinea	24	Malawi	38	Lesotho
11	Congo, Dem. Rep.	25	Uganda	39	Mauritius
12	Central Afr. Rep.	26	Tanzania	40	Cape Verde
13	Guinea-Bissau	27	Benin	41	Seychelles
14	Swaziland	28	Burkina Faso		
Least		MIDDLE		Most	

It was the 6th best out of 41 countries. Note that 8 of the top 10 are oil exporters.

Central Africa
East Africa
Southern Africa
West Africa

13.5 Imports Dependence in Services

mind over matter

Self-sufficiency in services trade was an improvement for Nigeria in 2003/06 over 1999/02.

That brought Nigeria from a below-average in Africa during 1999/02 to an above-average showing in 2003/06. But most of West Africa did better.

Yet, Nigeria was best among the oil economies, emphasizing how neglected the non-oil sectors of these countries are. At least in foreign trade is concerned.

	99-02	03-06
Self-comparison to Preceding Period		▲
Performance in Sub-Saharan Africa	▼	▲
Performance in West Africa	▼	▼
	Gambia, The	Cape Verde
	Cape Verde	Gambia, The
	Ghana	Sierra Leone
	Senegal	Ghana
	Benin	Benin
	Niger	Senegal
	Burkina Faso	Niger
	Sierra Leone	Burkina Faso
	Togo	**Nigeria**
	Guinea-Bissau	Liberia
	Nigeria	Guinea
	Guinea	Togo
	Mali	Guinea-Bissau
	Côte d'Ivoire	Mali
	Mauritania	Côte d'Ivoire
	Liberia	Mauritania
Performance among Oil-Exporters	▲	▲
	Sudan	**Nigeria**
	Nigeria	Cameroon
	Cameroon	Sudan
	Chad	Côte d'Ivoire
	Côte d'Ivoire	Chad
	Angola	Angola
	Congo, Rep.	Congo, Rep.
	Gabon	Gabon
	Equatorial Guinea	Equatorial Guinea

Primary Data: WTO, World Bank

▲	better = less imports dependent
▼	worse = more imports dependent
◁▷	no change *or* average

13.18

Net Services Exports per Person in West Africa during 2003/06

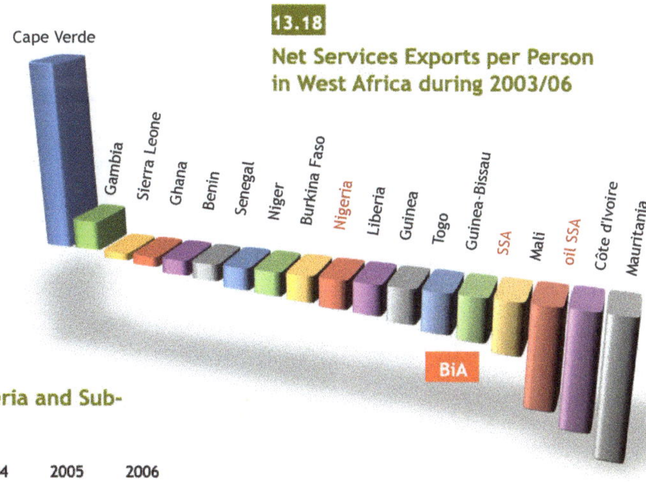

	$US
Cape Verde	107
Gambia, The	17
Sierra Leone	-4
Ghana	-6
Benin	-9
Senegal	-10
Niger	-13
Burkina Faso	-14
Nigeria	-15
Liberia	-17
Guinea	-18
Togo	-20
Guinea-Bissau	-24
SSA	-26
Mali	-30
oil SSA	-59
Côte d'Ivoire	-68
Mauritania	-82

Primary Data: WTO, World Bank

13.19

Net Services Exports per Person in Nigeria and Sub-Saharan Africa from 1999-2007

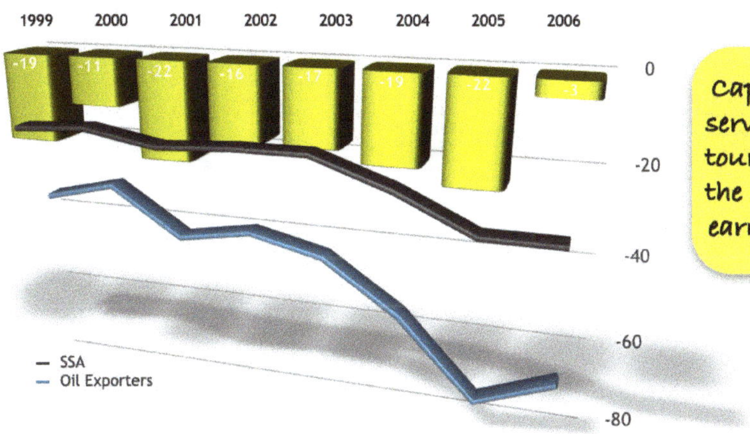

Cape verde's the top earner in services by a distance; through tourism mainly. Further down, the oil economies are the bottom earners, also by a distance.

Nigeria's trade deficit in services ended up lower in '06 than in '99, after shaky travel in-between. But better — again — than Africa and the oil group.

Services Imports Dependence per Person in Sub-Saharan Africa during 2003-06: Rankings

Rank	Country	Rank	Country	Rank	Country
1	Seychelles	15	Uganda	29	Zambia
2	Mauritius	16	Burundi	30	Central Afr. Rep.
3	Cape Verde	17	Malawi	31	Guinea-Bissau
4	Namibia	18	Rwanda	32	Mali
5	Gambia, The	19	Botswana	33	Cameroon
6	Kenya	20	Niger	34	Côte d' Ivoire
7	Tanzania	21	Burkina Faso	35	Swaziland
8	Ethiopia	22	Comoros	36	Chad
9	Sierra Leone	23	Mozambique	37	Angola
10	Congo, Dem. Rep.	24	Lesotho	38	Congo, Rep.
11	Madagascar	25	Nigeria	39	Gabon
12	Ghana	26	Guinea	40	Equatorial Guinea
13	Benin	27	South Africa	N/A	Eritrea
14	Senegal	28	Togo		
Least		MIDDLE		Most	

Central Africa
East Africa
Southern Africa
West Africa

13.6 Composition of Goods Exports and Imports

this is how these break down

Not much surprise about Nigeria's goods exports composition: 97% oil-related exports.

The surprises, perhaps, are Togo, Senegal, Cape Verde and Gambia, who have a good chunk of export earnings coming from the manufacturing sector.

It may not be unexpected that Nigeria's exports are skewed towards fuels & mining, but it is worrying that its agric. sector is dwarfed by agric. imports.

Besides Cape Verde (which has poor natural resources), Nigeria seems to be the only country that isn't self-sufficient in agriculture.

13.20

Composition of Goods Exports and Imports in West Africa during 2003/06

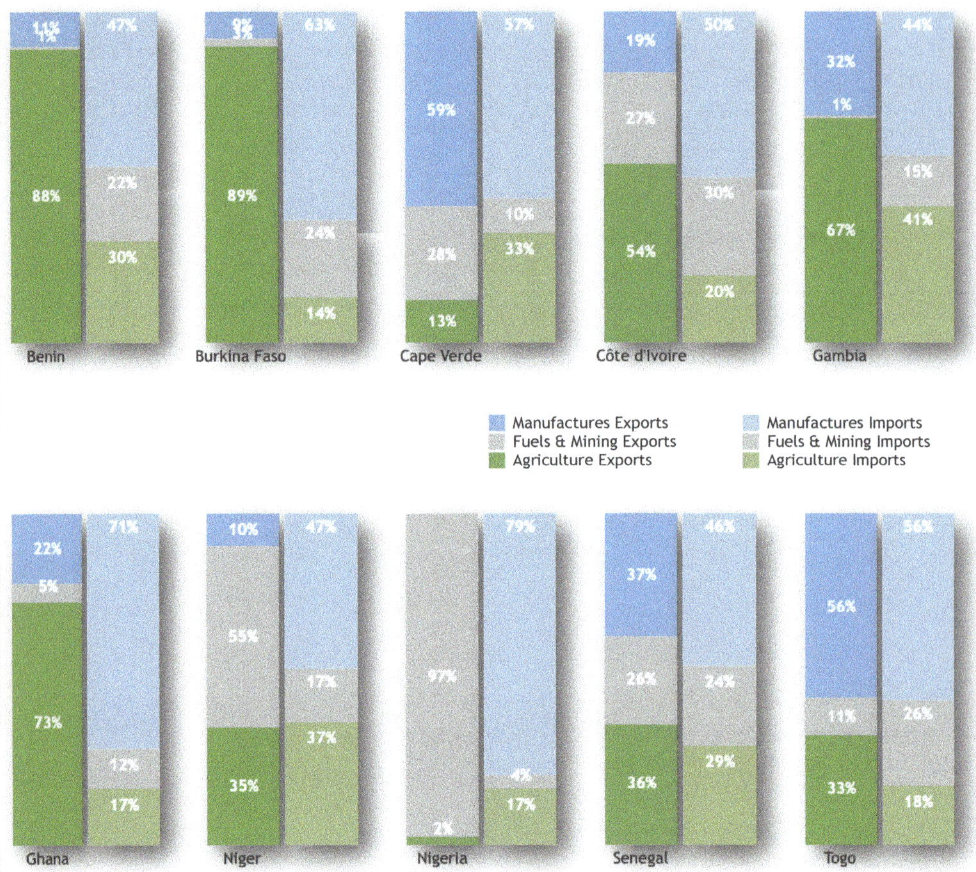

13.21

Primary Data: WTO

Composition of Goods Exports and Imports in Nigeria from 1999-2005

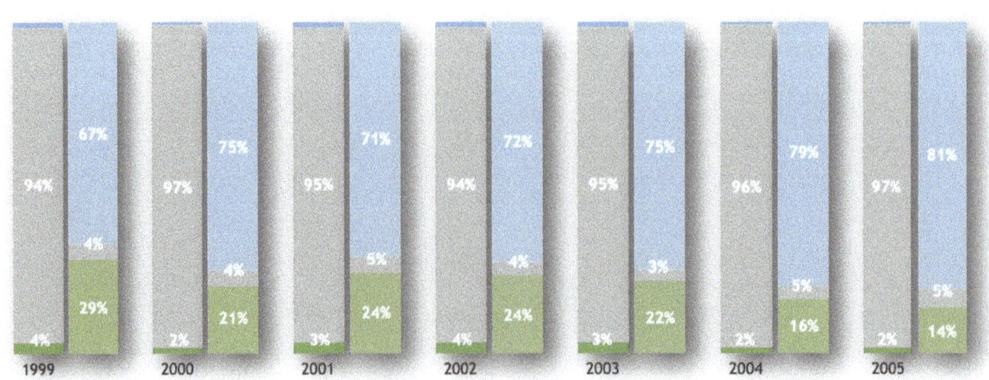

while these ones break down like so

13.22

Composition of Services Exports and Imports in West Africa during 2003/06

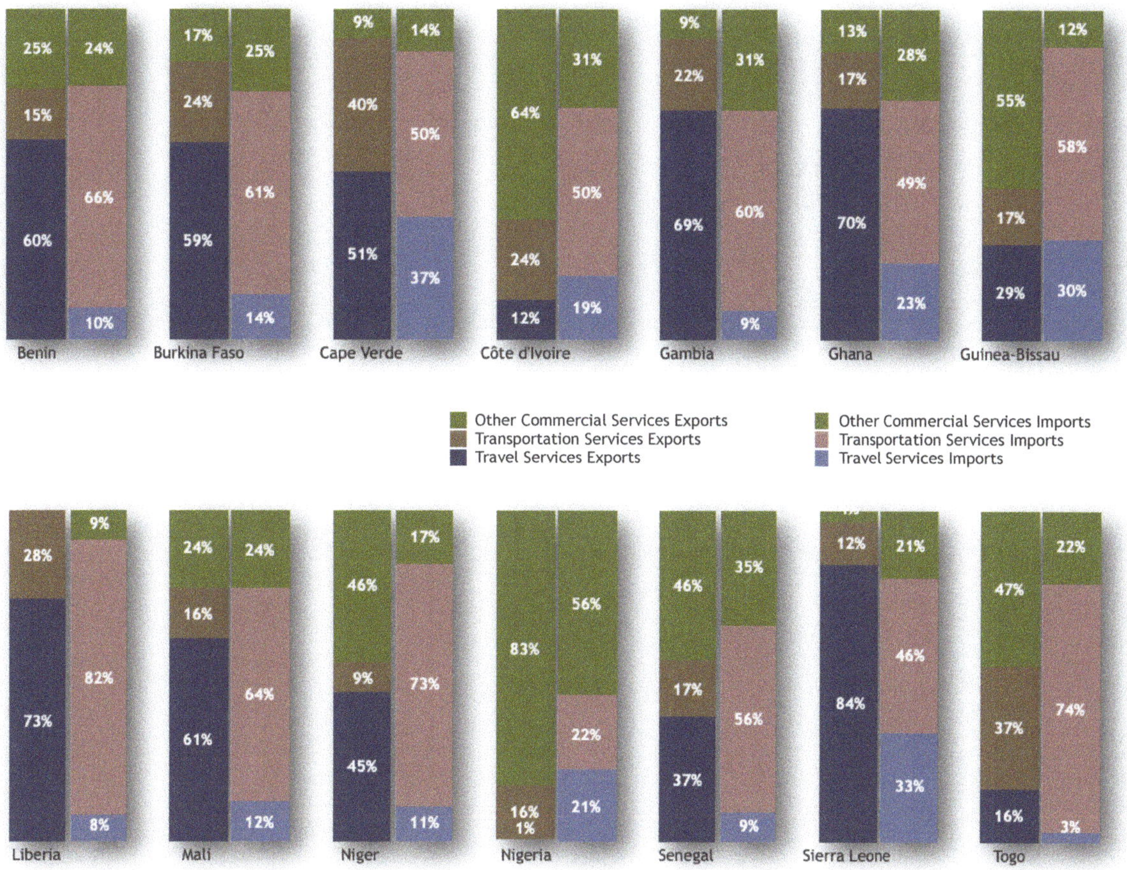

Primary Data: WTO

13.23

Composition of Services Exports and Imports in Nigeria from 1999-2005

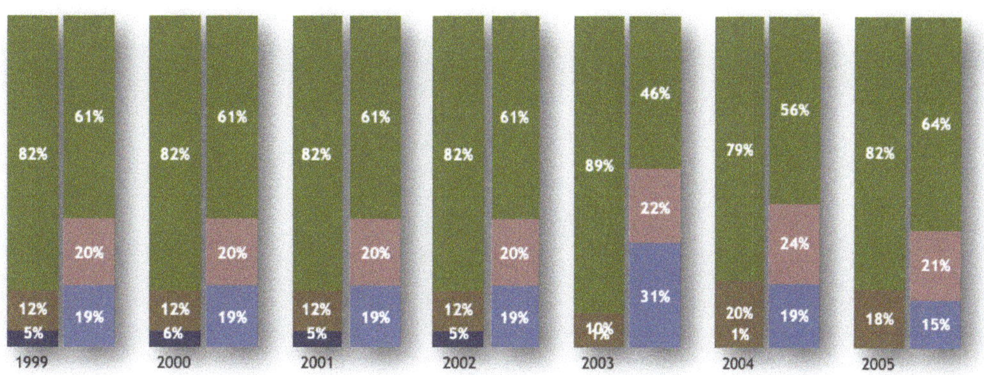

13.7 Foreign Reserves (months of imports)

we've got it stashed away

Ever-growing foreign reserves in Nigeria. Thanks to oil. And to some financial discipline, too: other oil exporters didn't do as well.

	97-02	03-06	07-08
Self-comparison to Preceding Period		▲	▲
Performance in Sub-Saharan Africa	▲	▲	▲
Performance in West Africa	▲	▲	▲
	Benin	Benin	**Nigeria**
	Guinea-Bissau	**Nigeria**	Benin
	Nigeria	Mali	Guinea-Bissau
	Gambia, The	Burkina Faso	Burkina Faso
	Burkina Faso	Guinea-Bissau	Mali
	Mali	Senegal	Sierra Leone
	Côte d'Ivoire	Gambia, The	Niger
	Senegal	Sierra Leone	Gambia, The
	Sierra Leone	Niger	Cape Verde
	Guinea	Ghana	Senegal
	Togo	Côte d'Ivoire	Togo
	Niger	Togo	Côte d'Ivoire
	Ghana	Cape Verde	Ghana
	Cape Verde	Guinea	Guinea
	Liberia	Liberia	Liberia
Performance among Oil-Exporters	▲	▲	▲
	Nigeria	**Nigeria**	**Nigeria**
	Côte d'Ivoire	Equatorial Guinea	Equatorial Guinea
	Chad	Côte d'Ivoire	Angola
	Angola	Cameroon	Cameroon
	Cameroon	Gabon	Congo, Rep.
	Congo, Rep.	Angola	Gabon
	Gabon	Congo, Rep.	Chad
	Equatorial Guinea	Chad	Côte d'Ivoire

Primary Data: IMF

▲	improved *or* better than average
▼	worsened *or* worse than average
◁▷	no change *or* average

After 2003, Nigeria seems to have taken off, swelling its foreign reserves holdings.

13.24

Foreign Reserves (as months of imports) in West Africa during 2003-06

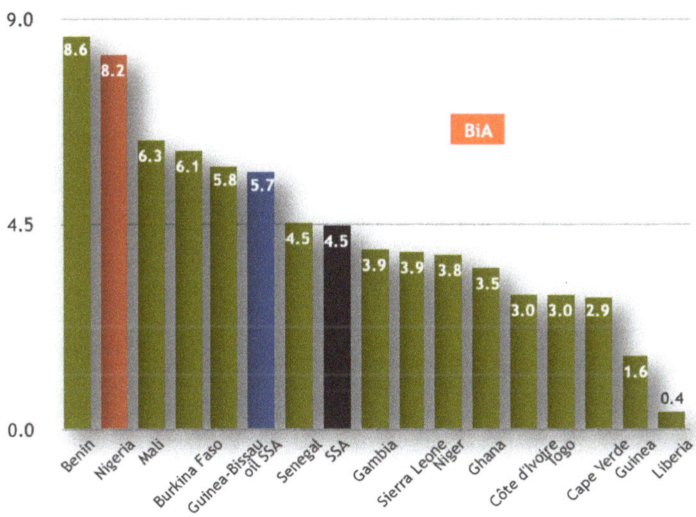

13.25

Foreign Reserves (as months of imports) in Nigeria and Sub-Saharan Africa from 1997 - 2008

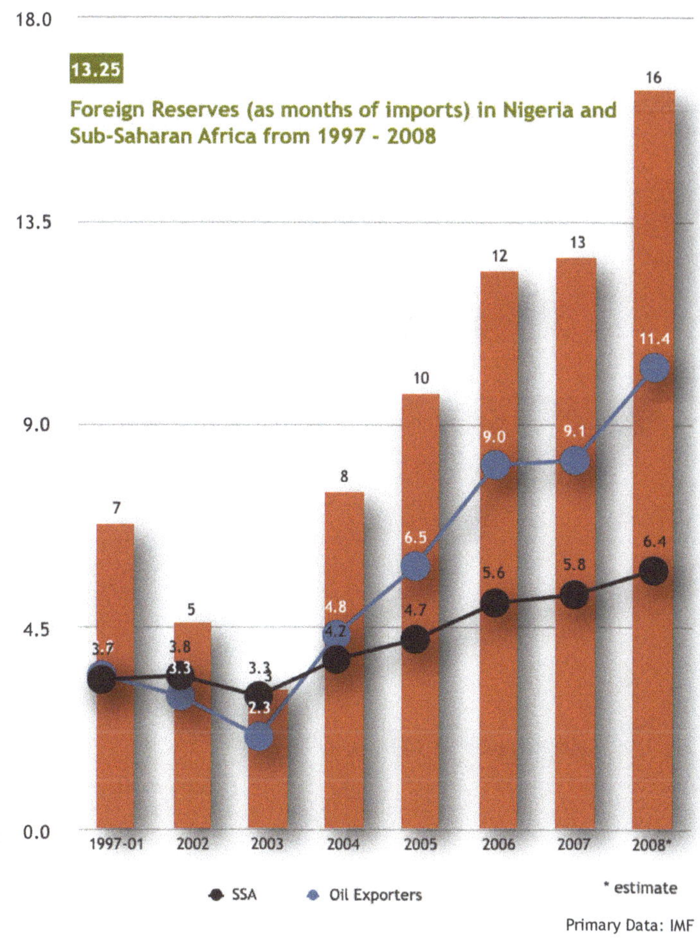

Foreign Reserves (as months of imports) in Sub-Saharan Africa during 2003-06: Rankings

Rank	Country
1	Botswana
2	Comoros
3	Benin
4	Nigeria
5	Tanzania
6	Uganda
7	Rwanda
8	Central Afr. Rep.
9	Mali
10	Burkina Faso
11	Guinea-Bissau
12	Equatorial Guinea
13	Mauritius

TOP

Rank	Country
14	Lesotho
15	Mozambique
16	Senegal
17	Burundi
18	Gambia, The
19	Ethiopia
20	Sierra Leone
21	Niger
22	Kenya
23	Ghana
24	Côte d' Ivoire
	Togo
25	Cameroon
26	Cape Verde
	Madagascar

MIDDLE

Rank	Country
27	Gabon
	South Africa
28	Angola
29	Zambia
30	Congo, Rep.
31	Swaziland
32	Namibia
33	Guinea
34	Malawi
35	Chad
36	Seychelles
37	Congo, Dem. Rep.
38	Eritrea

BOTTOM

Central Africa
East Africa
Southern Africa
West Africa

It had the 4th best reserves holdings in Africa during 2003-2006.

13.8 Foreign Debt (as % of GDP)

bills, bills, bills

	97-02	03-06	07-08
Self-comparison to Preceding Period		▲	▲
Performance in Sub-Saharan Africa	▼	▲	▲
Performance in West Africa	▲	▲	▲
	Cape Verde	**Nigeria**	**Nigeria**
	Burkina Faso	Benin	Sierra Leone
	Nigeria	Burkina Faso	Benin
	Senegal	Senegal	Niger
	Benin	Niger	Senegal
	Côte d'Ivoire	Cape Verde	Burkina Faso
	Niger	Mali	Ghana
	Togo	Côte d'Ivoire	Mali
	Guinea	Ghana	Cape Verde
	Mali	Togo	Côte d'Ivoire
	Ghana	Guinea	Guinea
	Gambia, The	Sierra Leone	Gambia, The
	Sierra Leone	Gambia, The	Togo
	Guinea-Bissau	Guinea-Bissau	Guinea-Bissau
	Liberia	Liberia	Liberia
Performance among Oil-Exporters	▲	▲	▲
	Equatorial Guinea	Equatorial Guinea	Equatorial Guinea
	Cameroon	**Nigeria**	**Nigeria**
	Chad	Angola	Cameroon
	Nigeria	Cameroon	Angola
	Angola	Chad	Gabon
	Gabon	Gabon	Chad
	Côte d'Ivoire	Côte d'Ivoire	Côte d'Ivoire
	Congo, Rep.	Congo, Rep.	Congo, Rep.

Primary Data: IMF

▲	better = less debt
▼	worse = more debt
◁▷	no change *or* average

Another impressive showing by Nigeria: small foreign debt compared to the continent, and to the other oil producers, also. Only Equatorial Guinea did better.

Nigeria is the least geared in West Africa: relatively little constraints of a debt burden.

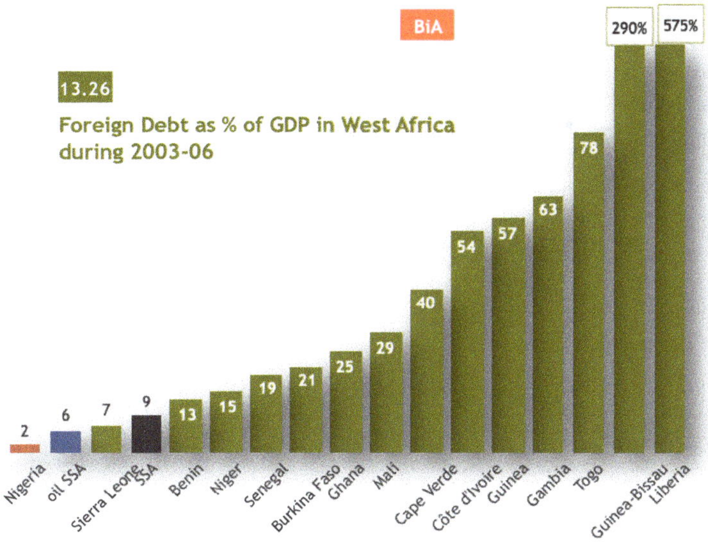

13.26 Foreign Debt as % of GDP in West Africa during 2003-06

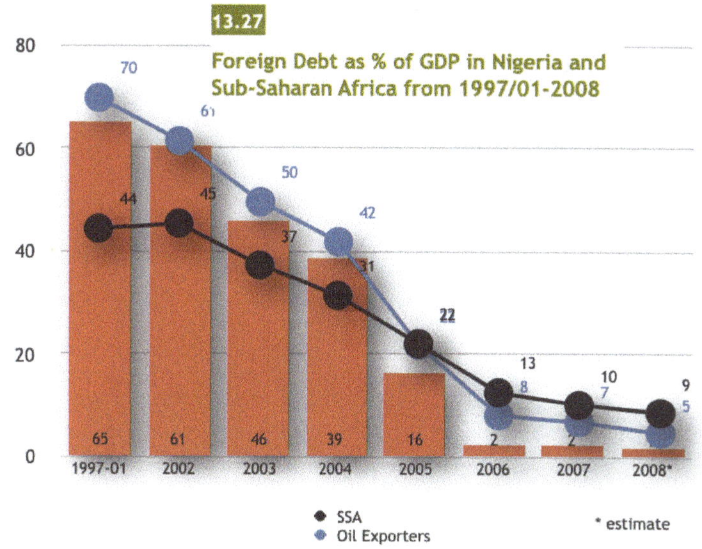

13.27 Foreign Debt as % of GDP in Nigeria and Sub-Saharan Africa from 1997/01-2008

Primary Data: IMF

+1-800-help

Remember, as saw in chapter 12 (Govt. Earning & Spending), foreign debt isn't necessarily a bad thing.

Likewise, negative trade balance.

It all depends on their levels and their reasons.

(Same applies even in the private sector. Recall that for endless years, Amazon never turned in a profit, only deficits.)

That's a strange one

You've just got to get the strategy right, otherwise the rest won't follow.

As a proportion of overall economy size, Nigeria had the 7th smallest debt portfolio in Africa.

Spectacular collapsing of its debt since 2001. But the trend was continent-wide: other nations were crashing their debt portfolios, too.

Foreign Debt as % of GDP in Sub-Saharan Africa during 2003-06: Rankings

Rank	Country	Rank	Country	Rank	Country
1	South Africa	15	Senegal	29	Eritrea
2	Botswana	16	Gabon	30	Comoros
3	Namibia	17	Tanzania	31	Zambia
4	Equatorial Guinea	18	Lesotho	32	Central Afr. Rep.
5	Mauritius	19	Niger	33	Togo
6	Swaziland	20	Cape Verde	34	Guinea
7	Nigeria	21	Mozambique	35	Malawi
8	Kenya	22	Mali	36	Sierra Leone
9	Angola	23	Uganda	37	Congo, Rep.
10	Cameroon	24	Ethiopia	38	Congo, Dem. Rep.
11	Benin	25	Rwanda	39	Gambia, The
12	Burkina Faso	26	Côte d' Ivoire	40	Burundi
13	Chad	27	Madagascar	41	Guinea-Bissau
14	Seychelles	28	Ghana		
	Least		MIDDLE		Most

Central Africa
East Africa
Southern Africa
West Africa

13.9 Foreign Debt (as $PPP per person)

beware

	97-02	03-06	07-08
Self-comparison to Preceding Period		▲	▲
Performance in Sub-Saharan Africa	▼	▼	▲
Performance in West Africa	▲	▲	▲
	Benin	Benin	**Nigeria**
	Guinea-Bissau	**Nigeria**	Benin
	Nigeria	Mali	Guinea-Bissau
	Gambia, The	Burkina Faso	Burkina Faso
	Burkina Faso	Guinea-Bissau	Mali
	Mali	Senegal	Sierra Leone
	Côte d'Ivoire	Gambia, The	Niger
	Senegal	Sierra Leone	Gambia, The
	Sierra Leone	Niger	Cape Verde
	Guinea	Ghana	Senegal
	Togo	Côte d'Ivoire	Togo
	Niger	Togo	Côte d'Ivoire
	Ghana	Cape Verde	Ghana
	Cape Verde	Guinea	Guinea
	Liberia	Liberia	Liberia
Performance among Oil-Exporters	▲	▲	▲
	Chad	**Nigeria**	**Nigeria**
	Nigeria	Chad	Cameroon
	Cameroon	Equatorial Guinea	Equatorial Guinea
	Côte d'Ivoire	Cameroon	Angola
	Angola	Côte d'Ivoire	Chad
	Equatorial Guinea	Angola	Côte d'Ivoire
	Congo, Rep.	Congo, Rep.	Congo, Rep.
	Gabon	Gabon	Gabon

Primary Data: IMF

Expressed as debt per person of population, Nigeria was behind the continent average in 03/06, but it did well in West Africa and within the oil league.

▲	better = less debt
▼	worse = more debt
◁▷	no change *or* average

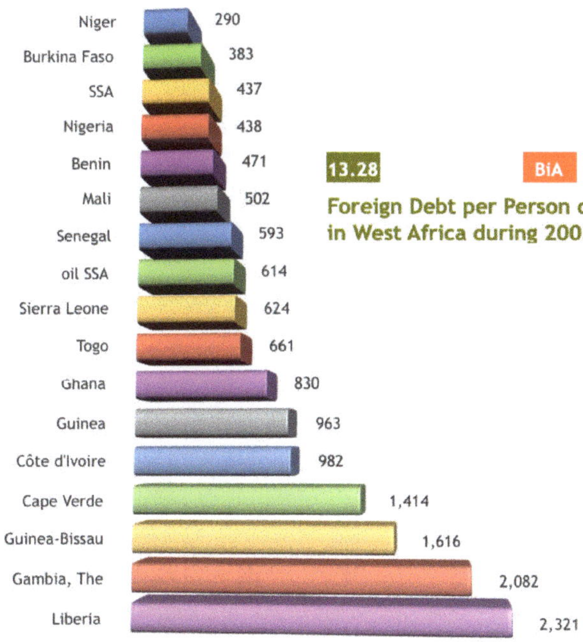

13.28 BiA

Foreign Debt per Person of Population in West Africa during 2003/06 ($PPP)

The collapsing debt burden would better the rest of the continent by a distance, after 2005.

13.29

Foreign Debt per Person of Population in Nigeria and Sub-Saharan Africa from 1997-2008 ($PPP)

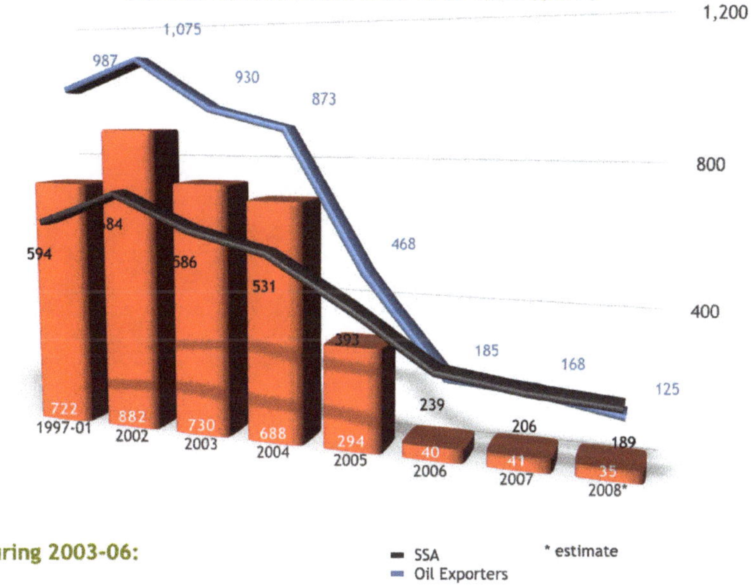

By either measure, % GDP or $ per person, Nigeria's debt baggage was among the 10 smallest in Africa.

Foreign Debt per Person of Population in Sub-Saharan Africa during 2003-06: Rankings

Rank	Country	Rank	Country	Rank	Country
1	South Africa	15	Chad	29	Ghana
2	Namibia	16	Lesotho	30	Comoros
3	Niger	17	Central Afr. Rep.	31	Zambia
4	Ethiopia	18	Equatorial Guinea	32	Guinea
5	Mozambique	19	Eritrea	33	Côte d' Ivoire
6	Congo, Dem. Rep.	20	Madagascar	34	Angola
7	Kenya	21	Botswana	35	Mauritius
8	Burkina Faso	22	Senegal	36	Cape Verde
9	Rwanda	23	Malawi	37	Guinea-Bissau
10	**Nigeria**	24	Cameroon	38	Gambia, The
11	Tanzania	25	Swaziland	39	Congo, Rep.
12	Benin	26	Sierra Leone	40	Gabon
13	Uganda	27	Burundi	41	Seychelles
14	Mali	28	Togo		
Least		MIDDLE		Most	

Primary Data: IMF

Central Africa
East Africa
Southern Africa
West Africa

13.10 Service of Foreign Debt (as % of exports)

paying up

Perhaps as a result of the drive to collapse debt burdens, Nigeria's debt repayments have been significantly high, in the years leading to 2006.

But it still does comparatively better than much of the continent, including the oil group.

	99-02	03-06
Self-comparison to Preceding Period		▲
Performance in Sub-Saharan Africa	▲	▲
Performance in West Africa	▲	▲
	Togo	Togo
	Nigeria	Mali
	Mali	Benin
	Mauritania	Ghana
	Niger	Sierra Leone
	Benin	**Nigeria**
	Senegal	Burkina Faso
	Burkina Faso	Guinea-Bissau
	Guinea	Niger
	Cape Verde	Guinea
	Ghana	Côte d'Ivoire
	Côte d'Ivoire	Senegal
	Guinea-Bissau	Cape Verde
	Gambia, The	Mauritania
	Sierra Leone	Gambia, The

Primary Data: AfDB

Performance among Oil-Exporters	99-02	03-06
	▲	▲
	Equatorial Guinea	Equatorial Guinea
	Sudan	Chad
	Congo, Rep.	Sudan
	Nigeria	**Nigeria**
	Cameroon	Congo, Rep.
	Gabon	Côte d'Ivoire
	Côte d'Ivoire	Cameroon
	Chad	Angola
	Angola	Gabon

▲	better = smaller debt service
▼	worse = larger debt service
◁▷	no change *or* average

13.30

Service of Foreign Debt as % of Exports in West Africa during 2003/06

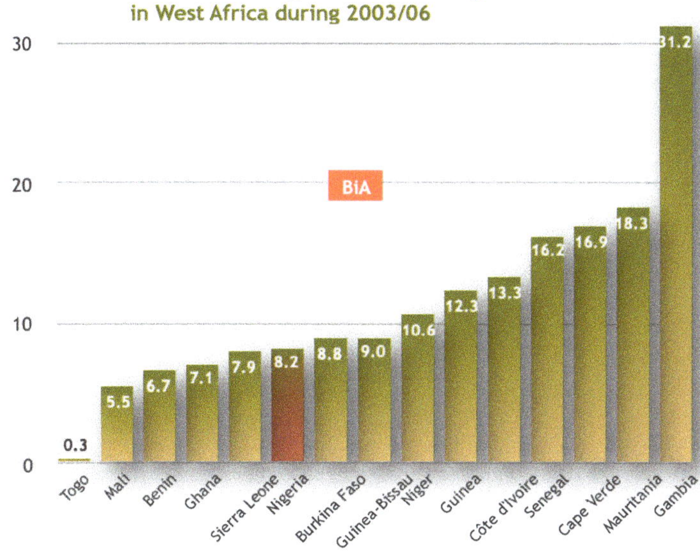

13.31

Service of Foreign Debt as % of Exports in Nigeria from 1999-2007

A massive outlay in 2005 to push a further climb-down in debt burden.

Service of Foreign Debt as % of Exports in Sub-Saharan Africa during 2003-06: Rankings

Rank	Country	Rank	Country	Rank	Country
1	Togo	15	Burkina Faso	29	Angola
2	Equatorial Guinea	16	Tanzania	30	Malawi
3	Namibia	17	Kenya	31	Senegal
4	Central Afr. Rep.	18	Guinea-Bissau	32	Cape Verde
5	Chad	19	Congo, Rep.	33	Rwanda
6	Mali	20	South Africa	34	Uganda
7	Benin	21	Zambia	35	Gabon
8	Ghana	22	Niger	36	Mozambique
9	Mauritius	23	Ethiopia	37	Gambia, The
10	Comoros	24	Seychelles	38	Madagascar
11	Sierra Leone	25	Guinea	39	Eritrea
12	Nigeria	26	Côte d' Ivoire	40	Burundi
13	Lesotho	27	Cameroon	N/A	Swaziland
14	Congo, Dem. Rep.	28	Botswana		
Least		MIDDLE		Most	

As a whole, during 2003-2006, Nigeria's debt repayment was easier to shoulder than most other countries'. upper-third performance.

Primary Data: AfDB

Central Africa
East Africa
Southern Africa
West Africa

13.11 Growth of Income & Growth of Debt

er... are we doing ok?

13.34

Build-up of Debt and Income in Nigeria and Sub-Saharan Africa from 2000-2006: 2000=100

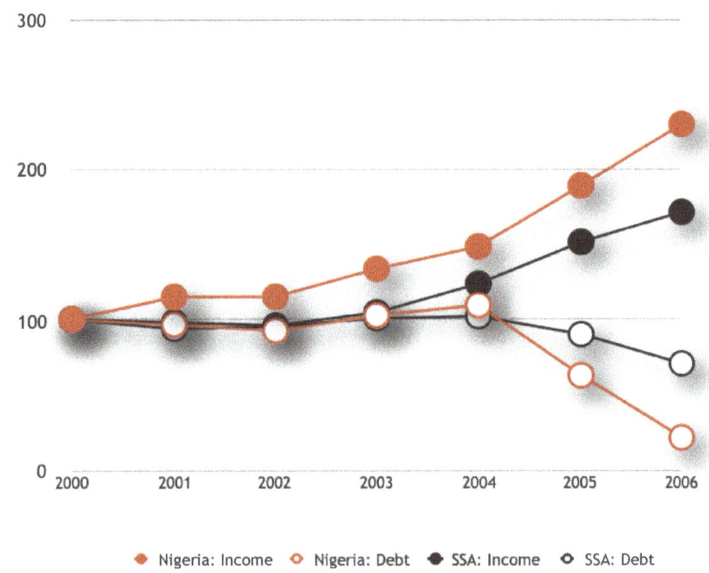

Something about 2005; when there seems to have been a concerted and continent-wide drive to lower debt profiles.

Excellent work by Nigeria, putting a gaping distance between its increasing earnings and falling debt.

13.32

Growth Rates of Debt and Income in West Africa during 2003/06 (%)

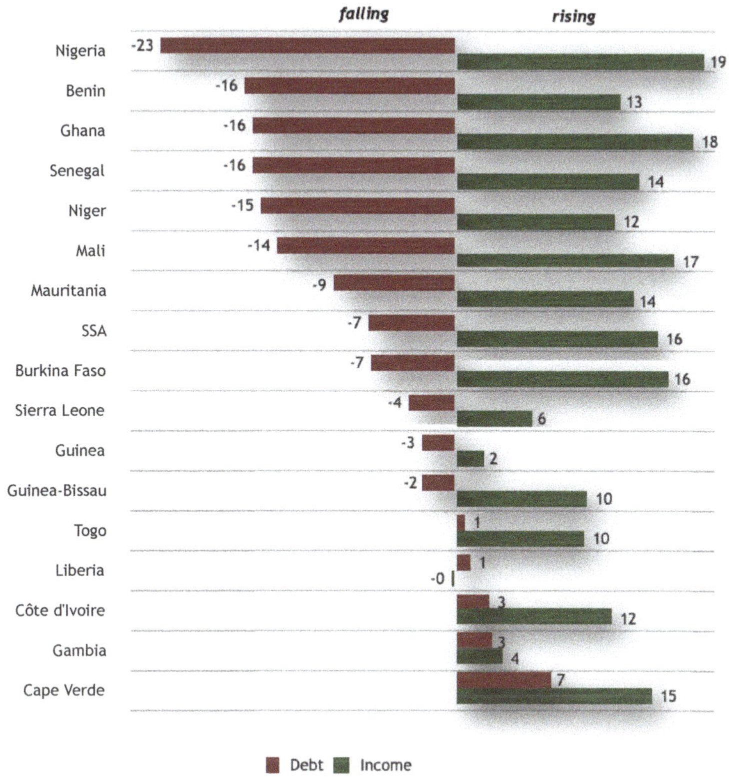

Primary Data: World Bank

13.33

Net Growth Rate of Debt and Income in West Africa during 2003/06 (%)

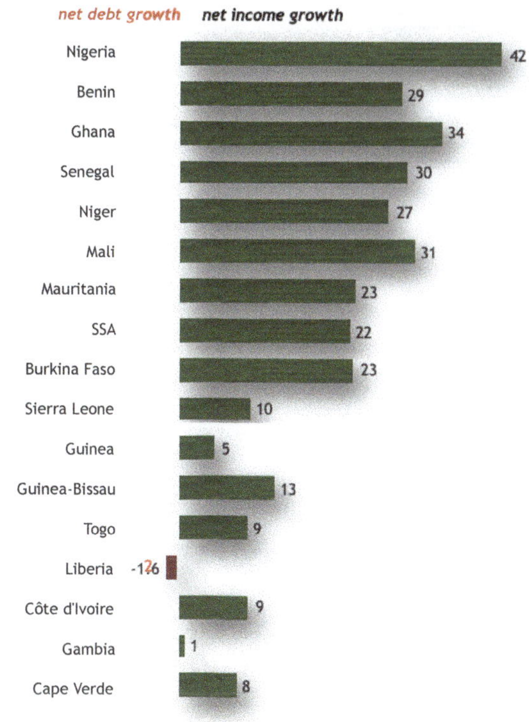

Nigeria out-did everyone else in West Africa. Fastest rate of debt climb-down and fastest rate of income build-up.

Ghana came in 2nd and Mali, 3rd.

Liberia was worst, understandably: it was picking itself up from zero after years of war. It needed both grants and loans to rebuild from scratch.

13.12 Aid Dependency (as % of GDP)

counting on Santa

	97-02	03-06	07-08
Self-comparison to Preceding Period		◁▷	◁▷
Performance in Sub-Saharan Africa	▲	▲	▲
Performance in West Africa	▲	▲	▲
	Nigeria	**Nigeria**	**Nigeria**
	Côte d'Ivoire	Côte d'Ivoire	Guinea
	Guinea	Guinea	Côte d'Ivoire
	Mali	Togo	Mali
	Senegal	Senegal	Senegal
	Togo	Mali	Togo
	Benin	Benin	Ghana
	Niger	Niger	Niger
	Burkina Faso	Burkina Faso	Benin
	Ghana	Ghana	Sierra Leone
	Cape Verde	Cape Verde	Burkina Faso
	Sierra Leone	Sierra Leone	Cape Verde
	Gambia, The	Gambia, The	Gambia, The
	Guinea-Bissau	Guinea-Bissau	Guinea-Bissau
	Liberia	Liberia	Liberia

Primary Data: IMF

It could be argued, of course, that Nigeria has no business with foreign aid because of its economic size and potential. It lives up to those expectations.

Performance among Oil-Exporters	97-02	03-06	07-08
	▲	▲	▲
	Nigeria	Gabon	Gabon
	Congo, Rep.	**Nigeria**	**Nigeria**
	Gabon	Côte d'Ivoire	Côte d'Ivoire
	Cameroon	Angola	Angola
	Côte d'Ivoire	Equatorial Guinea	Equatorial Guinea
	Angola	Congo, Rep.	Congo, Rep.
	Equatorial Guinea	Cameroon	Cameroon
	Chad	Chad	Chad

It was bettered within the oil bloc by Gabon.

▲	better = less dependence
▼	worse = more dependence
◁▷	no change *or* average

13.35

Foreign Aid as % of GDP in West Africa during 2003/06

Liberia's position here is understandable. Nigeria and Côte d'Ivoire look to have been net donors, not recipients.

13.36

Foreign Aid as % of GDP in Nigeria and Sub-Saharan Africa from 1999-2007

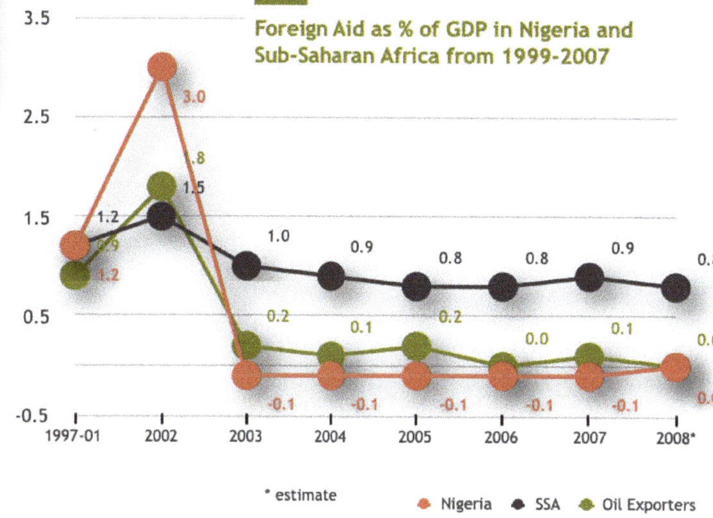

Foreign aid tightened up for the oil economies in 2003. For the rest of Africa, too, but not as sharply.

Foreign Aid as % of GDP in Sub-Saharan Africa during 2003-06: Rankings

Rank	Country	Rank	Country	Rank	Country
1	South Africa	15	Senegal	29	Ethiopia
2	Gabon	16	Mali	30	Sierra Leone
3	Nigeria	17	Madagascar	31	Congo, Dem. Rep.
4	Côte d' Ivoire	18	Seychelles	32	Uganda
5	Angola	19	Benin	33	Malawi
6	Kenya	20	Niger	34	Gambia, The
7	Mauritius	21	Burkina Faso	35	Guinea-Bissau
8	Equatorial Guinea	22	Central Afr. Rep.	36	Swaziland
9	Congo, Rep.	23	Tanzania	37	Namibia
10	Guinea	24	Chad	38	Rwanda
11	Cameroon	25	Ghana	39	Eritrea
12	Togo	26	Cape Verde	40	Burundi
13	Comoros	27	Mozambique	41	Lesotho
14	Zambia	28	Botswana		
Least		MIDDLE		Most	

6 of the 10 least aid recipients were oil exporters. Of these 10, South Africa, Gabon and Nigeria were net donors.

Primary Data: IMF

Central Africa
East Africa
Southern Africa
West Africa

13.13 Aid Dependency (as $PPP per person)

beggar thy neighbor

Primary Data: IMF

	97-02	03-06	07-08
Self-comparison to Preceding Period		▲	▼
Performance in Sub-Saharan Africa	▲	▲	▲
Performance in West Africa	▲	▲	▲

97-02	03-06	07-08
Nigeria	Nigeria	Nigeria
Côte d'Ivoire	Côte d'Ivoire	Guinea
Guinea	Guinea	Mali
Mali	Togo	Togo
Niger	Niger	Niger
Togo	Mali	Senegal
Senegal	Senegal	Sierra Leone
Sierra Leone	Burkina Faso	Côte d'Ivoire
Burkina Faso	Sierra Leone	Ghana
Benin	Benin	Benin
Ghana	Guinea-Bissau	Burkina Faso
Guinea-Bissau	Ghana	Guinea-Bissau
Gambia, The	Gambia, The	Liberia
Cape Verde	Liberia	Gambia, The
Liberia	Cape Verde	Cape Verde

In $ per person, Nigeria was a net donor, not recipient, during 2003-2006. By 2007-2008, it is still a net donor, but by a smaller margin.

Performance among Oil-Exporters

97-02	03-06	07-08
▲	▲	▲
Nigeria	Gabon	Angola
Cameroon	Nigeria	Nigeria
Congo, Rep.	Côte d'Ivoire	Equatorial Guinea
Côte d'Ivoire	Angola	Gabon
Gabon	Cameroon	Congo, Rep.
Angola	Congo, Rep.	Cameroon
Chad	Equatorial Guinea	Côte d'Ivoire
Equatorial Guinea	Chad	Chad

▲	better = less dependence
▼	worse = more dependence
◁▷	no change *or* average

13.37

Foreign Aid as $PPP per Person in West Africa during 2003/06

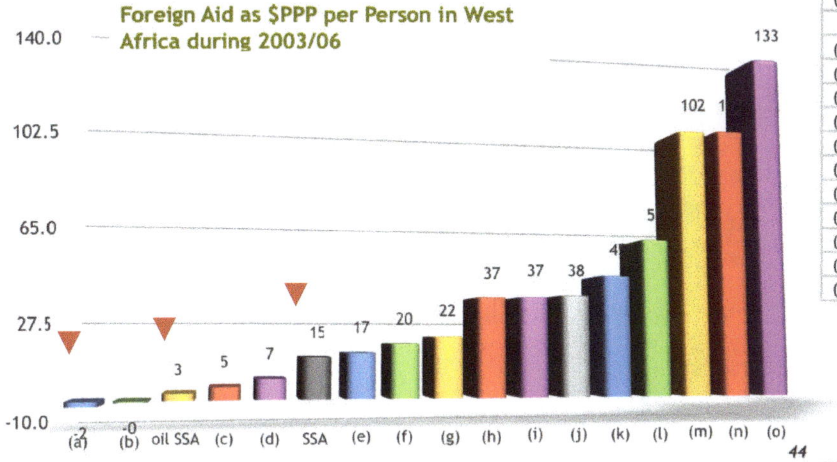

(a)	Nigeria	-2
(b)	Côte d'Ivoire	-0
	oil SSA	3
(c)	Guinea	5
(d)	Togo	7
	SSA	15
(e)	Niger	17
(f)	Mali	20
(g)	Senegal	22
(e)	Burkina Faso	37
(f)	Sierra Leone	37
(g)	Benin	38
(e)	Guinea-Bissau	45
(f)	Ghana	59
(g)	Gambia	102
(e)	Liberia	103
(f)	Cape Verde	133

13.38

Foreign Aid in Nigeria and Sub-Saharan Africa during 2003/06 as $PPP per Person

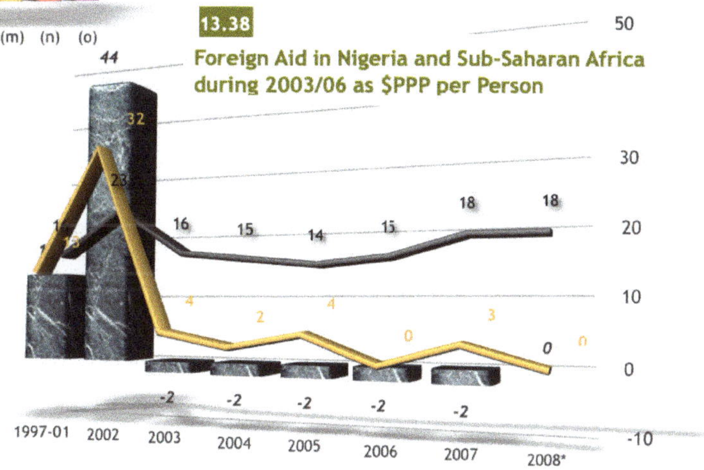

Besides Nigeria, the other net donors during 03/06 in Africa were South Africa and Gabon.

Foreign Aid in Sub-Saharan Africa as $PPP per Person during 2003-06: Rankings

Rank	Country	Rank	Country	Rank	Country
1	South Africa	15	Madagascar	29	Malawi
2	Gabon	16	Mali	30	Ghana
3	Nigeria	17	Senegal	31	Burundi
4	Côte d' Ivoire	18	Central Afr. Rep.	32	Uganda
5	Kenya	19	Mauritius	33	Rwanda
6	Angola	20	Tanzania	34	Gambia, The
7	Guinea	21	Burkina Faso	35	Eritrea
8	Togo	22	Sierra Leone	36	Cape Verde
9	Cameroon	23	Ethiopia	37	Lesotho
10	Congo, Rep.	24	Benin	38	Seychelles
11	Comoros	25	Equatorial Guinea	39	Swaziland
12	Zambia	26	Mozambique	40	Namibia
13	Niger	27	Guinea-Bissau	41	Botswana
14	Congo, Dem. Rep.	28	Chad		
Least		MIDDLE		Most	

By 07/08 there were a different 3: South Africa and Nigeria again, but Angola rather than Gabon.

Central Africa
East Africa
Southern Africa
West Africa

Primary Data: IMF

Leaders & Stragglers

we'll be needing some more, please

Self-Reliance Rankings: 2003-06

Nigeria turned out to be the most self-reliant in Africa during 2003-2006, beating South Africa — the only larger economy — who came in 4th.

Rank	Country	Rank	Country	Rank	Country
1	Nigeria	15	Ethiopia	29	Rwanda
2	Kenya	16	Angola	30	Ghana
3	Equatorial Guinea	17	Côte d' Ivoire	31	Congo, Rep.
4	South Africa	18	Namibia	32	Zambia
5	Benin	19	Congo, Dem. Rep.	33	Lesotho
6	Tanzania	20	Gabon	34	Guinea-Bissau
7	Mauritius	21	Togo	35	Seychelles
8	Niger	22	Senegal	36	Cape Verde
9	Mali	23	Chad	37	Malawi
10	Burkina Faso	24	Mozambique	38	Burundi
11	Central Afr. Rep.	25	Sierra Leone	39	Swaziland
12	Botswana	26	Madagascar	40	Gambia, The
13	Cameroon	27	Guinea	41	Eritrea
14	Comoros	28	Uganda		
TOP		MIDDLE		BOTTOM	

Central Africa
East Africa
Southern Africa
West Africa

Wrap-up: Self-Reliance

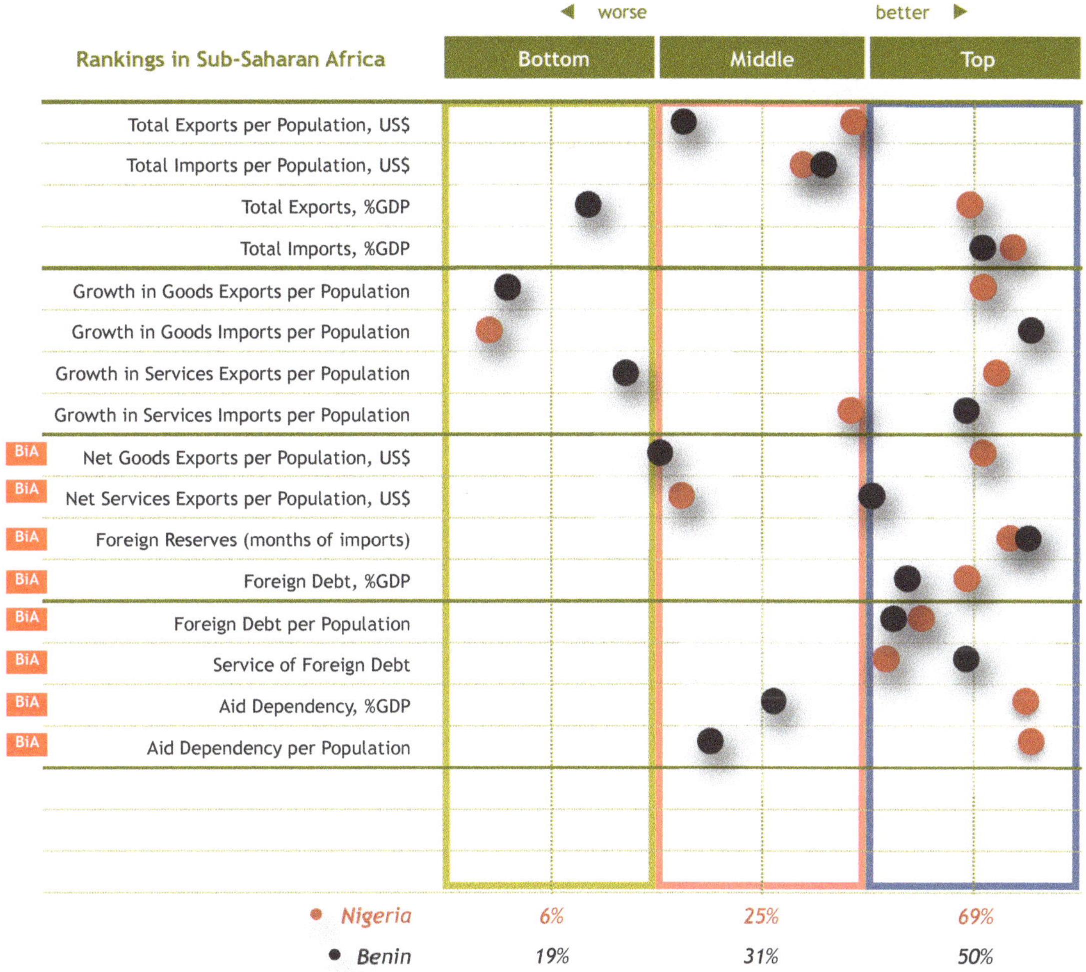

- This time, Nigeria tops West Africa and the entire Sub-Saharan Africa. The next best West Africa result is from Benin Republic, in 5th place on the continental table.
- It isn't difficult to see why Nigeria stands out: near 70% of all the indicator outcomes are in the top segment; only one of them turns up in the bottom segment of performance. Benin has three there.
- All Nigeria's "critical" indicators are top-bracket finishers, except one. The country relies comparatively little on foreign aid, and is not burdened by debt overhang. Its external trade is robust, even though much of it is due to oil.
- A lot still must be done to improve external trade and exports in the services sector.
- There is a precarious balance though, in the desire for imports. Nigeria manages to stay within reasonable range in its import levels per population, but it is growing those levels dangerously fast. That is the one area where it sank into the bottom segment of performance.

14. Investor Confidence

Primer

Investment is crucial to any economy. Economies literally thrive on the volume of investments they attract. Countries fall over themselves to create environments that would pull investment into various sectors. Investors will only sink funds where they expect to derive reasonable benefits and rewards. Governments would have to maintain a sane balance to make sure that consumer rights, for example, are well protected, otherwise business will, left to itself, be exploitative. Volume of investment is a strong sign of an economy's strength and viability.

Foreign Direct Investment (FDI)

The volume of foreign commitment to business enterprises in a host economy. It must be distinguished from acquisition of shares on a stock exchange which generally is taken not to be a firm investment commitment but could easily become "hot money": money withdrawn at the least notice and moved elsewhere. FDI generally involves the acquisition of "immovable assets" (e.g., factories, machinery) and the exercise of some managerial control. An increase in FDI would imply investor confidence in a host country's economic and social climate. By expressing FDI in terms of percentage of GDP, or per person of population, a more accurate picture of economic activity can be obtained. Otherwise the volume of FDI by itself, without reference to country size, could not be a meaningful evaluation.

The FDI figures shown are *net* flows. That is, the net of investment coming into the economy and the ones leaving it. That is why some figures are negative, indicating that there was a net exodus of foreign investment: more FDI leaving than entering, during the period.

Total Capital investment (TCI)

Refers to the aggregate total of Capital Investment in an economy (again, as distinct from stocks and shares), and so, comprises FDI and more. It is also known as Gross Fixed Capital Formation (GFCF). It may be split into various components to measure and evaluate its make-up.

It would, for example, be a further sign of confidence in the economy if the level of **Private** input into TCI is high or growing. The **Public** (government) component of TCI would not, for simply that fact, necessarily point to a robust economy, since the government's imperatives do not have to be confident expectations of a justifying return on investment.

FDI is part of the private component of this Total Capital Investment. The rest of this private component would be of "domestic origins", i.e., investors from the private sector, domiciled within that economy. In other words,

TCI = Private Investment + Public Investment

Private Investment = FDI + "Domestic Investment"

Domestic Credit to the Private Sector

This is another indicator of the level of business confidence in an economy; this time from the perspective of commercial institutions in the financial sector. The thinking being that these institutions would tend to lend money to business enterprises when they (the institutions) perceive the economic and business climate to be promising or vibrant.

Sources of Primary Data: AfDB, IMF, UNCTAD, World Bank

Charts

- **Wrap-up**

Tables

1999-2002; 2003-2006:

- *self-comparison to preceding period;*
- *performance in S-Saharan Africa;*
- *performance in West Africa;*
- *performance among oil-exporters;*

for:

FDI as % of GDP

FDI per Person

Growth in FDI per Person

FDI as % of Total Capital Investment

Total Capital Investment as % of GDP

Total Capital Investment per Person

Growth in TCI per Person

Private Component of TCI as % of GDP

Private Component of TCI as Investment per Person

Growth of Private Component of TCI

Domestic Credit to the Private Sector as % of GDP

Domestic Credit to the Private Sector in $PPP

Growth in Domestic Credit to the Private Sector

- FDI as % of GDP in Sub-Saharan Africa during 2003-06: Rankings
- FDI as US$ per Person in Sub-Saharan Africa during 2003-06: Rankings
- Annual Growth in FDI per Person in Sub-Saharan Africa during 2003-06: Rankings
- FDI as % of Total Capital Investment in Sub-Saharan Africa during 2003-06: Rankings
- Total Capital Investment as % of GDP in Sub-Saharan Africa during 2003-06: Rankings
- Total Capital Investment per Person in Sub-Saharan Africa during 2003-06: Rankings
- Growth in Total Capital Investment per Person in Sub-Saharan Africa during 2003-06: Rankings
- Private Component of Total Capital Investment as % of GDP in Sub-Saharan Africa during 2003-06: Rankings
- Private Component of TCI as Investment per Person ($PPP) in Sub-Saharan Africa during 2003-06: Rankings
- Growth of Private Component of Total Capital Investment per Person in Sub-Saharan Africa during 2003-06: Rankings
- Domestic Credit to the Private Sector as % of GDP in Sub-Saharan Africa during 2003-06: Rankings
- Domestic Credit to the Private Sector as $PPP in Sub-Saharan Africa during 2003-06: Rankings
- Growth in Domestic Credit to the Private Sector in Sub-Saharan Africa during 2003-06: Rankings
- **Investor Confidence Rankings: 2003-06**

14.1 FDI as % of GDP

shall we, shall we not?

	99-02	03-06
Self-comparison to Preceding Period		▲
Performance in Sub-Saharan Africa	▼	▲

Primary Data: UNCTAD

Performance in West Africa	99-02	03-06
	▲	▲
	Liberia	Mauritania
	Gambia, The	Gambia, The
	Cape Verde	Cape Verde
	Mauritania	**Nigeria**
	Mali	Sierra Leone
	Togo	Guinea
	Nigeria	Togo
	Côte d'Ivoire	Guinea-Bissau
	Ghana	Mali
	Senegal	Ghana
	Benin	Côte d'Ivoire
	Sierra Leone	Benin
	Guinea	Senegal
	Guinea-Bissau	Niger
	Burkina Faso	Burkina Faso
	Niger	Liberia

Nigeria improved on its 99-02 performance, during 03-06. It also did better than the Africa average; whereas it had done worse in 99-02.

Performance among Oil-Exporters	99-02	03-06
	▼	▼
	Equatorial Guinea	Equatorial Guinea
	Angola	Chad
	Chad	Sudan
	Congo, Rep.	Angola
	Sudan	Congo, Rep.
	Nigeria	**Nigeria**
	Côte d'Ivoire	Gabon
	Cameroon	Cameroon
	Gabon	Côte d'Ivoire

Nevertheless, it didn't match up to fellow exporters of crude oil, suggesting that there is still a lot of latent capacity for FDI in the economy.

▲	improved *or* better than average
▼	worsened *or* worse than average
◁▷	no change *or* average

14.1

FDI as % of GDP in West Africa during 2003-06

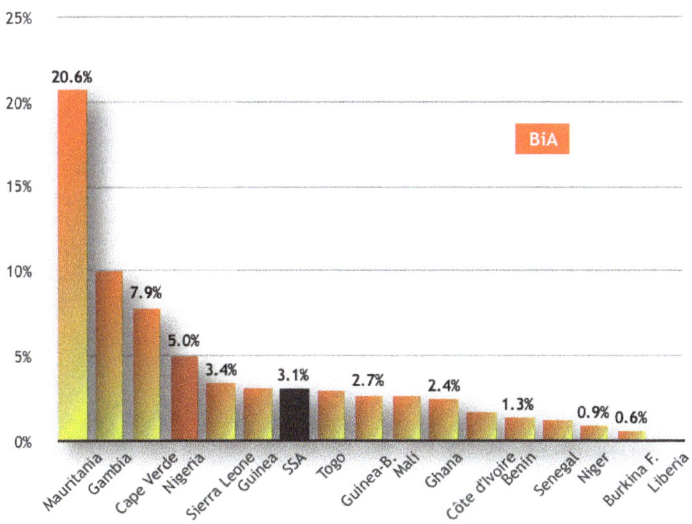

14.2

FDI as % of GDP in Nigeria and Sub-Saharan Africa from 1999 to 2007

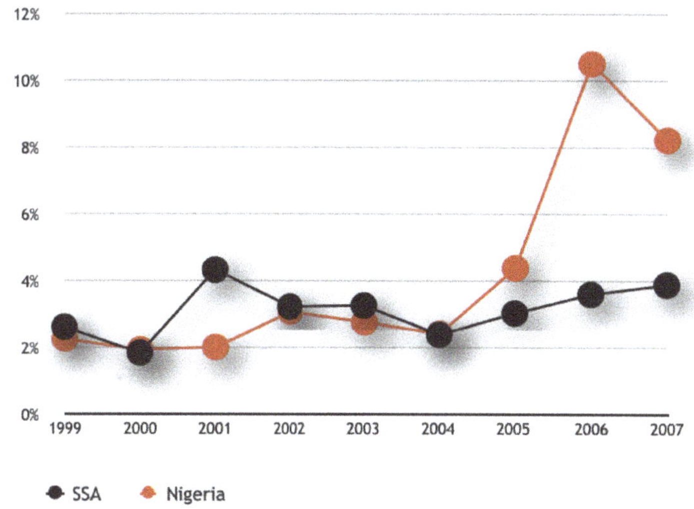

After 2004, FDI moved rapidly to fill that latent capacity. It dipped slightly in 2007, though.

Primary Data: UNCTAD

Central Africa
East Africa
Southern Africa
West Africa

FDI as % of GDP in Sub-Saharan Africa during 2003-06: Rankings

Rank	Country	Rank	Country	Rank	Country
1	Equatorial Guinea	15	Mozambique	29	Central Afr. Rep.
2	Chad	16	Tanzania	30	Senegal
3	Seychelles	17	Sierra Leone	31	Niger
4	Gambia, The	18	Guinea	32	Mauritius
5	Cape Verde	19	Malawi	33	South Africa
6	Angola	20	Togo	34	Burkina Faso
7	Congo, Rep.	21	Madagascar	35	Rwanda
8	Zambia	22	Guinea-Bissau	36	Eritrea
9	Nigeria	23	Mali	37	Kenya
10	Botswana	24	Gabon	38	Comoros
11	Namibia	25	Ghana	39	Congo, Dem. Rep.
12	Lesotho	26	Cameroon	40	Burundi
13	Ethiopia	27	Côte d' Ivoire	41	Swaziland
14	Uganda	28	Benin		
TOP		MIDDLE		BOTTOM	

Top-10 performance in Africa; the pack being led by oil exporters. Understandably; as they command foreign investment more easily than the other countries.

14.2 FDI per Person

	99-02	03-06
Self-comparison to Preceding Period		▲
Performance in Sub-Saharan Africa	▼	▲
Performance in West Africa	▲	▲
	Cape Verde	Cape Verde
	Gambia, The	Mauritania
	Liberia	**Nigeria**
	Mauritania	Gambia, The
	Côte d'Ivoire	Côte d'Ivoire
	Nigeria	Mali
	Mali	Ghana
	Togo	Guinea
	Senegal	Togo
	Ghana	Sierra Leone
	Benin	Senegal
	Sierra Leone	Benin
	Guinea	Guinea-Bissau
	Burkina Faso	Niger
	Guinea-Bissau	Burkina Faso
	Niger	Liberia
Performance among Oil-Exporters	▼	▼
	Equatorial Guinea	Equatorial Guinea
	Angola	Gabon
	Congo, Rep.	Congo, Rep.
	Chad	Chad
	Côte d'Ivoire	Angola
	Sudan	Sudan
	Cameroon	**Nigeria**
	Nigeria	Cameroon
	Gabon	Côte d'Ivoire

Primary Data: UNCTAD

▲	improved *or* better than average
▼	worsened *or* worse than average
◁▷	no change *or* average

Nigeria has commanded an increasing share of Africa's FDI, but still lies bottom of the oil exporters' league. untapped investment potential.

14.3

Share of West Africa and Nigeria in Total FDI of Sub-Saharan Africa (%): 1999 - 2007

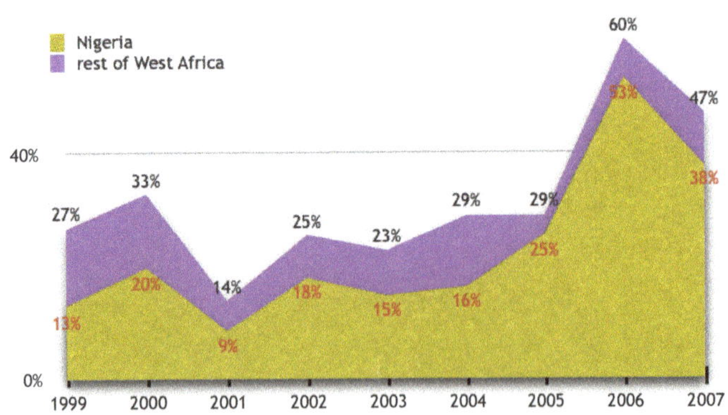

14.4

FDI as US$ per Person in West Africa during 2003-06

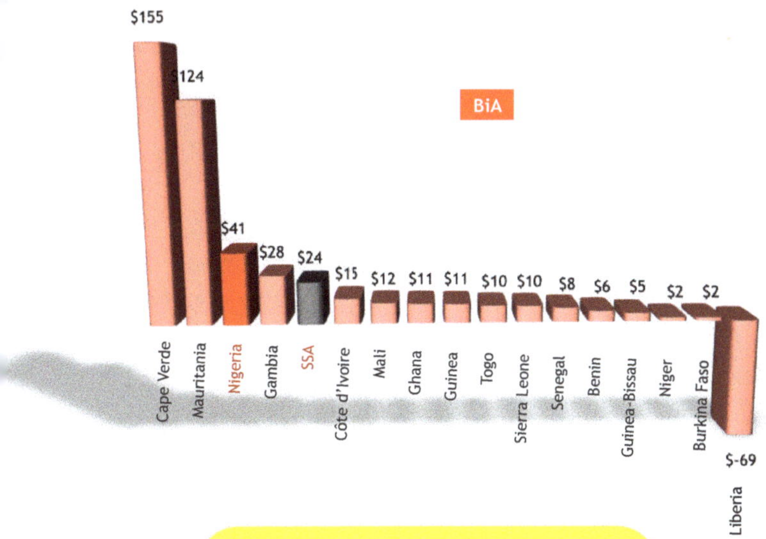

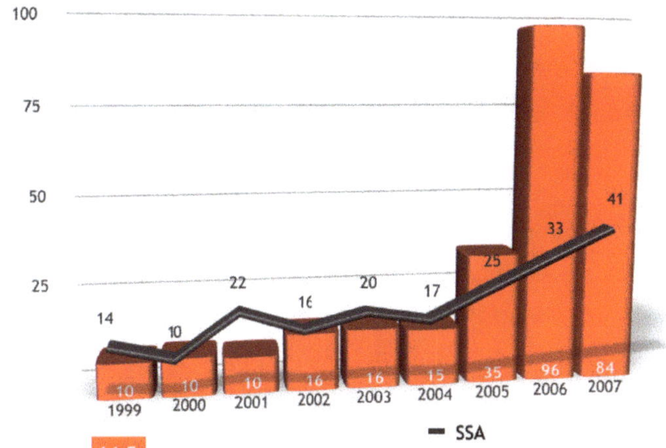

14.5

FDI as US$ per Person in Nigeria and Sub-Saharan Africa from 1999 to 2007

After 2004, Nigeria surpassed the Africa average for FDI per population. A dip in level in 2007, however.

Primary Data: UNCTAD

Central Africa
East Africa
Southern Africa
West Africa

FDI as US$ per Person in Sub-Saharan Africa during 2003-06: Rankings

Rank	Country	Rank	Country	Rank	Country
1	Equatorial Guinea	15	Gambia, The	29	Ethiopia
2	Seychelles	16	Cameroon	30	Guinea-Bissau
3	Botswana	17	Côte d' Ivoire	31	Malawi
4	Cape Verde	18	Mali	32	Central Afr. Rep.
5	Gabon	19	Ghana	33	Niger
6	Namibia	20	Tanzania	34	Burkina Faso
7	Congo, Rep.	21	Uganda	35	Kenya
8	Chad	22	Guinea	36	Rwanda
9	Angola	23	Mozambique	37	Eritrea
10	Mauritius	24	Togo	38	Comoros
11	**Nigeria**	25	Sierra Leone	39	Burundi
12	South Africa	26	Senegal	40	Congo, Dem. Rep.
13	Zambia	27	Madagascar	41	Swaziland
14	Lesotho	28	Benin		
TOP		MIDDLE		BOTTOM	

But it is beaten out of a Top-10 showing in Africa. Smaller countries like Namibia and Chad attracted more foreign money per population.

14.3 Growth in FDI per Person

who had the widest doors?

	99-02	03-06
Self-comparison to Preceding Period		▲
Performance in Sub-Saharan Africa	▼	▲
Performance in West Africa	▼	▲
	Sierra Leone	Liberia
	Mauritania	Sierra Leone
	Mali	Niger
	Guinea	Guinea-Bissau
	Cape Verde	Ghana
	Guinea-Bissau	Senegal
	Burkina Faso	Mauritania
	Senegal	**Nigeria**
	Niger	Benin
	Togo	Gambia, The
	Gambia, The	Guinea
	Nigeria	Burkina Faso
	Benin	Cape Verde
	Côte d'Ivoire	Togo
	Ghana	Côte d'Ivoire
	Liberia	Mali
Performance among Oil-Exporters	▼	▲
	Cameroon	Congo, Rep.
	Congo, Rep.	Gabon
	Chad	Equatorial Guinea
	Equatorial Guinea	**Nigeria**
	Angola	Sudan
	Sudan	Côte d'Ivoire
	Nigeria	Chad
	Côte d'Ivoire	Angola
	Gabon	Cameroon

14.6

Annual Growth in FDI per Person in West Africa during 2003-06 (%)

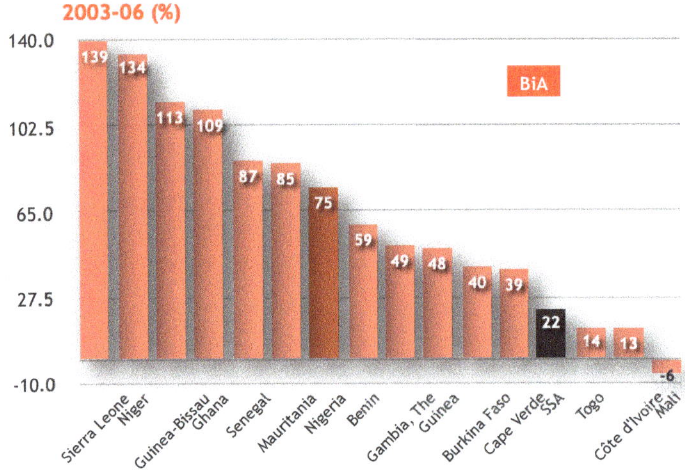

Primary Data: UNCTAD

A good showing by West Africa in general, where investment per person grew by more than the Africa average.

▲	improved *or* better than average
▼	worsened *or* worse than average
◁▷	no change *or* average

14.7

Annual Growth in FDI per Person in Nigeria and Sub-Saharan Africa from 2000-2007 (%)

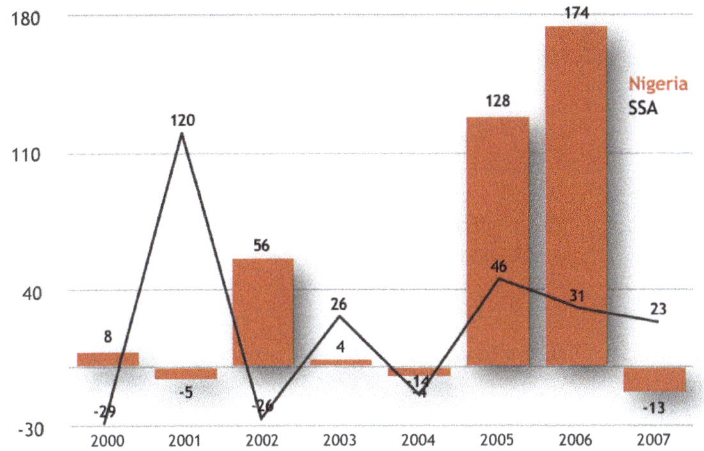

14.8

Build-up of FDI per Person in Nigeria and Sub-Saharan Africa from 2000-2007: 2000=100

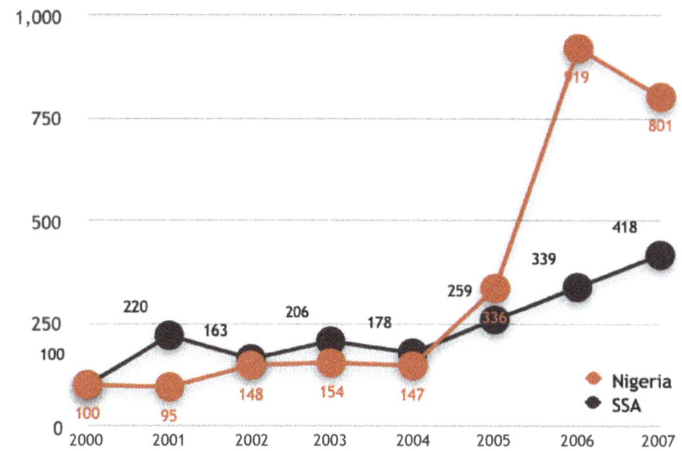

Primary Data: UNCTAD

Nigeria generally grew its FDI during 03-06, better than it did during the previous 4 yrs.

Nigeria's FDI per Population grew by 8 times from 2000 through 2007. The rest of Africa grew by 4 times.

Annual Growth in FDI per Person in Sub-Saharan Africa during 2003-06: Rankings

Rank	Country	Rank	Country	Rank	Country
1	Congo, Rep.	15	Benin	29	Togo
2	Gabon	16	Central Afr. Rep.	30	Côte d' Ivoire
3	South Africa	17	Kenya	31	Swaziland
4	Sierra Leone	18	Gambia, The	32	Comoros
5	Niger	19	Guinea	33	Tanzania
6	Guinea-Bissau	20	Seychelles	34	Botswana
7	Ghana	21	Burkina Faso	35	Burundi
8	Mauritius	22	Cape Verde	36	Mali
9	Rwanda	23	Lesotho	37	Chad
10	Senegal	24	Ethiopia	38	Angola
11	Equatorial Guinea	25	Namibia	39	Mozambique
12	Nigeria	26	Zambia	40	Cameroon
13	Malawi	27	Uganda	41	Congo, Dem. Rep.
14	Madagascar	28	Eritrea		
TOP		MIDDLE		BOTTOM	

However, it was behind more than 10 other countries, who did better.

Central Africa
East Africa
Southern Africa
West Africa

14.4 FDI as % of Total Capital Investment

pleased to work with you

+1-800-help

Why such a big fuss about FDI?

Mark of approval for country's policies and long-term direction. Investors will go where their money will see good — sustainable — returns.

Notice that every country, developed and developing, competes strenuously for foreign investment, because this means jobs, infrastructure, competitive advantage, long-term.

Remember, though: FDI is not the same as stock market investment: that one's fleeting and can be gone in 60 seconds; manufacturing plants and factories and buildings cannot.

	99-02	03-06
Self-comparison to Preceding Period		▼
Performance in Sub-Saharan Africa	▲	▲
Performance in West Africa	▲	▲
	Liberia	Sierra Leone
	Sierra Leone	Mauritania
	Gambia, The	**Nigeria**
	Nigeria	Gambia, The
	Togo	Cape Verde
	Mauritania	Guinea
	Cape Verde	Guinea-Bissau
	Côte d'Ivoire	Côte d'Ivoire
	Mali	Mali
	Ghana	Togo
	Benin	Ghana
	Senegal	Benin
	Guinea	Niger
	Guinea-Bissau	Senegal
	Niger	Burkina Faso
	Burkina Faso	Liberia
Performance among Oil-Exporters	▲	▲
	Angola	Equatorial Guinea
	Chad	Angola
	Equatorial Guinea	Chad
	Nigeria	**Nigeria**
	Congo, Rep.	Sudan
	Sudan	Congo, Rep.
	Côte d'Ivoire	Côte d'Ivoire
	Cameroon	Cameroon
	Gabon	Gabon

Primary Data: UNCTAD

▲	improved *or* better than average
▼	worsened *or* worse than average
◁▷	no change *or* average

14.9

FDI as % of Total Capital Investment in West Africa during 2003-06

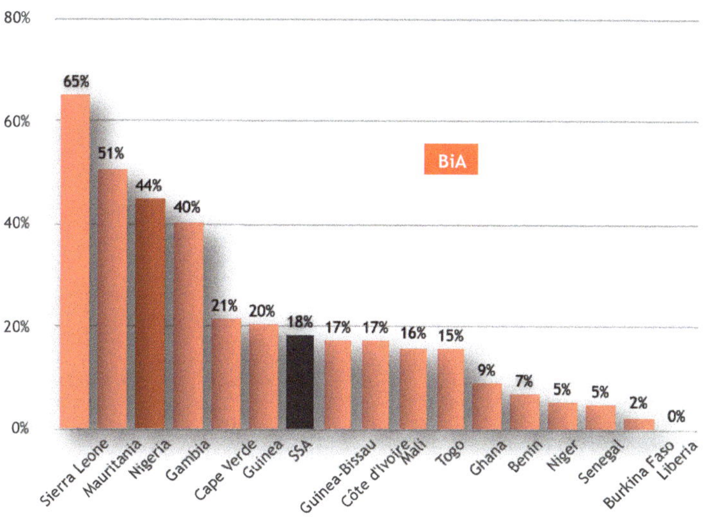

14.10

FDI as % of Total Capital Investment in Nigeria and Sub-Saharan Africa from 1999-2006

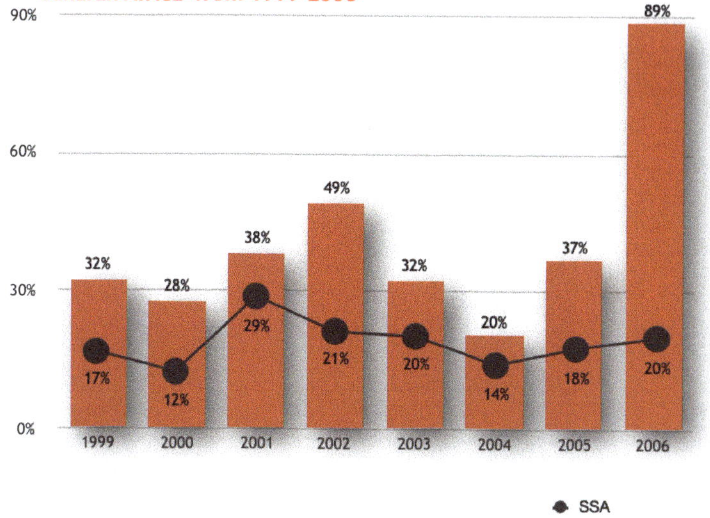

The FDI contribution to overall investment in Nigeria grew — even though in fits and starts — from 1999 through 2006.

FDI as % of Total Capital Investment in Sub-Saharan Africa during 2003-06: Rankings

Rank	Country	Rank	Country	Rank	Country
1	Seychelles	15	Botswana	29	Benin
2	Equatorial Guinea	16	Namibia	30	Niger
3	Sierra Leone	17	Guinea-Bissau	31	South Africa
4	Angola	18	Côte d' Ivoire	32	Senegal
5	Chad	19	Tanzania	33	Mauritius
6	Nigeria	20	Uganda	34	Rwanda
7	Gambia, The	21	Mozambique	35	Burkina Faso
8	Malawi	22	Mali	36	Comoros
9	Zambia	23	Togo	37	Eritrea
10	Congo, Rep.	24	Madagascar	38	Congo, Dem. Rep.
11	Central Afr. Rep.	25	Lesotho	39	Kenya
12	Ethiopia	26	Cameroon	40	Burundi
13	Cape Verde	27	Gabon	41	Swaziland
14	Guinea	28	Ghana		

TOP MIDDLE BOTTOM

Nigeria did better than average in Africa, in terms of FDI contribution to overall investment. Top-10.

Primary Data: UNCTAD

Central Africa
East Africa
Southern Africa
West Africa

14.5 Total Capital Investment as % of GDP

do the numbers bear that out?

+1-800-help

> Please remind me of the distinctions: Total capital inv., Private sector inv., Domestic inv.; it all gets confusing 🤔

> No problem.

> Private inv. is investment carried out by the private sector // Public inv. is investment carried out by the government sector // Foreign direct inv. (FDI) is investment from outside the country // Domestic inv. is investment by private sector based in the country.

> Total capital investment = Private inv. + Public inv. // Private investment = Foreign inv. (FDI) + Domestic inv.

> Capish?

> Muy bueno

03/06 was an improvement over the previous 4 yrs. But it still didn't bring Nigeria up to "standard". Worse performance than in most of the continent.

Primary Data: UNCTAD

	99-02	03-06
Self-comparison to Preceding Period		▲
Performance in Sub-Saharan Africa	▼	▼
Performance in West Africa	▼	▼
	Cape Verde	Mauritania
	Burkina Faso	Cape Verde
	Senegal	Ghana
	Ghana	Gambia, The
	Mauritania	Senegal
	Gambia, The	Burkina Faso
	Guinea	Benin
	Mali	Togo
	Benin	Mali
	Togo	Niger
	Guinea-Bissau	Guinea-Bissau
	Niger	Guinea
	Côte d'Ivoire	Liberia
	Nigeria	**Nigeria**
	Liberia	Côte d'Ivoire
	Sierra Leone	Sierra Leone
Performance among Oil-Exporters	▼	▼
	Equatorial Guinea	Equatorial Guinea
	Chad	Chad
	Gabon	Congo, Rep.
	Congo, Rep.	Gabon
	Sudan	Sudan
	Cameroon	Cameroon
	Angola	**Nigeria**
	Côte d'Ivoire	Angola
	Nigeria	Côte d'Ivoire

▲	improved *or* better than average
▼	worsened *or* worse than average
◁▷	no change *or* average

14.11

Total Capital Investment as % of GDP in West Africa during 2003-06

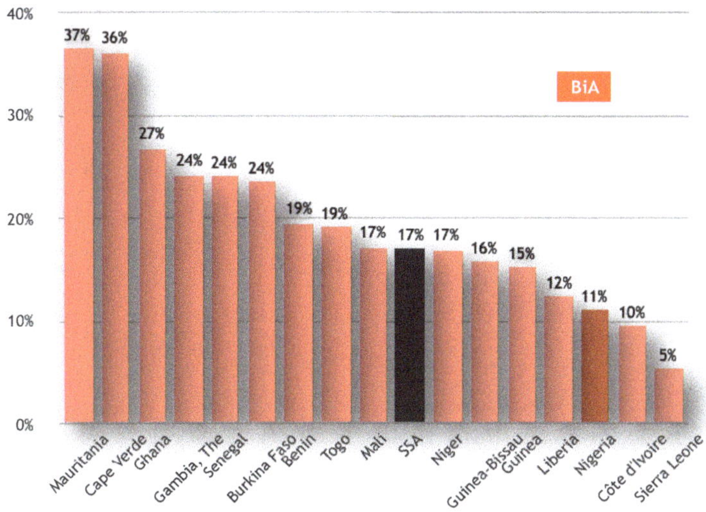

14.12

Total Capital Investment as % of GDP in Nigeria and Sub-Saharan Africa from 1999-2006

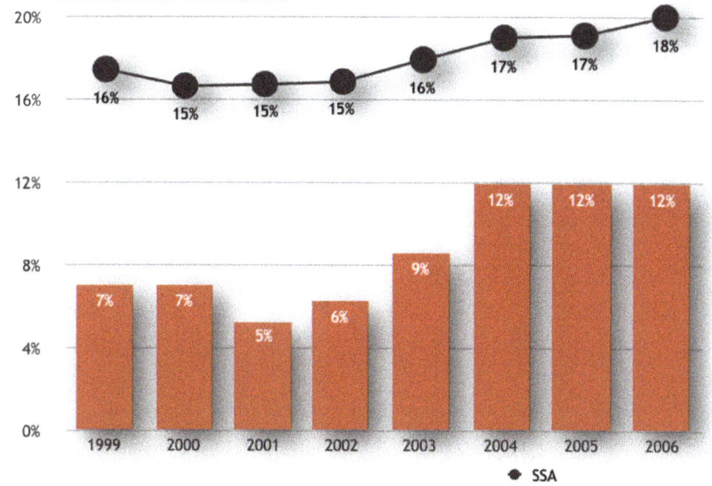

Huge chasm between Africa and Nigeria levels, but closing up towards 2006. Perhaps an indicator again that there's considerable unharnessed potential.

Total Capital Investment as % of GDP in Sub-Saharan Africa during 2003-06: Rankings

Rank	Country	Rank	Country	Rank	Country
1	Equatorial Guinea	15	Mauritius	29	Niger
2	Lesotho	16	Mozambique	30	South Africa
3	Cape Verde	17	Eritrea	31	Guinea-Bissau
4	Chad	18	Madagascar	32	Congo, Dem. Rep.
5	Ghana	19	Tanzania	33	Burundi
6	Namibia	20	Ethiopia	34	Guinea
7	Congo, Rep.	21	Rwanda	35	Nigeria
8	Zambia	22	Seychelles	36	Angola
9	Botswana	23	Benin	37	Comoros
10	Gambia, The	24	Cameroon	38	Côte d' Ivoire
11	Senegal	25	Togo	39	Malawi
12	Burkina Faso	26	Swaziland	40	Central Afr. Rep.
13	Gabon	27	Mali	41	Sierra Leone
14	Uganda	28	Kenya		
TOP		MIDDLE		BOTTOM	

Primary Data: UNCTAD

Central Africa
East Africa
Southern Africa
West Africa

14.6 Total Capital Investment per Person

home, sweet home?

	99-02	03-06
Self-comparison to Preceding Period		▲
Performance in Sub-Saharan Africa	▼	▼
Performance in West Africa	▼	▲

99-02	03-06
Cape Verde	Cape Verde
Senegal	Mauritania
Mauritania	Senegal
Côte d'Ivoire	Ghana
Guinea	Benin
Ghana	Burkina Faso
Benin	Côte d'Ivoire
Gambia, The	**Nigeria**
Burkina Faso	Mali
Mali	Gambia, The
Togo	Togo
Nigeria	Guinea
Guinea-Bissau	Niger
Niger	Guinea-Bissau
Liberia	Liberia
Sierra Leone	Sierra Leone

Primary Data: UNCTAD

Also when investment is measured in per capita terms, 03/06 was an improvement over 99/02. Despite that, Nigeria is at rock bottom among oil exporters.

	99-02	03-06
Performance among Oil-Exporters	▼	▼

99-02	03-06
Equatorial Guinea	Equatorial Guinea
Gabon	Gabon
Congo, Rep.	Congo, Rep.
Cameroon	Angola
Angola	Cameroon
Côte d'Ivoire	Sudan
Sudan	Chad
Chad	Côte d'Ivoire
Nigeria	**Nigeria**

▲	improved *or* better than average
▼	worsened *or* worse than average
◁▷	no change *or* average

14.13

Total Capital Investment per Person (US$) in West Africa during 2003-06

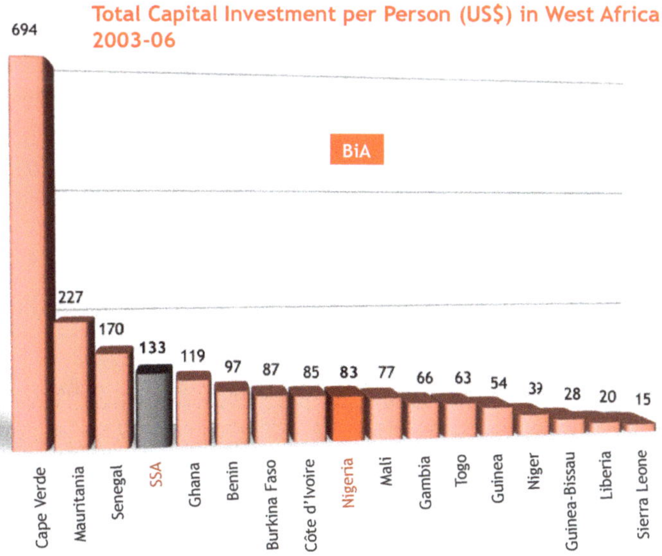

Looks like the Nigeria market can still absorb a lot more capital investment. It falls behind the continent average by a considerable gap.

14.14

Total Capital Investment per Person ($US) in Nigeria and Sub-Saharan Africa from 1999-2006

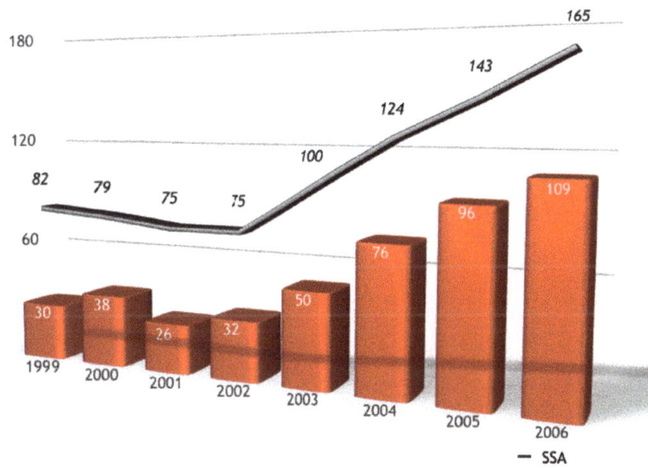

Total Capital Investment per Person in Sub-Saharan Africa during 2003-06: Rankings

Rank	Country	Rank	Country	Rank	Country
1	Equatorial Guinea	15	Zambia	29	Madagascar
2	Seychelles	16	Chad	30	Guinea
3	Gabon	17	Ghana	31	Comoros
4	Botswana	18	Benin	32	Eritrea
5	Mauritius	19	Kenya	33	Rwanda
6	South Africa	20	Burkina Faso	34	Niger
7	Namibia	21	Côte d' Ivoire	35	Guinea-Bissau
8	Cape Verde	22	Nigeria	36	Ethiopia
9	Swaziland	23	Mali	37	Congo, Dem. Rep.
10	Congo, Rep.	24	Uganda	38	Central Afr. Rep.
11	Lesotho	25	Mozambique	39	Burundi
12	Angola	26	Tanzania	40	Sierra Leone
13	Cameroon	27	Gambia, The	41	Malawi
14	Senegal	28	Togo		
TOP		MIDDLE		BOTTOM	

Primary Data: UNCTAD

Central Africa
East Africa
Southern Africa
West Africa

14.7 Growth in Total Capital Investment per Person

it's quite safe, actually

14.15

Growth in Total Capital Investment per Person (%) in West Africa during 2003-06

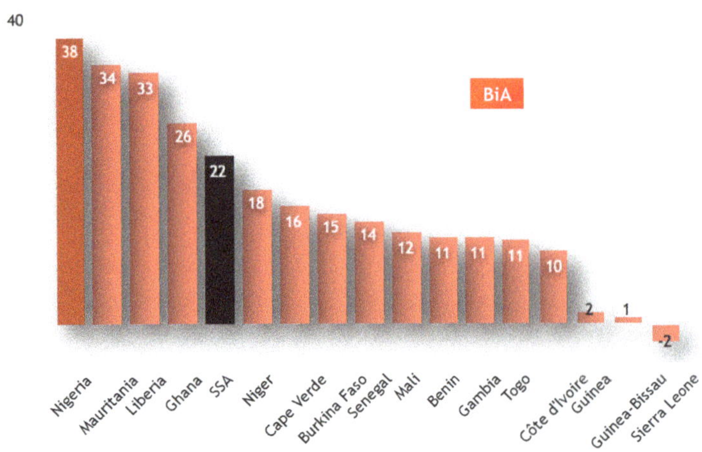

Signs of strong growth for Nigeria. Looks like it's trying to fill in the huge capacity vacuum.

	99-02	03-06
Self-comparison to Preceding Period		▲
Performance in Sub-Saharan Africa	▲	▲
Performance in West Africa	▲	▲

Primary Data: UNCTAD

99-02	03-06
Sierra Leone	**Nigeria**
Guinea-Bissau	Mauritania
Cape Verde	Liberia
Nigeria	Ghana
Benin	Niger
Mali	Cape Verde
Mauritania	Burkina Faso
Guinea	Senegal
Niger	Mali
Senegal	Benin
Burkina Faso	Gambia, The
Togo	Togo
Gambia, The	Côte d'Ivoire
Ghana	Guinea
Côte d'Ivoire	Guinea-Bissau
Liberia	Sierra Leone

Performance among Oil-Exporters	99-02	03-06
	◁▷	▲
	Chad	Equatorial Guinea
	Equatorial Guinea	Angola
	Sudan	**Nigeria**
	Cameroon	Sudan
	Nigeria	Congo, Rep.
	Gabon	Cameroon
	Congo, Rep.	Côte d'Ivoire
	Angola	Gabon
	Côte d'Ivoire	Chad

▲	improved *or* better than average
▼	worsened *or* worse than average
◁▷	no change *or* average

Africa has been getting a growing swathe of investment from about 2001.

14.16
Growth in Total Capital Investment per Person in Nigeria and Sub-Saharan Africa during 2003-06

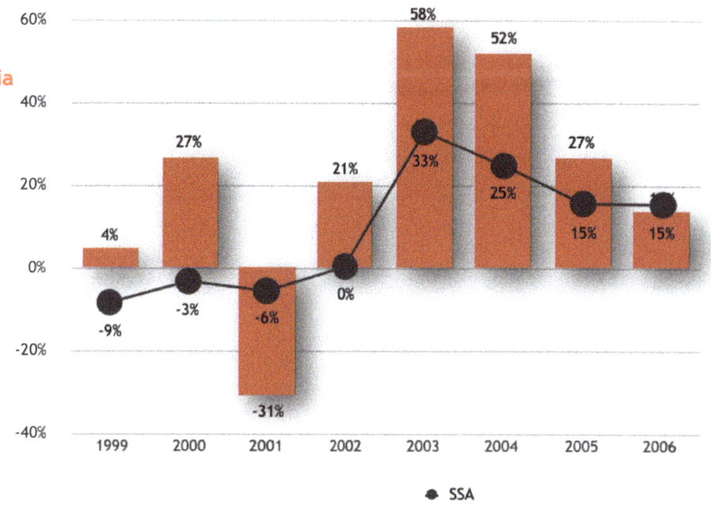

Nigeria's volume of capital investment per population almost tripled between 2000 and 2006, where Africa's doubled.

14.17
Build-up of Total Capital Investment per Person in Nigeria and Sub-Saharan Africa: 2000=100

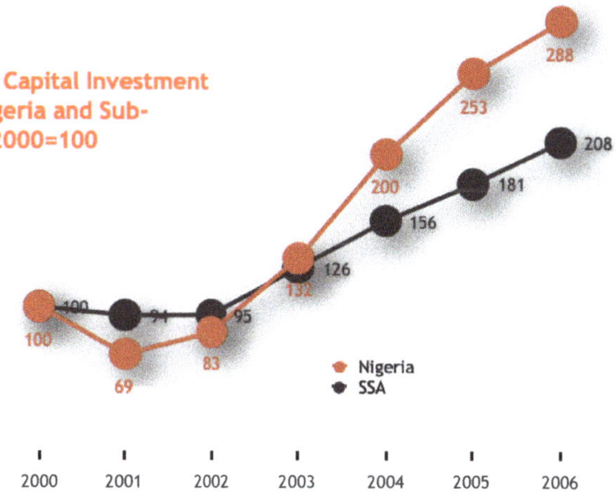

Both growth rates - Nigeria & Africa - were slowing significantly from 2003 levels, though.

Growth in Total Capital Investment per Person in Sub-Saharan Africa during 2003-06: Rankings

Rank	Country	Rank	Country	Rank	Country
1	Equatorial Guinea	15	Botswana	29	Rwanda
2	Angola	16	Mozambique	30	Mauritius
3	Seychelles	17	Uganda	31	Côte d' Ivoire
4	Nigeria	18	Madagascar	32	Ethiopia
5	Burundi	19	Cape Verde	33	Tanzania
6	Zambia	20	Kenya	34	Gabon
7	Congo, Dem. Rep.	21	Burkina Faso	35	Chad
8	Namibia	22	Cameroon	36	Eritrea
9	Congo, Rep.	23	Senegal	37	Guinea
10	South Africa	24	Comoros	38	Guinea-Bissau
11	Ghana	25	Mali	39	Central Afr. Rep.
12	Swaziland	26	Benin	40	Sierra Leone
13	Lesotho	27	Gambia, The	41	Malawi
14	Niger	28	Togo		
TOP		MIDDLE		BOTTOM	

But Nigeria's was the 4th fastest growing capital investment portfolio in Africa.

Primary Data: UNCTAD

Central Africa
East Africa
Southern Africa
West Africa

14.8 Private Component of TCI as % of GDP

this one's private...

	99-02	03-06
Self-comparison to Preceding Period		▼
Performance in Sub-Saharan Africa	▲	▼
Performance in West Africa	▲	▼
	Cape Verde	Cape Verde
	Ghana	Senegal
	Senegal	Ghana
	Nigeria	Burkina Faso
	Gambia, The	Gambia, The
	Mali	Mali
	Togo	Benin
	Burkina Faso	Niger
	Guinea	**Nigeria**
	Benin	Togo
	Côte d'Ivoire	Sierra Leone
	Niger	Guinea
	Mauritania	Côte d'Ivoire
	Sierra Leone	Mauritania
	Guinea-Bissau	Guinea-Bissau
Performance among Oil-Exporters	▼	▼
	Equatorial Guinea	Equatorial Guinea
	Chad	Chad
	Gabon	Gabon
	Cameroon	Sudan
	Sudan	Congo, Rep.
	Congo, Rep.	Cameroon
	Nigeria	**Nigeria**
	Angola	Côte d'Ivoire
	Côte d'Ivoire	Angola

Primary Data: AfDB

Most of Nigeria's capital investment seems to have come from the public sector (govt.), as overall TCI was growing, even though private investment fell.

Indeed, overwhelmingly so, when placed alongside other countries' proportions. Including the oil exporters'.

▲	improved *or* better than average
▼	worsened *or* worse than average
◁▷	no change *or* average

14.18

Private and Public Components of Total Capital Investment as % GDP in West Africa during 2003-06

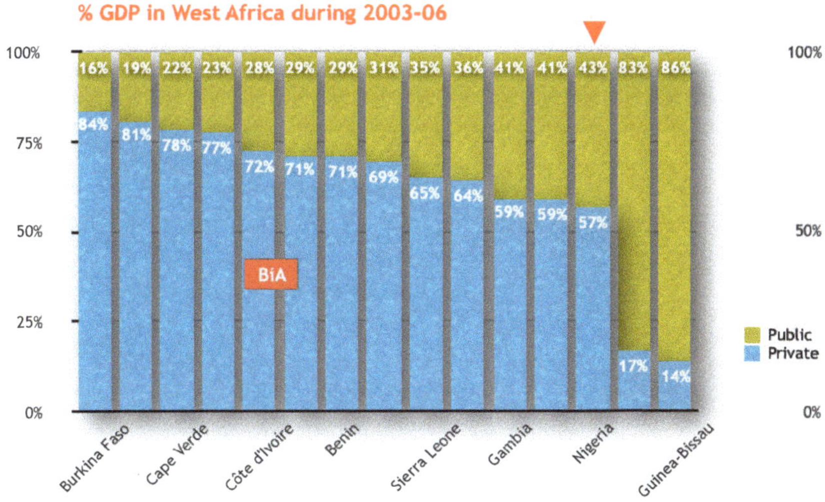

14.19

Private and Public Components of Total Capital Investment as % GDP in Nigeria: from 2000-07

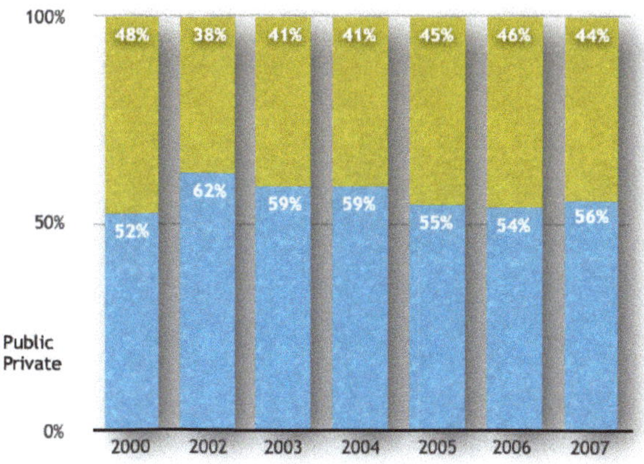

Primary Data: AfDB

The level of private sector involvement in Nigeria's capital investment generally revolved around the 50% mark, smaller than most of West Africa's.

... and that one over there's public

Also smaller than most of SSA. But difficult to say whether this reflects the level of private sector confidence.

Private Component of Total Capital Investment as % of GDP in Sub-Saharan Africa during 2003-06: Rankings

Rank	Country	Rank	Country	Rank	Country
1	Equatorial Guinea	15	South Africa	29	Swaziland
2	Cape Verde	16	Cameroon	30	Congo, Dem. Rep.
3	Botswana	17	Mauritius	31	Togo
4	Chad	18	Burkina Faso	32	Sierra Leone
5	Lesotho	19	Gambia, The	33	Ethiopia
6	Namibia	20	Mozambique	34	Guinea
7	Malawi	21	Mali	35	Côte d' Ivoire
8	Gabon	22	Benin	36	Comoros
9	Senegal	23	Niger	37	Central Afr. Rep.
10	Uganda	24	Tanzania	38	Eritrea
11	Seychelles	25	Kenya	39	Burundi
12	Congo, Rep.	26	Nigeria	40	Angola
13	Zambia	27	Rwanda	41	Guinea-Bissau
14	Ghana	28	Madagascar		
TOP		MIDDLE		BOTTOM	

Central Africa
East Africa
Southern Africa
West Africa

14.9 Private Component of TCI as Investment per Person

that's me, in the corner

In per-person measures of private sector participation, however, Nigeria looked good within West Africa.

But that wasn't enough to earn it satisfaction among the oil economies. They did considerably better, both sides of 2003.

	99-02	03-06
Self-comparison to Preceding Period		▲
Performance in Sub-Saharan Africa	▲	▲

Performance in West Africa	99-02	03-06
	▲	▲
	Cape Verde	Cape Verde
	Senegal	Senegal
	Nigeria	**Nigeria**
	Ghana	Ghana
	Benin	Benin
	Gambia, The	Gambia, The
	Côte d'Ivoire	Burkina Faso
	Guinea	Mali
	Burkina Faso	Côte d'Ivoire
	Mali	Mauritania
	Togo	Guinea
	Mauritania	Niger
	Niger	Togo
	Sierra Leone	Sierra Leone
	Guinea-Bissau	Guinea-Bissau

Primary Data: AfDB, IMF

Performance among Oil-Exporters	99-02	03-06
	▼	▼
	Gabon	Equatorial Guinea
	Equatorial Guinea	Gabon
	Congo, Rep.	Congo, Rep.
	Chad	Chad
	Cameroon	Sudan
	Sudan	Cameroon
	Angola	**Nigeria**
	Nigeria	Angola
	Côte d'Ivoire	Côte d'Ivoire

▲	improved *or* better than average
▼	worsened *or* worse than average
◁▷	no change *or* average

14.20

Private and Public Components of Total Capital Investment per Person ($PPP) in West Africa during 2003-06

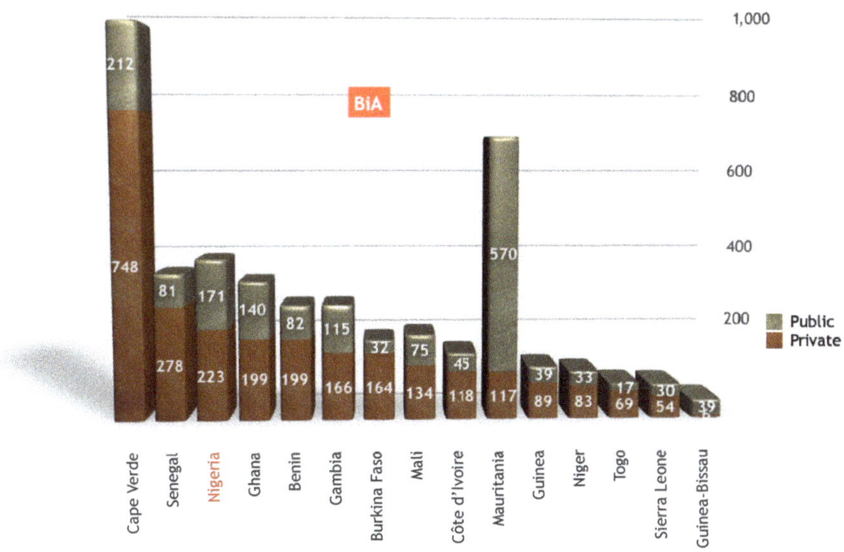

14.21

Private and Public Components of Total Capital Investment per Person in Nigeria ($PPP): from 2000-07

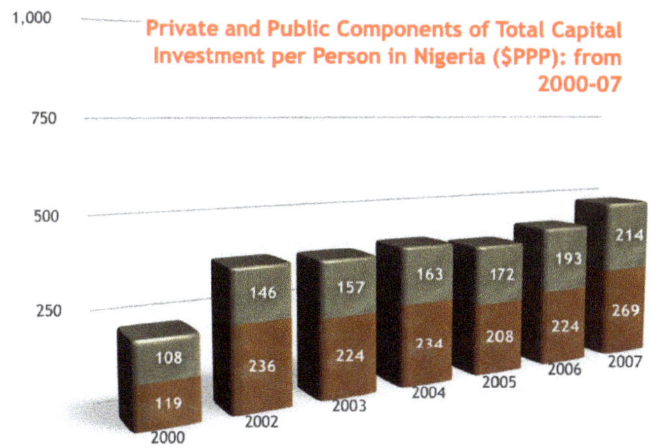

Primary Data: AfDB, IMF

Nigeria doubled the amount of capital invested per person, in both public and private-owned ventures, between 2000 & 2007.

Private Component of TCI as Investment per Person ($PPP) in Sub-Saharan Africa during 2003-06: Rankings

Rank	Country	Rank	Country	Rank	Country
1	Botswana	15	Nigeria	29	Mozambique
2	Equatorial Guinea	16	Ghana	30	Rwanda
3	Gabon	17	Benin	31	Guinea
4	Seychelles	18	Kenya	32	Niger
5	Mauritius	19	Zambia	33	Togo
6	South Africa	20	Gambia, The	34	Sierra Leone
7	Namibia	21	Burkina Faso	35	Ethiopia
8	Cape Verde	22	Uganda	36	Comoros
9	Congo, Rep.	23	Tanzania	37	Eritrea
10	Swaziland	24	Mali	38	Central Afr. Rep.
11	Chad	25	Angola	39	Congo, Dem. Rep.
12	Cameroon	26	Malawi	40	Burundi
13	Senegal	27	Côte d' Ivoire	41	Guinea-Bissau
14	Lesotho	28	Madagascar		
TOP		MIDDLE		BOTTOM	

But private sector participation looked healthier in several other countries. Nigeria made the middle category on the continent.

Primary Data: AfDB, IMF

Central Africa
East Africa
Southern Africa
West Africa

14.10 Growth of Private (& Public) Component of TCI

he can't wait

	99-02	03-06
Self-comparison to Preceding Period		▼
Performance in Sub-Saharan Africa	▲	▼
Performance in West Africa	▲	▼
	Sierra Leone	Guinea-Bissau
	Nigeria	Niger
	Togo	Sierra Leone
	Mauritania	Senegal
	Cape Verde	Burkina Faso
	Niger	Benin
	Gambia, The	Ghana
	Ghana	Mali
	Mali	Cape Verde
	Benin	Mauritania
	Côte d'Ivoire	Gambia, The
	Burkina Faso	Guinea
	Senegal	Côte d'Ivoire
	Guinea	**Nigeria**
	Guinea-Bissau	Togo

Primary Data: AfDB, IMF

Sharp deterioration in growth of private sector investment during 03/06, compared to the rest of West Africa. And to fellow oil exporters, too.

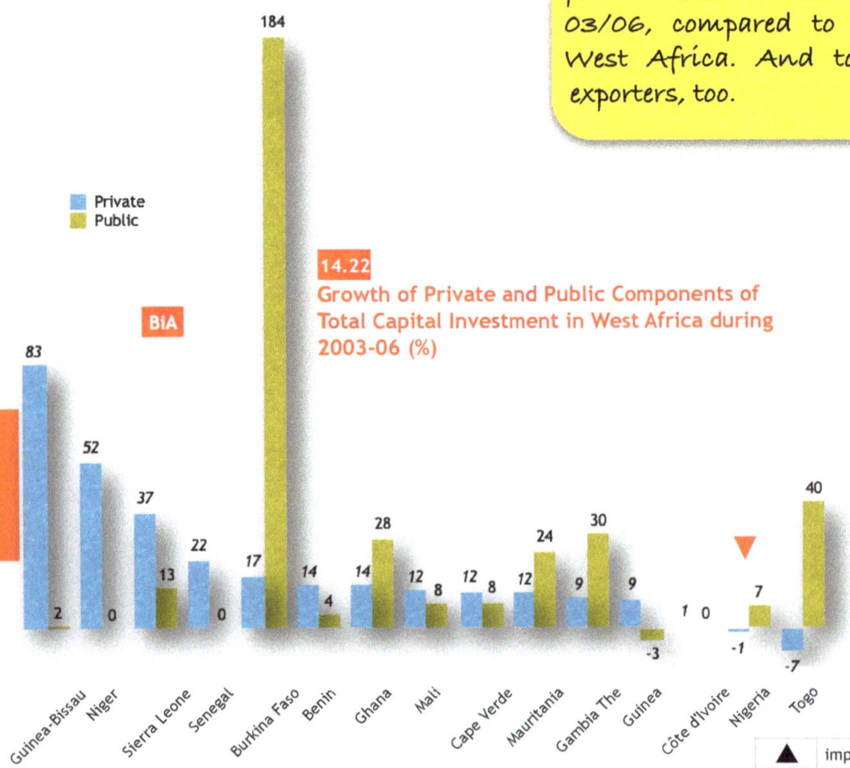

14.22 Growth of Private and Public Components of Total Capital Investment in West Africa during 2003-06 (%)

Performance among Oil-Exporters	99-02 ▲	03-06 ▼
	Chad	Equatorial Guinea
	Nigeria	Sudan
	Cameroon	Congo, Rep.
	Sudan	Côte d'Ivoire
	Gabon	Cameroon
	Congo, Rep.	Gabon
	Côte d'Ivoire	**Nigeria**
	Equatorial Guinea	Angola
	Angola	Chad

▲	improved *or* better than average
▼	worsened *or* worse than average
◁▷	no change *or* average

14.23

Growth of Private and Public Components of Total Capital Investment in Nigeria (%): from 2000-07

After sharp growth in 2000/02, subsequent yrs have struggled to even achieve a fifth of that pace in private investment growth. Similar story for public investment, too.

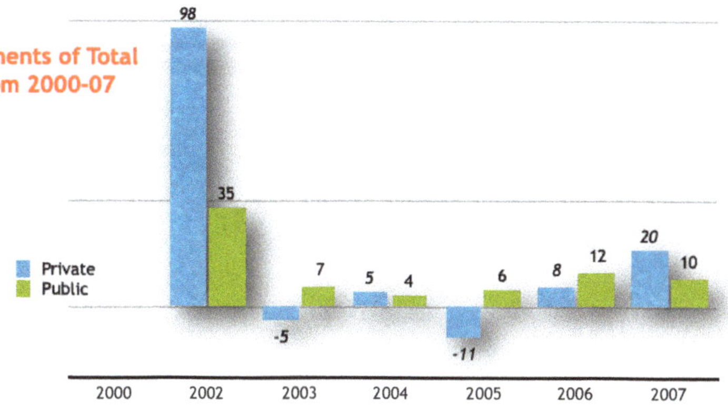

14.24

Build-up of Private and Public Components of Total Capital Investment in Nigeria 2000-07: 2000=100

The huge leap in 2002 masks the very poor showing during 2003-2007. Bottom position in the continent rankings.

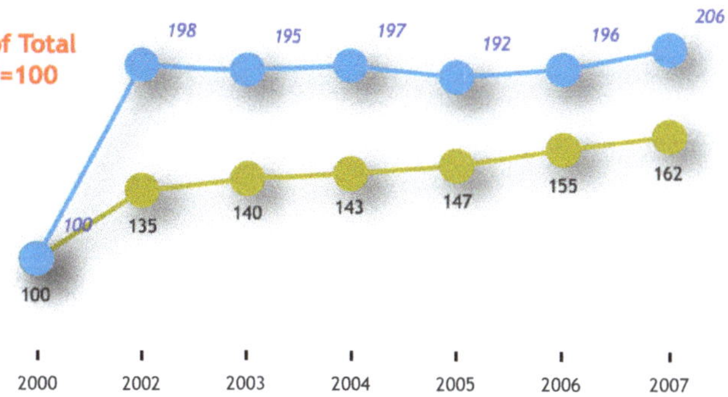

Growth of Private Component of Total Capital Investment per Person in Sub-Saharan Africa during 2003-06: Rankings

Rank	Country	Rank	Country	Rank	Country
1	Malawi	15	Benin	29	Congo, Rep.
2	Guinea-Bissau	16	Ghana	30	Comoros
3	Niger	17	Tanzania	31	Côte d' Ivoire
4	Burundi	18	Congo, Dem. Rep.	32	Cameroon
5	Sierra Leone	19	Mali	33	Botswana
6	Seychelles	20	Uganda	34	Gabon
7	Kenya	21	Cape Verde	35	Nigeria
8	Equatorial Guinea	22	Central Afr. Rep.	36	Swaziland
9	Zambia	23	Gambia, The	37	Togo
10	Madagascar	24	Guinea	38	Lesotho
11	Senegal	25	Mauritius	39	Angola
12	Namibia	26	Rwanda	40	Chad
13	Burkina Faso	27	Mozambique	41	Eritrea
14	South Africa	28	Ethiopia		
	TOP		MIDDLE		BOTTOM

Primary Data: AfDB, IMF

Central Africa
East Africa
Southern Africa
West Africa

14.11 Domestic Credit to the Private Sector as % of GDP

opening up the bank vaults

	99-02	03-06
Self-comparison to Preceding Period		▼
Performance in Sub-Saharan Africa	▼	▼

Performance in West Africa

99-02	03-06
▲	▲
Cape Verde	Cape Verde
Mauritania	Mauritania
Senegal	Senegal
Mali	Mali
Côte d'Ivoire	Togo
Nigeria	Burkina Faso
Togo	Benin
Gambia, The	**Nigeria**
Burkina Faso	Ghana
Ghana	Gambia, The
Benin	Côte d'Ivoire
Guinea-Bissau	Niger
Niger	Liberia
Guinea	Sierra Leone
Liberia	Guinea
Sierra Leone	Guinea-Bissau

Primary Data: WB, IMF

Level of credit from Nigeria's domestic financial institutions dropped to average within West Africa in 03/06.

Performance among Oil-Exporters

99-02	03-06
▲	▲
Côte d'Ivoire	**Nigeria**
Nigeria	Côte d'Ivoire
Gabon	Cameroon
Cameroon	Gabon
Congo, Rep.	Sudan
Chad	Angola
Equatorial Guinea	Equatorial Guinea
Angola	Chad
Sudan	Congo, Rep.

That average performance nonetheless was sufficient to put Nigeria on top of the other oil economies. Dismal performance by the group.

▲	improved *or* better than average
▼	worsened *or* worse than average
◁▷	no change *or* average

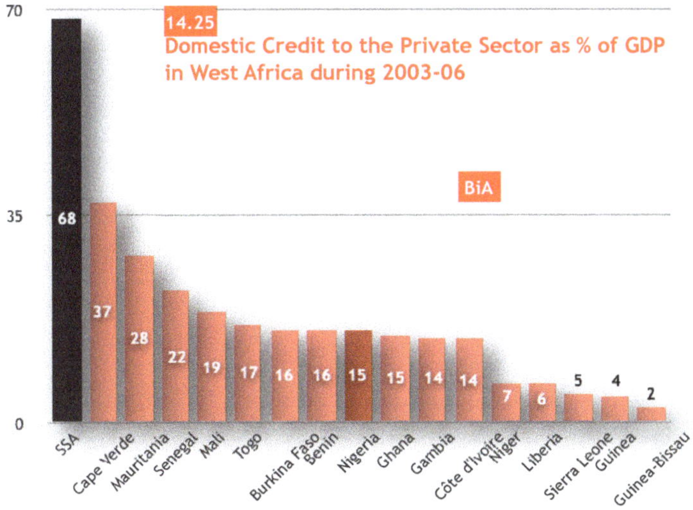

14.25
Domestic Credit to the Private Sector as % of GDP in West Africa during 2003-06

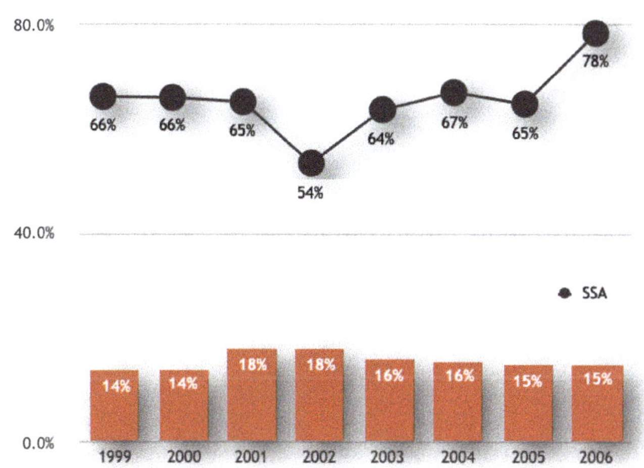

14.26
Domestic Credit to the Private Sector as % of GDP in Nigeria and Sub-Saharan Africa from 1999-2006

Huge gulf between the continent's and Nigeria's levels of private-sector investment participation.

It should be observed, though, that South Africa was responsible for the continent's high % average. Indeed, all the other 46 countries fell below that (weighted) average.

Domestic Credit to the Private Sector as % of GDP in Sub-Saharan Africa during 2003-06: Rankings

Rank	Country	Rank	Country	Rank	Country
1	South Africa	15	Burkina Faso	29	Lesotho
2	Mauritius	16	Benin	30	Mozambique
3	Namibia	17	Nigeria	31	Uganda
4	Cape Verde	18	Ghana	32	Niger
5	Seychelles	19	Gambia, The	33	Central Afr. Rep.
6	Eritrea	20	Côte d' Ivoire	34	Angola
7	Ethiopia	21	Rwanda	35	Sierra Leone
8	Kenya	22	Tanzania	36	Guinea
9	Burundi	23	Madagascar	37	Equatorial Guinea
10	Senegal	24	Cameroon	38	Chad
11	Swaziland	25	Gabon	39	Congo, Rep.
12	Botswana	26	Malawi	40	Guinea-Bissau
13	Mali	27	Comoros	41	Congo, Dem. Rep.
14	Togo	28	Zambia		
TOP		MIDDLE		BOTTOM	

Primary Data: WB, IMF

Central Africa
East Africa
Southern Africa
West Africa

14.12 Domestic Credit to the Private Sector in $PPP

perilous trips to the bank

	99-02	03-06
Self-comparison to Preceding Period		▲
Performance in Sub-Saharan Africa	▲	▲

Performance in West Africa	▲	▲
	Nigeria	Nigeria
	Côte d'Ivoire	Côte d'Ivoire
	Senegal	Senegal
	Ghana	Ghana
	Mali	Burkina Faso
	Burkina Faso	Mali
	Mauritania	Benin
	Benin	Mauritania
	Togo	Togo
	Guinea	Niger
	Cape Verde	Cape Verde
	Niger	Guinea
	Gambia, The	Gambia, The
	Sierra Leone	Sierra Leone
	Liberia	Liberia
	Guinea-Bissau	Guinea-Bissau

Primary Data: WB, IMF

Nigeria's excellent performance here isn't surprising, since this measures the volume of investment in itself, and not as a proportion of output or population.

Performance among Oil-Exporters	▲	▲
	Nigeria	Nigeria
	Côte d'Ivoire	Côte d'Ivoire
	Cameroon	Sudan
	Gabon	Angola
	Sudan	Cameroon
	Angola	Gabon
	Congo, Rep.	Equatorial Guinea
	Chad	Chad
	Equatorial Guinea	Congo, Rep.

It simply reflects the overall size of the economy.

▲	improved *or* better than average
▼	worsened *or* worse than average
◁▷	no change *or* average

14. Investor Confidence

14.27

Domestic Credit to the Private Sector in West Africa ($PPP millions) during 2003-06

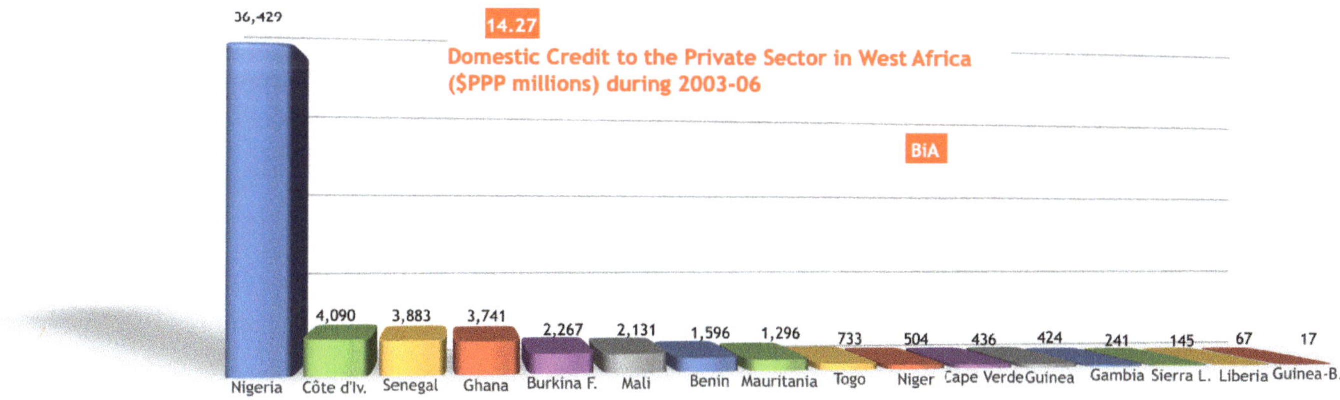

Primary Data: WB, IMF

The vol. of credit facilities has been increasing in Nigeria since 1999.

14.28

Domestic Credit to the Private Sector in Nigeria in $PPP (millions): from 1999-2006

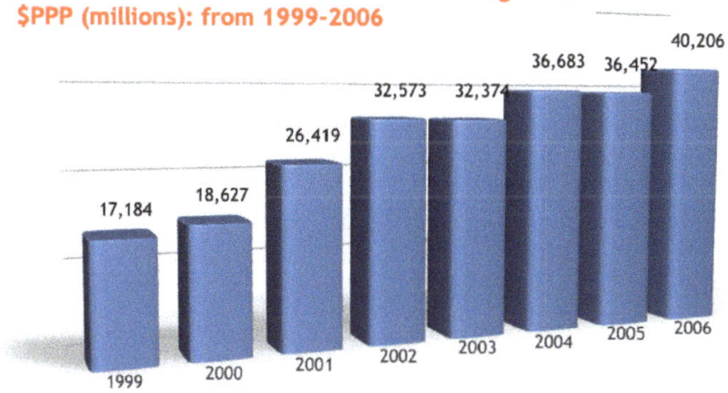

Central Africa
East Africa
Southern Africa
West Africa

Domestic Credit to the Private Sector as $PPP in Sub-Saharan Africa during 2003-06: Rankings

Rank	Country	Rank	Country	Rank	Country
1	South Africa	15	Mali	29	Equatorial Guinea
2	Nigeria	16	Uganda	30	Cape Verde
3	Kenya	17	Gabon	31	Chad
4	Ethiopia	18	Benin	32	Guinea
5	Mauritius	19	Madagascar	33	Seychelles
6	Namibia	20	Eritrea	34	Congo, Rep.
7	Côte d' Ivoire	21	Mozambique	35	Congo, Dem. Rep.
8	Botswana	22	Zambia	36	Gambia, The
9	Senegal	23	Swaziland	37	Lesotho
10	Tanzania	24	Rwanda	38	Central Afr. Rep.
11	Ghana	25	Malawi	39	Sierra Leone
12	Angola	26	Togo	40	Comoros
13	Cameroon	27	Burundi	41	Guinea-Bissau
14	Burkina Faso	28	Niger		
TOP		MIDDLE		BOTTOM	

The figures for 03/06
South Africa: $PPP 567bn
Nigeria: $PPP 36bn
Kenya: $PPP 12bn
Ethiopia: $PPP 11bn

Quite a distance between 1st and 2nd positions in vol. of investment. Volume thereafter gradually tapers from Ethiopia's 11 billion until Guinea-Bissau's 0.02 billion.

14.13 Growth in Domestic Credit to the Private Sector

dashing to the bank manager

Primary Data: WB, IMF

	99-02	03-06
Self-comparison to Preceding Period		▼
Performance in Sub-Saharan Africa	▲	▼

Performance in West Africa

99-02 ▲	03-06 ▼
Nigeria	Liberia
Sierra Leone	Guinea-Bissau
Benin	Niger
Gambia, The	Ghana
Mauritania	Sierra Leone
Ghana	Benin
Cape Verde	Togo
Senegal	Burkina Faso
Burkina Faso	Guinea
Niger	Cape Verde
Mali	Senegal
Guinea	Gambia, The
Guinea-Bissau	Mali
Côte d'Ivoire	**Nigeria**
Togo	Mauritania
Liberia	Côte d'Ivoire

Nigeria drops sharply on credit growth levels during 03/06 from 99/02. Eventual growth level worse than both the West Africa & continent average.

Surprisingly, that performance was still good enough to rank it high among the oil exporters. Their collective performance was poor, indeed.

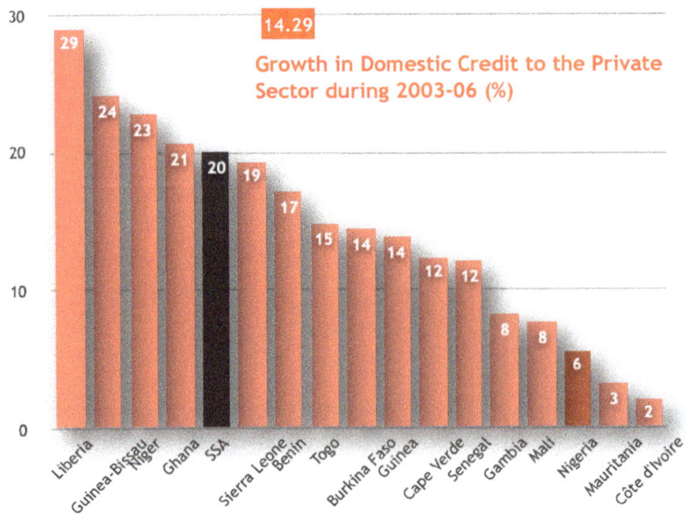

14.29 Growth in Domestic Credit to the Private Sector during 2003-06 (%)

Performance among Oil-Exporters

99-02 ▲	03-06 ▲
Sudan	Equatorial Guinea
Nigeria	Angola
Angola	**Nigeria**
Equatorial Guinea	Chad
Chad	Sudan
Cameroon	Congo, Rep.
Gabon	Cameroon
Côte d'Ivoire	Côte d'Ivoire
Congo, Rep.	Gabon

▲	improved *or* better than average
▼	worsened *or* worse than average
◁▷	no change *or* average

14.30
Growth in Domestic Credit to the Private Sector in Nigeria and Sub-Saharan Africa from 1999-2006

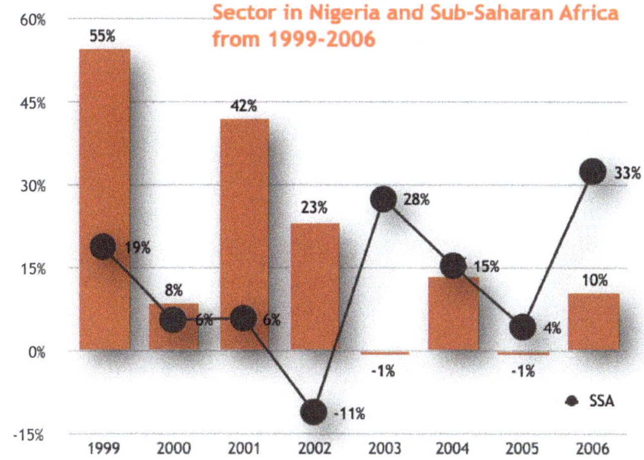

14.31
Build-up of Domestic Credit to the Private Sector in Nigeria and Sub-Saharan Africa from 2000-06: 2000=100

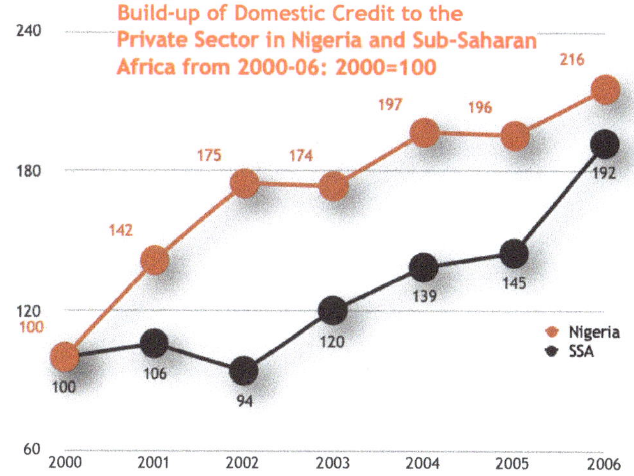

Nonetheless, Nigeria's domestic credit progress since 2000 is encouraging, outstripping the continent average.

Growth in Domestic Credit to the Private Sector in Sub-Saharan Africa during 2003-06: Rankings

Rank	Country	Rank	Country	Rank	Country
1	Mozambique	15	Rwanda	29	Gambia, The
2	Congo, Dem. Rep.	16	Namibia	30	Central Afr. Rep.
3	Equatorial Guinea	17	Togo	31	Mali
4	Malawi	18	Burkina Faso	32	Comoros
5	Angola	19	Mauritius	33	**Nigeria**
6	Tanzania	20	Ethiopia	34	Chad
7	Seychelles	21	Guinea	35	Lesotho
8	Guinea-Bissau	22	Uganda	36	Congo, Rep.
9	Niger	23	South Africa	37	Cameroon
10	Zambia	24	Kenya	38	Côte d' Ivoire
11	Swaziland	25	Cape Verde	39	Burundi
12	Ghana	26	Senegal	40	Eritrea
13	Sierra Leone	27	Madagascar	41	Gabon
14	Benin	28	Botswana		
TOP		MIDDLE		BOTTOM	

However, many other countries came off better, even if only by small margins.

Primary Data: WB, IMF

Central Africa
East Africa
Southern Africa
West Africa

Leaders & Stragglers

**wait!
we can
explain!!**

Investor Confidence Rankings: 2003-06

Rank	Country
1	Equatorial Guinea
2	Namibia
3	Cape Verde
4	Seychelles
5	South Africa
6	Zambia
7	Botswana
8	Mauritius
9	Ghana
10	Congo, Rep.
	Gabon
11	Gambia, The
12	Mali
	Senegal

TOP

Rank	Country
13	Angola
	Lesotho
14	Chad
15	Mozambique
16	Benin
	Tanzania
17	Ethiopia
	Nigeria
18	Burundi
19	Burkina Faso
20	Kenya
21	Uganda
22	Madagascar
23	Sierra Leone
24	Malawi

MIDDLE

Rank	Country
25	Guinea-Bissau
	Swaziland
26	Cameroon
27	Niger
28	Togo
29	Côte d' Ivoire
30	Guinea
31	Rwanda
32	Eritrea
33	Congo, Dem. Rep.
34	Central Afr. Rep.
35	Comoros

BOTTOM

- Central Africa
- East Africa
- Southern Africa
- West Africa

Ranked a joint 17th out of 35 positions (among 41 countries, though); investor confidence wasn't looking that hot in Nigeria.

Wrap-up: Investor Confidence

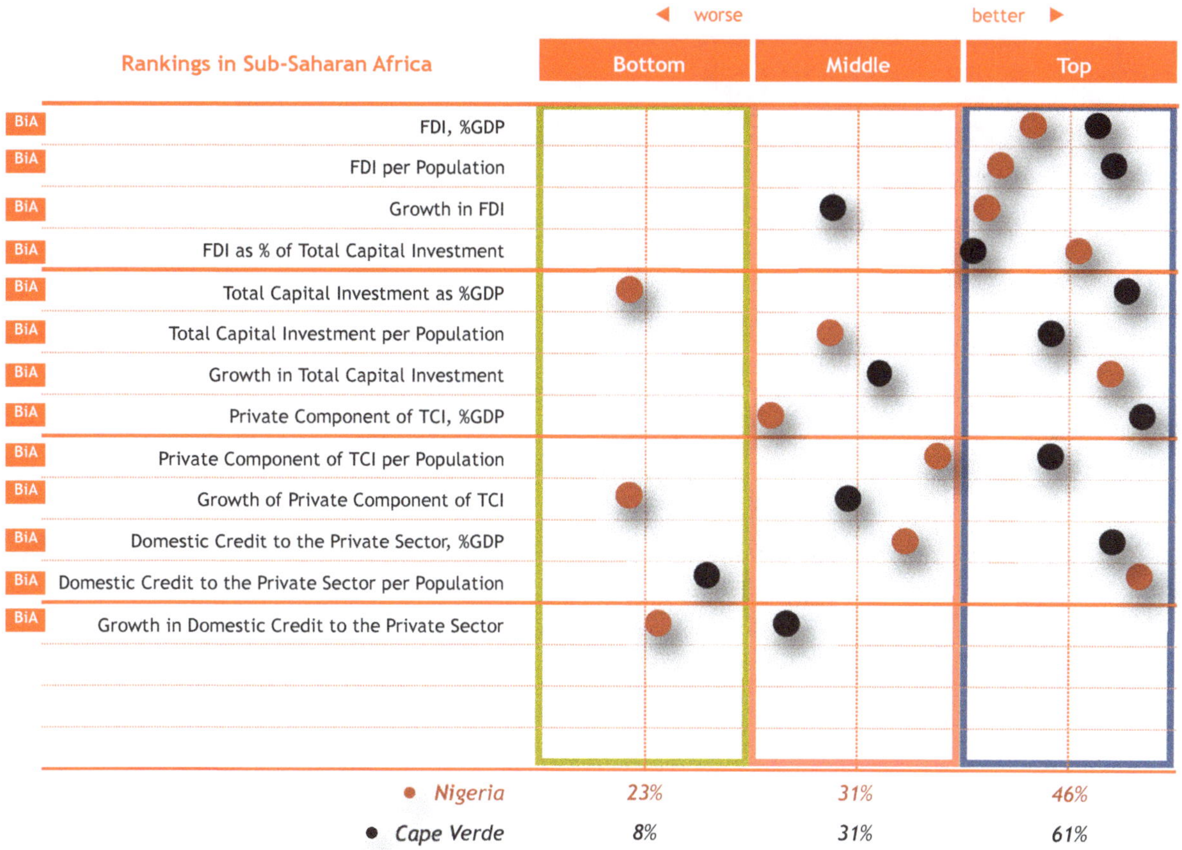

- Within West Africa, investors showed the most confidence in Cape Verde. The country was 3rd most favored on the continent. Nigeria was 7th out of the 14 countries of West Africa, and joint 17th on the continent.

- All the indicators here are critical. Cape Verde scored more top-bracket points than Nigeria (61% of the indicators, compared to Nigeria's 46%) and less bottom-bracket outcomes (8% against 23%).

- Within its own performance, Nigeria scored highest in the foreign investment areas; all the different FDI indicators ended up in the top-third. But when total investment is considered, the performance drops to average or middle-brackets.

- And so, it appears that the private (domestic) investment portion of Nigeria investment is not a robust performance and has the effect of dragging the overall (total) investment performance down.

- This may suggest that foreigners appear to have more confidence in the Nigerian economy than Nigerians themselves. FDI was more robust than private domestic investment. FDI was also growing considerably faster.

- A consolation, though, might be that it was easier to corner loans from Nigerian financial institutions than in many countries of Africa.

15. Regulatory Environment

do you sense bureaucracy?

Primer

This chapter attempts to quantify the ease or difficulty entailed in various critical business procedures for entrants into the particular country's economic structure. It involves data collated by the World Bank and the International Finance Corporation (IFC).

The different indicators are appropriately named and their meaning can be followed without difficulty. In this chapter, they comprise ten divisions, which are each broken into segments as shown below.

In the chapter sections which follow, the countries are ranked according to their relative performance. The World Bank/IFC explain that the data refer to the period between April 2007 and June 2008.

Ease of starting a business

Based on four segments:

- procedures – completed when the final document is submitted
- time – preregistration, registration and post-registration
- cost – as % of income per capita
- paid-in minimum capital – funds deposited in a bank or with a notary before registration

Ease of dealing with construction permits

Based on three segments:

- procedures – completed when final document is received (construction permits, inspections and utility connections included)
- time – number of days to build a warehouse in a main city
- cost – as % of income per capita

Ease of employing workers

Four segments:

- ease of hiring – fixed-term contracts, minimum wage regulations
- flexibility of hours – nonstandard work schedules, paid vacation days
- Ease of firing – mandatory legal requirements for dismissals for economic reasons
- firing cost – as weeks of salary; includes notice period and severance payments

Ease of registering property

Three segments:

- procedures – steps for encumbrance checking, deed and title transfer until property can be sold again or used as collateral
- time – days to transfer property between two companies in main city
- cost – as % of property value

Ease of getting credit

Two segments:

- strength-of-legal rights index – regulations on non-possessory security interests in movable property
- depth-of-credit information index – scope, quality and accessibility of credit information through public and private credit registries

Extent of investor protection

Three segments:

- extent-of-disclosure index – requirements on approval and disclosure of related-party transactions

- extent-of-director liability index – liability of CEO and board of directors in related-party transactions
- ease-of-shareholders suits index – type of evidence that can be collected before and during the trial

Ease of paying taxes

Three segments:

- payments – number of tax payments per year
- time – number of hours per year to prepare, file returns and pay taxes
- total tax rate – firm tax liability as % of profits before all taxes borne

Ease of external trade

Three segments:

- documents to export and import – all documents required by customs and other agencies
- time to export and import – document preparation, customs clearance and technical control, ports and terminal handling, inland transport and handling

Ease of enforcing contracts

Three segments:

- procedures – steps to file claim, obtain and enforce judgment
- time – days to resolve commercial sale dispute before courts
- cost – lawyer, court and enforcement costs as % of claim value

Ease of closing a business

One segment only:

- recovery rate (cents on the $US) – function of time, cost and other factors such as lending rate and the likelihood of the company continuing to operate

Ease of doing business

the eventual score and rank of the country across these indicators

Sources of Primary Data: AfDB, IMF, UNCTAD, World Bank

Charts

15.1 Ease of Starting a Business in West Africa: no. of days. 2009
15.2 Ease of Starting a Business in WA: no. of procedures. 2009

15.3 Ease of Dealing with Construction Permits in WA: no. of days. 2009
15.4 Ease of Dealing with Construction Permits in WA: no. of procedures. 2009

15.5 Ease of Employing Workers in WA: ease of hiring. 2009
15.6 Ease of Employing Workers in WA: flexibility of hours. 2009
15.7 Ease of Employing Workers in WA: ease of firing. 2009
15.8 Ease of Employing Workers in WA: cost of firing (no. of weeks' wages). 2009

15.9 Ease of Registering Property in WA: no. of procedures. 2009
15.10 Ease of Registering Property in WA: no. of days. 2009
15.11 Ease of Registering Property in WA: cost (% of property value). 2009

15.12 Extent of Investor Protection in WA: disclosure index. 2009
15.13 Extent of Investor Protection in WA: director liability index. 2009
15.14 Extent of Investor Protection in WA: shareholder suits index. 2009

15.15 Ease of Paying Taxes in WA: no. of payments. 2009
15.16 Ease of Paying Taxes in WA: time required (hours). 2009
15.17 Ease of Paying Taxes in WA: tax on profit (%). 2009
15.18 Ease of Paying Taxes in WA: labour tax & contributions (%). 2009
15.19 Ease of Paying Taxes in WA: other taxes. 2009
15.20 Ease of Paying Taxes in WA: total tax rate (%). 2009

15.21 Ease of External Trade in WA: cost to export 1 container (US$). 2009
15.22 Ease of External Trade in WA: cost to import 1 container (US$). 2009
15.23 Ease of External Trade in WA: no. of documents needed to export. 2009
15.24 Ease of External Trade in WA: no. of documents needed to import. 2009
15.25 Ease of External Trade in WA: time for export (days). 2009
15.26 Ease of External Trade in WA: time for import (days). 2009

15.27 Ease of Enforcing Contracts in WA: no. of procedures. 2009
15.28 Ease of Enforcing Contracts in WA: time in days. 2009
15.29 Ease of Enforcing Contracts in WA: cost (as % of debt in dispute). 2009

15.30 Ease of Closing a Business in WA: recovery rate (cents on the dollar). 2009

- **Wrap-up**

Tables

2008; 2009:
- *self-comparison to preceding period;*
- *performance in S-Saharan Africa;*
- *performance in West Africa;*
- *performance among oil-exporters;*

for:

Ease of Starting a Business

Ease of Dealing with Construction Permits

Ease of Employing Workers

Ease of Registering Property

Ease of Getting Credit

Extent of Investor Protection

Ease of Paying Taxes

Ease of External Trade

Ease of Enforcing Contracts

Ease of Closing a Business

- **Regulatory Environment Rankings: 2009**

15.1 Ease of Starting a Business: Rank

	2008	2009
Self-comparison to Preceding Period		▼
Performance in Sub-Saharan Africa	▲	▲
Performance in West Africa	▲	▲
	Nigeria	Sierra Leone
	Sierra Leone	Liberia
	Gambia, The	Nigeria
	Burkina Faso	Senegal
	Benin	Gambia, The
	Ghana	Burkina Faso
	Liberia	Ghana
	Mali	Mauritania
	Niger	Benin
	Côte d'Ivoire	Niger
	Cape Verde	Mali
	Senegal	Cape Verde
	Mauritania	Côte d'Ivoire
	Guinea	Guinea
	Togo	Togo
	Guinea-Bissau	Guinea-Bissau
Performance among Oil-Exporters	▲	▲
	Nigeria	Nigeria
	Sudan	Sudan
	Gabon	Gabon
	Congo, Rep.	Angola
	Côte d'Ivoire	Congo, Rep.
	Cameroon	Côte d'Ivoire
	Equatorial Guinea	Cameroon
	Angola	Equatorial Guinea
	Chad	Chad

Nigeria dropped from the easiest place to start a business in West Africa in 2008, to 3rd easiest in 2009, behind Sierra Leone and Liberia.

3	Sierra Leone
9	Liberia
10	Nigeria
11	Senegal
22	Gambia
16	Burkina Faso
22	Ghana
24	Mauritania
27	Benin
33	Niger
35	Mali
36	Cape Verde
38	Côte d'Ivoire
42	Guinea
44	Togo
46	Guinea-Bissau

2009 rankings of 47 Sub-Saharan Africa Countries

Source: World Bank, IFC

Those 2 countries perhaps displayed greater urgency in attracting business to their shores after difficult and protracted war years.

it's a breeze...

▲ improved *or* better than avera
▼ worsened *or* worse than avera
◁▷ no change *or* average

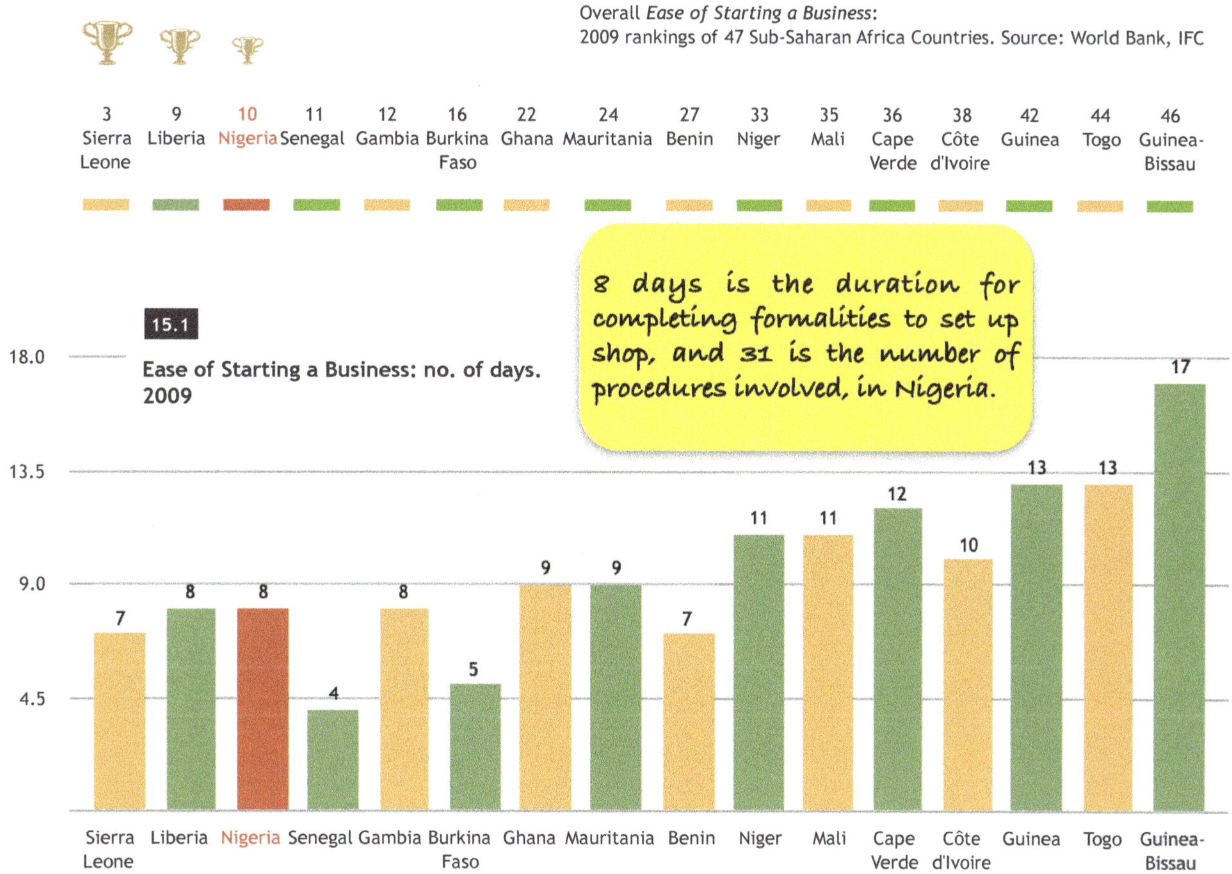

... right?

Fewer days in Senegal (4), Burkina Faso (5) and Benin (7). But Nigeria had fewer procedures than many in West Africa.

Source: World Bank, IFC

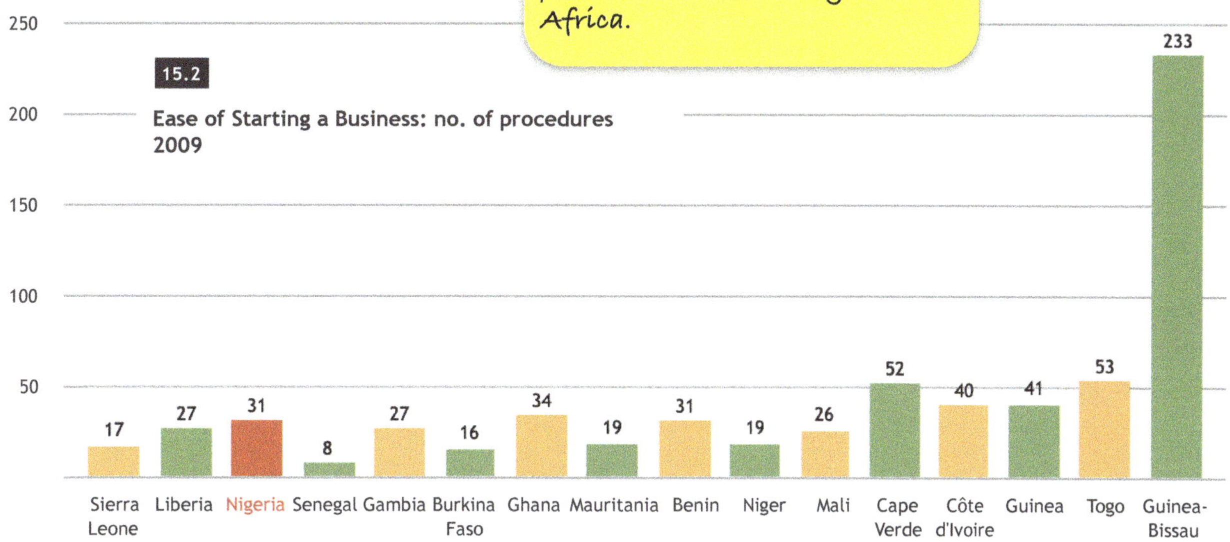

15.2 Ease of Dealing with Construction Permits: Rank

	2008	2009
Self-comparison to Preceding Period		▲
Performance in Sub-Saharan Africa	▼	▼

Performance in West Africa	2008	2009
	▼	▼
	Senegal	Gambia, The
	Gambia, The	Cape Verde
	Cape Verde	Burkina Faso
	Mali	Mali
	Guinea-Bissau	Guinea-Bissau
	Benin	Senegal
	Ghana	Benin
	Mauritania	Ghana
	Togo	Mauritania
	Sierra Leone	Togo
	Niger	**Nigeria**
	Côte d'Ivoire	Niger
	Guinea	Côte d'Ivoire
	Nigeria	Guinea
	Burkina Faso	Sierra Leone
	Liberia	Liberia

Performance among Oil-Exporters	2008	2009
	▼	▼
	Gabon	Gabon
	Congo, Rep.	Congo, Rep.
	Chad	Chad
	Equatorial Guinea	Equatorial Guinea
	Sudan	Angola
	Angola	Sudan
	Cameroon	**Nigeria**
	Côte d'Ivoire	Cameroon
	Nigeria	Côte d'Ivoire

▲	improved *or* better than average
▼	worsened *or* worse than average
◁▷	no change *or* average

nice word, that

Improvement in Nigeria from 2008 to 2009. But still below par in the continent and in West Africa, as well. Below par within the oil club also.

2009 rankings of 47 Sub-Saharan Africa Countries

Source: World Bank, IFC

12 Gambia	13 Cape Verde
19 Burkina Faso	19 Mali

20	Guinea-Bissau	33	Nigeria
22	Senegal	37	Niger
25	Benin	38	Côte d'Ivoire
29	Ghana	39	Guinea
29	Mauritania	40	Sierra Leone
30	Togo	44	Liberia

Overall *Ease of Dealing with Construction Permits*:
2009 rankings of 47 Sub-Saharan Africa Countries. Source: World Bank, IFC

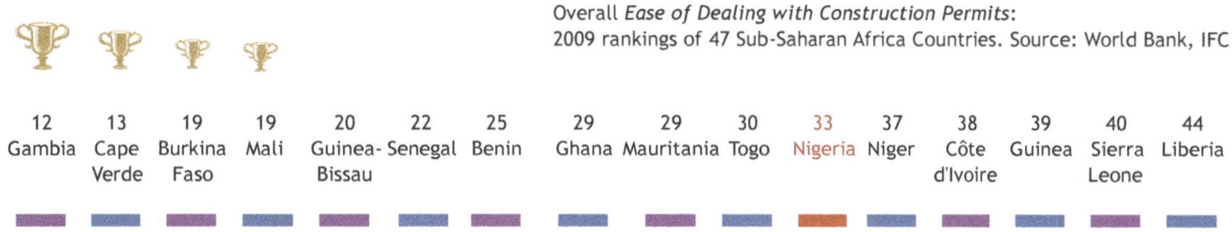

15.3

Ease of Dealing with Construction Permits: no. of days. 2009

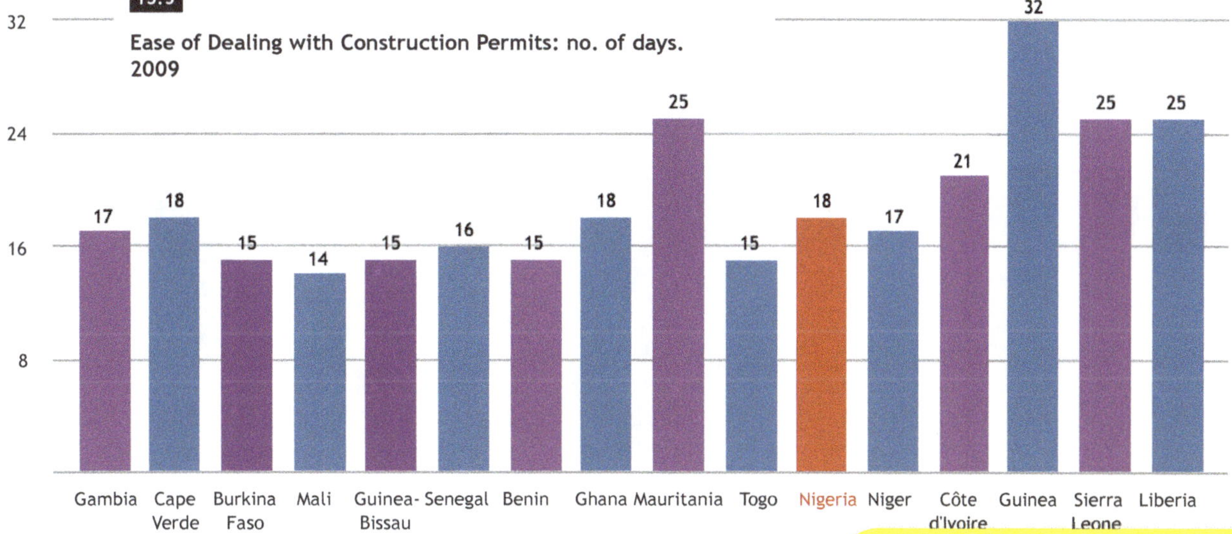

The reason for that is clearly seen here. Too many days of paperwork and too many procedures in Nigeria.

15.4

Ease of Dealing with Construction Permits: no. of procedures. 2009

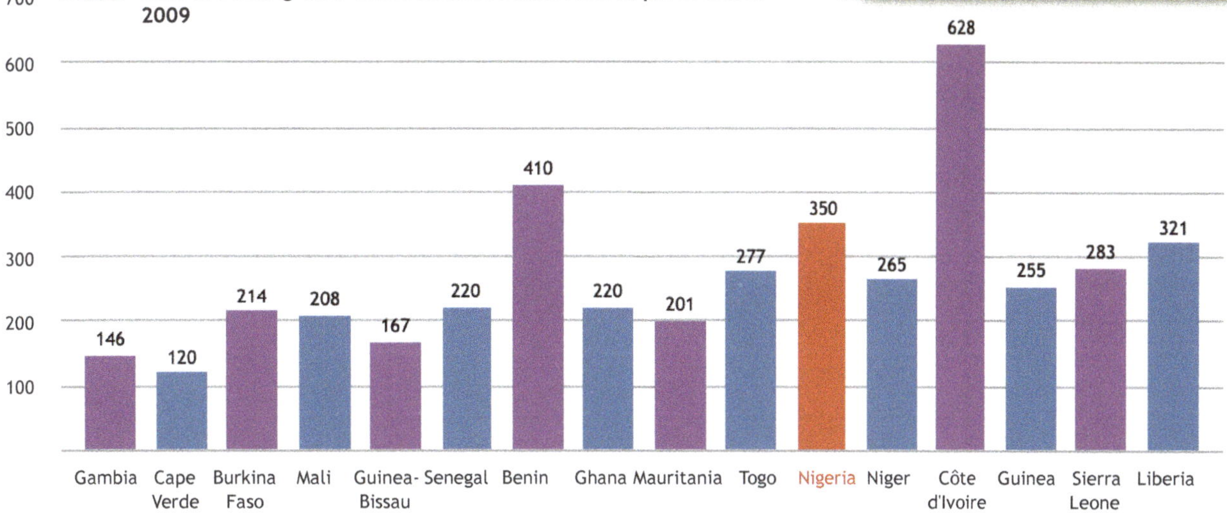

15.3 Ease of Employing Workers: Rank

2008	2009	
	▲	Self-comparison to Preceding Period
▲	▲	Performance in Sub-Saharan Africa

Performance in West Africa

2008	2009
▲	▲
Gambia, The	Nigeria
Nigeria	Gambia, The
Mali	Burkina Faso
Guinea	Mali
Liberia	Liberia
Côte d'Ivoire	Côte d'Ivoire
Benin	Guinea
Mauritania	Benin
Ghana	Mauritania
Cape Verde	Ghana
Togo	Togo
Burkina Faso	Senegal
Senegal	Niger
Niger	Cape Verde
Sierra Leone	Sierra Leone
Guinea-Bissau	Guinea-Bissau

Performance among Oil-Exporters

2008	2009
▲	▲
Nigeria	Nigeria
Côte d'Ivoire	Côte d'Ivoire
Cameroon	Cameroon
Chad	Chad
Sudan	Sudan
Gabon	Gabon
Congo, Rep.	Congo, Rep.
Angola	Angola
Equatorial Guinea	Equatorial Guinea

▲	improved *or* better than average
▼	worsened *or* worse than average
◁▷	no change *or* average

rules of engagement

Engaging staff in West Africa is easiest in Nigeria, the 2nd easiest on the continent.

2 Nigeria

5 Gambia

6 Burkina Faso

14	Mali
18	Liberia
19	Côte d'Ivoire
20	Guinea
21	Benin
23	Mauritania
31	Ghana
35	Togo
38	Senegal
39	Niger
40	Cape Verde
42	Sierra Leone
45	Guinea-Bissau

2009 rankings of 47 Sub-Saharan Africa Countries

Source: World Bank, IFC

Overall *Ease of Employing Workers*:
2009 rankings of 47 Sub-Saharan Africa Countries. Source: World Bank, IFC

2	5	6	14	18	19	20	21	23	31	35	38	39	40	42	45
Nigeria	Gambia	Burkina Faso	Mali	Liberia	Côte d'Ivoire	Guinea	Benin	Mauritania	Ghana	Togo	Senegal	Niger	Cape Verde	Sierra Leone	Guinea-Bissau

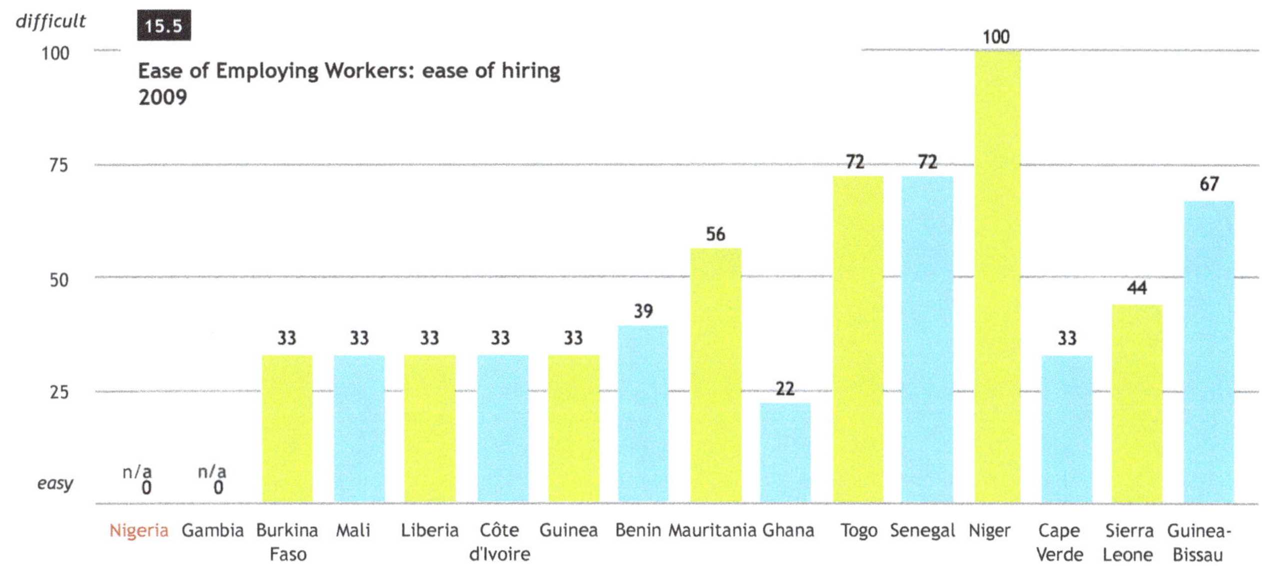

15.5 Ease of Employing Workers: ease of hiring 2009

No data for Nigeria here. But Niger is the most difficult country in which to hire people and Burkina Faso & Liberia have the most flexible working hours.

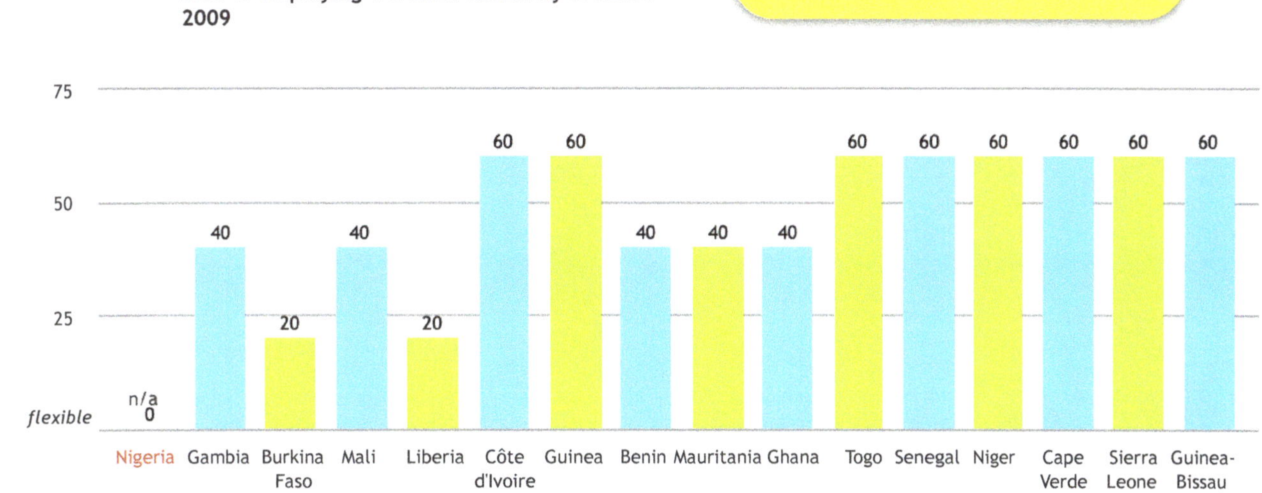

15.6 Ease of Employing Workers: flexibility of hours 2009

Overall *Ease of Employing Workers*:
2009 rankings of 47 Sub-Saharan Africa Countries. Source: World Bank, IFC

The numbers here show why Nigeria has that high rank. It is easier to disengage staff there than anywhere else in West Africa, except Burkina Faso.

15.7

Ease of Employing Workers: ease of firing 2009

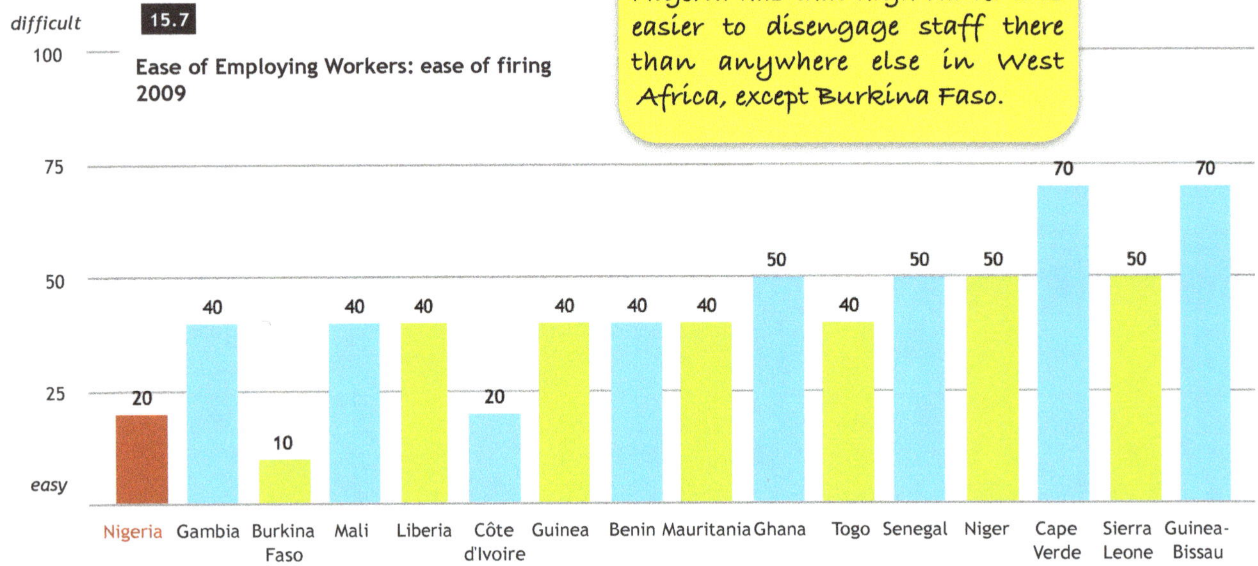

15.8

Ease of Employing Workers: cost of firing (no. of weeks' wages) 2009

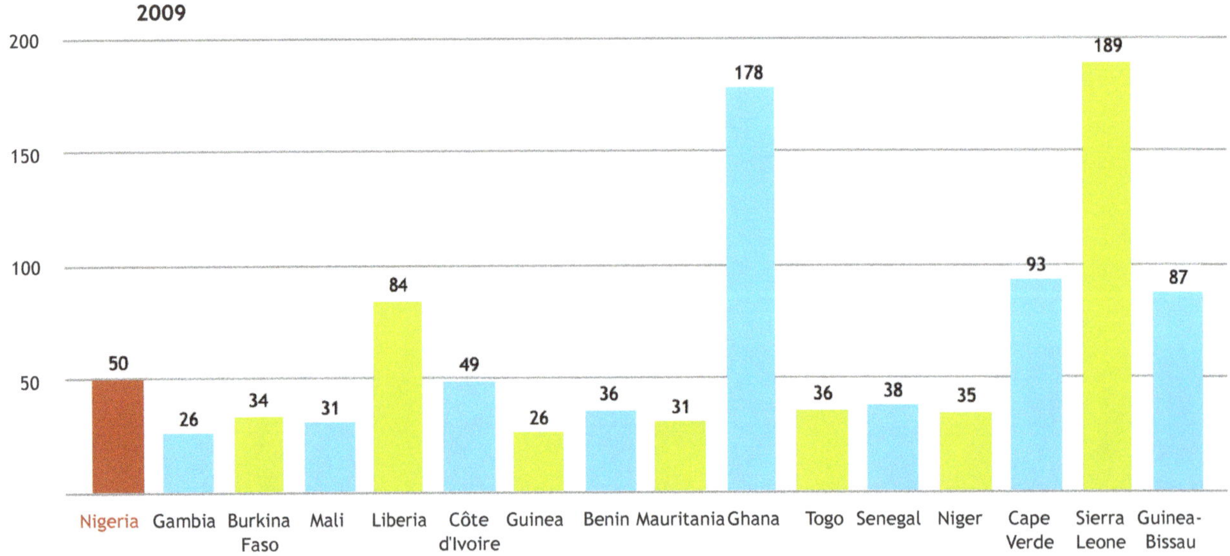

15.4 Ease of Registering Property: Rank

maybe there's a good reason

2008	2009	
	◁▷	Self-comparison to Preceding Period
▼	▼	Performance in Sub-Saharan Africa
▼	▼	Performance in West Africa
Ghana	Ghana	
Mauritania	Mauritania	
Niger	Niger	
Mali	Mali	
Benin	Gambia, The	
Cape Verde	Benin	
Gambia, The	Cape Verde	
Togo	Côte d'Ivoire	
Guinea	Burkina Faso	
Côte d'Ivoire	Togo	
Senegal	Guinea	
Guinea-Bissau	Senegal	
Liberia	Sierra Leone	
Burkina Faso	Guinea-Bissau	
Sierra Leone	Liberia	
Nigeria	Nigeria	

2008	2009	
▼	▼	Performance among Oil-Exporters
Sudan	Sudan	
Equatorial Guinea	Equatorial Guinea	
Chad	Chad	
Cameroon	Cameroon	
Gabon	Côte d'Ivoire	
Côte d'Ivoire	Gabon	
Angola	Congo, Rep.	
Congo, Rep.	Angola	
Nigeria	Nigeria	

A hassle to register property in Nigeria. Easier everywhere else in Sub-Saharan Africa.

2 Ghana

6 Mauritania

8 Niger

13	Mali	36	Guinea
15	Gambia	38	Senegal
16	Benin	39	Sierra Leone
17	Cape Verde	42	Guinea-Bissau
26	Côte d'Ivoire	44	Liberia
29	Burkina Faso	46	Nigeria
35	Togo		

2009 rankings of 47 Sub-Saharan Africa Countries

Source: World Bank, IFC

▲	improved *or* better than average
▼	worsened *or* worse than average
◁▷	no change *or* average

Overall *Ease of Registering Property*:
2009 rankings of 47 Sub-Saharan Africa Countries. Source: World Bank, IFC

2	Ghana
6	Mauritania
8	Niger
13	Mali
15	Gambia
16	Benin
17	Cape Verde
26	Côte d'Ivoire
29	Burkina Faso
35	Togo
36	Guinea
38	Senegal
39	Sierra Leone
42	Guinea-Bissau
44	Liberia
46	Nigeria

15.9

Ease of Registering Property: no. of procedures 2009

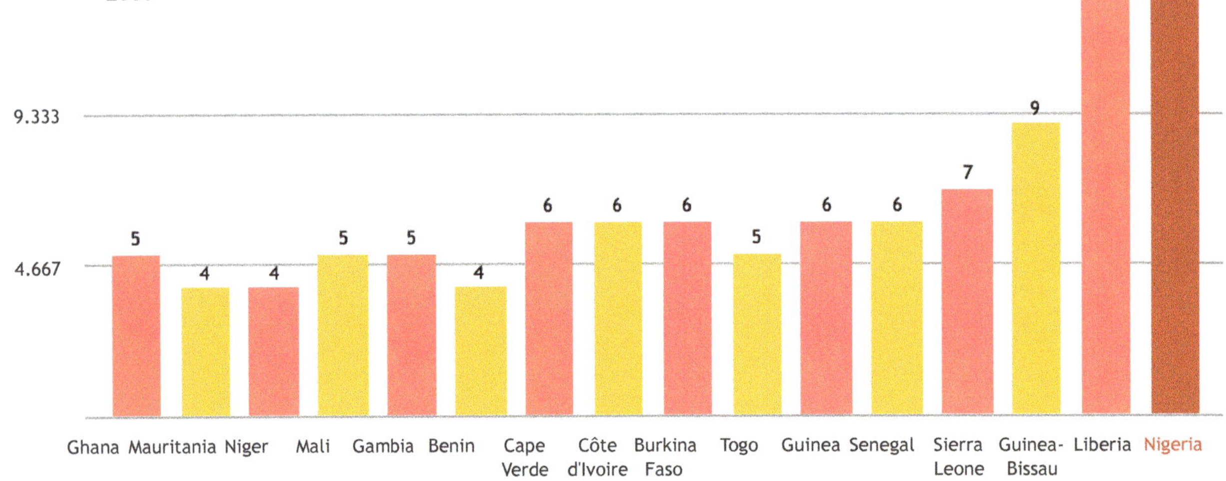

15.10

Ease of Registering Property: no. of days 2009

There are more procedures in Nigeria than anywhere else, although these take up less time than they do in several other countries.

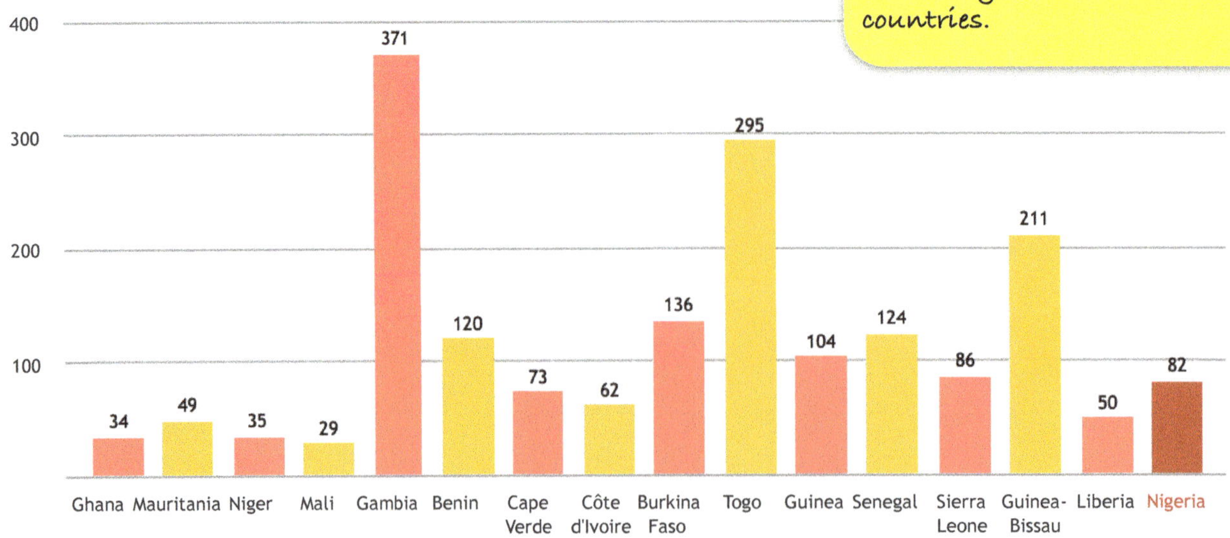

Overall *Ease of Registering Property*:
2009 rankings of 47 Sub-Saharan Africa Countries. Source: World Bank, IFC

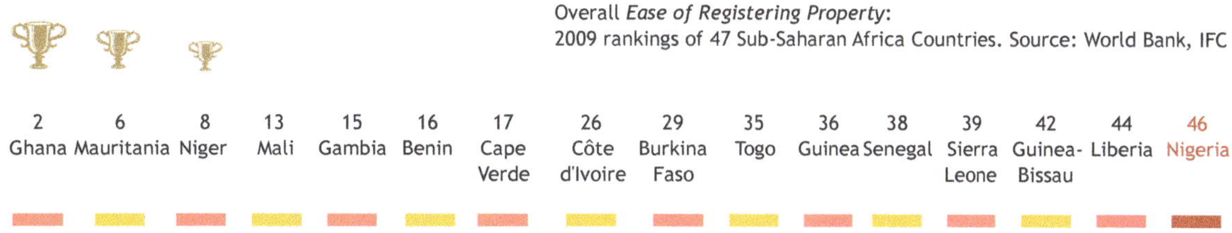

15.11

Ease of Registering Property: cost (% of property value) 2009

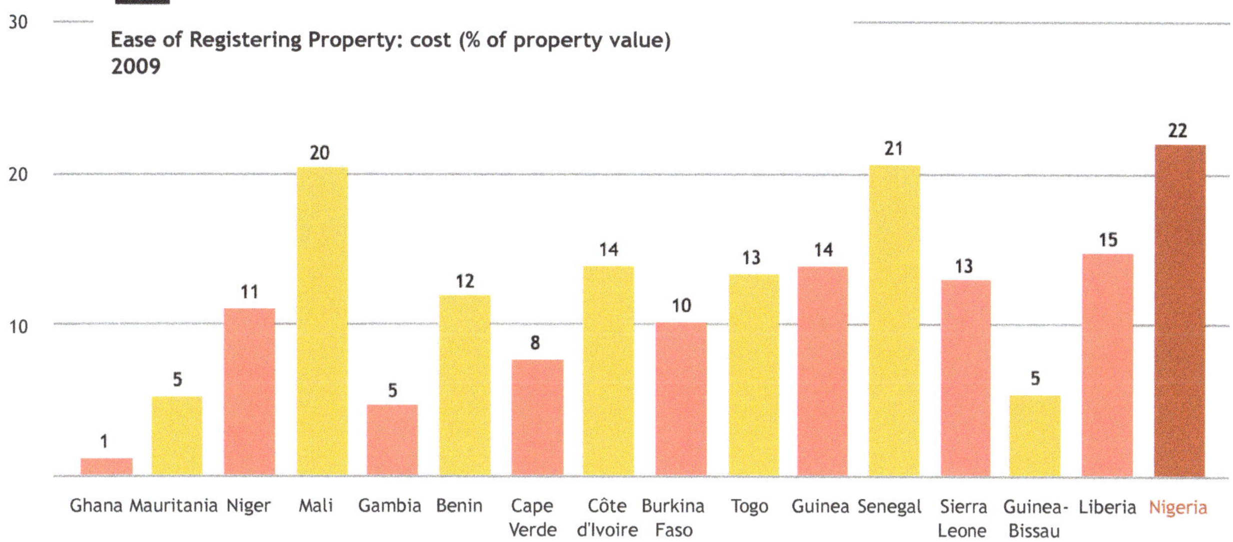

Costs involved in registration are the highest in West Africa and 3rd highest on the continent, after Zimbabwe (25%) and Chad (23%).

15.5 Ease of Getting Credit: Rank

2008	2009	
	▼	Self-comparison to Preceding Period
▲	▲	Performance in Sub-Saharan Africa
▲	▲	Performance in West Africa
Cape Verde	Nigeria	
Nigeria	Ghana	
Ghana	Cape Verde	
Benin	Gambia, The	
Burkina Faso	Liberia	
Mauritania	Benin	
Sierra Leone	Burkina Faso	
Gambia, The	Côte d'Ivoire	
Liberia	Guinea-Bissau	
Côte d'Ivoire	Mali	
Guinea-Bissau	Mauritania	
Mali	Niger	
Niger	Senegal	
Senegal	Sierra Leone	
Togo	Togo	
Guinea	Guinea	

2008	2009	
▲	▲	Performance among Oil-Exporters
Angola	Angola	
Nigeria	Nigeria	
Cameroon	Cameroon	
Congo, Rep.	Congo, Rep.	
Gabon	Equatorial Guinea	
Chad	Gabon	
Côte d'Ivoire	Sudan	
Equatorial Guinea	Chad	
Sudan	Côte d'Ivoire	

▲	improved *or* better than average
▼	worsened *or* worse than average
◁▷	no change *or* average

they'll be wanting your shoe size next

Banks and other financial institutions are more welcoming of your business in Nigeria: the best in West Africa; 6th best on the continent.

6 Nigeria	7 Ghana	8 Cape Verde
9 Gambia	10 Benin	11 Guinea
9 Liberia	10 Burkina Faso	
	10 Côte d'Ivoire	
	10 Guinea-Bissau	
	10 Mali	
	10 Mauritania	
	10 Niger	
	10 Senegal	
	10 Sierra Leone	
	10 Togo	

2009 rankings of 47 Sub-Saharan Africa Countries

Source: World Bank, IFC

15.6 Extent of Investor Protection: Rank

he's on your side. or isn't he?

Its arbitration institutions are 2nd best in West Africa (after Ghana) and 2nd best among the oil exporters, too. They were 4th best in Sub-Saharan Africa.

	2008	2009
Self-comparison to Preceding Period		◁▷
Performance in Sub-Saharan Africa	▲	▲
Performance in West Africa	▲	▲
	Ghana	Ghana
	Nigeria	Nigeria
	Sierra Leone	Sierra Leone
	Cape Verde	Cape Verde
	Guinea-Bissau	Guinea-Bissau
	Burkina Faso	Burkina Faso
	Liberia	Liberia
	Togo	Mauritania
	Mauritania	Togo
	Benin	Benin
	Côte d'Ivoire	Côte d'Ivoire
	Mali	Mali
	Niger	Niger
	Senegal	Senegal
	Gambia, The	Gambia, The
	Guinea	Guinea
Performance among Oil-Exporters	▲	▲
	Angola	Angola
	Nigeria	Nigeria
	Cameroon	Cameroon
	Chad	Chad
	Equatorial Guinea	Equatorial Guinea
	Sudan	Congo, Rep.
	Congo, Rep.	Côte d'Ivoire
	Côte d'Ivoire	Gabon
	Gabon	Sudan

3 Ghana

4 Nigeria
4 Sierra Leone

9 Cape Verde
9 Guinea-Bissau

10 Burkina Faso
10 Liberia
10 Mauritania
10 Togo

11 Benin
11 Côte d'Ivoire
11 Mali
11 Niger

12 Senegal
13 Gambia
13 Guinea

2009 rankings of 47 Sub-Saharan Africa Countries

Source: World Bank, IFC

▲	improved *or* better than average
▼	worsened *or* worse than average
◁▷	no change *or* average

Overall *Extent of Investor Protection*:
2009 rankings of 47 Sub-Saharan Africa Countries. Source: World Bank, IFC

3	4	4	9	9	10	10	10	10	11	11	11	11	12	13	13
Ghana	Nigeria	Sierra Leone	Cape Verde	Guinea-Bissau	Burkina Faso	Liberia	Mauritania	Togo	Benin	Côte d'Ivoire	Mali	Niger	Senegal	Gambia	Guinea

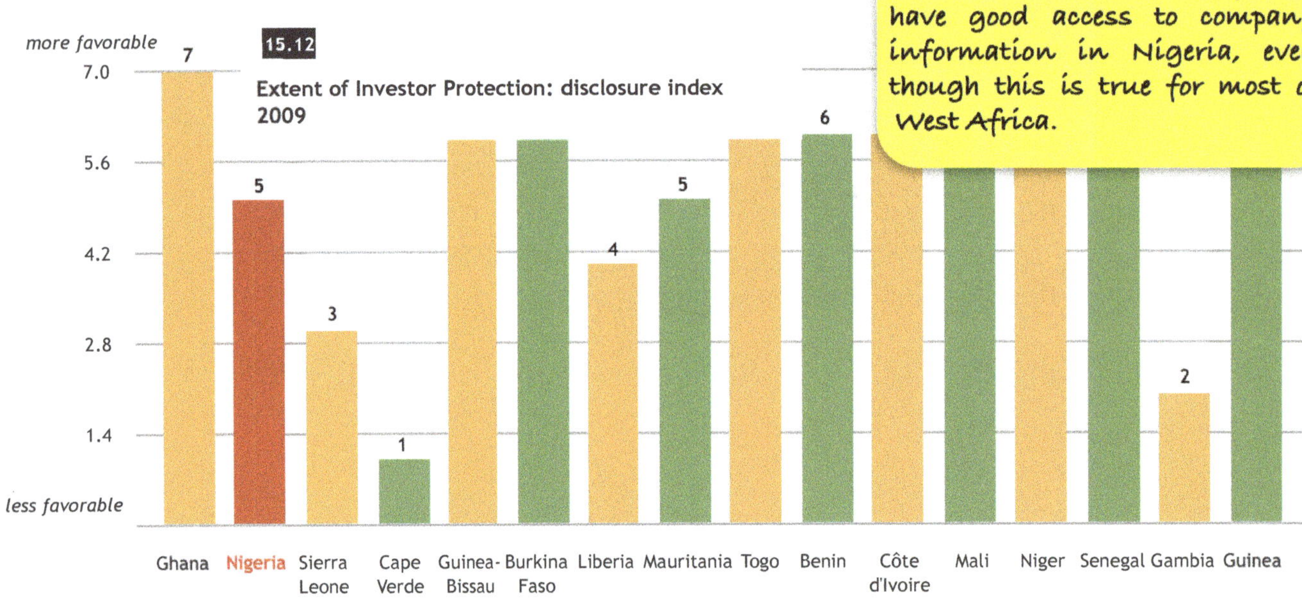

15.12 Extent of Investor Protection: disclosure index 2009

Shareholders and the public have good access to company information in Nigeria, even though this is true for most of West Africa.

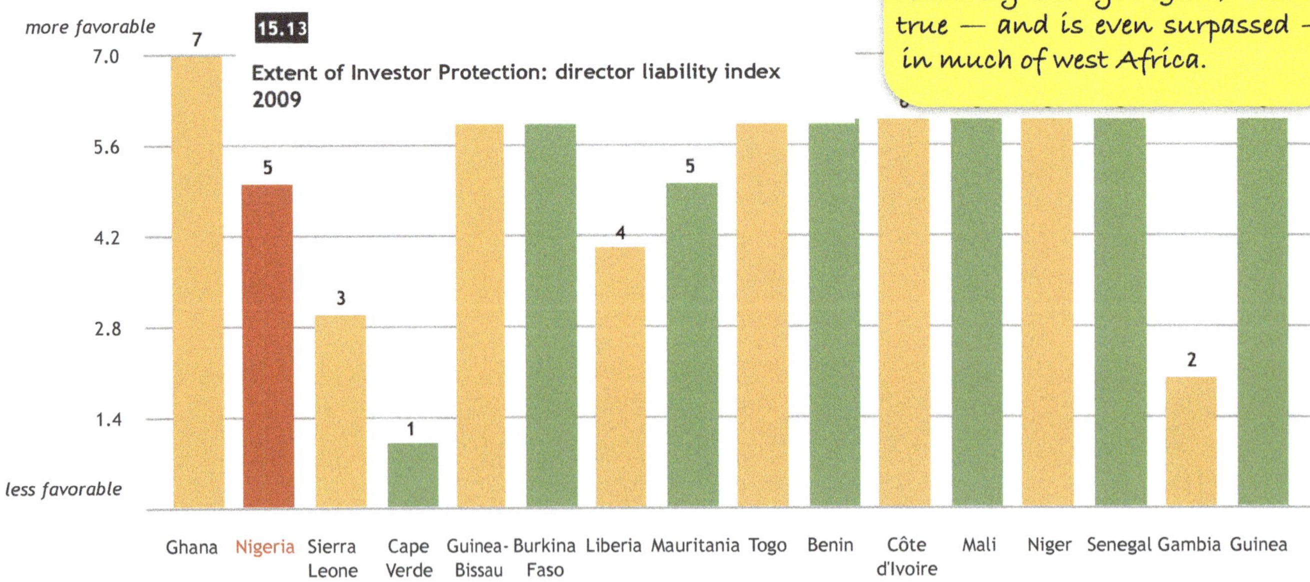

15.13 Extent of Investor Protection: director liability index 2009

Shareholders may also hold company directors accountable relatively easily. Again, this is true — and is even surpassed — in much of west Africa.

Overall *Extent of Investor Protection*:
2009 rankings of 47 Sub-Saharan Africa Countries. Source: World Bank, IFC

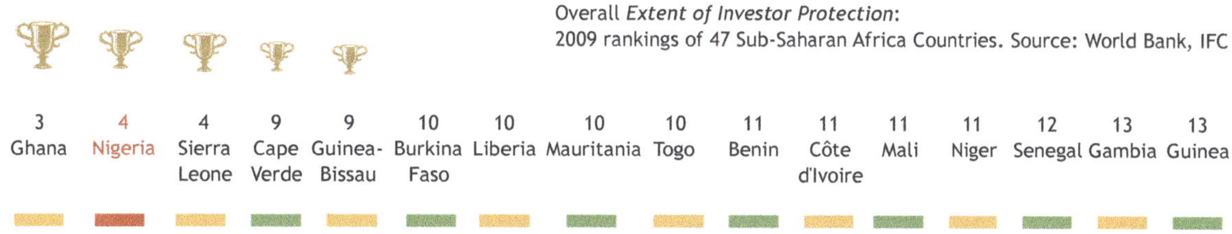

15.14

Extent of Investor Protection: shareholder suits index 2009

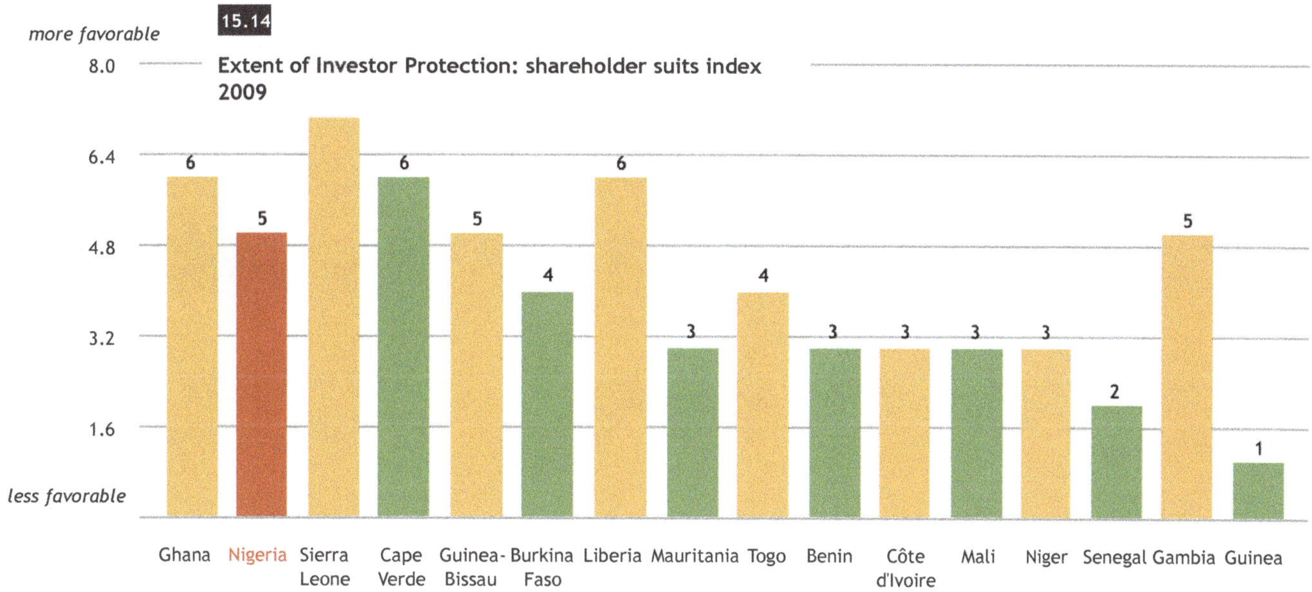

Should the parties opt for court resolution of disputes, evidence is gathered more easily in Nigeria than it is in 9 West African countries.

More easily than obtains in 16 countries of Sub-Saharan Africa.

15.7 Ease of Paying Taxes: Rank

two quick steps and it's done

2008	2009	
	▼	Self-comparison to Preceding Period
▲	▼	Performance in Sub-Saharan Africa

Performance in West Africa

2008 ▲	2009 ▲
Ghana	Liberia
Nigeria	Ghana
Guinea-Bissau	Cape Verde
Niger	Guinea-Bissau
Cape Verde	Niger
Liberia	**Nigeria**
Burkina Faso	Burkina Faso
Togo	Togo
Côte d'Ivoire	Côte d'Ivoire
Sierra Leone	Mali
Mali	Sierra Leone
Benin	Benin
Guinea	Guinea
Senegal	Senegal
Mauritania	Mauritania
Gambia, The	Gambia, The

Performance among Oil-Exporters

2008 ▲	2009 ▲
Sudan	Sudan
Gabon	Gabon
Nigeria	**Nigeria**
Angola	Angola
Chad	Chad
Equatorial Guinea	Côte d'Ivoire
Côte d'Ivoire	Equatorial Guinea
Cameroon	Cameroon
Congo, Rep.	Congo, Rep.

It is more difficult to comply with tax regulations in Nigeria than most places in Sub-Saharan Africa.

But still easier than is the case in most of the oil exporters.

12 Liberia

14 Ghana

24 Cape Verde

25	Guinea-Bissau
26	Niger
26	Nigeria
28	Burkina Faso
29	Togo
30	Côte d'Ivoire
33	Mali
36	Sierra Leone
38	Benin
39	Guinea
40	Senegal
42	Mauritania
43	Gambia

2009 rankings of 47 Sub-Saharan Africa Countries

Source: World Bank, IFC

▲	improved *or* better than average
▼	worsened *or* worse than average
◁▷	no change *or* average

Overall *Ease of Paying Taxes*:
2009 rankings of 47 Sub-Saharan Africa Countries. Source: World Bank, IFC

12	14	24	25	26	26	28	29	30	33	36	38	39	40	42	43
Liberia	Ghana	Cape Verde	Guinea-Bissau	Niger	Nigeria	Burkina Faso	Togo	Côte d'Ivoire	Mali	Sierra Leone	Benin	Guinea	Senegal	Mauritania	Gambia

15.15

Ease of Paying Taxes: no. of payments 2009

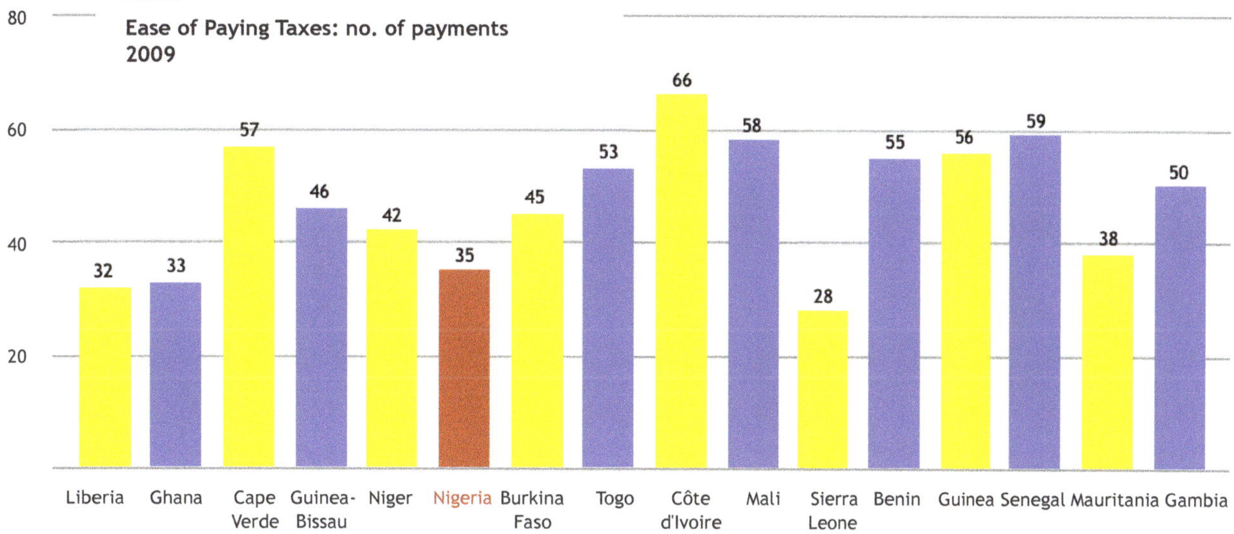

15.16

Ease of Paying Taxes: time required (hours) 2009

A major reason for that unflattering ranking would be the no. of hours that the tax procedures involve.

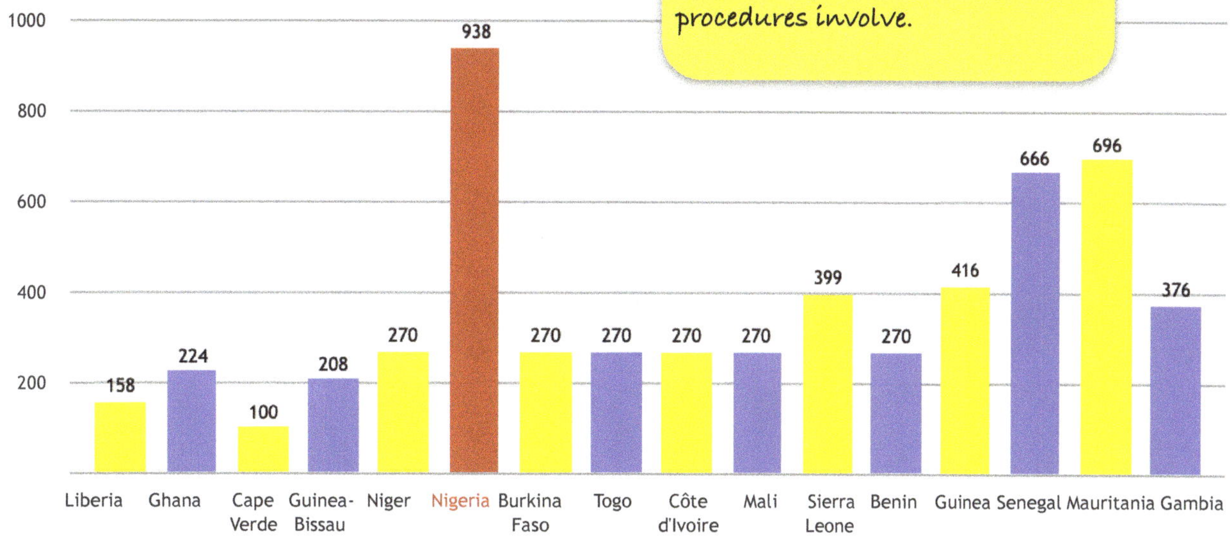

Overall *Ease of Paying Taxes*:
2009 rankings of 47 Sub-Saharan Africa Countries. Source: World Bank, IFC

12	14	24	25	26	26	28	29	30	33	36	38	39	40	42	43
Liberia	Ghana	Cape Verde	Guinea-Bissau	Niger	Nigeria	Burkina Faso	Togo	Côte d'Ivoire	Mali	Sierra Leone	Benin	Guinea	Senegal	Mauritania	Gambia

15.17

Ease of Paying Taxes: tax on profit (%) 2009

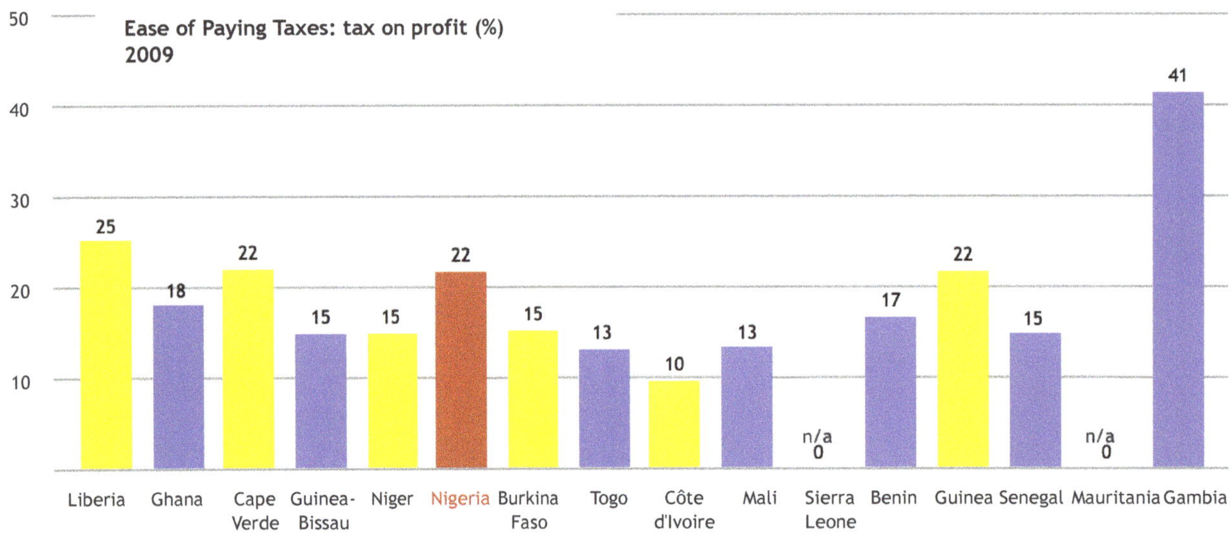

The various applicable tax rates, taken as a whole, compare more or less favorably with the rest of West Africa.

15.18

Ease of Paying Taxes: labour tax & contributions (%) 2009

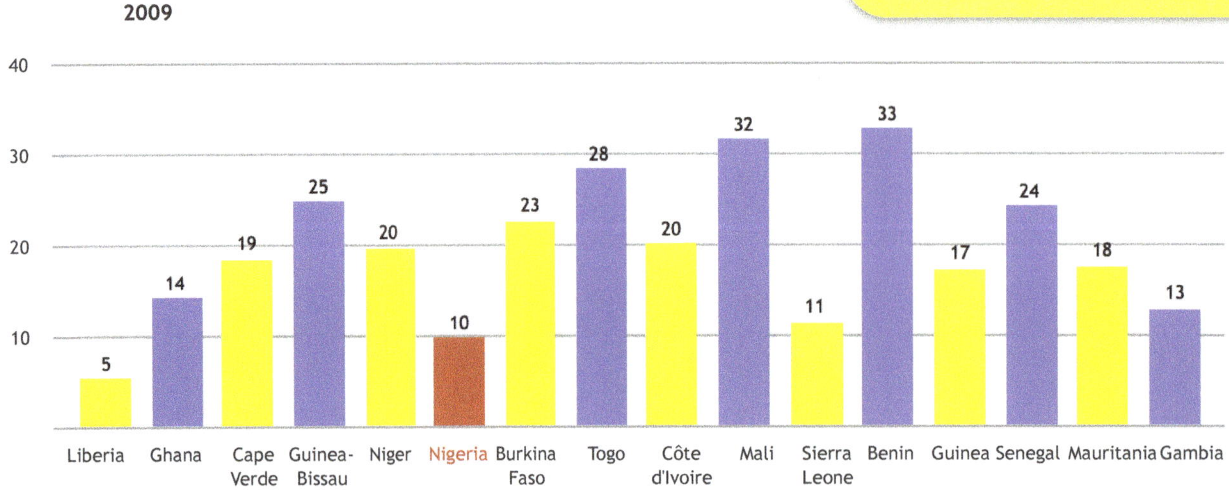

Overall *Ease of Paying Taxes*:
2009 rankings of 47 Sub-Saharan Africa Countries. Source: World Bank, IFC

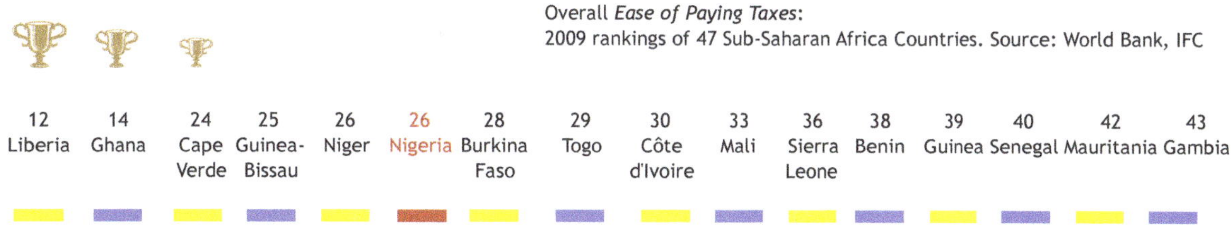

15.19

Ease of Paying Taxes: other taxes 2009

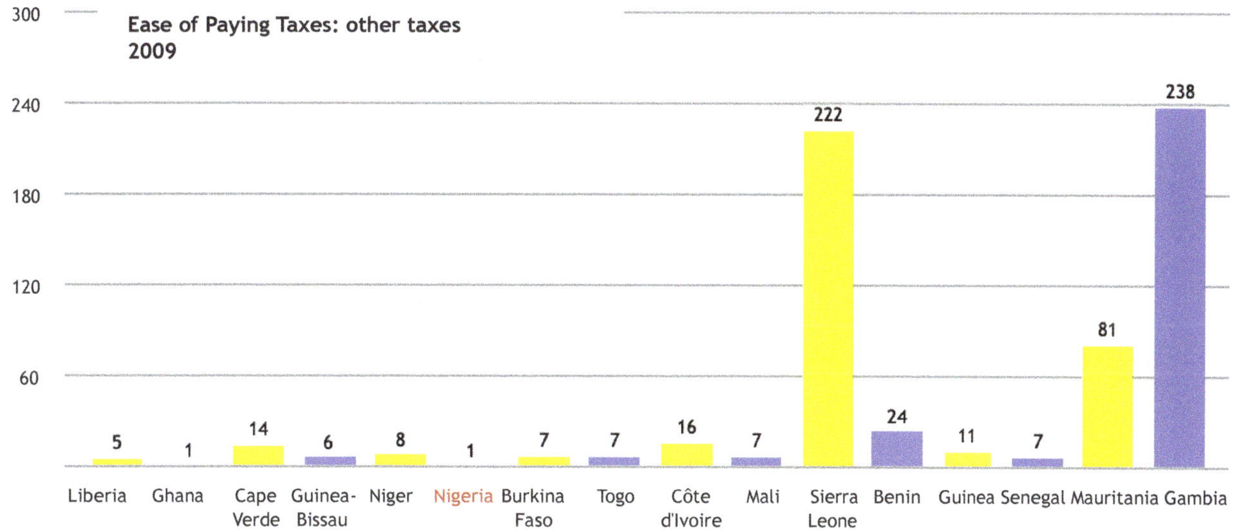

15.20

Ease of Paying Taxes: total tax rate (%) 2009

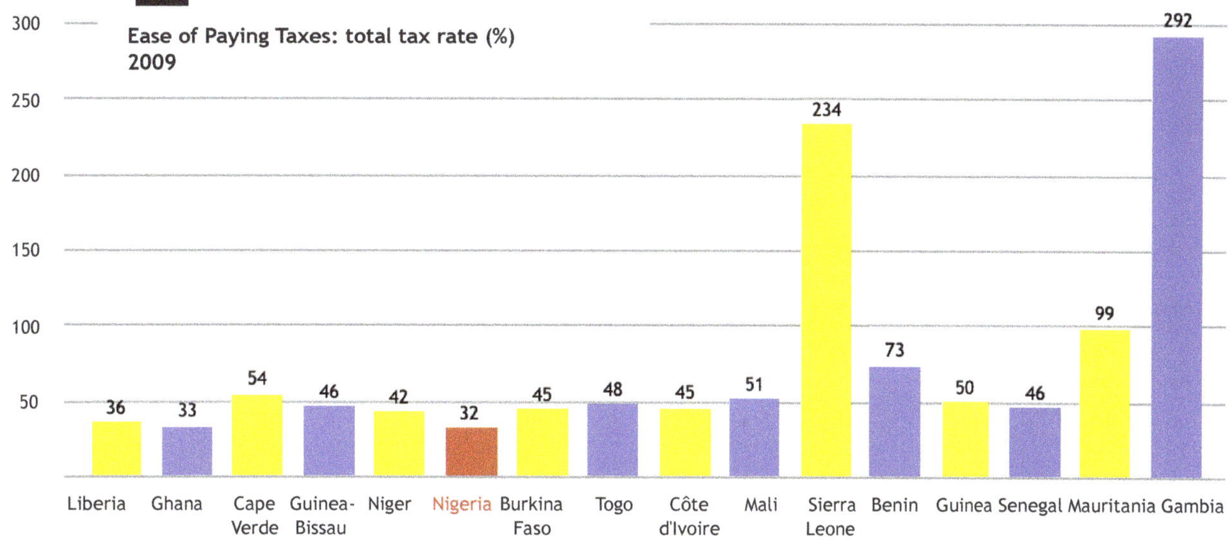

15.8 Ease of External Trade: Rank

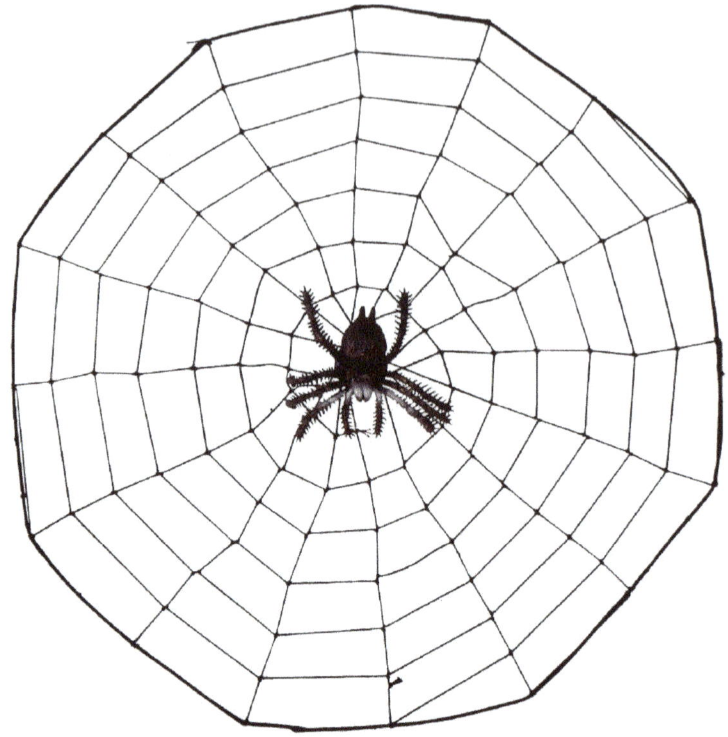

it's actually simpler elsewhere

2008	2009	
	◁▷	Self-comparison to Preceding Period
▲	▲	Performance in Sub-Saharan Africa
▼	▼	Performance in West Africa
Cape Verde	Cape Verde	
Ghana	Senegal	
Gambia, The	Gambia, The	
Togo	Ghana	
Liberia	Togo	
Guinea	Guinea	
Guinea-Bissau	Guinea-Bissau	
Benin	Liberia	
Sierra Leone	Benin	
Senegal	Sierra Leone	
Nigeria	Nigeria	
Côte d'Ivoire	Côte d'Ivoire	
Mauritania	Mauritania	
Mali	Mali	
Niger	Niger	
Burkina Faso	Burkina Faso	
▲	◁▷	Performance among Oil-Exporters
Gabon	Gabon	
Cameroon	Equatorial Guinea	
Equatorial Guinea	Cameroon	
Nigeria	Sudan	
Sudan	Nigeria	
Côte d'Ivoire	Côte d'Ivoire	
Chad	Chad	
Angola	Angola	
Congo, Rep.	Congo, Rep.	

23rd out of 47 gives Nigeria a shaky pass-mark in Africa, but not in West Africa & the oil bloc, where it is outflanked in the ease of exporting and importing.

Cape Verde, Senegal and Gambia are among the top 5 in Africa for ease of external trade. Ghana and Togo are in the top 10.

▲	improved *or* better than average
▼	worsened *or* worse than average
◁▷	no change *or* average

3 Cape Verde

4 Senegal

5 Gambia

6	Ghana
7	Togo
12	Guinea
13	Guinea-Bissau
14	Liberia
16	Benin
17	Sierra Leone
23	Nigeria
32	Côte d'Ivoire
33	Mauritania
38	Mali
41	Niger
44	Burkina Faso

2009 rankings of 47 Sub-Saharan Africa Countries

Source: World Bank, IFC

Overall *Ease of External Trade*:
2009 rankings of 47 Sub-Saharan Africa Countries. Source: World Bank, IFC

3	4	5	6	7	12	13	14	16	17	23	32	33	38	41	44
Cape Verde	Senegal	Gambia	Ghana	Togo	Guinea	Guinea-Bissau	Liberia	Benin	Sierra Leone	Nigeria	Côte d'Ivoire	Mauritania	Mali	Niger	Burkina Faso

15.21

Ease of External Trade: cost to export 1 container (US$)
2009

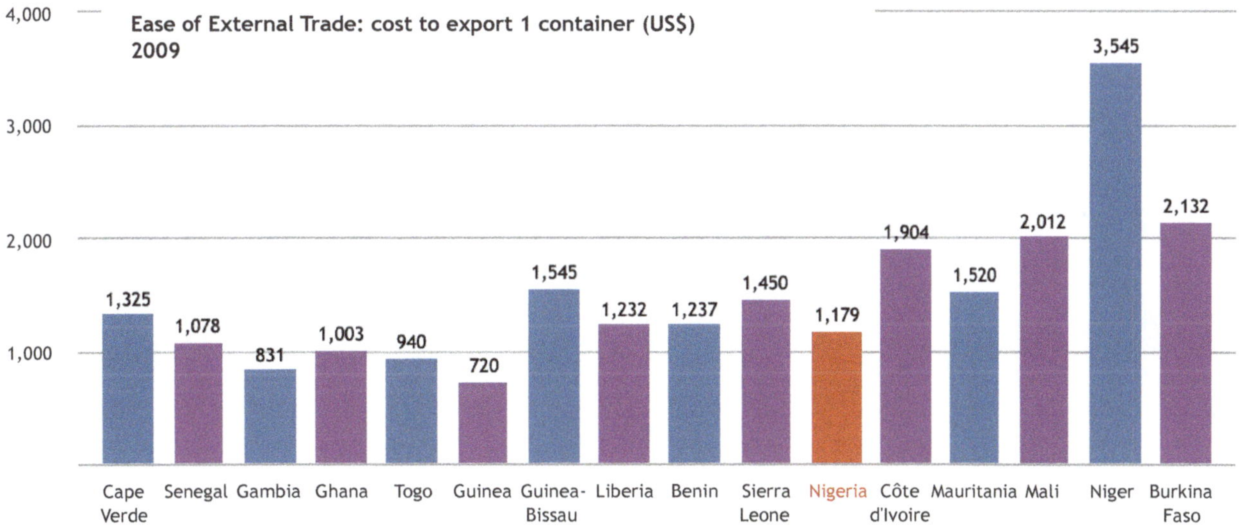

Handling charges for exports and imports are in the mid-range when compared to other West Africa.

15.22

Ease of External Trade: cost to import 1 container (US$)
2009

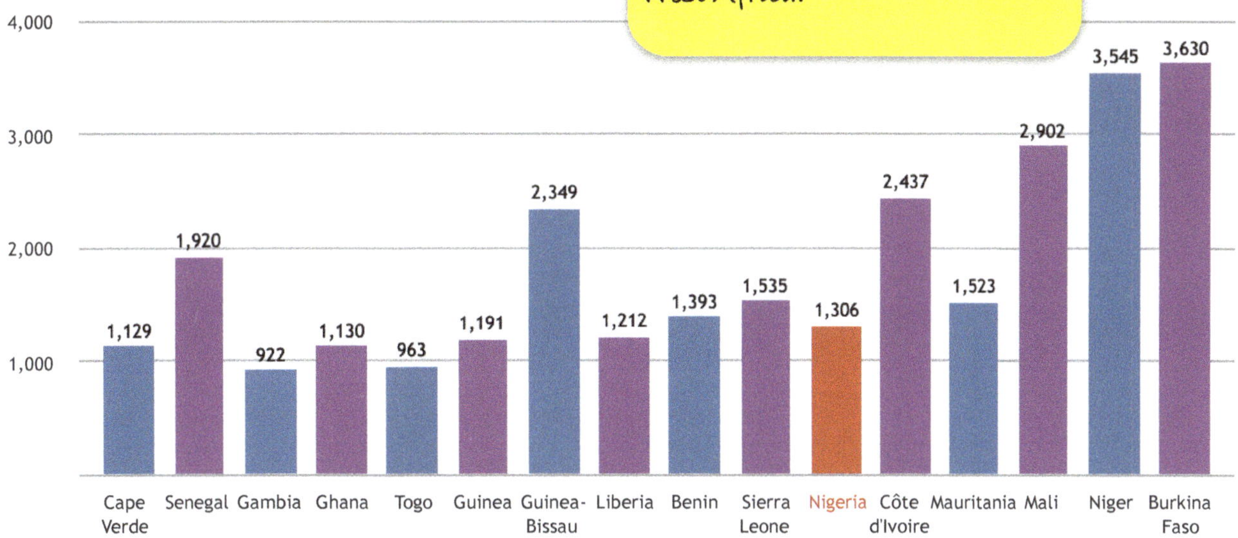

Overall *Ease of External Trade*:
2009 rankings of 47 Sub-Saharan Africa Countries. Source: World Bank, IFC

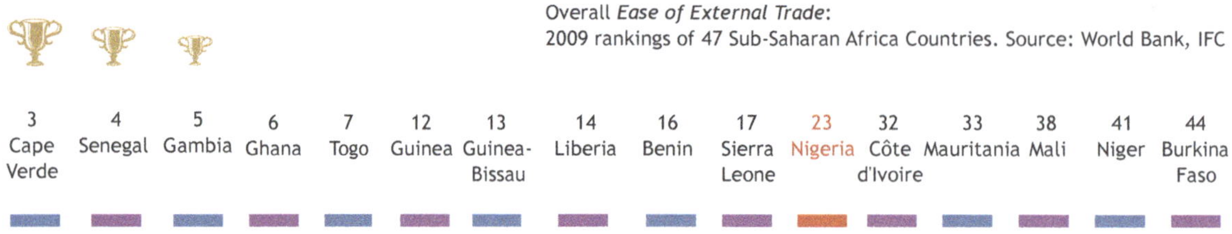

15.23

Ease of External Trade: no. of documents needed to export 2009

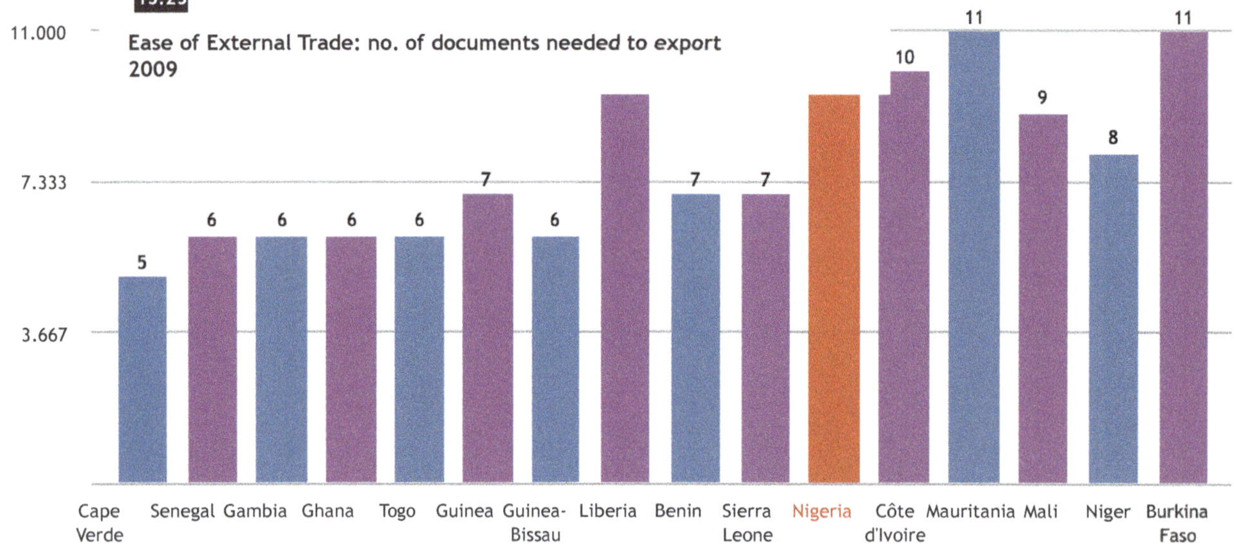

But paperwork is tedious.

15.24

Ease of External Trade: no. of documents needed to import 2009

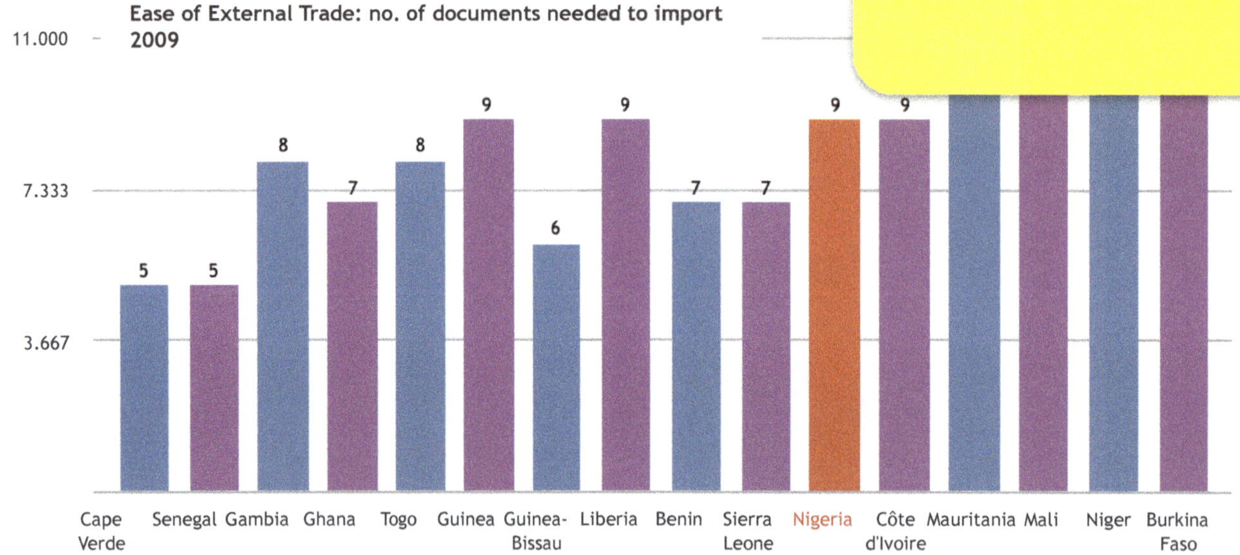

Overall *Ease of External Trade*:
2009 rankings of 47 Sub-Saharan Africa Countries. Source: World Bank, IFC

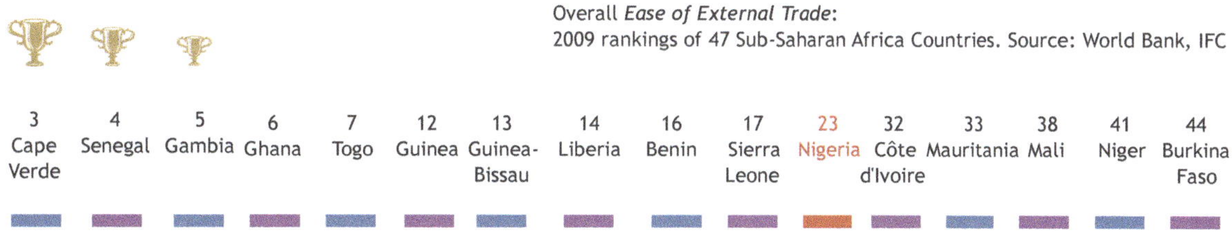

15.25

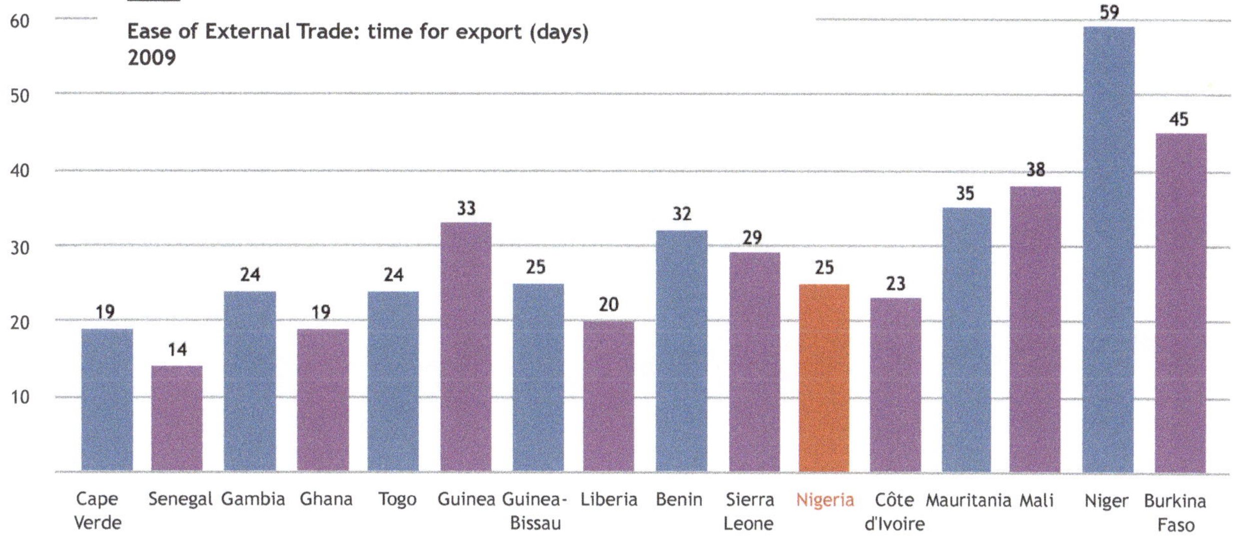

Ease of External Trade: time for export (days) 2009

In the end, through-put time is on the high side for both exports and imports processes.

15.26

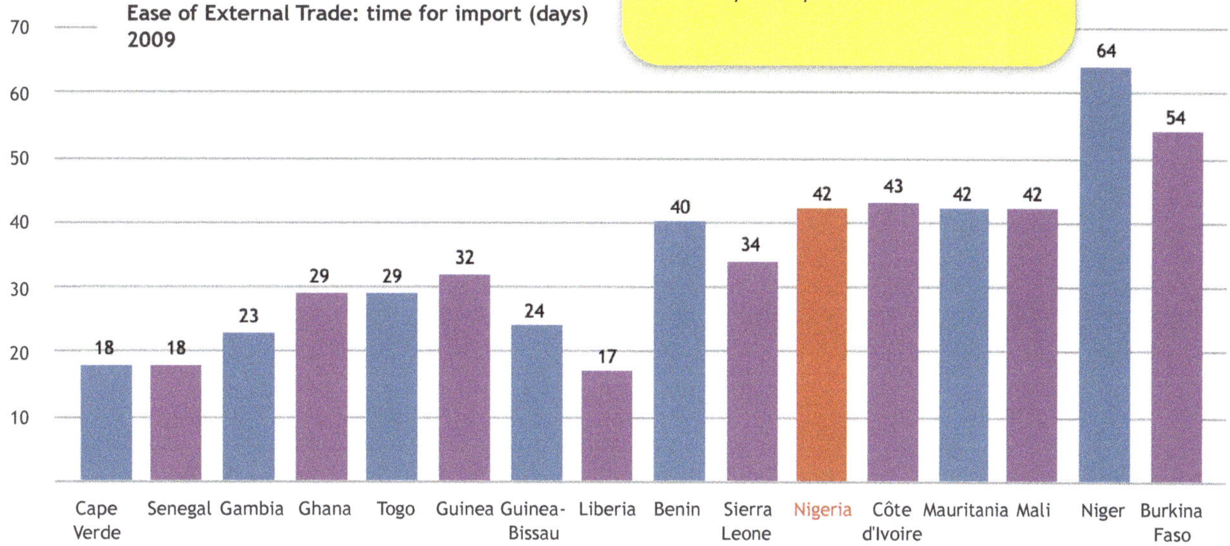

Ease of External Trade: time for import (days) 2009

15.9 Ease of Enforcing Contracts: Rank

2008	2009	
	◁▷	Self-comparison to Preceding Period
▲	▲	Performance in Sub-Saharan Africa
▲	▲	Performance in West Africa
Ghana	Cape Verde	
Cape Verde	Ghana	
Gambia, The	Gambia, The	
Mauritania	Mauritania	
Nigeria	Nigeria	
Burkina Faso	Burkina Faso	
Côte d'Ivoire	Côte d'Ivoire	
Guinea	Guinea	
Niger	Niger	
Guinea-Bissau	Guinea-Bissau	
Sierra Leone	Sierra Leone	
Senegal	Senegal	
Togo	Togo	
Mali	Mali	
Liberia	Liberia	
Benin	Benin	

she's on top of it

Business disputes usually reach suitable resolution in Nigeria. Cape Verde, Ghana & Gambia are again top finishers in West Africa, and in all Africa, too.

2008	2009	
▲	▲	Performance among Oil-Exporters
Equatorial Guinea	Equatorial Guinea	
Nigeria	Nigeria	
Côte d'Ivoire	Côte d'Ivoire	
Sudan	Sudan	
Gabon	Gabon	
Congo, Rep.	Congo, Rep.	
Chad	Chad	
Cameroon	Cameroon	
Angola	Angola	

▲	improved *or* better than average
▼	worsened *or* worse than average
◁▷	no change *or* average

2009 rankings of 47 Sub-Saharan Africa Countries

Source: World Bank, IFC

3 **Cape Verde**

5 **Ghana**

8 **Gambia**

14	Mauritania	28	Sierra Leone
16	Nigeria	30	Senegal
20	Burkina Faso	33	Togo
22	Côte d'Ivoire	36	Mali
24	Guinea	38	Liberia
25	Niger	45	Benin
27	Guinea-Bissau		

Overall *Ease of Enforcing Contracts*:
2009 rankings of 47 Sub-Saharan Africa Countries. Source: World Bank, IFC

3	Cape Verde
5	Ghana
8	Gambia
14	Mauritania
16	Nigeria
20	Burkina Faso
22	Côte d'Ivoire
24	Guinea
25	Niger
27	Guinea-Bissau
28	Sierra Leone
30	Senegal
33	Togo
36	Mali
38	Liberia
45	Benin

15.27

Ease of Enforcing Contracts: no. of procedures 2009

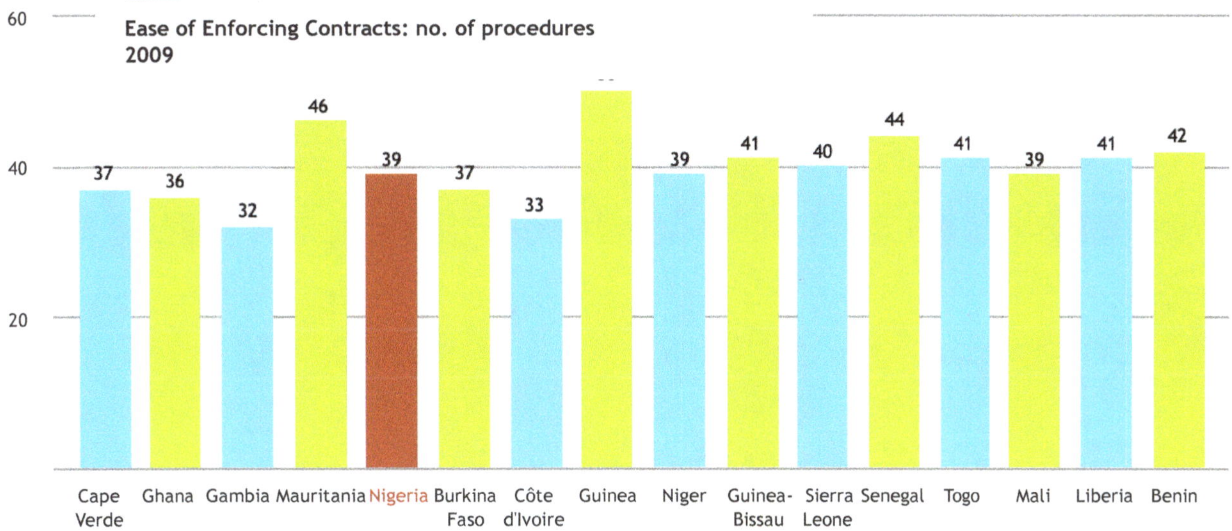

There's little separating West Africa's countries in no. of procedures involved. But in Nigeria it takes many days less than in a lot of West Africa.

15.28

Ease of Enforcing Contracts: time in days 2009

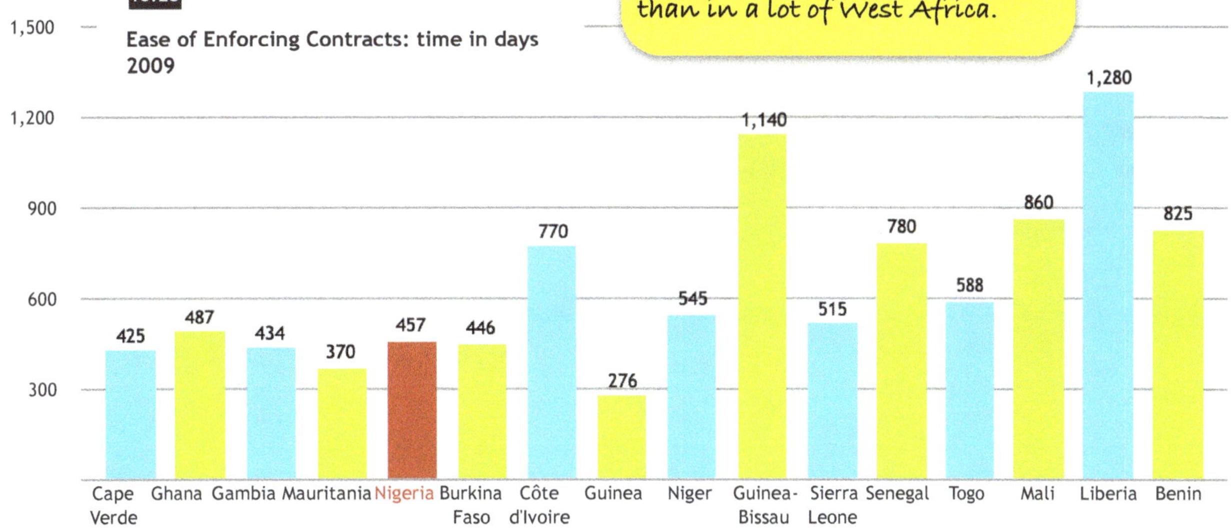

Overall *Ease of Enforcing Contracts*:
2009 rankings of 47 Sub-Saharan Africa Countries. Source: World Bank, IFC

3	5	8	14	16	20	22	24	25	27	28	30	33	36	38	45
Cape Verde	Ghana	Gambia	Mauritania	Nigeria	Burkina Faso	Côte d'Ivoire	Guinea	Niger	Guinea-Bissau	Sierra Leone	Senegal	Togo	Mali	Liberia	Benin

15.29

Ease of Enforcing Contracts: cost (as % of debt in dispute)
2009

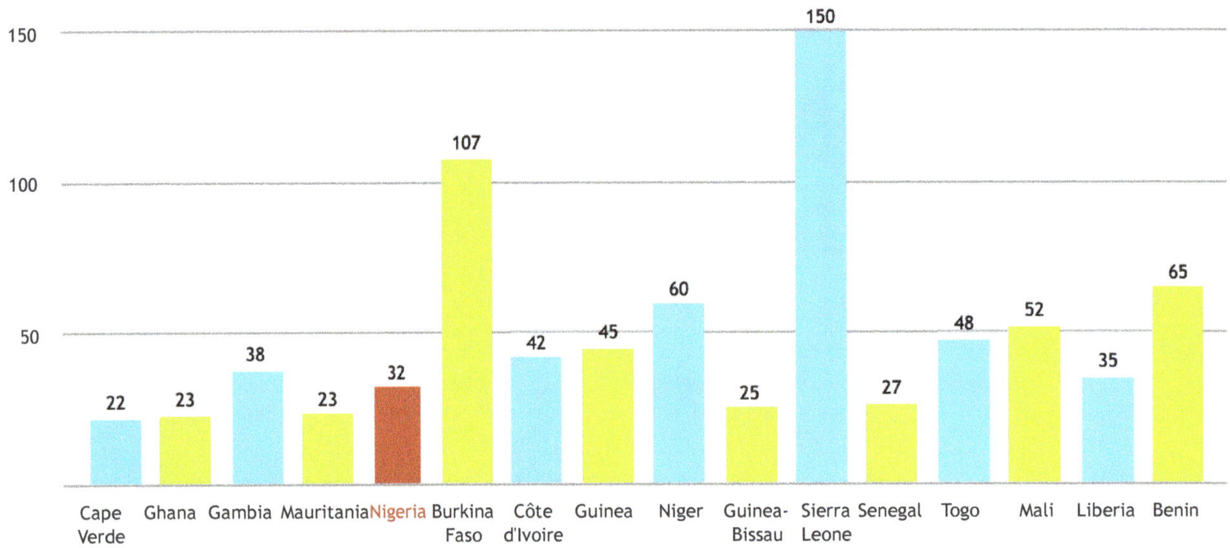

It also costs less than the West Africa average, in Nigeria, to bring the dispute to a resolution.

15.10 Ease of Closing a Business: Rank

2008	2009	
	◁▷	Self-comparison to Preceding Period
▲	▲	Performance in Sub-Saharan Africa
▲	▲	Performance in West Africa
Côte d'Ivoire	Côte d'Ivoire	
Senegal	Senegal	
Nigeria	Nigeria	
Togo	Togo	
Burkina Faso	Ghana	
Ghana	Guinea	
Benin	Burkina Faso	
Mali	Mali	
Guinea	Gambia, The	
Gambia, The	Benin	
Niger	Niger	
Sierra Leone	Sierra Leone	
Mauritania	Liberia	
Liberia	Mauritania	
Cape Verde	Cape Verde	
Guinea-Bissau	Guinea-Bissau	

To "up and go" is relatively easy in Nigeria, giving a picture somewhat of "hard to get in but easy to pull out". Tricky to say which one investors would prefer.

good-bye. it was a pleasure. honest.

2008	2009	
▲	▲	Performance among Oil-Exporters
Côte d'Ivoire	Côte d'Ivoire	
Nigeria	Nigeria	
Cameroon	Cameroon	
Congo, Rep.	Congo, Rep.	
Gabon	Gabon	
Angola	Angola	
Chad	Chad	
Equatorial Guinea	Equatorial Guinea	
Sudan	Sudan	

▲ improved *or* better than average
▼ worsened *or* worse than average
◁▷ no change *or* average

2009 rankings of 47 Sub-Saharan Africa Countries

Source: World Bank, IFC

5 Côte d'Ivoire

11 Senegal

13 Nigeria

14	Togo	28	Niger
16	Ghana	30	Sierra Leone
17	Guinea	31	Liberia
18	Burkina Faso	32	Mauritania
20	Mali	35	Cape Verde
22	Gambia	35	Guinea-Bissau
23	Benin		

Overall *Ease of Closing a Business*:
2009 rankings of 47 Sub-Saharan Africa Countries. Source: World Bank, IFC

5	11	13	14	16	17	18	20	22	23	28	30	31	32	35	35
Côte d'Ivoire	Senegal	Nigeria	Togo	Ghana	Guinea	Burkina Faso	Mali	Gambia	Benin	Niger	Sierra Leone	Liberia	Mauritania	Cape Verde	Guinea-Bissau

As though to press that point, you stand to recover more of your investment and costs in Nigeria than elsewhere, should you wish to pack and leave.

15.30

Ease of Closing a Business: recovery rate (cents on the dollar) 2009

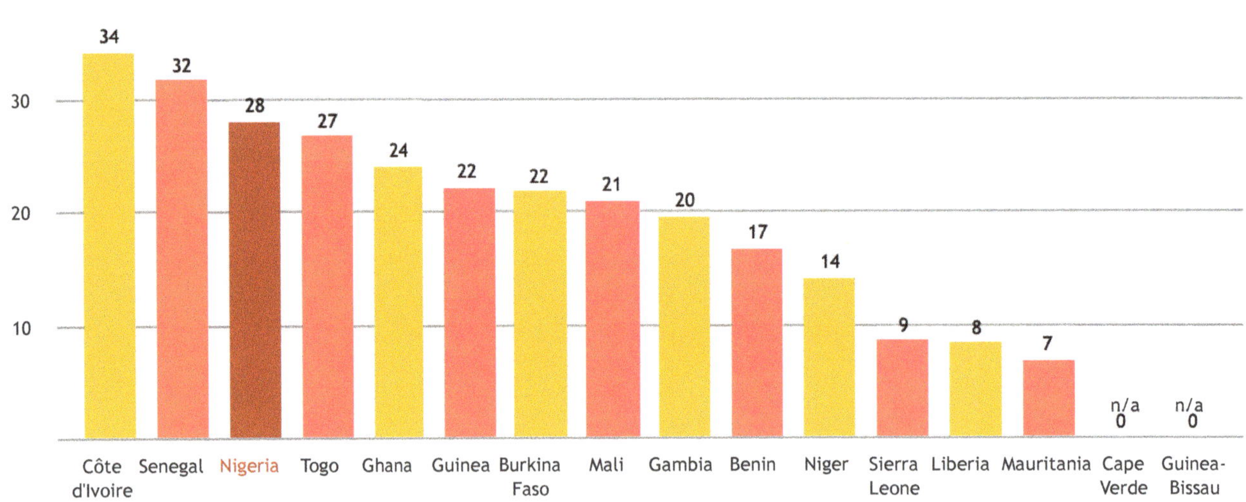

15.11 Ease of Doing Business: Rank

are you in for long nights?

Nigeria ends up in the upper-third of Sub-Saharan Afr. countries when ranked by the ease of business operations. Only bettered in West Afr. by Ghana.

2009 rankings of 47 Sub-Saharan Africa Countries

Source: World Bank, IFC

6	Ghana
12	Nigeria
15	Gambia
19	Cape Verde
22	Burkina Faso
23	Senegal
27	Sierra Leone
28	Liberia
30	Mauritania
31	Côte d'Ivoire
32	Togo
34	Mali
37	Benin
38	Guinea
39	Niger
45	Guinea-Bissau

	2008	2009
Self-comparison to Preceding Period		▼
Performance in Sub-Saharan Africa	▲	▲
Performance in West Africa	▲	▲
	Ghana	Ghana
	Nigeria	Nigeria
	Gambia, The	Gambia, The
	Cape Verde	Cape Verde
	Benin	Burkina Faso
	Côte d'Ivoire	Senegal
	Togo	Sierra Leone
	Mauritania	Liberia
	Mali	Mauritania
	Sierra Leone	Côte d'Ivoire
	Burkina Faso	Togo
	Senegal	Mali
	Guinea	Benin
	Niger	Guinea
	Liberia	Niger
	Guinea-Bissau	Guinea-Bissau
Performance among Oil-Exporters	▲	▲
	Nigeria	Nigeria
	Sudan	Sudan
	Gabon	Gabon
	Cameroon	Côte d'Ivoire
	Côte d'Ivoire	Cameroon
	Equatorial Guinea	Equatorial Guinea
	Angola	Angola
	Chad	Chad
	Congo, Rep.	Congo, Rep.

▲ improved *or* better than average
▼ worsened *or* worse than average
◁▷ no change *or* average

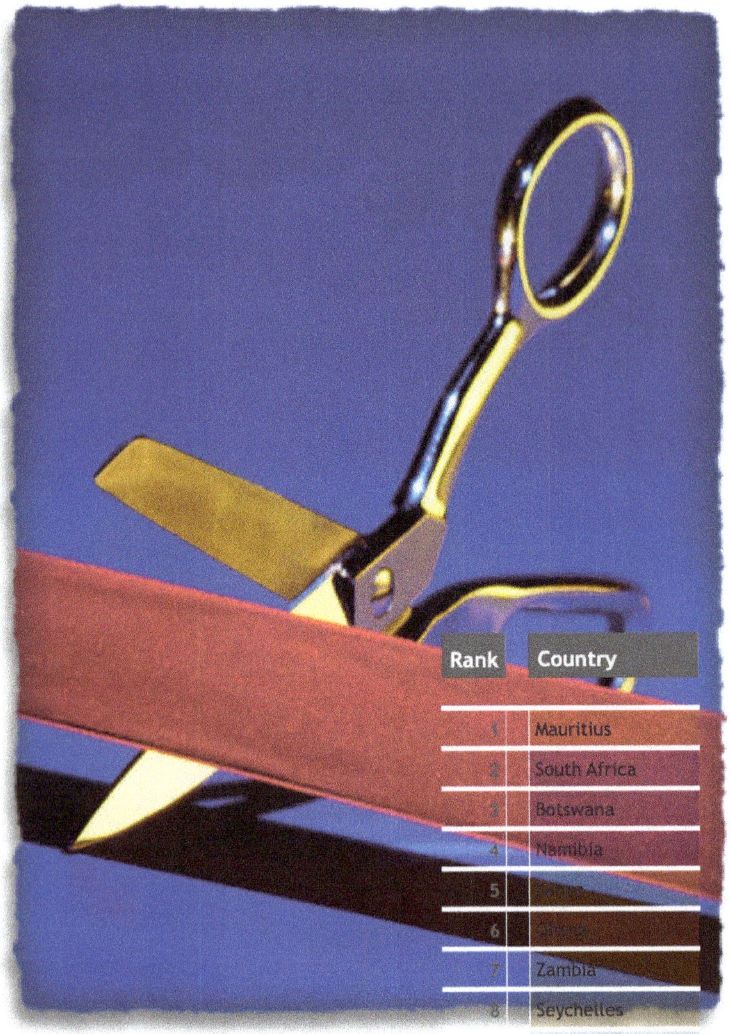

they've cut out the red tape

Regulatory Environment Rankings: 2009

Rank	Country
1	Mauritius
2	South Africa
3	Botswana
4	Namibia
5	Kenya
6	Ghana
7	Zambia
8	Seychelles
9	Swaziland
10	Uganda
11	Ethiopia
12	**Nigeria**
13	Lesotho
14	Tanzania
15	Gambia, The
16	Malawi
17	Rwanda
18	Mozambique
19	Cape Verde
20	Madagascar
21	Burkina Faso
22	Senegal
23	Gabon
24	Comoros
25	Sierra Leone
26	Côte d' Ivoire
27	Togo
28	Cameroon
29	Mali
30	Equatorial Guinea
31	Angola
32	Benin
33	Guinea
34	Niger
35	Eritrea
36	Chad
37	Burundi
38	Congo, Rep.
39	Guinea-Bissau
40	Central Afr. Rep.
41	Congo, Dem. Rep.

More Favorable — MIDDLE — Less Favorable

Of the top 10 in Sub-Saharan Africa, 5 are East African (including no. 1), 4 Southern African, and 1 West African: Ghana.

- Central Africa
- East Africa
- Southern Africa
- West Africa

Wrap-up: Regulatory Environment

- Mauritius, then Ghana, and then Nigeria, was the order of the top 3 finishers in West Africa. Mauritius was also the least constrained economy in Africa in which to do business. Ghana was 6th and Nigeria 12th. All 3 countries were the only West Africans in the top-brackets.

- Mauritius' performance was outstanding: 82% of the indicators ended up top-bracket. Nigeria had its majority in the mid-brackets (45%), but next highest was its top-bracket finishers (37%).

- Nigeria was excellent in the ease of starting a business, ease of employing workers, and in the legal and regulatory protection given to investors. But it was very poor at enabling registration of property. And it fared only marginally better in the construction department.

- Otherwise, on the whole, Nigeria was an enabling environment for business, compared to the rest of Sub-Saharan Africa: top-bracket finisher.

16. Business Friendliness

here's to us

Primer

This chapter attempts to encapsulate in figures the extent to which an economy has proven to be welcoming and stimulating for the conduct of business and investment. It relies on data gathered and presented by two groups: *The Heritage Foundation* in conjunction with the *Wall Street Journal* (through their Index of Economic Freedoms); and the *World Bank* (through its Worldwide Governance Indicators).

Index of Economic Freedom

The Heritage Foundation and The Wall Street Journal have been producing their Index of Economic Freedoms for many years. The methodology and scope have been adjusted and improved through this time. As they explain, the "2008 Index of Economic Freedom covers 162 countries across 10 specific factors of economic freedom (...) the higher the score on a factor, the lower the level of government interference in the economy (...) Taken together, they offer an empirical depiction of a country's degree of economic freedom (...) the key to creating an environment that allows a virtuous cycle of entrepreneurship, innovation, and sustained economic growth and development to flourish. Economies with higher levels of economic freedom enjoy higher living standards."

The 10 Factors of Economic Freedom as presented by them are:

- Business Freedom
- Trade Freedom
- Fiscal Freedom
- Government Size
- Monetary Freedom
- Investment Freedom
- Financial Freedom
- Property Rights
- Freedom from Corruption
- Labour Freedom

Tax Rates

The top tax rate on individual income, and the top tax rate on corporate income.

Quality of Governance

The World Bank, with the International Bank for Reconstruction and Development (IBRD), has been collating data about Governance practice throughout the world for a little over ten years now. They divide this set of indices into six areas:

Voice and Accountability

"The extent to which a country's citizens are able to participate in selecting their government, as well as freedom of expression, freedom of association, and a free media."

Political Stability and Absence of Violence

"Perceptions of the likelihood that the government will be destabilized or overthrown by unconstitutional or violent means, including domestic violence and terrorism."

Government Effectiveness

"The quality of public services, the quality of the civil service and the degree of its independence from political pressures, the quality of policy formulation and implementation, and the credibility of the government's commitment to such policies."

Regulatory Quality

"The ability of the government to formulate and implement sound policies and regulations that permit and promote private sector development."

Rule of Law

"The extent to which agents have confidence in and abide by the rules of society, and in particular the quality of contract enforcement, the police, and the courts, as well as the likelihood of crime and violence."

Control of Corruption

"The extent to which public power is exercised for private gain, including both petty and grand forms of corruption, as well as capture of the state by the elite and private interests."

In this chapter we have charted the progress, along the years, of the country in focus across the ranks in Sub-Saharan Africa, dividing the 48 countries into three bands of achievement: the top rank (top third: 1-16), middle rank (middle third: 17-32), and bottom rank (bottom third: 33-48).

(The quotations cited above – enclosed within marks – are as they are given by the agencies mentioned, in the following publications: *2008 Index of Economic Freedom* and *A Decade of Measuring the Quality of Governance*. None of the data in this chapter goes towards evaluating our BiA Index of Country Performance.)

Sources of Primary Data: The Heritage Foundation, The Wall Street Journal, the World Bank, IBRD.

Charts

- **Wrap-up**

Tables

2001-2004; 2005-2008:
- *self-comparison to preceding period;*
- *performance in S-Saharan Africa;*
- *performance in West Africa;*
- *performance among oil-exporters;*

for:

Index of Economic Freedoms: Rank

1998-2002; 2003-2006:
- *self-comparison to preceding period;*
- *performance in S-Saharan Africa;*
- *performance in West Africa;*
- *performance among oil-exporters;*

for:

Voice and Accountability: Rank

Political Stability: Rank

Government Effectiveness: Rank

Regulatory Quality: Rank

Rule of Law: Rank

Control of Corruption: Rank

2001-2004; 2005-2008:
- *rank out of 40 African countries over the 2 periods;*

for:

Index of Economic Freedoms

2003-2006; 1998-2002:
- *rank out of 48 African countries over the 2 periods;*

for:

Voice and Accountability: Rank

Political Stability: Rank

Government Effectiveness: Rank

Regulatory Quality: Rank

Rule of Law: Rank

Control of Corruption: Rank

- Personal Income Tax Rate: 2008
- Corporate Tax Rate: 2008

- **Business Friendliness Rankings: 2003-2008**

16.1 Index of Economic Freedoms: Rank

01-04	05-08	
	▲	Self-comparison to Preceding Period
▼	▼	Performance in Sub-Saharan Africa
▼	▼	Performance in West Africa
Mali	Cape Verde	
Senegal	Senegal	
Burkina Faso	Gambia, The	
Ghana	Ghana	
Cape Verde	Côte d'Ivoire	
Mauritania	Burkina Faso	
Côte d'Ivoire	Mauritania	
Benin	Mali	
Gambia, The	Guinea	
Guinea	Benin	
Niger	**Nigeria**	
Nigeria	Niger	
Togo	Togo	
Guinea-Bissau	Sierra Leone	
Sierra Leone	Guinea-Bissau	
▲	▲	Performance among Oil-Exporters
Gabon	Côte d'Ivoire	
Côte d'Ivoire	Gabon	
Cameroon	Cameroon	
Nigeria	**Nigeria**	
Equatorial Guinea	Equatorial Guinea	
Chad	Chad	
Congo, Rep.	Angola	
Angola	Congo, Rep.	

they won't shackle you

Not a good verdict. Nigeria improved during 2005-08, over the preceding 4 yrs; but it wasn't enough to match the rest of West Africa, nor the rest of Africa.

That it stayed above water among the oil economies is a sign of their poor rating on the conduciveness of their business and investment culture.

▲	improved *or* better than average
▼	worsened *or* worse than average
◁▷	no change *or* average

2008 rankings of 40 Sub-Saharan Africa Countries
Source: Heritage Foundation, Wall Street Journal

and they won't shackle it, either

16.1

Index of Economic Freedom: Nigeria's Ranking in SSA 1999-2008

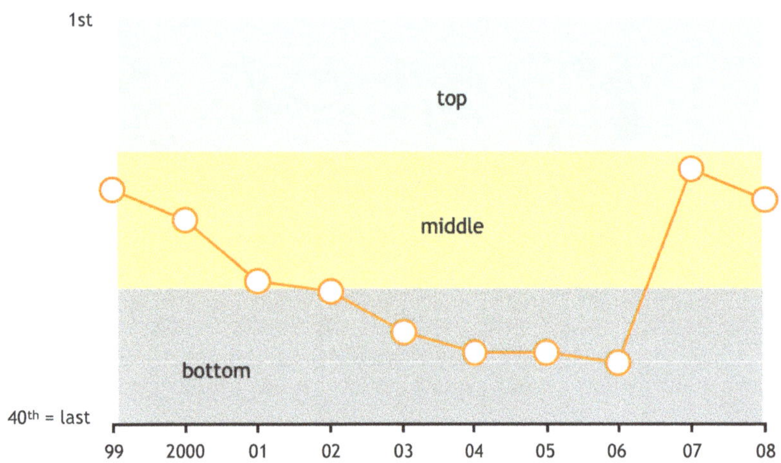

2008 rankings of 40 Sub-Saharan Africa Countries
Source: Heritage Foundation, Wall Street Journal

During 2002-2006 Nigeria fell deeper into the bottom tier in Africa. 2007 saw a leap into a high in the mid-tier. By 2008 it was dropping again.

now, that's worth celebrating

▲	moved up from 2001/04
▼	moved down from 2001/04
blank	no change from 2001/04

Index of Economic Freedom: Rankings

	Rank	2005-08	2001-04
	1	Botswana	Botswana
	2	Mauritius	Mauritius
▲	3	Uganda	Namibia
	4	South Africa	South Africa
▲	5	Madagascar	Uganda
▼	6	Namibia	Swaziland
▼	7	Swaziland	Mali
▲	8	Kenya	Senegal
▲	9	Cape Verde	Burkina Faso
▼	10	Senegal	Mozambique
▲	11	Gambia, The	Kenya
	12	Tanzania	Tanzania
▲	13	Ghana	Madagascar
▲	14	Zambia	Ghana
▲	15	Côte d' Ivoire	Zambia
▼	16	Burkina Faso	Gabon
▲	17	Mauritania	Cape Verde
▼	18	Mali	Central Afr. Rep.
▼	19	Mozambique	Djibouti
▲	20	Malawi	Mauritania
▲	21	Guinea	Côte d' Ivoire
▼	22	Gabon	Benin
▲	23	Cameroon	Gambia, The
▼	24	Benin	Guinea
▼	25	Djibouti	Malawi
▲	26	Nigeria	Cameroon
▲	27	Lesotho	Niger
▲	28	Equatorial Guinea	Ethiopia
▼	29	Central Afr. Rep.	Nigeria
▼	30	Ethiopia	Lesotho
▲	31	Rwanda	Equatorial Guinea
▼	32	Niger	Chad
▼	33	Chad	Rwanda
	34	Togo	Togo
▲	35	Sierra Leone	Congo, Rep.
▲	36	Burundi	Guinea-Bissau
▼	37	Guinea-Bissau	Sierra Leone
▲	38	Angola	Zimbabwe
▼	39	Congo, Rep.	Angola
▼	40	Zimbabwe	Burundi

Economic Freedom: 2005-08 was an improvement over 2001-04. Three places up. But still firmly rooted in Africa's bottom half.

Central Africa
East Africa
Southern Africa
West Africa

2008 rankings of 40 Sub-Saharan Africa Countries
Source: Heritage Foundation, Wall Street Journal

16.2 Personal Income Tax Rate: 2008

it's going to cost her

Tax on personal earnings is higher in most of Sub-Saharan Africa, than it is in Nigeria. At about 25%, Nigeria's is less than half of the highest (Chad: 65%).

It is near twice that of the lowest (Angola, Mauritius: 15%). The least in West Africa is Guinea-Bissau (20%), and the highest, Côte d'Ivoire (60%).

Source: Heritage Foundation

Ran	Country	%
1	Angola	15
1	Mauritius	15
2	Guinea-Bissau	20
3	Botswana	25
3	Ghana	25
3	Nigeria	25
4	Burkina Faso	30
4	Djibouti	30
4	Kenya	30
4	Madagascar	30
4	Sierra Leone	30
4	Tanzania	30
4	Uganda	30
5	Mozambique	32
6	Swaziland	33
7	Burundi	35
7	Cameroon	35
7	Equatorial Guinea	35
7	Ethiopia	35
7	Gambia, The	35
7	Lesotho	35
7	Namibia	35
7	Rwanda	35
7	Zambia	35
8	Benin	40
8	Guinea	40
8	Malawi	40
8	Mali	40
8	Mauritania	40
8	South Africa	40
9	Cape Verde	45
9	Niger	45
10	Zimbabwe	47.5
11	Central Afr. Rep.	50
11	Congo, Rep.	50
11	Gabon	50
11	Senegal	50
12	Togo	55
13	Côte d' Ivoire	60
14	Chad	65

16.3 Corporate Tax Rate: 2008

and it will cost you, too

Corporate tax is a closer call, with smaller differences. Nigeria at 30% is in the mid-range.

The lowest — again — is Mauritius (15%), and the highest — again — is Chad (40%).

Rank	Country	%
1	Mauritius	15
2	Botswana	25
2	Djibouti	25
2	Ghana	25
2	Guinea-Bissau	25
2	Lesotho	25
2	Mauritania	25
2	Senegal	25
3	South Africa	29
4	Cape Verde	30
4	Central Afr. Rep.	30
4	Ethiopia	30
4	Kenya	30
4	Madagascar	30
4	Malawi	30
4	Nigeria	30
4	Rwanda	30
4	Sierra Leone	30
4	Swaziland	30
4	Tanzania	30
4	Uganda	30
4	Zimbabwe	30
5	Mozambique	32
6	Angola	35
6	Burkina Faso	35
6	Burundi	35
6	Côte d' Ivoire	35
6	Equatorial Guinea	35
6	Gabon	35
6	Gambia, The	35
6	Guinea	35
6	Mali	35
6	Namibia	35
6	Niger	35
6	Zambia	35
7	Togo	37
8	Benin	38
8	Congo, Rep.	38
9	Cameroon	38.5
10	Chad	40

Source: Heritage Foundation

16.4 Voice and Accountability: Rank

tough getting yourself heard?

A poor Nigeria showing.
This indicator measures the influence the country's people have on their govt.

The oil bloc does poorly. Even Nigeria survives in the group, whereas it falls short within the rest of Africa. Perhaps oil and open govt. don't mix.

	1998-02	2003-06
Self-comparison to Preceding Period		▲
Performance in Sub-Saharan Africa	▼	▼
Performance in West Africa	▼	▼
	Cape Verde	Cape Verde
	Benin	Mali
	Mali	Ghana
	Senegal	Benin
	Ghana	Senegal
	Burkina Faso	Niger
	Mauritania	Burkina Faso
	Niger	Sierra Leone
	Gambia, The	Gambia, The
	Nigeria	Guinea-Bissau
	Guinea-Bissau	**Nigeria**
	Côte d'Ivoire	Mauritania
	Guinea	Liberia
	Togo	Guinea
	Sierra Leone	Togo
	Liberia	Côte d'Ivoire
Performance among Oil-Exporters	▲	▲
	Gabon	Gabon
	Chad	**Nigeria**
	Nigeria	Congo, Rep.
	Cameroon	Cameroon
	Côte d'Ivoire	Angola
	Angola	Chad
	Congo, Rep.	Côte d'Ivoire
	Equatorial Guinea	Equatorial Guinea
	Sudan	Sudan

▲	improved *or* better than average
▼	worsened *or* worse than average
◁▷	no change *or* average

Rankings of 48 Sub-Saharan Africa Countries
Source: IBRD, World Bank

Central Africa
East Africa
Southern Africa
North Africa
West Africa

▲	moved up from 98/02
▼	moved down from 98/02
blank	no change from 98/02

16.2

Voice and Accountability: Nigeria's Ranking in SSA. 1998-2006

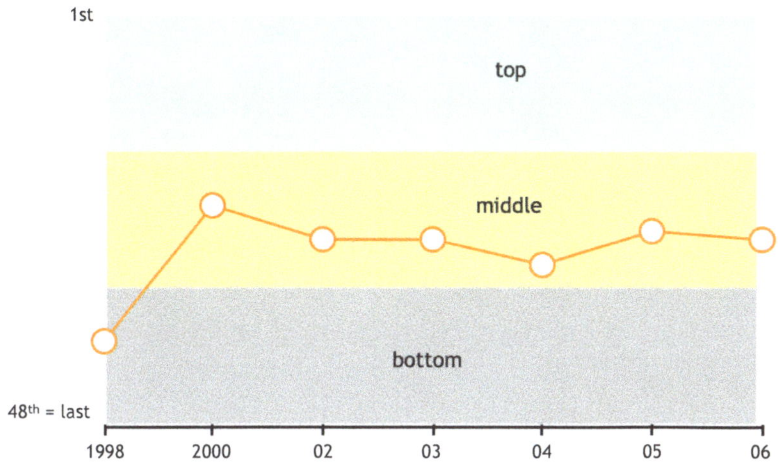

Nigeria stayed average on the continent; worse than many, but better than a number. Moved up one notch from 1998-2002 levels.

	Rank	2003-06	1998-2002
	1	Mauritius	Mauritius
	2	Botswana	Botswana
▲	3	South Africa	Cape Verde
▼	4	Cape Verde	South Africa
	5	Namibia	Namibia
▼	6	Mali	Sao Tome & Princ.
▼	7	Ghana	Benin
▼	8	Sao Tome & Princ.	Mali
	9	Seychelles	Seychelles
▼	10	Benin	Madagascar
	11	Senegal	Senegal
▲	12	Lesotho	Ghana
▼	13	Madagascar	Mozambique
▼	14	Mozambique	Malawi
▲	15	Kenya	Gabon
▲	16	Niger	Tanzania
▲	17	Zambia	Burkina Faso
▲	18	Comoros	Lesotho
▼	19	Tanzania	Zambia
▼	20	Burkina Faso	Comoros
▼	21	Malawi	Mauritania
▲	22	Sierra Leone	Central Afr. Rep.
▲	23	Gambia, The	Niger
▲	24	Guinea-Bissau	Kenya
▲	25	Uganda	Gambia, The
▼	26	Gabon	Djibouti
▲	27	**Nigeria**	Chad
▼	28	Djibouti	**Nigeria**
▼	29	Mauritania	Uganda
▲	30	Congo, Rep.	Ethiopia
▲	31	Cameroon	Guinea-Bissau
▲	32	Burundi	Cameroon
▼	33	Ethiopia	Côte d' Ivoire
▲	34	Liberia	Zimbabwe
▲	35	Angola	Guinea
▼	36	Guinea	Togo
▼	37	Chad	Sierra Leone
▲	38	Rwanda	Swaziland
▼	39	Central Afr. Rep.	Angola
▼	40	Swaziland	Liberia
▼	41	Togo	Congo, Rep.
▼	42	Côte d' Ivoire	Eritrea
▼	43	Zimbabwe	Rwanda
▲	44	Equatorial Guinea	Burundi
▲	45	Sudan	Equatorial Guinea
▲	46	Congo, Dem. Rep.	Sudan
	47	Somalia	Somalia
▼	48	Eritrea	Congo, Dem. Rep.

16.5 Political Stability: Rank

are you feeling the love?

Touchy topic in Nigeria: there are as many opinions as there are thinkers. Applying empirical methods as here, a poor outing again is the picture.

This time, Nigeria performs poorly within the oil club, too.

	1998-02	2003-06
Self-comparison to Preceding Period		▼
Performance in Sub-Saharan Africa	▼	▼
Performance in West Africa	▼	▼
	Cape Verde	Cape Verde
	Benin	Gambia, The
	Gambia, The	Benin
	Mali	Ghana
	Mauritania	Mali
	Ghana	Burkina Faso
	Burkina Faso	Senegal
	Togo	Mauritania
	Niger	Niger
	Senegal	Guinea-Bissau
	Côte d'Ivoire	Sierra Leone
	Guinea	Togo
	Guinea-Bissau	Guinea
	Nigeria	Liberia
	Sierra Leone	**Nigeria**
	Liberia	Côte d'Ivoire
Performance among Oil-Exporters	▼	▼
	Gabon	Gabon
	Equatorial Guinea	Equatorial Guinea
	Cameroon	Cameroon
	Côte d'Ivoire	Angola
	Congo, Rep.	Congo, Rep.
	Nigeria	Chad
	Chad	**Nigeria**
	Angola	Côte d'Ivoire
	Sudan	Sudan

▲	improved *or* better than average
▼	worsened *or* worse than average
◁▷	no change *or* average

Rankings of 48 Sub-Saharan Africa Countries
Source: IBRD, World Bank

- Central Africa
- East Africa
- Southern Africa
- North Africa
- West Africa

▲	moved up from 98/02
▼	moved down from 98/02
blank	no change from 98/02

	Rank	2003-06	1998-2002
▲	1	Botswana	Mauritius
▼	2	Mauritius	Seychelles
▼	3	Seychelles	Cape Verde
▼	4	Cape Verde	Botswana
▲	5	Namibia	Sao Tome & Princ.
▼	6	Sao Tome & Princ.	Benin
	7	Gambia, The	Gambia, The
▲	8	Lesotho	Mali
▼	9	Benin	Mauritania
▲	10	Ghana	Mozambique
▼	11	Mozambique	Comoros
	12	Gabon	Gabon
▼	13	Mali	Namibia
	14	Madagascar	Madagascar
▲	15	Zambia	Swaziland
▼	16	Swaziland	Lesotho
▲	17	Malawi	Ghana
	18	Burkina Faso	Burkina Faso
▲	19	South Africa	Equatorial Guinea
▼	20	Comoros	Tanzania
▼	21	Equatorial Guinea	Togo
▲	22	Senegal	Zambia
▼	23	Mauritania	Niger
▼	24	Tanzania	Malawi
▼	25	Niger	South Africa
	26	Cameroon	Cameroon
	27	Djibouti	Djibouti
▲	28	Guinea-Bissau	Senegal
▲	29	Sierra Leone	Côte d' Ivoire
▼	30	Togo	Ethiopia
▲	31	Eritrea	Kenya
▲	32	Rwanda	Guinea
▲	33	Angola	Guinea-Bissau
▼	34	Guinea	Eritrea
	35	Congo, Rep.	Congo, Rep.
▼	36	Kenya	**Nigeria**
▲	37	Central Afr. Rep.	Zimbabwe
	38	Chad	Chad
▲	39	Uganda	Central Afr. Rep.
▼	40	Ethiopia	Uganda
▼	41	Zimbabwe	Sierra Leone
▲	42	Liberia	Rwanda
▲	43	Burundi	Angola
▼	44	**Nigeria**	Liberia
▼	45	Côte d' Ivoire	Sudan
▼	46	Sudan	Burundi
▲	47	Congo, Dem. Rep.	Somalia
▼	48	Somalia	Congo, Dem. Rep.

16.3

Political Stability: Nigeria's Ranking in SSA. 1998-2006

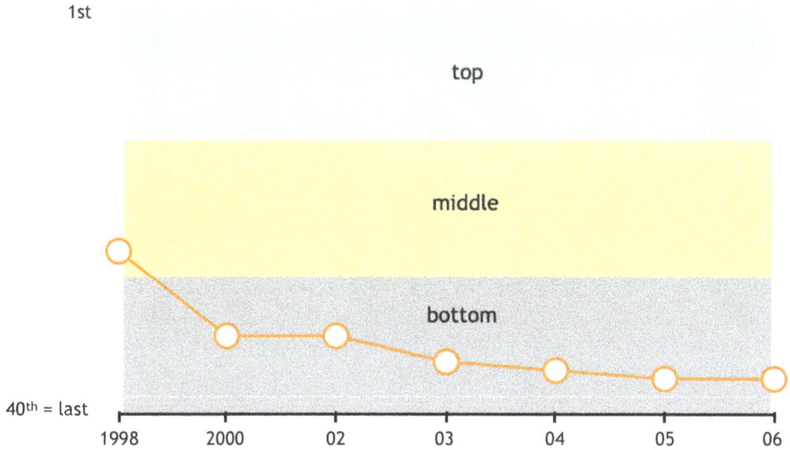

The trend isn't a pretty picture, either: gradual descent in rank, and entrenched in the bottom tier.

16.6 Government Effectiveness: Rank

the waiting game

Quality of governance in Nigeria improved across 1999-2006. Alas, not substantially enough to better other African countries.

But the oil economies did worse.

	1998-02	2003-06
Self-comparison to Preceding Period		▲
Performance in Sub-Saharan Africa	▼	▼
Performance in West Africa	▼	▼

1998-02	2003-06
Cape Verde	Cape Verde
Senegal	Senegal
Ghana	Ghana
Mauritania	Mauritania
Benin	Mali
Gambia, The	Benin
Burkina Faso	Gambia, The
Mali	Burkina Faso
Côte d'Ivoire	Niger
Guinea	**Nigeria**
Nigeria	Guinea
Togo	Sierra Leone
Niger	Côte d'Ivoire
Guinea-Bissau	Guinea-Bissau
Sierra Leone	Liberia
Liberia	Togo

Performance among Oil-Exporters	1998-02	2003-06
	◁▷	▲

1998-02	2003-06
Gabon	Gabon
Chad	Cameroon
Côte d'Ivoire	**Nigeria**
Cameroon	Angola
Nigeria	Chad
Sudan	Sudan
Angola	Congo, Rep.
Equatorial Guinea	Côte d'Ivoire
Congo, Rep.	Equatorial Guinea

▲	improved *or* better than average
▼	worsened *or* worse than average
◁▷	no change *or* average

Rankings of 48 Sub-Saharan Africa Countries
Source: IBRD, World Bank

Central Africa
East Africa
Southern Africa
North Africa
West Africa

▲	moved up from 98/02
▼	moved down from 98/02
blank	no change from 98/02

	Rank	2003-06	1998-2002
▲	1	Botswana	South Africa
▼	2	South Africa	Botswana
	3	Mauritius	Mauritius
	4	Namibia	Namibia
▲	5	Cape Verde	Seychelles
▼	6	Seychelles	Cape Verde
	7	Senegal	Senegal
	8	Ghana	Ghana
▲	9	Madagascar	Mauritania
	10	Lesotho	Lesotho
▼	11	Mauritania	Mozambique
▲	12	Mali	Benin
▼	13	Mozambique	Gabon
▲	14	Tanzania	Malawi
▼	15	Benin	Tanzania
▲	16	Uganda	Madagascar
▲	17	Gambia, The	Uganda
▼	18	Gabon	Gambia, The
▲	19	Burkina Faso	Sao Tome & Princ.
▲	20	Kenya	Swaziland
▲	21	Ethiopia	Burkina Faso
▼	22	Sao Tome & Princ.	Chad
▲	23	Rwanda	Kenya
▲	24	Djibouti	Mali
▼	25	Malawi	Côte d' Ivoire
▲	26	Niger	Cameroon
▼	27	Swaziland	Zambia
▼	28	Cameroon	Zimbabwe
▼	29	Zambia	Eritrea
▲	30	Nigeria	Djibouti
▼	31	Eritrea	Ethiopia
▲	32	Angola	Guinea
▼	33	Chad	Rwanda
▼	34	Guinea	Nigeria
▲	35	Sudan	Togo
▲	36	Sierra Leone	Niger
▲	37	Congo, Rep.	Sudan
▲	38	Burundi	Guinea-Bissau
▼	39	Côte d' Ivoire	Angola
▲	40	Equatorial Guinea	Comoros
▼	41	Guinea-Bissau	Equatorial Guinea
▼	42	Zimbabwe	Congo, Rep.
▲	43	Liberia	Burundi
▼	44	Togo	Sierra Leone
	45	Central Afr. Rep.	Central Afr. Rep.
▲	46	Congo, Dem. Rep.	Liberia
▼	47	Comoros	Congo, Dem. Rep.
	48	Somalia	Somalia

16.4

Government Effectiveness: Nigeria's Ranking in SSA. 1998-2006

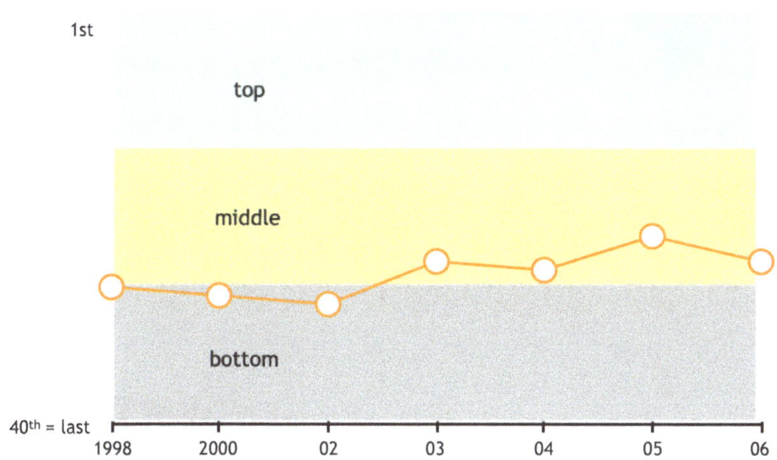

A hesitant climb in 2003 out of the bottom tier and into the average group. But not a confident resurgence; still teetered near the borderline.

16.7 Regulatory Quality: Rank

there's a watching umpire

Still no respite for Nigeria.

Poor regulation of private (and also, public) sector business practice.

Yet again, the oil economies do badly in Africa.

	1998-02	2003-06
Self-comparison to Preceding Period		▼
Performance in Sub-Saharan Africa	▼	▼
Performance in West Africa	▼	▼
	Burkina Faso	Mauritania
	Cape Verde	Cape Verde
	Benin	Ghana
	Senegal	Senegal
	Ghana	Burkina Faso
	Mali	Gambia, The
	Gambia, The	Benin
	Côte d'Ivoire	Mali
	Mauritania	Niger
	Guinea	Togo
	Niger	Côte d'Ivoire
	Togo	Guinea
	Nigeria	**Nigeria**
	Guinea-Bissau	Guinea-Bissau
	Sierra Leone	Sierra Leone
	Liberia	Liberia
Performance among Oil-Exporters	◁▷	◁▷
	Gabon	Gabon
	Côte d'Ivoire	Cameroon
	Cameroon	Côte d'Ivoire
	Chad	Chad
	Nigeria	**Nigeria**
	Congo, Rep.	Congo, Rep.
	Sudan	Sudan
	Equatorial Guinea	Angola
	Angola	Equatorial Guinea

▲	improved *or* better than average
▼	worsened *or* worse than average
◁▷	no change *or* average

Rankings of 48 Sub-Saharan Africa Countries
Source: IBRD, World Bank

- Central Africa
- East Africa
- Southern Africa
- North Africa
- West Africa

▲	moved up from 98/02
▼	moved down from 98/02
blank	no change from 98/02

	Rank	2003-06	1998-2002
	1	Botswana	Botswana
▲	2	South Africa	Mauritius
▼	3	Mauritius	Namibia
▼	4	Namibia	South Africa
	5	Uganda	Uganda
▲	6	Mauritania	Gabon
▲	7	Kenya	Burkina Faso
	8	Cape Verde	Cape Verde
▲	9	Ghana	Benin
	10	Senegal	Senegal
▲	11	Madagascar	Ghana
▼	12	Burkina Faso	Mali
▼	13	Gabon	Zambia
▲	14	Tanzania	Mozambique
	15	Gambia, The	Gambia, The
▼	16	Benin	Côte d' Ivoire
▼	17	Mali	Malawi
▼	18	Mozambique	Mauritania
▼	19	Malawi	Kenya
▲	20	Niger	Swaziland
	21	Lesotho	Lesotho
▲	22	Seychelles	Tanzania
▼	23	Swaziland	Madagascar
▼	24	Zambia	Guinea
▲	25	Rwanda	Cameroon
▼	26	Cameroon	Niger
▲	27	Sao Tome & Princ.	Togo
▲	28	Djibouti	Seychelles
▼	29	Togo	Sao Tome & Princ.
▼	30	Côte d' Ivoire	Eritrea
▲	31	Ethiopia	Djibouti
▼	32	Guinea	Chad
▼	33	Chad	Nigeria
▼	34	Nigeria	Rwanda
▲	35	Guinea-Bissau	Central Afr. Rep.
▲	36	Congo, Rep.	Ethiopia
▲	37	Sierra Leone	Comoros
▲	38	Sudan	Guinea-Bissau
▲	39	Burundi	Congo, Rep.
▲	40	Angola	Zimbabwe
▼	41	Central Afr. Rep.	Sudan
▲	42	Equatorial Guinea	Burundi
▼	43	Comoros	Sierra Leone
▼	44	Eritrea	Equatorial Guinea
▲	45	Congo, Dem. Rep.	Angola
	46	Liberia	Liberia
▼	47	Zimbabwe	Congo, Dem. Rep.
	48	Somalia	Somalia

16.5

Regulatory Quality: Nigeria's Ranking in SSA, 1998-2006

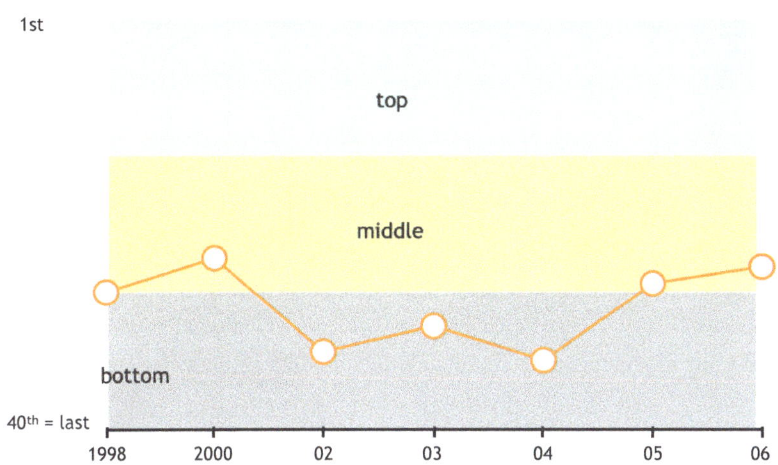

Things began to look up in Nigeria during 2005. But unclear how strong a break-out from the bottom that movement connoted.

16.8 Rule of Law: Rank

hopefully, more than a mantra

Rule of Law performance: not good news for Nigeria.
Better picture almost everywhere else in West Africa, and among the oil economies as well.

	1998-02	2003-06
Self-comparison to Preceding Period		▼
Performance in Sub-Saharan Africa	▼	▼
Performance in West Africa	▼	▼
	Cape Verde	Cape Verde
	Senegal	Mali
	Gambia, The	Gambia, The
	Ghana	Ghana
	Benin	Senegal
	Mauritania	Mauritania
	Mali	Burkina Faso
	Burkina Faso	Benin
	Togo	Niger
	Niger	Togo
	Côte d'Ivoire	Sierra Leone
	Guinea	Guinea-Bissau
	Nigeria	Guinea
	Sierra Leone	**Nigeria**
	Guinea-Bissau	Liberia
	Liberia	Côte d'Ivoire
Performance among Oil-Exporters	▼	▼
	Gabon	Gabon
	Chad	Cameroon
	Côte d'Ivoire	Chad
	Cameroon	Equatorial Guinea
	Equatorial Guinea	Congo, Rep.
	Nigeria	Angola
	Congo, Rep.	**Nigeria**
	Sudan	Sudan
	Angola	Côte d'Ivoire

▲	improved *or* better than average
▼	worsened *or* worse than average
◁▷	no change *or* average

Rankings of 48 Sub-Saharan Africa Countries
Source: IBRD, World Bank

Central Africa
East Africa
Southern Africa
North Africa
West Africa

▲	moved up from 98/02
▼	moved down from 98/02
blank	no change from 98/02

	Rank	2003-06	1998-2002
	1	Mauritius	Mauritius
▲	2	Botswana	Cape Verde
▼	3	Cape Verde	Seychelles
▼	4	Seychelles	Botswana
▲	5	South Africa	Namibia
▼	6	Namibia	South Africa
	7	Lesotho	Lesotho
▲	8	Mali	Senegal
	9	Gambia, The	Gambia, The
▲	10	Madagascar	Ghana
▼	11	Ghana	Benin
▼	12	Senegal	Gabon
▲	13	Malawi	Sao Tome & Princ.
▲	14	Tanzania	Eritrea
	15	Mauritania	Mauritania
▼	16	Sao Tome & Princ.	Madagascar
▲	17	Burkina Faso	Mali
▼	18	Gabon	Tanzania
▼	19	Benin	Malawi
	20	Zambia	Zambia
▼	21	Eritrea	Swaziland
▲	22	Uganda	Burkina Faso
▲	23	Mozambique	Togo
▲	24	Ethiopia	Uganda
▲	25	Rwanda	Mozambique
	26	Djibouti	Djibouti
▼	27	Swaziland	Ethiopia
	28	Niger	Niger
▲	29	Comoros	Chad
	30	Kenya	Kenya
▼	31	Togo	Zimbabwe
▲	32	Cameroon	Côte d' Ivoire
▲	33	Sierra Leone	Cameroon
▲	34	Burundi	Guinea
▲	35	Guinea-Bissau	Comoros
▼	36	Chad	Rwanda
	37	Equatorial Guinea	Equatorial Guinea
▼	38	Guinea	Nigeria
▲	39	Congo, Rep.	Sierra Leone
▲	40	Angola	Central Afr. Rep.
▼	41	Nigeria	Congo, Rep.
▲	42	Liberia	Guinea-Bissau
▲	43	Sudan	Burundi
▼	44	Côte d' Ivoire	Sudan
▼	45	Central Afr. Rep.	Angola
▼	46	Zimbabwe	Liberia
	47	Congo, Dem. Rep.	Congo, Dem. Rep.
	48	Somalia	Somalia

16.6

Rule of Law: Nigeria's Ranking in SSA. 1998-2006

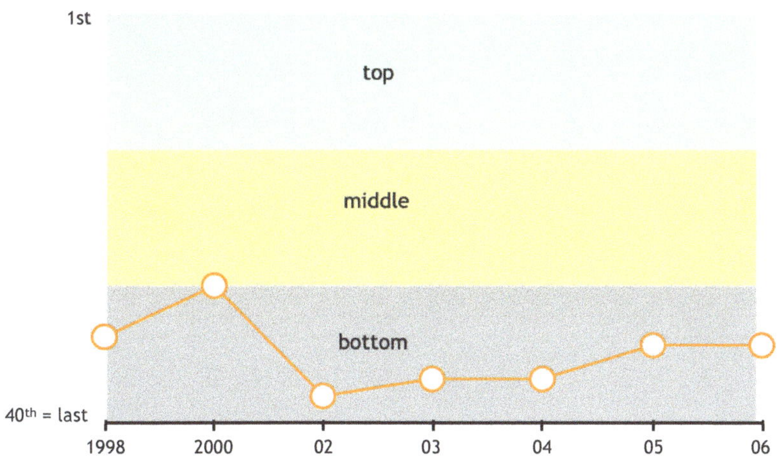

Brief climb-out attempt in 2000. Then a fall, back onto the bottom tier. During 03/06, only Liberia and Côte d'Ivoire did worse in West Africa.

16.9 Control of Corruption: Rank

disappearing act

Another tetchy topic, and another poor Nigeria showing. There was a cleaner climate everywhere else in West Africa.

	1998-02	2003-06
Self-comparison to Preceding Period		▼
Performance in Sub-Saharan Africa	▼	▼
Performance in West Africa	▼	▼
	Cape Verde	Cape Verde
	Burkina Faso	Burkina Faso
	Mauritania	Mauritania
	Senegal	Ghana
	Ghana	Senegal
	Gambia, The	Mali
	Mali	Gambia, The
	Côte d'Ivoire	Benin
	Togo	Togo
	Benin	Guinea
	Guinea	Niger
	Sierra Leone	Sierra Leone
	Guinea-Bissau	Guinea-Bissau
	Niger	Liberia
	Nigeria	Côte d'Ivoire
	Liberia	**Nigeria**
Performance among Oil-Exporters	▼	▼
	Côte d'Ivoire	Gabon
	Gabon	Cameroon
	Chad	Congo, Rep.
	Sudan	Côte d'Ivoire
	Congo, Rep.	Angola
	Cameroon	Chad
	Nigeria	Sudan
	Angola	**Nigeria**
	Equatorial Guinea	Equatorial Guinea

▲	improved *or* better than average
▼	worsened *or* worse than average
◁▷	no change *or* average

Rankings of 48 Sub-Saharan Africa Countries
Source: IBRD, World Bank

- Central Africa
- East Africa
- Southern Africa
- North Africa
- West Africa

▲	moved up from 98/02
▼	moved down from 98/02
blank	no change from 98/02

	Rank	2003-06	1998-2002
	1	Botswana	Botswana
▲	2	South Africa	Eritrea
▲	3	Cape Verde	South Africa
	4	Mauritius	Mauritius
	5	Seychelles	Seychelles
	6	Namibia	Namibia
▲	7	Madagascar	Cape Verde
	8	Burkina Faso	Burkina Faso
▲	9	Lesotho	Mauritania
▼	10	Eritrea	Swaziland
▼	11	Mauritania	Lesotho
▲	12	Ghana	Madagascar
	13	Senegal	Senegal
▲	14	Mali	Sao Tome & Princ.
▲	15	Rwanda	Ghana
▼	16	Swaziland	Gambia, The
▼	17	Gambia, The	Ethiopia
▲	18	Mozambique	Mali
▼	19	Ethiopia	Côte d' Ivoire
▲	20	Gabon	Malawi
▼	21	Sao Tome & Princ.	Gabon
▲	22	Tanzania	Togo
▲	23	Djibouti	Benin
▼	24	Benin	Mozambique
▲	25	Uganda	Rwanda
▼	26	Malawi	Guinea
▲	27	Comoros	Djibouti
▼	28	Togo	Chad
▲	29	Zambia	Sierra Leone
▼	30	Guinea	Zimbabwe
▲	31	Kenya	Zambia
▲	32	Cameroon	Guinea-Bissau
▲	33	Niger	Uganda
▲	34	Burundi	Sudan
▲	35	Congo, Rep.	Comoros
▼	36	Sierra Leone	Niger
▼	37	Guinea-Bissau	Tanzania
▲	38	Liberia	Kenya
▼	39	Côte d' Ivoire	Congo, Rep.
▲	40	Angola	Burundi
▲	41	Central Afr. Rep.	Cameroon
▼	42	Chad	Central Afr. Rep.
▼	43	Sudan	Nigeria
▼	44	Zimbabwe	Angola
▼	45	Nigeria	Somalia
	46	Congo, Dem. Rep.	Congo, Dem. Rep.
▲	47	Equatorial Guinea	Liberia
▼	48	Somalia	Equatorial Guinea

16.7

Control of Corruption: Nigeria's Ranking in SSA. 1998-2006

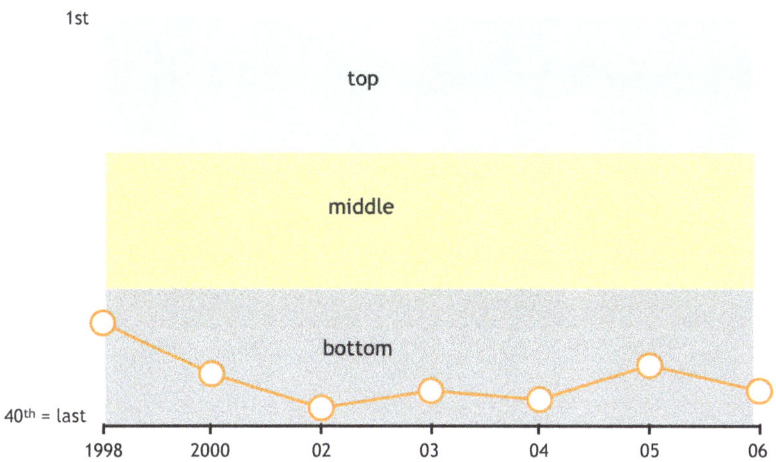

Stranded at the bottom.

Leaders & Stragglers

Never mind the red, it's mostly green

Business Friendliness Rankings: 2003-08

Rank	Country
1	Mauritius
2	Botswana
3	South Africa
4	Cape Verde
5	Namibia
6	Ghana
7	Madagascar
8	Senegal
9	Lesotho
10	Mali
11	Tanzania
12	Burkina Faso
13	Mozambique

TOP

Rank	Country
14	Gambia, The
15	Uganda
16	Kenya
17	Benin
18	Malawi
19	Swaziland
20	Zambia
21	Gabon
22	Rwanda
23	Niger
24	Ethiopia
25	Guinea-Bissau

MIDDLE

Rank	Country
26	Cameroon
27	Sierra Leone
28	**Nigeria**
29	Guinea
30	Angola
31	Togo
32	Equatorial Guinea
33	Burundi
34	Côte d' Ivoire
35	Congo, Rep.
36	Central Afr. Rep.
37	Chad
n/a	Comoros
n/a	Congo, Dem. Rep.
n/a	Eritrea
n/a	Seychelles

BOTTOM

Central Africa
East Africa
Southern Africa
West Africa

Many parameters here have already been represented in previous sections, so this end-table outcome doesn't go towards the final definitive rankings.

But it is still worth noting that Nigeria is 4th from bottom in West Africa & needs to make its business environment more endearing to stakeholders.

Cape Verde, Ghana, Senegal & Mali are the most business friendly environments in West Africa and count among the top 10 in Sub-Saharan Africa.

Wrap-up: Business Friendliness

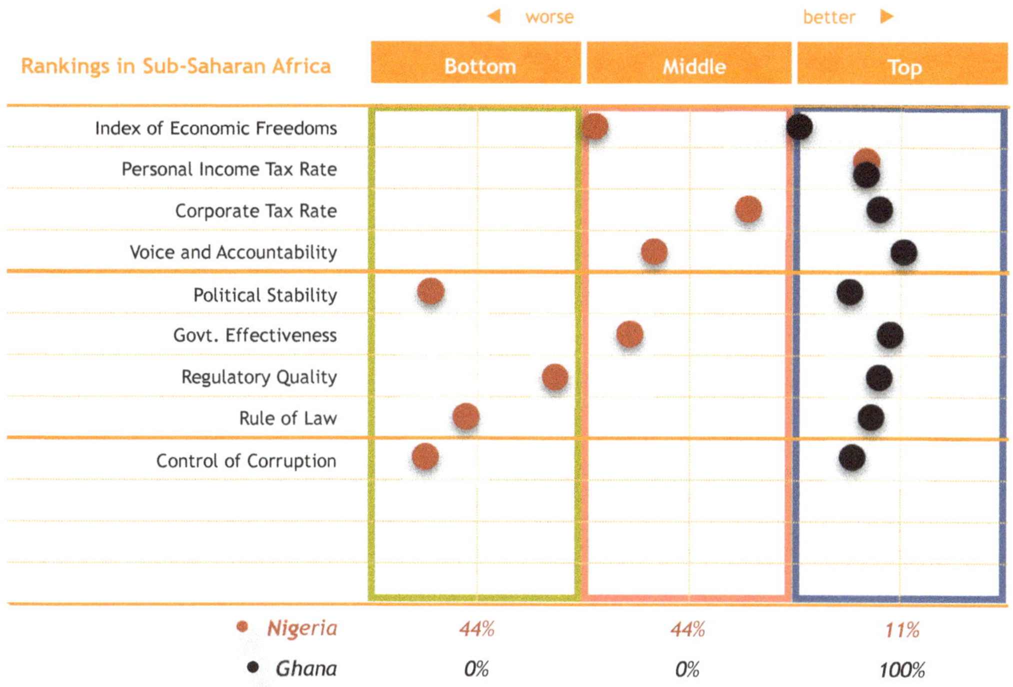

- Comparing Nigeria with Ghana this time, the reason for the gulf in friendliness ranking is easy to see. Ghana scores top-bracket performance in every area. Nigeria ends up mainly in the middle and bottom-brackets.

- Nigeria does best in level of personal income tax, followed by level of company taxes. But it is dragged down by very poor scores for political environment, rule of law and control of corruption.

- Ghana outdoes Nigeria in every measure and does best in voice & accountability. Then government effectiveness and company tax rates.

17. The Final Ratings

and the winners are...

Primer

The BiA Ranking and BiA Rating

This final chapter brings all the preceding analyses to a culmination. It assesses 41 Sub-Saharan Africa economies (out of 48) across 56 critical socio-economic indicators among the 200 employed for this compilation – the so-called BiA [Be-eye-ay] indicators. The outcome is the BiA Rankings and Ratings.

All 48 Sub-Saharan Africa economies are involved in this study, but 7 of the economies were missing data among the critical 56 indicators. They are Djibouti, Liberia, Mauritania, São Tomé & Príncipe, Somalia, Sudan and Zimbabwe. And so, they are not included in the ensuing BiA ranking and ratings.

(Note, though, that appendix B, which follows this chapter is exhaustive and carries individual tables for near all indicators employed in this study, including the 56 critical indices, showing how all the countries with that specific data available, stack up. Hence, wherever their data is at hand, the 7 countries absent from the final rankings, are also shown there, in the position they occupy according to their performance, although without final assigned ratings.)

Methodology

The procedure for this final rankings is straightforward: each of the book's main chapters ends with a final table-ranking of performance across the critical indicators in that chapter. The aggregate scores across these critical indicators, through all the main chapters, are evaluated, and rankings derived from the countries' relative performance positions. These are the *BiA Rankings*.

BiA Ratings range from one star to five stars, out of five. The country aggregate scores go from 0 for worst performance, to 10 for best performance. That range is divided into 5 equal sections, that is: 0 to 1.99, 2 to 3.99, 4 to 5.99, 6 to 7.99 and 8 to 10. These divisions carry the ratings of 1, 2, 3, 4 and 5 stars, respectively; all out of the maximum 5. A 5-star rating would mean "excellent", down to a 1-star rating meaning "worst".

Assessments, not Final Say

Please note that the BiA rankings and ratings are purely assessments according to a specific body of indicators and specific methods of evaluation, and they have been well described in the main chapters of this volume and in its appendices. They are not hard-and-fast apportionments, and do not attempt to recommend a particular country for specific business purposes.

Nonetheless, they are intended as a guide, while decisions or steps taken would be the responsibility of the business owners themselves. The *BiA Rankings* and *Ratings*, however, do have the immense advantage of being entirely transparent, so that where the user is familiar with aspects of a specific economy, they may feel comfortable to make allowances for that country's good or poor performance in a particular area, and effectively attach a weight to an indicator different from the equal weighting assigned across them in the BiA evaluation. The user may thereby make appropriate allowances for countries' performances in coming to a business decision, should they so wish.

(Please note that BiA Index, BiA Rank & BiA Rating are covered by extant patent, trademark and copyright laws.)

Tables

17.1 BiA Ranking by Rank

Rank	Country	Rating
1	Botswana	★★★★☆
2	South Africa	★★★★☆
3	Namibia	★★★★☆
4	Mauritius	★★★★☆
5	Cape Verde	★★★★☆
6	Equatorial Guinea	★★★★☆
7	Seychelles	★★★★☆
8	Ghana	★★★☆☆
9	Gabon	★★★☆☆
10	**Nigeria**	★★★☆☆
11	Senegal	★★★☆☆
12	Kenya	★★★☆☆
13	Tanzania	★★★☆☆
14	Angola	★★★☆☆

TOP

- Central Africa
- East Africa
- Southern Africa
- West Africa

Rank	Country	Rating
15	Swaziland	★★★☆☆
16	Lesotho	★★★☆☆
17	Uganda	★★★☆☆
18	Zambia	★★★☆☆
19	Gambia, The	★★★☆☆
20	Benin	★★★☆☆
21	Burkina Faso	★★★☆☆
22	Cameroon	★★★☆☆
23	Madagascar	★★★☆☆
24	Congo, Rep.	★★★☆☆
25	Ethiopia	★★★☆☆
26	Mali	★★★☆☆
27	Mozambique	★★★☆☆
28	Malawi	★★★☆☆

MIDDLE

Rank	Country	Rating
29	Chad	★★★☆☆
30	Rwanda	★★★☆☆
31	Togo	★★★☆☆
32	Côte d' Ivoire	★★★☆☆
33	Niger	★★☆☆☆
34	Sierra Leone	★★☆☆☆
35	Comoros	★★☆☆☆
36	Guinea	★★☆☆☆
37	Congo, Dem. Rep.	★★☆☆☆
38	Central Afr. Rep.	★★☆☆☆
39	Guinea-Bissau	★★☆☆☆
40	Eritrea	★★☆☆☆
41	Burundi	★★☆☆☆

BOTTOM

There are no 5-star finishers. But neither are there any 1-stars. Instead, the 41 countries breakdown like this: 7 4-stars, 25 3-stars & 9 2-stars.

Central Africa & East Africa have 2 countries each in the top-10. The bottom-10 has 2 Central Africans, 3 East Africans, & 5 West Africans.

Nigeria is in 10th place, & is the 3rd highest ranked West African country after Cape Verde & Ghana.

The top-10 involve countries from all 4 sub-regions, with the smallest, Southern Africa, and one of the largest, West Africa, leading with 3 countries each.

The 3 Southerners make up the top-3 places.

Africa's best 3 performers are Botswana, South Africa & Namibia, all Southern Africans. They are followed by Mauritius, Cape Verde, & Equatorial Guinea.

17.2 BiA Ranking by Rating

Rank	Country	Score	Rating
1	Botswana	6.985	★★★★☆
2	South Africa	6.941	★★★★☆
3	Namibia	6.779	★★★★☆
4	Mauritius	6.535	★★★★☆
5	Cape Verde	6.299	★★★★☆
6	Equatorial Guinea	6.275	★★★★☆
7	Seychelles	6.207	★★★★☆

7 countries: 17%

Central Africa
East Africa
Southern Africa
West Africa

Rank	Country	Score	Rating
8	Ghana	5.738	★★★☆☆
9	Gabon	5.696	★★★☆☆
10	Nigeria	5.548	★★★☆☆
11	Senegal	5.504	★★★☆☆
12	Kenya	5.461	★★★☆☆
13	Tanzania	5.37	★★★☆☆
14	Angola	5.283	★★★☆☆
15	Swaziland	5.096	★★★☆☆
16	Lesotho	5.025	★★★☆☆
17	Uganda	4.998	★★★☆☆
18	Zambia	4.985	★★★☆☆
19	Gambia, The	4.919	★★★☆☆
20	Benin	4.91	★★★☆☆
21	Burkina Faso	4.902	★★★☆☆
22	Cameroon	4.901	★★★☆☆
23	Madagascar	4.809	★★★☆☆
24	Congo, Rep.	4.759	★★★☆☆
25	Ethiopia	4.721	★★★☆☆
26	Mali	4.715	★★★☆☆
27	Mozambique	4.685	★★★☆☆
28	Malawi	4.528	★★★☆☆
29	Chad	4.452	★★★☆☆
30	Rwanda	4.402	★★★☆☆
31	Togo	4.235	★★★☆☆
32	Côte d' Ivoire	4.146	★★★☆☆

25 countries: 61%

Rank	Country	Score	Rating
33	Niger	3.738	★★☆☆☆
34	Sierra Leone	3.701	★★☆☆☆
35	Comoros	3.689	★★☆☆☆
36	Guinea	3.335	★★☆☆☆
37	Congo, Dem. Rep.	3.161	★★☆☆☆
38	Central Afr. Rep.	2.951	★★☆☆☆
39	Guinea-Bissau	2.935	★★☆☆☆
40	Eritrea	2.866	★★☆☆☆
41	Burundi	2.638	★★☆☆☆

9 countries: 22%

East and West Africa have the same number of countries among the 41: 14 each. And they break down across the 3 rating categories differently:

	4-stars	3-stars	2-stars
East	14%	64%	22%
West	7%	64%	29%

A large majority of the 41 countries fall into the 3-star rating category (61%), followed by the 2-star (22%), then the 4-star superior finishers (17%).

17.3 BiA Ranking by Country

Rank	Country	Rating
14	Angola	★★★☆☆
20	Benin	★★★☆☆
1	Botswana	★★★★☆
21	Burkina Faso	★★★☆☆
41	Burundi	★★☆☆☆
22	Cameroon	★★★☆☆
5	Cape Verde	★★★★☆
38	Central Afr. Rep.	★★☆☆☆
29	Chad	★★★☆☆
35	Comoros	★★☆☆☆
37	Congo, Dem. Rep.	★★☆☆☆
24	Congo, Rep.	★★★☆☆
32	Côte d' Ivoire	★★★☆☆
6	Equatorial Guinea	★★★★☆
40	Eritrea	★★☆☆☆
25	Ethiopia	★★★☆☆
9	Gabon	★★★☆☆
19	Gambia, The	★★★☆☆
8	Ghana	★★★☆☆
36	Guinea	★★☆☆☆
39	Guinea-Bissau	★★☆☆☆

Rank	Country	Rating
12	Kenya	★★★☆☆
16	Lesotho	★★★☆☆
23	Madagascar	★★★☆☆
28	Malawi	★★★☆☆
26	Mali	★★★☆☆
4	Mauritius	★★★★☆
27	Mozambique	★★★☆☆
3	Namibia	★★★★☆
33	Niger	★★☆☆☆
10	Nigeria	★★★☆☆
30	Rwanda	★★★☆☆
11	Senegal	★★★☆☆
7	Seychelles	★★★★☆
34	Sierra Leone	★★☆☆☆
2	South Africa	★★★★☆
15	Swaziland	★★★☆☆
13	Tanzania	★★★☆☆
31	Togo	★★★☆☆
17	Uganda	★★★☆☆
18	Zambia	★★★☆☆

- Central Africa
- East Africa
- Southern Africa
- West Africa

nice country, that

17.4 BiA Ranking by Sub-Region

Rank	Country	Rating
6	Equatorial Guinea	★★★★☆
9	Gabon	★★★☆☆
14	Angola	★★★☆☆
22	Cameroon	★★★☆☆
24	Congo, Rep.	★★★☆☆
29	Chad	★★★☆☆
37	Congo, Dem. Rep.	★★☆☆☆
38	Central Afr. Rep.	★★☆☆☆

CENTRAL AFRICA

Rank	Country	Rating
5	Cape Verde	★★★★☆
8	Ghana	★★★☆☆
10	Nigeria	★★★☆☆
11	Senegal	★★★☆☆
19	Gambia, The	★★★☆☆
20	Benin	★★★☆☆
21	Burkina Faso	★★★☆☆
26	Mali	★★★☆☆
31	Togo	★★★☆☆
32	Côte d' Ivoire	★★★☆☆
33	Niger	★★☆☆☆
34	Sierra Leone	★★☆☆☆
36	Guinea	★★☆☆☆
39	Guinea-Bissau	★★☆☆☆

WEST AFRICA

Rank	Country	Rating
4	Mauritius	★★★★☆
7	Seychelles	★★★★☆
12	Kenya	★★★☆☆
13	Tanzania	★★★☆☆
17	Uganda	★★★☆☆
18	Zambia	★★★☆☆
23	Madagascar	★★★☆☆
25	Ethiopia	★★★☆☆
27	Mozambique	★★★☆☆
28	Malawi	★★★☆☆
30	Rwanda	★★★☆☆
35	Comoros	★★☆☆☆
40	Eritrea	★★☆☆☆
41	Burundi	★★☆☆☆

EAST AFRICA

Rank	Country	Rating
1	Botswana	★★★★☆
2	South Africa	★★★★☆
3	Namibia	★★★★☆
15	Swaziland	★★★☆☆
16	Lesotho	★★★☆☆

SOUTHERN AFRICA

The top 6 economies in Central Africa - out of 8 - are oil exporters.

Not so in West Africa, where there are 2 oil exporters — Nigeria & Côte d'Ivoire — and they end up far apart. Quite likely a result of the civil war in Côte d'Ivoire.

All the sub-regions, save Southern Africa, have their countries spanning across three tiers of performance: 4-star, 3-star and 2-star.

Only Southern Africa has a majority of its countries chalking up a 4-star rating. It is the smallest sub-region, though.

	4-stars	3-stars	2-stars
Central	12%	63%	25%
East	14%	64%	22%
Southern	60%	40%	0%
West	7%	64%	29%

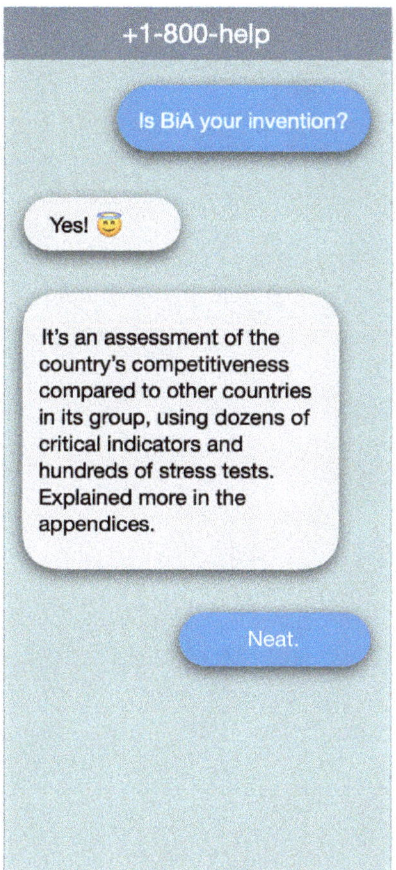
+1-800-help
Is BiA your invention?
Yes!
It's an assessment of the country's competitiveness compared to other countries in its group, using dozens of critical indicators and hundreds of stress tests. Explained more in the appendices.
Neat.

Part III

Appendices

A BiA Index & Rankings & Ratings

The BiA [be-eye-ay] Index is an assessment of the economic and business environment prevailing in the countries that make up Sub-Saharan Africa. The letters stand for **B**usiness in **A**frica and it is the first assessment and innovation of the sort.

The index ranges from zero to 10, representing worst and best, and it expresses the countries' performance across an array of relevant parameters, evaluated over the latest continuous four years with definitive data, within the preceding 6 years in the build-up to the index's reference year. In other words, BiA 2009-2010 considers country performance across 2003 to 2009, using any continuous four years during the period with confirmed and not provisional data. This is done with a view to presenting accurate scenarios and persisting trends that are of importance to investors, businesses, governments and other myriad purposes for which a clear and concise picture of the region's economic and social situation is crucial.

56 "Critical" Indicators

A total of 56 "critical" macro and socio-economic indices are employed, selected from the 200 involved in the in-depth compilation of country analyses in the book. All of them are taken from the latest data held by various leading multilateral agencies like the World Bank and the World Health Organization, that is available at the time of evaluation. The sources of these indicators are always identified.

In almost every case, these indices are analyzed and adapted to enable a comparative evaluation of each country in the context of the sub-continent. So, for example, rather than use just size of GDP outright for cross-country comparisons, GDP per person of population is applied, instead. That is a more accurate measure of country output; what is being assessed there is the efficiency with which the country deploys its resources and factors of production in producing the volume of GDP. Otherwise, countries like Nigeria and South Africa would stand out for the sheer volume of their GDP, whereas, when that performance is rated across their populations, South Africa ranks considerably higher than Nigeria, in terms of GDP per person of population. That ranking shows that economic productivity in South Africa is more efficient and robust.

The same applies to Foreign Direct Investment (FDI), Manufacturing Output, etc. They are all better evaluated as a proportion of either the overall size of the economy (percentage of GDP) or its population (per person). In effect, ratios are the important parameters for comparison.

11 Specific Areas

These 56 indicators come from the same 11 areas of assessment into which we have split the countries' broad spectrum of economic and national life, as would interest the business practitioner or other user of the index:

- General size
- Quality of life
- Economic strength
- Economic productivity
- Government earning and spending
- Spending on health
- Purchasing power
- Self-reliance
- Investor confidence
- Regulatory environment
- Business friendliness

Methodology

(This is protected by relevant patent, copyright and trademark laws.)

All the countries are ranked for each of the 56 indices, based on their performance in the specific area during four years leading to the BiA publication year. So, for instance, 'BiA 2009-2010' involves the countries' performance with respect to each index, across the latest 4 contiguous years of definitive data between 2003 and 2009. The same four years are applied for the same indicator across all the countries, so that every country's performance is evaluated for the same base years.

The highest ranking would imply the best performing, and the lowest the worst performing, of the 48 countries that make up Sub-Saharan Africa. In the end, each country's aggregate ranking across the entire spectrum of 56 indices would be its BiA index for that reference year.

It is clear, therefore, that BiA is not an absolute scoring of country performance, but is instead an assessment of the country's performance relative to others in the Sub-Saharan Africa region. In other words, while a country may perform well or poorly in a given sector, its overall relative score would help express its performance in a total context, which – in the end – is usually what matters for investors and businesses.

41 of the Continent's 48 Countries

However, not every country had sufficient data available for a BiA evaluation. Our criterion was that missing data must not constitute more than 5% of the total applied; in this case, 3 out of 56. Domestic data from the individual countries (usually their Office of Statistics and Central Banks) was deliberately avoided, as this was not likely to provide a satisfactory common and objective basis for cross-country comparison and assessment. It was important to use external and "detached" assessors, which the multilaterals like the IMF, World Bank, UNICEF and so on, suitably represent.

7 of the 48 countries ended up outside the scope of BiA 2009-2010, for insufficient data. They are: Djibouti, Liberia, Mauritania, Sao Tome & Principe, Somalia, Sudan and Zimbabwe. However, these seven countries are assessed in every indicator for which they had data, and their performance can be gleaned from the respective indicator ranking tables supplied in the body of the book and in appendix B.

Unequivocal, yet Flexible

It should be borne in mind, though, that while the BiA Index is a wide-spanning comparative assessment of country performance, other factors about a particular country that ranks poorly (whether out of the 41 included or the 7 omitted) might still recommend them for whatever purpose the investor or user is concerned with. Their specific performance in a particular area can be seen in the rest of the book and might very well be a deciding factor.

One advantage of our BiA Index is that its procedure is transparent, and its user may choose to adapt it further to their needs by assigning a weight or level of importance to particular areas different from that which the index itself assumed. (So far, the 56 indices carry equal weighting; this will be adjusted as appropriate over subsequent BiA editions.)

To the best of our knowledge, there isn't yet anywhere else, as comprehensive and rigorous a ranking as the BiA Index, None provides a level comparable to its in-depth macro and socio-economy wide comparative evaluations of country performance in Africa.

B1 performance tables – region overview

Surface Area

largest	1	Sudan
	2	Congo, Dem. Rep.
	3	Chad
	4	Niger
	5	Angola
	6	Mali
	7	South Africa
	8	Ethiopia
	9	Mauritania
	10	Tanzania
	11	Nigeria
	12	Namibia
	13	Mozambique
	14	Zambia
	15	Somalia
	16	Central African Rep.
	17	Madagascar
	18	Botswana
	19	Kenya
	20	Cameroon
	21	Zimbabwe
	22	Congo, Rep.
	23	Cote d'Ivoire
	24	Burkina Faso
	25	Gabon
	26	Guinea
	27	Uganda
	28	Ghana
	29	Senegal
	30	Malawi
	31	Eritrea
	32	Benin
	33	Liberia
	34	Sierra Leone
	35	Togo
	36	Guinea-Bissau
	37	Lesotho
	38	Equatorial Guinea
	39	Burundi
	40	Rwanda
	41	Djibouti
	42	Swaziland
	43	Gambia, The
	44	Cape Verde
	45	Comoros
	46	Mauritius
	47	Sao Tome & Principe
	48	Seychelles
smallest		

Population

IMF estimates

		2009
largest	1	Nigeria
	2	Ethiopia
	3	Congo, Dem. Rep.
	4	South Africa
	5	Tanzania
	6	Sudan
	7	Kenya
	8	Uganda
	9	Ghana
	10	Mozambique
	11	Cameroon
	12	Cote d'Ivoire
	13	Madagascar
	14	Angola
	15	Burkina Faso
	16	Niger
	17	Malawi
	18	Mali
	19	Senegal
	20	Zambia
	21	Guinea
	22	Chad
	23	Rwanda
	24	Benin
	25	Burundi
	26	Togo
	27	Sierra Leone
	28	Eritrea
	29	Central African Rep.
	30	Liberia
	31	Congo, Rep.
	32	Mauritania
	33	Lesotho
	34	Namibia
	35	Guinea-Bissau
	36	Gambia, The
	37	Botswana
	38	Gabon
	39	Mauritius
	40	Equatorial Guinea
	41	Swaziland
	42	Djibouti
	43	Comoros
	44	Cape Verde
	45	Sao Tome & Principe
	46	Seychelles
	n/a	Somalia
	n/a	Zimbabwe
smallest		

Population Density

UNPD estimates

		2005-2010
most dense	1	Mauritius
	2	Comoros
	3	Rwanda
	4	Burundi
	5	Sao Tome & Principe
	6	Nigeria
	7	Gambia, The
	8	Cape Verde
	9	Uganda
	10	Malawi
	11	Togo
	12	Ghana
	13	Sierra Leone
	14	Benin
	15	Ethiopia
	16	Lesotho
	16	Swaziland
	17	Kenya
	18	Senegal
	19	Cote d'Ivoire
	20	Burkina Faso
	21	Guinea-Bissau
	22	Tanzania
	23	Eritrea
	24	South Africa
	25	Cameroon
	25	Guinea
	26	Djibouti
	27	Liberia
	28	Zimbabwe
	29	Madagascar
	30	Congo, Dem. Rep.
	30	Mozambique
	31	Equatorial Guinea
	32	Zambia
	33	Sudan
	34	Angola
	34	Somalia
	35	Congo, Rep.
	36	Niger
	37	Mali
	38	Chad
	39	Central African Rep.
	40	Gabon
	41	Botswana
	41	Mauritania
	42	Namibia
least dense	n/a	Seychelles

Urban Population

UNPD estimates

		2005-2010
largest	1	Nigeria
	2	South Africa
	3	Congo, Dem. Rep.
	4	Sudan
	5	Ethiopia
	6	Ghana
	7	Cameroon
	8	Tanzania
	9	Angola
	10	Cote d'Ivoire
	11	Kenya
	12	Mozambique
	13	Madagascar
	14	Senegal
	15	Zimbabwe
	16	Zambia
	17	Uganda
	18	Mali
	19	Benin
	20	Guinea
	21	Somalia
	22	Burkina Faso
	23	Chad
	24	Togo
	25	Malawi
	26	Niger
	27	Congo, Rep.
	28	Liberia
	29	Sierra Leone
	30	Rwanda
	31	Central African Rep.
	32	Mauritania
	33	Gabon
	34	Botswana
	35	Eritrea
	36	Gambia, The
	37	Burundi
	38	Namibia
	39	Djibouti
	40	Mauritius
	41	Guinea-Bissau
	42	Lesotho
	43	Cape Verde
	44	Swaziland
	45	Comoros
	46	Equatorial Guinea
	47	Sao Tome & Principe
	48	Seychelles
smallest		

Urban % of Total Population

UNPD estimates

		2005-2010
highest	1	Djibouti
	2	Gabon
	3	Congo, Rep.
	4	South Africa
	5	Sao Tome & Principe
	6	Liberia
	7	Cape Verde
	8	Botswana
	9	Cameroon
	10	Angola
	11	Gambia, The
	12	Seychelles
	13	Ghana
	14	Cote d'Ivoire
	15	Nigeria
	16	Sudan
	17	Mauritius
	18	Senegal
	19	Togo
	20	Benin
	21	Mauritania
	22	Equatorial Guinea
	23	Central African Rep.
	24	Sierra Leone
	25	Zimbabwe
	26	Namibia
	27	Mozambique
	28	Somalia
	29	Zambia
		SSA average
	30	Guinea
	31	Congo, Dem. Rep.
	32	Mali
	33	Guinea-Bissau
	34	Madagascar
	35	Comoros
	36	Chad
	37	Tanzania
	38	Lesotho
	39	Swaziland
	40	Kenya
	41	Eritrea
	42	Burkina Faso
	43	Malawi
	44	Rwanda
	45	Ethiopia
	46	Niger
	47	Uganda
lowest	48	Burundi

Growth Rate of Urban Population

UNPD estimates

		2005-2010
highest	1	Burundi
	2	Liberia
	3	Eritrea
	4	Malawi
	5	Congo, Dem. Rep.
	6	Burkina Faso
	7	Mali
	8	Chad
	9	Angola
	9	Uganda
	10	Togo
	11	Sudan
	11	Ethiopia
	12	Rwanda
	13	Tanzania
	14	Somalia
	15	Gambia, The
	16	Mozambique
	17	Benin
	18	Kenya
	19	Niger
	20	Madagascar
	21	Nigeria
		SSA average
	22	Guinea
	23	Lesotho
	24	Ghana
	24	Cape Verde
	25	Cameroon
	26	Guinea-Bissau
	27	Cote d'Ivoire
	28	Senegal
	29	Mauritania
	30	Sao Tome & Principe
	31	Namibia
	32	Sierra Leone
	33	Equatorial Guinea
	34	Congo, Rep.
	35	Comoros
	36	Botswana
	37	Zambia
	38	Central African Rep.
	39	Zimbabwe
	40	Djibouti
	41	Gabon
	42	Swaziland
	43	Seychelles
	44	South Africa
lowest	45	Mauritius

Rural Population

UNPD estimates

		2005-2010
largest	1	Nigeria
	2	Ethiopia
	3	Congo, Dem. Rep.
	4	Tanzania
	5	Kenya
	6	Uganda
	7	Sudan
	8	South Africa
	9	Madagascar
	10	Mozambique
	11	Niger
	12	Burkina Faso
	13	Ghana
	14	Malawi
	15	Cote d'Ivoire
	16	Mali
	17	Zimbabwe
	18	Cameroon
	19	Rwanda
	20	Chad
	21	Burundi
	22	Zambia
	23	Angola
	24	Senegal
	25	Guinea
	26	Somalia
	27	Benin
	28	Eritrea
	29	Togo
	30	Sierra Leone
	31	Central African Rep.
	32	Mauritania
	33	Liberia
	34	Lesotho
	35	Congo, Rep.
	36	Namibia
	37	Guinea-Bissau
	38	Swaziland
	39	Botswana
	40	Gambia, The
	41	Mauritius
	42	Comoros
	43	Equatorial Guinea
	44	Cape Verde
	45	Gabon
	46	Djibouti
	47	Sao Tome & Principe
	48	Seychelles
smallest		

Rural % of Total Population

UNPD estimates

		2005-2010
highest	1	Burundi
	2	Uganda
	3	Niger
	4	Ethiopia
	5	Rwanda
	6	Malawi
	7	Burkina Faso
	8	Eritrea
	9	Kenya
	10	Swaziland
	11	Lesotho
	12	Tanzania
	13	Chad
	14	Comoros
	15	Madagascar
	16	Guinea-Bissau
	17	Mali
	18	Congo, Dem. Rep.
	19	Guinea
	20	Zambia
		SSA average
	21	Somalia
	22	Mozambique
	23	Namibia
	24	Zimbabwe
	25	Sierra Leone
	26	Central African Rep.
	27	Equatorial Guinea
	28	Mauritania
	29	Benin
	30	Togo
	31	Senegal
	32	Mauritius
	33	Sudan
	34	Nigeria
	35	Cote d'Ivoire
	36	Ghana
	37	Seychelles
	38	Gambia, The
	39	Angola
	40	Cameroon
	41	Botswana
	42	Cape Verde
	43	Liberia
	44	Sao Tome & Principe
	45	South Africa
	46	Congo, Rep.
	47	Gabon
lowest	48	Djibouti

Growth Rate of Rural Population

UNPD estimates

	2005-2010	
highest	1	Burundi
	2	Niger
	3	Uganda
	4	Guinea-Bissau
	5	Liberia
	6	Eritrea
	7	Rwanda
	8	Burkina Faso
	8	Comoros
	9	Benin
	10	Kenya
	11	Congo, Dem. Rep.
	12	Chad
	13	Somalia
	14	Madagascar
	15	Mali
	15	Mauritania
	16	Ethiopia
	17	Equatorial Guinea
	18	Senegal
	19	Malawi
	20	Tanzania
	21	Zambia
		SSA average
	22	Central African Rep.
	23	Sierra Leone
	24	Togo
	25	Guinea
	26	Congo, Rep.
	27	Nigeria
	28	Mozambique
	29	Angola
	29	Gambia, The
	30	Mauritius
	31	Sudan
	32	Cote d'Ivoire
	33	Ghana
	34	Cape Verde
	35	Namibia
	36	Swaziland
	37	Zimbabwe
	38	Cameroon
	39	Lesotho
	40	Sao Tome & Principe
	41	Seychelles
	42	Botswana
	43	South Africa
	44	Djibouti
lowest	45	Gabon

GDP $PPP

IMF estimates

	2009	
largest	1	South Africa
	2	Nigeria
	3	Angola
	4	Sudan
	5	Ethiopia
	6	Kenya
	7	Tanzania
	8	Cameroon
	9	Ghana
	10	Cote d'Ivoire
	11	Uganda
	12	Botswana
	13	Senegal
	14	Congo, Dem. Rep.
	15	Gabon
	16	Madagascar
	17	Mozambique
	18	Burkina Faso
	19	Zambia
	20	Equatorial Guinea
	21	Chad
	22	Congo, Rep.
	23	Mauritius
	24	Mali
	25	Benin
	26	Malawi
	27	Guinea
	28	Namibia
	29	Niger
	30	Rwanda
	31	Mauritania
	32	Swaziland
	33	Togo
	34	Sierra Leone
	35	Eritrea
	36	Lesotho
	37	Central African Rep.
	38	Burundi
	39	Gambia, The
	40	Djibouti
	41	Cape Verde
	42	Liberia
	43	Seychelles
	44	Guinea-Bissau
	45	Comoros
	46	Sao Tome & Principe
	n/a	Somalia
	n/a	Zimbabwe
smallest		

Economic Productivity

Primary data: IMF

	2009	
highest	1	Botswana
	2	Seychelles
	3	Gabon
	4	Equatorial Guinea
	5	Mauritius
	6	South Africa
	7	Angola
	8	Namibia
	9	Swaziland
	10	Congo, Rep.
	11	Cape Verde
	12	Sudan
	13	Djibouti
	14	Nigeria
	15	Mauritania
	16	Cameroon
	17	Cote d'Ivoire
	18	Senegal
	19	Kenya
	20	Sao Tome & Principe
	21	Chad
	22	Benin
	23	Ghana
	24	Gambia, The
	25	Zambia
	26	Tanzania
	27	Lesotho
	28	Burkina Faso
	29	Madagascar
	30	Comoros
	31	Guinea
	32	Mali
	33	Uganda
	34	Rwanda
	35	Mozambique
	36	Ethiopia
	37	Malawi
	38	Togo
	39	Central African Rep.
	40	Eritrea
	41	Sierra Leone
	42	Niger
	43	Guinea-Bissau
	44	Burundi
	45	Liberia
	46	Congo, Dem. Rep.
	n/a	Somalia
	n/a	Zimbabwe
lowest		

Female % of the Labour Force

World Bank

	2006	
highest	1	Mozambique
	2	Burundi
	3	Rwanda
	4	Malawi
	5	Tanzania
	6	Mali
	7	Uganda
	8	Madagascar
	9	Ghana
	10	Guinea
	11	Burkina Faso
	12	Chad
	13	Central African Rep.
	14	Angola
	15	Ethiopia
	16	Kenya
	17	Namibia
	18	Zimbabwe
	19	Lesotho
	20	Gabon
	21	Zambia
	22	Niger
		SSA average
	23	Congo, Dem. Rep.
	24	Senegal
	25	Eritrea
	26	Gambia, The
	27	Guinea-Bissau
	28	Botswana
	29	Congo, Rep.
	30	Comoros
	31	Liberia
	32	Cameroon
	33	Djibouti
	34	Somalia
	35	Mauritania
	36	Sierra Leone
	37	Benin
	38	South Africa
	39	Equatorial Guinea
	40	Togo
	41	Mauritius
	42	Nigeria
	43	Cape Verde
	44	Swaziland
	45	Cote d'Ivoire
	46	Sao Tome & Principe
	47	Sudan
lowest	n/a	Seychelles

	Human Development Index UNDP			Life Expectancy Primary data: UNICEF			Under-5 Child Mortality Primary data: UNICEF	
	2003-2005			2003-2006			2003-2006	
high	1	Seychelles	*high life*	1	Mauritius	*least*	1	Seychelles
development	2	Mauritius	*expecta*	2	Cape Verde	*deaths*	2	Mauritius
index	3	Cape Verde	*ncy*	3	Sao Tome & Principe		3	Cape Verde
	4	South Africa		4	Comoros		4	Namibia
	5	Gabon		5	Ghana		5	South Africa
	6	Equatorial Guinea		6	Senegal		6	Comoros
	7	Namibia		6	Sudan		7	Eritrea
	7	São Tomé & Príncipe		7	Gambia, The		8	Sudan
	8	Botswana		8	Madagascar		9	Gabon
	9	Comoros		9	Mauritania		10	Lesotho
	10	Ghana		10	Gabon		11	Ghana
	11	Congo, Rep.		11	Eritrea		12	Congo, Rep.
	12	Sudan		12	Togo		12	Sao Tome & Principe
	13	Madagascar		13	Benin		13	Botswana
	14	Swaziland		14	Guinea		14	Madagascar
	15	Cameroon		15	Congo, Rep.		14	Kenya
	16	Lesotho		16	Djibouti		15	Zimbabwe
	17	Togo		17	Mali		16	Gambia, The
	17	Uganda		18	Burkina Faso		17	Senegal
	18	Mauritania		18	Ethiopia		17	Djibouti
	19	Zimbabwe		18	Uganda		17	Togo
	20	Djibouti		19	Kenya		18	Tanzania
		SSA average		20	Niger		19	Uganda
	21	Kenya		21	South Africa		20	Mauritania
	22	Gambia, The		22	Namibia		21	Mozambique
	23	Senegal		22	Somalia		22	Malawi
	24	Eritrea		23	Cameroon		23	Benin
	24	Nigeria			SSA average		24	Cameroon
	25	Guinea		24	Tanzania		25	Ethiopia
	26	Rwanda		25	Equatorial Guinea		26	Guinea
	27	Angola		25	Nigeria		27	Swaziland
	28	Tanzania		26	Chad			SSA average
	29	Benin		27	Côte d'Ivoire		28	Côte d'Ivoire
	30	Côte d'Ivoire		27	Guinea-Bissau		29	Zambia
	31	Malawi		28	Burundi		30	Central African Rep.
	32	Zambia		29	Congo, Dem. Rep.		31	Burundi
	33	Congo, Dem. Rep.		30	Rwanda		32	Equatorial Guinea
	34	Burundi		31	Liberia		33	Rwanda
	35	Mozambique		32	Malawi		34	Nigeria
	36	Ethiopia		33	Angola		35	Burkina Faso
	37	Central African Rep.		33	Mozambique		36	Guinea-Bissau
	37	Chad		34	Central African Rep.		37	Chad
	38	Guinea-Bissau		35	Sierra Leone		38	Congo, Dem. Rep.
	39	Mali		36	Botswana		38	Somalia
	40	Burkina Faso		37	Zambia		39	Mali
	41	Niger		38	Zimbabwe		40	Liberia
low	42	Sierra Leone	*low life*	39	Lesotho		41	Niger
development	n/a	Liberia	*expecta*	40	Swaziland	*most*	42	Angola
index	n/a	Somalia	*ncy*	n/a	Seychelles	*deaths*	43	Sierra Leone

% of 1-yr olds Immunised against Measles

Primary data: UNICEF

	Rank	2003-2006
highest	1	Seychelles
	2	Mauritius
	3	Tanzania
	4	Botswana
	5	Gambia, The
	6	Rwanda
	7	Sao Tome & Principe
	8	Uganda
	9	Eritrea
	10	Benin
	11	Zambia
	12	Zimbabwe
	13	Ghana
	13	South Africa
	14	Burkina Faso
	15	Malawi
	16	Mali
	17	Lesotho
	18	Mozambique
	19	Burundi
	20	Kenya
	21	Liberia
	22	Comoros
	23	Guinea-Bissau
	23	Swaziland
	23	Togo
	24	Namibia
	25	Senegal
	25	Sierra Leone
	26	Niger
	27	Cape Verde
	28	Cameroon
		SSA average
	29	Congo, Dem. Rep.
	30	Djibouti
	30	Mauritania
	31	Guinea
	32	Sudan
	33	Ethiopia
	34	Congo, Rep.
	35	Madagascar
	36	Côte d'Ivoire
	37	Gabon
	38	Angola
	39	Equatorial Guinea
	40	Nigeria
	41	Chad
	42	Somalia
lowest	43	Central African Rep.

% of 1-yr olds Immunised against Tuberculosis

Primary data: UNICEF

	Rank	2003-2006
highest	1	Benin
	1	Botswana
	1	Seychelles
	2	Sao Tome & Principe
	3	South Africa
	4	Mauritius
	5	Zimbabwe
	6	Malawi
	7	Gambia, The
	7	Ghana
	8	Burkina Faso
	9	Zambia
	10	Eritrea
	10	Tanzania
	10	Uganda
	11	Togo
	12	Rwanda
	12	Senegal
	13	Lesotho
	14	Gabon
	15	Kenya
	16	Mozambique
	17	Namibia
	18	Mauritania
	18	Swaziland
	19	Burundi
	19	Sierra Leone
	20	Guinea-Bissau
	21	Guinea
	22	Comoros
	23	Cameroon
	24	Congo, Dem. Rep.
		SSA average
	25	Congo, Rep.
	26	Cape Verde
	26	Mali
	27	Ethiopia
	28	Niger
	29	Equatorial Guinea
	30	Madagascar
	31	Djibouti
	32	Central African Rep.
	33	Liberia
	34	Angola
	35	Côte d'Ivoire
	36	Sudan
	37	Somalia
	38	Nigeria
lowest	39	Chad

% of Population with Access to Safe Water

Primary data: UNICEF

	Rank	2004-2006
highest	1	Mauritius
	2	Botswana
	3	Gabon
	3	Seychelles
	4	Namibia
	5	Comoros
	6	South Africa
	7	Côte d'Ivoire
	8	Gambia, The
	9	Zimbabwe
	10	Cape Verde
	11	Burundi
	11	Lesotho
	11	Sao Tome & Principe
	12	Senegal
	13	Ghana
	14	Malawi
	14	Rwanda
	15	Djibouti
	16	Sudan
	17	Benin
	17	Uganda
	18	Cameroon
	19	Central African Rep.
	20	Liberia
	20	Swaziland
	20	Tanzania
	21	Burkina Faso
	21	Kenya
	22	Eritrea
	23	Guinea-Bissau
	24	Congo, Rep.
	24	Zambia
	25	Sierra Leone
	26	Angola
	26	Mauritania
	27	Togo
	28	Nigeria
	29	Guinea
	29	Madagascar
	29	Mali
	30	Congo, Dem. Rep.
	30	Niger
	31	Equatorial Guinea
	31	Mozambique
	32	Chad
	33	Somalia
	34	Ethiopia
lowest		

% of Population with Access to Sanitation

Primary data: UNICEF

	Rank	2004-2006
highest	1	Mauritius
	2	Djibouti
	3	South Africa
	4	Malawi
	5	Senegal
	6	Zambia
	7	Equatorial Guinea
	7	Gambia, The
	7	Zimbabwe
	8	Cameroon
	9	Swaziland
	10	Tanzania
	11	Mali
	12	Nigeria
	13	Cape Verde
	13	Kenya
	13	Uganda
	14	Botswana
	14	Rwanda
	15	Sierra Leone
	16	Côte d'Ivoire
	16	Lesotho
	17	Burundi
	17	Gabon
	18	Guinea-Bissau
	18	Togo
	19	Madagascar
	19	Mauritania
	19	Sudan
	20	Benin
	20	Comoros
	21	Mozambique
	22	Angola
	23	Congo, Dem. Rep.
	24	Central African Rep.
	24	Congo, Rep.
	24	Liberia
	25	Somalia
	26	Namibia
	26	Sao Tome & Principe
	27	Ghana
	27	Guinea
	28	Burkina Faso
	28	Ethiopia
	28	Niger
	29	Chad
	29	Eritrea
	n/a	Seychelles
lowest		

Total Number of Phone Subscribers (fixed & mobile) per 100 persons of Population

ITU

	Rank	2007
highest	1	Mauritius
	2	Seychelles
	3	Cape Verde
	4	South Africa
	5	Botswana
	6	Namibia
	7	Sao Tome & Principe
	8	Gambia, The
	9	Nigeria
	10	Swaziland
	11	Lesotho
	12	Gabon
	13	Zimbabwe
	14	Comoros
	15	Senegal
	16	Equatorial Guinea
		SSA average
	17	Ghana
	18	Djibouti
	19	Côte d'Ivoire
	20	Togo
	21	Malawi
	22	Benin
	23	Somalia
	24	Mauritania
	25	Ethiopia
	26	Sudan
	27	Eritrea
	28	Cameroon
	29	Zambia
	30	Kenya
	31	Burkina Faso
	32	Mali
	33	Madagascar
	34	Angola
	35	Tanzania
	36	Uganda
	37	Burundi
	38	Congo, Rep.
	39	Guinea
	39	Mozambique
	40	Central African Rep.
	41	Guinea-Bissau
	42	Rwanda
	43	Niger
	44	Chad
	45	Congo, Dem. Rep.
	n/a	Liberia
lowest	n/a	Sierra Leone

Number of Mobile Phone Subscribers per 100 persons of Population

ITU

	2007	
highest	1	Seychelles
	2	Gabon
	3	South Africa
	4	Botswana
	5	Mauritius
	6	Gambia, The
	7	Equatorial Guinea
	8	Mauritania
	9	Namibia
	10	Côte d'Ivoire
	11	Congo, Rep.
	12	Senegal
	13	Swaziland
	14	Ghana
	15	Kenya
	16	Cape Verde
	17	Nigeria
	18	Cameroon
	19	Lesotho
	20	Zambia
	21	Benin
	22	Tanzania
	23	Mali
	24	Angola
	25	Sudan
	26	Sao Tome & Principe
		SSA average
	27	Togo
	28	Guinea-Bissau
	29	Mozambique
	30	Liberia
	31	Uganda
	32	Sierra Leone
	33	Madagascar
	34	Burkina Faso
	35	Congo, Dem. Rep.
	36	Zimbabwe
	37	Chad
	38	Malawi
	39	Rwanda
	40	Somalia
	41	Niger
	42	Djibouti
	43	Comoros
	44	Central African Rep.
	45	Burundi
	46	Guinea
	47	Ethiopia
lowest	48	Eritrea

Total Adult Literacy Rate

AfDB

	2007	
highest	1	Zimbabwe
	2	Equatorial Guinea
	3	Kenya
	4	South Africa
	5	Congo, Rep.
	6	Mauritius
	7	Namibia
	8	Lesotho
	9	Swaziland
	10	Zambia
	11	Botswana
	12	Tanzania
	13	Cape Verde
	14	Ghana
	15	Cameroon
	16	Rwanda
	17	Uganda
	18	Nigeria
	19	Djibouti
	19	Madagascar
	20	Congo, Dem. Rep.
	21	Malawi
	22	Togo
	23	Sudan
	24	Eritrea
	25	Liberia
	26	Comoros
	27	Central African Rep.
	28	Burundi
	29	Côte d'Ivoire
	30	Chad
	31	Mozambique
	32	Ethiopia
	32	Guinea-Bissau
	33	Benin
	34	Gambia, The
	35	Senegal
	36	Mauritania
	37	Mali
	38	Burkina Faso
	39	Niger
	n/a	Gabon
	n/a	Angola
	n/a	Guinea
	n/a	Sao Tome & Principe
	n/a	Seychelles
	n/a	Sierra Leone
	n/a	Somalia
lowest		

Number of Internet Users per 100 persons of Population

ITU

	2007	
highest	1	Seychelles
	2	Mauritius
	3	Sao Tome & Principe
	4	South Africa
	5	Zimbabwe
	6	Kenya
	7	Nigeria
	8	Senegal
	9	Uganda
	10	Cape Verde
	11	Gambia, The
	12	Gabon
	13	Togo
	14	Namibia
	15	Botswana
	16	Zambia
	17	Swaziland
	18	Sudan
		SSA average
	19	Lesotho
	20	Ghana
	21	Comoros
	22	Guinea-Bissau
	23	Cameroon
	24	Eritrea
	25	Congo, Rep.
	26	Benin
	27	Côte d'Ivoire
	28	Equatorial Guinea
	29	Djibouti
	30	Somalia
	31	Rwanda
	32	Malawi
	32	Tanzania
	33	Mauritania
	34	Mozambique
	35	Mali
	36	Burundi
	37	Angola
	37	Chad
	38	Burkina Faso
	39	Madagascar
	40	Guinea
	41	Congo, Dem. Rep.
	42	Ethiopia
	43	Central African Rep.
	44	Niger
	45	Sierra Leone
lowest	n/a	Liberia

Number of Personal Computers per 100 persons of Population

AfDB

	2006	
highest	1	Seychelles
	2	Mauritius
	3	Namibia
	4	Sudan
	5	Cape Verde
	6	South Africa
	7	Zimbabwe
	8	Botswana
	9	Sao Tome & Principe
	10	Swaziland
	11	Gabon
	12	Togo
	13	Mauritania
	14	Djibouti
		Africa average
	15	Senegal
	16	Gambia, The
	17	Equatorial Guinea
	18	Côte d'Ivoire
	19	Uganda
	20	Kenya
	20	Mozambique
	21	Zambia
	22	Cameroon
	23	Tanzania
	24	Somalia
	25	Nigeria
	26	Angola
	26	Burundi
	27	Comoros
	28	Eritrea
	29	Benin
	30	Ghana
	31	Madagascar
	32	Congo, Rep.
	33	Guinea
	34	Mali
	35	Ethiopia
	36	Central African Rep.
	37	Burkina Faso
	38	Rwanda
	39	Guinea-Bissau
	39	Malawi
	40	Chad
	41	Lesotho
	41	Niger
	42	Congo, Dem. Rep.
	n/a	Liberia
lowest	n/a	Sierra Leone

Net Migration per Population

UNPD

	2000-2005	
people mostly coming into the country	1	Sierra Leone
	2	Eritrea
	3	Burundi
	4	Chad
	5	Gambia, The
	6	Somalia
	7	Benin
	8	Angola
	9	Botswana
	10	Mauritania
	11	Burkina Faso
	12	Gabon
	13	Rwanda
	14	South Africa
	15	Guinea-Bissau
	16	Kenya
	17	Cameroon
	18	Ghana
	18	Djibouti
	19	Equatorial Guinea
	20	Mauritius
	21	Uganda
	22	Madagascar
	22	Namibia
	22	Togo
	23	Mozambique
	23	Nigeria
		SSA average
	23	Ethiopia
	23	Malawi
	24	Niger
	25	Congo, Rep.
	26	Congo, Dem. Rep.
	27	Swaziland
	28	Zimbabwe
	29	Zambia
	30	Senegal
	30	Tanzania
	31	Cape Verde
	31	Central African Rep.
	32	Mali
	33	Comoros
	34	Sudan
	35	Lesotho
	36	Côte d'Ivoire
	37	Liberia
	38	Sao Tome & Principe
	39	Guinea
people mostly leaving the country	n/a	Seychelles

		GDP $PPP IMF	GDP $PPP IMF	GDP $PPP IMF
		1999-2002	2003-2006	2007-2010
largest	1	South Africa	South Africa	South Africa
	2	Nigeria	Nigeria	Nigeria
	3	Sudan	Sudan	Angola
	4	Kenya	Angola	Sudan
	5	Angola	Kenya	Ethiopia
	6	Ethiopia	Ethiopia	Kenya
	7	Tanzania	Tanzania	Tanzania
	8	Cameroon	Cameroon	Cameroon
	9	Côte d'Ivoire	Côte d'Ivoire	Ghana
	10	Ghana	Ghana	Côte d'Ivoire
	11	Uganda	Uganda	Uganda
	12	Botswana	Botswana	Botswana
	13	Gabon	Senegal	Senegal
	14	Senegal	Gabon	Congo, Dem. Rep.
	15	Madagascar	Congo, Dem. Rep.	Gabon
	16	Congo, Dem. Rep.	Madagascar	Madagascar
	17	Burkina Faso	Burkina Faso	Mozambique
	18	Zambia	Mozambique	Burkina Faso
	19	Mauritius	Chad	Zambia
	20	Mozambique	Zambia	Equatorial Guinea
	21	Congo, Rep.	Equatorial Guinea	Chad
	22	Mali	Mauritius	Mauritius
	23	Guinea	Congo, Rep.	Congo, Rep.
	24	Benin	Mali	Mali
	25	Chad	Benin	Benin
	26	Namibia	Guinea	Malawi
	27	Malawi	Namibia	Guinea
	28	Niger	Malawi	Namibia
	29	Equatorial Guinea	Niger	Niger
	30	Rwanda	Rwanda	Rwanda
	31	Swaziland	Mauritania	Mauritania
	32	Mauritania	Swaziland	Swaziland
	33	Togo	Togo	Togo
	34	Eritrea	Eritrea	Sierra Leone
	35	Zimbabwe	Sierra Leone	Eritrea
	36	Central African Rep.	Central African Rep.	Lesotho
	37	Lesotho	Lesotho	Central African Rep.
	38	Burundi	Burundi	Burundi
	39	Sierra Leone	Zimbabwe	Gambia, The
	40	Gambia, The	Gambia, The	Zimbabwe
	41	Liberia	Djibouti	Djibouti
	42	Djibouti	Cape Verde	Cape Verde
	43	Seychelles	Seychelles	Liberia
	44	Cape Verde	Liberia	Seychelles
	45	Guinea-Bissau	Guinea-Bissau	Guinea-Bissau
	46	Comoros	Comoros	Comoros
	47	São Tomé & Príncipe	São Tomé & Príncipe	São Tomé & Príncipe
	n/a	Somalia	Somalia	Somalia
smallest				

GDP per Person $PPP

Primary data: IMF

		1999-2002
largest	1	Seychelles
	2	Gabon
	3	Botswana
	4	Mauritius
	5	South Africa
	6	Equatorial Guinea
	7	Swaziland
	8	Namibia
	9	Congo, Rep.
	10	Angola
	11	Cape Verde
	12	Djibouti
	13	Cameroon
	14	Côte d'Ivoire
	15	Mauritania
		SSA average
	16	Sudan
	17	Senegal
	18	Kenya
	19	Nigeria
	20	Benin
	21	São Tomé & Príncipe
	22	Ghana
	23	Lesotho
	24	Comoros
	25	Gambia, The
	26	Guinea
	27	Chad
	28	Zambia
	29	Burkina Faso
	30	Eritrea
	31	Tanzania
	32	Mali
	33	Madagascar
	34	Uganda
	35	Togo
	36	Central African Rep.
	37	Rwanda
	38	Malawi
	39	Mozambique
	40	Niger
	41	Guinea-Bissau
	42	Ethiopia
	43	Liberia
	44	Sierra Leone
	45	Burundi
	46	Zimbabwe
	47	Congo, Dem. Rep.
smallest	n/a	Somalia

GDP per Person $PPP

Primary data: IMF

		2003-2006
largest	1	Seychelles
	2	Botswana
	3	Gabon
	4	Equatorial Guinea
	5	Mauritius
	6	South Africa
	7	Namibia
	8	Swaziland
	9	Angola
	10	Congo, Rep.
	11	Cape Verde
	12	Djibouti
	13	Cameroon
	14	Nigeria
	15	Mauritania
		SSA average
	16	Sudan
	17	Côte d'Ivoire
	18	Senegal
	19	Chad
	20	Kenya
	21	Benin
	22	São Tomé & Príncipe
	23	Ghana
	24	Zambia
	25	Gambia, The
	26	Lesotho
	27	Burkina Faso
	28	Comoros
	29	Tanzania
	30	Guinea
	31	Mali
	32	Madagascar
	33	Uganda
	34	Eritrea
	35	Rwanda
	36	Togo
	37	Mozambique
	38	Malawi
	39	Central African Rep.
	40	Ethiopia
	41	Niger
	42	Sierra Leone
	43	Guinea-Bissau
	44	Burundi
	45	Liberia
	46	Congo, Dem. Rep.
	47	Zimbabwe
smallest	n/a	Somalia

GDP per Person $PPP

Primary data: IMF

		2007-2010
largest	1	Botswana
	2	Seychelles
	3	Gabon
	4	Equatorial Guinea
	5	Mauritius
	6	South Africa
	7	Angola
	8	Namibia
	9	Swaziland
	10	Congo, Rep.
	11	Cape Verde
	12	Djibouti
	13	Sudan
	14	Nigeria
		SSA average
	15	Cameroon
	16	Mauritania
	17	Côte d'Ivoire
	18	Senegal
	19	Kenya
	20	Chad
	21	São Tomé & Príncipe
	22	Benin
	23	Ghana
	24	Gambia, The
	25	Zambia
	26	Tanzania
	27	Lesotho
	28	Burkina Faso
	29	Madagascar
	30	Comoros
	31	Guinea
	32	Mali
	33	Uganda
	34	Rwanda
	35	Mozambique
	36	Ethiopia
	37	Malawi
	38	Togo
	39	Eritrea
	40	Central African Rep.
	41	Sierra Leone
	42	Niger
	43	Guinea-Bissau
	44	Burundi
	45	Liberia
	46	Congo, Dem. Rep.
	47	Zimbabwe
smallest	n/a	Somalia

Growth in GDP per Person

Primary data: IMF

		2000-2002
largest	1	Equatorial Guinea
	2	Sierra Leone
	3	Nigeria
	4	Botswana
	5	Mozambique
	6	Sudan
	7	Cape Verde
	8	Angola
	9	Chad
	10	Mauritius
	11	Tanzania
	12	São Tomé & Príncipe
		SSA average
	13	Congo, Rep.
	14	South Africa
	15	Namibia
	16	Uganda
	17	Mali
	18	Ethiopia
	19	Zambia
	20	Ghana
	21	Benin
	22	Burkina Faso
	23	Cameroon
	24	Guinea
	25	Liberia
	26	Senegal
	27	Rwanda
	28	Niger
	29	Lesotho
	30	Comoros
	31	Gambia, The
	32	Djibouti
	33	Kenya
	34	Mauritania
	35	Seychelles
	36	Swaziland
	37	Central African Rep.
	38	Burundi
	39	Gabon
	40	Malawi
	41	Madagascar
	42	Côte d'Ivoire
	43	Togo
	44	Eritrea
	45	Congo, Dem. Rep.
	46	Zimbabwe
	47	Guinea-Bissau
smallest	n/a	Somalia

Growth in GDP per Person

Primary data: IMF

		2003-2006
largest	1	Chad
	2	Equatorial Guinea
	3	Angola
	4	Madagascar
	5	Ethiopia
	6	Botswana
	7	Sierra Leone
	8	Sudan
	9	Mozambique
	10	Mauritania
	11	Tanzania
	12	Nigeria
	13	Cape Verde
	14	South Africa
	15	Namibia
	16	Rwanda
	17	Malawi
		SSA average
	18	Congo, Dem. Rep.
	19	Gambia, The
	20	São Tomé & Príncipe
	21	Ghana
	22	Zambia
	23	Mauritius
	24	Mali
	25	Congo, Rep.
	26	Burkina Faso
	27	Kenya
	28	Togo
	29	Senegal
	30	Uganda
	31	Niger
	32	Swaziland
	33	Lesotho
	34	Djibouti
	35	Benin
	36	Burundi
	37	Cameroon
	38	Comoros
	39	Gabon
	40	Central African Rep.
	41	Guinea-Bissau
	42	Côte d'Ivoire
	43	Guinea
	44	Seychelles
	45	Eritrea
	46	Liberia
	47	Zimbabwe
smallest	n/a	Somalia

appendix B3: performance tables — economic strength

Growth in GDP per Person

Primary data: IMF

	Rank	2007-2010
largest	1	Angola
	2	Sudan
	3	Congo, Dem. Rep.
	4	Botswana
	5	Ethiopia
	6	Tanzania
	7	Liberia
	8	Cape Verde
	9	Malawi
	10	Mauritius
	11	Equatorial Guinea
	12	Nigeria
	13	Madagascar
	14	Mozambique
		SSA average
	15	Ghana
	16	Congo, Rep.
	17	Djibouti
	18	Seychelles
	19	São Tomé & Príncipe
	20	Sierra Leone
	21	Gambia, The
	22	Namibia
	23	Rwanda
	24	Zambia
	25	Lesotho
	26	South Africa
	27	Burundi
	28	Uganda
	29	Senegal
	30	Burkina Faso
	31	Central African Rep.
	32	Kenya
	33	Gabon
	34	Mauritania
	35	Côte d'Ivoire
	36	Benin
	37	Mali
	38	Cameroon
	39	Guinea
	40	Niger
	41	Togo
	42	Swaziland
	43	Guinea-Bissau
	44	Comoros
	45	Eritrea
	46	Chad
	n/a	Zimbabwe
smallest	n/a	Somalia

GNI per Person

World Bank

	Rank	1992-2002
largest	1	Seychelles
	2	Gabon
	3	Botswana
	4	Mauritius
	5	Equatorial Guinea
	6	South Africa
	7	Swaziland
	8	Namibia
	9	Angola
	10	Cape Verde
	11	Congo, Rep.
	12	Djibouti
	13	Cameroon
	14	Côte d'Ivoire
	15	Mauritania
	16	Lesotho
		SSA average
	17	Senegal
	18	Kenya
	19	Sudan
	20	Nigeria
	21	Benin
	22	Comoros
	23	Guinea
	24	Ghana
	25	Zambia
	26	Gambia, The
	27	Burkina Faso
	28	Chad
	29	Mali
	30	Madagascar
	31	Tanzania
	32	Eritrea
	32	Togo
	32	Uganda
	33	Central African Rep.
	34	Malawi
	35	Rwanda
	36	Niger
	37	Ethiopia
	38	Mozambique
	39	Guinea-Bissau
	40	Sierra Leone
	41	Burundi
	42	Liberia
	43	Congo, Dem. Rep.
	n/a	São Tomé & Príncipe
	n/a	Somalia
smallest	n/a	Zimbabwe

GNI per Person

World Bank

	Rank	2003-2006
largest	1	Seychelles
	2	Equatorial Guinea
	3	Gabon
	4	Botswana
	5	Mauritius
	6	South Africa
	7	Namibia
	8	Swaziland
	9	Angola
	10	Cape Verde
	11	Congo, Rep.
	12	Djibouti
	13	Cameroon
	14	Mauritania
	15	Lesotho
	16	Sudan
		SSA average
	17	Côte d'Ivoire
	18	Senegal
	19	Kenya
	20	Nigeria
	21	Benin
	22	Ghana
	23	Chad
	23	Comoros
	24	Guinea
	25	Zambia
	26	Burkina Faso
	27	Gambia, The
	28	Mali
	29	Tanzania
	30	Uganda
	31	Madagascar
	32	Togo
	33	Eritrea
	34	Rwanda
	35	Central African Rep.
	36	Malawi
	37	Mozambique
	38	Niger
	39	Sierra Leone
	40	Ethiopia
	41	Guinea-Bissau
	42	Burundi
	43	Congo, Dem. Rep.
	43	Liberia
	n/a	São Tomé & Príncipe
	n/a	Somalia
smallest	n/a	Zimbabwe

Growth in GNI per Person

Primary data: World Bank

	Rank	2000-2002
largest	1	Equatorial Guinea
	2	Sierra Leone
	3	Liberia
	4	Angola
	5	Sudan
	6	Mozambique
	7	Congo, Rep.
	8	Mauritius
	9	Tanzania
	10	Namibia
	11	Ethiopia
	12	Cape Verde
	13	Botswana
	14	Rwanda
	15	Mauritania
	16	Zambia
	17	Uganda
	18	Guinea
	19	Benin
	20	South Africa
	21	Ghana
	22	Chad
	23	Mali
	24	Cameroon
	25	Burkina Faso
		SSA average
	26	Comoros
	27	Senegal
	28	Lesotho
	29	Djibouti
	30	Niger
	31	Gambia, The
	32	Gabon
	33	Kenya
	34	Burundi
	35	Central African Rep.
	36	Togo
	37	Swaziland
	38	Guinea-Bissau
	39	Seychelles
	40	Nigeria
	41	Congo, Dem. Rep.
	42	Madagascar
	43	Côte d'Ivoire
	44	Malawi
	45	Eritrea
	n/a	São Tomé & Príncipe
	n/a	Somalia
smallest	n/a	Zimbabwe

Growth in GNI per Person

Primary data: World Bank

	Rank	2003-2006
largest	1	Equatorial Guinea
	2	Angola
	3	Sudan
	4	Chad
	5	Botswana
	6	Nigeria
	7	Ethiopia
	8	Djibouti
	9	Lesotho
	10	Ghana
	11	Sierra Leone
	12	Tanzania
	13	Congo, Dem. Rep.
	14	Madagascar
	15	South Africa
	16	Gambia, The
	17	Mauritius
	18	Burkina Faso
	19	Mozambique
		SSA average
	20	Malawi
	21	Cape Verde
	22	Mali
	23	Kenya
	24	Namibia
	25	Congo, Rep.
	26	Mauritania
	27	Senegal
	28	Cameroon
	29	Uganda
	30	Rwanda
	31	Zambia
	32	Swaziland
	33	Niger
	34	Guinea
	35	Seychelles
	36	Benin
	37	Togo
	38	Comoros
	39	Guinea-Bissau
	40	Côte d'Ivoire
	41	Central African Rep.
	42	Burundi
	43	Eritrea
	44	Gabon
	45	Liberia
	n/a	São Tomé & Príncipe
	n/a	Somalia
smallest	n/a	Zimbabwe

Real GDP Growth

IMF

		1999-2002
highest	1	Equatorial Guinea
	2	Liberia
	3	Sierra Leone
	4	Nigeria
	5	Mozambique
	6	Cape Verde
	7	Rwanda
	8	Botswana
	9	Uganda
	10	Angola
	11	Sudan
	12	Tanzania
	13	Ethiopia
	14	Benin
	15	Burkina Faso
	16	Chad
		SSA average
	17	São Tomé & Príncipe
	18	Mauritius
	19	Cameroon
	20	Ghana
	21	Mali
	22	Namibia
	23	Guinea
	24	Senegal
	25	Gambia, The
	26	Zambia
	27	Congo, Rep.
	28	South Africa
	29	Mauritania
	30	Niger
	31	Comoros
	32	Guinea-Bissau
	33	Djibouti
	34	Kenya
	35	Swaziland
	36	Lesotho
	37	Seychelles
	38	Central African Rep.
	39	Burundi
	40	Madagascar
	41	Malawi
	42	Eritrea
	43	Togo
	44	Côte d'Ivoire
	45	Gabon
	46	Congo, Dem. Rep.
	47	Zimbabwe
lowest	n/a	Somalia

Real GDP Growth

IMF

		2003-2006
highest	1	Chad
	2	Angola
	3	Equatorial Guinea
	4	Nigeria
	5	Sierra Leone
	6	Mozambique
	7	Ethiopia
	8	Sudan
	9	Tanzania
	10	Mauritania
	11	Congo, Dem. Rep.
	12	Madagascar
	13	Gambia, The
	14	Cape Verde
	15	Burkina Faso
		SSA average
	16	São Tomé & Príncipe
	17	Ghana
	18	Zambia
	19	Uganda
	20	Mali
	21	Botswana
	22	Senegal
	23	Niger
	24	Malawi
	25	Kenya
	26	Namibia
	27	South Africa
	28	Congo, Rep.
	29	Rwanda
	30	Lesotho
	31	Mauritius
	32	Djibouti
	33	Benin
	34	Cameroon
	35	Togo
	36	Swaziland
	37	Burundi
	38	Guinea
	39	Gabon
	40	Comoros
	41	Guinea-Bissau
	42	Côte d'Ivoire
	43	Eritrea
	44	Central African Rep.
	45	Seychelles
	46	Liberia
	47	Zimbabwe
lowest	n/a	Somalia

Real GDP Growth

IMF

		2007-2010
highest	1	Angola
	2	Liberia
	3	Sudan
	4	Congo, Dem. Rep.
	5	Ethiopia
	6	Equatorial Guinea
	7	Tanzania
	8	Nigeria
	9	Madagascar
	10	Cape Verde
	11	Congo, Rep.
	12	Ghana
	13	Mozambique
	14	Malawi
	15	Uganda
	16	Djibouti
		SSA average
	17	Sierra Leone
	18	Gambia, The
	19	São Tomé & Príncipe
	20	Zambia
	21	Rwanda
	22	Mauritius
	23	Senegal
	24	Lesotho
	25	Burundi
	26	Benin
	27	Burkina Faso
	28	Botswana
	29	Central African Rep.
	30	Mauritania
	31	Namibia
	32	Seychelles
	33	South Africa
	34	Mali
	35	Kenya
	36	Cameroon
	37	Niger
	38	Guinea
	39	Gabon
	40	Côte d'Ivoire
	41	Togo
	42	Guinea-Bissau
	43	Eritrea
	44	Swaziland
	45	Comoros
	46	Chad
	47	Zimbabwe
lowest	n/a	Somalia

Inflation

IMF

		1999-2002
lowest rate	1	Ethiopia
	2	Gabon
	3	Djibouti
	4	Burkina Faso
	5	Rwanda
	6	Senegal
	7	Niger
	8	Congo, Rep.
	9	Cape Verde
	10	Central African Rep.
	11	Mali
	12	Uganda
	13	Togo
	14	Côte d'Ivoire
	15	Benin
	16	Cameroon
	17	Chad
	18	Guinea-Bissau
	19	Comoros
	20	Gambia, The
	21	Seychelles
	22	Guinea
	23	Equatorial Guinea
	24	Mauritius
	25	Mauritania
	26	Kenya
	27	Tanzania
	28	South Africa
	29	Botswana
	30	Sierra Leone
	31	Swaziland
	32	Lesotho
	33	Burundi
	34	Sudan
	35	Namibia
	36	São Tomé & Príncipe
	37	Mozambique
	38	Madagascar
	39	Liberia
	40	Nigeria
		SSA average
	41	Eritrea
	42	Ghana
	43	Zambia
	44	Malawi
	45	Zimbabwe
	46	Angola
highest rate	47	Congo, Dem. Rep.
	n/a	Somalia

Inflation

IMF

		2003-2006
lowest rate	1	Gabon
	2	Guinea-Bissau
	3	Mali
	4	Senegal
	5	Cape Verde
	6	Niger
	7	Seychelles
	8	Cameroon
	9	Togo
	10	Chad
	11	Burkina Faso
	12	Côte d'Ivoire
	13	Benin
	14	Djibouti
	15	Central African Rep.
	16	Congo, Rep.
	17	Comoros
	18	South Africa
	19	Namibia
	20	Mauritius
	21	Tanzania
	22	Swaziland
	23	Equatorial Guinea
	24	Lesotho
	25	Uganda
	26	Liberia
	27	Sudan
	28	Mauritania
		SSA average
	29	Burundi
	30	Botswana
	31	Rwanda
	32	Gambia, The
	33	Madagascar
	34	Ethiopia
	35	Sierra Leone
	36	Mozambique
	37	Kenya
	38	Malawi
	39	Congo, Dem. Rep.
	40	Nigeria
	41	São Tomé & Príncipe
	42	Ghana
	43	Zambia
	44	Eritrea
	45	Guinea
	46	Angola
highest rate	47	Zimbabwe
	n/a	Somalia

Inflation

IMF

lowest rate

	2007-2010
1	Chad
2	Cameroon
3	Niger
4	Benin
5	Mali
6	Central African Rep.
7	Burkina Faso
8	Côte d'Ivoire
9	Comoros
10	Guinea-Bissau
11	Congo, Rep.
12	Cape Verde
13	Togo
14	Senegal
15	Gabon
16	Djibouti
17	Equatorial Guinea
18	Gambia, The
19	Uganda
20	Mozambique
21	Tanzania
22	Mauritania
23	Sudan
24	Rwanda
25	South Africa
26	Namibia
27	Malawi
28	Botswana
	SSA average
29	Zambia
30	Lesotho
31	Madagascar
32	Swaziland
33	Nigeria
34	Burundi
35	Ghana
36	Kenya
37	Mauritius
38	Liberia
39	Angola
40	Eritrea
41	Sierra Leone
42	Seychelles
43	São Tomé & Príncipe
44	Guinea
45	Congo, Dem. Rep.
46	Ethiopia
47	Zimbabwe

highest rate

Exchange Rate Stability

Primary data: IMF

most stable

	1999-2006
1	Liberia
2	Seychelles
3	Sudan
4	Ethiopia
5	Botswana
6	Lesotho
7	Swaziland
8	South Africa
9	Namibia
10	Djibouti
11	Mauritius
12	Eritrea
13	Gambia, The
14	Kenya
15	Cape Verde
16	Senegal
17	Cameroon
18	Benin
19	Niger
20	Côte d'Ivoire
21	Burkina Faso
22	Mali
23	Guinea-Bissau
24	Central African Rep.
25	Comoros
26	Malawi
27	Togo
28	Nigeria
29	Mauritania
30	Angola
31	Gabon
32	Rwanda
33	Chad
34	Tanzania
35	Congo, Rep.
36	Burundi
37	Uganda
38	Equatorial Guinea
39	Congo, Dem. Rep.
40	Madagascar
41	Zimbabwe
42	Sierra Leone
43	Guinea
44	Zambia
45	São Tomé & Príncipe
46	Ghana
47	Mozambique
n/a	Somalia

least stable

Exchange Rate Stability

Primary data: IMF

most stable

	2003-2010
1	Liberia
2	Sudan
3	Lesotho
4	Swaziland
5	Botswana
6	South Africa
7	Gambia, The
8	Namibia
9	Seychelles
10	Ethiopia
11	Eritrea
12	Mauritius
13	Cape Verde
14	Cameroon
15	Comoros
16	Benin
17	Guinea-Bissau
18	Mali
19	Djibouti
20	Central African Rep.
21	Kenya
22	Burkina Faso
23	Senegal
24	Niger
25	Côte d'Ivoire
26	Togo
27	Malawi
28	Angola
29	Nigeria
30	Mauritania
31	Chad
32	Rwanda
33	Gabon
34	Tanzania
35	Congo, Rep.
36	Burundi
37	Congo, Dem. Rep.
38	Equatorial Guinea
39	Uganda
40	Madagascar
41	Sierra Leone
42	Zambia
43	Guinea
44	Ghana
45	Mozambique
46	São Tomé & Príncipe
47	Zimbabwe
n/a	Somalia

least stable

Productivity Index

Primary data: IMF

		1999-2002
highest	1	Seychelles
	2	Gabon
	3	Botswana
	4	Mauritius
	5	South Africa
	6	Equatorial Guinea
	7	Swaziland
	8	Namibia
	9	Congo, Rep.
	10	Angola
	11	Cape Verde
	12	Djibouti
	13	Cameroon
	14	Côte d'Ivoire
	15	Mauritania
		SSA=1.00
	16	Sudan
	17	Senegal
	18	Kenya
	19	Nigeria
	20	Benin
	21	São Tomé & Príncipe
	22	Ghana
	23	Lesotho
	24	Comoros
	25	Gambia, The
	26	Guinea
	27	Chad
	28	Zambia
	29	Burkina Faso
	30	Eritrea
	31	Tanzania
	32	Mali
	33	Madagascar
	34	Uganda
	35	Togo
	36	Central African Rep.
	37	Rwanda
	38	Malawi
	39	Niger
	40	Mozambique
	41	Guinea-Bissau
	42	Ethiopia
	43	Liberia
	44	Sierra Leone
	45	Burundi
	46	Zimbabwe
	47	Congo, Dem. Rep.
lowest	n/a	Somalia

Productivity Index

Primary data: IMF

		2003-2006
highest	1	Seychelles
	2	Botswana
	3	Gabon
	4	Equatorial Guinea
	5	Mauritius
	6	South Africa
	7	Namibia
	8	Swaziland
	9	Angola
	10	Congo, Rep.
	11	Cape Verde
	12	Djibouti
	13	Cameroon
	14	Nigeria
	15	Mauritania
		SSA=1.00
	16	Sudan
	17	Côte d'Ivoire
	18	Senegal
	19	Chad
	20	Kenya
	21	Benin
	22	São Tomé & Príncipe
	23	Ghana
	24	Zambia
	25	Gambia, The
	26	Lesotho
	27	Burkina Faso
	28	Comoros
	29	Tanzania
	30	Guinea
	31	Mali
	32	Madagascar
	33	Uganda
	34	Eritrea
	35	Rwanda
	36	Togo
	37	Mozambique
	38	Malawi
	39	Central African Rep.
	40	Niger
	41	Ethiopia
	42	Sierra Leone
	43	Guinea-Bissau
	44	Burundi
	45	Liberia
	46	Congo, Dem. Rep.
	47	Zimbabwe
lowest	n/a	Somalia

Productivity Index

Primary data: IMF

		2007-2010
highest	1	Botswana
	2	Seychelles
	3	Gabon
	4	Equatorial Guinea
	5	Mauritius
	6	South Africa
	7	Angola
	8	Namibia
	9	Swaziland
	10	Congo, Rep.
	11	Cape Verde
	12	Djibouti
	13	Sudan
	14	Nigeria
		SSA=1.00
	15	Cameroon
	16	Mauritania
	17	Côte d'Ivoire
	18	Senegal
	19	Kenya
	20	Chad
	21	São Tomé & Príncipe
	22	Benin
	23	Ghana
	24	Gambia, The
	25	Zambia
	26	Tanzania
	27	Lesotho
	28	Burkina Faso
	29	Madagascar
	30	Comoros
	31	Guinea
	32	Mali
	33	Uganda
	34	Rwanda
	35	Mozambique
	36	Ethiopia
	37	Malawi
	38	Togo
	39	Eritrea
	40	Central African Rep.
	41	Sierra Leone
	42	Niger
	43	Guinea-Bissau
	44	Burundi
	45	Liberia
	46	Congo, Dem. Rep.
	n/a	Somalia
lowest	n/a	Zimbabwe

appendix B4: performance tables — economic productivity

Size of Services Sector as % of Total Economy

World Bank

		2003-2006
largest	1	Djibouti
	2	Cape Verde
	3	Seychelles
	4	South Africa
	5	Mauritius
	6	São Tomé & Príncipe
	7	Zimbabwe
	8	Namibia
	9	Senegal
	10	Eritrea
	11	Madagascar
	12	Benin
	13	Gambia, The
	14	Kenya
		SSA
	15	Côte d'Ivoire
	16	Guinea
	17	Cameroon
	18	Zambia
	19	Uganda
	20	Mozambique
	21	Mauritania
	22	Malawi
	23	Botswana
	24	Niger
	25	Burundi
	26	Swaziland
	27	Lesotho
	28	Burkina Faso
	29	Ethiopia
	30	Sudan
	31	Mali
	32	Rwanda
	33	Ghana
	34	Tanzania
	35	Comoros
	36	Gabon
	37	Togo
	38	Chad
	39	Sierra Leone
	40	Central African Rep.
	41	Congo, Rep.
	42	Congo, Dem. Rep.
	43	Guinea-Bissau
	44	Nigeria
	45	Angola
	46	Liberia
	47	Equatorial Guinea
smallest	n/a	Somalia

Productivity in Agriculture as % of GDP

World Bank

		1999-2002
highest	1	Liberia
	2	Guinea-Bissau
	3	Central African Rep.
	4	Sierra Leone
	5	Congo, Dem. Rep.
	6	Comoros
	7	Ethiopia
	8	Tanzania
	9	Sudan
	10	Rwanda
	11	Burundi
	12	Chad
	13	Mali
	14	Niger
	15	Malawi
	16	Togo
	17	Benin
	18	Uganda
	19	Ghana
	20	Gambia, The
	21	Kenya
	22	Burkina Faso
	23	Nigeria
	24	Madagascar
	25	Mauritania
	26	Mozambique
	27	Côte d'Ivoire
	28	Zambia
	29	Cameroon
	30	Guinea
	31	São Tomé & Príncipe
		SSA average
	32	Senegal
	33	Eritrea
	34	Zimbabwe
	35	Lesotho
	36	Swaziland
	37	Namibia
	38	Cape Verde
	39	Equatorial Guinea
	40	Mauritius
	41	Angola
	42	Gabon
	43	Congo, Rep.
	44	South Africa
	45	Djibouti
	46	Seychelles
	47	Botswana
lowest	n/a	Somalia

Productivity in Agriculture as % of GDP

World Bank

		2003-2006
highest	1	Liberia
	2	Guinea-Bissau
	3	Central African Rep.
	4	Comoros
	5	Congo, Dem. Rep.
	6	Sierra Leone
	7	Ethiopia
	8	Tanzania
	9	Togo
	10	Rwanda
	11	Niger
	12	Burundi
	13	Ghana
	14	Mali
	15	Malawi
	16	Sudan
	17	Uganda
	18	Gambia, The
	19	Benin
	20	Burkina Faso
	21	Madagascar
	22	Kenya
	23	Mozambique
	24	Chad
	25	Côte d'Ivoire
	26	Zambia
	27	Mauritania
	28	Nigeria
	29	Cameroon
	30	São Tomé & Príncipe
	31	Zimbabwe
	32	Guinea
	33	Eritrea
	34	Lesotho
	35	Senegal
		SSA average
	36	Swaziland
	37	Namibia
	38	Cape Verde
	39	Angola
	40	Mauritius
	41	Gabon
	42	Congo, Rep.
	43	Equatorial Guinea
	44	Djibouti
	45	South Africa
	46	Seychelles
	47	Botswana
lowest	n/a	Somalia

Productivity in Agriculture as $PPP per Person

IMF, World Bank

		1999-2002
highest	1	Gabon
	2	Sudan
	3	Swaziland
	4	Mauritius
	5	Comoros
	6	Equatorial Guinea
	7	Seychelles
	8	Benin
	9	Mauritania
	10	Kenya
	11	Cameroon
	12	Chad
	13	Côte d'Ivoire
	14	Namibia
	15	Nigeria
	16	Tanzania
	17	Ghana
	18	Central African Rep.
	19	Gambia, The
	20	Mali
	21	Burkina Faso
	22	Liberia
	23	Guinea-Bissau
		SSA average
	24	Rwanda
	25	Uganda
	26	Togo
	27	Botswana
	28	South Africa
	29	Senegal
	30	Malawi
	31	Madagascar
	32	São Tomé & Príncipe
	33	Ethiopia
	34	Zambia
	35	Guinea
	36	Niger
	37	Cape Verde
	38	Sierra Leone
	39	Angola
	40	Congo, Rep.
	41	Lesotho
	42	Eritrea
	43	Burundi
	44	Mozambique
	45	Congo, Dem. Rep.
	46	Djibouti
	47	Zimbabwe
lowest	n/a	Somalia

Productivity in Agriculture as $PPP per Person

IMF, World Bank

		2003-2006
highest	1	Gabon
	2	Sudan
	3	Mauritius
	4	Comoros
	5	Swaziland
	6	Namibia
	7	Tanzania
	8	Ghana
	9	Benin
	10	Seychelles
	11	Equatorial Guinea
	12	Cameroon
	13	Kenya
	14	Nigeria
	15	Mauritania
	16	Côte d'Ivoire
	17	Central African Rep.
	18	Chad
	19	Gambia, The
	20	Burkina Faso
	21	Mali
	22	Angola
	23	Rwanda
	24	Togo
	25	Botswana
	26	Ethiopia
	27	Guinea-Bissau
		SSA average
	28	Uganda
	29	Sierra Leone
	30	São Tomé & Príncipe
	31	Madagascar
	32	Zambia
	33	Senegal
	34	South Africa
	35	Niger
	36	Malawi
	37	Cape Verde
	38	Liberia
	39	Mozambique
	40	Lesotho
	41	Guinea
	42	Congo, Rep.
	43	Eritrea
	44	Congo, Dem. Rep.
	45	Burundi
	46	Djibouti
	47	Zimbabwe
lowest	n/a	Somalia

appendix B4: performance tables — economic productivity

Growth in Agriculture Productivity

IMF, World Bank

	Rank	1999-2002
highest	1	São Tomé & Príncipe
	2	Comoros
	3	Mozambique
	4	Seychelles
	5	South Africa
	6	Zambia
	7	Tanzania
	8	Liberia
	9	Namibia
	10	Nigeria
	11	Gambia, The
	12	Chad
	13	Ghana
	14	Sierra Leone
	15	Sudan
	16	Burkina Faso
	17	Djibouti
	18	Central African Rep.
	19	Mauritius
		SSA average
	20	Malawi
	21	Lesotho
	22	Togo
	23	Guinea
	24	Benin
	25	Côte d'Ivoire
	26	Madagascar
	27	Rwanda
	28	Niger
	29	Kenya
	30	Cameroon
	31	Congo, Dem. Rep.
	32	Ethiopia
	33	Angola
	34	Botswana
	35	Senegal
	36	Mauritania
	37	Uganda
	38	Burundi
	39	Mali
	40	Cape Verde
	41	Swaziland
	42	Guinea-Bissau
	43	Gabon
	44	Equatorial Guinea
	45	Congo, Rep.
	46	Zimbabwe
	47	Eritrea
lowest	n/a	Somalia

Growth in Agriculture Productivity

IMF, World Bank

	Rank	2003-2006
highest	1	Angola
	2	Cape Verde
	3	Ethiopia
	4	Gambia, The
	5	Eritrea
	6	Togo
	7	Mozambique
	8	Tanzania
	9	Ghana
	10	Mali
	11	Sierra Leone
	12	Namibia
	13	Madagascar
	14	Zimbabwe
	15	Rwanda
	16	Uganda
	17	Senegal
	18	Zambia
	19	Niger
	20	Guinea-Bissau
	21	Lesotho
	22	Burkina Faso
	23	Djibouti
	24	Malawi
	25	Congo, Dem. Rep.
	26	Botswana
	27	Kenya
	28	Benin
	29	Nigeria
	30	Central African Rep.
	31	São Tomé & Príncipe
	32	Seychelles
	33	Sudan
		SSA average
	34	Comoros
	35	Cameroon
	36	Mauritius
	37	Burundi
	38	Swaziland
	39	Côte d'Ivoire
	40	Gabon
	41	South Africa
	42	Congo, Rep.
	43	Chad
	44	Guinea
	45	Mauritania
	46	Liberia
	47	Equatorial Guinea
lowest	n/a	Somalia

Productivity in Industry as % of GDP

World Bank

	Rank	1999-2002
highest	1	Equatorial Guinea
	2	Angola
	3	Congo, Rep.
	4	Botswana
	5	Gabon
	6	Swaziland
	7	Nigeria
	8	Lesotho
	9	Cameroon
	10	South Africa
	11	Guinea
	12	Mauritius
		SSA average
	13	Namibia
	14	Seychelles
	15	Mauritania
	16	Sierra Leone
	17	Zambia
	18	Ghana
	19	Senegal
	20	Côte d'Ivoire
	21	Eritrea
	22	Mozambique
	23	Zimbabwe
	24	Mali
	25	Burkina Faso
	26	Rwanda
	27	Uganda
	28	Congo, Dem. Rep.
	29	Sudan
	30	Burundi
	31	Malawi
	32	Togo
	33	Niger
	34	Kenya
	35	São Tomé & Príncipe
	36	Cape Verde
	37	Central African Rep.
	38	Tanzania
	39	Djibouti
	40	Madagascar
	41	Benin
	42	Ethiopia
	43	Gambia, The
	44	Chad
	45	Guinea-Bissau
	46	Comoros
	47	Liberia
lowest	n/a	Somalia

Productivity in Industry as % of GDP

World Bank

	Rank	2003-2006
highest	1	Equatorial Guinea
	2	Angola
	3	Congo, Rep.
	4	Gabon
	5	Nigeria
	6	Botswana
	7	Swaziland
	8	Chad
	9	Lesotho
	10	Guinea
	11	Mauritania
		SSA average
	12	Cameroon
	13	South Africa
	14	Zambia
	15	Namibia
	16	Mauritius
	17	Seychelles
	18	Mozambique
	19	Sudan
	20	Congo, Dem. Rep.
	21	Ghana
	22	Sierra Leone
	23	Eritrea
	24	Côte d'Ivoire
	25	Senegal
	26	Mali
	27	Zimbabwe
	28	Togo
	29	Burkina Faso
	30	Rwanda
	31	Uganda
	32	São Tomé & Príncipe
	33	Burundi
	34	Malawi
	35	Kenya
	36	Cape Verde
	37	Niger
	38	Tanzania
	39	Djibouti
	40	Madagascar
	41	Central African Rep.
	42	Liberia
	43	Ethiopia
	44	Gambia, The
	45	Benin
	46	Guinea-Bissau
	47	Comoros
lowest	n/a	Somalia

Productivity in Industry as $PPP per Person

IMF, World Bank

	Rank	1992-2002
highest	1	Gabon
	2	Botswana
	3	Equatorial Guinea
	4	Seychelles
	5	Mauritius
	6	South Africa
	7	Congo, Rep.
	8	Angola
	9	Swaziland
	10	Namibia
	11	Cameroon
	12	Nigeria
		SSA average
	13	Mauritania
	14	Lesotho
	15	Côte d'Ivoire
	16	Cape Verde
	17	Senegal
	18	Guinea
	19	Djibouti
	20	Sudan
	21	Ghana
	22	Zambia
	23	Kenya
	24	Eritrea
	25	Burkina Faso
	26	São Tomé & Príncipe
	27	Mali
	28	Benin
	29	Uganda
	30	Gambia, The
	31	Tanzania
	32	Rwanda
	33	Chad
	34	Mozambique
	35	Togo
	36	Comoros
	37	Central African Rep.
	38	Madagascar
	39	Malawi
	40	Sierra Leone
	41	Niger
	42	Ethiopia
	43	Guinea-Bissau
	44	Burundi
	45	Zimbabwe
	46	Congo, Dem. Rep.
	47	Liberia
lowest	n/a	Somalia

Productivity in Industry as $PPP per Person

IMF, World Bank

	Rank	2003-2006
highest	1	Equatorial Guinea
	2	Gabon
	3	Botswana
	4	Seychelles
	5	Mauritius
	6	Angola
	7	South Africa
	8	Congo, Rep.
	9	Swaziland
	10	Namibia
	11	Nigeria
	12	Chad
	13	Cameroon
	14	Mauritania
		SSA average
	15	Lesotho
	16	Sudan
	17	Cape Verde
	18	Côte d'Ivoire
	19	Senegal
	20	Guinea
	21	Zambia
	22	Djibouti
	23	Ghana
	24	Kenya
	25	São Tomé & Príncipe
	26	Burkina Faso
	27	Mali
	28	Eritrea
	29	Benin
	30	Mozambique
	31	Tanzania
	32	Togo
	33	Uganda
	34	Rwanda
	35	Gambia, The
	36	Sierra Leone
	37	Madagascar
	38	Comoros
	39	Malawi
	40	Niger
	41	Central African Rep.
	42	Ethiopia
	43	Congo, Dem. Rep.
	44	Burundi
	45	Guinea-Bissau
	46	Zimbabwe
	47	Liberia
lowest	n/a	Somalia

Growth in Industry Productivity

IMF, World Bank

	Rank	1999-2002
highest	1	Equatorial Guinea
	2	Mali
	3	Nigeria
	4	Sudan
	5	Congo, Rep.
	6	Angola
	7	São Tomé & Príncipe
	8	Mozambique
	9	Uganda
	10	Sierra Leone
	11	Burkina Faso
	12	Ethiopia
	13	Chad
	14	Botswana
	15	Seychelles
	16	Cape Verde
	17	Namibia
	18	Tanzania
		SSA average
	19	Cameroon
	20	Rwanda
	21	Senegal
	22	Mauritius
	23	South Africa
	24	Benin
	25	Djibouti
	26	Lesotho
	27	Gambia, The
	28	Ghana
	29	Guinea
	30	Burundi
	31	Swaziland
	32	Eritrea
	33	Mauritania
	34	Niger
	35	Gabon
	36	Kenya
	37	Comoros
	38	Zambia
	39	Madagascar
	40	Togo
	41	Côte d'Ivoire
	42	Guinea-Bissau
	43	Congo, Dem. Rep.
	44	Malawi
	45	Central African Rep.
	46	Zimbabwe
	47	Liberia
lowest	n/a	Somalia

Growth in Industry Productivity

IMF, World Bank

	Rank	2003-2006
highest	1	Chad
	2	Mauritania
	3	Liberia
	4	Sudan
	5	Nigeria
	6	São Tomé & Príncipe
	7	Congo, Dem. Rep.
	8	Equatorial Guinea
	9	Togo
	10	Zambia
	11	Angola
	12	Madagascar
	13	Mozambique
	14	Cape Verde
	15	Malawi
	16	Congo, Rep.
	17	Tanzania
	18	Sierra Leone
	19	Ethiopia
	20	Botswana
	21	Kenya
	22	Gabon
	23	Burkina Faso
	24	Rwanda
	25	Ghana
	26	Namibia
		SSA average
	27	Côte d'Ivoire
	28	Djibouti
	29	Guinea
	30	Lesotho
	31	Burundi
	32	South Africa
	33	Niger
	34	Swaziland
	35	Cameroon
	36	Comoros
	37	Benin
	38	Senegal
	39	Mauritius
	40	Mali
	41	Gambia, The
	42	Central African Rep.
	43	Zimbabwe
	44	Uganda
	45	Guinea-Bissau
	46	Seychelles
	47	Eritrea
lowest	n/a	Somalia

Productivity in Manufacturing as $US per Person

AfDB, World Bank

	Rank	1999-2002
highest	1	Seychelles
	2	Mauritius
	3	South Africa
	4	Swaziland
	5	Namibia
	6	Gabon
	7	Botswana
	8	Côte d'Ivoire
	9	Cameroon
	10	Lesotho
	11	Zimbabwe
	12	Cape Verde
	13	Senegal
	14	Kenya
	15	Congo, Rep.
	16	Mauritania
	17	Zambia
	18	Burkina Faso
	19	Sudan
	20	Mozambique
	21	Benin
	22	Tanzania
	23	Madagascar
	24	Ghana
	25	Uganda
	26	Central African Rep.
	27	Togo
	28	Eritrea
	29	Angola
	30	Guinea-Bissau
	31	Djibouti
	32	Mali
	33	Comoros
	34	Malawi
	35	Rwanda
	36	São Tomé & Príncipe
	37	Gambia, The
	38	Guinea
	39	Nigeria
	40	Burundi
	41	Niger
	42	Ethiopia
	43	Equatorial Guinea
	44	Sierra Leone
	45	Congo, Dem. Rep.
	46	Chad
	n/a	Liberia
	n/a	Somalia
lowest		

Productivity in Manufacturing as $US per Person

AfDB, World Bank

	Rank	2003-2006
highest	1	Seychelles
	2	Mauritius
	3	South Africa
	4	Swaziland
	5	Namibia
	6	Gabon
	7	Botswana
	8	Cameroon
	9	Côte d'Ivoire
	10	Lesotho
	11	Cape Verde
	12	Senegal
	13	Congo, Rep.
	14	Zimbabwe
	15	Kenya
	16	Mozambique
	17	Zambia
	18	Burkina Faso
	19	Tanzania
	20	Benin
	21	Angola
	22	Sudan
	23	Ghana
	24	Togo
	25	Mauritania
	26	Madagascar
	27	Uganda
	28	Eritrea
	29	Djibouti
	30	Rwanda
	31	Mali
	32	Nigeria
	33	Comoros
	34	Central African Rep.
	35	Malawi
	36	Guinea-Bissau
	37	Gambia, The
	38	Guinea
	39	São Tomé & Príncipe
	40	Burundi
	41	Niger
	42	Equatorial Guinea
	43	Ethiopia
	44	Sierra Leone
	45	Congo, Dem. Rep.
	46	Chad
	n/a	Liberia
	n/a	Somalia
lowest		

appendix B4: performance tables — economic productivity

Productivity in Other Industry as $US per Person

AfDB, World Bank

	1999-2002	
highest	1	Equatorial Guinea
	2	Gabon
	3	Botswana
	4	Seychelles
	5	Congo, Rep.
	6	Angola
	7	South Africa
	8	Namibia
	9	Mauritius
	10	Nigeria
	11	Cape Verde
	12	Guinea
	13	Lesotho
	14	Djibouti
	15	Swaziland
	16	Cameroon
	17	Mauritania
	18	Sudan
	19	São Tomé & Príncipe
	20	Mali
	21	Zambia
	22	Ghana
	23	Senegal
	24	Côte d'Ivoire
	25	Tanzania
	26	Zimbabwe
	27	Comoros
	28	Mozambique
	29	Central African Rep.
	30	Uganda
	31	Togo
	32	Kenya
	33	Gambia, The
	34	Eritrea
	35	Sierra Leone
	36	Burkina Faso
	37	Benin
	38	Rwanda
	39	Congo, Dem. Rep.
	40	Niger
	41	Ethiopia
	42	Malawi
	43	Burundi
	44	Chad
	45	Guinea-Bissau
	46	Madagascar
	n/a	Liberia
	n/a	Somalia
lowest		

Productivity in Other Industry as $US per Person

AfDB, World Bank

	2003-2006	
highest	1	Equatorial Guinea
	2	Gabon
	3	Botswana
	4	Congo, Rep.
	5	Angola
	6	South Africa
	7	Namibia
	8	Mauritius
	9	Nigeria
	10	Cape Verde
	11	Lesotho
	12	Guinea
	13	Djibouti
	14	Mauritania
	15	Swaziland
	16	Sudan
	17	Cameroon
	18	Zambia
	19	São Tomé & Príncipe
	20	Mali
	21	Ghana
	22	Chad
	23	Senegal
	24	Tanzania
	25	Côte d'Ivoire
	26	Mozambique
	27	Sierra Leone
	28	Uganda
	29	Comoros
	30	Togo
	31	Central African Rep.
	32	Kenya
	33	Gambia, The
	34	Burkina Faso
	35	Rwanda
	36	Benin
	37	Zimbabwe
	38	Eritrea
	39	Congo, Dem. Rep.
	40	Ethiopia
	41	Niger
	42	Malawi
	43	Burundi
	44	Guinea-Bissau
	45	Madagascar
	45	Seychelles
	n/a	Liberia
	n/a	Somalia
lowest		

Growth in Manufacturing Productivity

AfDB, World Bank

	1999-2002	
highest	1	Mozambique
	2	Equatorial Guinea
	3	Congo, Rep.
	4	Togo
	5	Angola
	6	Burkina Faso
	7	Uganda
	8	Guinea
	9	Cameroon
	10	Nigeria
	11	Benin
	12	Tanzania
	13	Lesotho
	14	Seychelles
	15	Ethiopia
	16	Zambia
	17	Ghana
	18	Mauritius
	19	Namibia
	20	South Africa
	21	Gabon
	22	Comoros
	23	Sierra Leone
	24	Senegal
	25	Botswana
	26	Burundi
	27	Central African Rep.
	28	Mali
	29	Gambia, The
	30	Swaziland
	31	Cape Verde
	32	Rwanda
	33	São Tomé & Príncipe
	34	Eritrea
	35	Djibouti
	36	Kenya
	37	Madagascar
	38	Congo, Dem. Rep.
	39	Niger
	40	Mauritania
	41	Malawi
	42	Guinea-Bissau
	43	Côte d'Ivoire
	44	Chad
	45	Sudan
	46	Zimbabwe
	n/a	Liberia
	n/a	Somalia
lowest		

Growth in Manufacturing Productivity

AfDB, World Bank

	2003-2006	
highest	1	Equatorial Guinea
	2	Angola
	3	Mozambique
	4	Tanzania
	5	Congo, Rep.
	6	Congo, Dem. Rep.
	7	Nigeria
	8	Cape Verde
	9	Madagascar
	10	Rwanda
	11	Togo
	12	Burkina Faso
	13	Zambia
	14	Malawi
	15	Kenya
	16	Ethiopia
	17	Ghana
	18	South Africa
	19	Djibouti
	20	Uganda
	21	Gabon
	22	Burundi
	23	Botswana
	24	Sudan
	25	Swaziland
	26	Comoros
	27	Mali
	28	Eritrea
	29	Cameroon
	30	Gambia, The
	31	Namibia
	32	Chad
	33	Niger
	34	Central African Rep.
	35	Mauritius
	36	Lesotho
	37	Benin
	38	Guinea
	39	São Tomé & Príncipe
	40	Mauritania
	41	Côte d'Ivoire
	42	Guinea-Bissau
	43	Sierra Leone
	44	Senegal
	45	Seychelles
	46	Zimbabwe
	n/a	Liberia
	n/a	Somalia
lowest		

Growth in Other Industry Productivity

AfDB, World Bank

	1999-2002	
highest	1	Equatorial Guinea
	2	Guinea-Bissau
	3	Sudan
	4	Chad
	5	Mali
	6	Burkina Faso
	7	Mozambique
	8	Mauritius
	9	Botswana
	10	Tanzania
	11	Uganda
	12	Cape Verde
	13	Angola
	14	Gambia, The
	15	Ethiopia
	16	Burundi
	17	Senegal
	18	Rwanda
	19	Central African Rep.
	20	Guinea
	21	Swaziland
	22	São Tomé & Príncipe
	23	Zambia
	24	Lesotho
	25	Seychelles
	26	Ghana
	27	Congo, Dem. Rep.
	28	Djibouti
	29	Namibia
	30	Mauritania
	31	Eritrea
	32	Comoros
	33	Benin
	34	Sierra Leone
	35	South Africa
	36	Malawi
	37	Kenya
	38	Côte d'Ivoire
	39	Congo, Rep.
	40	Niger
	41	Nigeria
	42	Togo
	43	Cameroon
	44	Gabon
	45	Zimbabwe
	46	Madagascar
	n/a	Liberia
	n/a	Somalia
lowest		

appendix B4: performance tables – economic productivity

Growth in Other Industry Productivity

AfDB, World Bank

		2003-2006
highest	1	Chad
	2	Sudan
	3	Equatorial Guinea
	4	Sierra Leone
	5	Malawi
	6	Mauritania
	7	Zambia
	8	Namibia
	9	Burundi
	10	Mozambique
	11	Angola
	12	Tanzania
	13	Rwanda
	14	Burkina Faso
	15	Lesotho
	16	Uganda
	17	Congo, Dem. Rep.
	18	Côte d'Ivoire
	19	Nigeria
	20	Cape Verde
	21	Ethiopia
	22	Senegal
	23	São Tomé & Príncipe
	24	Botswana
	25	Djibouti
	26	Togo
	27	Ghana
	28	South Africa
	29	Gambia, The
	30	Mauritius
	31	Benin
	32	Kenya
	33	Congo, Rep.
	34	Niger
	35	Guinea
	36	Central African Rep.
	37	Madagascar
	38	Swaziland
	39	Mali
	40	Gabon
	41	Comoros
	42	Eritrea
	43	Cameroon
	44	Guinea-Bissau
	45	Zimbabwe
	46	Seychelles
	n/a	Liberia
	n/a	Somalia
lowest		

Productivity in Services as % of GDP

World Bank

		1999-2002
highest	1	Djibouti
	2	Cape Verde
	3	Seychelles
	4	South Africa
	5	São Tomé & Príncipe
	6	Mauritius
	7	Zimbabwe
	8	Namibia
	9	Eritrea
	10	Senegal
	11	Madagascar
	12	Gambia, The
	13	Côte d'Ivoire
	14	Zambia
	15	Mozambique
	16	Kenya
		SSA average
	17	Benin
	18	Guinea
	19	Chad
	20	Togo
	21	Cameroon
	22	Mauritania
	23	Malawi
	24	Uganda
	25	Niger
	26	Burkina Faso
	27	Gabon
	28	Lesotho
	29	Comoros
	30	Ethiopia
	31	Botswana
	32	Burundi
	33	Swaziland
	34	Ghana
	35	Tanzania
	36	Rwanda
	37	Sudan
	38	Mali
	39	Guinea-Bissau
	40	Central African Rep.
	41	Congo, Rep.
	42	Congo, Dem. Rep.
	43	Nigeria
	44	Angola
	45	Sierra Leone
	46	Liberia
	47	Equatorial Guinea
lowest	n/a	Somalia

Productivity in Services as % of GDP

World Bank

		2003-2006
highest	1	Djibouti
	2	Cape Verde
	3	Seychelles
	4	South Africa
	5	Mauritius
	6	São Tomé & Príncipe
	7	Namibia
	8	Senegal
	9	Eritrea
	10	Zimbabwe
	11	Madagascar
	12	Benin
	13	Gambia, The
	14	Kenya
		SSA average
	15	Côte d'Ivoire
	16	Guinea
	17	Cameroon
	18	Zambia
	19	Uganda
	20	Mozambique
	21	Mauritania
	22	Malawi
	23	Botswana
	24	Niger
	25	Burundi
	26	Swaziland
	27	Lesotho
	28	Burkina Faso
	29	Ethiopia
	30	Sudan
	31	Mali
	32	Rwanda
	33	Ghana
	34	Tanzania
	35	Comoros
	36	Gabon
	37	Togo
	38	Chad
	39	Sierra Leone
	40	Central African Rep.
	41	Congo, Rep.
	42	Congo, Dem. Rep.
	43	Guinea-Bissau
	44	Angola
	45	Nigeria
	46	Liberia
	47	Equatorial Guinea
lowest	n/a	Somalia

Productivity in Services as $PPP per Person

IMF, World Bank

		1999-2002
highest	1	Seychelles
	2	Gabon
	3	Mauritius
	4	South Africa
	5	Botswana
	6	Namibia
	7	Cape Verde
	8	Swaziland
	9	Djibouti
	10	Côte d'Ivoire
	11	Congo, Rep.
	12	Cameroon
	13	Senegal
		SSA average
	14	São Tomé & Príncipe
	15	Kenya
	16	Mauritania
	17	Angola
	18	Benin
	19	Gambia, The
	20	Sudan
	21	Eritrea
	22	Zambia
	23	Guinea
	24	Chad
	25	Madagascar
	26	Lesotho
	27	Comoros
	28	Ghana
	29	Burkina Faso
	30	Tanzania
	31	Togo
	32	Uganda
	33	Nigeria
	34	Mali
	35	Equatorial Guinea
	36	Mozambique
	37	Malawi
	38	Rwanda
	39	Niger
	40	Ethiopia
	41	Central African Rep.
	42	Guinea-Bissau
	43	Zimbabwe
	44	Burundi
	45	Sierra Leone
	46	Liberia
	47	Congo, Dem. Rep.
lowest	n/a	Somalia

Productivity in Services as $PPP per Person

IMF, World Bank

		2003-2006
highest	1	Seychelles
	2	Mauritius
	3	Botswana
	4	South Africa
	5	Gabon
	6	Namibia
	7	Cape Verde
	8	Swaziland
	9	Djibouti
	10	Congo, Rep.
	11	Cameroon
		SSA average
	12	Senegal
	13	Angola
	14	Côte d'Ivoire
	15	Mauritania
	16	São Tomé & Príncipe
	17	Kenya
	18	Benin
	19	Sudan
	20	Gambia, The
	21	Zambia
	22	Madagascar
	23	Guinea
	24	Lesotho
	25	Eritrea
	26	Ghana
	27	Burkina Faso
	28	Chad
	29	Comoros
	30	Uganda
	31	Nigeria
	32	Tanzania
	33	Equatorial Guinea
	34	Mali
	35	Mozambique
	36	Malawi
	37	Rwanda
	38	Niger
	39	Togo
	40	Ethiopia
	41	Central African Rep.
	42	Sierra Leone
	43	Burundi
	44	Guinea-Bissau
	45	Zimbabwe
	46	Congo, Dem. Rep.
	47	Liberia
lowest	n/a	Somalia

Growth in Services Productivity

IMF, World Bank

		1999-2002
highest	1	Sierra Leone
	2	São Tomé & Príncipe
	3	Uganda
	4	Cape Verde
	5	Ethiopia
	6	Equatorial Guinea
	7	Botswana
	8	Mozambique
	9	Nigeria
	10	Mauritius
	11	Mauritania
	12	Benin
	13	Burkina Faso
	14	Guinea-Bissau
	15	Zambia
	16	Tanzania
	17	Sudan
	18	Mali
	19	Ghana
	20	Senegal
	21	Chad
	22	Central African Rep.
		SSA average
	23	Guinea
	24	Rwanda
	25	Cameroon
	26	South Africa
	27	Niger
	28	Burundi
	29	Kenya
	30	Liberia
	31	Namibia
	32	Gambia, The
	33	Zimbabwe
	34	Swaziland
	35	Seychelles
	36	Eritrea
	37	Djibouti
	38	Angola
	39	Lesotho
	40	Madagascar
	41	Malawi
	42	Côte d'Ivoire
	43	Congo, Dem. Rep.
	44	Comoros
	45	Congo, Rep.
	46	Togo
	47	Gabon
lowest	n/a	Somalia

Growth in Services Productivity

IMF, World Bank

		2003-2006
highest	1	Madagascar
	2	Botswana
	3	Sierra Leone
	4	Angola
	5	Sudan
		SSA average
	6	Mauritius
	7	South Africa
	8	Ethiopia
	9	Namibia
	10	Swaziland
	11	Malawi
	12	Rwanda
	13	Mali
	14	Cape Verde
	15	Tanzania
	16	Uganda
	17	Senegal
	18	Mozambique
	19	Burundi
	20	Congo, Dem. Rep.
	21	Kenya
	22	Burkina Faso
	23	São Tomé & Príncipe
	24	Benin
	25	Ghana
	26	Djibouti
	27	Lesotho
	28	Niger
	29	Gambia, The
	30	Cameroon
	31	Guinea
	32	Seychelles
	33	Mauritania
	34	Comoros
	35	Zambia
	36	Nigeria
	37	Côte d'Ivoire
	38	Central African Rep.
	39	Guinea-Bissau
	40	Congo, Rep.
	41	Liberia
	42	Equatorial Guinea
	43	Togo
	44	Eritrea
	45	Gabon
	46	Chad
	47	Zimbabwe
lowest	n/a	Somalia

Fiscal Balance as % of GDP (IMF)

greatest balance

	1997-2002		2003-2006		2007-2008
1	Equatorial Guinea	1	Equatorial Guinea	1	São Tomé & Príncipe
2	Botswana	2	Cameroon	2	Equatorial Guinea
3	Gabon	3	Congo, Rep.	3	Congo, Rep.
4	Benin	4	Gabon	4	Lesotho
5	Senegal	5	Niger	5	Sierra Leone
6	Cameroon	6	Mali	6	Gabon
7	Tanzania	7	Madagascar	7	Botswana
8	Central African Rep.	8	Lesotho	8	Angola
9	Kenya	9	Nigeria	9	Nigeria
9	Swaziland	10	Botswana	10	Cameroon
10	Côte d'Ivoire	11	Angola	11	Chad
11	Rwanda	12	Zambia	12	Liberia
12	South Africa		SSA average	13	Namibia
13	Nigeria	13	Burkina Faso		SSA average
14	Togo	14	Liberia	14	South Africa
	SSA average	15	Swaziland	15	Burundi
15	Comoros	16	Central African Rep.	16	Central African Rep.
15	Guinea	17	Rwanda	17	Congo, Dem. Rep.
16	Namibia	18	São Tomé & Príncipe	18	Guinea
17	Mali	19	Sierra Leone	19	Côte d'Ivoire
17	Uganda	20	South Africa	20	Gambia, The
18	Burkina Faso	21	Togo	21	Swaziland
18	Lesotho	22	Seychelles	22	Rwanda
19	Niger	23	Benin	23	Benin
20	Mozambique	24	Kenya	24	Malawi
21	Madagascar	25	Chad	25	Zambia
22	Burundi	26	Côte d'Ivoire	26	Niger
23	Zambia	26	Uganda	27	Comoros
24	Congo, Dem. Rep.	27	Comoros	27	Togo
25	Chad	28	Namibia	28	Uganda
25	Mauritius	29	Tanzania	29	Mauritius
26	Gambia, The	30	Malawi	30	Ethiopia
27	Ethiopia	31	Mozambique	31	Cape Verde
28	Malawi	32	Senegal	32	Kenya
29	Congo, Rep.	33	Congo, Dem. Rep.	33	Tanzania
30	Ghana	34	Ghana	34	Mali
31	Zimbabwe	35	Guinea	35	Madagascar
32	Sierra Leone	36	Burundi	36	Guinea-Bissau
33	Cape Verde	37	Ethiopia	37	Senegal
34	Guinea-Bissau	38	Cape Verde	38	Burkina Faso
35	Seychelles	39	Mauritius	39	Mozambique
36	Angola	40	Zimbabwe	40	Ghana
37	São Tomé & Príncipe	41	Gambia, The	41	Seychelles
38	Eritrea	42	Guinea-Bissau	42	Eritrea
n/a	Djibouti	43	Eritrea	43	Zimbabwe
n/a	Liberia	n/a	Djibouti	n/a	Djibouti
n/a	Mauritania	n/a	Mauritania	n/a	Mauritania
n/a	Somalia	n/a	Somalia	n/a	Somalia
n/a	Sudan	n/a	Sudan	n/a	Sudan

least balance

Fiscal Balance as $PPP per Person

Primary data: IMF

	1997-2002	
largest	1	Equatorial Guinea
	2	Gabon
	3	Botswana
	4	Benin
	5	Senegal
	6	Central African Rep.
	7	Tanzania
	8	Congo, Dem. Rep.
	9	Rwanda
	10	Burundi
	11	Cameroon
	12	Kenya
	13	Togo
	14	Niger
	15	Mozambique
	16	Zimbabwe
	17	Uganda
	18	Côte d'Ivoire
	19	Mali
	20	Nigeria
	21	Ethiopia
	22	Madagascar
	23	Guinea
	24	Comoros
	25	Burkina Faso
	26	Sierra Leone
	27	Lesotho
		SSA average
	28	Malawi
	29	Zambia
	30	Chad
	31	Swaziland
	32	Gambia, The
	33	Guinea-Bissau
	34	Ghana
	35	Namibia
	36	South Africa
	37	São Tomé & Príncipe
	38	Congo, Rep.
	39	Cape Verde
	40	Eritrea
	41	Angola
	42	Mauritius
	43	Seychelles
	n/a	Djibouti
	n/a	Liberia
	n/a	Mauritania
	n/a	Somalia
smallest	n/a	Sudan

Fiscal Balance as $PPP per Person

Primary data: IMF

	2003-2006	
largest	1	Equatorial Guinea
	2	Gabon
	3	Botswana
	4	Congo, Rep.
	5	Cameroon
	6	Angola
	7	Nigeria
	8	Lesotho
	9	Madagascar
	10	Mali
	11	Niger
	12	Zambia
	13	Swaziland
		SSA average
	14	Burkina Faso
	15	Liberia
	16	Central African Rep.
	17	Sierra Leone
	18	Rwanda
	19	São Tomé & Príncipe
	20	Togo
	21	Congo, Dem. Rep.
	22	Zimbabwe
	23	Burundi
	24	Uganda
	25	Malawi
	26	Benin
	27	Mozambique
	28	Comoros
	29	Chad
	30	Kenya
	31	Ethiopia
	32	Côte d'Ivoire
	33	Tanzania
	34	Guinea
	35	Ghana
	36	Senegal
	37	Guinea-Bissau
	38	Gambia, The
	39	South Africa
	40	Namibia
	41	Eritrea
	42	Cape Verde
	43	Seychelles
	44	Mauritius
	n/a	Djibouti
	n/a	Mauritania
	n/a	Somalia
smallest	n/a	Sudan

Fiscal Balance as $PPP per Person

Primary data: IMF

	2007-2008	
largest	1	Equatorial Guinea
	2	Gabon
	3	São Tomé & Príncipe
	4	Botswana
	5	Congo, Rep.
	6	Angola
	7	Lesotho
	8	Nigeria
	9	Namibia
	10	South Africa
	11	Cameroon
	12	Sierra Leone
	13	Chad
		SSA average
	14	Liberia
	15	Central African Rep.
	16	Burundi
	17	Congo, Dem. Rep.
	18	Guinea
	19	Rwanda
	20	Côte d'Ivoire
	21	Gambia, The
	22	Malawi
	23	Niger
	24	Benin
	25	Togo
	26	Zimbabwe
	27	Guinea-Bissau
	28	Comoros
	29	Zambia
	30	Ethiopia
	31	Uganda
	32	Mali
	33	Swaziland
	34	Madagascar
	35	Tanzania
	36	Mozambique
	37	Kenya
	38	Eritrea
	39	Burkina Faso
	40	Senegal
	41	Ghana
	42	Cape Verde
	43	Mauritius
	44	Seychelles
	n/a	Djibouti
	n/a	Mauritania
	n/a	Somalia
smallest	n/a	Sudan

Govt. Earnings - incl. Grants - as % of GDP

IMF

	1997-2002	
highest	1	Lesotho
	2	Seychelles
	3	Angola
	4	Namibia
	5	Botswana
	6	Eritrea
	7	São Tomé & Príncipe
	8	Swaziland
	9	Gabon
	10	Cape Verde
	11	Congo, Rep.
	12	Gambia, The
	13	Guinea-Bissau
	14	Zimbabwe
	15	Burundi
	16	Equatorial Guinea
	17	Malawi
	18	South Africa
		SSA average
	19	Ghana
	20	Nigeria
	21	Zambia
	22	Kenya
	23	Rwanda
	24	Mauritius
	25	Ethiopia
	26	Senegal
	27	Uganda
	28	Côte d'Ivoire
	29	Benin
	30	Sierra Leone
	31	Mozambique
	32	Togo
	33	Mali
	34	Burkina Faso
	35	Comoros
	36	Cameroon
	37	Tanzania
	38	Central African Rep.
	39	Guinea
	40	Niger
	41	Madagascar
	42	Chad
	43	Congo, Dem. Rep.
	n/a	Djibouti
	n/a	Liberia
	n/a	Mauritania
	n/a	Somalia
lowest	n/a	Sudan

Govt. Earnings - incl. Grants - as % of GDP

IMF

	2003-2006	
highest	1	Lesotho
	2	São Tomé & Príncipe
	3	Seychelles
	4	Liberia
	5	Botswana
	6	Swaziland
	7	Namibia
	8	Eritrea
	9	Angola
	10	Burundi
	11	Equatorial Guinea
	12	Congo, Rep.
	13	Zimbabwe
	14	Gabon
	15	Gambia, The
	16	Cape Verde
	17	Ghana
	18	Guinea-Bissau
	19	Malawi
	20	Rwanda
		SSA average
	21	South Africa
	22	Ethiopia
	23	Nigeria
	24	Kenya
	25	Uganda
	26	Senegal
	27	Mauritius
	28	Mozambique
	29	Mali
	30	Benin
	31	Zambia
	32	Sierra Leone
	33	Togo
	34	Cameroon
	35	Côte d'Ivoire
	36	Congo, Dem. Rep.
	37	Comoros
	38	Burkina Faso
	39	Chad
	40	Tanzania
	41	Niger
	42	Madagascar
	43	Guinea
	44	Central African Rep.
	n/a	Djibouti
	n/a	Mauritania
	n/a	Somalia
lowest	n/a	Sudan

Govt. Earnings - incl. Grants - as % of GDP

IMF

	2007-2008	
highest	1	Lesotho
	2	Swaziland
	3	São Tomé & Príncipe
	4	Liberia
	5	Seychelles
	6	Namibia
	7	Botswana
	8	Congo, Rep.
	9	Equatorial Guinea
	10	Burundi
	11	Angola
	12	Guinea-Bissau
	13	Malawi
	14	Gambia, The
	15	Gabon
	16	Zimbabwe
	17	Cape Verde
	18	Mozambique
	19	Ghana
	19	South Africa
	20	Eritrea
		SSA average
	21	Rwanda
	22	Chad
	23	Senegal
	24	Zambia
	25	Benin
	26	Côte d'Ivoire
	27	Kenya
	28	Congo, Dem. Rep.
	29	Mauritius
	30	Ethiopia
	31	Cameroon
	32	Mali
	33	Togo
	33	Uganda
	34	Nigeria
	35	Tanzania
	36	Burkina Faso
	37	Niger
	38	Comoros
	39	Sierra Leone
	40	Guinea
	41	Central African Rep.
	42	Madagascar
	n/a	Djibouti
	n/a	Mauritania
	n/a	Somalia
lowest	n/a	Sudan

Govt. Spending as % of GDP

IMF

	1997-2002	
highest	1	Eritrea
	2	Angola
	3	Seychelles
	4	São Tomé & Príncipe
	5	Lesotho
	6	Cape Verde
	7	Botswana
	8	Guinea-Bissau
	9	Namibia
	10	Congo, Rep.
	11	Zimbabwe
	12	Gabon
	13	Zambia
	14	Malawi
	15	Swaziland
	16	Ghana
	17	South Africa
	18	Gambia, The
		SSA average
	19	Burundi
	19	Mauritius
	20	Mozambique
	21	Ethiopia
	22	Sierra Leone
	23	Nigeria
	24	Burkina Faso
	24	Kenya
	25	Comoros
	26	Mali
	27	Uganda
	28	Rwanda
	29	Côte d'Ivoire
	30	Senegal
	31	Niger
	32	Chad
	33	Benin
	34	Madagascar
	35	Equatorial Guinea
	36	Togo
	37	Guinea
	38	Central African Rep.
	39	Cameroon
	40	Tanzania
	41	Congo, Dem. Rep.
	n/a	Djibouti
	n/a	Liberia
	n/a	Mauritania
	n/a	Somalia
lowest	n/a	Sudan

Govt. Spending as % of GDP

IMF

	2003-2006	
highest	1	Eritrea
	2	Seychelles
	3	São Tomé & Príncipe
	4	Lesotho
	5	Guinea-Bissau
	6	Zimbabwe
	7	Burundi
	8	Angola
	9	Botswana
	10	Cape Verde
	11	Namibia
	12	Swaziland
	13	Ghana
	14	Malawi
	15	Gambia, The
	16	Congo, Rep.
	17	Zambia
	18	Mozambique
	19	South Africa
	20	Mauritius
	21	Ethiopia
	22	Sierra Leone
	23	Senegal
	24	Mali
	25	Rwanda
		SSA average
	26	Kenya
	27	Gabon
	28	Madagascar
	28	Uganda
	29	Burkina Faso
	30	Comoros
	31	Benin
	32	Côte d'Ivoire
	33	Niger
	34	Tanzania
	35	Equatorial Guinea
	36	Togo
	37	Congo, Dem. Rep.
	38	Guinea
	39	Chad
	40	Nigeria
	41	Cameroon
	42	Central African Rep.
	n/a	Djibouti
	n/a	Liberia
	n/a	Mauritania
	n/a	Somalia
lowest	n/a	Sudan

Govt. Earnings as $PPP per Person

Primary data: IMF

	1997-2002	
highest	1	Seychelles
	2	Gabon
	3	Botswana
	4	Namibia
	5	South Africa
	6	Mauritius
	7	Swaziland
	8	Angola
	9	Equatorial Guinea
	10	Congo, Rep.
	11	Lesotho
	12	Cape Verde
	13	São Tomé & Príncipe
	14	Eritrea
		SSA average
	15	Côte d'Ivoire
	16	Kenya
	17	Gambia, The
	18	Cameroon
	19	Nigeria
	20	Senegal
	21	Benin
	22	Ghana
	23	Zambia
	24	Comoros
	25	Malawi
	26	Burkina Faso
	27	Guinea-Bissau
	28	Rwanda
	29	Uganda
	30	Guinea
	31	Mali
	32	Togo
	33	Tanzania
	34	Chad
	35	Ethiopia
	36	Central African Rep.
	37	Madagascar
	38	Mozambique
	39	Burundi
	40	Zimbabwe
	41	Niger
	42	Sierra Leone
	43	Congo, Dem. Rep.
	n/a	Djibouti
	n/a	Liberia
	n/a	Mauritania
	n/a	Somalia
lowest	n/a	Sudan

Govt. Earnings as $PPP per Person

Primary data: IMF

	2003-2006	
highest	1	Seychelles
	2	Botswana
	3	Equatorial Guinea
	4	Gabon
	5	South Africa
	6	Mauritius
	7	Swaziland
	8	Namibia
	9	Angola
	10	Congo, Rep.
	11	Lesotho
	12	São Tomé & Príncipe
	13	Cape Verde
		SSA average
	14	Nigeria
	15	Cameroon
	16	Ghana
	17	Eritrea
	18	Gambia, The
	19	Senegal
	20	Kenya
	21	Côte d'Ivoire
	22	Benin
	23	Chad
	24	Zambia
	25	Rwanda
	26	Mali
	27	Comoros
	28	Burkina Faso
	29	Malawi
	30	Uganda
	31	Tanzania
	32	Liberia
	33	Mozambique
	34	Ethiopia
	35	Togo
	36	Guinea
	37	Burundi
	38	Guinea-Bissau
	39	Madagascar
	40	Sierra Leone
	41	Niger
	42	Central African Rep.
	43	Zimbabwe
	44	Congo, Dem. Rep.
	n/a	Djibouti
	n/a	Mauritania
	n/a	Somalia
lowest	n/a	Sudan

Govt. Earnings as $PPP per Person

Primary data: IMF

	Rank	2007-2008
highest	1	Seychelles
	2	Botswana
	3	Equatorial Guinea
	4	Gabon
	5	Swaziland
	6	Namibia
	7	South Africa
	8	Mauritius
	9	Angola
	10	Congo, Rep.
	11	Lesotho
	12	São Tomé & Príncipe
	13	Cape Verde
		SSA average
	14	Cameroon
	15	Gambia, The
	16	Nigeria
	17	Chad
	18	Ghana
	19	Senegal
	20	Côte d'Ivoire
	21	Kenya
	22	Benin
	23	Zambia
	24	Malawi
	25	Tanzania
	26	Mozambique
	27	Rwanda
	28	Burkina Faso
	29	Mali
	30	Liberia
	31	Eritrea
	32	Uganda
	33	Comoros
	34	Ethiopia
	35	Guinea-Bissau
	36	Togo
	37	Guinea
	38	Burundi
	39	Madagascar
	40	Niger
	41	Sierra Leone
	42	Central African Rep.
	43	Congo, Dem. Rep.
	44	Zimbabwe
	n/a	Djibouti
	n/a	Mauritania
	n/a	Somalia
lowest	n/a	Sudan

Govt. Spending as $PPP per Person

Primary data: IMF

	Rank	1997-2002
highest	1	Seychelles
	2	Gabon
	3	Botswana
	4	Mauritius
	5	South Africa
	6	Angola
	7	Namibia
	8	Swaziland
	9	Congo, Rep.
	10	Equatorial Guinea
	11	Cape Verde
	12	Eritrea
	13	São Tomé & Príncipe
	14	Lesotho
		SSA average
	15	Côte d'Ivoire
	16	Kenya
	17	Zambia
	18	Nigeria
	19	Ghana
	20	Cameroon
	21	Gambia, The
	22	Senegal
	23	Comoros
	24	Benin
	25	Burkina Faso
	26	Guinea-Bissau
	27	Chad
	28	Malawi
	29	Guinea
	30	Mali
	31	Uganda
	32	Madagascar
	33	Rwanda
	34	Togo
	35	Mozambique
	36	Ethiopia
	37	Tanzania
	38	Central African Rep.
	39	Niger
	40	Sierra Leone
	41	Zimbabwe
	42	Burundi
	43	Congo, Dem. Rep.
	n/a	Djibouti
	n/a	Liberia
	n/a	Mauritania
	n/a	Somalia
lowest	n/a	Sudan

Govt. Spending as $PPP per Person

Primary data: IMF

	Rank	2003-2006
highest	1	Seychelles
	2	Botswana
	3	Gabon
	4	Mauritius
	5	South Africa
	6	Equatorial Guinea
	7	Namibia
	8	Swaziland
	9	Angola
	10	Congo, Rep.
	11	Cape Verde
	12	São Tomé & Príncipe
	13	Lesotho
	14	Eritrea
		SSA average
	15	Ghana
	16	Senegal
	17	Kenya
	18	Côte d'Ivoire
	19	Gambia, The
	20	Zambia
	21	Cameroon
	22	Nigeria
	23	Benin
	24	Burkina Faso
	25	Chad
	26	Mali
	27	Comoros
	28	Malawi
	29	Tanzania
	30	Madagascar
	31	Guinea-Bissau
	32	Rwanda
	33	Uganda
	34	Mozambique
	35	Guinea
	36	Ethiopia
	37	Sierra Leone
	38	Togo
	39	Burundi
	40	Niger
	41	Central African Rep.
	42	Zimbabwe
	43	Congo, Dem. Rep.
	n/a	Djibouti
	n/a	Liberia
	n/a	Mauritania
	n/a	Somalia
lowest	n/a	Sudan

Growth in Govt. Earnings per Person

Primary data: IMF

	Rank	2003-2006
highest	1	Liberia
	2	Equatorial Guinea
	3	São Tomé & Príncipe
	4	Chad
	5	Congo, Dem. Rep.
	6	Mozambique
	7	Congo, Rep.
	8	Swaziland
	9	Burundi
	10	Sierra Leone
	11	Angola
	12	Botswana
	13	Mali
	14	Nigeria
	15	Lesotho
	16	Ghana
	17	Madagascar
	18	Ethiopia
	19	Malawi
	20	Tanzania
	21	Cameroon
		SSA average
	22	Niger
	23	Cape Verde
	24	South Africa
	25	Rwanda
	26	Namibia
	27	Senegal
	28	Mauritius
	29	Central African Rep.
	30	Uganda
	31	Benin
	32	Burkina Faso
	33	Seychelles
	34	Gambia, The
	35	Guinea-Bissau
	36	Togo
	37	Kenya
	38	Guinea
	39	Zambia
	40	Comoros
	41	Zimbabwe
	42	Côte d'Ivoire
	43	Gabon
	44	Eritrea
	n/a	Djibouti
	n/a	Mauritania
	n/a	Somalia
lowest	n/a	Sudan

Growth in Govt. Earnings per Person

Primary data: IMF

	Rank	2007-2008
highest	1	Guinea-Bissau
	2	Gambia, The
	3	Tanzania
	4	São Tomé & Príncipe
	5	Mozambique
	6	Lesotho
	7	Rwanda
	8	Ethiopia
	9	Zambia
	10	Nigeria
	11	Mauritius
	12	Ghana
	13	Swaziland
	14	Chad
	15	Burkina Faso
	16	Malawi
	17	Madagascar
	18	Côte d'Ivoire
	19	Benin
	20	Congo, Dem. Rep.
	21	Liberia
	22	South Africa
	23	Niger
		SSA average
	24	Namibia
	25	Angola
	26	Guinea
	27	Togo
	28	Botswana
	29	Senegal
	30	Uganda
	31	Cape Verde
	32	Kenya
	33	Cameroon
	34	Mali
	35	Congo, Rep.
	36	Comoros
	37	Equatorial Guinea
	38	Gabon
	39	Sierra Leone
	40	Central African Rep.
	41	Seychelles
	42	Burundi
	43	Eritrea
	44	Zimbabwe
	n/a	Djibouti
	n/a	Mauritania
	n/a	Somalia
lowest	n/a	Sudan

appendix B5: performance tables — govt. earnings & spending

Current Account Balance as % of GDP
IMF

	Rank	1999-2002
largest	1	Gabon
	2	Botswana
	3	Namibia
	4	Mauritius
	5	Zimbabwe
	6	Côte d'Ivoire
	7	South Africa
	8	Comoros
	9	Kenya
	10	Nigeria
	11	Central African Rep.
	12	Swaziland
		SSA average
	13	Gambia, The
	14	Congo, Dem. Rep.
	15	Cameroon
	16	Congo, Rep.
	17	Djibouti
	18	Eritrea
	19	Guinea
	20	Madagascar
	21	Ethiopia
	22	Mauritania
	23	Senegal
	24	Burundi
	25	Tanzania
	26	Ghana
	27	Sierra Leone
	28	Uganda
	29	Niger
	30	Rwanda
	31	Togo
	32	Benin
	33	Mali
	34	Malawi
	35	Angola
	36	Liberia
	37	Sudan
	38	Burkina Faso
	39	Cape Verde
	40	Guinea-Bissau
	41	Mozambique
	42	Seychelles
	43	Zambia
	44	São Tomé & Príncipe
	45	Lesotho
	46	Equatorial Guinea
	47	Chad
smallest	n/a	Somalia

Current Account Balance as % of GDP
IMF

	Rank	2003-2006
largest	1	Gabon
	2	Botswana
	3	Angola
	4	Namibia
	5	Congo, Rep.
	6	Nigeria
	7	Côte d'Ivoire
	8	Eritrea
	9	Swaziland
	10	Kenya
	11	Mauritius
		SSA average
	12	Cameroon
	13	Mozambique
	14	Djibouti
	15	Central African Rep.
	16	Congo, Dem. Rep.
	17	South Africa
	18	Uganda
	19	Guinea-Bissau
	20	Togo
	21	Ghana
	22	Guinea
	23	Rwanda
	24	Tanzania
	25	Comoros
	26	Lesotho
	27	Ethiopia
	28	Sierra Leone
	29	Benin
	30	Mali
	31	Zimbabwe
	32	Senegal
	33	Madagascar
	34	Niger
	35	Cape Verde
	36	Malawi
	37	Zambia
	38	Burundi
	39	Gambia, The
	40	Burkina Faso
	41	Sudan
	42	Seychelles
	43	Equatorial Guinea
	44	Liberia
	45	Chad
	46	São Tomé & Príncipe
	47	Mauritania
smallest	n/a	Somalia

Current Account Balance as % of GDP
IMF

	Rank	2007-2010
largest	1	Gabon
	2	Namibia
	3	Angola
	4	Botswana
	5	Lesotho
	6	Nigeria
	7	Congo, Rep.
	8	Guinea-Bissau
	9	Equatorial Guinea
	10	Côte d'Ivoire
	11	Cameroon
	12	Zimbabwe
	13	Swaziland
		SSA average
	14	Comoros
	15	Malawi
	16	Chad
	17	Kenya
	18	Eritrea
	19	Zambia
	20	Ethiopia
	21	Sierra Leone
	22	Benin
	23	Central African Rep.
	24	Mauritius
	25	Mali
	26	Uganda
	27	Togo
	28	South Africa
	29	Sudan
	30	Ghana
	31	Tanzania
	32	Rwanda
	33	Mozambique
	34	Guinea
	35	Senegal
	36	Burkina Faso
	37	Gambia, The
	38	Mauritania
	39	Niger
	40	Burundi
	41	Cape Verde
	42	Congo, Dem. Rep.
	43	Madagascar
	44	Djibouti
	45	Liberia
	46	São Tomé & Príncipe
	47	Seychelles
smallest	n/a	Somalia

Debt Service as % of GNI
AfDB, World Bank

	Rank	1999-2002
highest	1	Equatorial Guinea
	2	Eritrea
	3	Uganda
	4	Rwanda
	5	Central African Rep.
	6	Niger
	7	Togo
	8	Sudan
	9	Botswana
	10	Burkina Faso
	11	Mozambique
	12	Comoros
	13	Chad
	14	South Africa
	15	Ethiopia
	16	Tanzania
	17	Djibouti
	18	Congo, Rep.
	19	Swaziland
	20	Benin
	21	Burundi
	22	Madagascar
	23	Malawi
	24	Sierra Leone
	25	Cameroon
	26	Zimbabwe
	27	Mali
	28	Cape Verde
	29	Kenya
	30	Guinea
	31	Ghana
	32	Gambia, The
	33	Senegal
	34	Zambia
	35	Nigeria
	36	Seychelles
	37	Mauritius
	38	Lesotho
	39	Mauritania
	40	Côte d'Ivoire
	41	Guinea-Bissau
	42	Gabon
	43	Angola
	n/a	Congo, Dem. Rep.
	n/a	Liberia
	n/a	Namibia
	n/a	São Tomé & Príncipe
	n/a	Somalia
lowest		

Debt Service as % of GNI
AfDB, World Bank

	Rank	2003-2006
highest	1	Togo
	2	Equatorial Guinea
	3	Zimbabwe
	4	Botswana
	5	Tanzania
	6	Mozambique
	7	Burkina Faso
	8	Côte d'Ivoire
	9	Ethiopia
	10	Comoros
	11	Niger
	12	Rwanda
	13	South Africa
	14	Chad
	15	Uganda
	16	Central African Rep.
	17	Madagascar
	18	Sudan
	19	Benin
	20	Mali
	21	Swaziland
	22	Sierra Leone
	23	Eritrea
	24	Djibouti
	25	Ghana
	26	Kenya
	27	Malawi
	28	Cameroon
	29	Senegal
	30	Cape Verde
	31	Mauritania
	32	Mauritius
	33	Guinea
	34	Gabon
	35	Congo, Rep.
	36	Lesotho
	37	Zambia
	38	Gambia, The
	39	Burundi
	40	Nigeria
	41	Seychelles
	42	Guinea-Bissau
	43	Angola
	n/a	Congo, Dem. Rep.
	n/a	Liberia
	n/a	Namibia
	n/a	São Tomé & Príncipe
	n/a	Somalia
lowest		

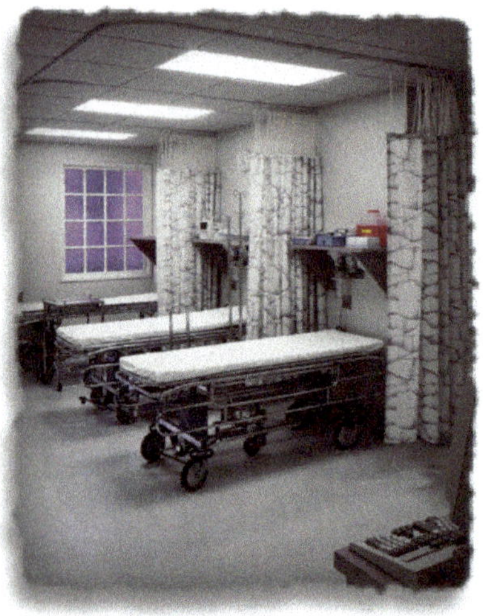

Total Expenditure on Health as % of GDP

World Bank

		2000-2002
largest	1	South Africa
	2	São Tomé & Príncipe
	3	Malawi
	4	Zimbabwe
	5	Uganda
	6	Namibia
	7	Ghana
	8	Lesotho
	9	Djibouti
	9	Chad
	10	Mali
	11	Zambia
		SSA average
	12	Swaziland
	13	Guinea-Bissau
	14	Guinea
	15	Gambia, The
	16	Ethiopia
	17	Gabon
	18	Seychelles
	19	Mozambique
	20	Cape Verde
	20	Burkina Faso
	21	Nigeria
	22	Togo
	23	Cameroon
	23	Eritrea
	24	Benin
	25	Senegal
	26	Botswana
	27	Kenya
	28	Rwanda
	28	Côte d'Ivoire
	29	Sierra Leone
	30	Tanzania
	30	Central African Rep.
	31	Mauritius
	32	Niger
	33	Burundi
	34	Liberia
	35	Congo, Dem. Rep.
	35	Sudan
	36	Madagascar
	37	Mauritania
	38	Angola
	39	Comoros
	40	Equatorial Guinea
	41	Congo, Rep.
smallest	n/a	Somalia

Total Expenditure on Health as % of GDP

World Bank

		2003-2006
largest	1	Malawi
	2	Zimbabwe
	3	São Tomé & Príncipe
	4	Rwanda
	5	Namibia
	5	South Africa
	6	Botswana
	7	Uganda
	8	Burundi
	9	Zambia
	10	Djibouti
	11	Lesotho
	12	Swaziland
	13	Burkina Faso
	14	Seychelles
	15	Ghana
	16	Togo
		SSA average
	17	Congo, Dem. Rep.
	18	Guinea-Bissau
	19	Guinea
	20	Mali
	21	Senegal
	22	Tanzania
	22	Chad
	23	Gambia, The
	24	Cape Verde
	25	Benin
	25	Sierra Leone
	26	Niger
	27	Gabon
	28	Mozambique
	29	Kenya
	29	Cameroon
	30	Liberia
	31	Ethiopia
	32	Mauritius
	33	Central African Rep.
	33	Nigeria
	34	Côte d'Ivoire
	35	Sudan
	36	Eritrea
	37	Madagascar
	38	Comoros
	39	Mauritania
	40	Congo, Rep.
	41	Angola
	42	Equatorial Guinea
smallest	n/a	Somalia

Total Govt. Expenditure on Health as % of GDP

World Bank

		2000-2002
largest	1	São Tomé & Príncipe
	2	Malawi
	3	Lesotho
	4	Namibia
	5	Djibouti
	6	Seychelles
	7	Gabon
	8	Cape Verde
	9	Swaziland
	10	Zambia
	11	Mozambique
	12	South Africa
	13	Zimbabwe
	14	Ethiopia
	15	Eritrea
	16	Botswana
	17	Chad
	18	Ghana
		SSA average
	19	Mali
	20	Benin
	21	Angola
	22	Madagascar
	23	Mauritius
	24	Sierra Leone
	25	Burkina Faso
	26	Gambia, The
	27	Kenya
	28	Uganda
	29	Niger
	30	Rwanda
	31	Mauritania
	32	Equatorial Guinea
	33	Senegal
	34	Tanzania
	35	Central African Rep.
	36	Guinea-Bissau
	37	Nigeria
	38	Comoros
	39	Congo, Rep.
	40	Cameroon
	41	Liberia
	42	Togo
	43	Sudan
	44	Côte d'Ivoire
	45	Guinea
	46	Burundi
	47	Congo, Dem. Rep.
smallest	n/a	Somalia

Total Govt. Expenditure on Health as % of GDP

World Bank

	2003-2006	
largest	1	Malawi
	2	Zimbabwe
	3	São Tomé & Príncipe
	4	Rwanda
	5	Namibia
	6	South Africa
	7	Botswana
	8	Uganda
	9	Burundi
	10	Zambia
	11	Djibouti
	12	Lesotho
	13	Swaziland
	14	Burkina Faso
	15	Seychelles
	16	Ghana
	17	Togo
		SSA average
	18	Congo, Dem. Rep.
	19	Guinea-Bissau
	20	Guinea
	21	Mali
	22	Senegal
	23	Tanzania
	24	Chad
	25	Gambia, The
	26	Cape Verde
	27	Benin
	28	Sierra Leone
	29	Niger
	30	Gabon
	31	Mozambique
	32	Kenya
	33	Cameroon
	34	Liberia
	35	Ethiopia
	36	Mauritius
	37	Central African Rep.
	38	Nigeria
	39	Côte d'Ivoire
	40	Sudan
	41	Eritrea
	42	Madagascar
	43	Comoros
	44	Mauritania
	45	Congo, Rep.
	46	Angola
	47	Equatorial Guinea
smallest	n/a	Somalia

Total Private Expenditure on Health as % of GDP

World Bank

	2000-2002	
largest	1	Uganda
	2	South Africa
	3	Guinea
	4	Zimbabwe
	5	Ghana
	6	Guinea-Bissau
	7	Togo
	8	Mali
	9	Cameroon
	10	Chad
		SSA average
	11	Nigeria
	12	Gambia, The
	13	Côte d'Ivoire
	14	Congo, Dem. Rep.
	15	Burundi
	16	Malawi
	17	Senegal
	18	Burkina Faso
	19	Zambia
	20	Kenya
	21	Benin
	22	Liberia
	23	Central African Rep.
	24	Sudan
	25	Swaziland
	26	Namibia
	27	Ethiopia
	28	Tanzania
	29	Rwanda
	30	Sierra Leone
	31	Eritrea
	32	Djibouti
	33	Botswana
	34	Mauritius
	35	Niger
	36	Lesotho
	37	Mozambique
	38	Gabon
	39	São Tomé & Príncipe
	40	Seychelles
	41	Madagascar
	42	Comoros
	43	Cape Verde
	44	Congo, Rep.
	45	Mauritania
	46	Equatorial Guinea
	47	Angola
smallest	n/a	Somalia

Total Private Expenditure on Health as % of GDP

World Bank

	2003-2006	
largest	1	Burundi
	2	Uganda
	3	South Africa
	4	Guinea
	5	Zimbabwe
	6	Congo, Dem. Rep.
	7	Togo
	8	Namibia
	9	Guinea-Bissau
	10	Ghana
	11	Rwanda
	12	Cameroon
		SSA average
	13	Malawi
	14	Liberia
	15	Mali
	16	Côte d'Ivoire
	17	Senegal
	18	Sierra Leone
	19	Nigeria
	20	Burkina Faso
	21	Lesotho
	22	Zambia
	23	Chad
	24	Central African Rep.
	25	Sudan
	26	Kenya
	27	Benin
	28	Swaziland
	29	Tanzania
	30	Niger
	31	Eritrea
	32	Mauritius
	33	Gambia, The
	34	Djibouti
	35	Ethiopia
	36	Botswana
	37	Mozambique
	38	Seychelles
	39	Gabon
	40	Comoros
	41	Madagascar
	42	São Tomé & Príncipe
	43	Cape Verde
	44	Congo, Rep.
	45	Mauritania
	46	Equatorial Guinea
	47	Angola
smallest	n/a	Somalia

Total Expenditure on Health per Person $PPP

Primary data: WHO

	2000-2002	
largest	1	South Africa
	2	Seychelles
	3	Mauritius
	4	Namibia
	5	Botswana
	6	Gabon
	7	Swaziland
	8	Equatorial Guinea
	9	Cape Verde
	10	Zimbabwe
	11	Lesotho
	12	Uganda
	13	Guinea
	14	Ghana
	15	Kenya
	16	São Tomé & Príncipe
	17	Côte d'Ivoire
	18	Djibouti
	19	Cameroon
	20	Rwanda
	21	Togo
	22	Zambia
	23	Mali
	24	Senegal
	25	Burkina Faso
	26	Central African Rep.
	27	Gambia, The
	28	Nigeria
	29	Guinea-Bissau
	30	Mauritania
	31	Angola
	32	Mozambique
	33	Sudan
	34	Chad
	35	Benin
	35	Malawi
	36	Eritrea
	37	Sierra Leone
	38	Madagascar
	39	Congo, Rep.
	39	Liberia
	40	Comoros
	41	Tanzania
	42	Niger
	43	Ethiopia
	44	Burundi
	45	Congo, Dem. Rep.
	n/a	Somalia
smallest		

Total Expenditure on Health per Person $PPP

Primary data: WHO

	2003-2006	
largest	1	South Africa
	2	Seychelles
	3	Botswana
	4	Mauritius
	5	Namibia
	6	Swaziland
	7	Gabon
	8	Equatorial Guinea
	9	Cape Verde
	10	Zimbabwe
	11	Rwanda
	12	Uganda
	13	São Tomé & Príncipe
	14	Lesotho
	15	Guinea
	16	Kenya
	17	Ghana
	18	Djibouti
	19	Burkina Faso
	20	Cameroon
	21	Senegal
	22	Togo
	23	Malawi
	24	Zambia
	25	Côte d'Ivoire
	26	Mali
	27	Gambia, The
	28	Central African Rep.
	28	Sudan
	29	Angola
	30	Mozambique
	31	Nigeria
	32	Mauritania
	33	Benin
	34	Chad
	35	Sierra Leone
	36	Guinea-Bissau
	37	Tanzania
	38	Eritrea
	39	Liberia
	40	Madagascar
	41	Comoros
	42	Congo, Rep.
	43	Niger
	44	Ethiopia
	45	Congo, Dem. Rep.
	46	Burundi
	n/a	Somalia
smallest		

	Total Govt. Expenditure on Health per Person $PPP		Total Govt. Expenditure on Health per Person $PPP		Total Private Expenditure on Health per Person $PPP		Total Private Expenditure on Health per Person $PPP		Govt. Expenditure on Health as % of Total Govt. Expenditure
	Primary data: WHO		Primary data: WHO		Primary data: WHO		Primary data: WHO		Primary data: WHO
	1999-2002		2003-2006		2000-2002		2003-2006		1999-2002
	largest		*largest*		*largest*		*largest*		*highest*
1	Seychelles	1	Seychelles	1	South Africa	1	South Africa	1	Gabon
2	South Africa	2	Botswana	2	Mauritius	2	Mauritius	2	Namibia
3	Namibia	3	South Africa	3	Seychelles	3	Seychelles	3	Benin
4	Gabon	4	Mauritius	4	Swaziland	4	Botswana	4	Malawi
5	Mauritius	5	Namibia	5	Namibia	5	Swaziland	5	Chad
6	Botswana	6	Swaziland	6	Botswana	6	Namibia	6	Tanzania
7	Swaziland	7	Equatorial Guinea	7	Zimbabwe	7	Guinea	7	Djibouti
8	Equatorial Guinea	8	Gabon	8	Guinea	8	Uganda	8	Mozambique
9	Cape Verde	9	Cape Verde	9	Uganda	9	Zimbabwe	9	Equatorial Guinea
10	São Tomé & Príncipe	10	São Tomé & Príncipe	10	Gabon	10	Gabon	10	Niger
11	Lesotho	11	Rwanda	11	Côte d'Ivoire	11	Equatorial Guinea	11	Madagascar
12	Zimbabwe	12	Lesotho	12	Ghana	12	Rwanda	12	Swaziland
13	Djibouti	13	Djibouti	13	Lesotho	13	Ghana	13	Zambia
14	Kenya	14	Zimbabwe	14	Cameroon	14	Cameroon	14	Cape Verde
15	Angola	15	Malawi	15	Cape Verde	15	Lesotho	14	Mali
16	Ghana	16	Kenya	16	Kenya	16	Togo	15	Ethiopia
17	Zambia	16	Burkina Faso	17	Togo	17	Kenya	16	Ghana
18	Uganda	17	Angola	18	Equatorial Guinea	18	Côte d'Ivoire	17	Burkina Faso
19	Mauritania	18	Uganda	19	Guinea-Bissau	19	Cape Verde	18	Central African Rep.
20	Rwanda	19	Gambia, The	20	Mali	20	Senegal	19	Uganda
21	Mozambique	20	Zambia	20	Senegal	21	Burkina Faso	20	Zimbabwe
22	Gambia, The	21	Ghana	21	Rwanda	22	Sudan	21	Rwanda
23	Malawi	22	Mozambique	22	Nigeria	23	Central African Rep.	22	South Africa
24	Mali	23	Mali	23	Burkina Faso	24	Nigeria	23	Botswana
25	Burkina Faso	23	Mauritania	24	Central African Rep.	25	Mali	24	São Tomé & Príncipe
25	Central African Rep.	24	Senegal	25	Sudan	26	Zambia	25	Senegal
26	Senegal	25	Benin	26	Gambia, The	27	Guinea-Bissau	26	Gambia, The
26	Madagascar	26	Cameroon	27	Djibouti	28	Chad	27	Cameroon
27	Côte d'Ivoire	27	Liberia	28	Zambia	29	Eritrea	28	Mauritius
28	Benin	28	Sierra Leone	29	Chad	30	Djibouti	29	Comoros
29	Cameroon	29	Central African Rep.	30	Eritrea	31	Gambia, The	30	Seychelles
30	Guinea	29	Madagascar	31	Benin	32	Benin	30	Sudan
31	Eritrea	30	Tanzania	32	Liberia	33	Sierra Leone	31	Liberia
31	Sierra Leone	31	Sudan	33	Sierra Leone	34	São Tomé & Príncipe	32	Sierra Leone
32	Congo, Rep.	32	Comoros	34	Tanzania	35	Malawi	33	Lesotho
33	Chad	33	Togo	35	Malawi	36	Tanzania	34	Kenya
34	Comoros	34	Chad	36	São Tomé & Príncipe	37	Mozambique	35	Togo
35	Nigeria	35	Côte d'Ivoire	36	Mozambique	38	Congo, Rep.	36	Mauritania
36	Togo	36	Guinea	37	Mauritania	39	Mauritania	37	Côte d'Ivoire
36	Niger	36	Congo, Rep.	38	Congo, Rep.	40	Comoros	38	Guinea
37	Sudan	37	Nigeria	38	Comoros	41	Liberia	39	Congo, Rep.
38	Liberia	38	Niger	39	Burundi	42	Madagascar	40	Guinea-Bissau
38	Tanzania	39	Guinea-Bissau	40	Madagascar	42	Niger	41	Nigeria
39	Ethiopia	39	Eritrea	40	Niger	43	Burundi	42	Angola
40	Guinea-Bissau	40	Ethiopia	40	Congo, Dem. Rep.	44	Congo, Dem. Rep.	43	Eritrea
41	Burundi	41	Congo, Dem. Rep.	41	Ethiopia	45	Ethiopia	44	Burundi
42	Congo, Dem. Rep.	42	Burundi	42	Angola	46	Angola	45	Congo, Dem. Rep.
n/a	Somalia	n/a	Somalia	n/a	Somalia	n/a	Somalia	n/a	Somalia
	smallest		*smallest*		*smallest*		*smallest*		*lowest*

Govt. Expenditure on Health as % of Total Govt. Expenditure (Primary data: WHO) 2003-2006 (highest → lowest)		Out-of-Pocket Expenditure as % of Total Health Expenditure (Primary data: WHO) 1999-2002 (smallest → largest)		Out-of-Pocket Expenditure as % of Total Health Expenditure (Primary data: WHO) 2003-2006 (smallest → largest)		Out-of-Pocket Expenditure as % of Private Health Expenditure (Primary data: WHO) 1999-2002 (smallest → largest)		Out-of-Pocket Expenditure as % of Private Health Expenditure (Primary data: WHO) 2003-2006 (smallest → largest)	
1	Rwanda	1	Namibia	1	Namibia	1	South Africa	1	Namibia
2	Liberia	2	South Africa	2	Botswana	2	Namibia	2	South Africa
3	Malawi	3	Botswana	3	Malawi	3	Botswana	3	Botswana
4	Botswana	4	Mozambique	4	South Africa	4	Mozambique	4	Malawi
5	Burkina Faso	5	Seychelles	5	São Tomé & Príncipe	5	Swaziland	5	Mozambique
6	Gabon	6	Swaziland	6	Mozambique	6	Malawi	6	Swaziland
7	São Tomé & Príncipe	7	São Tomé & Príncipe	7	Swaziland	7	Rwanda	7	Rwanda
8	Djibouti	8	Malawi	8	Seychelles	8	Zimbabwe	8	Uganda
9	Benin	9	Madagascar	9	Angola	9	Madagascar	9	Zimbabwe
10	Mali	10	Rwanda	10	Equatorial Guinea	10	Uganda	10	Madagascar
11	Cape Verde	11	Cape Verde	11	Rwanda	11	Guinea-Bissau	11	Seychelles
12	Namibia	12	Gabon	12	Madagascar	12	Seychelles	12	Eritrea
13	Tanzania	13	Equatorial Guinea	13	Cape Verde	13	Eritrea	13	Guinea-Bissau
14	Mozambique	14	Angola	14	Djibouti	14	Lesotho	14	Lesotho
15	Zambia	15	Zimbabwe	15	Gambia, The	15	Mauritius	15	Gambia, The
16	Swaziland	16	Mauritania	16	Gabon	16	Zambia	16	Zambia
17	Central African Rep.	17	Djibouti	17	Lesotho	17	Ghana	17	Equatorial Guinea
18	Gambia, The	18	Lesotho	18	Zimbabwe	18	Kenya	18	Ghana
19	Niger	19	Zambia	19	Zambia	19	Ethiopia	19	Kenya
20	Ethiopia	20	Mauritius	20	Ethiopia	20	Tanzania	20	Mauritius
21	Cameroon	21	Eritrea	21	Mauritania	21	Equatorial Guinea	21	Ethiopia
22	Uganda	22	Ethiopia	22	Uganda	22	Gambia, The	22	Tanzania
23	Seychelles	23	Uganda	23	Mauritius	23	Niger	23	Togo
24	Chad	24	Niger	24	Tanzania	24	Togo	24	Niger
24	South Africa	25	Kenya	25	Liberia	25	Côte d'Ivoire	25	Côte d'Ivoire
25	Madagascar	26	Congo, Rep.	26	Niger	26	Senegal	26	Senegal
26	Mauritius	27	Gambia, The	27	Burkina Faso	27	Nigeria	27	Nigeria
27	Zimbabwe	28	Comoros	28	Kenya	28	Cameroon	28	Burkina Faso
28	Comoros	29	Tanzania	29	Eritrea	29	Burkina Faso	29	Cameroon
29	Lesotho	30	Guinea-Bissau	30	Comoros	30	Central African Rep.	30	Central African Rep.
30	Sierra Leone	31	Ghana	31	Guinea-Bissau	31	Chad	31	Chad
31	Senegal	32	Benin	32	Benin	32	Sudan	32	Sudan
32	Equatorial Guinea	33	Sierra Leone	33	Sierra Leone	33	Djibouti	33	Djibouti
33	Ghana	34	Burkina Faso	34	Ghana	34	Liberia	34	Liberia
34	Congo, Dem. Rep.	35	Central African Rep.	35	Mali	35	Guinea	35	Mali
35	Sudan	36	Senegal	36	Congo, Rep.	36	Mali	36	Guinea
36	Togo	37	Liberia	37	Chad	37	Cape Verde	37	Cape Verde
37	Kenya	38	Chad	38	Senegal	38	Benin	38	Benin
38	Guinea	39	Mali	39	Central African Rep.	39	Angola	39	Angola
39	Angola	40	Nigeria	40	Sudan	39	Burundi	39	Burundi
40	Mauritania	41	Togo	41	Nigeria	39	Comoros	39	Comoros
41	Côte d'Ivoire	42	Côte d'Ivoire	42	Togo	39	Congo, Dem. Rep.	39	Congo, Dem. Rep.
41	Guinea-Bissau	43	Cameroon	43	Côte d'Ivoire	39	Congo, Rep.	39	Congo, Rep.
42	Eritrea	44	Sudan	44	Congo, Dem. Rep.	39	Gabon	39	Gabon
43	Congo, Rep.	45	Burundi	45	Cameroon	39	Mauritania	39	Mauritania
44	Nigeria	46	Guinea	46	Burundi	39	São Tomé & Príncipe	39	São Tomé & Príncipe
45	Burundi	47	Congo, Dem. Rep.	47	Guinea	39	Sierra Leone	39	Sierra Leone
n/a	Somalia	n/a	Somalia	n/a	Somalia	n/a	Somalia	n/a	Somalia

performance tables – purchasing power

Govt. Consumption as $PPP per Person (IMF, World Bank)

	Rank	1999-2002
highest	1	Seychelles
	2	Botswana
	3	Gabon
	4	South Africa
	5	Angola
	6	Mauritius
	7	Namibia
	8	Swaziland
	9	Eritrea
	10	Congo, Rep.
	11	Cape Verde
	12	Nigeria
		SSA average
	13	Mauritania
	14	Kenya
	15	Lesotho
	16	Senegal
	17	Cameroon
	18	Comoros
	19	Benin
	20	Gambia, The
	21	Côte d'Ivoire
	22	Burkina Faso
	23	Zambia
	24	Sudan
	25	Ghana
	26	Uganda
	27	Ethiopia
	28	Malawi
	29	Mali
	30	Central African Rep.
	31	Chad
	32	Tanzania
	33	Rwanda
	34	Niger
	35	Togo
	36	Guinea-Bissau
	37	Guinea
	38	Burundi
	39	Madagascar
	40	Sierra Leone
	41	Mozambique
	42	Zimbabwe
	43	Congo, Dem. Rep.
	44	Equatorial Guinea
	n/a	Djibouti
	n/a	Liberia
	n/a	São Tomé & Príncipe
lowest	n/a	Somalia

Govt. Consumption as $PPP per Person (IMF, World Bank)

	Rank	2003-2006
highest	1	Botswana
	2	Seychelles
	3	South Africa
	4	Mauritius
	5	Namibia
	6	Angola
	7	Swaziland
	8	Gabon
	9	Congo, Rep.
	10	Eritrea
	11	Nigeria
	12	Mauritania
	13	Cape Verde
		SSA average
	14	Sudan
	15	Equatorial Guinea
	16	Kenya
	17	Senegal
	18	Cameroon
	19	Benin
	20	Ghana
	21	Lesotho
	22	Burkina Faso
	23	Tanzania
	24	Zambia
	25	Côte d'Ivoire
	26	Gambia, The
	27	Uganda
	28	Comoros
	29	Malawi
	30	Rwanda
	31	Ethiopia
	32	Chad
	33	Mali
	34	Madagascar
	35	Sierra Leone
	36	Burundi
	37	Central African Rep.
	38	Togo
	39	Mozambique
	40	Niger
	41	Guinea-Bissau
	42	Guinea
	43	Zimbabwe
	44	Congo, Dem. Rep.
	n/a	Djibouti
	n/a	Liberia
	n/a	São Tomé & Príncipe
lowest	n/a	Somalia

Household Consumption as $PPP per Person (IMF, World Bank)

	Rank	1999-2002
highest	1	Seychelles
	2	Gabon
	3	Mauritius
	4	South Africa
	5	Botswana
	6	Swaziland
	7	Cape Verde
	8	Namibia
	9	Mauritania
	10	Cameroon
	11	Côte d'Ivoire
	12	Sudan
	13	Benin
	14	Congo, Rep.
	15	Senegal
	16	Lesotho
	17	Kenya
		SSA average
	18	Chad
	19	Angola
	20	Ghana
	21	Comoros
	22	Guinea
	23	Burkina Faso
	24	Gambia, The
	25	Zambia
	26	Tanzania
	27	Eritrea
	28	São Tomé & Príncipe
	29	Madagascar
	30	Nigeria
	31	Togo
	32	Mali
	33	Uganda
	34	Rwanda
	35	Central African Rep.
	36	Malawi
	37	Guinea-Bissau
	38	Niger
	39	Mozambique
	40	Ethiopia
	41	Sierra Leone
	42	Burundi
	43	Congo, Dem. Rep.
	44	Zimbabwe
	n/a	Djibouti
	n/a	Liberia
	n/a	São Tomé & Príncipe
lowest	n/a	Somalia

	Household Consumption as $PPP per Person (IMF, World Bank) 2003-2006		Govt. Consumption as % of GDP (World Bank) 1999-2002		Govt. Consumption as % of GDP (World Bank) 2003-2006		Household Consumption as % of GDP (World Bank) 1999-2002		Household Consumption as % of GDP (World Bank) 2003-2006	
highest	1	Seychelles	1	Eritrea	1	Eritrea	1	Lesotho	1	Cape Verde
	2	Gabon	2	Angola	2	Botswana	2	Cape Verde	2	Malawi
	3	Mauritius	3	Botswana	3	Angola	3	Guinea-Bissau	3	Central African Rep.
	4	South Africa	4	Namibia	4	Namibia	4	Sierra Leone	4	Lesotho
	5	Botswana	5	Seychelles	5	Seychelles	5	Chad	5	Congo, Dem. Rep.
	6	Cape Verde	6	Nigeria	6	Swaziland	6	Togo	6	Guinea
	7	Swaziland	7	Swaziland	7	Nigeria	7	Burundi	7	Comoros
	8	Namibia	8	Ethiopia	8	Burundi	8	Congo, Dem. Rep.	7	Sierra Leone
	9	Mauritania	9	Burundi	8	Zimbabwe	9	Rwanda	8	Guinea-Bissau
	10	Angola	10	South Africa	9	Mauritania	10	Malawi	9	Togo
	11	Cameroon	11	Lesotho	10	South Africa	11	Comoros	10	Rwanda
	12	Sudan		SSA average		SSA average	12	Ghana	11	Madagascar
	13	Senegal	12	Cape Verde	11	Kenya	13	Benin	12	Ethiopia
	14	Congo, Rep.	13	Kenya	12	Malawi	14	Tanzania	13	Burundi
	15	Côte d'Ivoire	14	Comoros	13	Ethiopia	15	Madagascar	14	Eritrea
	16	Benin	15	Congo, Rep.	14	Congo, Rep.	16	Niger	15	Mauritania
	17	Kenya	16	Malawi	15	Lesotho	17	Mauritania	16	Niger
	18	Equatorial Guinea	17	Mauritania	16	Sudan	18	Burkina Faso	17	Ghana
		SSA average	18	Sierra Leone	17	Ghana	19	Sudan	18	Mali
	19	Lesotho	19	Uganda	18	Uganda	20	Guinea	19	Burkina Faso
	20	Ghana	20	Zimbabwe	19	Guinea-Bissau	21	Mozambique	20	Benin
	21	Comoros	21	Gambia, The	20	Mauritius	22	Uganda	21	Senegal
	22	Chad	22	Gabon	21	Benin	23	Central African Rep.	22	Gambia, The
	23	Guinea	23	Senegal	22	Senegal	23	Ethiopia	23	Uganda
	24	Burkina Faso	24	Niger	23	Rwanda	24	Mali	24	Tanzania
	25	Gambia, The	25	Mauritius	24	Cape Verde	25	Senegal	25	Kenya
	26	Tanzania	26	Burkina Faso	25	Sierra Leone	26	Zambia	26	Sudan
	27	Madagascar	27	Guinea-Bissau	26	Tanzania	27	Eritrea	27	Mozambique
	28	Mali	28	Zambia	27	Burkina Faso	28	Gambia, The	28	Cameroon
	29	Zambia	29	Central African Rep.	28	Zambia	29	Zimbabwe	29	Côte d'Ivoire
	30	Nigeria	30	Benin	29	Niger	30	Kenya	30	Zimbabwe
	31	Eritrea	31	Rwanda	30	Central African Rep.	31	Swaziland	31	Swaziland
	32	Uganda	32	Mali	31	Comoros	32	Côte d'Ivoire	32	Mauritius
	33	Rwanda	33	Ghana	32	Gambia, The	33	Cameroon	33	Zambia
	34	Togo	34	Mozambique	33	Cameroon		SSA average	34	South Africa
	35	Malawi	35	Cameroon	34	Mozambique	34	Mauritius	35	Gabon
	36	Central African Rep.	35	Togo	35	Togo	35	South Africa	36	Chad
	37	Sierra Leone	36	Tanzania	36	Madagascar	36	Namibia		SSA average
	38	Ethiopia	37	Sudan	37	Mali	37	Gabon	37	Seychelles
	39	Mozambique	38	Madagascar	38	Côte d'Ivoire	38	Seychelles	38	Namibia
	40	Niger	39	Chad	39	Gabon	39	Nigeria	39	Angola
	41	Guinea-Bissau	40	Côte d'Ivoire	40	Congo, Dem. Rep.	40	Congo, Rep.	40	Nigeria
	42	Burundi	41	Congo, Dem. Rep.	41	Guinea	41	Angola	41	Congo, Rep.
	43	Congo, Dem. Rep.	42	Guinea	42	Chad	42	Botswana	42	Botswana
	44	Zimbabwe	n/a	Equatorial Guinea	43	Equatorial Guinea	n/a	Equatorial Guinea	43	Equatorial Guinea
	n/a	Djibouti	n/a	Djibouti	n/a	Djibouti	n/a	Djibouti	n/a	Djibouti
	n/a	Liberia	n/a	Liberia	n/a	Liberia	n/a	Liberia	n/a	Liberia
	n/a	São Tomé & Príncipe	n/a	São Tomé & Príncipe	n/a	São Tomé & Príncipe	n/a	São Tomé & Príncipe	n/a	São Tomé & Príncipe
lowest	n/a	Somalia	n/a	Somalia	n/a	Somalia	n/a	Somalia	n/a	Somalia

Growth in Govt. Consumption

IMF, World Bank

	Rank	1999-2002
highest	1	Nigeria
	2	Sierra Leone
	3	Ethiopia
	4	Angola
	5	Guinea
	6	Sudan
	7	Chad
	8	Mozambique
	9	Benin
	10	Botswana
	11	Tanzania
	12	Mauritania
	13	Uganda
	14	Guinea-Bissau
	15	Rwanda
	16	Senegal
	17	Cape Verde
	18	Cameroon
		SSA average
	19	Mauritius
	20	Burkina Faso
	21	Burundi
	22	Côte d'Ivoire
	23	South Africa
	24	Gambia, The
	25	Comoros
	26	Ghana
	27	Kenya
	28	Central African Rep.
	29	Madagascar
	30	Zambia
	31	Namibia
	32	Congo, Rep.
	33	Niger
	34	Malawi
	35	Swaziland
	36	Eritrea
	37	Seychelles
	38	Mali
	39	Lesotho
	40	Zimbabwe
	41	Togo
	42	Congo, Dem. Rep.
	43	Gabon
	n/a	Equatorial Guinea
	n/a	Djibouti
	n/a	Liberia
	n/a	São Tomé & Príncipe
lowest	n/a	Somalia

Growth in Govt. Consumption

IMF, World Bank

	Rank	2003-2006
highest	1	Burundi
	2	Sudan
	3	Congo, Dem. Rep.
	4	Guinea-Bissau
	5	Ghana
	6	Mali
	7	Tanzania
	8	Swaziland
	9	Gabon
	10	Madagascar
	11	Mauritania
	12	Malawi
	13	Benin
	14	Cape Verde
	15	Mauritius
	16	Senegal
	17	Rwanda
	18	Togo
	19	Eritrea
	20	South Africa
	21	Mozambique
	22	Zimbabwe
		SSA average
	23	Seychelles
	24	Botswana
	25	Burkina Faso
	26	Uganda
	27	Kenya
	28	Cameroon
	29	Namibia
	30	Niger
	31	Chad
	32	Côte d'Ivoire
	33	Sierra Leone
	34	Nigeria
	35	Lesotho
	36	Gambia, The
	37	Central African Rep.
	38	Ethiopia
	39	Zambia
	40	Congo, Rep.
	41	Angola
	42	Guinea
	43	Comoros
	44	Equatorial Guinea
	n/a	Djibouti
	n/a	Liberia
	n/a	São Tomé & Príncipe
lowest	n/a	Somalia

Growth in Household Consumption

IMF, World Bank

	Rank	1999-2002
highest	1	Angola
	2	Gabon
	3	Sierra Leone
	4	Cape Verde
	5	Mozambique
	6	Burkina Faso
	7	Chad
	8	Malawi
	9	Ethiopia
	10	Seychelles
	11	Mauritius
	12	Mali
	13	Mauritania
	14	Guinea
	15	Botswana
	16	Senegal
	17	Ghana
	18	Uganda
	19	Benin
	20	Namibia
	21	Cameroon
	22	South Africa
	23	Zimbabwe
	24	Sudan
	25	Gambia, The
	26	Nigeria
	27	Burundi
	28	Eritrea
	29	Rwanda
	30	Niger
		SSA average
	31	Tanzania
	32	Kenya
	33	Zambia
	34	Comoros
	35	Central African Rep.
	36	Togo
	37	Lesotho
	38	Madagascar
	39	Guinea-Bissau
	40	Swaziland
	41	Congo, Dem. Rep.
	42	Côte d'Ivoire
	43	Congo, Rep.
	n/a	Equatorial Guinea
	n/a	Djibouti
	n/a	Liberia
	n/a	São Tomé & Príncipe
lowest	n/a	Somalia

Growth in Household Consumption

IMF, World Bank

	Rank	2003-2006
highest	1	Gabon
	2	Ethiopia
	3	Madagascar
	4	Botswana
	5	Cape Verde
	6	Mauritius
	7	Sierra Leone
	8	Central African Rep.
	9	South Africa
	10	Kenya
	11	Ghana
	12	Gambia, The
	13	Malawi
	14	Tanzania
	15	Angola
	16	Congo, Rep.
	17	Mali
	18	Sudan
	19	Comoros
	20	Congo, Dem. Rep.
	21	Swaziland
	22	Rwanda
	23	Senegal
	24	Burkina Faso
	25	Mozambique
	26	Mauritania
	27	Guinea
	28	Uganda
	29	Togo
	30	Seychelles
	31	Niger
	32	Namibia
	33	Côte d'Ivoire
		SSA average
	34	Cameroon
	35	Benin
	36	Zambia
	37	Burundi
	38	Lesotho
	39	Nigeria
	40	Chad
	41	Guinea-Bissau
	42	Eritrea
	43	Zimbabwe
	44	Equatorial Guinea
	n/a	Djibouti
	n/a	Liberia
	n/a	São Tomé & Príncipe
lowest	n/a	Somalia

Total Exports per Person $US

WTO

		1999-2002
greatest	1	Seychelles
	2	Equatorial Guinea
	3	Mauritius
	4	Gabon
	5	Botswana
	6	Swaziland
	7	Namibia
	8	South Africa
	9	Congo, Rep.
	10	Angola
	11	Côte d'Ivoire
	12	Cape Verde
		SSA average
	13	Nigeria
	14	Lesotho
	15	Cameroon
	16	Mauritania
	17	Djibouti
	18	Senegal
	19	Ghana
	20	Zambia
	21	São Tomé & Príncipe
	22	Guinea
	23	Kenya
	24	Comoros
	25	Togo
	26	Mali
	27	Benin
	28	Madagascar
	29	Gambia, The
	30	Sudan
	31	Mozambique
	32	Guinea-Bissau
	33	Tanzania
	34	Central African Rep.
	35	Malawi
	36	Niger
	37	Uganda
	38	Chad
	39	Burkina Faso
	40	Congo, Dem. Rep.
	41	Ethiopia
	42	Rwanda
	43	Sierra Leone
	44	Burundi
	n/a	Eritrea
	n/a	Liberia
	n/a	Somalia
smallest	n/a	Zimbabwe

Total Exports per Person $US

WTO

		2003-2006
greatest	1	Equatorial Guinea
	2	Seychelles
	3	Gabon
	4	Mauritius
	5	Botswana
	6	Swaziland
	7	Angola
	8	Congo, Rep.
	9	South Africa
	10	Namibia
	11	Cape Verde
	12	Côte d'Ivoire
	13	Lesotho
	14	Nigeria
		SSA average
	15	Mauritania
	16	Chad
	17	Cameroon
	18	Zambia
	19	Senegal
	20	Djibouti
	21	Ghana
	22	São Tomé & Príncipe
	23	Kenya
	24	Togo
	25	Mali
	26	Sudan
	27	Mozambique
	28	Guinea
	29	Benin
	30	Comoros
	31	Madagascar
	32	Tanzania
	33	Gambia, The
	34	Guinea-Bissau
	35	Malawi
	36	Burkina Faso
	37	Uganda
	38	Niger
	39	Sierra Leone
	40	Congo, Dem. Rep.
	41	Central African Rep.
	42	Ethiopia
	43	Rwanda
	44	Burundi
	n/a	Eritrea
	n/a	Liberia
	n/a	Somalia
smallest	n/a	Zimbabwe

Total Imports per Person $US

WTO

		1999-2002
smallest	1	Congo, Dem. Rep.
	2	Burundi
	3	Ethiopia
	4	Rwanda
	5	Niger
	6	Sierra Leone
	7	Central African Rep.
	8	Guinea-Bissau
	9	Tanzania
	10	Burkina Faso
	11	Malawi
	12	Sudan
	13	Uganda
	14	Madagascar
	15	Mozambique
	16	Guinea
	17	Nigeria
	18	Kenya
	19	Benin
	20	Mali
	21	Chad
	22	Togo
	23	Comoros
	24	Zambia
	25	Gambia, The
	26	Cameroon
		SSA average
	27	Ghana
	28	Senegal
	29	Mauritania
	30	Côte d'Ivoire
	31	São Tomé & Príncipe
	32	Djibouti
	33	Angola
	34	Lesotho
	35	Congo, Rep.
	36	South Africa
	37	Cape Verde
	38	Namibia
	39	Swaziland
	40	Gabon
	41	Botswana
	42	Mauritius
	43	Equatorial Guinea
	44	Seychelles
	n/a	Eritrea
	n/a	Liberia
	n/a	Somalia
greatest	n/a	Zimbabwe

appendix B8: performance tables – self-reliance

Total Imports per Person $US

WTO

	2003-2006	
smallest	1	Congo, Dem. Rep.
	2	Burundi
	3	Rwanda
	4	Ethiopia
	5	Central African Rep.
	6	Sierra Leone
	7	Niger
	8	Guinea-Bissau
	9	Uganda
	10	Malawi
	11	Tanzania
	12	Guinea
	13	Madagascar
	14	Burkina Faso
	15	Mozambique
	16	Benin
	17	Nigeria
	18	Gambia, The
	19	Kenya
	20	Mali
	21	Sudan
	22	Togo
	23	Cameroon
	24	Chad
	25	Comoros
	26	Zambia
	27	Ghana
		SSA average
	28	Senegal
	29	Côte d'Ivoire
	30	Djibouti
	31	São Tomé & Príncipe
	32	Mauritania
	33	Lesotho
	34	Angola
	35	Congo, Rep.
	36	Cape Verde
	37	Namibia
	38	South Africa
	39	Gabon
	40	Botswana
	41	Swaziland
	42	Mauritius
	43	Equatorial Guinea
	44	Seychelles
	n/a	Eritrea
	n/a	Liberia
	n/a	Somalia
greatest	n/a	Zimbabwe

Goods Exports per Person $US

WTO

	1999-2002	
greatest	1	Equatorial Guinea
	2	Seychelles
	3	Gabon
	4	Botswana
	5	Mauritius
	6	Swaziland
	7	South Africa
	8	Congo, Rep.
	9	Namibia
	10	Angola
	11	Côte d'Ivoire
	12	Nigeria
	13	Lesotho
	14	Mauritania
		SSA average
	15	Cameroon
	16	Senegal
	17	Zambia
	18	Ghana
	19	Guinea
	20	Togo
	21	Mali
	22	Kenya
	23	Benin
	24	Sudan
	25	Madagascar
	26	Djibouti
	27	Guinea-Bissau
	28	Central African Rep.
	29	Malawi
	30	Mozambique
	31	Comoros
	32	Niger
	33	Cape Verde
	34	Chad
	35	Tanzania
	36	São Tomé & Príncipe
	37	Burkina Faso
	38	Uganda
	39	Congo, Dem. Rep.
	40	Gambia, The
	41	Rwanda
	42	Ethiopia
	43	Burundi
	44	Sierra Leone
	n/a	Eritrea
	n/a	Liberia
	n/a	Somalia
smallest	n/a	Zimbabwe

Goods Exports per Person $US

WTO

	2003-2006	
greatest	1	Equatorial Guinea
	2	Seychelles
	3	Gabon
	4	Botswana
	5	Swaziland
	6	Mauritius
	7	Angola
	8	Congo, Rep.
	9	South Africa
	10	Namibia
	11	Côte d'Ivoire
	12	Lesotho
	13	Nigeria
		SSA average
	14	Chad
	15	Mauritania
	16	Zambia
	17	Cameroon
	18	Senegal
	19	Ghana
	20	Sudan
	21	Togo
	22	Mali
	23	Guinea
	24	Kenya
	25	Mozambique
	26	Benin
	27	Djibouti
	28	Madagascar
	29	Guinea-Bissau
	30	Tanzania
	31	Malawi
	32	Niger
	33	Burkina Faso
	34	Congo, Dem. Rep.
	35	Cape Verde
	36	Central African Rep.
	37	São Tomé & Príncipe
	38	Comoros
	39	Sierra Leone
	40	Uganda
	41	Rwanda
	42	Ethiopia
	43	Burundi
	44	Gambia, The
	n/a	Eritrea
	n/a	Liberia
	n/a	Somalia
smallest	n/a	Zimbabwe

Goods Imports per Person $US

WTO

	1999-2002	
smallest	1	Congo, Dem. Rep.
	2	Burundi
	3	Ethiopia
	4	Rwanda
	5	Central African Rep.
	6	Sierra Leone
	7	Niger
	8	Guinea-Bissau
	9	Tanzania
	10	Malawi
	11	Sudan
	12	Madagascar
	13	Uganda
	14	Burkina Faso
	15	Mozambique
	16	Nigeria
	17	Guinea
	18	Chad
	19	Mali
	20	Benin
	21	Comoros
	22	Kenya
	23	Cameroon
	24	Zambia
	25	Togo
	26	Gambia, The
		SSA average
	27	Ghana
	28	Mauritania
	29	Côte d'Ivoire
	30	Senegal
	31	Congo, Rep.
	32	São Tomé & Príncipe
	33	Angola
	34	Djibouti
	35	Lesotho
	36	Cape Verde
	37	South Africa
	38	Gabon
	39	Namibia
	40	Swaziland
	41	Botswana
	42	Equatorial Guinea
	43	Mauritius
	44	Seychelles
	n/a	Eritrea
	n/a	Liberia
	n/a	Somalia
greatest	n/a	Zimbabwe

Goods Imports per Person $US

WTO

	2003-2006	
smallest	1	Burundi
	2	Congo, Dem. Rep.
	3	Central African Rep.
	4	Rwanda
	5	Ethiopia
	6	Guinea-Bissau
	7	Niger
	8	Sierra Leone
	9	Uganda
	10	Malawi
	11	Tanzania
	12	Madagascar
	13	Guinea
	14	Burkina Faso
	15	Chad
	16	Benin
	17	Mozambique
	18	Nigeria
	19	Mali
	20	Gambia, The
	21	Sudan
	22	Cameroon
	23	Kenya
	24	Comoros
	25	Togo
	26	Zambia
		SSA average
	27	Ghana
	28	Côte d'Ivoire
	29	Senegal
	30	São Tomé & Príncipe
	31	Djibouti
	32	Congo, Rep.
	33	Mauritania
	34	Angola
	35	Lesotho
	36	Cape Verde
	37	Gabon
	38	Namibia
	39	South Africa
	40	Botswana
	41	Swaziland
	42	Mauritius
	43	Equatorial Guinea
	44	Seychelles
	n/a	Eritrea
	n/a	Liberia
	n/a	Somalia
greatest	n/a	Zimbabwe

appendix B8: performance tables — self-reliance

Services Exports per Person $US

WTO

		1999-2002
greatest	1	Seychelles
	2	Mauritius
	3	Cape Verde
	4	Botswana
	5	Namibia
	6	Gabon
	7	Swaziland
	8	South Africa
	9	Djibouti
	10	São Tomé & Príncipe
	11	Comoros
	12	Gambia, The
	13	Congo, Rep.
	14	Cameroon
	15	Senegal
	16	Equatorial Guinea
	17	Côte d'Ivoire
	18	Ghana
	19	Kenya
		SSA average
	20	Tanzania
	21	Benin
	22	Lesotho
	23	Madagascar
	24	Mozambique
	25	Angola
	26	Nigeria
	27	Mauritania
	28	Mali
	29	Zambia
	30	Togo
	31	Uganda
	32	Sierra Leone
	33	Ethiopia
	34	Guinea
	35	Rwanda
	36	Malawi
	37	Niger
	38	Chad
	39	Guinea-Bissau
	40	Burkina Faso
	41	Central African Rep.
	42	Sudan
	43	Congo, Dem. Rep.
	44	Burundi
	n/a	Eritrea
	n/a	Liberia
	n/a	Somalia
smallest	n/a	Zimbabwe

Services Exports per Person $US

WTO

		2003-2006
greatest	1	Seychelles
	2	Mauritius
	3	Cape Verde
	4	Botswana
	5	Swaziland
	6	Namibia
	7	South Africa
	8	Djibouti
	9	Gabon
	10	São Tomé & Príncipe
	11	Equatorial Guinea
	12	Congo, Rep.
	13	Comoros
	14	Gambia, The
	15	Senegal
	16	Cameroon
	17	Ghana
		SSA average
	18	Kenya
	19	Côte d'Ivoire
	20	Angola
	21	Nigeria
	22	Tanzania
	23	Lesotho
	24	Benin
	25	Mauritania
	26	Madagascar
	27	Togo
	28	Mali
	29	Zambia
	30	Mozambique
	31	Uganda
	32	Sierra Leone
	33	Ethiopia
	34	Burkina Faso
	35	Rwanda
	36	Niger
	37	Chad
	38	Guinea
	39	Guinea-Bissau
	40	Malawi
	41	Congo, Dem. Rep.
	42	Central African Rep.
	43	Sudan
	44	Burundi
	n/a	Eritrea
	n/a	Liberia
	n/a	Somalia
smallest	n/a	Zimbabwe

Services Imports per Person $US

WTO

		1999-2002
smallest	1	Burundi
	2	Congo, Dem. Rep.
	3	Ethiopia
	4	Burkina Faso
	5	Niger
	6	Rwanda
	7	Malawi
	8	Sudan
	9	Sierra Leone
	10	Tanzania
	11	Uganda
	12	Guinea-Bissau
	13	Kenya
	14	Lesotho
	15	Togo
	16	Guinea
	17	Madagascar
	18	Central African Rep.
	19	Ghana
	20	Benin
	21	Mozambique
	22	Nigeria
	23	Zambia
	24	Mali
		SSA average
	25	Senegal
	26	Comoros
	27	Chad
	28	Gambia, The
	29	Cameroon
	30	São Tomé & Príncipe
	31	Mauritania
	32	Côte d'Ivoire
	33	Djibouti
	34	South Africa
	35	Namibia
	36	Angola
	37	Swaziland
	38	Cape Verde
	39	Congo, Rep.
	40	Botswana
	41	Mauritius
	42	Gabon
	43	Equatorial Guinea
	44	Seychelles
	n/a	Eritrea
	n/a	Liberia
	n/a	Somalia
greatest	n/a	Zimbabwe

Services Imports per Person $US

WTO

		2003-2006
smallest	1	Congo, Dem. Rep.
	2	Burundi
	3	Ethiopia
	4	Sierra Leone
	5	Malawi
	6	Niger
	7	Rwanda
	8	Guinea
	9	Burkina Faso
	10	Uganda
	11	Kenya
	12	Tanzania
	13	Central African Rep.
	14	Madagascar
	15	Guinea-Bissau
	16	Mozambique
	17	Benin
	18	Gambia, The
	19	Zambia
	20	Lesotho
	21	Togo
	22	Sudan
	23	Ghana
	24	Mali
	25	Nigeria
	26	Senegal
		SSA average
	27	Comoros
	28	Cameroon
	29	Djibouti
	30	Côte d'Ivoire
	31	Mauritania
	32	São Tomé & Príncipe
	33	Chad
	34	Namibia
	35	South Africa
	36	Angola
	37	Swaziland
	38	Cape Verde
	39	Congo, Rep.
	40	Botswana
	41	Gabon
	42	Mauritius
	43	Equatorial Guinea
	44	Seychelles
	n/a	Eritrea
	n/a	Liberia
	n/a	Somalia
greatest	n/a	Zimbabwe

Total Exports as % of GDP

World Bank, WTO

		1999-2002
largest	1	Equatorial Guinea
	2	Swaziland
	3	Angola
	4	Congo, Rep.
	5	Seychelles
	6	Mauritius
	7	Gabon
	8	Botswana
	9	Namibia
	10	Nigeria
	11	Côte d'Ivoire
	12	Ghana
	13	Lesotho
	14	Mauritania
		SSA average
	15	Togo
	16	Zambia
	17	Guinea-Bissau
	18	Mali
	19	South Africa
	20	Senegal
	21	Malawi
	22	Madagascar
	23	Cameroon
	24	Guinea
	25	Benin
	26	Cape Verde
	27	Congo, Dem. Rep.
	28	Kenya
	29	Comoros
	30	Mozambique
	31	Gambia, The
	32	Djibouti
	33	Niger
	34	Tanzania
	35	Central African Rep.
	36	Chad
	37	São Tomé & Príncipe
	38	Sudan
	39	Uganda
	40	Ethiopia
	41	Burkina Faso
	42	Sierra Leone
	43	Burundi
	44	Rwanda
	n/a	Eritrea
	n/a	Liberia
	n/a	Somalia
smallest	n/a	Zimbabwe

Total Exports as % of GDP

World Bank, WTO

	2003-2006	
largest	1	Swaziland
	2	Equatorial Guinea
	3	Seychelles
	4	Congo, Rep.
	5	Angola
	6	Mauritius
	7	Nigeria
	8	Gabon
	9	Lesotho
	10	Côte d'Ivoire
	11	Botswana
	12	Chad
	13	Namibia
	14	Ghana
	15	Togo
	16	Mauritania
		SSA average
	17	Mozambique
	18	Zambia
	19	Congo, Dem. Rep.
	20	Guinea-Bissau
	21	Cape Verde
	22	South Africa
	23	Madagascar
	24	Mali
	25	Senegal
	26	Guinea
	27	Kenya
	28	Tanzania
	29	Cameroon
	30	Gambia, The
	31	Malawi
	32	Djibouti
	33	Benin
	34	Sierra Leone
	35	São Tomé & Príncipe
	36	Niger
	37	Sudan
	38	Uganda
	39	Ethiopia
	40	Comoros
	41	Burkina Faso
	42	Central African Rep.
	43	Rwanda
	44	Burundi
	n/a	Eritrea
	n/a	Liberia
	n/a	Somalia
smallest	n/a	Zimbabwe

Total Imports as % of GDP

World Bank, WTO

	1999-2002	
smallest	1	Sudan
	2	Rwanda
	3	Central African Rep.
	4	Congo, Dem. Rep.
	5	Burundi
	6	Tanzania
	7	Cameroon
	8	Guinea
	9	Ethiopia
	10	South Africa
	11	Burkina Faso
	12	Niger
	13	Kenya
	14	Nigeria
	15	Uganda
	16	Madagascar
		SSA average
	17	Comoros
	18	Sierra Leone
	19	Gabon
	20	Côte d'Ivoire
	21	Benin
	22	Guinea-Bissau
	23	Mozambique
	24	Malawi
	25	Zambia
	26	Senegal
	27	Botswana
	28	Djibouti
	29	Mali
	30	São Tomé & Príncipe
	31	Togo
	32	Mauritania
	33	Congo, Rep.
	34	Gambia, The
	35	Namibia
	36	Ghana
	37	Chad
	38	Cape Verde
	39	Mauritius
	40	Angola
	41	Equatorial Guinea
	42	Seychelles
	43	Swaziland
	44	Lesotho
	n/a	Eritrea
	n/a	Liberia
	n/a	Somalia
largest	n/a	Zimbabwe

Total Imports as % of GDP

World Bank, WTO

	2003-2006	
smallest	1	Central African Rep.
	2	Cameroon
	3	Rwanda
	4	Sudan
	5	Nigeria
	6	Guinea
	7	Benin
	8	Burkina Faso
	9	Gabon
	10	South Africa
	11	Niger
	12	Uganda
	13	Kenya
	14	Tanzania
		SSA average
	15	Sierra Leone
	16	Comoros
	17	Congo, Dem. Rep.
	18	Botswana
	19	Côte d'Ivoire
	20	Mali
	21	Zambia
	22	Madagascar
	23	Ethiopia
	24	Malawi
	25	Senegal
	26	Burundi
	27	Guinea-Bissau
	28	Angola
	29	Mozambique
	30	Chad
	31	Namibia
	32	Congo, Rep.
	33	Djibouti
	34	Equatorial Guinea
	35	Ghana
	36	São Tomé & Príncipe
	37	Gambia, The
	38	Togo
	39	Cape Verde
	40	Mauritius
	41	Mauritania
	42	Swaziland
	43	Lesotho
	44	Seychelles
	n/a	Eritrea
	n/a	Liberia
	n/a	Somalia
largest	n/a	Zimbabwe

Goods Exports as % of GDP

World Bank, WTO

	1999-2002	
largest	1	Equatorial Guinea
	2	Angola
	3	Swaziland
	4	Congo, Rep.
	5	Gabon
	6	Botswana
	7	Nigeria
	8	Côte d'Ivoire
	9	Mauritius
	10	Namibia
	11	Lesotho
	12	Mauritania
	13	Seychelles
	14	Ghana
	15	Guinea-Bissau
	16	Togo
	17	Zambia
		SSA average
	18	Mali
	19	South Africa
	20	Malawi
	21	Guinea
	22	Senegal
	23	Congo, Dem. Rep.
	24	Madagascar
	25	Cameroon
	26	Benin
	27	Central African Rep.
	28	Kenya
	29	Niger
	30	Mozambique
	31	Chad
	32	Sudan
	33	Tanzania
	34	Uganda
	35	Burkina Faso
	36	Comoros
	37	Ethiopia
	38	Burundi
	39	Djibouti
	40	São Tomé & Príncipe
	41	Rwanda
	42	Gambia, The
	43	Sierra Leone
	44	Cape Verde
	n/a	Eritrea
	n/a	Liberia
	n/a	Somalia
smallest	n/a	Zimbabwe

Goods Exports as % of GDP

World Bank, WTO

	2003-2006	
largest	1	Equatorial Guinea
	2	Swaziland
	3	Congo, Rep.
	4	Angola
	5	Gabon
	6	Nigeria
	7	Lesotho
	8	Côte d'Ivoire
	9	Chad
	10	Seychelles
	11	Botswana
	12	Mauritius
	13	Namibia
	14	Mauritania
	15	Togo
		SSA average
	16	Ghana
	17	Zambia
	18	Mozambique
	19	Congo, Dem. Rep.
	20	Guinea-Bissau
	21	Guinea
	22	Mali
	23	South Africa
	24	Malawi
	25	Madagascar
	26	Senegal
	27	Cameroon
	28	Kenya
	29	Sudan
	30	Niger
	31	Benin
	32	Tanzania
	33	Sierra Leone
	34	Central African Rep.
	35	Uganda
	36	Burkina Faso
	37	Ethiopia
	38	Burundi
	39	Djibouti
	40	Rwanda
	41	Comoros
	42	São Tomé & Príncipe
	43	Gambia, The
	44	Cape Verde
	n/a	Eritrea
	n/a	Liberia
	n/a	Somalia
smallest	n/a	Zimbabwe

Goods Imports as % of GDP

World Bank, WTO

		1999-2002
smallest	1	Central African Rep.
	2	Rwanda
	3	Sudan
	4	Cameroon
	5	Congo, Dem. Rep.
	6	Tanzania
	7	Gabon
	8	Guinea
	9	Burundi
	10	Ethiopia
	11	Nigeria
	12	Niger
	13	Sierra Leone
	14	Madagascar
	15	Comoros
	16	Burkina Faso
	17	South Africa
	18	Uganda
	19	Kenya
	20	Congo, Rep.
	21	Côte d'Ivoire
		SSA average
	22	Guinea-Bissau
	23	Benin
	24	Mozambique
	25	Zambia
	26	Malawi
	27	Mali
	28	Botswana
	29	Senegal
	30	Djibouti
	31	São Tomé & Príncipe
	32	Mauritania
	33	Angola
	34	Equatorial Guinea
	35	Togo
	36	Gambia, The
	37	Chad
	38	Cape Verde
	39	Namibia
	40	Mauritius
	41	Ghana
	42	Seychelles
	43	Swaziland
	44	Lesotho
	n/a	Eritrea
	n/a	Liberia
	n/a	Somalia
largest	n/a	Zimbabwe

Goods Imports as % of GDP

World Bank, WTO

		2003-2006
smallest	1	Central African Rep.
	2	Cameroon
	3	Gabon
	4	Rwanda
	5	Nigeria
	6	Sudan
	7	Chad
	8	Benin
	9	Guinea
	10	Congo, Rep.
	11	Burkina Faso
	12	Niger
	13	Uganda
	14	Comoros
	15	Tanzania
	16	South Africa
		SSA average
	17	Sierra Leone
	18	Côte d'Ivoire
	19	Angola
	20	Kenya
	21	Mali
	22	Botswana
	23	Congo, Dem. Rep.
	24	Guinea-Bissau
	25	Madagascar
	26	Ethiopia
	27	Equatorial Guinea
	28	Burundi
	29	Zambia
	30	Senegal
	31	Malawi
	32	Mozambique
	33	Djibouti
	34	Namibia
	35	São Tomé & Príncipe
	36	Cape Verde
	37	Ghana
	38	Mauritius
	39	Gambia, The
	40	Togo
	41	Mauritania
	42	Seychelles
	43	Swaziland
	44	Lesotho
	n/a	Eritrea
	n/a	Liberia
	n/a	Somalia
largest	n/a	Zimbabwe

Services Exports as % of GDP

World Bank, WTO

		1999-2002
largest	1	Seychelles
	2	Mauritius
	3	Cape Verde
	4	Gambia, The
	5	Comoros
	6	Djibouti
	7	Swaziland
	8	São Tomé & Príncipe
	9	Ghana
	10	Namibia
	11	Tanzania
	12	Mozambique
	13	Madagascar
	14	Senegal
	15	Cameroon
	16	Kenya
	17	Botswana
	18	Benin
	19	Ethiopia
	20	Congo, Rep.
	21	Sierra Leone
		SSA average
	22	Côte d'Ivoire
	23	Mali
	24	Lesotho
	25	South Africa
	26	Togo
	27	Nigeria
	28	Zambia
	29	Uganda
	30	Gabon
	31	Mauritania
	32	Rwanda
	33	Angola
	34	Malawi
	35	Guinea-Bissau
	36	Niger
	37	Chad
	38	Congo, Dem. Rep.
	39	Guinea
	40	Burkina Faso
	41	Equatorial Guinea
	42	Central African Rep.
	43	Sudan
	44	Burundi
	n/a	Eritrea
	n/a	Liberia
	n/a	Somalia
smallest	n/a	Zimbabwe

Services Exports as % of GDP

World Bank, WTO

		2003-2006
largest	1	Seychelles
	2	Cape Verde
	3	Mauritius
	4	Gambia, The
	5	Djibouti
	6	São Tomé & Príncipe
	7	Swaziland
	8	Tanzania
	9	Comoros
	10	Ghana
	11	Madagascar
	12	Namibia
	13	Botswana
	14	Kenya
	15	Ethiopia
	16	Senegal
	17	Togo
	18	Sierra Leone
	19	Nigeria
	20	Mozambique
	21	Cameroon
	22	Uganda
		SSA average
	23	Benin
	24	South Africa
	25	Congo, Rep.
	26	Mali
	27	Côte d'Ivoire
	28	Lesotho
	29	Mauritania
	30	Rwanda
	31	Zambia
	32	Congo, Dem. Rep.
	33	Niger
	34	Burkina Faso
	35	Guinea-Bissau
	36	Gabon
	37	Malawi
	38	Angola
	39	Chad
	40	Guinea
	41	Equatorial Guinea
	42	Central African Rep.
	43	Burundi
	44	Sudan
	n/a	Eritrea
	n/a	Liberia
	n/a	Somalia
smallest	n/a	Zimbabwe

Services Imports as % of GDP

World Bank, WTO

		1999-2002
smallest	1	Burundi
	2	South Africa
	3	Sudan
	4	Burkina Faso
	5	Kenya
	6	Lesotho
	7	Congo, Dem. Rep.
	8	Guinea
	9	Rwanda
	10	Ethiopia
	11	Niger
	12	Tanzania
		SSA average
	13	Benin
	14	Uganda
	15	Senegal
	16	Botswana
	17	Nigeria
	18	Ghana
	19	Togo
	20	Namibia
	21	Cameroon
	22	Malawi
	23	Zambia
	24	Comoros
	25	Central African Rep.
	26	Madagascar
	27	Djibouti
	28	Sierra Leone
	29	São Tomé & Príncipe
	30	Côte d'Ivoire
	31	Mozambique
	32	Guinea-Bissau
	33	Mali
	34	Gambia, The
	35	Mauritania
	36	Gabon
	37	Swaziland
	38	Mauritius
	39	Cape Verde
	40	Chad
	41	Seychelles
	42	Congo, Rep.
	43	Angola
	44	Equatorial Guinea
	n/a	Eritrea
	n/a	Liberia
	n/a	Somalia
largest	n/a	Zimbabwe

Services Imports as % of GDP

World Bank, WTO

	Rank	2003-2006
smallest	1	Kenya
	2	South Africa
	3	Guinea
	4	Sudan
	5	Burkina Faso
	6	Lesotho
	7	Namibia
	8	Benin
	9	Zambia
	10	Sierra Leone
	11	Congo, Dem. Rep.
	12	Malawi
	13	Niger
	14	Botswana
		SSA average
	15	Central African Rep.
	16	Nigeria
	17	Tanzania
	18	Cameroon
	19	Rwanda
	20	Senegal
	21	Uganda
	22	Ethiopia
	23	Madagascar
	24	Mozambique
	25	Ghana
	26	Djibouti
	27	Mali
	28	Comoros
	29	Côte d'Ivoire
	30	Gambia, The
	31	Burundi
	32	Togo
	33	Gabon
	34	Swaziland
	35	Guinea-Bissau
	36	Mauritania
	37	São Tomé & Príncipe
	38	Mauritius
	39	Angola
	40	Cape Verde
	41	Equatorial Guinea
	42	Chad
	43	Congo, Rep.
	44	Seychelles
	n/a	Eritrea
	n/a	Liberia
	n/a	Somalia
largest	n/a	Zimbabwe

Growth in Goods Exports

World Bank, WTO

	Rank	2000-2002
largest	1	Sierra Leone
	2	Eritrea
	3	Mozambique
	4	Sudan
	5	Equatorial Guinea
	6	São Tomé & Príncipe
	7	Comoros
	8	Lesotho
	9	Tanzania
	10	Angola
	11	Seychelles
	12	Congo, Rep.
	13	Mali
	14	Zimbabwe
	15	Nigeria
	16	Congo, Dem. Rep.
	17	Djibouti
	18	Rwanda
		SSA average
	19	Côte d'Ivoire
	20	Mauritius
	21	Kenya
	22	South Africa
	23	Guinea
	24	Cameroon
	25	Swaziland
	26	Gambia, The
	27	Togo
	28	Ghana
	29	Guinea-Bissau
	30	Zambia
	31	Benin
	32	Madagascar
	33	Senegal
	34	Central African Rep.
	35	Gabon
	36	Ethiopia
	37	Burkina Faso
	38	Cape Verde
	39	Botswana
	40	Niger
	41	Malawi
	42	Uganda
	43	Namibia
	44	Mauritania
	45	Chad
	46	Burundi
	47	Liberia
smallest	n/a	Somalia

Growth in Goods Exports

World Bank, WTO

	Rank	2003-2006
largest	1	Chad
	2	Mauritania
	3	Zambia
	4	Sierra Leone
	5	Equatorial Guinea
	6	Angola
	7	Nigeria
	8	Sudan
	9	Mozambique
	10	Congo, Rep.
	11	Namibia
	12	Swaziland
		SSA average
	13	Burkina Faso
	14	Rwanda
	15	Gabon
	16	Madagascar
	17	Lesotho
	18	Ethiopia
	19	Ghana
	20	South Africa
	21	Uganda
	22	Congo, Dem. Rep.
	23	Cameroon
	24	Botswana
	25	Cape Verde
	26	Burundi
	27	Seychelles
	28	Niger
	29	Tanzania
	30	Mali
	31	Djibouti
	32	Côte d'Ivoire
	33	Kenya
	34	Guinea
	35	Togo
	36	Senegal
	37	Mauritius
	38	Malawi
	39	Guinea-Bissau
	40	Benin
	41	Central African Rep.
	42	Gambia, The
	43	Zimbabwe
	44	Liberia
	45	São Tomé & Príncipe
	46	Eritrea
	47	Comoros
smallest	n/a	Somalia

Growth in Goods Imports

World Bank, WTO

	Rank	2000-2002
smallest	1	Liberia
	2	Côte d'Ivoire
	3	Ghana
	4	Uganda
	5	São Tomé & Príncipe
	6	Zimbabwe
	7	Gambia, The
	8	Botswana
	9	Swaziland
	10	Namibia
	11	Central African Rep.
	12	Togo
	13	Benin
	14	Lesotho
	15	Rwanda
	16	Nigeria
	17	Mauritius
	18	Comoros
	19	Congo, Rep.
	20	Djibouti
	21	Madagascar
	22	Eritrea
		SSA average
	23	Tanzania
	24	Malawi
	25	Burkina Faso
	26	Seychelles
	27	Niger
	28	South Africa
	29	Burundi
	30	Mali
	31	Cape Verde
	32	Kenya
	33	Ethiopia
	34	Guinea-Bissau
	35	Gabon
	36	Angola
	37	Guinea
	38	Senegal
	39	Mozambique
	40	Cameroon
	41	Mauritania
	42	Equatorial Guinea
	43	Zambia
	44	Sudan
	45	Congo, Dem. Rep.
	46	Sierra Leone
	47	Chad
largest	n/a	Somalia

Growth in Goods Imports

World Bank, WTO

	Rank	2003-2006
smallest	1	Eritrea
	2	Chad
	3	Benin
	4	Sierra Leone
	5	Zimbabwe
	6	Guinea
	7	Gambia, The
	8	Guinea-Bissau
	9	Cameroon
	10	Malawi
	11	Senegal
	12	Djibouti
	13	Central African Rep.
	14	Mauritius
	15	Botswana
	16	Mozambique
	17	Gabon
	18	Niger
	19	Mali
	20	Lesotho
	21	Cape Verde
	22	Burkina Faso
	23	Seychelles
	24	Rwanda
	25	Namibia
	26	Comoros
	27	Côte d'Ivoire
	28	Kenya
	29	Togo
	30	Uganda
		SSA average
	31	Angola
	32	São Tomé & Príncipe
	33	Ghana
	34	Congo, Dem. Rep.
	35	Zambia
	36	Tanzania
	37	South Africa
	38	Swaziland
	39	Congo, Rep.
	40	Ethiopia
	41	Nigeria
	42	Liberia
	43	Burundi
	44	Madagascar
	45	Sudan
	46	Mauritania
	47	Equatorial Guinea
largest	n/a	Somalia

Growth in Services Exports

World Bank, WTO

		2000-2002
largest	1	Sudan
	2	Swaziland
	3	Nigeria
	4	Sierra Leone
	5	Guinea
	6	Cameroon
	7	Guinea-Bissau
	8	Congo, Dem. Rep.
	9	Burundi
	10	Mauritania
	11	Mali
	12	Equatorial Guinea
	13	Angola
	14	Tanzania
	15	Niger
	16	Botswana
	17	Cape Verde
	18	Chad
	19	Togo
	20	Burkina Faso
	21	Mozambique
	22	Djibouti
	23	Ghana
	24	Seychelles
		SSA average
	25	Mauritius
	26	Zambia
	27	Ethiopia
	28	Congo, Rep.
	29	Uganda
	30	Senegal
	31	Malawi
	32	Kenya
	33	Côte d'Ivoire
	34	South Africa
	35	Namibia
	36	Madagascar
	37	Benin
	38	Lesotho
	39	São Tomé & Príncipe
	40	Gambia, The
	41	Central African Rep.
	42	Comoros
	43	Gabon
	n/a	Eritrea
	n/a	Liberia
	n/a	Rwanda
	n/a	Somalia
smallest	n/a	Zimbabwe

Growth in Services Exports

World Bank, WTO

		2003-2006
largest	1	Angola
	2	Burkina Faso
	3	Sudan
	4	Swaziland
	5	Equatorial Guinea
	6	Nigeria
	7	São Tomé & Príncipe
	8	Congo, Dem. Rep.
	9	Togo
	10	South Africa
	11	Cape Verde
	12	Kenya
	13	Gabon
	14	Ghana
	15	Central African Rep.
		SSA average
	16	Chad
	17	Guinea-Bissau
	18	Uganda
	19	Zambia
	20	Madagascar
	21	Namibia
	22	Burundi
	23	Ethiopia
	24	Mauritania
	25	Malawi
	26	Lesotho
	27	Botswana
	28	Comoros
	29	Niger
	30	Congo, Rep.
	31	Benin
	32	Tanzania
	33	Senegal
	34	Gambia, The
	35	Mauritius
	36	Seychelles
	37	Sierra Leone
	38	Côte d'Ivoire
	39	Djibouti
	40	Cameroon
	41	Mozambique
	42	Mali
	43	Guinea
	n/a	Eritrea
	n/a	Liberia
	n/a	Rwanda
	n/a	Somalia
smallest	n/a	Zimbabwe

Growth in Services Imports

World Bank, WTO

		2000-2002
smallest	1	Namibia
	2	Guinea
	3	Tanzania
	4	Gambia, The
	5	Central African Rep.
	6	Gabon
	7	Djibouti
	8	Benin
	9	Sierra Leone
	10	South Africa
	11	Ghana
	12	Burkina Faso
	13	Lesotho
	14	Botswana
	15	Niger
	16	Comoros
	17	Senegal
	18	Congo, Rep.
	19	Mali
	20	São Tomé & Príncipe
	21	Côte d'Ivoire
	22	Togo
	23	Mauritius
		SSA average
	24	Ethiopia
	25	Kenya
	26	Zambia
	27	Malawi
	28	Guinea-Bissau
	29	Congo, Dem. Rep.
	30	Cape Verde
	31	Uganda
	32	Angola
	33	Mauritania
	34	Seychelles
	35	Equatorial Guinea
	36	Nigeria
	37	Mozambique
	38	Madagascar
	39	Swaziland
	40	Cameroon
	41	Burundi
	42	Chad
	43	Sudan
	n/a	Eritrea
	n/a	Liberia
	n/a	Rwanda
	n/a	Somalia
largest	n/a	Zimbabwe

Growth in Services Imports

World Bank, WTO

		2003-2006
smallest	1	Sierra Leone
	2	Malawi
	3	Madagascar
	4	Cameroon
	5	Mozambique
	6	Central African Rep.
	7	Benin
	8	Guinea
	9	Côte d'Ivoire
	10	Seychelles
	11	Djibouti
	12	Mali
	13	Zambia
	14	Gabon
	15	Nigeria
	16	Botswana
	17	Senegal
	18	Cape Verde
	19	Uganda
	20	Mauritius
	21	Lesotho
	22	Mauritania
	23	Congo, Dem. Rep.
	24	Tanzania
	25	Niger
	26	Togo
	27	Guinea-Bissau
	28	Swaziland
	29	Namibia
	30	Ethiopia
	31	Kenya
		SSA average
	32	Chad
	33	Comoros
	34	Gambia, The
	35	Angola
	36	Ghana
	37	South Africa
	38	Equatorial Guinea
	39	Burkina Faso
	40	Congo, Rep.
	41	Sudan
	42	São Tomé & Príncipe
	43	Burundi
	n/a	Eritrea
	n/a	Liberia
	n/a	Rwanda
	n/a	Somalia
largest	n/a	Zimbabwe

Imports Dependence in Goods (Net Goods Exports per Person)

World Bank, WTO

		1999-2002
least dependent	1	Equatorial Guinea
	2	Gabon
	3	Congo, Rep.
	4	Botswana
	5	Angola
	6	Côte d'Ivoire
	7	Nigeria
	8	South Africa
		SSA average
	9	Guinea
	10	Central African Rep.
	11	Cameroon
	12	Congo, Dem. Rep.
	13	Guinea-Bissau
	14	Zimbabwe
	15	Sudan
	16	Madagascar
	17	Niger
	18	Burundi
	19	Ethiopia
	20	Malawi
	21	Zambia
	22	Mali
	23	Rwanda
	24	Mauritania
	25	Tanzania
	26	Sierra Leone
	27	Togo
	28	Uganda
	29	Burkina Faso
	30	Benin
	31	Mozambique
	32	Kenya
	33	Liberia
	34	Chad
	35	Swaziland
	36	Senegal
	37	Comoros
	38	Ghana
	39	Gambia, The
	40	Eritrea
	41	Namibia
	42	São Tomé & Príncipe
	43	Djibouti
	44	Lesotho
	45	Mauritius
most dependent	46	Cape Verde
	47	Seychelles
	n/a	Somalia

appendix B8: performance tables – self-reliance

Imports Dependence in Goods (Net Goods Exports per Person)

World Bank, WTO

least dependent

	2003-2006
1	Equatorial Guinea
2	Gabon
3	Congo, Rep.
4	Angola
5	Botswana
6	Nigeria
7	Côte d'Ivoire
8	Chad
	SSA average
9	Cameroon
10	Guinea
11	Congo, Dem. Rep.
12	Central African Rep.
13	Guinea-Bissau
14	Swaziland
15	Zimbabwe
16	Niger
17	Burundi
18	Rwanda
19	Zambia
20	Mozambique
21	Sierra Leone
22	Sudan
23	Mali
24	Ethiopia
25	Madagascar
26	Malawi
27	Uganda
28	Tanzania
29	Benin
30	Liberia
31	Burkina Faso
32	Togo
33	Kenya
34	Ghana
35	Eritrea
36	Comoros
37	Senegal
38	Gambia, The
39	Mauritania
40	South Africa
41	Namibia
42	Djibouti
43	São Tomé & Príncipe
44	Lesotho
45	Mauritius
46	Cape Verde
47	Seychelles
n/a	Somalia

most dependent

Imports Dependence in Services (Net Services Exports per Person)

World Bank, WTO

least dependent

	1999-2002
1	Seychelles
2	Mauritius
3	Djibouti
4	Comoros
5	São Tomé & Príncipe
6	Gambia, The
7	Kenya
8	Tanzania
9	Cape Verde
10	Ethiopia
11	Ghana
12	Burundi
13	Congo, Dem. Rep.
14	Lesotho
15	Senegal
16	Benin
17	Niger
18	Madagascar
19	Rwanda
20	Burkina Faso
21	Sierra Leone
22	Mozambique
23	Uganda
24	Malawi
25	South Africa
26	Togo
27	Sudan
28	Guinea-Bissau
	SSA average
29	Nigeria
30	Cameroon
31	Guinea
32	Zambia
33	Namibia
34	Central African Rep.
35	Mali
36	Chad
37	Côte d'Ivoire
38	Mauritania
39	Swaziland
40	Botswana
41	Angola
42	Congo, Rep.
43	Gabon
44	Equatorial Guinea
n/a	Eritrea
n/a	Liberia
n/a	Somalia
n/a	Zimbabwe

most dependent

Imports Dependence in Services (Net Services Exports per Person)

World Bank, WTO

least dependent

	2003-2006
1	Seychelles
2	Mauritius
3	Cape Verde
4	Namibia
5	Djibouti
6	Gambia, The
7	Kenya
8	Tanzania
9	Ethiopia
10	Sierra Leone
11	Congo, Dem. Rep.
12	Madagascar
13	Ghana
14	Benin
15	Senegal
16	Uganda
17	Burundi
18	Malawi
19	Rwanda
20	Botswana
21	Niger
22	Burkina Faso
23	Comoros
24	Mozambique
25	Lesotho
26	Nigeria
27	Guinea
28	South Africa
29	Togo
30	Zambia
31	Central African Rep.
32	Guinea-Bissau
33	São Tomé & Príncipe
	SSA average
34	Mali
35	Cameroon
36	Sudan
37	Côte d'Ivoire
38	Mauritania
39	Swaziland
40	Chad
41	Angola
42	Congo, Rep.
43	Gabon
44	Equatorial Guinea
n/a	Eritrea
n/a	Liberia
n/a	Somalia
n/a	Zimbabwe

most dependent

Foreign Reserves (as Months of Imports)

IMF

most number of months

	1997-2002
1	Botswana
2	Comoros
3	Benin
4	Central African Rep.
5	Uganda
6	Lesotho
7	Guinea-Bissau
8	Nigeria
9	Gambia, The
10	Mozambique
11	Burkina Faso
12	Rwanda
12	Tanzania
13	Mali
14	Burundi
15	São Tomé & Príncipe
16	Mauritius
	SSA average
17	Ethiopia
17	Malawi
18	Côte d'Ivoire
18	Kenya
18	Senegal
18	Sierra Leone
18	Swaziland
19	Madagascar
20	Guinea
21	Togo
22	Chad
23	South Africa
24	Namibia
24	Niger
25	Zambia
26	Ghana
27	Eritrea
28	Angola
28	Cape Verde
28	Congo, Dem. Rep.
29	Cameroon
29	Seychelles
30	Zimbabwe
31	Congo, Rep.
31	Gabon
32	Equatorial Guinea
n/a	Djibouti
n/a	Liberia
n/a	Mauritania
n/a	Somalia
n/a	Sudan

least number of months

Foreign Reserves (as Months of Imports)

IMF

most number of months

	2003-2006
1	Botswana
2	Comoros
3	Benin
4	Nigeria
5	Tanzania
6	Uganda
7	Rwanda
8	Central African Rep.
9	Mali
10	Burkina Faso
11	Guinea-Bissau
12	Equatorial Guinea
13	Mauritius
14	Lesotho
15	Mozambique
16	São Tomé & Príncipe
17	Senegal
	SSA average
18	Burundi
19	Gambia, The
20	Ethiopia
21	Sierra Leone
22	Niger
23	Kenya
24	Ghana
25	Côte d'Ivoire
25	Togo
26	Cameroon
27	Cape Verde
27	Madagascar
28	Gabon
28	South Africa
29	Angola
30	Zambia
31	Congo, Rep.
32	Swaziland
33	Namibia
34	Guinea
35	Malawi
36	Chad
37	Seychelles
38	Congo, Dem. Rep.
39	Zimbabwe
40	Liberia
41	Eritrea
n/a	Djibouti
n/a	Mauritania
n/a	Somalia
n/a	Sudan

least number of months

appendix B8: performance tables — self-reliance

Foreign Reserves (as Months of Imports)

IMF

most number of months (top) / *least number of months* (bottom)

	2007-2008
1	Botswana
2	Nigeria
3	Benin
4	Comoros
5	Equatorial Guinea
6	Uganda
7	Lesotho
8	Guinea-Bissau
9	Angola
10	Rwanda
	SSA average
11	Burkina Faso
12	Cameroon
13	Mali
14	São Tomé & Príncipe
15	Tanzania
16	Congo, Rep.
17	Sierra Leone
18	Niger
19	Mozambique
20	Gambia, The
21	Gabon
22	Cape Verde
23	Senegal
24	Burundi
24	Mauritius
25	Kenya
26	Chad
27	South Africa
27	Swaziland
28	Togo
29	Zambia
30	Côte d'Ivoire
31	Namibia
32	Madagascar
33	Ghana
34	Malawi
35	Central African Rep.
36	Ethiopia
37	Guinea
38	Zimbabwe
39	Seychelles
40	Liberia
41	Congo, Dem. Rep.
42	Eritrea
n/a	Djibouti
n/a	Mauritania
n/a	Somalia
n/a	Sudan

Foreign Debt as % of GDP

IMF

smallest (top) / *largest* (bottom)

	1997-2002
1	Namibia
2	South Africa
3	Botswana
4	Swaziland
5	Mauritius
6	Seychelles
7	Zimbabwe
8	Kenya
9	Eritrea
10	Equatorial Guinea
	SSA average
11	Cape Verde
12	Burkina Faso
13	Uganda
14	Cameroon
15	Chad
16	Ethiopia
16	Nigeria
17	Angola
18	Senegal
19	Lesotho
20	Benin
21	Gabon
22	Tanzania
23	Rwanda
24	Côte d'Ivoire
25	Central African Rep.
26	Mozambique
27	Niger
28	Togo
29	Guinea
30	Mali
31	Comoros
32	Madagascar
33	Ghana
34	Gambia, The
35	Malawi
36	Burundi
37	Sierra Leone
38	Congo, Rep.
39	Zambia
40	Congo, Dem. Rep.
41	São Tomé & Príncipe
42	Guinea-Bissau
43	Liberia
n/a	Djibouti
n/a	Mauritania
n/a	Somalia
n/a	Sudan

Foreign Debt as % of GDP

IMF

smallest (top) / *largest* (bottom)

	2003-2006
1	South Africa
2	Botswana
3	Namibia
4	Equatorial Guinea
5	Mauritius
6	Swaziland
7	Nigeria
	SSA average
8	Kenya
9	Angola
10	Cameroon
11	Benin
12	Burkina Faso
13	Chad
14	Seychelles
15	Senegal
16	Gabon
17	Tanzania
18	Lesotho
19	Niger
20	Zimbabwe
21	Cape Verde
22	Mozambique
23	Mali
24	Uganda
25	Ethiopia
26	Rwanda
27	Côte d'Ivoire
28	Madagascar
29	Ghana
30	Eritrea
31	Comoros
32	Zambia
33	Central African Rep.
34	Togo
35	Guinea
36	Malawi
37	Sierra Leone
38	Congo, Rep.
39	Congo, Dem. Rep.
40	Gambia, The
41	Burundi
42	São Tomé & Príncipe
43	Guinea-Bissau
44	Liberia
n/a	Djibouti
n/a	Mauritania
n/a	Somalia
n/a	Sudan

Foreign Debt as % of GDP

IMF

smallest (top) / *largest* (bottom)

	2007-2008
1	Equatorial Guinea
2	South Africa
3	Nigeria
4	Botswana
5	Cameroon
6	Namibia
7	Angola
8	Zambia
9	Sierra Leone
10	Mauritius
	SSA average
11	Swaziland
12	Ethiopia
13	Benin
14	Uganda
15	Niger
16	Tanzania
17	Rwanda
18	Kenya
19	Gabon
20	Senegal
21	Zimbabwe
22	Burkina Faso
23	Malawi
24	Ghana
25	Madagascar
26	Chad
27	Mali
28	Mozambique
29	Seychelles
30	Lesotho
31	Cape Verde
32	Congo, Dem. Rep.
33	Comoros
34	Côte d'Ivoire
35	Guinea
36	Congo, Rep.
37	Eritrea
38	Gambia, The
39	Central African Rep.
40	Togo
41	São Tomé & Príncipe
42	Burundi
43	Guinea-Bissau
44	Liberia
n/a	Djibouti
n/a	Mauritania
n/a	Somalia
n/a	Sudan

Foreign Debt as $PPP per Person

Primary data: IMF

smallest (top) / *largest* (bottom)

	1997-2002
1	Zimbabwe
2	Namibia
3	South Africa
4	Ethiopia
5	Eritrea
6	Uganda
7	Rwanda
8	Mozambique
9	Burundi
10	Niger
11	Kenya
12	Burkina Faso
13	Central African Rep.
14	Tanzania
15	Chad
16	Sierra Leone
17	Swaziland
18	Congo, Dem. Rep.
	SSA average
19	Togo
20	Lesotho
21	Mali
22	Nigeria
23	Malawi
24	Benin
25	Botswana
26	Madagascar
27	Senegal
28	Guinea
29	Comoros
30	Cameroon
31	Cape Verde
32	Ghana
33	Côte d'Ivoire
34	Gambia, The
35	Angola
36	Mauritius
37	Zambia
38	Equatorial Guinea
39	Guinea-Bissau
40	Seychelles
41	São Tomé & Príncipe
42	Congo, Rep.
43	Gabon
n/a	Liberia
n/a	Djibouti
n/a	Mauritania
n/a	Somalia
n/a	Sudan

appendix B8: performance tables — self-reliance

Foreign Debt as $PPP per Person

Primary data: IMF

		2003-2006
smallest	1	Zimbabwe
	2	South Africa
	3	Namibia
	4	Niger
	5	Ethiopia
	6	Mozambique
	7	Congo, Dem. Rep.
	8	Kenya
	9	Burkina Faso
		SSA average
	10	Rwanda
	11	Nigeria
	12	Tanzania
	13	Benin
	14	Uganda
	15	Mali
	16	Chad
	17	Lesotho
	18	Central African Rep.
	19	Equatorial Guinea
	20	Eritrea
	21	Madagascar
	22	Botswana
	23	Senegal
	24	Malawi
	25	Cameroon
	26	Swaziland
	27	Sierra Leone
	28	Burundi
	29	Togo
	30	Ghana
	31	Comoros
	32	Zambia
	33	Guinea
	34	Côte d'Ivoire
	35	Angola
	36	Mauritius
	37	Cape Verde
	38	Guinea-Bissau
	39	Gambia, The
	40	Liberia
	41	São Tomé & Príncipe
	42	Congo, Rep.
	43	Gabon
	44	Seychelles
	n/a	Djibouti
	n/a	Mauritania
	n/a	Somalia
largest	n/a	Sudan

Foreign Debt as $PPP per Person

Primary data: IMF

		2007-2008
smallest	1	Nigeria
	2	Sierra Leone
	3	Zambia
	4	Ethiopia
	5	Niger
	6	Cameroon
	7	Uganda
	8	Rwanda
	9	Equatorial Guinea
	10	Congo, Dem. Rep.
	11	South Africa
	12	Malawi
	13	Tanzania
		SSA average
	14	Benin
	15	Burkina Faso
	16	Mozambique
	17	Kenya
	18	Madagascar
	19	Namibia
	20	Mali
	21	Senegal
	22	Angola
	23	Ghana
	24	Chad
	25	Eritrea
	26	Botswana
	27	Central African Rep.
	28	Lesotho
	29	Burundi
	30	Swaziland
	31	Comoros
	32	Guinea
	33	Togo
	34	Gambia, The
	35	Côte d'Ivoire
	36	Mauritius
	37	Cape Verde
	38	Guinea-Bissau
	39	São Tomé & Príncipe
	40	Liberia
	41	Congo, Rep.
	42	Gabon
	43	Seychelles
	44	Zimbabwe
	n/a	Djibouti
	n/a	Mauritania
	n/a	Somalia
largest	n/a	Sudan

Service of Foreign Debt as % of Exports

AfDB

		1999-2002
lowest	1	Equatorial Guinea
	2	Namibia
	3	Togo
	4	Central African Rep.
	5	Comoros
	6	Djibouti
	7	Sudan
	8	Mauritius
	9	Congo, Rep.
	10	Nigeria
	11	Mali
	12	Mauritania
	13	Cameroon
	14	Niger
	15	Zimbabwe
	16	Benin
	17	Seychelles
	18	Senegal
	19	Zambia
	20	South Africa
	21	Burkina Faso
	22	Guinea
	23	Eritrea
	24	Cape Verde
	25	Ghana
	26	Madagascar
	27	Gabon
	28	Kenya
	29	Lesotho
	30	Côte d'Ivoire
	31	Chad
	32	Malawi
	33	Botswana
	34	Uganda
	35	Tanzania
	36	Guinea-Bissau
	37	Gambia, The
	38	Rwanda
	39	São Tomé & Príncipe
	40	Angola
	41	Congo, Dem. Rep.
	42	Mozambique
	43	Sierra Leone
	44	Ethiopia
	45	Burundi
	n/a	Liberia
	n/a	Somalia
	n/a	Swaziland
highest		

Service of Foreign Debt as % of Exports

AfDB

		2003-2006
lowest	1	Togo
	2	Equatorial Guinea
	3	Namibia
	4	Central African Rep.
	5	Chad
	6	Mali
	7	Benin
	8	Ghana
	9	Sudan
	10	Mauritius
	11	Comoros
	12	Sierra Leone
	13	Nigeria
	14	Djibouti
	15	Lesotho
	16	Congo, Dem. Rep.
	17	Burkina Faso
	18	Tanzania
	19	Kenya
	20	Guinea-Bissau
	21	Congo, Rep.
	22	South Africa
	23	Zambia
	24	Niger
	25	Zimbabwe
	26	Ethiopia
	27	Seychelles
	28	Guinea
	29	Côte d'Ivoire
	30	Cameroon
	31	Botswana
	32	Angola
	33	Malawi
	34	Senegal
	35	Cape Verde
	36	Mauritania
	37	Rwanda
	38	Uganda
	39	Gabon
	40	Mozambique
	41	Gambia, The
	42	Madagascar
	43	Eritrea
	44	São Tomé & Príncipe
	45	Burundi
	n/a	Liberia
	n/a	Somalia
	n/a	Swaziland
highest		

Growth in Foreign Debt per Person

Primary data: World Bank

		1999-2002
slowest	1	Mozambique
	2	Guinea-Bissau
	3	Ethiopia
	4	Congo, Dem. Rep.
	5	Angola
	6	Côte d'Ivoire
	7	Gabon
	8	Equatorial Guinea
	9	Mali
	10	Cameroon
	11	Kenya
	12	Zimbabwe
		SSA average
	13	Mauritania
	14	Tanzania
	15	Guinea
	16	Botswana
	17	Zambia
	18	Uganda
	19	Nigeria
	20	Lesotho
	21	Senegal
	22	Congo, Rep.
	23	Liberia
	24	Madagascar
	25	Mauritius
	26	South Africa
	27	Niger
	28	Sudan
	29	Rwanda
	30	Togo
	31	Burkina Faso
	32	Sierra Leone
	33	Swaziland
	34	Benin
	35	Burundi
	36	Ghana
	37	Djibouti
	38	Chad
	39	Malawi
	40	Comoros
	41	Gambia, The
	42	Central African Rep.
	43	Seychelles
	44	Cape Verde
	45	Eritrea
	n/a	Namibia
	n/a	São Tomé & Príncipe
fastest	n/a	Somalia

appendix B8: performance tables — self-reliance

Growth in Foreign Debt per Person

Primary data: World Bank

		2003-2006
slowest	1	Nigeria
	2	Madagascar
	3	Cameroon
	4	Zambia
	5	Ethiopia
	6	Rwanda
	7	Malawi
	8	Uganda
	9	Benin
	10	Ghana
	11	Senegal
	12	Niger
	13	Mali
	14	Mozambique
	15	Tanzania
	16	Mauritania
		SSA average
	17	Burkina Faso
	18	Botswana
	19	Sierra Leone
	20	Guinea
	21	Central African Rep.
	22	Guinea-Bissau
	23	Comoros
	24	Kenya
	25	Congo, Dem. Rep.
	26	Equatorial Guinea
	27	Lesotho
	28	Burundi
	29	Angola
	30	Sudan
	31	Togo
	32	Liberia
	33	Côte d'Ivoire
	34	Gambia, The
	35	Congo, Rep.
	36	Mauritius
	37	Gabon
	38	Chad
	39	Zimbabwe
	40	Eritrea
	41	Cape Verde
	42	Djibouti
	43	South Africa
	44	Swaziland
	45	Seychelles
	n/a	Namibia
	n/a	São Tomé & Príncipe
fastest	n/a	Somalia

Aid Dependency (Foreign Aid as % of GDP)

IMF

		1997-2002
lowest	1	South Africa
	2	Nigeria
	3	Mauritius
	4	Congo, Rep.
	5	Gabon
	6	Cameroon
	6	Kenya
	7	Côte d'Ivoire
	8	Zimbabwe
	9	Madagascar
	10	Angola
		SSA average
	11	Guinea
	12	Equatorial Guinea
	13	Mali
	13	Zambia
	14	Senegal
	14	Seychelles
	15	Comoros
	16	Togo
	17	Benin
	17	Niger
	18	Burkina Faso
	18	Chad
	19	Ghana
	20	Botswana
	21	Central African Rep.
	22	Ethiopia
	23	Tanzania
	24	Congo, Dem. Rep.
	25	Mozambique
	26	Uganda
	27	Burundi
	28	Cape Verde
	29	Malawi
	30	Sierra Leone
	31	Swaziland
	32	Gambia, The
	33	Rwanda
	34	Eritrea
	35	Namibia
	36	Guinea-Bissau
	37	Lesotho
	38	São Tomé & Príncipe
	n/a	Liberia
	n/a	Djibouti
	n/a	Mauritania
	n/a	Somalia
highest	n/a	Sudan

Aid Dependency (Foreign Aid as % of GDP)

IMF

		2003-2006
lowest	1	South Africa
	2	Gabon
	3	Nigeria
	4	Côte d'Ivoire
	5	Angola
	6	Kenya
	7	Mauritius
	8	Equatorial Guinea
	9	Congo, Rep.
	10	Guinea
	11	Cameroon
	12	Zimbabwe
		SSA average
	13	Togo
	14	Comoros
	15	Zambia
	16	Senegal
	17	Mali
	18	Madagascar
	19	Seychelles
	20	Benin
	21	Niger
	22	Burkina Faso
	23	Central African Rep.
	23	Tanzania
	24	Chad
	25	Ghana
	26	Cape Verde
	27	Mozambique
	28	Botswana
	29	Ethiopia
	30	Sierra Leone
	31	Congo, Dem. Rep.
	32	Uganda
	33	Malawi
	34	Gambia, The
	35	Guinea-Bissau
	36	Swaziland
	37	Namibia
	38	Rwanda
	39	Eritrea
	40	Burundi
	41	Lesotho
	42	São Tomé & Príncipe
	43	Liberia
	n/a	Djibouti
	n/a	Mauritania
	n/a	Somalia
highest	n/a	Sudan

Aid Dependency (Foreign Aid as % of GDP)

IMF

		2007-2008
lowest	1	South Africa
	2	Angola
	3	Nigeria
	4	Equatorial Guinea
	5	Gabon
	6	Kenya
	7	Congo, Rep.
	8	Guinea
	9	Madagascar
	9	Mauritius
	10	Zimbabwe
		SSA average
	11	Cameroon
	12	Côte d'Ivoire
	12	Mali
	12	Senegal
	13	Togo
	14	Eritrea
	15	Chad
	15	Seychelles
	16	Comoros
	17	Zambia
	18	Ghana
	18	Niger
	19	Benin
	20	Central African Rep.
	20	Tanzania
	21	Sierra Leone
	22	Burkina Faso
	23	Congo, Dem. Rep.
	24	Cape Verde
	25	Uganda
	26	Ethiopia
	27	Botswana
	28	Gambia, The
	29	Mozambique
	30	Rwanda
	31	Malawi
	32	Namibia
	33	Guinea-Bissau
	34	Burundi
	35	Swaziland
	36	São Tomé & Príncipe
	37	Liberia
	38	Lesotho
	n/a	Djibouti
	n/a	Mauritania
	n/a	Somalia
highest	n/a	Sudan

Aid Dependency (Foreign Aid as $PPP per Person)

Primary data: IMF

		1999-2002
lowest	1	South Africa
	2	Nigeria
	3	Zimbabwe
	4	Kenya
	5	Cameroon
	6	Congo, Rep.
	7	Côte d'Ivoire
	8	Madagascar
	9	Mauritius
	10	Guinea
	11	Congo, Dem. Rep.
	12	Mali
	13	Niger
		SSA average
	14	Togo
	15	Zambia
	16	Ethiopia
	17	Burundi
	18	Comoros
	19	Central African Rep.
	20	Senegal
	21	Gabon
	22	Mozambique
	23	Angola
	24	Sierra Leone
	25	Burkina Faso
	26	Chad
	27	Benin
	28	Tanzania
	29	Ghana
	30	Malawi
	31	Uganda
	32	Rwanda
	33	Guinea-Bissau
	34	Equatorial Guinea
	35	Eritrea
	36	Gambia, The
	37	Cape Verde
	38	Lesotho
	39	São Tomé & Príncipe
	40	Seychelles
	41	Swaziland
	42	Botswana
	43	Namibia
	n/a	Liberia
	n/a	Djibouti
	n/a	Mauritania
	n/a	Somalia
highest	n/a	Sudan

Aid Dependency (Foreign Aid as $PPP per Person)

Primary data: IMF

		2003-2006
lowest	1	South Africa
	2	Gabon
	3	Nigeria
	4	Côte d'Ivoire
	5	Zimbabwe
	6	Kenya
	7	Angola
	8	Guinea
	9	Togo
	10	Cameroon
	11	Congo, Rep.
	12	Comoros
		SSA average
	13	Zambia
	14	Niger
	15	Congo, Dem. Rep.
	16	Madagascar
	17	Mali
	18	Senegal
	19	Central African Rep.
	20	Mauritius
	21	Tanzania
	22	Burkina Faso
	23	Sierra Leone
	24	Ethiopia
	25	Benin
	26	Equatorial Guinea
	27	Mozambique
	28	Guinea-Bissau
	29	Chad
	30	Malawi
	31	Ghana
	32	Burundi
	33	Uganda
	34	Rwanda
	35	Gambia, The
	36	Liberia
	37	Eritrea
	38	Cape Verde
	39	Lesotho
	40	São Tomé & Príncipe
	41	Seychelles
	42	Swaziland
	43	Namibia
	44	Botswana
	n/a	Djibouti
	n/a	Mauritania
	n/a	Somalia
highest	n/a	Sudan

Aid Dependency (Foreign Aid as $PPP per Person)

Primary data: IMF

		2007-2008
lowest	1	South Africa
	2	Angola
	3	Nigeria
	4	Zimbabwe
	5	Kenya
	6	Guinea
	7	Madagascar
	8	Equatorial Guinea
	9	Gabon
	10	Congo, Rep.
	11	Congo, Dem. Rep.
	12	Mali
	13	Togo
	14	Eritrea
		SSA average
	15	Niger
	16	Cameroon
	17	Central African Rep.
	18	Senegal
	19	Sierra Leone
	20	Côte d'Ivoire
	21	Comoros
	22	Zambia
	23	Chad
	24	Ghana
	25	Tanzania
	26	Benin
	27	Burkina Faso
	28	Uganda
	29	Mauritius
	30	Ethiopia
	31	Guinea-Bissau
	32	Burundi
	33	Mozambique
	34	Rwanda
	35	Malawi
	36	Liberia
	37	Gambia, The
	38	Cape Verde
	39	São Tomé & Príncipe
	40	Seychelles
	41	Lesotho
	42	Namibia
	43	Swaziland
	44	Botswana
	n/a	Djibouti
	n/a	Mauritania
	n/a	Somalia
highest	n/a	Sudan

FDI as % of GDP

UNCTAD

		1999-2002
largest	1	Equatorial Guinea
	2	Angola
	3	Chad
	4	Liberia
	5	Gambia, The
	6	Congo, Rep.
	7	Seychelles
	8	Mozambique
	9	São Tomé & Príncipe
	10	Cape Verde
	11	Swaziland
	12	Namibia
	13	Eritrea
	14	Mauritania
	15	Zambia
	16	Sudan
	17	Tanzania
	18	Lesotho
	19	Mali
	20	Togo
		SSA average
	21	Uganda
	22	Ethiopia
	23	Botswana
	24	Nigeria
	25	Côte d'Ivoire
	26	Ghana
	27	South Africa
	28	Malawi
	29	Cameroon
	30	Mauritius
	31	Madagascar
	32	Senegal
	33	Benin
	34	Sierra Leone
	35	Congo, Dem. Rep.
	36	Guinea
	37	Guinea-Bissau
	38	Djibouti
	39	Burkina Faso
	40	Zimbabwe
	41	Niger
	42	Rwanda
	43	Burundi
	44	Central African Rep.
	45	Kenya
	46	Comoros
	47	Somalia
smallest	48	Gabon

FDI as % of GDP

UNCTAD

		2003-2006
largest	1	Equatorial Guinea
	2	São Tomé & Príncipe
	3	Mauritania
	4	Chad
	5	Seychelles
	6	Gambia, The
	7	Djibouti
	8	Sudan
	9	Cape Verde
	10	Angola
	11	Congo, Rep.
	12	Zambia
	13	Nigeria
	14	Botswana
	15	Namibia
	16	Lesotho
	17	Ethiopia
	18	Uganda
	19	Mozambique
	20	Tanzania
	21	Sierra Leone
	22	Guinea
		SSA average
	23	Malawi
	24	Togo
	25	Madagascar
	26	Guinea-Bissau
	27	Mali
	28	Gabon
	29	Ghana
	30	Cameroon
	31	Zimbabwe
	32	Côte d'Ivoire
	33	Benin
	34	Central African Rep.
	35	Somalia
	36	Senegal
	37	Niger
	38	Mauritius
	39	South Africa
	40	Burkina Faso
	41	Rwanda
	42	Eritrea
	43	Kenya
	44	Comoros
	45	Congo, Dem. Rep.
	46	Burundi
	47	Swaziland
smallest	48	Liberia

FDI as $US per Person

Primary data: UNCTAD

		1999-2002
largest	1	Equatorial Guinea
	2	Seychelles
	3	Angola
	4	Namibia
	5	Cape Verde
	6	Swaziland
	7	Botswana
	8	Mauritius
	9	Congo, Rep.
	10	South Africa
	11	Chad
	12	Gambia, The
	13	Liberia
	14	São Tomé & Príncipe
	15	Mauritania
	16	Lesotho
		SSA average
	17	Mozambique
	18	Côte d'Ivoire
	19	Sudan
	20	Zambia
	21	Cameroon
	22	Nigeria
	23	Tanzania
	24	Mali
	25	Eritrea
	26	Togo
	27	Senegal
	28	Ghana
	29	Uganda
	30	Benin
	31	Djibouti
	32	Madagascar
	33	Malawi
	34	Sierra Leone
	35	Guinea
	36	Ethiopia
	37	Zimbabwe
	38	Kenya
	39	Congo, Dem. Rep.
	40	Burkina Faso
	41	Guinea-Bissau
	42	Central African Rep.
	43	Rwanda
	44	Niger
	45	Comoros
	46	Burundi
	47	Somalia
smallest	48	Gabon

FDI as $US per Person

Primary data: UNCTAD

		2003-2006
largest	1	Equatorial Guinea
	2	Seychelles
	3	Botswana
	4	Cape Verde
	5	Gabon
	6	Namibia
	7	Mauritania
	8	São Tomé & Príncipe
	9	Congo, Rep.
	10	Djibouti
	11	Chad
	12	Angola
	13	Sudan
	14	Mauritius
	15	Nigeria
	16	South Africa
	17	Zambia
	18	Lesotho
	19	Gambia, The
		SSA average
	20	Cameroon
	21	Côte d'Ivoire
	22	Mali
	23	Ghana
	24	Tanzania
	25	Uganda
	26	Guinea
	27	Mozambique
	28	Togo
	29	Sierra Leone
	30	Senegal
	31	Madagascar
	32	Benin
	33	Ethiopia
	34	Guinea-Bissau
	35	Malawi
	36	Central African Rep.
	37	Somalia
	38	Zimbabwe
	39	Niger
	40	Burkina Faso
	41	Kenya
	42	Rwanda
	43	Eritrea
	44	Comoros
	45	Burundi
	46	Congo, Dem. Rep.
	47	Swaziland
smallest	48	Liberia

Growth of FDI per Person

Primary data: UNCTAD

		1999-2002
fastest	1	Sierra Leone
	2	Mauritania
	3	Mali
	4	Guinea
	5	Cameroon
	6	Congo, Rep.
	7	Botswana
	8	Kenya
	9	Comoros
	10	Mauritius
	11	Namibia
	12	Chad
	13	South Africa
	14	Cape Verde
	15	Guinea-Bissau
	16	Equatorial Guinea
	17	Central African Rep.
	18	Zimbabwe
	19	Burkina Faso
	20	Rwanda
	21	Malawi
	22	Madagascar
	23	Zambia
	24	Tanzania
	25	Congo, Dem. Rep.
	26	Senegal
	27	Niger
	28	Angola
	29	Ethiopia
	30	Togo
	31	Mozambique
	32	Swaziland
	33	Somalia
		SSA average
	34	Gambia, The
	35	Seychelles
	36	Sudan
	37	Nigeria
	38	Uganda
	39	Lesotho
	40	Djibouti
	41	São Tomé & Príncipe
	42	Benin
	43	Côte d'Ivoire
	44	Ghana
	45	Eritrea
	46	Liberia
	47	Gabon
slowest	48	Burundi

Growth of FDI per Person

Primary data: UNCTAD

		2003-2006
fastest	1	Liberia
	2	Congo, Rep.
	3	Zimbabwe
	4	Gabon
	5	Djibouti
	6	South Africa
	7	Sierra Leone
	8	Niger
	9	São Tomé & Príncipe
	10	Guinea-Bissau
	11	Ghana
	12	Mauritius
	13	Somalia
	14	Rwanda
	15	Senegal
	16	Equatorial Guinea
	17	Mauritania
	18	Nigeria
	19	Malawi
	20	Madagascar
	21	Benin
	22	Central African Rep.
	23	Kenya
	24	Gambia, The
	25	Sudan
	26	Guinea
	27	Seychelles
	28	Burkina Faso
	29	Cape Verde
	30	Lesotho
	31	Ethiopia
	32	Namibia
		SSA average
	33	Zambia
	34	Uganda
	35	Eritrea
	36	Togo
	37	Côte d'Ivoire
	38	Swaziland
	39	Comoros
	40	Tanzania
	41	Botswana
	42	Burundi
	43	Mali
	44	Chad
	45	Angola
	46	Mozambique
	47	Cameroon
slowest	48	Congo, Dem. Rep.

FDI as % of Total Capital Investment

UNCTAD

		1999-2002
highest	1	Liberia
	2	Angola
	3	Sierra Leone
	4	Chad
	5	Gambia, The
	6	Equatorial Guinea
	7	Nigeria
	8	Congo, Rep.
	9	Mozambique
	10	Swaziland
	11	Seychelles
	12	Namibia
	13	Tanzania
	14	Sudan
	15	Zambia
	16	Togo
	17	Mauritania
	18	Cape Verde
	19	Côte d'Ivoire
		SSA average
	20	São Tomé & Príncipe
	21	Mali
	22	Eritrea
	23	Malawi
	24	South Africa
	25	Uganda
	26	Congo, Dem. Rep.
	27	Ethiopia
	28	Madagascar
	29	Botswana
	30	Cameroon
	31	Ghana
	32	Benin
	33	Lesotho
	34	Mauritius
	35	Senegal
	36	Burundi
	37	Zimbabwe
	38	Central African Rep.
	39	Guinea
	40	Djibouti
	41	Guinea-Bissau
	42	Niger
	43	Rwanda
	44	Comoros
	45	Burkina Faso
	46	Kenya
	47	Somalia
lowest	48	Gabon

FDI as % of Total Capital Investment

UNCTAD

		2003-2006
highest	1	Seychelles
	2	Equatorial Guinea
	3	Sierra Leone
	4	Zimbabwe
	5	Angola
	6	Mauritania
	7	Chad
	8	Djibouti
	9	Nigeria
	10	São Tomé & Príncipe
	11	Sudan
	12	Gambia, The
	13	Malawi
	14	Zambia
	15	Congo, Rep.
	16	Central African Rep.
	17	Ethiopia
	18	Cape Verde
	19	Guinea
	20	Botswana
	21	Namibia
		SSA average
	22	Guinea-Bissau
	23	Côte d'Ivoire
	24	Tanzania
	25	Uganda
	26	Mozambique
	27	Mali
	28	Togo
	29	Madagascar
	30	Lesotho
	31	Cameroon
	32	Gabon
	33	Ghana
	34	Benin
	35	Somalia
	36	Niger
	37	South Africa
	38	Senegal
	39	Mauritius
	40	Rwanda
	41	Burkina Faso
	42	Comoros
	43	Eritrea
	44	Congo, Dem. Rep.
	45	Kenya
	46	Burundi
	47	Swaziland
lowest	48	Liberia

appendix B9: performance tables — investor confidence

Total Capital Investment as % of GDP

UNCTAD

		1999-2002
highest	1	Equatorial Guinea
	2	Lesotho
	3	São Tomé & Príncipe
	4	Cape Verde
	5	Chad
	6	Seychelles
	7	Eritrea
	8	Gabon
	9	Botswana
	10	Burkina Faso
	11	Mauritius
	12	Senegal
	13	Mozambique
	14	Ghana
	15	Congo, Rep.
	16	Namibia
	17	Swaziland
	18	Mauritania
	19	Somalia
	20	Gambia, The
	21	Ethiopia
	22	Uganda
	23	Guinea
	24	Mali
	25	Zambia
	26	Benin
	27	Sudan
	28	Cameroon
	29	Rwanda
	30	Djibouti
	31	Tanzania
	32	Kenya
	33	Angola
	34	Togo
	35	Guinea-Bissau
	36	Madagascar
		SSA average
	37	South Africa
	38	Niger
	39	Malawi
	40	Côte d'Ivoire
	41	Comoros
	42	Zimbabwe
	43	Central African Rep.
	44	Burundi
	45	Congo, Dem. Rep.
	46	Nigeria
	47	Liberia
lowest	48	Sierra Leone

Total Capital Investment as % of GDP

UNCTAD

		2003-2006
highest	1	Equatorial Guinea
	2	São Tomé & Príncipe
	3	Lesotho
	4	Mauritania
	5	Cape Verde
	6	Chad
	7	Ghana
	8	Namibia
	9	Congo, Rep.
	10	Zambia
	11	Botswana
	12	Gambia, The
	13	Senegal
	14	Burkina Faso
	15	Gabon
	16	Uganda
	17	Mauritius
	18	Mozambique
	19	Sudan
	20	Eritrea
	21	Madagascar
	22	Tanzania
	23	Ethiopia
	24	Somalia
	25	Rwanda
	26	Seychelles
	27	Benin
	28	Djibouti
	29	Cameroon
	30	Togo
	31	Swaziland
	32	Mali
	33	Kenya
		SSA average
	34	Niger
	35	South Africa
	36	Guinea-Bissau
	37	Congo, Dem. Rep.
	38	Burundi
	39	Guinea
	40	Liberia
	41	Nigeria
	42	Angola
	43	Comoros
	44	Côte d'Ivoire
	45	Malawi
	46	Central African Rep.
	47	Sierra Leone
lowest	48	Zimbabwe

Total Capital Investment as $US per Person

Primary data: UNCTAD

		1999-2002
largest	1	Seychelles
	2	Equatorial Guinea
	3	Gabon
	4	Mauritius
	5	Botswana
	6	Cape Verde
	7	South Africa
	8	Namibia
	9	Swaziland
	10	Congo, Rep.
	11	Lesotho
	12	Djibouti
	13	São Tomé & Príncipe
	14	Senegal
	15	Cameroon
	16	Angola
	17	Mauritania
	18	Côte d'Ivoire
		SSA average
	19	Guinea
	20	Kenya
	21	Ghana
	22	Sudan
	23	Benin
	24	Chad
	25	Zambia
	26	Gambia, The
	27	Somalia
	28	Burkina Faso
	29	Mali
	30	Eritrea
	31	Mozambique
	32	Tanzania
	33	Uganda
	34	Zimbabwe
	35	Togo
	36	Madagascar
	37	Rwanda
	38	Comoros
	39	Nigeria
	40	Guinea-Bissau
	41	Central African Rep.
	42	Niger
	43	Ethiopia
	44	Malawi
	45	Liberia
	46	Sierra Leone
	47	Burundi
smallest	48	Congo, Dem. Rep.

Total Capital Investment as $US per Person

Primary data: UNCTAD

		2003-2006
largest	1	Equatorial Guinea
	2	Seychelles
	3	Gabon
	4	Botswana
	5	Mauritius
	6	South Africa
	7	Namibia
	8	Cape Verde
	9	Swaziland
	10	Congo, Rep.
	11	Lesotho
	12	Mauritania
	13	São Tomé & Príncipe
	14	Angola
	15	Cameroon
	16	Senegal
	17	Djibouti
	18	Zambia
	19	Sudan
		SSA average
	20	Chad
	21	Ghana
	22	Benin
	23	Kenya
	24	Burkina Faso
	25	Côte d'Ivoire
	26	Nigeria
	27	Mali
	28	Uganda
	29	Mozambique
	30	Tanzania
	31	Gambia, The
	32	Togo
	33	Madagascar
	34	Somalia
	35	Guinea
	36	Comoros
	37	Eritrea
	38	Rwanda
	39	Niger
	40	Guinea-Bissau
	41	Ethiopia
	42	Liberia
	43	Congo, Dem. Rep.
	44	Central African Rep.
	45	Burundi
	46	Sierra Leone
	47	Malawi
smallest	48	Zimbabwe

Growth of Total Capital Investment per Person

Primary data: UNCTAD

		1999-2002
fastest	1	Sierra Leone
	2	Chad
	3	Guinea-Bissau
	4	Congo, Dem. Rep.
	5	Equatorial Guinea
	6	Zambia
	7	Sudan
	8	Cameroon
	9	Cape Verde
	10	Mozambique
	11	Tanzania
	12	Djibouti
	13	Nigeria
	14	São Tomé & Príncipe
	15	Benin
	16	Madagascar
	17	Mali
	18	Mauritania
	19	Guinea
	20	Mauritius
	21	Burundi
	22	Niger
	23	Senegal
	24	Burkina Faso
	25	Ethiopia
	26	Togo
	27	Somalia
	28	Seychelles
	29	Botswana
	30	Uganda
	31	Kenya
	32	Gambia, The
	33	Malawi
	34	Gabon
		SSA average
	35	Rwanda
	36	Eritrea
	37	Namibia
	38	Central African Rep.
	39	Swaziland
	40	Comoros
	41	Ghana
	42	South Africa
	43	Congo, Rep.
	44	Lesotho
	45	Angola
	46	Côte d'Ivoire
	47	Liberia
slowest	48	Zimbabwe

Growth of Total Capital Investment per Person

Primary data: UNCTAD

		2003-2006
highest	1	Equatorial Guinea
	2	Angola
	3	Seychelles
	4	Nigeria
	5	Burundi
	6	Mauritania
	7	Zambia
	8	São Tomé & Príncipe
	9	Liberia
	10	Congo, Dem. Rep.
	11	Sudan
	12	Namibia
	13	Congo, Rep.
	14	South Africa
	15	Ghana
		SSA average
	16	Swaziland
	17	Lesotho
	18	Niger
	19	Botswana
	20	Mozambique
	21	Uganda
	22	Madagascar
	23	Cape Verde
	24	Kenya
	25	Burkina Faso
	26	Cameroon
	27	Senegal
	28	Comoros
	29	Mali
	30	Benin
	31	Gambia, The
	32	Togo
	33	Rwanda
	34	Mauritius
	35	Côte d'Ivoire
	36	Ethiopia
	37	Tanzania
	38	Gabon
	39	Chad
	40	Eritrea
	41	Djibouti
	42	Guinea
	43	Guinea-Bissau
	44	Somalia
	45	Central African Rep.
	46	Sierra Leone
	47	Malawi
lowest	48	Zimbabwe

Public Investment as % of GDP

AfDB

		2000-2002
highest	1	Mauritania
	2	Eritrea
	3	Ethiopia
	4	Mozambique
	5	Seychelles
	6	Nigeria
	7	Lesotho
	8	Malawi
	9	Zambia
	10	Chad
	11	Botswana
	12	Niger
	13	Cape Verde
	14	Guinea-Bissau
	15	Congo, Rep.
	16	Ghana
	17	Swaziland
	18	Mauritius
	18	Tanzania
	19	Madagascar
	19	Angola
	20	Namibia
	20	Benin
	21	Mali
	22	Kenya
	23	Senegal
	24	Gambia, The
	25	Uganda
	26	Rwanda
	27	Burkina Faso
	28	Comoros
	29	Equatorial Guinea
	29	Sierra Leone
	30	Central African Rep.
	31	Guinea
	32	Gabon
	33	Burundi
	34	Djibouti
	35	Côte d'Ivoire
	36	Sudan
	37	South Africa
	38	Togo
	39	Cameroon
	40	Congo, Dem. Rep.
	n/a	Liberia
	n/a	São Tomé & Príncipe
	n/a	Somalia
	n/a	Zimbabwe
lowest		

Public Investment as % of GDP

AfDB

		2003-2006
highest	1	Mauritania
	2	Eritrea
	3	Lesotho
	4	Ethiopia
	5	Ghana
	6	Tanzania
	7	Gambia, The
	8	Equatorial Guinea
	8	Djibouti
	9	Nigeria
	10	Madagascar
	11	Mauritius
	12	Zambia
	13	Guinea-Bissau
	14	Burundi
	15	Chad
	16	Rwanda
	17	Mali
	18	Cape Verde
	19	Swaziland
	20	Botswana
	21	Congo, Rep.
	22	Namibia
	23	Angola
	24	Gabon
	25	Benin
	26	Niger
	27	Senegal
	28	Seychelles
	29	Sierra Leone
	30	Uganda
	30	Mozambique
	31	Comoros
	32	Kenya
	33	Sudan
	34	Guinea
	35	Cameroon
	36	Congo, Dem. Rep.
	37	Burkina Faso
	37	Central African Rep.
	38	Côte d'Ivoire
	39	Togo
	40	South Africa
	41	Malawi
	n/a	Liberia
	n/a	São Tomé & Príncipe
	n/a	Somalia
	n/a	Zimbabwe
lowest		

Private Investment as % of GDP

AfDB

		2000-2002
highest	1	Equatorial Guinea
	2	Lesotho
	3	Chad
	4	Botswana
	5	Cape Verde
	6	Mozambique
	7	Gabon
	8	Cameroon
	9	Mauritius
	9	Sudan
	10	Congo, Rep.
	11	Seychelles
	12	Ghana
	13	Uganda
	14	Senegal
	15	Namibia
	16	Nigeria
	17	Gambia, The
	17	South Africa
	18	Mali
	19	Togo
	20	Burkina Faso
	20	Swaziland
	21	Guinea
	22	Benin
	22	Rwanda
	23	Tanzania
	24	Zambia
	25	Madagascar
	26	Kenya
	27	Ethiopia
	28	Eritrea
	29	Angola
	29	Côte d'Ivoire
	30	Djibouti
	31	Comoros
	32	Congo, Dem. Rep.
	33	Niger
	34	Mauritania
	35	Central African Rep.
	36	Sierra Leone
	37	Malawi
	38	Burundi
	39	Guinea-Bissau
	n/a	Liberia
	n/a	São Tomé & Príncipe
	n/a	Somalia
	n/a	Zimbabwe
lowest		

Private Investment as % of GDP

AfDB

		2003-2006
highest	1	Equatorial Guinea
	2	Cape Verde
	3	Botswana
	4	Chad
	5	Lesotho
	6	Namibia
	7	Malawi
	8	Gabon
	9	Senegal
	10	Sudan
	11	Uganda
	12	Seychelles
	13	Congo, Rep.
	14	Zambia
	15	Ghana
	16	South Africa
	17	Cameroon
	18	Mauritius
	19	Burkina Faso
	20	Gambia, The
	21	Mozambique
	22	Mali
	23	Benin
	24	Niger
	25	Tanzania
	26	Kenya
	27	Nigeria
	28	Rwanda
	29	Djibouti
	30	Madagascar
	31	Swaziland
	32	Congo, Dem. Rep.
	33	Togo
	34	Sierra Leone
	35	Ethiopia
	36	Guinea
	37	Côte d'Ivoire
	38	Mauritania
	39	Comoros
	40	Central African Rep.
	41	Eritrea
	42	Burundi
	43	Angola
	44	Guinea-Bissau
	n/a	Liberia
	n/a	São Tomé & Príncipe
	n/a	Somalia
	n/a	Zimbabwe
lowest		

appendix B9: performance tables — investor confidence

Rank	Public Investment as $PPP per Person (AfDB, IMF) 2000-2002	Public Investment as $PPP per Person (AfDB, IMF) 2003-2006	Private Investment as $PPP per Person (AfDB, IMF) 2000-2002	Private Investment as $PPP per Person (AfDB, IMF) 2003-2006	Growth of Public Investment per Person (AfDB, IMF) 2002
	largest	*largest*	*largest*	*largest*	*fastest*
1	Seychelles	Equatorial Guinea	Botswana	Botswana	Equatorial Guinea
2	Botswana	Botswana	Gabon	Equatorial Guinea	Cameroon
3	Mauritius	Mauritius	Seychelles	Gabon	Burkina Faso
4	Gabon	Gabon	Equatorial Guinea	Seychelles	Congo, Dem. Rep.
5	Equatorial Guinea	Seychelles	Mauritius	Mauritius	Zambia
6	Swaziland	Mauritania	South Africa	South Africa	Botswana
7	Mauritania	Swaziland	Cape Verde	Namibia	Senegal
8	Congo, Rep.	Namibia	Namibia	Cape Verde	Gambia, The
9	Namibia	Angola	Swaziland	Congo, Rep.	Djibouti
10	Angola	Congo, Rep.	Congo, Rep.	Swaziland	Comoros
11	South Africa	Cape Verde	Lesotho	Chad	Mali
12	Cape Verde	Djibouti	Chad	Sudan	Cape Verde
13	Nigeria	South Africa	Cameroon	Cameroon	Lesotho
14	Eritrea	Nigeria	Sudan	Senegal	Chad
15	Lesotho	Lesotho	Angola	Djibouti	Mozambique
16	Zambia	Ghana	Senegal	Lesotho	Sudan
17	Chad	Eritrea	Nigeria	Nigeria	Nigeria
18	Ghana	Chad	Ghana	Ghana	Congo, Rep.
19	Senegal	Gambia, The	Benin	Benin	Angola
20	Kenya	Tanzania	Gambia, The	Kenya	Tanzania
21	Benin	Zambia	Côte d'Ivoire	Zambia	Ethiopia
22	Djibouti	Madagascar	Guinea	Gambia, The	Sierra Leone
23	Ethiopia	Benin	Burkina Faso	Burkina Faso	Benin
24	Mozambique	Senegal	Kenya	Uganda	Guinea-Bissau
25	Tanzania	Mali	Mozambique	Tanzania	Mauritania
26	Gambia, The	Ethiopia	Djibouti	Mali	Gabon
27	Malawi	Sudan	Zambia	Angola	Niger
28	Burkina Faso	Rwanda	Uganda	Malawi	Côte d'Ivoire
29	Comoros	Cameroon	Mali	Côte d'Ivoire	Namibia
30	Côte d'Ivoire	Kenya	Tanzania	Mauritania	Eritrea
31	Mali	Comoros	Togo	Madagascar	Mauritius
32	Madagascar	Côte d'Ivoire	Rwanda	Mozambique	Central African Rep.
33	Niger	Uganda	Mauritania	Rwanda	South Africa
34	Guinea	Guinea-Bissau	Eritrea	Guinea	Uganda
35	Uganda	Guinea	Madagascar	Niger	Swaziland
36	Sudan	Mozambique	Comoros	Togo	Burundi
37	Guinea-Bissau	Niger	Ethiopia	Sierra Leone	Rwanda
38	Rwanda	Burkina Faso	Central African Rep.	Ethiopia	Guinea
39	Central African Rep.	Sierra Leone	Niger	Comoros	Seychelles
40	Cameroon	Burundi	Malawi	Eritrea	Ghana
41	Sierra Leone	Central African Rep.	Sierra Leone	Central African Rep.	Malawi
42	Togo	Togo	Congo, Dem. Rep.	Congo, Dem. Rep.	Kenya
43	Burundi	Congo, Dem. Rep.	Burundi	Burundi	Madagascar
44	Congo, Dem. Rep.	Malawi	Guinea-Bissau	Guinea-Bissau	Togo
n/a	Liberia	Liberia	Liberia	Liberia	Liberia
n/a	São Tomé & Príncipe	São Tomé & Príncipe	São Tomé & Príncipe	São Tomé & Príncipe	São Tomé & Príncipe
n/a	Somalia	Somalia	Somalia	Somalia	Somalia
n/a	Zimbabwe	Zimbabwe	Zimbabwe	Zimbabwe	Zimbabwe
	smallest	*smallest*	*smallest*	*smallest*	*slowest*

appendix B9: performance tables — investor confidence

Growth of Public Investment per Person

AfDB, IMF

		2003-2006
fastest	1	Malawi
	2	Guinea-Bissau
	3	Djibouti
	4	Niger
	5	Burundi
	6	Sierra Leone
	7	Seychelles
	8	Kenya
	9	Equatorial Guinea
	10	Zambia
	11	Madagascar
	12	Senegal
	13	Namibia
	14	Burkina Faso
	15	South Africa
	16	Benin
	17	Ghana
	18	Tanzania
	19	Congo, Dem. Rep.
	20	Mali
	21	Uganda
	22	Cape Verde
	23	Mauritania
	24	Sudan
	25	Central African Rep.
	26	Gambia, The
	27	Guinea
	28	Mauritius
	29	Rwanda
	30	Mozambique
	31	Ethiopia
	32	Congo, Rep.
	33	Comoros
	34	Côte d'Ivoire
	35	Cameroon
	36	Botswana
	37	Gabon
	38	Nigeria
	39	Swaziland
	40	Togo
	41	Lesotho
	42	Angola
	43	Chad
	44	Eritrea
	n/a	Liberia
	n/a	São Tomé & Príncipe
	n/a	Somalia
	n/a	Zimbabwe
slowest		

Growth of Private Investment per Person

AfDB, IMF

		2002
fastest	1	Chad
	2	Sierra Leone
	3	Congo, Dem. Rep.
	4	Eritrea
	5	Nigeria
	6	Togo
	7	Mauritania
	8	Botswana
	9	Ethiopia
	10	Tanzania
	11	Cape Verde
	12	Burundi
	13	Seychelles
	14	Cameroon
	15	Rwanda
	16	Sudan
	17	Niger
	18	Uganda
	19	South Africa
	20	Namibia
	21	Gabon
	22	Gambia, The
	23	Madagascar
	24	Zambia
	25	Swaziland
	26	Congo, Rep.
	27	Ghana
	28	Djibouti
	29	Lesotho
	30	Mali
	31	Mozambique
	32	Comoros
	33	Central African Rep.
	34	Benin
	35	Côte d'Ivoire
	36	Kenya
	37	Burkina Faso
	38	Senegal
	39	Mauritius
	40	Equatorial Guinea
	41	Angola
	42	Malawi
	43	Guinea
	44	Guinea-Bissau
	n/a	Liberia
	n/a	São Tomé & Príncipe
	n/a	Somalia
	n/a	Zimbabwe
slowest		

Growth of Private Investment per Person

AfDB, IMF

		2003-2006
fastest	1	Malawi
	2	Guinea-Bissau
	3	Djibouti
	4	Niger
	5	Burundi
	6	Sierra Leone
	7	Seychelles
	8	Kenya
	9	Equatorial Guinea
	10	Zambia
	11	Madagascar
	12	Senegal
	13	Namibia
	14	Burkina Faso
	15	South Africa
	16	Benin
	17	Ghana
	18	Tanzania
	19	Congo, Dem. Rep.
	20	Mali
	21	Uganda
	22	Cape Verde
	23	Mauritania
	24	Sudan
	25	Central African Rep.
	26	Gambia, The
	27	Guinea
	28	Mauritius
	29	Rwanda
	30	Mozambique
	31	Ethiopia
	32	Congo, Rep.
	33	Comoros
	34	Côte d'Ivoire
	35	Cameroon
	36	Botswana
	37	Gabon
	38	Nigeria
	39	Swaziland
	40	Togo
	41	Lesotho
	42	Angola
	43	Chad
	44	Eritrea
	n/a	Liberia
	n/a	São Tomé & Príncipe
	n/a	Somalia
	n/a	Zimbabwe
slowest		

Domestic Credit to the Private Sector as % of GDP

IMF, World Bank

		1999-2002
largest	1	South Africa
		SSA average
	2	Mauritius
	3	Namibia
	4	Eritrea
	5	Cape Verde
	6	Zimbabwe
	7	Ethiopia
	8	Djibouti
	9	Mauritania
	10	Kenya
	11	Burundi
	12	Senegal
	13	Mali
	14	Seychelles
	15	Botswana
	16	Côte d'Ivoire
	17	Nigeria
	18	Togo
	19	Gambia, The
	20	Lesotho
	21	Swaziland
	22	Burkina Faso
	23	Ghana
	24	Benin
	25	Gabon
	26	Mozambique
	27	Rwanda
	28	Cameroon
	29	Madagascar
	30	Comoros
	31	Zambia
	32	Uganda
	33	Congo, Rep.
	34	Malawi
	35	Guinea-Bissau
	36	Tanzania
	37	Central African Rep.
	38	São Tomé & Príncipe
	39	Niger
	40	Guinea
	41	Chad
	42	Equatorial Guinea
	43	Liberia
	44	Angola
	45	Sudan
	46	Sierra Leone
	47	Congo, Dem. Rep.
smallest	n/a	Somalia

Domestic Credit to the Private Sector as % of GDP

IMF, World Bank

		2003-2006
largest	1	South Africa
		SSA average
	2	Mauritius
	3	Namibia
	4	Cape Verde
	5	Seychelles
	6	Eritrea
	7	São Tomé & Príncipe
	8	Mauritania
	8	Zimbabwe
	9	Ethiopia
	10	Kenya
	11	Burundi
	12	Senegal
	13	Djibouti
	14	Swaziland
	15	Botswana
	16	Mali
	17	Togo
	18	Burkina Faso
	19	Benin
	20	Nigeria
	21	Ghana
	22	Gambia, The
	23	Côte d'Ivoire
	24	Rwanda
	25	Tanzania
	26	Madagascar
	27	Cameroon
	28	Gabon
	29	Malawi
	30	Comoros
	31	Zambia
	32	Lesotho
	33	Mozambique
	34	Uganda
	35	Niger
	36	Central African Rep.
	37	Liberia
	38	Sudan
	39	Angola
	40	Sierra Leone
	41	Guinea
	42	Equatorial Guinea
	43	Chad
	44	Congo, Rep.
	45	Guinea-Bissau
	46	Congo, Dem. Rep.
smallest	n/a	Somalia

Domestic Credit to the Private Sector as $PPP

IMF, World Bank

largest

Rank	1999-2002
1	South Africa
2	Nigeria
3	Kenya
4	Ethiopia
5	Mauritius
6	Côte d'Ivoire
7	Namibia
8	Cameroon
9	Botswana
10	Senegal
11	Ghana
12	Gabon
13	Mali
14	Tanzania
15	Burkina Faso
16	Sudan
17	Angola
18	Madagascar
19	Uganda
20	Eritrea
21	Mauritania
22	Benin
23	Mozambique
24	Zimbabwe
25	Zambia
26	Togo
27	Congo, Rep.
28	Rwanda
29	Burundi
30	Swaziland
31	Malawi
32	Djibouti
33	Lesotho
34	Guinea
35	Cape Verde
36	Chad
37	Niger
38	Seychelles
39	Gambia, The
40	Equatorial Guinea
41	Central African Rep.
42	Congo, Dem. Rep.
43	Sierra Leone
44	Comoros
45	Liberia
46	Guinea-Bissau
47	São Tomé & Príncipe
n/a	Somalia

smallest

Domestic Credit to the Private Sector as $PPP

IMF, World Bank

largest

Rank	2003-2006
1	South Africa
2	Nigeria
3	Kenya
4	Ethiopia
5	Mauritius
6	Namibia
7	Côte d'Ivoire
8	Botswana
9	Senegal
10	Tanzania
11	Ghana
12	Sudan
13	Angola
14	Cameroon
15	Burkina Faso
16	Mali
17	Uganda
18	Gabon
19	Benin
20	Madagascar
21	Mauritania
22	Eritrea
23	Mozambique
24	Zambia
25	Swaziland
26	Rwanda
27	Malawi
28	Togo
29	Zimbabwe
30	Burundi
31	Niger
32	Equatorial Guinea
33	Cape Verde
34	Chad
35	Guinea
36	Seychelles
37	Congo, Rep.
38	Djibouti
39	Congo, Dem. Rep.
40	Gambia, The
41	Lesotho
42	Central African Rep.
43	Sierra Leone
44	Liberia
45	São Tomé & Príncipe
46	Comoros
47	Guinea-Bissau
n/a	Somalia

smallest

Growth of Domestic Credit to the Private Sector

IMF, World Bank

fastest

Rank	1999-2002
1	Sudan
2	Nigeria
3	Angola
4	Sierra Leone
5	Equatorial Guinea
6	Benin
7	Botswana
8	Gambia, The
9	Tanzania
10	Uganda
11	Mauritania
12	Burundi
13	Rwanda
14	Ghana
15	Ethiopia
16	Seychelles
17	São Tomé & Príncipe
18	Chad
19	Cameroon
20	Cape Verde
21	Senegal
22	Burkina Faso
23	Niger
24	Central African Rep.
25	Mali
26	South Africa
27	Mauritius
28	Comoros
29	Gabon
30	Zambia
	SSA average
31	Namibia
32	Swaziland
33	Madagascar
34	Guinea
35	Zimbabwe
36	Lesotho
37	Guinea-Bissau
38	Kenya
39	Côte d'Ivoire
40	Malawi
41	Togo
42	Mozambique
43	Congo, Rep.
n/a	Congo, Dem. Rep.
n/a	Djibouti
n/a	Eritrea
n/a	Liberia
n/a	Somalia

slowest

Growth of Domestic Credit to the Private Sector

IMF, World Bank

fastest

Rank	2003-2006
1	Mozambique
2	São Tomé & Príncipe
4	Equatorial Guinea
5	Malawi
6	Angola
7	Tanzania
9	Seychelles
10	Guinea-Bissau
11	Niger
12	Zambia
13	Swaziland
14	Ghana
	SSA average
15	Sierra Leone
16	Benin
17	Rwanda
18	Namibia
19	Togo
20	Burkina Faso
21	Mauritius
22	Ethiopia
23	Guinea
24	Uganda
25	South Africa
26	Kenya
27	Cape Verde
28	Senegal
29	Madagascar
30	Botswana
31	Gambia, The
32	Central African Rep.
33	Mali
34	Comoros
35	Nigeria
36	Chad
37	Sudan
38	Mauritania
39	Lesotho
40	Congo, Rep.
41	Cameroon
42	Côte d'Ivoire
43	Burundi
45	Gabon
46	Zimbabwe
n/a	Congo, Dem. Rep.
n/a	Eritrea
n/a	Liberia
n/a	Djibouti
n/a	Somalia

slowest

Ease of Starting a Business

IFC/ World Bank

	2008	
easiest	1	Mauritius
	2	Seychelles
	3	South Africa
	4	Madagascar
	5	Rwanda
	6	Nigeria
	7	Zambia
	8	Sierra Leone
	9	Gambia, The
	10	Sudan
	10	Tanzania
	11	Botswana
	12	Namibia
	13	Burkina Faso
	14	Ethiopia
	15	Malawi
	16	Kenya
	17	Uganda
	18	Burundi
	19	Mozambique
	20	Lesotho
	20	São Tomé & Príncipe
	21	Benin
	22	Ghana
	23	Central African Rep.
	24	Liberia
	25	Swaziland
	26	Zimbabwe
	27	Comoros
	28	Congo, Dem. Rep.
	29	Gabon
	30	Mali
	31	Niger
	32	Congo, Rep.
	33	Côte d'Ivoire
	34	Cape Verde
	35	Senegal
	36	Cameroon
	37	Djibouti
	38	Mauritania
	39	Guinea
	40	Equatorial Guinea
	41	Angola
	42	Eritrea
	43	Togo
	44	Chad
	45	Guinea-Bissau
	n/a	Somalia
toughest		

Ease of Starting a Business

IFC/ World Bank

	2009	
easiest	1	Mauritius
	2	South Africa
	3	Sierra Leone
	4	Madagascar
	5	Rwanda
	6	Seychelles
	7	Zambia
	8	Botswana
	9	Liberia
	10	Nigeria
	11	Senegal
	12	Gambia, The
	13	Sudan
	14	Kenya
	14	Tanzania
	15	Namibia
	16	Burkina Faso
	17	Ethiopia
	18	Malawi
	19	Lesotho
	20	Uganda
	21	São Tomé & Príncipe
	22	Ghana
	23	Burundi
	24	Mauritania
	25	Mozambique
	26	Gabon
	27	Benin
	28	Central African Rep.
	29	Swaziland
	30	Congo, Dem. Rep.
	31	Angola
	32	Congo, Rep.
	33	Niger
	34	Comoros
	35	Mali
	36	Cape Verde
	37	Zimbabwe
	38	Côte d'Ivoire
	39	Cameroon
	40	Djibouti
	41	Equatorial Guinea
	42	Guinea
	43	Eritrea
	44	Togo
	45	Chad
	46	Guinea-Bissau
	n/a	Somalia
toughest		

Ease of Dealing with Construction Permits

IFC/World Bank

	2008	
easiest	1	Kenya
	2	Swaziland
	3	Namibia
	4	Mauritius
	5	Gabon
	6	South Africa
	7	Seychelles
	8	Comoros
	9	Ethiopia
	10	Senegal
	11	Congo, Rep.
	12	Chad
	13	Gambia, The
	14	Cape Verde
	15	Uganda
	16	Equatorial Guinea
	17	Djibouti
	18	Mali
	18	Guinea-Bissau
	19	São Tomé & Príncipe
	20	Malawi
	21	Botswana
	22	Benin
	23	Rwanda
	24	Sudan
	25	Central African Rep.
	26	Angola
	27	Congo, Dem. Rep.
	28	Madagascar
	29	Ghana
	30	Mauritania
	31	Togo
	32	Lesotho
	33	Mozambique
	34	Zambia
	35	Sierra Leone
	36	Cameroon
	37	Niger
	38	Côte d'Ivoire
	39	Guinea
	40	Nigeria
	41	Burkina Faso
	42	Tanzania
	43	Burundi
	44	Zimbabwe
	45	Liberia
	46	Eritrea
	n/a	Somalia
toughest		

Ease of Dealing with Construction Permits

IFC/World Bank

	2009	
easiest	1	Kenya
	2	Swaziland
	3	Mauritius
	4	Namibia
	5	South Africa
	6	Seychelles
	7	Ethiopia
	8	Gabon
	9	Comoros
	10	Congo, Rep.
	11	Chad
	12	Gambia, The
	13	Cape Verde
	14	Uganda
	15	Equatorial Guinea
	16	Rwanda
	17	Djibouti
	18	Madagascar
	19	Burkina Faso
	19	Mali
	20	Guinea-Bissau
	21	São Tomé & Príncipe
	22	Senegal
	23	Botswana
	24	Angola
	25	Benin
	26	Sudan
	27	Central African Rep.
	28	Congo, Dem. Rep.
	29	Ghana
	29	Mauritania
	30	Togo
	31	Zambia
	32	Lesotho
	33	Nigeria
	34	Mozambique
	35	Cameroon
	36	Malawi
	37	Niger
	38	Côte d'Ivoire
	39	Guinea
	40	Sierra Leone
	41	Tanzania
	42	Burundi
	43	Zimbabwe
	44	Liberia
	45	Eritrea
	n/a	Somalia
toughest		

Ease of Employing Workers

IFC/World Bank

	2008	
easiest	1	Uganda
	2	Gambia, The
	3	Nigeria
	4	Namibia
	5	Swaziland
	6	Eritrea
	7	Mauritius
	8	Kenya
	9	Lesotho
	10	Botswana
	11	Mali
	12	Ethiopia
	13	Malawi
	14	South Africa
	15	Rwanda
	16	Seychelles
	17	Burundi
	17	Guinea
	18	Liberia
	19	Côte d'Ivoire
	20	Benin
	21	Mauritania
	22	Cameroon
	23	Zambia
	24	Zimbabwe
	25	Djibouti
	26	Chad
	27	Ghana
	28	Sudan
	29	Cape Verde
	30	Togo
	31	Central African Rep.
	32	Madagascar
	33	Tanzania
	34	Burkina Faso
	35	Comoros
	36	Senegal
	37	Niger
	38	Mozambique
	39	Gabon
	40	Congo, Rep.
	41	Sierra Leone
	42	Congo, Dem. Rep.
	43	Angola
	44	Guinea-Bissau
	45	Equatorial Guinea
	46	São Tomé & Príncipe
	n/a	Somalia
toughest		

Ease of Employing Workers

IFC/World Bank

	2009	
easiest	1	Uganda
	2	Nigeria
	3	Namibia
	4	Swaziland
	5	Gambia, The
	6	Burkina Faso
	7	Lesotho
	8	Mauritius
	9	Eritrea
	10	Kenya
	11	Burundi
	12	Botswana
	13	Rwanda
	14	Mali
	15	Ethiopia
	16	Malawi
	17	South Africa
	18	Liberia
	19	Côte d'Ivoire
	20	Guinea
	21	Benin
	22	Seychelles
	23	Mauritania
	24	Cameroon
	25	Zimbabwe
	26	Zambia
	27	Djibouti
	28	Chad
	29	Tanzania
	30	Sudan
	31	Ghana
	32	Central African Rep.
	33	Madagascar
	34	Gabon
	35	Togo
	36	Mozambique
	37	Comoros
	38	Senegal
	39	Niger
	40	Cape Verde
	41	Congo, Rep.
	42	Sierra Leone
	43	Angola
	44	Congo, Dem. Rep.
	45	Guinea-Bissau
	46	Equatorial Guinea
	47	São Tomé & Príncipe
	n/a	Somalia
toughest		

Ease of Registering Property

IFC/World Bank

	2008	
easiest	1	Ghana
	2	Sudan
	3	Botswana
	4	Seychelles
	5	Mauritania
	6	Equatorial Guinea
	7	Niger
	8	South Africa
	9	Zimbabwe
	10	Comoros
	11	Malawi
	12	Mali
	13	Central African Rep.
	14	Benin
	15	Kenya
	16	Burundi
	17	Chad
	18	Zambia
	19	Mozambique
	20	Cape Verde
	21	Namibia
	22	Djibouti
	23	Lesotho
	24	Gambia, The
	25	Cameroon
	26	Rwanda
	27	Congo, Dem. Rep.
	28	Swaziland
	29	São Tomé & Príncipe
	30	Ethiopia
	31	Gabon
	32	Togo
	33	Guinea
	34	Mauritius
	34	Côte d'Ivoire
	35	Senegal
	36	Eritrea
	37	Tanzania
	38	Uganda
	39	Guinea-Bissau
	40	Madagascar
	41	Angola
	42	Liberia
	43	Congo, Rep.
	44	Burkina Faso
	45	Sierra Leone
	46	Nigeria
	n/a	Somalia
toughest		

Ease of Registering Property

IFC/World Bank

	2009	
easiest	1	Botswana
	2	Ghana
	3	Sudan
	4	Seychelles
	5	Rwanda
	6	Mauritania
	7	Equatorial Guinea
	8	Niger
	9	Zimbabwe
	10	South Africa
	11	Zambia
	12	Comoros
	13	Mali
	14	Malawi
	15	Gambia, The
	16	Kenya
	16	Benin
	17	Cape Verde
	18	Burundi
	19	Mauritius
	20	Namibia
	21	Chad
	22	Central African Rep.
	23	Djibouti
	24	Lesotho
	25	Cameroon
	26	Côte d'Ivoire
	27	Tanzania
	28	Madagascar
	29	Burkina Faso
	30	Mozambique
	31	São Tomé & Príncipe
	32	Congo, Dem. Rep.
	33	Swaziland
	34	Ethiopia
	35	Togo
	36	Guinea
	37	Gabon
	38	Senegal
	39	Sierra Leone
	40	Eritrea
	41	Uganda
	42	Guinea-Bissau
	43	Congo, Rep.
	44	Liberia
	45	Angola
	46	Nigeria
	n/a	Somalia
toughest		

Ease of Getting Credit

IFC/World Bank

		2008
easiest	1	Kenya
	2	Botswana
	2	South Africa
	3	Namibia
	3	Swaziland
	4	Cape Verde
	5	Angola
	5	Malawi
	5	Nigeria
	6	Ethiopia
	6	Mauritius
	6	Mozambique
	6	Zambia
	6	Zimbabwe
	7	Benin
	7	Burkina Faso
	7	Cameroon
	7	Central African Rep.
	7	Congo, Rep.
	7	Gabon
	7	Ghana
	7	Lesotho
	7	Mauritania
	7	São Tomé & Príncipe
	7	Sierra Leone
	7	Tanzania
	8	Chad
	8	Côte d'Ivoire
	8	Djibouti
	8	Equatorial Guinea
	8	Gambia, The
	8	Guinea
	8	Guinea-Bissau
	8	Liberia
	8	Mali
	8	Niger
	8	Senegal
	8	Sudan
	8	Togo
	9	Comoros
	9	Congo, Dem. Rep.
	9	Eritrea
	9	Rwanda
	9	Seychelles
	9	Uganda
	10	Burundi
	11	Madagascar
	n/a	Somalia
toughest		

Ease of Getting Credit

IFC/World Bank

		2009
easiest	1	South Africa
	2	Kenya
	3	Namibia
	4	Botswana
	4	Swaziland
	5	Zambia
	6	Angola
	6	Lesotho
	6	Malawi
	6	Mauritius
	6	Nigeria
	6	Tanzania
	6	Zimbabwe
	7	Ghana
	7	Uganda
	8	Cape Verde
	8	Ethiopia
	8	Mozambique
	9	Cameroon
	9	Central African Rep.
	9	Congo, Rep.
	9	Equatorial Guinea
	9	Gabon
	9	Gambia, The
	9	Liberia
	9	Sudan
	10	Benin
	10	Burkina Faso
	10	Chad
	10	Côte d'Ivoire
	10	Guinea-Bissau
	10	Mali
	10	Mauritania
	10	Niger
	10	Rwanda
	10	Senegal
	10	Sierra Leone
	10	Togo
	11	Burundi
	11	Comoros
	11	Congo, Dem. Rep.
	11	Guinea
	11	São Tomé & Príncipe
	11	Seychelles
	12	Djibouti
	12	Eritrea
	12	Madagascar
	n/a	Somalia
toughest		

Extent of Investor Protection

IFC/World Bank

		2008
best	1	South Africa
	2	Mauritius
	3	Ghana
	3	Mozambique
	4	Angola
	4	Madagascar
	4	Nigeria
	4	Seychelles
	5	Malawi
	5	Namibia
	5	Zambia
	6	Kenya
	6	Tanzania
	7	Eritrea
	7	Sierra Leone
	8	Botswana
	8	Cameroon
	8	Ethiopia
	8	Zimbabwe
	9	Cape Verde
	9	Central African Rep.
	9	Chad
	9	Comoros
	9	Guinea-Bissau
	9	São Tomé & Príncipe
	9	Uganda
	10	Burkina Faso
	10	Liberia
	10	Togo
	11	Equatorial Guinea
	11	Lesotho
	11	Mauritania
	11	Sudan
	12	Benin
	12	Burundi
	12	Congo, Dem. Rep.
	12	Congo, Rep.
	12	Côte d'Ivoire
	12	Gabon
	12	Mali
	12	Niger
	13	Senegal
	14	Gambia, The
	14	Guinea
	14	Rwanda
	15	Djibouti
	16	Swaziland
	n/a	Somalia
worst		

Extent of Investor Protection

IFC/World Bank

		2009
best	1	South Africa
	2	Mauritius
	3	Botswana
	3	Ghana
	3	Mozambique
	4	Angola
	4	Madagascar
	4	Nigeria
	4	Seychelles
	4	Sierra Leone
	5	Malawi
	5	Namibia
	5	Zambia
	6	Kenya
	6	Tanzania
	7	Eritrea
	8	Cameroon
	8	Ethiopia
	8	Zimbabwe
	9	Cape Verde
	9	Central African Rep.
	9	Chad
	9	Comoros
	9	Guinea-Bissau
	9	Uganda
	10	Burkina Faso
	10	Equatorial Guinea
	10	Lesotho
	10	Liberia
	10	Mauritania
	10	Togo
	11	Benin
	11	Burundi
	11	Congo, Dem. Rep.
	11	Congo, Rep.
	11	Côte d'Ivoire
	11	Gabon
	11	Mali
	11	Niger
	11	São Tomé & Príncipe
	11	Sudan
	12	Senegal
	13	Gambia, The
	13	Guinea
	13	Rwanda
	14	Djibouti
	15	Swaziland
	n/a	Somalia
worst		

Ease of Paying Taxes

IFC/World Bank

		2008
easiest	1	Mauritius
	2	Botswana
	3	Ethiopia
	4	Zambia
	5	Seychelles
	6	Swaziland
	7	Comoros
	8	Namibia
	9	Lesotho
	10	Rwanda
	11	Djibouti
	12	Uganda
	13	Sudan
	14	South Africa
	15	Mozambique
	16	Ghana
	17	Malawi
	18	Madagascar
	19	Gabon
	20	Eritrea
	21	Tanzania
	22	Nigeria
	23	Burundi
	24	Guinea-Bissau
	25	Niger
	26	Cape Verde
	27	Liberia
	28	Angola
	29	Chad
	30	Burkina Faso
	31	Equatorial Guinea
	32	Togo
	33	Côte d'Ivoire
	34	Zimbabwe
	35	Sierra Leone
	36	Congo, Dem. Rep.
	37	Mali
	38	São Tomé & Príncipe
	39	Kenya
	40	Benin
	41	Guinea
	42	Senegal
	43	Cameroon
	44	Mauritania
	45	Gambia, The
	46	Central African Rep.
	47	Congo, Rep.
	n/a	Somalia
toughest		

Ease of Paying Taxes

IFC/World Bank

easiest

Rank	2009
1	Mauritius
2	Botswana
3	South Africa
4	Ethiopia
5	Zambia
6	Seychelles
7	Swaziland
8	Lesotho
9	Comoros
10	Rwanda
11	Malawi
12	Liberia
13	Djibouti
14	Ghana
15	Sudan
16	Uganda
17	Mozambique
18	Madagascar
19	Namibia
20	Gabon
21	Eritrea
22	Tanzania
23	Burundi
24	Cape Verde
25	Guinea-Bissau
26	Niger
26	Nigeria
27	Angola
27	Chad
28	Burkina Faso
29	Togo
30	Côte d'Ivoire
31	São Tomé & Príncipe
32	Congo, Dem. Rep.
33	Mali
34	Zimbabwe
35	Kenya
36	Sierra Leone
37	Equatorial Guinea
38	Benin
39	Guinea
40	Senegal
41	Cameroon
42	Mauritania
43	Gambia, The
44	Central African Rep.
45	Congo, Rep.
n/a	Somalia

toughest

Ease of External Trade

IFC/World Bank

easiest

Rank	2008
1	Mauritius
2	Cape Verde
3	Ghana
4	Djibouti
5	Gambia, The
6	Togo
7	Seychelles
8	São Tomé & Príncipe
9	Liberia
10	Tanzania
11	Guinea
12	Gabon
13	Guinea-Bissau
14	Comoros
15	Benin
16	Madagascar
17	Lesotho
18	Sierra Leone
19	Cameroon
20	Equatorial Guinea
21	South Africa
22	Senegal
23	Nigeria
24	Mozambique
25	Uganda
26	Sudan
27	Namibia
28	Botswana
29	Swaziland
30	Côte d'Ivoire
31	Kenya
32	Ethiopia
33	Mauritania
34	Congo, Dem. Rep.
35	Chad
36	Eritrea
37	Zambia
38	Malawi
39	Mali
40	Niger
41	Angola
42	Rwanda
43	Burundi
44	Zimbabwe
45	Burkina Faso
46	Congo, Rep.
47	Central African Rep.
n/a	Somalia

toughest

Ease of External Trade

IFC/World Bank

easiest

Rank	2009
1	Mauritius
2	Djibouti
3	Cape Verde
4	Senegal
5	Gambia, The
6	Ghana
7	Togo
8	São Tomé & Príncipe
9	Seychelles
10	Tanzania
11	Madagascar
12	Guinea
13	Guinea-Bissau
14	Liberia
15	Gabon
16	Benin
16	Comoros
17	Sierra Leone
18	Equatorial Guinea
19	Cameroon
20	Sudan
21	Mozambique
22	Lesotho
23	Nigeria
24	Uganda
25	South Africa
26	Kenya
27	Botswana
28	Namibia
29	Ethiopia
30	Zambia
31	Swaziland
32	Côte d'Ivoire
33	Mauritania
34	Chad
35	Congo, Dem. Rep.
36	Zimbabwe
37	Eritrea
38	Mali
39	Malawi
40	Rwanda
41	Niger
42	Burundi
43	Angola
44	Burkina Faso
45	Central African Rep.
46	Congo, Rep.
n/a	Somalia

toughest

Ease of Enforcing Contracts

IFC/World Bank

easiest

Rank	2008
1	Namibia
2	Tanzania
3	Rwanda
4	Ghana
5	Eritrea
6	Cape Verde
7	Gambia, The
8	Seychelles
9	Equatorial Guinea
10	Zimbabwe
11	Ethiopia
12	Mauritius
13	South Africa
14	Zambia
15	Mauritania
16	Nigeria
17	Botswana
18	Lesotho
19	Kenya
20	Burkina Faso
21	São Tomé & Príncipe
22	Uganda
23	Côte d'Ivoire
24	Guinea
25	Swaziland
26	Niger
27	Malawi
28	Guinea-Bissau
29	Mozambique
30	Sierra Leone
31	Sudan
32	Gabon
33	Burundi
33	Senegal
34	Madagascar
35	Comoros
36	Togo
37	Congo, Rep.
38	Mali
39	Djibouti
40	Liberia
41	Benin
42	Chad
43	Central African Rep.
44	Cameroon
45	Congo, Dem. Rep.
46	Angola
n/a	Somalia

toughest

Ease of Enforcing Contracts

IFC/World Bank

easiest

Rank	2009
1	Tanzania
2	Namibia
3	Cape Verde
4	Rwanda
5	Ghana
6	Eritrea
7	Seychelles
8	Gambia, The
9	Equatorial Guinea
10	Mauritius
11	Zimbabwe
12	Ethiopia
13	South Africa
14	Mauritania
15	Zambia
16	Nigeria
17	Botswana
18	Lesotho
19	Kenya
20	Burkina Faso
21	Uganda
22	Côte d'Ivoire
22	Mozambique
23	Swaziland
24	Guinea
25	Niger
26	Malawi
27	Guinea-Bissau
28	Sierra Leone
29	Sudan
30	Senegal
31	Gabon
32	Comoros
33	Togo
34	Madagascar
35	Congo, Rep.
36	Mali
37	Djibouti
38	Liberia
39	Chad
40	Central African Rep.
41	Burundi
42	São Tomé & Príncipe
43	Cameroon
44	Congo, Dem. Rep.
45	Benin
46	Angola
n/a	Somalia

toughest

	Ease of Closing a Business IFC/World Bank 2008	Ease of Closing a Business IFC/World Bank 2009	Overall Ease of Doing Business IFC/World Bank 2008	Overall Ease of Doing Business IFC/World Bank 2009
easiest	1 Botswana	1 Botswana	1 Mauritius	1 Mauritius
	2 Namibia	2 Uganda	2 South Africa	2 South Africa
	3 Uganda	3 Namibia	3 Namibia	3 Botswana
	4 Swaziland	4 Swaziland	4 Botswana	4 Namibia
	5 Lesotho	5 Côte d'Ivoire	5 Kenya	5 Kenya
	6 Mauritius	6 Lesotho	6 Ghana	6 Ghana
	7 South Africa	7 Mauritius	7 Seychelles	7 Zambia
	8 Ethiopia	8 South Africa	8 Swaziland	8 Seychelles
	9 Côte d'Ivoire	9 Ethiopia	9 Ethiopia	9 Swaziland
	10 Senegal	10 Kenya	10 Nigeria	10 Uganda
	11 Kenya	11 Senegal	11 Zambia	11 Ethiopia
	12 Zambia	12 Zambia	12 Uganda	12 Nigeria
	13 Nigeria	13 Nigeria	13 Lesotho	13 Lesotho
	14 Togo	14 Togo	14 Malawi	14 Tanzania
	15 Burkina Faso	15 Cameroon	15 Tanzania	15 Gambia, The
	16 Cameroon	16 Ghana	16 Gambia, The	16 Malawi
	17 Ghana	17 Guinea	17 Cape Verde	17 Rwanda
	18 Benin	18 Burkina Faso	18 Mozambique	18 Mozambique
	19 Mali	19 Tanzania	19 Sudan	19 Cape Verde
	20 Tanzania	20 Mali	20 Gabon	20 Madagascar
	21 Congo, Rep.	21 Congo, Rep.	21 Djibouti	21 Sudan
	22 Guinea	22 Gambia, The	22 Comoros	22 Burkina Faso
	23 Gambia, The	23 Benin	23 Madagascar	23 Senegal
	24 Djibouti	24 Djibouti	24 Rwanda	24 Gabon
	25 Gabon	25 Mozambique	25 Benin	25 Djibouti
	26 Niger	26 Gabon	26 Zimbabwe	26 Comoros
	27 Mozambique	27 Malawi	27 Cameroon	27 Sierra Leone
	28 Malawi	28 Niger	28 Côte d'Ivoire	28 Liberia
	29 Angola	29 Angola	29 Togo	29 Zimbabwe
	30 Sierra Leone	30 Sierra Leone	30 Mauritania	30 Mauritania
	31 Mauritania	31 Liberia	31 Mali	31 Côte d'Ivoire
	32 Liberia	32 Mauritania	32 Sierra Leone	32 Togo
	33 Congo, Dem. Rep.	33 Congo, Dem. Rep.	33 Burkina Faso	33 Cameroon
	34 Zimbabwe	34 Zimbabwe	34 Senegal	34 Mali
	35 Burundi	35 Burundi	35 São Tomé & Príncipe	35 Equatorial Guinea
	35 Cape Verde	35 Cape Verde	36 Equatorial Guinea	36 Angola
	35 Central African Rep.	35 Central African Rep.	37 Guinea	37 Benin
	35 Chad	35 Chad	38 Angola	38 Guinea
	35 Comoros	35 Comoros	39 Niger	39 Niger
	35 Equatorial Guinea	35 Equatorial Guinea	40 Liberia	40 Eritrea
	35 Eritrea	35 Eritrea	41 Eritrea	41 Chad
	35 Guinea-Bissau	35 Guinea-Bissau	42 Chad	42 São Tomé & Príncipe
	35 Madagascar	35 Madagascar	43 Burundi	43 Burundi
	35 Rwanda	35 Rwanda	44 Congo, Rep.	44 Congo, Rep.
	35 São Tomé & Príncipe	35 São Tomé & Príncipe	45 Guinea-Bissau	45 Guinea-Bissau
	35 Seychelles	35 Seychelles	46 Central African Rep.	46 Central African Rep.
	35 Sudan	35 Sudan	47 Congo, Dem. Rep.	47 Congo, Dem. Rep.
	n/a Somalia	n/a Somalia	n/a Somalia	n/a Somalia
toughest				

B11 performance tables – business friendliness

	Index of Economic Freedom The Heritage Foundation & The Wall Street Journal		Index of Economic Freedom The Heritage Foundation & The Wall Street Journal		Individual Income Tax Rate The Heritage Foundation & The Wall Street Journal
	2001-2004		2005-2008		2008
best 1	Botswana	best 1	Botswana	lowest 1	Angola
2	Mauritius	2	Mauritius	1	Mauritius
3	Namibia	3	Uganda	2	Guinea-Bissau
4	South Africa	4	South Africa	3	Botswana
5	Uganda	5	Madagascar	3	Ghana
6	Swaziland	6	Namibia	3	Nigeria
7	Mali	7	Swaziland	4	Burkina Faso
8	Senegal	8	Kenya	4	Djibouti
9	Burkina Faso	9	Cape Verde	4	Kenya
10	Mozambique	10	Senegal	4	Madagascar
11	Kenya	11	Gambia, The	4	Sierra Leone
12	Tanzania	12	Tanzania	4	Tanzania
13	Madagascar	13	Ghana	4	Uganda
14	Ghana	14	Zambia	5	Mozambique
15	Zambia	15	Côte d'Ivoire	6	Swaziland
16	Gabon	16	Burkina Faso	7	Burundi
17	Cape Verde	17	Mauritania	7	Cameroon
18	Central African Rep.	18	Mali	7	Equatorial Guinea
19	Djibouti	19	Mozambique	7	Ethiopia
20	Mauritania	20	Malawi	7	Gambia, The
21	Côte d'Ivoire	21	Guinea	7	Lesotho
22	Benin	22	Gabon	7	Namibia
23	Gambia, The	23	Cameroon	7	Rwanda
24	Guinea	24	Benin	7	Zambia
25	Malawi	25	Djibouti	8	Benin
26	Cameroon	26	Nigeria	8	Guinea
27	Niger	27	Lesotho	8	Malawi
28	Ethiopia	28	Equatorial Guinea	8	Mali
29	Nigeria	29	Central African Rep.	8	Mauritania
30	Lesotho	30	Ethiopia	8	South Africa
31	Equatorial Guinea	31	Rwanda	9	Cape Verde
32	Chad	32	Niger	9	Niger
33	Rwanda	33	Chad	10	Zimbabwe
34	Togo	34	Togo	11	Central African Rep.
35	Congo, Rep.	35	Sierra Leone	11	Congo, Rep.
36	Guinea-Bissau	36	Burundi	11	Gabon
37	Sierra Leone	37	Guinea-Bissau	11	Senegal
38	Zimbabwe	38	Angola	12	Togo
39	Angola	39	Congo, Rep.	13	Côte d'Ivoire
39	Burundi	40	Zimbabwe	14	Chad
n/a	Comoros	n/a	Comoros	n/a	Comoros
n/a	Congo, Dem. Rep.	n/a	Congo, Dem. Rep.	n/a	Congo, Dem. Rep.
n/a	Eritrea	n/a	Eritrea	n/a	Eritrea
n/a	Liberia	n/a	Liberia	n/a	Liberia
n/a	São Tomé & Príncipe	n/a	São Tomé & Príncipe	n/a	São Tomé & Príncipe
n/a	Seychelles	n/a	Seychelles	n/a	Seychelles
n/a	Somalia	n/a	Somalia	n/a	Somalia
n/a	Sudan	n/a	Sudan	n/a	Sudan
worst		worst		highest	

appendix B11: performance tables — business friendliness

Corporate Tax Rate

The Heritage Foundation & The Wall Street Journal

		2008
low	1	Mauritius
	2	Botswana
	2	Djibouti
	2	Ghana
	2	Guinea-Bissau
	2	Lesotho
	2	Mauritania
	2	Senegal
	3	South Africa
	4	Cape Verde
	4	Central African Rep.
	4	Ethiopia
	4	Kenya
	4	Madagascar
	4	Malawi
	4	Nigeria
	4	Rwanda
	4	Sierra Leone
	4	Swaziland
	4	Tanzania
	4	Uganda
	4	Zimbabwe
	5	Mozambique
	6	Angola
	6	Burkina Faso
	6	Burundi
	6	Côte d'Ivoire
	6	Equatorial Guinea
	6	Gabon
	6	Gambia, The
	6	Guinea
	6	Mali
	6	Namibia
	6	Niger
	6	Zambia
	7	Togo
	8	Benin
	8	Congo, Rep.
	9	Cameroon
	10	Chad
	n/a	Comoros
	n/a	Congo, Dem. Rep.
	n/a	Eritrea
	n/a	Liberia
	n/a	São Tomé & Príncipe
	n/a	Seychelles
	n/a	Somalia
	n/a	Sudan
high		

Voice and Accountability

World Bank

		1998-2002
best	1	Mauritius
	2	Botswana
	3	Cape Verde
	4	South Africa
	5	Namibia
	6	São Tomé & Príncipe
	7	Benin
	8	Mali
	9	Seychelles
	10	Madagascar
	11	Senegal
	12	Ghana
	13	Mozambique
	14	Malawi
	15	Gabon
	16	Tanzania
	17	Burkina Faso
	18	Lesotho
	19	Zambia
	20	Comoros
	21	Mauritania
	22	Central African Rep.
	23	Niger
	24	Kenya
	25	Gambia, The
	26	Djibouti
	27	Chad
	28	Nigeria
	29	Uganda
	30	Ethiopia
	31	Guinea-Bissau
	32	Cameroon
	33	Côte d'Ivoire
	34	Zimbabwe
	35	Guinea
	36	Togo
	37	Sierra Leone
	38	Swaziland
	39	Angola
	40	Liberia
	41	Congo, Rep.
	42	Eritrea
	43	Rwanda
	44	Burundi
	45	Equatorial Guinea
	46	Sudan
	47	Somalia
	48	Congo, Dem. Rep.
worst		

Voice and Accountability

World Bank

		2003-2008
best	1	Mauritius
	2	Botswana
	3	South Africa
	4	Cape Verde
	5	Namibia
	6	Mali
	7	Ghana
	8	São Tomé & Príncipe
	9	Seychelles
	10	Benin
	11	Senegal
	12	Lesotho
	13	Madagascar
	14	Mozambique
	15	Kenya
	16	Niger
	17	Zambia
	18	Comoros
	19	Tanzania
	20	Burkina Faso
	21	Malawi
	22	Sierra Leone
	23	Gambia, The
	24	Guinea-Bissau
	25	Uganda
	26	Gabon
	27	Nigeria
	28	Djibouti
	29	Mauritania
	30	Congo, Rep.
	31	Cameroon
	32	Burundi
	33	Ethiopia
	34	Liberia
	35	Angola
	36	Guinea
	37	Chad
	38	Rwanda
	39	Central African Rep.
	40	Swaziland
	41	Togo
	42	Côte d'Ivoire
	43	Zimbabwe
	44	Equatorial Guinea
	45	Sudan
	46	Congo, Dem. Rep.
	47	Somalia
	48	Eritrea
worst		

Political Stability

World Bank

		1998-2002
best	1	Mauritius
	2	Seychelles
	3	Cape Verde
	4	Botswana
	5	São Tomé & Príncipe
	6	Benin
	7	Gambia, The
	8	Mali
	9	Mauritania
	10	Mozambique
	11	Comoros
	12	Gabon
	13	Namibia
	14	Madagascar
	15	Swaziland
	16	Lesotho
	17	Ghana
	18	Burkina Faso
	19	Equatorial Guinea
	20	Tanzania
	21	Togo
	22	Zambia
	23	Niger
	24	Malawi
	25	South Africa
	26	Cameroon
	27	Djibouti
	28	Senegal
	29	Côte d'Ivoire
	30	Ethiopia
	31	Kenya
	32	Guinea
	33	Guinea-Bissau
	34	Eritrea
	35	Congo, Rep.
	36	Nigeria
	37	Zimbabwe
	38	Chad
	39	Central African Rep.
	40	Uganda
	41	Sierra Leone
	42	Rwanda
	43	Angola
	44	Liberia
	45	Sudan
	46	Burundi
	47	Somalia
	48	Congo, Dem. Rep.
worst		

Political Stability

World Bank

		2003-2006
best	1	Botswana
	2	Mauritius
	3	Seychelles
	4	Cape Verde
	5	Namibia
	6	São Tomé & Príncipe
	7	Gambia, The
	8	Lesotho
	9	Benin
	10	Ghana
	11	Mozambique
	12	Gabon
	13	Mali
	14	Madagascar
	15	Zambia
	16	Swaziland
	17	Malawi
	18	Burkina Faso
	19	South Africa
	20	Comoros
	21	Equatorial Guinea
	22	Senegal
	23	Mauritania
	24	Tanzania
	25	Niger
	26	Cameroon
	27	Djibouti
	28	Guinea-Bissau
	29	Sierra Leone
	30	Togo
	31	Eritrea
	32	Rwanda
	33	Angola
	34	Guinea
	35	Congo, Rep.
	36	Kenya
	37	Central African Rep.
	38	Chad
	39	Uganda
	40	Ethiopia
	41	Zimbabwe
	42	Liberia
	43	Burundi
	44	Nigeria
	45	Côte d'Ivoire
	46	Sudan
	47	Congo, Dem. Rep.
	48	Somalia
worst		

appendix B11: performance tables – business friendliness

	Rank	Govt. Effectiveness (World Bank)	Govt. Effectiveness (World Bank)	Regulatory Quality (World Bank)	Regulatory Quality (World Bank)	Rule of Law (World Bank)
		1998-2002	2003-2006	1998-2002	2003-2006	1998-2002
best	1	South Africa	Botswana	Botswana	Botswana	Mauritius
	2	Botswana	South Africa	Mauritius	South Africa	Cape Verde
	3	Mauritius	Mauritius	Namibia	Mauritius	Seychelles
	4	Namibia	Namibia	South Africa	Namibia	Botswana
	5	Seychelles	Cape Verde	Uganda	Uganda	Namibia
	6	Cape Verde	Seychelles	Gabon	Mauritania	South Africa
	7	Senegal	Senegal	Burkina Faso	Kenya	Lesotho
	8	Ghana	Ghana	Cape Verde	Cape Verde	Senegal
	9	Mauritania	Madagascar	Benin	Ghana	Gambia, The
	10	Lesotho	Lesotho	Senegal	Senegal	Ghana
	11	Mozambique	Mauritania	Ghana	Madagascar	Benin
	12	Benin	Mali	Mali	Burkina Faso	Gabon
	13	Gabon	Mozambique	Zambia	Gabon	São Tomé & Príncipe
	14	Malawi	Tanzania	Mozambique	Tanzania	Eritrea
	15	Tanzania	Benin	Gambia, The	Gambia, The	Mauritania
	16	Madagascar	Uganda	Côte d'Ivoire	Benin	Madagascar
	17	Uganda	Gambia, The	Malawi	Mali	Mali
	18	Gambia, The	Gabon	Mauritania	Mozambique	Tanzania
	19	São Tomé & Príncipe	Burkina Faso	Kenya	Malawi	Malawi
	20	Swaziland	Kenya	Swaziland	Niger	Zambia
	21	Burkina Faso	Ethiopia	Lesotho	Lesotho	Swaziland
	22	Chad	São Tomé & Príncipe	Tanzania	Seychelles	Burkina Faso
	23	Kenya	Rwanda	Madagascar	Swaziland	Togo
	24	Mali	Djibouti	Guinea	Zambia	Uganda
	25	Côte d'Ivoire	Malawi	Cameroon	Rwanda	Mozambique
	26	Cameroon	Niger	Niger	Cameroon	Djibouti
	27	Zambia	Swaziland	Togo	São Tomé & Príncipe	Ethiopia
	28	Zimbabwe	Cameroon	Seychelles	Djibouti	Niger
	29	Eritrea	Zambia	São Tomé & Príncipe	Togo	Chad
	30	Djibouti	Nigeria	Eritrea	Côte d'Ivoire	Kenya
	31	Ethiopia	Eritrea	Djibouti	Ethiopia	Zimbabwe
	32	Guinea	Angola	Chad	Guinea	Côte d'Ivoire
	33	Rwanda	Chad	Nigeria	Chad	Cameroon
	34	Nigeria	Guinea	Rwanda	Nigeria	Guinea
	35	Togo	Sudan	Central African Rep.	Guinea-Bissau	Comoros
	36	Niger	Sierra Leone	Ethiopia	Congo, Rep.	Rwanda
	37	Sudan	Congo, Rep.	Comoros	Sierra Leone	Equatorial Guinea
	38	Guinea-Bissau	Burundi	Guinea-Bissau	Sudan	Nigeria
	39	Angola	Côte d'Ivoire	Congo, Rep.	Burundi	Sierra Leone
	40	Comoros	Equatorial Guinea	Zimbabwe	Angola	Central African Rep.
	41	Equatorial Guinea	Guinea-Bissau	Sudan	Central African Rep.	Congo, Rep.
	42	Congo, Rep.	Zimbabwe	Burundi	Equatorial Guinea	Guinea-Bissau
	43	Burundi	Liberia	Sierra Leone	Comoros	Burundi
	44	Sierra Leone	Togo	Equatorial Guinea	Eritrea	Sudan
	45	Central African Rep.	Central African Rep.	Angola	Congo, Dem. Rep.	Angola
	46	Liberia	Congo, Dem. Rep.	Liberia	Liberia	Liberia
	47	Congo, Dem. Rep.	Comoros	Congo, Dem. Rep.	Zimbabwe	Congo, Dem. Rep.
worst	48	Somalia	Somalia	Somalia	Somalia	Somalia

Rank	Rule of Law (World Bank) 2003-2006	Control of Corruption (World Bank) 1998-2002	Control of Corruption (World Bank) 2003-2006
best 1	Mauritius	Botswana	Botswana
2	Botswana	Eritrea	South Africa
3	Cape Verde	South Africa	Cape Verde
4	Seychelles	Mauritius	Mauritius
5	South Africa	Seychelles	Seychelles
6	Namibia	Namibia	Namibia
7	Lesotho	Cape Verde	Madagascar
8	Mali	Burkina Faso	Burkina Faso
9	Gambia, The	Mauritania	Lesotho
10	Madagascar	Swaziland	Eritrea
11	Ghana	Lesotho	Mauritania
12	Senegal	Madagascar	Ghana
13	Malawi	Senegal	Senegal
14	Tanzania	São Tomé & Príncipe	Mali
15	Mauritania	Ghana	Rwanda
16	São Tomé & Príncipe	Gambia, The	Swaziland
17	Burkina Faso	Ethiopia	Gambia, The
18	Gabon	Mali	Mozambique
19	Benin	Côte d'Ivoire	Ethiopia
20	Zambia	Malawi	Gabon
21	Eritrea	Gabon	São Tomé & Príncipe
22	Uganda	Togo	Tanzania
23	Mozambique	Benin	Djibouti
24	Ethiopia	Mozambique	Benin
25	Rwanda	Rwanda	Uganda
26	Djibouti	Guinea	Malawi
27	Swaziland	Djibouti	Comoros
28	Niger	Chad	Togo
29	Comoros	Sierra Leone	Zambia
30	Kenya	Zimbabwe	Guinea
31	Togo	Zambia	Kenya
32	Cameroon	Guinea-Bissau	Cameroon
33	Sierra Leone	Uganda	Niger
34	Burundi	Sudan	Burundi
35	Guinea-Bissau	Comoros	Congo, Rep.
36	Chad	Niger	Sierra Leone
37	Equatorial Guinea	Tanzania	Guinea-Bissau
38	Guinea	Kenya	Liberia
39	Congo, Rep.	Congo, Rep.	Côte d'Ivoire
40	Angola	Burundi	Angola
41	Nigeria	Cameroon	Central African Rep.
42	Liberia	Central African Rep.	Chad
43	Sudan	Nigeria	Sudan
44	Côte d'Ivoire	Angola	Zimbabwe
45	Central African Rep.	Somalia	Nigeria
46	Zimbabwe	Congo, Dem. Rep.	Congo, Dem. Rep.
47	Congo, Dem. Rep.	Liberia	Equatorial Guinea
48	Somalia	Equatorial Guinea	Somalia
worst			

	General-Size (IMF, World Bank, UNPD)		Quality of Life (UNDP, UNICEF, AfDB, ITU, UNPD)		Economic Strength (IMF, World Bank)
	2009		2003-2007		2003-2006
top 1	Nigeria	1	Mauritius	1	Equatorial Guinea
2	South Africa	2	Seychelles	2	Cape Verde
3	Ethiopia	3	Cape Verde	3	Chad
4	Kenya	4	South Africa	4	Botswana
4	Tanzania	5	Gambia, The	5	South Africa
5	Angola	6	Namibia	6	Senegal
5	Congo, Dem. Rep.	7	Botswana	7	Mauritius
5	Ghana	8	Gabon	8	Angola
6	Cameroon	9	Comoros	9	Namibia
6	Uganda	10	Senegal	10	Burkina Faso
7	Cote d'Ivoire	11	Ghana	11	Mali
8	Mozambique	12	Togo	12	Nigeria
9	Madagascar	13	Uganda	13	Cameroon
10	Senegal	14	Kenya	14	Tanzania
11	Burkina Faso	15	Eritrea	15	Congo, Rep.
12	Zambia	16	Swaziland	16	Gabon
13	Mali	17	Benin	17	Seychelles
14	Chad	18	Tanzania	18	Lesotho
14	Malawi	19	Lesotho	19	Madagascar
15	Niger	20	Cameroon	20	Ethiopia
16	Botswana	21	Nigeria	21	Benin
17	Guinea	22	Equatorial Guinea	22	Swaziland
18	Benin	23	Congo, Rep.	23	Gambia, The
19	Gabon	24	Madagascar	24	Kenya
20	Congo, Rep.	25	Zambia	25	Ghana
21	Rwanda	26	Cote d'Ivoire	26	Sierra Leone
22	Equatorial Guinea	27	Malawi	27	Mozambique
22	Togo	28	Mozambique	28	Cote d'Ivoire
23	Mauritius	29	Guinea	29	Niger
23	Namibia	30	Rwanda	30	Uganda
23	Sierra Leone	31	Burundi	31	Togo
24	Burundi	32	Mali	32	Comoros
24	Eritrea	33	Ethiopia	33	Zambia
25	Central African Rep.	34	Burkina Faso	34	Rwanda
26	Lesotho	35	Guinea-Bissau	35	Congo, Dem. Rep.
27	Swaziland	36	Angola	36	Malawi
28	Gambia, The	37	Niger	37	Guinea-Bissau
29	Guinea-Bissau	38	Congo, Dem. Rep.	38	Central African Rep.
30	Cape Verde	39	Chad	39	Guinea
31	Comoros	40	Central African Rep.	40	Burundi
31	Seychelles	41	Sierra Leone	41	Eritrea
n/a	Djibouti	n/a	Djibouti	n/a	Djibouti
n/a	Liberia	n/a	Liberia	n/a	Liberia
n/a	Mauritania	n/a	Mauritania	n/a	Mauritania
n/a	São Tomé & Príncipe	n/a	São Tomé & Príncipe	n/a	São Tomé & Príncipe
n/a	Somalia	n/a	Somalia	n/a	Somalia
n/a	Sudan	n/a	Sudan	n/a	Sudan
n/a	Zimbabwe	n/a	Zimbabwe	n/a	Zimbabwe
bottom					

	Economic Productivity		Govt. Earnings & Spending		Spending on Health		Purchasing Power		Self-Reliance
	AfDB, IMF, World Bank		AfDB, IMF, World Bank		World Bank, WHO		IMF, World Bank		AfDB, IMF, World Bank, WTO
	2003-2006		2003-2006		2003-2006		2003-2006		2003-2006
top 1	Angola	top 1	Equatorial Guinea	top 1	Botswana	top 1	Cape Verde	top 1	Nigeria
2	Namibia	2	Botswana	2	Namibia	2	Gabon	2	Kenya
3	Botswana	3	Swaziland	3	Malawi	3	Mauritius	3	Equatorial Guinea
4	Mauritius	4	Angola	4	Rwanda	4	Madagascar	4	South Africa
5	Cape Verde	4	Congo, Rep.	5	South Africa	5	Comoros	5	Benin
6	Swaziland	4	Lesotho	6	Swaziland	6	South Africa	6	Tanzania
7	Gabon	5	Seychelles	7	Seychelles	7	Central African Rep.	7	Mauritius
8	Seychelles	6	Namibia	8	Uganda	8	Ghana	8	Niger
9	South Africa	7	Ghana	9	Zambia	9	Malawi	9	Mali
10	Ghana	8	Nigeria	10	Lesotho	10	Botswana	10	Burkina Faso
10	Tanzania	8	South Africa	11	Mozambique	11	Sierra Leone	11	Central African Rep.
11	Nigeria	9	Cape Verde	12	Burkina Faso	12	Kenya	12	Botswana
12	Kenya	10	Burundi	13	Gambia, The	13	Ethiopia	13	Cameroon
12	Equatorial Guinea	11	Gabon	14	Cape Verde	14	Guinea	14	Comoros
13	Madagascar	12	Mauritius	15	Gabon	15	Senegal	15	Ethiopia
14	Cameroon	13	Chad	16	Mauritius	16	Swaziland	16	Angola
15	Senegal	13	Mozambique	17	Equatorial Guinea	17	Gambia, The	17	Cote d'Ivoire
16	Zambia	14	Gambia, The	18	Ghana	18	Lesotho	18	Namibia
17	Benin	14	Malawi	19	Tanzania	19	Mali	19	Congo, Dem. Rep.
18	Burkina Faso	15	Mali	20	Mali	20	Angola	20	Gabon
19	Cote d'Ivoire	16	Eritrea	21	Madagascar	21	Tanzania	21	Togo
20	Chad	17	Cameroon	22	Kenya	22	Rwanda	22	Senegal
21	Congo, Rep.	17	Rwanda	23	Guinea-Bissau	23	Burkina Faso	23	Chad
21	Gambia, The	18	Senegal	24	Benin	24	Seychelles	24	Mozambique
22	Mali	19	Ethiopia	25	Ethiopia	25	Congo, Dem. Rep.	25	Sierra Leone
23	Mozambique	20	Kenya	26	Togo	26	Benin	26	Madagascar
24	Ethiopia	20	Sierra Leone	27	Niger	27	Congo, Rep.	27	Guinea
24	Rwanda	21	Benin	28	Senegal	28	Togo	28	Uganda
25	Lesotho	21	Congo, Dem. Rep.	29	Cameroon	29	Cameroon	29	Rwanda
26	Sierra Leone	22	Uganda	30	Central African Rep.	30	Cote d'Ivoire	30	Ghana
27	Togo	23	Guinea-Bissau	31	Chad	31	Namibia	31	Congo, Rep.
28	Comoros	24	Tanzania	32	Eritrea	32	Uganda	32	Zambia
28	Malawi	25	Zambia	33	Guinea	33	Niger	33	Lesotho
29	Uganda	26	Cote d'Ivoire	34	Angola	34	Eritrea	34	Guinea-Bissau
30	Guinea	26	Madagascar	35	Sierra Leone	35	Guinea-Bissau	35	Seychelles
31	Eritrea	27	Burkina Faso	36	Cote d'Ivoire	36	Mozambique	36	Cape Verde
32	Congo, Dem. Rep.	28	Niger	37	Comoros	37	Burundi	37	Malawi
33	Niger	28	Togo	38	Nigeria	38	Zambia	38	Burundi
34	Central African Rep.	29	Comoros	39	Congo, Dem. Rep.	39	Chad	39	Swaziland
35	Burundi	30	Central African Rep.	40	Burundi	40	Equatorial Guinea	40	Gambia, The
36	Guinea-Bissau	31	Guinea	41	Congo, Rep.	41	Nigeria	41	Eritrea
n/a	Djibouti	n/a	Djibouti	n/a	Djibouti	n/a	Djibouti	n/a	Djibouti
n/a	Liberia	n/a	Liberia	n/a	Liberia	n/a	Liberia	n/a	Liberia
n/a	Mauritania	n/a	Mauritania	n/a	Mauritania	n/a	Mauritania	n/a	Mauritania
n/a	São Tomé & Príncipe	n/a	São Tomé & Príncipe	n/a	São Tomé & Príncipe	n/a	São Tomé & Príncipe	n/a	São Tomé & Príncipe
n/a	Somalia	n/a	Somalia	n/a	Somalia	n/a	Somalia	n/a	Somalia
n/a	Sudan	n/a	Sudan	n/a	Sudan	n/a	Sudan	n/a	Sudan
n/a	Zimbabwe	n/a	Zimbabwe	n/a	Zimbabwe	n/a	Zimbabwe	n/a	Zimbabwe
bottom		bottom		bottom		bottom		bottom	

	Investor Confidence AfDB, IMF, UNCTAD, World Bank 2003-2006		Regulatory Environment AfDB, IMF, UNCTAD, World Bank 2009
top 1	Equatorial Guinea	top 1	Mauritius
2	Seychelles	2	South Africa
3	Namibia	3	Botswana
4	Cape Verde	4	Namibia
5	Botswana	5	Kenya
6	South Africa	6	Ghana
7	Zambia	7	Zambia
8	Ghana	8	Seychelles
9	Mauritius	9	Swaziland
10	Congo, Rep.	10	Uganda
11	Senegal	11	Ethiopia
12	Nigeria	12	Nigeria
13	Gabon	13	Lesotho
14	Gambia, The	14	Tanzania
15	Lesotho	15	Gambia, The
15	Uganda	16	Malawi
16	Angola	17	Rwanda
17	Chad	18	Mozambique
18	Tanzania	19	Cape Verde
19	Benin	20	Madagascar
20	Burkina Faso	21	Burkina Faso
21	Kenya	22	Senegal
22	Malawi	23	Gabon
23	Mozambique	24	Comoros
24	Madagascar	25	Sierra Leone
25	Ethiopia	26	Côte d'Ivoire
26	Mali	27	Togo
27	Cameroon	28	Cameroon
28	Niger	29	Mali
29	Swaziland	30	Equatorial Guinea
30	Sierra Leone	31	Angola
31	Togo	32	Benin
32	Cote d'Ivoire	33	Guinea
32	Rwanda	34	Niger
33	Guinea	35	Eritrea
33	Guinea-Bissau	36	Chad
34	Burundi	37	Burundi
35	Congo, Dem. Rep.	38	Congo, Rep.
36	Central African Rep.	39	Guinea-Bissau
37	Eritrea	40	Central African Rep.
38	Comoros	41	Congo, Dem. Rep.
n/a	Djibouti	n/a	Djibouti
n/a	Liberia	n/a	Liberia
n/a	Mauritania	n/a	Mauritania
n/a	São Tomé & Príncipe	n/a	São Tomé & Príncipe
n/a	Somalia	n/a	Somalia
n/a	Sudan	n/a	Sudan
n/a bottom	Zimbabwe	n/a bottom	Zimbabwe

www.ingramcontent.com/pod-product-compliance
Lightning Source LLC
LaVergne TN
LVHW070845210926
848482LV00016B/873
9780956452610